MOON

GRAND EUROPEAN JOURNEYS

40 UNFORGETTABLE TRIPS BY ROAD, RAIL, SEA & MORE

LUCAS PETERS

GRAND EUROPEAN JOURNEYS

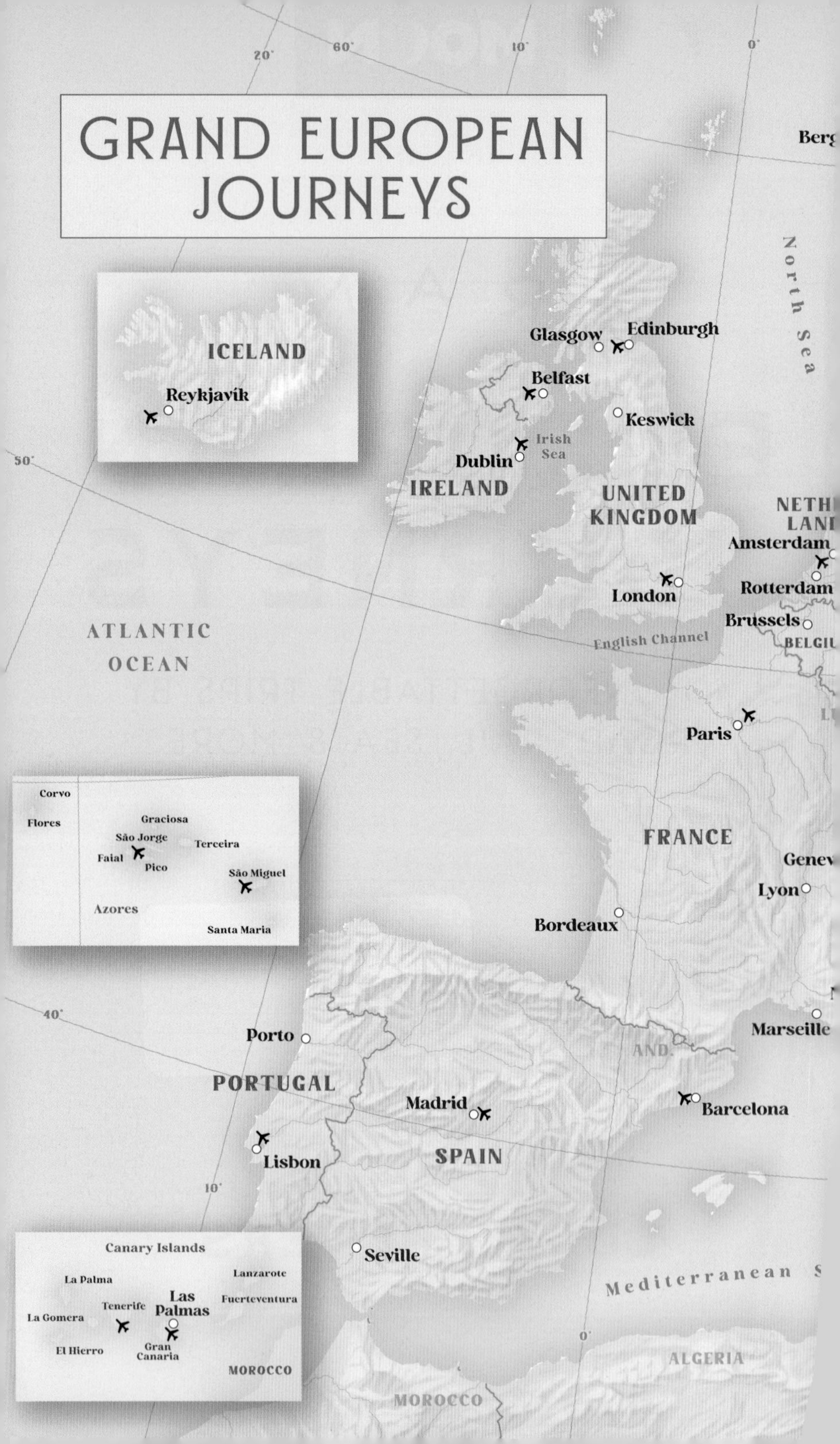

ICELAND
Reykjavík

Glasgow
Edinburgh
Belfast
Keswick
Irish Sea
Dublin
IRELAND
UNITED KINGDOM
NETH
LAN
Amsterdam
Rotterdam
London
Brussels
BELGIU
English Channel
North Sea
Berg
ATLANTIC OCEAN
Paris
FRANCE
Genev
Lyon
Bordeaux
Marseille
AND.
Porto
PORTUGAL
Madrid
Barcelona
Lisbon
SPAIN
Seville
Mediterranean S
ALGERIA
MOROCCO

Corvo
Flores
Graciosa
São Jorge
Terceira
Faial
Pico
São Miguel
Azores
Santa Maria

Canary Islands
La Palma
Lanzarote
Las Palmas
Tenerife
Fuerteventura
La Gomera
El Hierro
Gran Canaria
MOROCCO

20°
60°
10°
0°
50°
40°
10°
0°

FINLAND
NORWAY
Oslo
Stockholm
Tallinn
ESTONIA
Svolvær
Norwegian Sea
NORWAY
LATVIA
Riga
SWEDEN
DENMARK
Baltic Sea
LITHUANIA
Oslo
Stockholm
Copenhagen
RUSSIA
Vilnius
SWEDEN
Rostock
BELARUS
Warsaw
Berlin
POLAND
UKRAINE
GERMANY
Prague
Frankfurt
CZECHIA
SLOVAKIA
MOL.
Munich
Vienna
Budapest
ROMANIA
Zürich
AUSTRIA
HUNGARY
SWITZ.
Ljubljana
SLO.
Zagreb
Venice
Bucharest
Milan
CROATIA
Black Sea
ITALY
BOS. & HERZ.
SERBIA
BULGARIA
Florence
Adriatic Sea
KOS.
MONT.
NO. MACE.
Rome
ALB.
Naples
Aegean Sea
TURKEY
GREECE
Athens
TUNISIA
MALTA
© MOON.COM

CONTENTS

WELCOME TO EUROPE 7

CITY HOPPING . . . 41

top, a café at night in Paris; middle, Tower Bridge in London; bottom, gondola in the canal waters of Venice; right, train in the Alps

ROAD TRIPS . . 225

OUTDOOR ADVENTURES. . 351

ON THE WATER 481

CLASSIC RAIL TRIPS AND MORE 597

Welcome to Europe

The dream of Europe can take infinite forms.

It may be browsing in the markets of quaint hilltop villages or seeing iconic masterpieces in storied art museums. It may be marveling at the opulence of grand palaces or sipping a glass of white wine on a sunny plaza. From majestic mountains to glittering coastlines, bustling cities to sleepy hamlets, each European country and region has its own reverie-worthy charm and character. Connecting them—whether by rail, road, water, or your own two feet—is key to manifesting the dream into a journey.

Perhaps no mode of transportation is as synonymous with Europe as trains. Traveling by train on its extensive rail network is comfortable and eco-friendly—and often mind-blowingly scenic. Whether you're trundling through the Swiss Alps, hopping between Spanish cities, or traversing the continent from west to east, train journeys offer a window into the heart of Europe.

Sometimes realizing your European dream calls for the flexibility offered by a car. Coastal drives and winding mountain passes beckon those seeking the freedom of a road trip. Active travelers might dream of trekking through the Dolomites or biking among the windmills of the Netherlands. Cycling and hiking trips are unparalleled ways to experience Europe's natural beauty up close. And the seas, oceans, and rivers that shaped Europe's place in the world are plied by ferries as well as cruise ships, offering a unique perspective on the shores where they berth.

However you choose to link the various parts of your dream of Europe, taking one journey may very well lead to another—and another. Europe offers a wealth of unforgettable trips, whether it's your first or your fortieth.

1. Sipping an apero and watching the world go by at a **Paris café** (page 60).

TOP 10 EXPERIENCES

2. Road tripping to waterfalls on **Iceland's Ring Road** (page 237).

3. Hiking the **Pathway of the Gods** on the Amalfi Coast (page 546).

4. Catching a live **trad music session** in Dublin (page 358).

5. Cycling or cruising past the **Kinderdijk windmills** (page 505).

6. Relaxing in the healing waters of **Budapest's thermal baths** (page 200).

7. Ridng the **Bernina Express** train through the Alps (page 657).

8. Watching the sunrise over the Mediterranean on the island of **Santorini** (page 564).

9. Absorbing the exquisite palace and gardens of the **Alhambra** (page 135).

10. Stepping into a fairy tale at **Neuschwanstein** (page 317).

TYPES OF JOURNEYS

CITY HOPPING

The ultimate international urban adventures, these journeys combine 2-3 historic European cities in grand fashion.

ROAD TRIPS

If you fancy the freedom of the open road, check out some of the most iconic road trips Europe has to offer.

OUTDOOR ADVENTURES

These inspiring itineraries will take you hiking and cycling into the pastoral countryside and up into the high peaks of the continent.

ON THE WATER

Whether river cruising through the interior of the continent or island hopping on Mediterranean ferries, you'll no doubt find more than a few great beaches.

CLASSIC RAIL TRIPS AND MORE

Classic rail rides throughout Europe make the most of your Eurail pass, connecting vast swaths of the continent in just a few short days.

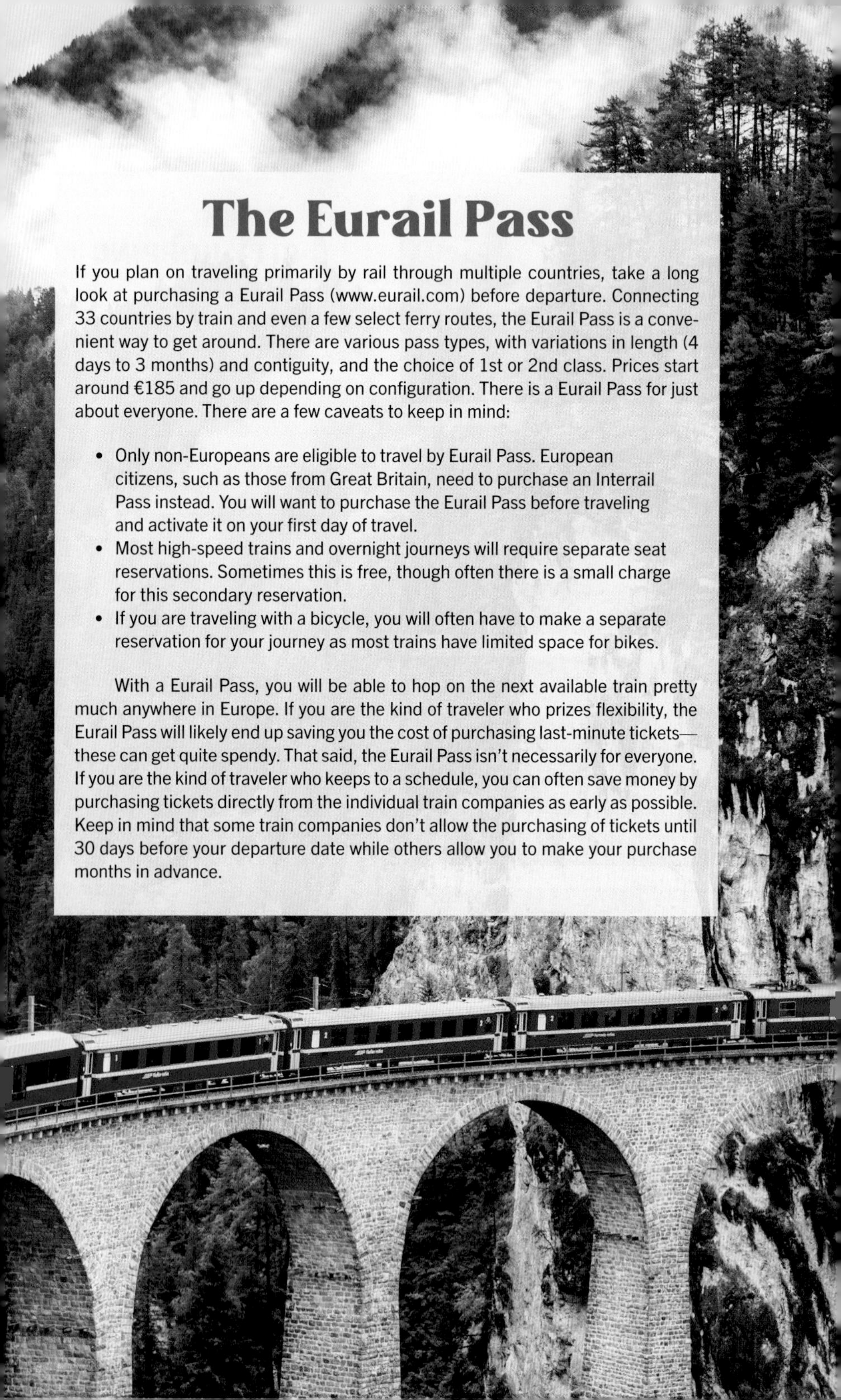

The Eurail Pass

If you plan on traveling primarily by rail through multiple countries, take a long look at purchasing a Eurail Pass (www.eurail.com) before departure. Connecting 33 countries by train and even a few select ferry routes, the Eurail Pass is a convenient way to get around. There are various pass types, with variations in length (4 days to 3 months) and contiguity, and the choice of 1st or 2nd class. Prices start around €185 and go up depending on configuration. There is a Eurail Pass for just about everyone. There are a few caveats to keep in mind:

- Only non-Europeans are eligible to travel by Eurail Pass. European citizens, such as those from Great Britain, need to purchase an Interrail Pass instead. You will want to purchase the Eurail Pass before traveling and activate it on your first day of travel.
- Most high-speed trains and overnight journeys will require separate seat reservations. Sometimes this is free, though often there is a small charge for this secondary reservation.
- If you are traveling with a bicycle, you will often have to make a separate reservation for your journey as most trains have limited space for bikes.

With a Eurail Pass, you will be able to hop on the next available train pretty much anywhere in Europe. If you are the kind of traveler who prizes flexibility, the Eurail Pass will likely end up saving you the cost of purchasing last-minute tickets—these can get quite spendy. That said, the Eurail Pass isn't necessarily for everyone. If you are the kind of traveler who keeps to a schedule, you can often save money by purchasing tickets directly from the individual train companies as early as possible. Keep in mind that some train companies don't allow the purchasing of tickets until 30 days before your departure date while others allow you to make your purchase months in advance.

BEST JOURNEYS FOR FIRST-TIMERS

If you are looking forward to your first journey to Europe, start here! With a great mix of bucket-list highlights and local insider knowledge, these are ideal for travel debutantes to the continent.

LONDON AND PARIS

City Hopping

Pairing two of the world's most iconic cities, this experience is a must for first-timers and old hats alike.

ROME, FLORENCE, AND VENICE

City Hopping

For many, Italy is Europe at its finest. Why not start your exploration with three of its most quintessential cities?

THE GREEK ISLANDS

On the Water

Paired with the ancient city of Athens, this journey offers a mix of historic urban settings, sunny beaches, and impossibly gorgeous islands.

Eiffel Tower, Paris

PARIS TO BUCHAREST

Classic Rail Trips and More

All aboard for the ultimate train trip for the ultimate first-time explorer. Set foot in a minimum of five countries, sampling a vast variety of cuisine and cultures, and marveling at phenomenal landscapes along the way.

CAMINO DE SANTIAGO

Outdoor Adventures

This medieval pilgrimage route takes you on foot through an incredible countryside. This is a true bucket-list experience for first-time travelers and those looking to include a longer trek in Europe for the first time.

Trevi Fountain, Rome

Eating and Drinking Your Way Through Europe

Dining in Europe is an exquisitely exciting experience for your tastebuds and your cultural palate. Discover a wide variety of cuisines and traditions across the continent; from the delicately delicious pizzas of Italy to the succulent seafood of France and hearty stews of Hungary, there is something for everyone. Each country and region has its own unique culinary heritage. In most countries, meals are typically relaxed and leisurely with a focus on enjoying the company of friends and family. The use of fresh, locally grown, high-quality ingredients is a common theme throughout.

COFFEE AND CAFÉS

The cafés of Europe. Is there any more quintessentially European experience than lingering a little too long at your local café, enjoying your choice of caffeinated beverage, watching the passersby darting to and fro, taking a moment perhaps to jot down that odd thought in your travel journal or draw a little memory of the morning in your sketchbook? Probably not. To get local, try these particular coffees in their noted locales.

- **Trieste:** The musical **capo in b** is, in fact, short for cappuccino in bicchiere (a drinking glass), a staple of café culture in Trieste. Somewhere between a macchiato and schiumato, this is a must-have beverage for coffee lovers of all stripes. This espresso concoction, dolloped with frothy milk, is so locally famous there is even a yearly competition to determine the capo in b champion.
- **Naxos:** The **kafeneios** of Greece are a local institution. More than cafés, these are Greek coffeehouses (traditionally a sort of boys club)—warm and inviting, and part of the local life. Enjoy a cup of strong Greek-styled coffee, and take your time. It's not unusual for a Greek coffee break to run over an hour.
- **Amsterdam:** Cafés like the **Aepjen** showcase the long, often seedy, history of Amsterdam's café culture. Tuck in from the cold under the wood beams and sip on a filtered coffee as most do in Amsterdam.
- **Paris:** It would be almost impossible to not visit one of the many historic cafés, such as **Café Flore** or **Les Deux Magots,** in the city that practically invented café culture. Enjoy your café crème on the sidewalk on a sunny day for a true slice of Parisian life.

PASTRIES

The buttery, flaky, sheer deliciousness of a French croissant is a wonder to behold. You would be forgiven for making this your go-to breakfast every morning. However, it's not the only delightful breakfast pastry you'll find in Europe.

- **Paris:** Although you can find all sorts of world-class, Michelin-starred restaurants in the City of Light, there is perhaps no greater pleasure than crunching into a perfectly baked **croissant,** buttery fireworks exploding in your mouth as you linger over breakfast at a neighborhood café.
- **Vienna:** Thought to be the home of the croissant (literally "crescent" in French), you'll find **Viennese crescents** in bakeries and cafés throughout the city, as well as all sorts of other pastries. Opt for an **apfelstrudel** or **topfenstrudel,** or maybe just order the whole lot!

- **Zagreb:** Enjoy an apple-stuffed **burek pastry** at a café in Croatia's capital city. Pair it with a yogurt, like the locals.
- **Madrid:** There is perhaps nothing quite as Spanish as dipping a piping hot **churro** into a cup of impossibly thick hot chocolate for breakfast.

PIZZA

In Italy, you´ll find some of the best pizzas in the world. Typically with deliciously crispy, thin crusts and featuring high-quality toppings, pizza is usually enjoyed at a local, casual pizzeria or as a quick pick-me-up street food.

- **Rome:** The capital of Italy is known for its **pizza al taglio** (pizza by the slice), which adds a touch of Rome-ance to that artichoke- or prosciutto-topped slice of goodness.
- **Naples:** Considered the birthplace of pizza, this is a pizza-lover's Mecca. Enjoy a slice or two of the classic of classics: **pizza Margherita** with savory tomato sauce, creamy mozzarella, and fresh basil, and finished with a drizzle of fine Italian olive oil.

CHEESE

The range of cheeses made in Europe is truly staggering. Specialties vary from region to region, as do ways to eat them. Memorable cheese experiences abound in Europe, but here are a few to get you started.

- **Geneva:** Cheese **fondue** is a French-Swiss classic and just the thing to warm you up after a cool walk through the old town of Geneva. Though fondue is best enjoyed in winter, you will be excused if you order it out of season.
- **Chamonix:** If you have never enjoyed **raclette**—a dish of cheese that you grill at your own table, generally paired with potatoes and charcuterie—just know that there is perhaps no more enjoyable feeling that filling up on all the cheese you can possibly enjoy before or after a day of trekking on Mont Blanc.
- **Spain: Queso manchego,** a semi-hard cured cheese, typically kept in olive oil, is a tapas staple throughout the country. Order it with your vino tinto or cerveza of choice and enjoy.
- **Italy:** Throughout the country, large bowls of grated **parmesan** are served with your pasta dishes, while **burrata** and prosciutto appetizer salads are commonplace, and oh-so-delish. If your journey takes you through Tuscany and Umbria, be sure to stop in at an agriturismo for locally made cheeses.

SAUSAGES

Throughout the continent, you'll find sausages that are cured, dried, smoked, and frozen, made of cow, poultry, or pork, and spiced in a seemingly infinite variety. In Germany alone, there is thought to be more than 1,500 types of sausage.

- **Berlin:** Enjoy your **currywurst** as a street food or in any number of greasy spoons found through the hip German capital. This currylicious street food is a staple for true Berliners. Grilled pork sausage meets flavor heaven with a healthy dollop of spicy, curry-infused ketchup.
- **Trieste:** Closer in regional cuisine to Slovenia than Italy, the multicultural city

of Trieste offers dishes such as **jota soup** (sauerkraut, beans, potatoes, and sausage) and **cevapcici** (a minced sausage dish). These staples of the local diet show the influence of years of Austro-Hungarian rule.

- **Reykjavík: Hot dogs** are a street food par excellence in Iceland and wildly popular. Pile on a not-so-healthy heap of pickled mayo and crispy fried onions like the locals for the full Icelandic gustatory experience.

DUMPLINGS

The most typical dumpling is a savory affair, stuffed with potatoes, farmer cheese, and onions. However, these days, you can find nearly endless varieties with various stuffed meats (particularly ground beef) as well as sweet dumplings filled with strawberry, blueberry, or plum. Dumplings are a staple throughout Eastern Europe, where you'll find endless varieties.

- **Warsaw:** There is perhaps no greater joy than digging into a **pierogi** (or five) of your choice after a big day of walking around the historical center of Warsaw. Tuck into a low-key local spot for the most authentic of pierogi dumpling experiences.
- **Tallinn: Bear dumplings** are exactly what you think they might be: potato dumplings filled with ground bear meat, a marker of a long history of Russian influence.
- **Vilnius:** Served in the shape of a blimp, the Lithunian version of a **potato dumpling** is more varied than many of its counterparts. There are countless vegan and vegetarian options available these days, typically with a mushroom base.

SEAFOOD

Europe is surrounded by the ice-cold saltwater of the North Atlantic and the warm waters of the Mediterranean, not to mention the many lakes and rivers that criss-cross the continent. With an abundance of seafood from a variety of sources, you will find plenty of locally caught and/or farmed seafood options throughout your journey.

- **French Riviera:** A traditional fish stew from Marseille, **bouillabaisse** is a quintessential French seafood dish. What gives bouillabaisse its shockingly high price and equally impressive flavor is the venomous rascasse (red scorpionfish), a rockfish only found in the Mediterranean. Recipes vary widely, but this fisherman's staple typically includes a mix of fish and shellfish with leeks, onions, tomatoes, and garlic.
- **Lofoten Islands:** A typical Norwegian staple, **tørrfisk** is wild-caught cod, dried and cured. Known as Lofoten stockfish, nothing quite says Norway like this local specialty. There is even a museum you can visit dedicated to this.
- **Dalmatian Coast:** Enjoy a wonderfully light **crzi rižot,** a black risotto made with fresh cuttlefish or squid, which lends the risotto its inky blackness. Smile big for your friends afterward as the natural pigment tends to stick around. Wash it down with a crisp white Dalmatian wine.
- **Budapest: Szeged** is a fish soup with lots of paprika and hot peppers, warming you up from the inside on a chill Hungarian night. This is a staple enjoyed anywhere in the country, though perhaps most romantically along the Danube.
- **Brighton:** You'll find the requisite **fish and chips** on pub menus throughout the UK, though the pubs of Brighton somehow just get it better than the rest.

BEER

From the crisp lagers of Germany to the complex ales of Belgium and rich stouts of Ireland, each country in Europe seems to have its own unique brewing tradition. Some of the oldest beers in the world are still brewed by traditional methods. Enjoying a pint (or a boot!) of beer in Europe is a great way to experience local culture and to savor the many different flavors and aromas that the continent has to offer.

- **Dublin:** Famous for its rich, creamy **stout beer,** especially Guinness, which is brewed at the St. James's Gate brewery. Whether you take a brewery tour to learn about the history and brewing process at the Gravity Bar or belly up to the local pub to try some different types of stouts, either way you're in for a lively experience.
- **Munich:** There is maybe no more authentic Bavarian experience than an afternoon in a wonderfully festive **beer hall.** The more famous beer halls, such as Hofbräuhaus, offer a selection of beers brewed in-house. Traditional Bavarian staples, such as pretzels, sausages, and roast chicken, are always available.
- **Brussels:** You could go anywhere in Belgium for a fantastic pint of beer, but only in Brussels can you choose from more than 2,000 available beers, a world record proudly held by Brussels Delirium Café. You are sure to find just the right style of beer for you, though sipping a **Belgium-style Trappist ale** should be top of the list.
- **Cologne:** A unique beer with a protected heritage status, a true **Kölsch** beer can only be brewed within a 50-km (31-mi) radius of the German city of Cologne.

WINE

There is perhaps no beverage more associated with Europe than wine. From the world-famous wineries of Bordeaux (France) and Tuscany (Italy) to lesser known, but equally impressive, regions like Ribera del Duero and Priorat (both in Spain), each wine region offers different grapes and wine styles that have been honed throughout centuries and are specific to that place.

- **Lyon:** If France is the home of fine cuisine, Lyon is the beating heart within it. Pair any of the amazing French eats you'll find here with an equally phenomenal vintage of a **Rhone Valley wine.**
- **Montalcino:** If you haven't tasted a rich glass of **Tuscan red** in Tuscany, you are missing out. As tried-and-true and on-the-beaten-path as wine tasting gets, this is the Italian version of Napa Valley and shouldn't be missed by any wine lover.
- **Bordeaux:** Sipping on a velvety rich **Cabernet Sauvignon** in Bordeaux in the midst of a lush vineyard is as quintessentially European as one could hope for, and one of the few experiences where the hype actually undersells the experience.
- **Tenerife:** A singular wine tasting event, **plate,** the banana wine of the Canary Islands, is crisper and lighter white wine than you might imagine, and is best enjoyed on a warm Canary day.

BEST JOURNEYS FOR FAMILIES

In part because Europe boasts some of the world's most delicious food, incredible sites, and iconic museums, it is a prime destination for families. In most major cities you'll find friendly neighborhood play parks for the younger set, while for older kids, seeing some real history up close and personal (as opposed to reading dry textbooks) can be just the thing to inspire a lifelong learner.

FRENCH RIVIERA

Classic Rail Trips and More

The Riviera might be synonymous with glitz and glamour, but with a series of wonderful beaches and an easy railway to facilitate travel, it is a winner for families traveling with the younger set as well.

HOLLAND JUNCTION NETWORK

Outdoor Adventures

The Netherlands seems almost set up specifically for families that love to cycle. With flat easy stretches of well-marked paths and kid-friendly favorites, like the Scheveningen Beach and Pier, you'll find something for everyone in the family on this active excursion.

ROMANTISCHE STRASSE

Road Trips

Nothing quite brings to life a childhood storybook like the Black Forest, medieval fortresses, and the castle that inspired the House of Mouse, the Neuschwanstein Castle. If you're a road-tripping family, it doesn't get any better.

SOUTH OF ENGLAND TO NORTH OF FRANCE

On the Water

Delve into some real-world history on this journey spanning two countries. Highlights include Stonehenge, the Bayeux Tapestry, and the D-Day Landing Beaches of World War II. Bring that dry history class to life for your young, budding historian.

BARCELONA AND MARDRID

City Hopping

With a series of incredible museums, awe-inspiring architecture, tasty eats, and Mediterranean beaches found in two easily connected urban hubs, this journey offers a perfect balance of learning and fun.

left, Romantische Strasse, Germany; right, Park Güell, Barcelona

Make It a Greener Trip

You can explore the continent while minimizing your impact on the environment. Make eco-conscious choices about transportation, accommodations, and activities that reduce carbon emissions and minimize waste. Be mindful of waste reduction and recycling, and support local communities and economies wherever you go. Not only will this make your journey more sustainable, but also you'll find yourself forging relationships with locals, and enjoying higher-quality goods and foods. While you experience the beauty of Europe, do your part to contribute to its preservation for the generations of travelers and pilgrims to come.

- **Travel by train, bus, bike, or foot.** Traveling on public transportation, or on your own steam, is much more carbon-friendly than renting a car or taking taxis.
- **Bring a reusable water bottle and shopping bag.** Pack smart. Bring a filtered water bottle and reusable shopping bag to use throughout your journey. Most European cities have plenty of water fountains and refill stations, and you can use your shopping bag for everything from souvenir shopping to toting picnic fixings from the local market.
- **Stay more than one night.** Staying at a hotel for only one night means that rooms need to be cleaned and linens washed each day. Also, look for hotels and accommodations than have implemented sustainable practices, such as solar power and recycling programs.
- **Research before you go.** Learn about local environmental issues before you go and find ways to minimize your impact while traveling.
- **Support sustainable businesses.** Keep an eye out for tour companies, restaurants, shops, and accommodations that prioritize sustainability.
- **Be mindful of your waste.** Be a conscious consumer. You may not be able to go full zero-waste, but understanding what happens to things you throw away and recycle can help you make greener decisions.
- **Offset your carbon footprint.** Consider offsetting your carbon footprint by purchasing carbon credits or investing in carbon offset programs.

BEST VIEWS

LAGO DI BRAIES

Alta Via 1: Dolomite High Route

The reflections of the Dolomite Mountains and surrounding green forest rippling across this aquamarine lake create a magical effect. There is maybe not a prettier start to a hike in all of Europe.

ARC DE TRIOMPHE

London and Paris

It's impossible not to be swept away by the charm of Paris. Every street in the historic city center seems to bring with it the best view, but for a bird's-eye view, consider the Arc de Triomphe where you can enjoy spectacular views over the entire city.

BRAN CASTLE

Transylvania

The setting of this behemoth 14th-century castle in the Transylvanian countryside is nothing short of spectacular. For a truly vampiric experience, consider a short walk at the foot of the fortress as the moon rises.

LA SAGRADA FAMÍLIA

Barcelona and Madrid

For a true bird's-eye view over Barcelona and the Mediterranean, climb the many, many stairs to the soaring towers of the architect Antoni Gaudi's masterpiece, the cathedral of La Sagrada Família.

DOURO HISTORIC STEAM TRAIN

The Douro Line

The view from your historic steam train window as it chugs through the Portuguese countryside, paired with local wine and music, is not to be missed.

COL DE LA SEIGNE

Tour du Mont Blanc

This is one of those views you really have to work for, and it is all the more magical for it. Witness the majesty of Mont Blanc from this summit on your fourth day of hiking the Tour du Mont Blanc.

VERNAZZA

Cinque Terre

You could maybe include all of the Cinque Terre on a list of best views; this series of five small Italian villages is just so colorful and beautifully set against the blue Mediterranean and green hills. But the village of Vernazza takes the cake.

JÖKULSÁRLÓN (GLACIER LAGOON)

Iceland's Ring Road

Take in the glaring white and ethereal glacial blues that surround you as you witness the calving of the Breiðamerkurjökull glacier. This spectacular setting puts you face to face with the planet's climate crisis.

Lago di Braies, Italy

Literary References

Everywhere you turn in Europe, it seems like you can find the muse of some writer or the setting of a great story. You can virtually take a stroll through your favorite book, or make a point to wander down a particular street or take in a view that has inspired some of your favorite writers. Here are a few favorites to get you started on your own literary exploration of Europe.

KRONBORG CASTLE

Copenhagen to Oslo

This is the setting of Shakespeare's *Hamlet.* One glance up at this imposing Danish fortress and you'll understand just how picture-perfect a backdrop it is for one of the Bard's finest tragedies.

ANNE FRANK HOUSE

Amsterdam, Brussels, and Bruges

The Diary of Anne Frank is required reading for high schoolers everywhere. On a trip to Amsterdam, you can visit the annex where the real Anne Frank and her family hid from Nazis and she penned her heartfelt diary.

CHARLES BRIDGE

Prague, Vienna, and Budapest

You'll find homages to Prague's literary master, Franz Kafka, nearly everywhere, though all it takes is a glance at the Danube River cutting through the city beneath this bridge to recall Gregor Samsa's longing as a bug looking out toward a freedom he could never have.

LES DEUX MAGOTS

London and Paris

Alongside Brasserie Lipp and Café Flore, Les Deux Magots forms a literary holy trinity of Parisian cafés that have hosted reclusive writers and sparring philosophers for centuries. Ernest Hemingway, James Joyce, Simone de Beauvoir, and Richard Wright are just a few of the authors who frequented this famous Saint-Germain café.

THE BLACK FOREST

Rhine River Cruise

Germany's mythic Black Forest is perhaps best known as the setting of many of the fairy tales told by the Brothers Grimm, with the most famous of those being Little Red Riding Hood.

TRANSYLVANIA

There may not be a region of Europe as synonymous with a single literary character as Transylvania is with Count Dracula.

BEST MUSEUMS

THE LOUVRE

London and Paris

Paris is dotted with incredible museums, but none is as iconic as the sprawling Louvre. See the Mona Lisa and Venus de Milo, and then carefully choose from the thousands more essential artworks housed in this former palace; it's impossible to visit the entire museum in one day.

THE UFFIZI GALLERY

Rome, Florence, and Venice

You may feel like a walk through Florence is already like visiting a giant open-air museum, but don't miss the world-class Uffizi Gallery, which features an extensive collection of Italian Renaissance masters.

THE VATICAN MUSEUMS

Rome, Florence, and Venice

The Raphael Rooms showcasing some of the Italian Renaissance master's finest paintings and Michelangelo's divine Sistine Chapel are just a couple of the highlights of this vast complex.

THE RIJKSMUSEUM

Amsterdam, Brussels, and Bruges

Rembrandt. Vermeer. Hals. If you are seeking the Dutch Masters, there is no finer museum in the world. Kick off your exploration of Amsterdam with some of the world's greatest art treasures.

The Rijksmuseum, Amsterdam

THE PERGAMON MUSEUM

Berlin, Warsaw, and Krakow

Of the many museums found on Berlin's "Museum Island," Pergamon takes der kuchen for its vast collection of antiquities, including the Ishtar Gate of Babylon and the Pergamon Alter, from which it derives its name.

PRADO MUSEUM

Barcelona and Madrid

With an extensive collection of art spanning the 12th-19th centuries, the Prado is one of Europe's most important museums and is a must-see while visiting Madrid.

KUNSTHISTORISCHES MUSEUM

Prague, Vienna, and Budapest

Take a walk through time from the dusty tombs of ancient Egypt to the gilded splendor of the baroque in Austria's largest collection of art and antiquities.

VILLAGE MUSEUM

Paris to Bucharest

For a more realistic stroll through another era, head to the Village Museum in Bucharest's King Mihai I Park, where you'll find more than 300 buildings that re-create Romania's storied countryside.

BEST SMALL TOWNS AND VILLAGES

Step out of the urban city centers of Europe, and in every country you will be rewarded with villages and hamlets in places where, as cliche as it may seem, time really does seem to stand still.

FÁSKRÚÐSFJÖRÐUR

Iceland's Ring Road

This charming Icelandic village is one of the most unique in the country for its historical connections to French fishermen.

ROTHENBURG

Romantische Strasse

It is almost unfair to pick one of the medieval villages along Germany's Romantische Strasse, which winds through the storied Black Forest, but nothing is maybe as romantic as walking the cobblestone streets of Rothenburg at dusk.

LAVACOLLA

Camino de Santiago

You'll find this medieval Spanish village on the edge of a eucalyptus forest, the perfect backdrop for the penultimate night before your arrival in Santiago de Compostela.

PYRGOS

The Greek Islands

The whitewashed former capital of Santorini, one of the Greek Islands, is one of the most pristine medieval villages, and perhaps the prettiest.

FLÅM

The Bergen Line

The Aurlandsfjord of Flåm fingers forth, an unforgettable Nordic fantasia carved into the Nordic countryside.

GRASMERE

England's Lake District

The word quaint does not begin to describe William Wordsworth's former home in the Lake District. Perhaps that's why he turned to poetry. You should be forgiven if you start speaking in sonnets.

TODI

Tuscany and Umbria

It is truly hard to pick just one Italian village. Though you could pick any of the five villages of Cinque Terre or pretty much anywhere in Tuscany, the Umbrian village of Todi has a special charm to it, most likely because it is much less touched by tourism.

TRAKAI

Vilnius, Riga, and Tallinn

All it takes is a short 30-minute bus ride from Vilnius to be plunged into the colorful village life of Lithuania in Trakai. While here, make sure to visit the castle on the lake, which is about as romantic as it sounds.

Flåm village in Norway

The European Lifestyle

What is the European lifestyle? It is difficult to pinpoint, and it varies greatly from region to region. Still, we know it when we see it. As diverse as Europe can be, here are a few not-to-be-missed experiences to help you immerse yourself in local culture during your journey.

MARKETS

Whether you are staying in a short-term rental or just assembling some picnic fixin's, make sure to do your shopping at the local markets. This is Europe at its finest where you can find seasonal legumes as well as local specialties.

GEZELLIGHEID AND HYGGE

When in the Netherlands, relax your thoughts and be "happy and at ease," in the truest sense of gezelligheid, a complex feeling that is most sensed when with friends, old or new, in a social space, like a café or club. The spirit of gezelligheid has been exported across Europe, alongside its Danish counterpart, hygge—a sort of warm, cozy feeling. Hygge has been adopted by interior designers worldwide, and you'll see it echoed throughout many places for social gatherings.

PUBS

You will find various pubs scattered throughout Europe, though the most quintessential pubs are found in the UK and Ireland. This is where locals meet up for a pint, share a laugh with friends, and occasionally enjoy a bit of music. If the local football (soccer) club is playing, expect a full house.

WHERE IS THE AC?

No air conditioning? Get used to it and dress appropriately. Europeans, by and large, have an aversion to air conditioning. In hotter climes, for centuries traditional buildings were constructed with a natural, cool air flow. In places that historically have experienced moderate summers, the heat was maybe inconvenient for a week or two, though things are shifting with climate change.

KNOW YOUR GREETINGS

Though by and large Europeans are not as smile-happy as North Americans tend to be, they usually do expect a friendly greeting. Before directing your question to the shopkeeper or giving your order to the waiter, do your best to wish that person "good day" or "good evening." It pays to know your bonjours, guten tags, and buenos diases.

DON'T RUSH THE MEAL

Throughout Europe, meals are times to share with friends and family. You'll see fewer people on their phones and tablets, and more conversation happening. In restaurants, your waiter will not be rushing to greet you or to deliver the bill; this is simply another way to give you space to enjoy the moment. Take advantage of this time and get into the flow of a longer lunch or dinner.

DRESSING THE PART

There is a certain way of dressing more European, and it doesn't involve jeans and a T-shirt, let alone pajamas and flip-flops. Don't worry too much about fitting in; you really don't have to nor should you feel any pressure to. But if you do want to feel more European, why not look the part? Take a look at what most people tend to wear and take your cues accordingly. Europeans, on the whole, both men and women, tend to take a bit more time to pick the right outfit and put themselves together before stepping out.

PUBLIC TRANSPORTATION

There is perhaps no better way to gauge the mood of a city than to hop on its popular form of public transportation during rush hour (which, for what it's worth, is nearly always 8-9am, no matter where you are in Europe). Here you will literally rub shoulders with locals while quickly, expediently, almost magically finding yourself in another part of the city.

GRAND TOURS

Most, if not all, of the journeys presented in this guide can be mixed and matched for an adventure all your own. For those who have bit more time or want to enjoy a rail trip *and* a road trip, here are a few suggested ways to knit selected journeys together for an even deeper experience.

ACROSS THE CHANNEL

Number of Days: 12

Go across the English Channel twice—once by train and once by boat—and experience two of Europe's most famous capitals, as well as the Gothic masterpiece of Mont-Saint-Michel, the historic beaches of Normandy, the mystery of Stonehenge, and the seaside fun of Brighton.

London and Paris

Start your exploration of Europe with two days in London, followed by three days in Paris, with a 2.5-hour train ride in between (page 44).

North of France to South of England

From Paris, you can connect via bus or train to Mont-Saint-Michel, where you can begin following the entire **South of England to North of France** journey in reverse. After winding your way along the Normandy coast, catch the ferry from Ouistreham back to British soil, where you'll discover the lively waterfronts that have made the English Channel so iconic (page 484).

AROUND THE ADRIATIC

Number of Days: 16

Make a full exploration of the countries dotting the Adriatic Sea, from Croatia, through Slovenia, and onto Italy with plenty of national parks, urban centers, and gorgeous beaches along the way.

Dubrovnik to Zadar

Take the **Magistrala Coastal Road** journey in reverse, beginning in Dubrovnik and ending in Zadar—a memorable nine-day road trip (page 331).

Zagreb, Ljubljana, and Trieste

From Zadar, you'll continue through Croatia, cutting inland to city-hop through the vibrant urban centers of Zagreb and Ljubljana, and back along the Adriatic Sea to Trieste (page 205).

Venice

End your exploration of the Adriatic Sea along the storied canals of Venice, which gives you the option of continuing on to Florence and Rome in the reverse of the **Rome, Florence, and Venice** route (page 139).

AN EXTENDED EUROPEAN JOURNEY

Number of Days: 20

Using the natural stops along the train ride from Paris to Bucharest, extend your European tour with some deeper dives into different regions as well as some different travel styles, hiking and road-tripping your way across the continent. This trip is perfect for those with a few weeks (or longer) to travel.

Dalmatia, Croatia

top, Dubrovnik's Old Town, Croatia; bottom, Grand Canal, Venice

(top to bottom) Mont-Saint-Michel, France; Reichstag building, Berlin; Belvedere Palace, Vienna; Alhambra Palace in Spain

Rhine River Cruise

Fly into Paris, then take the train to Strasbourg—which is the first stop on the epic Paris-Bucharest rail trip. There, you can connect with a three-day Rhine River Cruise ending in Basel, Switzerland (page 503).

Romantische Strasse

From Basel, take the train to Würzburg and follow this fairy-tale road trip, ending in Munich (page 307).

Vienna, Budapest, and Bucharest

From Munich, you'll be back on track with the **Paris to Bucharest** train route, stopping in Vienna and Budapest before reaching Bucharest (page 600).

Transylvania

End this European exploration with an adventurous road trip through the Transylvanian countryside, beginning in the Romanian capital city of Bucharest. Rent a car and plunge deep into the heart of mythic history (page 320).

NORTHERN EUROPEAN LOOP

Number of Days: 25

Cycle from Copenhagen to Berlin before boarding the train and looping through the northeastern corner of Europe, ending in the fashion-forward Finnish capital of Helsinki.

Copenhagen to Berlin

Kick off this epic route by cycling through Denmark and north Germany to the capital of Berlin (page 389).

Berlin, Krakow, and Warsaw

Do the Berlin, Warsaw, and Krakow journey slightly out of order, heading directly to Krakow, and ending in the Polish capital city of Warsaw (page 162).

Vilnius, Riga, and Tallinn

From Warsaw, connect to Vilnius. Swoop through the less-visited northeast corner

hikers walking in Val Ferret along the Tour du Mont Blanc

of Europe, with the option to end in Helsinki (page 688).

THE IBERIAN PENINSULA

Number of Days: 16

This deep dive will take you across the entire Iberian Peninsula. Start in Spain, in the vibrant Mediterranean city of Barcelona before catching the high-speed train to Madrid, then into magical Andalusia, before ending in Porto, Portugal, for a charming ride on the rails of the picturesque Douro Line.

Barcelona and Madrid

Begin this journey in the Catalan Capital of Barcelona before heading inland to Madrid, the political capital of Spain (page 99).

Granada, Córdoba, and Sevilla

From Madrid, take the high-speed train to Granada, where you can follow the **Sevilla, Córdoba, and Granada** itinerary in reverse, basking in the warmth of Andalusia (page 117).

The Douro Line

You can take a short flight from Sevilla to connect with Porto. From there, hop on the Douro Line to explore some of Portugal's finest countryside (page 663).

AN ITALIAN ADVENTURE

Number of Days: 24

To savor the entire country of Italy, consider linking together several journeys—in whole or in part—to create one grand tour of one of Europe's most diverse and incredible countries.

Milan

Begin this route by touring the bustling city of Milan, Italy's economic hub, as in **The Alps** route (page 648). If you have even more time and love the outdoors, consider adding the **Dolomite High Route** (page 439).

Cinque Terre

From Milan, it's an easy jaunt south to the Cinque Terre, where you can follow this picturesque route along the Mediterranean (page 423).

Florence

From the end of the Cinque Terre journey, head south to Florence and pick up the middle of the **Rome, Florence, and Venice** journey (page 150).

Tuscany and Umbria

From Florence, the rolling hills of the Tuscan and Umbrian countryside call for a road trip (page 289).

Rome

After your side trip through Tuscany and Umbria, continue on to Rome and soak in the historic capital (page 141).

Naples, Capri, and the Amalfi Coast

Keep heading south to explore the picturesque coastline and friendly Mediterranean waters of southern Italy (page 536).

EXTENDED ALPINE JOURNEY

Number of Days: 15

If it's the mountains you are craving, add these journeys together for a full exploration of the French, Swiss, and Italian Alps.

The Alps

Begin your journey by exploring the scenic railways between Milan and Geneva, taking the cities in the reverse order of the Alps journey (page 648).

Tour du Mont Blanc

From Geneva, head to Chamonix to start the Tour du Mont Blanc. It's one thing to see the Alps. It's quite another to devote a week to trekking through the quaint pastures and majestic views that make the TMB such a bucket-list multiday hike for nature lovers around the world (page 405).

A MEDITERRANEAN ODYSSEY

Number of Days: 30

You won't quite follow the meandering trail of Odysseus and his storied 10-year journey around the Mediterranean, but combining several routes over a few weeks will definitely give you the sense of an odyssey as you connect the different shores of this vast sea.

Barcelona

Begin in Barcelona, following the corresponding part of the **Barcelona and Madrid** route. Here is where you can first get your feet wet along the playas of the Mediterranean (page 99).

Marseilles

From Barcelona, connect by train to Marseilles in the south of France, where you could detour up the **Rhone Valley** to art-inspiring towns like Arles and Avignon (page 618).

The French Riviera

From Marseilles, reverse the French Riviera rail trip: Begin in Cannes (an easy rail connection with Marseilles) and end in Nice (page 634).

Cinque Terre

Leaving Nice, you can connect by rail through Genoa to the train that runs along the Cinque Terre (page 423).

Naples and the Amalfi Coast

Another rail trip sends you farther south, via Rome, to Naples where you can ferry around the Bay of Naples and the majestic Amalfi Coast (page 536).

The Greek Islands

From Naples, regular direct flights connect with Athens, making it possible to end your odyssey in the home of Odysseus himself, on the whitewashed islands of Greece (page 552).

JOURNEYS AT A GLANCE

CITY HOPPING	Number of Days	Countries	Best Season	Top 3 Experiences	Page
London and Paris	5	England, France	year-round	• Borough Market • West End show • Apero at a Paris café	44
Edinburgh and Glasgow	4	Scotland	spring and summer	• Hiking up Arthur's Seat • Live music • Kelvingrove Art Gallery and Museum	65
Amsterdam, Brussels, and Bruges	5	Netherlands, Belgium	spring and summer	• Gezelligheid at a brown bar • Brussels' Grand Place • Belfry of Bruges	81
Barcelona and Madrid	5	Spain	spring and fall	• Sampling Spanish cuisine at Mercat de la Boqueria • La Sagrada Família • Art at the Prado	99
Sevilla, Córdoba, and Granada	7	Spain	spring and fall	• Attending a flamenco performance • Architecture of Mezquita-Cathedral of Córdoba • The Alhambra's Gardens of the Generalife	117
Rome, Florence, and Venice	7	Italy	spring and fall	• Michelangelo's Sistine Chapel • Climbing Florence's Duomo • Views of Venice's Grand Canal	139
Berlin, Warsaw, and Krakow	7	Germany, Poland	summer	• East Side Gallery • Listening to Chopin • Confronting the past at Auschwitz	162
Prague, Vienna, and Budapest	7	Czech Republic, Austria, Hungary	spring to fall	• Castle experience at Vyšehrad Complex • Schönbrunn Palace • Budapest's thermal baths	184
Zagreb, Ljubljana, and Trieste	5	Croatia, Slovenia, Italy	spring and early summer	• Local produce at Dolac Market • City planning in Ljubljana • Capo in b in Trieste	205

ROAD TRIPS	Number of Days	Countries	Best Season	Top 3 Experiences	Page
Iceland's Ring Road	9	Iceland	summer	• Gullfoss waterfall • Glacial lake of Jökulsárlón • Whale-watching	228
Causeway Coast	2	Northern Ireland	summer	• Black Taxi Tour • Carrick-a-Rede Rope Bridge • Cliffside Dunluce Castle	246
The North Coast 500	7	Scotland	spring and summer	• Windswept Badbea • Driving the Drumbeg Road • Kayaking on Loch Ness	256
Lofoten	5	Norway	summer and early fall	• Surfing in Norway's far north • Hiking up Reinebringen • End of the road at Å	268
Bordeaux and the Pyrenees	4	France	late spring to early fall	• Elegant city center of Bordeaux • Sampling Bordeaux wine • Candlelit procession to the Sanctuary of Notre-Dame de Lourdes	279
Tuscany and Umbria	6	Italy	spring	• Views of the Italian countryside • Wine tasting • Art history at Basilica di San Francesco	289
Romantische Strasse	4	Germany	spring and fall	• Nightwatchman Tour • Rothenburg's Christmas Market • Fairy-tale Neuschwanstein Castle	307
Transylvania	4	Romania	summer	• Bran Castle and its connection to Dracula • Winding through Transfăgărășan Road • Soaking at Therme Bucuresti	320
The Magistrala Coastal Road	9	Croatia, Montenegro	early summer and early fall	• Waterfalls of Krka National Park • Roman monument of Diocletian's Palace • Walking along Dubrovnik's city walls	331

OUTDOOR ADVENTURES	Number of Days	Countries	Best Season	Top 3 Experiences	Page
Dublin and the Wicklow Way	5	Ireland	late spring and summer	• Trad music in Dublin • Ruins at Glendalough • Glenmalure's glacial valley	354
England's Lake District	6	England	spring to early fall	• Kayaking Windermere Lake • England's tallest mountain, Scafell Pike • England's tallest waterfall, Aira Force	364
Holland Junction Network	3	Netherlands	spring and summer	• Dutch apple pie • Listening to the waves at Scheveningen Beach • Architecture of the Cube Houses	377
Copenhagen to Berlin by Bike	9	Denmark, Germany	summer	• White cliffs of Møns Klint • Scenic Mecklenburg Lake District • Selfie in front of Brandenburg Gate	389
Tour du Mont Blanc	8	France, Italy, Switzerland	summer	• Mont Blanc views at Col de la Seigne • Pastoral Les Bovines route • Picnic at Lac Blanc	405
Cinque Terre	3	Italy	late spring and summer	• Sunset tour off the Cinque Terre • Wine tour at Azienda Agricola Cheo • Pesto-making at Nessun Dorma	423
Alta Via 1: Dolomite High Route	9	Italy	summer	• Alpine scenery of Lago di Braies • Preserved World War I tunnels at Galleria Lagazuoi • Waking up above the clouds	439
Camino de Santiago	7	Spain	spring to fall	• Views at Castro de Castromaior • Camino history at Iglesia de Santa María de Melide • Finishing the trek at Catedral de Santiago de Compostela	459

ON THE WATER	Number of Days	Countries	Best Season	Top 3 Experiences	Page
South of England to North of France	5	England, France	spring	• Portsmouth's Historic Dockyard • Remembering D-Day at Omaha Beach • Majesty of Mont-Saint-Michel	484
Rhine River Cruise	8	Netherlands, Germany, France, Switzerland	spring and fall	• Windmills of Kinderdijk • Climbing Cologne Cathedral tower • Drinks of the Rhine region	503
Copenhagen to Oslo	7	Denmark, Norway	spring to fall	• Biking over the Cykelslangen • Kronborg Castle, of *Hamlet* fame • Nobel Peace Center	519
Naples, Capri, and the Amalfi Coast	7	Italy	spring and summer	• Capri boat tour • Hiking the Pathway of the Gods • Seclusion of Santa Croce Beach	536
The Greek Islands	7	Greece	spring to early fall	• Delos Archaeological Site • Art and sun at Alyko Beach • Sunrise in Oia	552
The Canary Islands	5	Spain	year-round	• Year-round beaches • Spain's tallest mountain, El Teide • Forests of Garajonay National Park	568
The Azores	7	Portugal	late spring to early fall	• Views of Sete Cidades Lake • Summiting Mount Pico • Atlantic vistas at Rosais Point	581

CLASSIC RAIL TRIPS AND MORE	Number of Days	Countries	Best Season	Top 3 Experiences	Page
Paris to Bucharest	11	France, Germany, Austria, Hungary, Romania	year-round	• Fairy-tale town of La Petite France • Beer in a boot at Hofbräuhaus • Bucharest's Victory Avenue	600
The Rhone Valley	6	France	spring and fall	• French cuisine in Lyon • Architecture and history of Palais des Papes • Camargue wildlife safari	618
The French Riviera	4	France, Monaco	year-round	• Walking down Promenade des Anglais • People-watching on Place du Casino • Sunset drinks in Juan-les-Pins	634
The Alps	6	Switzerland, Italy	summer	• Horology history at Patek Phillipe Museum • Bernina Express train • Da Vinci's *The Last Supper*	648
The Douro Line	4	Portugal	summer and fall	• Port wine tasting • Douro Historic Steam Train • Côa Valley Archaeological Park	663
The Bergen Line	4	Norway	late spring and summer	• Flåm Railway • Nærøyfjord cruise • Voss Gondol	675
Vilnius, Riga, and Tallinn	7	Lithuania, Estonia, Latvia	late spring to early fall	• Day trip to Trakai Island and Castle • Riga canal cruise • Tallinn's Old Town	688

CITY HOPPING

CITY HOPPING
EDINBURGH AND GLASGOW
Glasgow
Edinburgh
UNITED KINGDOM
Irish Sea
IRELAND
North Sea
AMSTERDAM, BRUSSELS, AND BRUGES
Amsterdam
Bruges
Brussels
London
English Channel
BELGIUM
LONDON AND PARIS
Paris
ATLANTIC OCEAN
FRANCE
Bay of Biscay
BARCELONA AND MADRID
AND.
PORTUGAL
Madrid
Barcelona
SPAIN
SEVILLA, CÓRDOBA, AND GRANADA
Córdoba
Sevilla
Granada
© MOON.COM
MOROCCO
ALGERIA
20°
10°
0°
60°
50°
40°

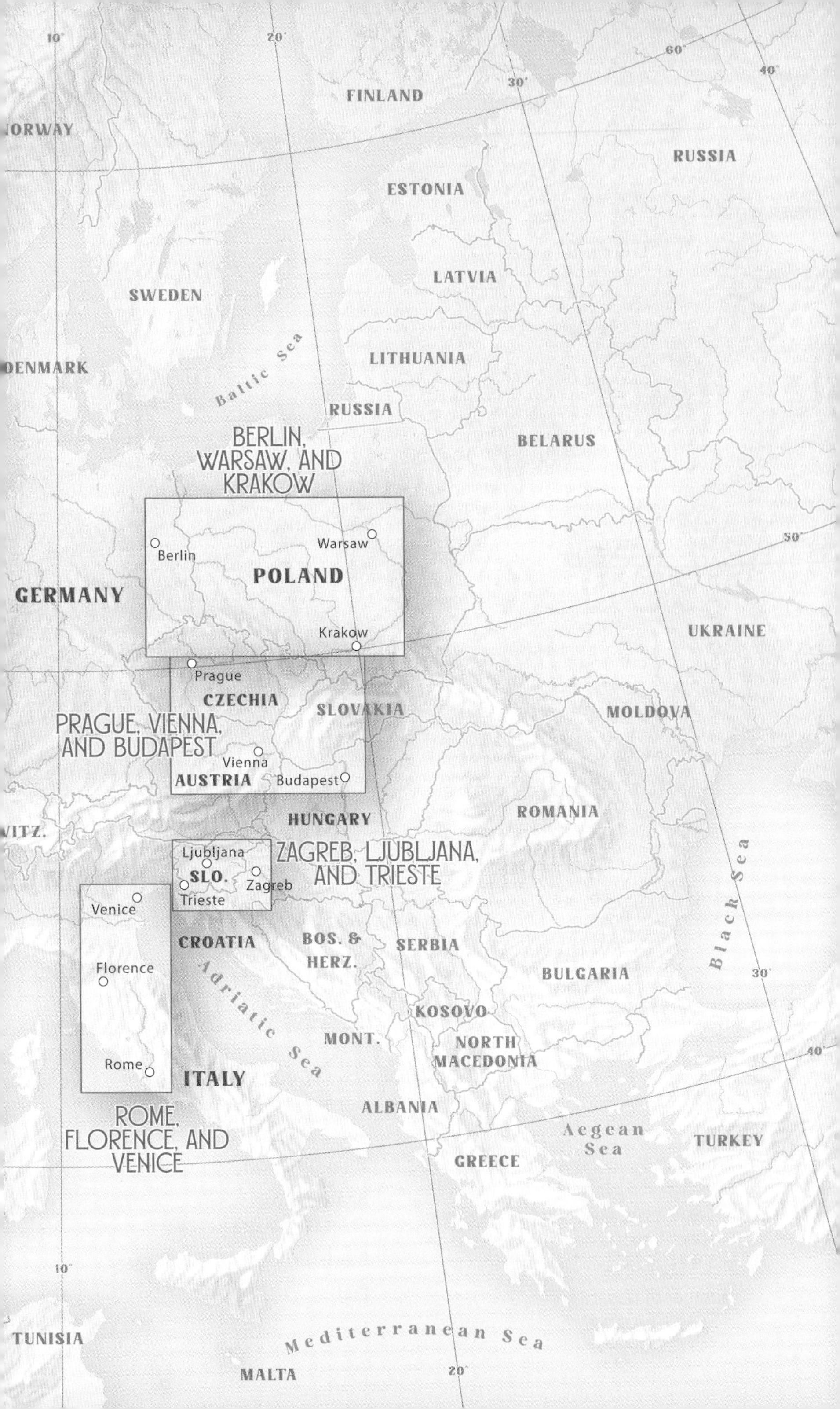

FINLAND
NORWAY
RUSSIA
ESTONIA
LATVIA
SWEDEN
Baltic Sea
DENMARK
LITHUANIA
RUSSIA
BELARUS
BERLIN, WARSAW, AND KRAKOW
Berlin
Warsaw
POLAND
GERMANY
Krakow
UKRAINE
Prague
CZECHIA
SLOVAKIA
MOLDOVA
PRAGUE, VIENNA, AND BUDAPEST
Vienna
AUSTRIA
Budapest
HUNGARY
ROMANIA
SWITZ.
Ljubljana
ZAGREB, LJUBLJANA, AND TRIESTE
SLO.
Zagreb
Trieste
Venice
CROATIA
BOS. & HERZ.
SERBIA
Black Sea
Florence
Adriatic Sea
BULGARIA
KOSOVO
MONT.
NORTH MACEDONIA
Rome
ITALY
ALBANIA
ROME, FLORENCE, AND VENICE
Aegean Sea
TURKEY
GREECE
TUNISIA
Mediterranean Sea
MALTA

LONDON AND PARIS

Why Go: From cozy pubs to outdoor cafés, from red double-decker buses to art-nouveau metro signs, and from Big Ben to the Eiffel Tower, London and Paris are on just about every European traveler's wish list.

Number of Days: 5

Total Distance: 490 km (305 mi)

Seasons: Year-round, except August, when many businesses in Paris close

Start: London

End: Paris

Two of the world's greatest cities, London and Paris, are located less than three hours' train ride from one another, making for one of the best city-hopping trips on Earth. Despite their proximity and intertwined histories, these two urban centers could hardly be more different. Compare, for example, the Day-Glo freneticism of Piccadilly Circus to the laid-back languor of backstreet bistros, or London's melting pot of different architectural styles to Paris's uniform Haussmann blocks, or a pint of lager to a bottle of burgundy. Visiting both cities provides a whirlwind lesson in those dramatic differences, and it's a trip you'll never forget. What's more, this route is extremely straightforward because both destinations are major international flight hubs, and, of course, are connected by that undersea marvel of modern travel the Eurostar.

TOP 3

★ Smelling and tasting your way through **Borough Market,** where dozens of stalls cook up British and global flavors under an elegant Victorian roof (page 48).

★ Catching a show at the **West End,** whether it's a musical that has been running for decades, the latest smash hit play, or a reimagining of Shakespeare (page 52).

★ Enjoying **an apero at a Paris café,** a quintessentially Parisian—and European—experience (page 60).

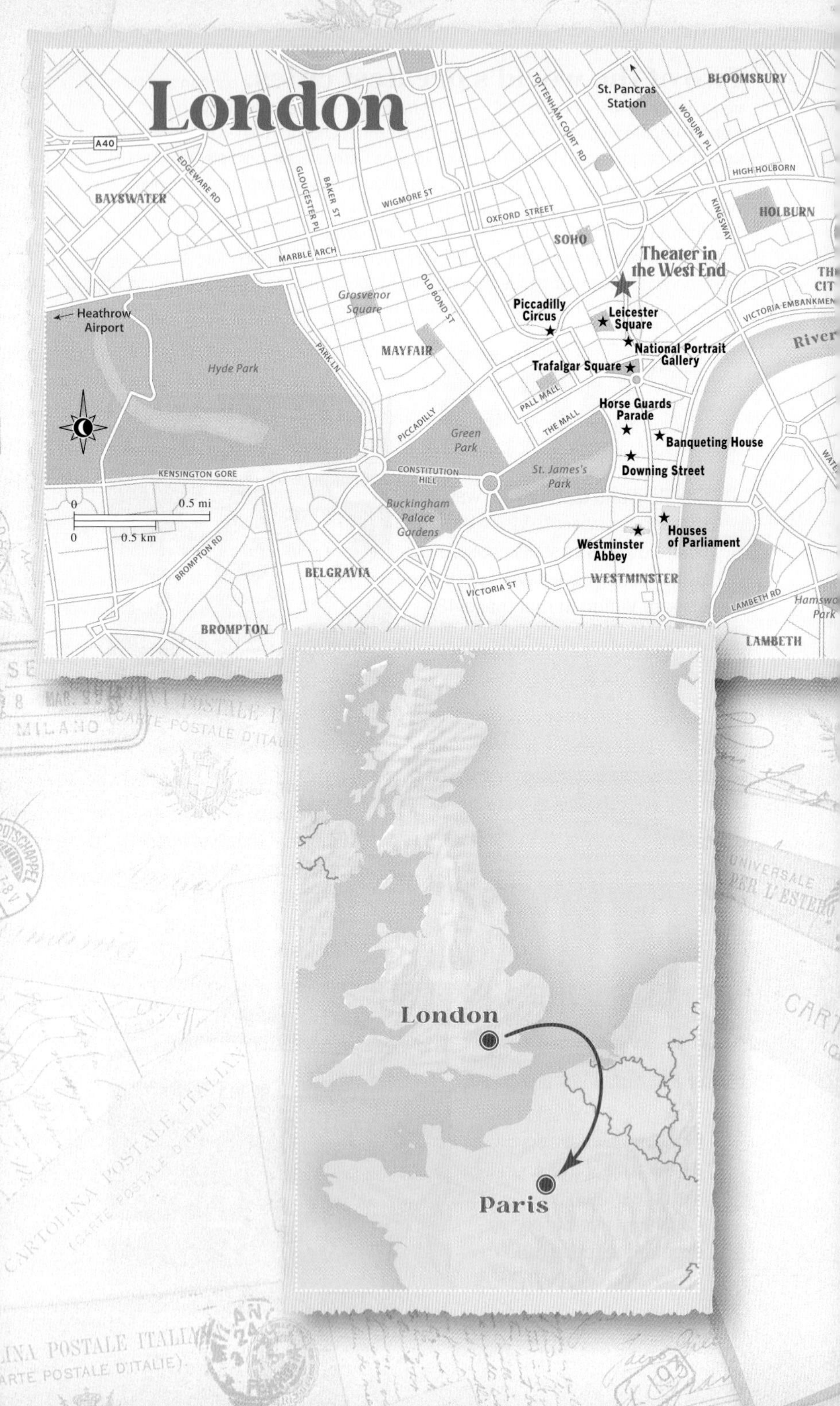

London
A40
BAYSWATER
EDGEWARE RD
GLOUCESTER PL
BAKER ST
WIGMORE ST
OXFORD STREET
TOTTENHAM COURT RD
St. Pancras Station
BLOOMSBURY
WOBURN PL
HIGH HOLBORN
KINGSWAY
HOLBURN
SOHO
MARBLE ARCH
Theater in the West End
Grosvenor Square
OLD BOND ST
Piccadilly Circus
Leicester Square
VICTORIA EMBANKMENT
Heathrow Airport
PARK LN
MAYFAIR
National Portrait Gallery
Hyde Park
Trafalgar Square
PALL MALL
THE MALL
Horse Guards Parade
PICCADILLY
Green Park
Banqueting House
Downing Street
KENSINGTON GORE
CONSTITUTION HILL
St. James's Park
0
0.5 mi
0
0.5 km
Buckingham Palace Gardens
Houses of Parliament
Westminster Abbey
BROMPTON RD
BELGRAVIA
WESTMINSTER
VICTORIA ST
LAMBETH RD
BROMPTON
LAMBETH
London
Paris

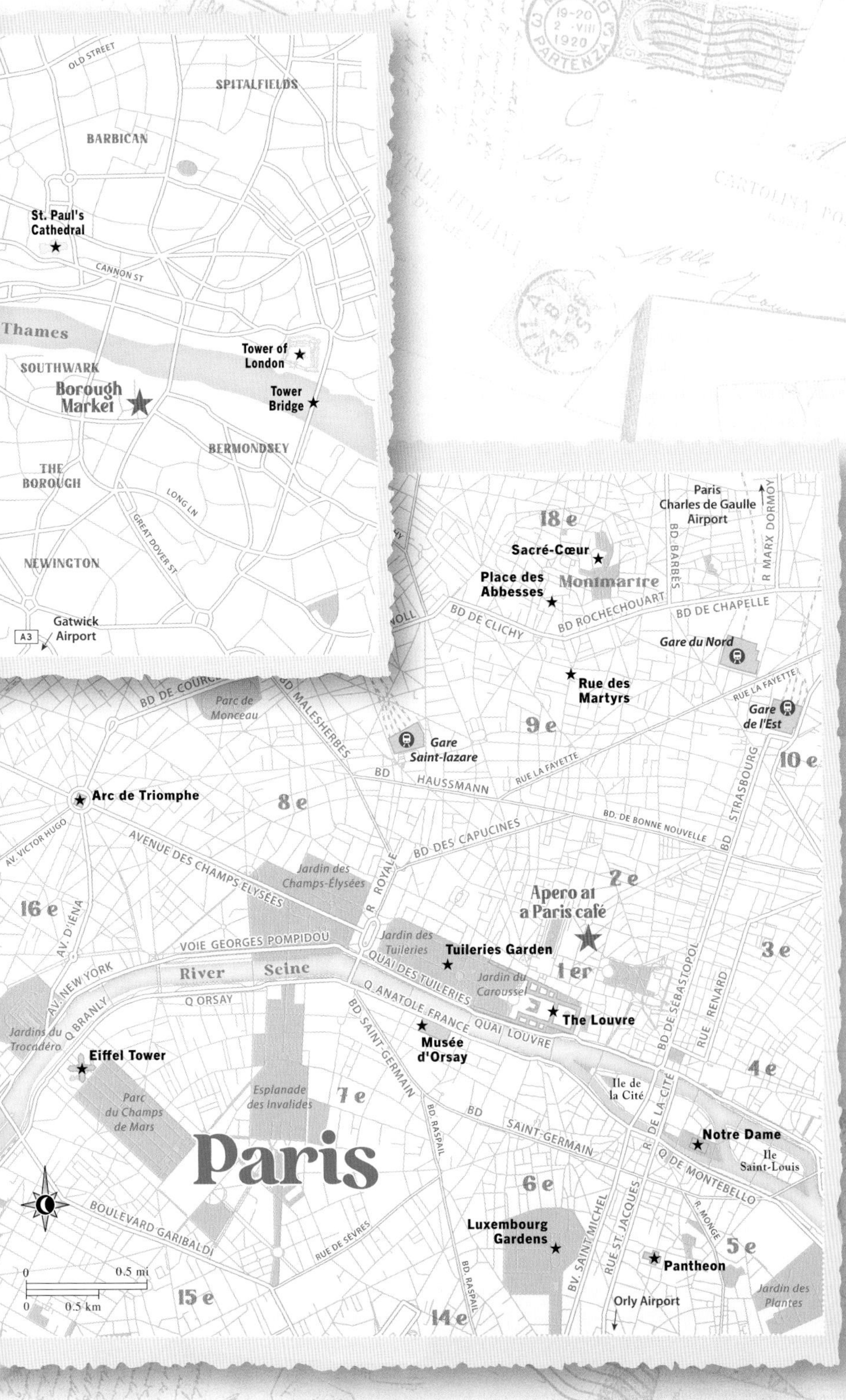

OLD STREET
SPITALFIELDS
BARBICAN
St. Paul's Cathedral
CANNON ST
Thames
Tower of London
SOUTHWARK
Borough Market
Tower Bridge
BERMONDSEY
THE BOROUGH
LONG LN
GREAT DOVER ST
NEWINGTON
A3
Gatwick Airport
Paris Charles de Gaulle Airport
18 e
Sacré-Cœur
Place des Abbesses
Montmartre
BD BARBÈS
R MARX DORMOY
BD DE CLICHY
BD ROCHECHOUART
BD DE CHAPELLE
Gare du Nord
Rue des Martyrs
RUE LA FAYETTE
Gare de l'Est
BD DE COURCELLES
Parc de Monceau
BD MALESHERBES
Gare Saint-lazare
9 e
10 e
BD HAUSSMANN
RUE LA FAYETTE
Arc de Triomphe
8 e
BD. DE BONNE NOUVELLE
BD STRASBOURG
AV. VICTOR HUGO
AVENUE DES CHAMPS ELYSÉES
BD DES CAPUCINES
R ROYALE
Jardin des Champs-Élysées
2 e
Apero at a Paris café
16 e
AV. D'IÉNA
VOIE GEORGES POMPIDOU
Jardin des Tuileries
Tuileries Garden
3 e
River Seine
AV. NEW YORK
QUAI DES TUILERIES
Jardin du Carousel
1 er
Q ORSAY
Q BRANLY
Q. ANATOLE FRANCE
QUAI LOUVRE
The Louvre
BD DE SÉBASTOPOL
RUE RENARD
Jardins du Trocadéro
BD SAINT-GERMAIN
Musée d'Orsay
Eiffel Tower
4 e
Ile de la Cité
Parc du Champs de Mars
Esplanade des Invalides
7 e
BD. RASPAIL
BD SAINT-GERMAIN
R DE LA CITÉ
Notre Dame
Ile Saint-Louis
Paris
6 e
Q DE MONTEBELLO
R. MONGE
BOULEVARD GARIBALDI
RUE DE SÈVRES
Luxembourg Gardens
BV. SAINT MICHEL
RUE ST. JACQUES
5 e
Pantheon
0
0.5 mi
0
0.5 km
15 e
BD. RASPAIL
14 e
Orly Airport
Jardin des Plantes
MILANO 19-20 2 - VIII 1920 PARTENZA
CARTOLINA POSTALE

London

Where to Stay: Southwark, one of London's eastern neighborhoods, which are its oldest

Arrive by: Plane to either London Heathrow or London Gatwick

DAY 1

★ 1. Breakfast at Borough Market

8 Southwark St.; tel. 020 7407 1002; 10am-5pm Mon.-Thurs., 10am-6pm Fri., 8am-5pm Sat., 10am-2pm Sun.

The best way to fortify any day in the British capital, this glorious produce market has been feeding hungry Londoners since the 12th century at least. Its current wrought iron covering was built in the mid-1800s. Make your way into the market sampling whatever morsels the eager stallholders thrust your way; it's worth making at least one full turn of the market, tasting cheese, sampling oysters, and smelling truffles, before settling on anything in particular.

2. Tower Bridge

Tower Bridge Rd.; tel. 020 7403 3761; www.towerbridge.org.uk; engine room and walkway open 9:30am-6pm daily; adults £10.60, children £5.40

With your hunger satisfied, head east toward the **Queen's Walk,** the pedestrianized Thames quayside built to celebrate Elizabeth II's Silver Jubilee. To get here, head down Montague Close, follow the road under the southern end of **London Bridge** to reach Tooley Street, and turn left into the Hay's Galleria shopping complex. Upon exiting the other side, the Thames, the City of London, and the museum ship the HMS *Belfast* (www.iwm.org.uk/visits/hms-belfast) open out before you, and you'll see the Tower Bridge looming proudly to the right. One of London's most iconic monuments, this neo-Gothic bascule bridge was built in the late 19th century, ingeniously allowing a crossing point in the east of London without disrupting river traffic.

Tower Bridge

Key Reservations

As some of the most visited cities in the world, both London and Paris have robust tourist infrastructures, which means you don't have to worry about booking too far ahead in terms of hotels, and all the restaurants listed below have a fast enough turnaround that there's no need to reserve a table.

WEST END SHOWS

If there's a specific West End play you want to see, book at least two weeks ahead to make sure to get a ticket at the price you want. If not, discount tickets can be snapped up on the day from booths around Leicester Square.

Eiffel Tower

EIFFEL TOWER

It's well worth booking a couple of days ahead to go up the Eiffel Tower; you will be given an e-ticket and allotted time slot, so you can escape the worst of queues.

PARIS MUSEUM PASS

www.parismuseumpass.fr; 2-day pass €52

This itinerary only includes three museums covered by the Paris Museum Pass, but if you plan to visit one more—such as the Musée de l'Orangerie in the Tuileries (page 604)—within the two days, it may be worth purchasing this popular pass to save money and avoid some of the lines.

THE EUROSTAR

Be sure to book your Eurostar tickets well in advance in order to keep the price down. Try to avoid traveling on the weekends to get the best deal.

3. Tower of London

www.hrp.org.uk/tower-of-london; 10am-5:30pm Sun.-Mon. and 9am-5:30pm Tues.-Sat. Mar.-Oct., 10am-4:30pm Sun.-Mon. and 9am-4:30pm Tues.-Sat. Nov.-Feb.; adults £29.90, children £16.90

Walk across the Tower Bridge to the Tower of London, founded by William the Conqueror in 1066. By turns a royal residence, a castle, a treasury, the country's mint, and a much-feared prison, the "Tower" refers to a whole complex of buildings centered around the eponymous White Tower structure. Home to the British Royal family's crown jewels, the red-smocked Beefeater guards, and countless ravens, it's an essential stop on any London itinerary. Allow around three hours for a worthwhile tour.

There's a whole street of restaurants and cafés west of the Tower's walls. Try the **Byward Kitchen & Bar** (Byward St.; tel. 020 7481 3533; www.bywardkitchenandbar.com; 9:30am-5pm Wed.-Sun.; lunch from £9), with a modern and inexpensive menu in a trendy and relaxed setting.

4. St. Paul's Cathedral

St. Paul's Churchyard; tel. 020 7246 8350; www.stpauls.co.uk; 8:30am-4:30pm Mon.-Sat.; adults

£21, children £9 (discount if booked ahead), check website to attend services for free

You'll walk through the City of London, where this sprawling metropolis began, en route to St. Paul's Cathedral, recognized the world over for its Christopher Wren-designed dome. There's been a church on this site since 604 CE, though the current building was constructed after London's Great Fire in the late 1600s. Famous British luminaries buried here include the Duke of Wellington, Admiral Lord Horatio Nelson, and William Blake; the ticket also allows access to the famous "whispering gallery" on the inside rim of the dome, and all the way up to the spire, which offers splendid views of London. An hour is enough to do the building justice.

5. Dinner at Ye Olde Cheshire Cheese

145 Fleet St.; tel. 020 7353 6170; noon-11pm Mon.-Sat.; entrées from £10

Just a short walk from St. Paul's down Fleet Street, Ye Olde Cheshire Cheese has been pulling pints since the 17th century and has served a veritable who's who of the London literary scene: Samuel Johnson, Charles Dickens, G. K. Chesterton, even Mark Twain dropped in here once upon a time. Enormous, wood paneled, and warren-y, Ye Olde Cheshire Cheese can be cavernous or cozy by turns, with inexpensive, own-brand beer and satisfying, old-fashioned food.

DAY 2

1. Uber Boat by Thames Clippers

London Bridge City Pier, London Bridge Walk; www.thamesclippers.com; boats every 20 minutes, see website for timetable; £7.30

There are few better ways to get around London than by boat. After another breakfast in Borough Market—make it hearty, perhaps the Great British breakfast at **Maria's Market Café** (The Market Porter, 9 Stoney St.; tel. 020 7407 1002; https://boroughmarket.org.uk/traders/marias-market-cafe; 10am-5pm Mon.-Thurs., 10am-6pm Fri., 8am-5pm Sat., 10am-2pm Sun.; breakfast from £6)—find

left, St. Paul's Cathedral; right, National Portrait Gallery

WATCH

Amelie: The whimsical adventures of Amelie Poulin, based mainly in Paris's hilltop Montmartre neighborhood, offer a portrait of Parisian life that effervesces with hyper-real charm, yet often comes closer to the city's reality than some cynics might suspect.

Sherlock: There are plenty of brilliant movies set in London, but few capture as broad an image of the capital as this series starring Benedict Cumberbatch. Updating the adventures of Baker Street's most famous resident, the series presents the modern city with all its grit and frenetic charm.

READ

A Moveable Feast by Ernest Hemingway: Even the French love American writer Ernest Hemmingway's memoir, which looks with rose-tinted hindsight at Paris during the 1920s, when it was a playground for the hard-partying artists and writers whose work went on to remake the world.

White Teeth by Zadie Smith: Few books conjure the wild multiplicity of London better than this astonishing debut about the coming together of two multi-racial families in the city across the latter half of the 20th century—as exuberant and digressive as the capital itself.

LISTEN

Grime: The last truly major music genre to have come out of London, Grime is a form of rap that emerged from a combination of jungle, dance hall, and hip-hop. Artists to check out include Stormzy, Skepta, and Lady Leshurr.

Coffee Break French: This charming, relaxed podcast, hosted by a Scottish guy called Mark, is one of the most approachable language courses on the market, with lessons for all levels, including absolute beginners.

your way to London Bridge pier and hop on a boat. Speed down the river to Westminster. You'll see the City and St. Paul's on your right, and Shakespeare's Globe, the Tate Modern, and the London Eye on your left, and pass under the Millennium Footbridge, Blackfriars, and Waterloo on your way. You'll disembark at Westminster pier, in plain sight of the Houses of Parliament.

2. Westminster Walk

From Westminster pier, an easy 20-minute walk will take you past much of the major apparatus of the British state. You can't miss the **Houses of Parliament,** its striking, instantly recognizable Gothic revival architecture dominating the river edge. Built in the mid-19th century after an earlier parliament building burned down, its most iconic feature is, of course, the Clock Tower, erroneously referred to as **Big Ben** (this is actually the nickname for the clock's main bell). In front of the building is Parliament square, base for a permanent coterie of protestors, news broadcasters, and statues of many of the major figures of British political history.

Westminster Abbey sits on the south side of the square. Dedicated to Saint Peter, construction on this Gothic building started in the 11th century, and it's where every English monarch has been crowned and buried since

1066. Resisting the urge to join the queues to the abbey (there's just so much to do in London!); it's time to make your way up Whitehall, passing **The Cenotaph** (Britain's national war memorial), the entrance to **Downing Street** (residence of British prime ministers, restricted for tourists), **Banqueting House** (the last remnant of the renaissance Palace of Whitehall), and the entrance to **Horse Guards Parade,** continually guarded by two mounted members of the household cavalry in full military regalia. Conclude your walk in **Trafalgar Square,** dominated by a statue of Lord Admiral Horatio Nelson, famous for his victory at the Battle of Trafalgar.

3. National Portrait Gallery

St. Martin's Pl.; tel. 020 7306 0055; www.npg.org.uk; 10am-6pm Sat.-Wed., 10am-9pm Thurs.-Fri.; free

There's a mind-boggling number of free museums to visit in London, which can make deciding which ones are worthy of your time a tricky business. The National Portrait Gallery, at the northeastern corner of Trafalgar Square, is an excellent bet, offering both an engaging journey through history and a fantastic artistic experience in one. Home to the largest collection of portraits in the world, it features contemporary images of just about every major figure to strut across the stage of British culture and politics in the past 1,000 years. Stare into the eyes of Anne Boleyn, the Bronte sisters, JMW Turner, and many more.

4. Piccadilly Circus

From the National Portrait gallery, head north up the theater- and bookshop-lined Charring Cross Road, right into the heart of the West End. Make a left into the always busy Leicester Square, home of London's biggest cinemas. (If you haven't done so already, now is a good time to buy cheap theater tickets for the evening from the last-minute **Leicester Square Box Office.**) Press on to the other side of the square and you'll emerge into Piccadilly Circus, the iconic junction dominated by flashing lights and centered around the delicate Shaftesbury Memorial Fountain, commonly referred to as "Eros."

5. High Tea at Fortnum & Mason

181 Piccadilly, St. James's; tel. 020 7734 8040; www.fortnumandmason.com; 10am-7pm Mon.-Sat., 11:30am-6pm Sun.

South, then west from Piccadilly on Piccadilly Street, Fortnum & Mason ranks among the most venerable department stores in London. Founded in 1707, it boasts stately staircases and plush red carpets that positively burst with luxury. The **food hall** is an excellent place to buy souvenirs that bring a taste of England back home. For now, stop for a spot of high tea. The fourth floor **Diamond Jubilee Tea Salon** offers some of the best in the capital. It's not cheap (£60 per person), but it's well worth it, including a wide variety of posh crustless sandwiches, scones, and bite-sized savory delights—plus tea, of course.

★ 6. Night Out at the Theater in the West End

Aim to finish your tea by about 6:15pm, then step out onto Piccadilly Street and hail one of London's famous black cabs to get you to the theater. Easily, one of London's best experiences, this is both about the show you go to see, and the true experience of a night out. Most of the theaters in the West End were built in the 19th century, and their walls positively exhale history. Gathering in the bar before or during the interval of a show is a tradition with actors all the way back through Lawrence Olivier to the days of the Victorian stage. Dress tends to be smart casual, and you'll find yourself surrounded by people similarly "up in town" for the night, whether from the London suburbs or farther afield. The atmosphere is almost always one of anticipation and excited chatter.

(clockwise from top) the Westminster Walk; Piccadilly Circus; Horse Guards Parade

West End Theatre

London has been synonymous with theater since the days of Shakespeare, and its famous West End district had its origins not long after. Always a popular entertainment, theater nevertheless long had a less than salubrious reputation, and the large theater houses began to spring up here precisely because it was once one of the poorer, cheaper areas of the city. The very oldest, still-running theatre in London, the **Theatre Royal** on Drury Lane, was established way back in 1663, though it was not until the 19th century that the West End secured its position as the capital's home for popular theater par excellence.

Today, there are no fewer than 39 theatres in the 21-square-km (8.3-square-mi) area bordered by Oxford Street to the north, the Strand to the south, Chancery Lane to the east, and Regent Street to the west. Every night they play host to a roster of both long-running and new musicals and plays, with many of the world's most famous actors commonly treading their historic boards. Among the most famous, and deeply ensconced, are the musicals *Les Miserables* and *The Phantom of the Opera,* as well as the Agatha Christie play *The Mousetrap,* which opened in 1952 and has the reputation as the world's longest running play.

BUYING TICKETS

There are numerous ways to buy tickets, including through individual theatre websites, discount box offices on **Leicester Square** (42 Cranbourn St.; tel. 020 7087 2999; www.lsbo.co.uk; 10am-7pm Mon.-Sat.; tickets from £20), and at the theaters themselves. Ticket prices vary widely, though it's always a good idea to book well in advance to get the price and seat that you want, especially with the popular short-run plays.

Many theaters release a number of discount tickets the morning of the performance itself, putting even the biggest-name shows within everyone's reach. Numbers of these are limited, though, and acquiring them means turning up in person and queuing before the box offices open (usually at 10am). For the most popular shows it's worth turning up at 9am or earlier. This also gives you a chance to meet your fellow theatergoers and can become as much a part of the experience as actually going to the shows themselves.

Paris

DAY 3

Where to Stay: Latin Quarter, classic Paris with lots of cafés. Great for an aimless stroll and well-connected to more distant sights.

Arrive by: Eurostar from London St. Pancras Station to Paris Gare du Nord (2.5 hours)

1. Traveling in Style on the Eurostar

St. Pancras International Station, Euston Rd., London; tel. 020 7843 7688; https://stpancras.com; open 24 hours

In the morning, head to **St. Pancras,** where you catch the Eurostar to Paris. There are few better ways to start a journey to the city of romance than with flutes of champagne right at the station itself, letting the tastes of France come to meet you at the concourse bar. And if you feel like something special for your grand arrival, visit **Terminus Nord** (23 Rue de Dunkerque; tel. 01 42 85 05 15; www.terminusnord.com; 6:45am-midnight Mon.-Sat., 7am-11pm Sun.; six oysters from €13), a venerable and always bustling brasserie directly opposite Paris's Gare du Nord with particularly good oysters. Note that the time zone in Paris is one hour later than in London.

top, St. Pancras Station; bottom, Notre Dame

2. Notre Dame

6 Parvis Notre-Dame-Pl. Jean-Paul II; tel. 01 42 34 56 10; www.notredamedeparis.fr; currently closed to the public

Take a taxi to your hotel in the Latin Quarter (20-30 minutes depending on traffic; there's a taxi rank directly outside the front of Gare du Nord; €15). Once you've deposited your bags at your hotel, it's time to get to know your neighborhood. The Latin Quarter has long been Paris's university district; its name derives from the student population, which used to converse in Latin. Start in front of the Fontaine St Michel, built in 1860 at the same time as Napoleon III's remodeling of the city, then head east down the narrow Rue de la Huchette, part of a complex of alleys just back from the Seine. Pop out on the Rue du Petit Pont, which you cross to get to Rue de la Bûcherie.

Hard to miss, Paris's most famous church rises high across the river to your left. It is still being rebuilt after the fire in 2019. Off-limits to visitors for the foreseeable future, there's still something magical about seeing this masterpiece of Gothic architecture being worked on. Construction of the building began in 1163, and truly has been the norm rather than the exception ever since. Getting to see what it looks like when a cathedral is being built is as good a way as any to travel through time.

3. Pantheon

Place du Panthéon; tel. 01 44 32 18 00; www.paris-pantheon.fr; 10am-6pm Oct.-Mar., 10am-6:30pm Apr.-Sept.; adults €11.50, under 18 free

Carry on east through the leafy Square

Regional Cuisine

LONDON

- **Beer and Pub Grub:** A great British institution, pubs in London can nevertheless prove a little hit-or-miss. When you find a good one, there are few better places on Earth to spend an afternoon drinking. Among the best are the family-run **Seven Stars** (53 Carey St.) in Lincoln's Inn Fields; the warren-y, ancient **Ye Olde Cheshire Cheese** (145 Fleet St.) off Fleet Street; and the riverside **Anchor** (34 Park St.), not far from Borough Market. For the true British experience, forego the larger in lieu of traditional English ale. Mostly locally brewed, they are served warm and flat, but don't let that put you off, as they're also delicious, offer an authentic flavor of the British past, and are mostly of a low enough alcohol content that you can drink several and hardly notice. Food in pubs is of the simple, traditional variety and must be ordered at the bar. If in doubt of what to order, fish-and-chips is usually a reliable bet.
- **The Full English:** With eggs, sausage, bacon, black pudding, fried bread, mushrooms, and beans, the full English breakfast remains resolutely popular across the capital (with good vegetarian options also on offer). **Maria's Market Café** (The Market Porter, 9 Stoney St.) at Borough Market is a good choice, but frankly searching out the best full English in London misses the point. It is a cheap, everyday dish that you'll find in its most authentic form in whatever "greasy spoon caff" is closest to you when you need it—identifiable by their molded plastic seating, unpretentious decor, and low, low prices. Pay a fiver for enough food to feed an army, unfurl one of the complimentary tabloid papers, and enjoy!
- **High Tea:** Scones, small sandwiches, and sweet patisserie treats served on a tiered platter, and of course a steaming pot of loose-leaf tea; this is the very last word in British refinement. It has its origins in the 18th century as a meal taken in the early afternoon by the British upper classes when their servants were away, precisely because it was easy to prepare. The **Ritz Hotel** (150 Piccadilly, St. James's) is one the most famous places serving high tea. If you plan to go here, book ahead!
- **Indian, Pakistani, and Bangladeshi Food:** A product of Britain's colonial heritage, food from the subcontinent is now thoroughly ensconced

Rene Viviani, home to the oldest tree in Paris, leaving at its southeastern corner to take the Rue Lagrange to the Boulevard Saint-Germain. Cross over the crossroads onto Rue Monge, and then make an almost immediate right onto the Rue de la Montagne Sainte Geneviève. Following this winding road for about five minutes uphill will take you through the delightful Place Jacqueline De Romilly surrounded by student cafés and past **Saint-Étienne-du-Mont** (Place Sainte-Geneviève; tel. 01 43 54 11 79; www.saintetiennedumont.fr), one of the most unusual and splendid churches of Paris.

You'll eventually reach the Pantheon. Built as a church during the reign of Louis XV, this towering neoclassical edifice modeled after the Pantheon in Rome has long since been co-opted as the secular resting place for the great men and women of the French Republic. It's

in the country's national cuisine. Curry houses abound in London, with a particular constancy around East London's **Brick Lane.** With their starched white tablecloths and heavy silver cutlery, they offer a great sense of occasion, often at a reasonable price. The food tends to be creamier and meatier than in south Asia, exemplified by Chicken Tikka Masala, a curry invented in Britain that now frequently ranks as the nation's favorite dish.

PARIS

- **The Formule:** In France, a meal is so much more than just food; it's a ritual. In the cafés and bistros across Paris, menus offer three-part deals, including starter, main, and desert. If you have the time, it's worth taking advantage of these, for they offer both the best deals and the freshest ingredients. The classic is probably to start with an egg mayonnaise, chase it with an order of steak frites (which will often come bathed in a sauce, so hold the ketchup), and finish it all off with a crème brûlée.
- **Baked Goods:** One of Paris's crowning glories, its bakeries are the most numerous kind of artists workshops across the city. For prices that are almost criminally low, on almost every street corner you can enjoy some of the best breads, croissants, and pastries anywhere in the world. There are a few consistently famous ones, but the real trick if you want the very best is to Google the results of the "concours de la meilleure baguette de Paris," where the champion **baguettes** are awarded for any particular year (there are similar awards for croissants and other baked goods that you can search for, too). Competition is almost unbelievably stiff, but winning barely affects the prices at all.
- **Apero:** A drink and a time to drink that is also a state of mind, apero is taken just as afternoon slips into evening. The apero can be anything from a pint of beer to a pastis, and is usually served with a light snack, such as dried sausage or olives. It makes the perfect precursor to an evening's dining and is best characterized by the sense of anticipation it imparts. Pull up a chair in a Montmartre café and you can combine it with some top-rate people watching, too. And while there's no technical definition to the kinds of drinks you can enjoy it with, the archetypal apero is probably a **kir:** a delicious mix of white wine and black currant liquor.

also home to an example of a Foucault's Pendulum—a device invented by 19th-century physicist Léon Foucault to prove the rotation of the Earth—swinging suspended from inside its dome.

4. Luxembourg Gardens

tel. 01 42 34 20 00; www.senat.fr/visite/jardin/index.html; open daily, hours change according to daylight, see website for details; free

Directly down the Rue Soufflot from the Pantheon, the Luxembourg Gardens are the pinnacle of horticultural refinement, their geometric lawns and flower beds and elegant paths of crushed stone designed at the behest of Marie de Medici in the early 1600s. Relax on the pond-side iron chairs, or watch the chess games played daily in the park's southwest corner. The large, elaborate building to the north is the **Palais de Luxembourg,** home of the French senate, and don't miss the **Fontaine de Medici** in its shadow.

(top to bottom) Luxembourg Gardens; the Louvre; Arc de Triomphe; Eiffel Tower

5. Dinner at Le Perraudin

157 Rue Saint-Jacques; tel. 01 46 33 15 75; https://leperraudin.fr; noon-2pm and 7pm-10pm Mon.-Sat.; beef bourguignon €20

The city is awash with bistros and restaurants, and Le Perraudin is among the best in the Latin Quarter—once favored by no less a French celebrity than the philosopher Roland Barthes. With its gingham tablecloths and wood fixtures, it's as traditional as a song by Edith Piaf, offering a wonderful beef bourguignon at an affordable price.

DAY 4

1. Tuileries Garden

7:30am-7:30pm daily; free

After grabbing a morning croissant and coffee at a traditional Parisian café like **Brasserie La Contrescarpe** (57 Rue Lacépède; tel. 01 43 36 82 88; www.facebook.com/Brasserie-la-Contrescarpe-476066745888070; 8am-2am daily; croissant and café crème €5), hop on the Metro to Place de la Concorde. Paris's largest public square is centered around an obelisk from Luxor, gifted to the French by Egypt in 1829. Stroll east through the Tuileries. Created by Catherine de Medici, these were originally the gardens to the Tuileries Palace, though they have been open to the public for more than 300 years. Keep your eyes peeled for the nonchalantly brilliant sculptures and the goats used to prune the grass. There are also a couple of cafés—a little overpriced, but great for a coffee on a sunny day.

2. The Louvre

Rue de Rivoli; tel. 01 40 20 50 50; www.louvre.fr; 9am-6pm Wed.-Mon., 9am-9:45pm Fri.; adults advance online ticket €17, adults on-site ticket €15, under 18 or under 26 from EEA members free

Dodge the queues to the world's most famous museum by not lining up outside I. M. Pei's glass pyramid, but rather descend on one of the staircases either side of the mini-Arc du Triomphe du

TO TAKE *Home*

MEN'S CLOTHING AND ACCESSORIES

Just a block away from London's Savile Row, south, then west from Piccadilly, on **Jermyn Street** you'll find every article of clothing associated with the "English gentleman," from shirt makers to fine leather shoe shops, milliners, and luxury barbers. If a new suit is not in the cards, £42 can hardly be better spent than on a traditional hot towel wet shave at **Geo F. Trumpers** (1 Duke of York St., St. James's, London; tel. 020 7734 6553; www.trumpers.com; 9am-5:30pm Mon.-Fri., 9am-5pm Sat.; shaves from £42).

TAXIDERMY

For something truly unique, head to **Deyrolle** (46 Rue du Bac, Paris; tel. 01 42 22 30 07; www.deyrolle.com; 10am-7pm Mon.-Sat.), a taxidermy store founded in the 1830s. The second floor of this shop is effectively one of the best free museums in Paris, boasting a whole menagerie of stuffed animals, from polar bears to peacocks. And if you want to walk away with a souvenir pin-mounted butterfly or a leopard's head, you can (expect something in the latter category to be quite expensive, though).

Carousel located on the rise where the Tuileries ends. From here, you can reach the museum's central underground atrium space from which its three wings extend.

Originally the French Royal Palace, then made home to a number of artists' workshops under Louis XIV, the Louvre was opened as a public museum during the French Revolution, then had its collection substantially increased under Napoleon and the subsequent rise of French colonialism. Likely, you're going to want to see the big hitters, which means following the signs to the Mona Lisa, the Venus de Milo, and the Egyptian collection. The Louvre's real joy, however, is found in its less crowded sections, which in almost any other museum in the world would be front and center of the show. Give yourself at least three hours for a proper self-guided Louvre experience, grabbing a snack at the central court's **café** to keep up your energy. This a museum that really benefits from a guided tour; **Paris Muse** (https://parismuse.com) offers one of the best.

3. Arc de Triomphe

Place Charles de Gaulle; tel. 01 55 37 73 77; www.paris-arc-de-triomphe.fr; 10am-10:30pm daily; adults €12, under 18 and under 26 from EU member states free

Technically, the **Champs-Élysées,** aka Paris's most famous shopping street, starts at the western edge of the Place de la Concorde, but much of the road is just park-lined avenue, and though it's perfectly possible to walk, it's more than 1.6 km (1 mi) long and not the most stimulating walk in the French capital. Better to get on Line 1 at the Tuileries metro station and ride up to **Georges V.** From there, all the flagship fashion stores you could want are a stone's throw away, as is the Arc de Triomphe.

Ironically, the world's most famous triumphal arch was commissioned by Napoleon to celebrate his victory at the battle of Austerlitz, but by the time it was finished Napoleon had lost the war and was dead. Well, it did take more than 30 years to build, and at 50 m (164 ft) high, the structure remains an awe-inspiring piece of architecture, and it has a viewing platform on the top that offers some of the best views of Paris, not to mention the automotive ballet on the anarchic roundabout below.

4. The Eiffel Tower

Champ de Mars, 5 Avenue Anatole; tel. 0892 70 12 39; 9:30am-10:30pm daily; elevator to top adults €26.80, ages 12-24 €13.40, ages 4-11 €6.70, under 4 free (stair/elevator options also available)

Wander down the Avenue Kleber from the Arc de Triomphe's giddying roundabout, and you will reach the Place de Trocadéro, and from there cross the river to the Eiffel Tower (unsurprisingly, you really can't miss it!). The singular most iconic structure in all of France was built as part of the 1889 World's Fair, with the express intention of being the tallest building in the world at the time. It was famously only meant to be temporary—and almost as famously loved and loathed at the time in almost equal measure. Now, the Paris skyline would be unimaginable without it. Going up is a ton of fun—it's worth taking the steps if you're not too tired, as it's cheaper, avoids queues, and gives a general sense of gathering grandeur as you get higher. Note the public-access steps only reach level 2, so you'll have to combine them with the elevators if you want to go all the way up. Expect the visit to take a little more than two hours. Booking ahead is essential.

If you're feeling peckish after you're visit, head south on the Champs de Mars to the delightful, pedestrianized **Rue Cler,** a slice of classic Paris lined by market stalls and a number of good cafés.

TOP EXPERIENCE

★ 5. Apero at the Deux Magots

6 Pl. Saint-Germain des Prés; tel. 01 45 48 55 25; www.lesdeuxmagots.fr; 7:30am-midnight daily; kir €9

Retrace your steps back on the Avenue de la Motte-Picquet, then carry on following it in the same direction you were until you reach the Esplanade des Invalides, another expansive green space that aprons away from the spectacular gold dome of the Saint Louis Cathedral and **Hotel les Invalides,** a military hospital from the 1700s that is now a museum dedicated to France's military history and houses the tomb of the Napoleon Bonaparte. Make your way east along the charming, narrow Rue de Grenelle, rejoining the Boulevard Saint-Germain, when you'll reach the holy trinity of Parisian cafés: Brasserie Lipp, Café Flore, and Les Deux Magots. These famous watering holes of artists, writers, and philosophers since the turn of the 20th century still do a fine job of conjuring up the artistic spirit. Les Deux Magots with its large terrace is best among them for an apero, or end-of-day drink.

6. Dinner at Bouillon République

39 Boulevard du Temple; tel. 01 42 59 69 31; https://bouillonlesite.com; noon-midnight daily; mains from €8

Once you've been to your home-base for a breather, head out to the Bouillon République. Opened in 2021, it's based on the 19th-century model of bouillons: huge eating houses dedicated to keeping their quality high and their prices low. A three-course meal here plus wine isn't going to set you back much more than €30. Situated on the premises of an old Alsatian restaurant, they've kept a delicious sauerkraut dish on the menu, and the upstairs has some stunning wood panel inlays reminiscent of that Germanic corner of France. The only downside is that you can expect at least a half-hour wait if you arrive any time after 7:30pm.

DAY 5

1. Musée d'Orsay

1 Rue de la Légion d'Honneur; tel. 01 40 49 48 14; www.musee-orsay.fr; 9:30am-6pm Tues.-Wed. and Fri.-Sun., 9:30am-9.45pm Thurs.; adults €16; under 18 or EU residents under 26 free

(clockwise from top) Musée d'Orsay; Sacré-Coeur; Montmartre

Home to the largest collection of Impressionist and post-Impressionist paintings in the world, the Musée d'Orsay opened its doors in 1986, built on the premises of a turn-of-the-century train station, and it is one of the absolute musts of any visit to Paris. Indeed, if you must choose between here and the Louvre, the Musée d'Orsay may have the edge, as it's more representative of French art and artistic movements. Alas, there's no secret way to jump the queues here, so your best tactic is to turn up early. Allow three hours for your visit.

2. Rue des Martyrs

A street south of the d'Orsay, you'll find Solferino Metro, which takes you up on the Line 12 (through some of Paris's more elegant metro stations) to the Notre-Dame-de-Lorette and the Rue des Martyrs. One of the liveliest, most picturesque streets in Paris, the Rue des Martyrs is a feast for the eyes and other senses, starting with a bountiful fruit seller and continuing past some of the best butchers, boulangeries, and other specialty food stores in the city.

3. Walking Montmartre

With its winding cobbled streets, smaller scale, and distinctly bohemian air, Montmartre offers something quite different from the rest of Paris. It became a hot spot for bohemians, with artists like Modigliani, Van Gogh, and Picasso taking up residence there. It remains a fantastic neighborhood to wander around, so long as you don't mind the occasional incline. **Place des Abbesses,** a cobbled square with its own carousel and frequent boutique-y market stalls, is a good place to aim for. On the northern side of the square is the entrance to a small public garden, decorated by the popular ***Mur des Je T'aime***—a mural with the words "I love you" written out in 250 different languages. Continuing northwest along the Rue des Abbesses will take you past a remarkable concentration of excellent cafés as well as the **Grenier à Pain** boulangerie (38 Rue des Abbesses; tel. 01 46 06 41 81; https://legrenierapain.com; 7:30am-7:30pm Thurs.-Mon.; baguettes €1.30), frequent winner of the best baguette in Paris and other awards. After around 150 yards, the Rue des Abbesses splits into the Rue Lepic, climbing and curving around to the right. As it does this, keep your eyes peeled for the plaque on the buildings on the right that announces them as the **residence of Vincent Van Gogh** back when he lived in this district in the 19th century.

4. Sacré-Coeur

35 Rue du Chevalier de la Barre; tel. 01 53 41 89 00; www.sacre-coeur-montmartre.com; 10am-7pm daily; free

Rue Lepic, which horseshoes back on itself, takes you past two wooden windmills, the first real, the second a reconstruction to indicate the **Moulin de la Gallette,** a famous artists' hangout in the 19th century, immortalized in a painting by Renoir. From the windmills, keep heading east into the bustling tourist heart of Montmartre, Place du Tertre, where local artists are willing to paint your portrait or draw your caricature for a price. On the other side of the square, the road starts to curve right and a stunning view of Paris opens out before of you. Follow this road to the steps of the Sacré-Coeur church (it's the big white one that looks like a wedding cake; you can't miss it!), where you can sit down for a well-earned rest and admire the view, perhaps buying a beer from one of the street hawkers.

5. Dinner at Polidor

41 Rue Monsieur le Prince; tel. 01 43 26 95 34; www.polidor.com; noon-3pm and 7pm-midnight daily; set menu €22

After touching base at your hotel, head back out to the Polidor, one of the most beautiful, most traditional looking restaurants left in Paris, with its zinc bar, gingham tablecloths, and filigreed walls. The menu is solid French fare and won't break the bank, and the atmosphere is reliably warm and welcoming. A great spot for a final meal at the end of your holiday.

TRANSPORTATION

Air

The third biggest international airport in the world, **Heathrow Airport** (Longford; tel. 0 844 335 1801; www.heathrow.com) is relatively close to London's center. London's second biggest airport is **Gatwick Airport** (Horley, Gatwick; www.gatwick-airport.com), 47 km (29.5 mi) south of the city center.

Paris's largest airport is **Charles de Gaulle** (95700 Roissy-en-France; tel. 1 70 36 39 50; www.parisaeroport.fr/roissy-charles-de-gaulle), situated just to the north of the city. A little more than 16 km (10 mi) to the south of Paris's center is the capital's second-largest air hub, **Paris Orly** (94390 Orly; tel. 0 892 56 39 50; www.parisaeroport.fr/orly).

Train

The **Eurostar** (tel. 01233 617575; www.eurostar.com) between London and Paris (2.5 hours), which runs under the English Channel, is one of the highlights of the trip. Be aware that you need to treat it a bit more like boarding a flight than a train, turning up an hour in advance of your departure for baggage and passport checks. It runs straight from St. Pancras in the heart of London to Gare du Nord in Paris. Prices start at €44/£37 one-way, but in general expect to pay closer to twice that with costs increasing significantly the closer to the date you book, on weekends, and during busier times of year.

- **St. Pancras** (Euston Rd., London; https://stpancras.com): London's only international station, situated in the north of the city, is where you catch the Eurostar for Paris.
- **Gare du Nord** (Rue de Dunkerque, Paris; www.sncf.com): This north central Paris station sits just below Montmartre. It is the French end of the Eurostar track, and serves the north of the country as well as Belgium and Holland.

Eurostar

Public Transport

London

From red double-decker buses to black cabs to tube trains, using the most iconic public transport system in the world is a quintessential experience. A single journey on a **bus** is £1.65 and starts from £2.50 on the **tube.** Buying tickets is easy: As long as you have a contactless credit card, all you need do is "tap" through the ticket barriers or onto buses—be sure that you use another card-reader machine to "tap" out when you complete your journey. If you don't have a contactless card, you can buy physical tickets (more expensive, with single fares starting at £6.20). It's a better value to purchase a day- or week-long travel card (from £14.40 and £38.40, respectively). Alternatively, you can buy an Oyster card (£5) from the ticket booths at most larger stations, which can then be topped up with cash at the same rate as a contactless credit or debit card. More details can be found on the **Transport for London** website (https://tfl.gov.uk).

The famous **black cabs,** meanwhile, with their highly trained drivers who have brains like Google Maps, are also priced high, starting at around £7 per mile.

Primarily a commuting service used by Londoners, the **Thames Clippers** (www.thamesclippers.com) are something of a tourist hack on the capital (as is riding around on the top deck of buses). Prices on these boats depend on which zones you are traveling through, just like the tube, starting at £5.20 and going up to £14.70 for maximum journey length. There's no need to book ahead, and again just like the tube, you merely tap in when getting on board.

Paris

The most important thing to know about the Paris transport system is that there are effectively two subway networks: the mostly inner-city **Metro,** designated by a large M, and the much larger **RER,** designated by its own acronym. The Metro is very straightforward to navigate. Ticket prices on all lines in central Paris are €1.90. The easiest way of saving money on tickets is buying "carnets" of 10 at a time, costing €16.90. These can also be used on the city's **buses,** which tend have more discursive routes and run later into the night.

- Edinburgh and Glasgow (page 65)
- Amsterdam, Brussels, and Bruges (page 81)
- England's Lake District (page 364)
- South of England to North of France (page 484)
- Paris to Bucharest (page 600)

Getting Back

Fly back home or to your next destination from one of the Paris airports, or take the Eurostar back to London. It is possible to take a 1.25-hour flight from Paris to London, but considering travel times to and from the airports, the train is the better option.

EDINBURGH AND GLASGOW

Why Go: In Edinburgh and Glasgow, eminent museums and galleries, boundary-pushing art shows, lively music, and world-class comedy give you a sense of the beating heart of urban Scotland.

Number of Days: 4

Total Distance: 76 km (46 mi)

Seasons: Spring and summer

Start: Edinburgh

End: Glasgow

A trip to Scotland's two largest cities offers a good sense of the country's character, a combination of the good looks, history, and intrigue of Edinburgh and the buzzy, post-industrial reinvention of Glasgow.

Each year, millions of travelers descend on the medieval city of Edinburgh to see the same noble buildings that have been capturing visitors' imaginations for centuries. They walk the historic Royal Mile, from ancient Edinburgh Castle all the way down to the Palace of Holyroodhouse, the queen's official home in Edinburgh. All this gloomy beauty is contradicted by its jovial atmosphere, perhaps best seen in its welcoming pubs.

It may not be as visually arresting as Edinburgh, but what Glasgow lacks in old-world charm it makes up for with culture, from its exceptional museums to its architecture. Glasgow's world-leading live music venues and working-class roots make this one of the most authentic cities you're likely to encounter.

TOP 3

★ Hiking up **Arthur's Seat,** the summit of a group of hills to the east of Edinburgh's center, for panoramic views and a calm retreat from city life (page 67).

★ Hearing **live music**—from traditional pub sessions to rock 'n' roll clubs, you haven't experienced Scotland until you've heard it sing (page 73).

Soaking up art and natural history in Glasgow's **Kelvingrove Art Gallery and Museum**, set in a stunning late-Victorian building that looks more like a palace than a museum (page 77).

Edinburgh

Where to Stay: Old Town or New Town

Arrive by: Plane to Edinburgh Airport or train from London to Edinburgh Waverly Station

DAY 1

Edinburgh's city center is split into two distinct areas: the Old Town and the New Town, divided by Princes Street Gardens. Spend your first day in Old Town, south of the garden, the oldest part of the city, home to the city's most iconic attractions.

★ 1. Hike to Arthur's Seat

Queen's Dr.; www.walkhighlands.co.uk/lothian/arthurs-seat.shtml

Visitors to Edinburgh can't avoid the gaze of Arthur's Seat, a hill left by a volcanic eruption 350 million years ago. It looms over the city to the east from its position 251 m (822 ft) above sea level in the serene 260-hectare (640-acre) **Holyrood Park.** Some say Arthur's Seat looks like a reclining lion, hence its nickname The Lion. Ascending to the summit is a rite of passage, and hiking up early in the morning is often quietest. From the top, you'll get overarching views of the city, all the way to Leith and the Firth of Forth. In total, it should take you 2-2.5 hours cover the 4.75 km (3 mi) to the summit and back.

2. Palace of Holyroodhouse and the Royal Mile

Canongate, Royal Mile; tel. 0303 123 7306; www.royalcollection.org.uk/visit/palace-of-holyroodhouse; 9:30am-6pm Thurs.-Mon. Apr.-Oct., 9:30am-4:30pm Thurs.-Mon. Nov.-Mar.; adults £16.50, under 17 £9.50, under 5 free, family £42.50

After your hike, head to the Palace of Holyroodhouse at the foot of Holyrood Park, which has been the principal home of the kings and queens of Scotland since the 16th century. On a tour of the grand, classical-style palace, dating mostly to the 17th century, you'll learn about the royal history of Edinburgh, from Mary,

Arthur's Seat

Water of Leith
QUEEN ST
NEW TOWN
Georgian House
PRINCES ST
WEST END
Edinburgh Castle
Edinburgh Airport
FOUNTAINBRIDGE
0 500 yds
0 500 m
BYRES RD
UNIVERSITY AVE
GREAT WESTERN RD
University of Glasgow
Kelvingrove Art Gallery and Museum
KELVIN WAY
Kelvingrove Park
M8
Islay Inn
Park Bar
Teuchter's Triangle
Ben Nevis
ARGYLE ST
RENFREW ST
BATH ST
PITT ST
CENTRE
Glasgow Queen Street
ST VINCENT ST
George Square
WELLINGTON ST
Glasgow Central
The Lighthouse
ARGYLE ST
Glasgow
River Clyde
PACIFIC DR
BROOMIELAW
Festival Park
M8
CLYDE ST
River Clyde
Glasgow Airport
BRIDGE ST

Edinburgh
LONDON RD
Scottish National Portrait Gallery
CALTON
Palace of Holyroodhouse
Scottish National Gallery
Edinburgh Waverley Train Station
QUEEN'S DR
St. Margaret's Loch
The Royal Mile
St. Giles' Cathedral
Edinburgh's Camera Obscura
Salisbury Crags
OLD TOWN
Sandy Bell's
Holyrood Park
SOUTHSIDE
Arthur's Seat
TOLLCROSS
CLERK ST
SPRINGBURN RD
0 500 yds
0 500 m
M8
ROYSTON RD
Glasgow
Edinburgh
Glasgow Cathedral
Necropolis
GEORGE ST
City Chambers
MERCHANT CITY
DUKE ST
Barrowland Ballroom
GALLOWGATE
SALTMARKET
LONDON RD
ABERCROMBY ST

Key Reservations

EDINBURGH

The Stand Comedy Club

- **Edinburgh Castle**
- Tickets for a show at **The Stand Comedy Club**
- Popular restaurants like **The Witchery by the Castle**
- If you are planning to visit Edinburgh during **Hogmanay** (New Year's) or the **Edinburgh Festivals** (Aug.)—the Edinburgh International Festival and the Edinburgh Festival Fringe, among others—try to book accommodations around six months in advance.

GLASGOW

- **University of Glasgow** tours

Queen of Scots, to Bonnie Prince Charlie. Afterward, have a pick-me-up in the **Café at the Palace** (tel. 0131 652 3685; www.rct.uk/visit/palace-of-holyroodhouse/cafe-at-the-palace; noon-4pm Thurs.-Mon. Apr.-Oct., noon-3pm Thurs.-Mon. Nov.-Mar.; afternoon tea £21 per person) in the Mews Courtyard.

The Palace of Holyroodhouse sits at one end of the famous Royal Mile (which, strictly speaking, is a Scots mile, slightly longer than an English mile), with Edinburgh Castle at the other. The epicenter of the Old Town, this thoroughfare is home to some of the city's most historic buildings, including **St. Giles' Cathedral** (High St., Royal Mile; tel. 0131 226 0674; www.stgilescathedral.org.uk; 9am-7pm Mon.-Fri., 9am-5pm Sat., 1pm-5pm Sun. Apr.-Oct., 9am-5pm Mon.-Sat., 1pm-5pm Sun. Nov.-Mar.; free, donation encouraged), a popular place of worship since medieval times; and **Edinburgh's Camera Obscura** (549 Castlehill; tel. 0131 226 3709; www.camera-obscura.co.uk; 9am-10pm daily July-Aug., 9:30am-8pm daily Sept.-Oct. and Apr.-Jun., 10am-7pm daily Nov.-Mar.; adults £15.50, ages 5-15 £11.50, under 5 free), today home to all kinds of high-tech optical illusions, but actually one of the city's oldest purpose-built tourist attractions.

The Royal Mile is easy to walk and should take no more than 20 minutes, but allow 1-2 hours if you want to stop by some of the attractions or pop into one of the many shops en route.

3. Dinner and a Tour at Edinburgh Castle

Castlehill; tel. 0131 225 9846; www.edinburgh-castle.scot; 9:30am-6pm daily Apr.-Sept., 9:30am-5pm daily Oct.-Mar.; adults £18.50 at gate/£17 in advance, children £11.50 at gate/£10.20 in advance, concessions £15/£13.60

High atop an old craggy volcano that has been home to a hill fort for the past 2,000 years, Scotland's most recognizable landmark can be seen from all parts of the city. But you really must pass the castle walls to appreciate this icon of Scottish history; inside there's a vast complex of historic buildings, interconnected by a series of batteries. Throughout its 900-year history the castle has served a variety of purposes: It has been a royal palace, an arsenal, a gun foundry, infantry

(clockwise from top) Edinburgh Castle; Palace of Holyroodhouse; Royal Mile

Distilled Delights

Whisky is to Scotland what beer is to England, with different regions bringing their own flavors and the tradition of distilling going back centuries. However, whisky isn't the only drink produced here—70 percent of the gin produced in the UK is made in Scotland, where it's the fastest-growing spirit.

Though whisky production famously takes place in more rural parts of Scotland, like the Highlands, Speyside, and the Isle of Islay, there are a number of great ways to try it in Edinburgh and Glasgow. Gin and tonic is also a popular drink of choice in many bars, and gin distilleries are quietly opening in cities all across the country.

SCOTCH WHISKY EXPERIENCE, EDINBURGH

354 Castlehill; tel. 0131 220 0441; www.scotchwhiskyexperience.co.uk; 10am-5pm daily; Silver Tour £15.50, Gold Tour £27

This visitor attraction on the Royal Mile—part museum, part tasting room—is bit touristy, but it's also fun; you're bound to walk away a bit more knowledgeable and perhaps a tad squiffy. All visitors must join one of the tours, which start aboard a bizarre but totally absorbing barrel ride that takes you on a visual journey through the history of Scotch, followed by tastings.

PICKERING'S GIN DISTILLERY, EDINBURGH

1 Summerhall; tel. 0131 290 2124; www.pickeringsgin.com; office 9am-5pm Mon.-Fri., tours Thurs.-Sun.; tours £15

In 2013, Pickering's became Edinburgh's first exclusive gin distillery to open in the city for more than 150 years, and everything is done on-site, from the distilling right through to the bottling and shipping. A tour (allow 1.5 hours) will begin in the buzzing Royal Dick bar (open to visitors outside tour times, too) with a gin and tonic to sip on as you're taken through to see the two copper stills and the bottling room before being taken back to the bar for some more tasting.

CLYDESIDE DISTILLERY, GLASGOW

The Old Pump House, Queen's Dock; tel. 0141 212 1401; www.theclydeside.com; 11am-5pm Wed.-Sun., tours on the hour, last tour 4pm; adults £15

This whisky distillery may have opened as recently as 2017, but it uses traditional techniques, such as hand-distilling to create its single malt. The ambition here is personal. Visitors on the main distillery tour (which lasts an hour) will hear all about the history of the whisky industry in Glasgow and be able to sample three drams from across Scotland.

★ Live Music in Edinburgh and Glasgow

While music in contemporary Scotland is a melting pot of styles—from techno to thrashing guitar music, pop, and classical—folk music has long been at Scotland's heart. At pubs in Glasgow and Edinburgh, regular traditional music nights feature fiddles, accordions, and guitars as well as occasional singing—from laments to more rousing sing-a-longs—and the odd bagpipe.

- **Sandy Bell's:** Squeeze yourself into this busy Edinburgh bar where there is fantastic folk music every night of the week (page 73).
- **Barrowland Ballroom:** Set in a 1930s music hall, this slightly kitsch and utterly retro venue in Glasgow's East End is like a time machine back to the heady days of early rock 'n' roll (page 77).
- **Teuchter's Triangle:** While there are lots of pubs around Glasgow where you can hear Scottish folk, nowhere does it better than the trio of pubs that make up what is known as the Teuchter's Triangle in the West End (page 78).

barracks, and even a prison. Join one of the free **tours** (usually running every half hour, and lasting 30-45 minutes) to hear tales of bloodshed and bitter rivalries, and to view the famous Honours of Scotland (crown jewels).

Have dinner at the legendary **The Witchery by the Castle** (352 Castlehill, Royal Mile; tel. 0131 225 5613; www.thewitchery.com; noon-10:30pm daily, afternoon tea 3pm-4pm Mon.-Fri.; entrées from £25), a rich baroque dining room that's one of the most romantic places to dine in the city, just at the foot of Castlehill (book well ahead).

4. Live Music at Sandy Bell's

25 Forrest Rd.; tel. 0131 225 2751; www.sandybells.co.uk; noon-1am Mon.-Sat., 12:30pm-midnight Sun.

Round off your evening at Sandy Bell's pub, a 10-minute walk from The Witchery by the Castle and the most renowned spot in the city for traditional Scottish and Irish folk music sessions. Nightly evening sessions include fiddles, guitars, flutes, and "mouthies" (harmonicas) from 9:30pm, and there are afternoon sessions on Saturday and Sunday at 2pm and 4pm, respectively. Locals embrace the in-the-know tourists who find themselves here, and the atmosphere is amiable and loud.

DAY 2

Spend your second day in the New Town, seeing a different side of the city. This section of Edinburgh was mostly built in the 18th century to escape overcrowding in the Old Town, and is full of splendid Georgian architecture.

1. Scottish National Gallery

The Mound; tel. 0131 624 6200; www.nationalgalleries.org; 10am-5pm daily; free

Start your morning at the Scottish National Gallery, set in the lovely **Princes Street Gardens** (Princes St.; 7am-6pm Nov.-Mar., 7am-7pm Mar.-Apr. and Oct., 7am-8pm Apr.-May and Sept., 7am-10pm May-Aug.), a popular place for Edinburghers to stroll. This exciting gallery is home to world-class collections of Renaissance art, British landscape paintings, and Scottish works, with pieces by Ramsay, Wilkie, McTaggart, and Raeburn.

2. Georgian House

7 Charlotte Sq.; tel. 0131 225 2160; www.nts.org.uk; 10am-4pm Apr.-Oct.; adults £10, concessions £8, family £19.50

Walk 20 minutes to **Charlotte Square,** a dignified 18th-century plaza that's the crowning glory of New Town. The mirrored palace-fronted edifices to the north and south, together with the statuesque sphinxes guarding the roofs, lend a resplendent air. Drop in or at least take your photo in front of the Georgian House, a perfectly preserved 18th-century townhouse, now a museum. It has been restored with period furniture, paintings, and silverware, as well as a glimpse into what life was like "below stairs" for the servants of the house.

Stop for lunch at the cozy **Cambridge Bar** (20 Young St.; tel. 0131 226 2120; www.thecambridgebar.co.uk; food served noon-10pm daily; entrées from £3.25), which serves homemade burgers with a dizzying number of options for toppings.

3. Scottish National Portrait Gallery

1 Queen St.; tel. 0131 624 6200; www.nationalgalleries.org; 10am-5pm daily; free

After lunch, visit another branch of the Scottish National Gallery to see some of Scotland's most recognizable faces, housed in one of the city's most magnificent buildings, a neo-Gothic palace built of red sandstone. It's a chance to see some of the men and women who have shaped Scotland, from William Wallace to Sir Walter Scott. Make your way here via **George Street,** one of the city's more salubrious shopping areas.

4. Seafood Feast

Take advantage of the fruits of the nearby Firth of Forth at the casual, centrally located **Mussel Inn** (61-65 Rose St.; tel. 0843 289 2481; www.mussel-inn.com; noon-3pm and 5pm-10pm daily; entrées £7.60), where the pots of mussels are hugely popular. After dinner, pop into the ornate Circle Bar in the **Café Royal** (19 West Register St.; tel. 0131 556 1884; www.caferoyaledinburgh.com; 11am-10pm daily) for a digestif, and then head to the beautiful Parisian-style oyster bar upstairs.

WATCH

Trainspotting: This 1996 cult favorite movie, directed by Danny Boyle, takes place in Edinburgh but was filmed mostly in Glasgow.

READ

44 Scotland Street by Alexander McCall Smith: For some gentle satire and a little leg-pulling directed at some of the snobbery and whims found in the residents of an upmarket urban street (it's set in Edinburgh's New Town), this first in a series of books is a lovely, warm introduction to the capital.

LISTEN

"Flower of Scotland" is one of the unofficial national anthems of Scotland (the others being "Scotland the Brave" and "Scots Wha Hae"). It's sung with gusto at weddings and sporting celebrations.

Eddi Reader is one of the best contemporary artists who performs folk songs. Her repertoire includes great versions of some Burns songs—her 2003 *Sings the Songs of Burns* album is excellent—including **"Red Red Rose,"** a beautiful ballad.

5. The Stand Comedy Club

5 York Pl.; tel. 0131 558 7272; www.thestand.co.uk; 7:30pm-midnight Mon.-Wed., 7pm-midnight Thurs., 6pm-midnight Fri.-Sat., 12:30pm-3:30pm and 7:30pm-midnight Sun., box office 10am-7pm Mon.-Fri. and noon-7pm Sat.; tickets £3-15

The Scots are famous for their wry sense of humor, often born from working-class roots, and given the freedom and fuel to flourish by the rise of the Edinburgh Fringe Festival. End your night with a riotous introduction to Scottish comedy at The Stand Comedy Club, a five-minute walk from Café Royal. There's comedy every night of the week, but tickets, particularly for the much-lauded Saturday night show, do sell out, so book a few days before.

Glasgow

Where to Stay: City Centre or Merchant City

Arrive by: Train from Edinburgh Waverley to Glasgow Central or Glasgow Queen Street (1 hour)

DAY 3

Spend your day visiting some of the major sights, mostly clustered in and around the City Centre and the medieval East End, home to some of the city's oldest surviving buildings.

1. City Chambers

George Sq.; tel. 0141 287 4018; www.glasgow.gov.uk; 9am-5pm Mon.-Fri., tours 10:30am and 2:30pm Mon.-Fri.; free

In **George Square,** Glasgow's principal plaza and civic heart, the City Chambers were opened by Queen Victoria in 1888. The opulent building was designed to showcase the wealth and power of Glasgow—built mostly on tobacco and shipbuilding—to the rest of the world. The star of the show is the three-story Italian white marble staircase, the largest of its kind in the world. You'll also see the actual chambers where the council sits, and the Banqueting Hall, where guests such as Nelson Mandela have been hosted.

2. Glasgow Cathedral and the Necropolis

Castle St.; tel. 0141 552 8198; www.glasgowcathedral.org; 10am-4pm Mon.-Sat. (closed for lunch 1pm-2pm) and 1pm-4pm Sun.; free, donation welcome

Take the 15-minute walk east to Glasgow Cathedral, the city's oldest building and one of the most impressive, best-preserved pre-Reformation churches in the

George Square

Charles Rennie Mackintosh

Glasgow Style architecture is pretty much synonymous with one man: Charles Rennie Mackintosh (1868-1928). Challenging the very staid Victorian expectations of how buildings should be, he created some of the city's most exquisite edifices. After winning an architecture competition, he received commissions for many buildings throughout Glasgow, all of which exhibited a progressive modern style characterized by decoration, similar to art nouveau. The **Glasgow School of Art** (167 Renfrew St.) was widely considered Mackintosh's masterpiece, but unfortunately little remains of it following two terrible fires. Happily, there are other ways to see Glasgow through the lens of this architect and designer.

- Today, the Mackintosh-designed **Lighthouse** is the best place to understand the mark Mackintosh left on Glasgow, especially at the permanent Mackintosh Interpretation Centre housed within it (page 76).
- Be immersed in Mackintosh's aesthetic at **Mackintosh at the Willow,** where he and his wife, Margaret Macdonald, had a hand in every design (page 77).
- The Mackintosh House at the **Hunterian Museum** (University of Glasgow, Gilbert Scott Building; tel. 0141 330 4221; www.gla.ac.uk/hunterian; 10am-5pm Tues.-Sat.; adult £8, concessions £6) re-creates the home of Mackintosh and his wife. Among the displays is his personal writing desk, one of his most luxurious creations.
- The **Charles Rennie Mackintosh Society** (www.crmsociety.com/tours-events/specialmackintosh-tours) now offers walking tours of the city centre on most Fridays at 2pm, starting at the Mackintosh at the Willow.
- **House for an Art Lover** (Bellahouston Park, 10 Dumbreck Road; tel. 0141 353 4770; www.houseforanartlover.co.uk; 10am-5pm daily, but subject to change; adult £6.50, child £5) is an art gallery and exhibition space built from Mackintosh's designs long after his death.

whole of Scotland—it's the only cathedral on the Scottish mainland that survived the Scottish Reformation without losing its roof. Its gray stone and central spire have darkened with age and are adorned with dozens of arched windows, many of stained glass that colors the light of the long interior nave.

Stroll up behind the cathedral to the "city of the dead," the Necropolis (www.glasgownecropolis.org; always open; free). This sprawling cemetery dates back to 1832, when it was built as a burial place for the rich merchants of the city, and many of the tombs and monuments feature an extravagant Greco-Egyptian style. From the Victorian cemetery's lofty position, you can enjoy some of the best views of Glasgow's skyline.

After your tour of the cemetery, come back to the world of the living with a burger and brew at nearby **Drygate Brewery** (85 Drygate; tel. 0141 212 8815; www.drygate.com; 5pm-midnight Mon.-Thurs., noon-midnight Fri.-Sun.; tours £10).

3. The Lighthouse

11 Mitchell Ln.; tel. 0141 276 5365; www.thelighthouse.co.uk; 10:30am-5pm Mon.-Sat., noon-5pm Sun.; free

Designed by Charles Rennie Mackintosh

in his first public commission, this building is today home to **Scotland's National Centre for Design and Architecture.** It's one big creative space where you are free to wander. The permanent Mackintosh Interpretation Centre tells the story of the building, Mackintosh's part in it, and how it was transformed into what you see today. A highlight of the building is undoubtedly the exposed stonework of the tower, which gives the Lighthouse its name and can be ascended via a dizzying spiral staircase. It's a 20-minute walk from Drygate Brewery.

Continue your Mackintosh tour with a late afternoon tea at the newly restored **Mackintosh at the Willow** (215-217 Sauchiehall St.; tel. 0141 204 1903; www.mackintoshatthewillow.com; tea rooms 11am-5pm daily, afternoon tea noon-4:30pm; afternoon tea £23.95, Salon de Luxe afternoon tea £45), a 15-minute walk from the Lighthouse. Mackintosh and his wife designed everything for this restaurant, from the chairs to the menus. The famously opulent Salon de Luxe boasts original Mackintosh stained-glass doors with purple paneling and leaded frieze.

4. Barrowland Ballroom

244 Gallowgate; tel. 0141 552 4601; https://barrowland-ballroom.co.uk; times vary, but often 7pm-11pm

If you're not totally worn out from your day of sightseeing, after recharging a bit at your hotel, put on your dancing shoes and head to the East End for a night of revelry at the legendary Barrowland Ballroom. Everyone from David Bowie to The Clash, U2, and the Foo Fighters have performed here, attracted no doubt by the famous sprung dance floor, fantastic acoustics, and faded glamour.

DAY 4

Head to the hip West End for a morning of art and history followed by an afternoon of vintage shopping and good food.

★ 1. Kelvingrove Art Gallery and Museum

Argyle St.; tel. 0141 276 9599; www.glasgowlife.org.uk; 10am-5pm Mon.-Thurs. and Sat., 11am-5pm Fri. and Sun.; free (some temporary exhibits may charge)

Set within the lovely Kelvingrove Park, the handsome red sandstone Kelvingrove Art Gallery and Museum is one of the city's

left, The Lighthouse; right, Kelvingrove Art Gallery and Museum

Regional Cuisine

Scotland is quite rightly famed for its national dishes such as haggis, but over the last decade Scottish cuisine has become increasingly focused on food provenance, and local fare now takes pride of place on menus, from Aberdeen Angus beef to shellfish still salty from the sea.

- **Haggis:** A dish of spiced sheep's heart, liver, and lungs, which tastes a lot nicer than it sounds.
- **Neeps and Tatties:** A traditional side dish of mashed rutabaga and potatoes.
- **Salmon:** With miles and miles of coastline, it is fitting that seafood now features heavily on menus throughout Scotland. Be especially sure to try Scottish wild salmon, ideally smoked.

most popular attractions. Inside, there are 22 galleries displaying some 8,000 objects. One side of the museum features art galleries, including as the foremost collection of works by the Glasgow Boys, a group of late 19th-century artists who eschewed formal painting techniques to paint rural scenes. The other side focuses on natural history and world culture. The **Kelvingrove organ** in the center hall is also a highlight; attending one of the daily organ recitals (1pm Mon.-Sat., 3pm Sun.) is highly recommended.

For lunch, walk 15 minutes to cobbled Ashton Lane and see if the **Ubiquitous Chip** (12 Ashton Ln.; tel. 0141 334 5007; www.ubiquitouschip.co.uk; noon-1am daily; entrées £11, brasserie £7.45), one of Glasgow's most popular restaurants, lives up to its reputation, with food showcasing the best of Scotland, from homemade haggis to Orkney smoked salmon.

2. University of Glasgow

University Ave.; www.gla.ac.uk/explore/visit/attractions; guided tours 2pm Tues.-Sun.; guided tours adults £10, children £5, concessions £8, under 5 free, family ticket £25

A 10-minute walk away, take the afternoon tour around the grounds of the neo-Gothic University of Glasgow, which some say inspired J. K. Rowling's Hogwarts. With its crow-stepped gables, pointed turrets, and conspicuous spire that can be seen for miles around, it attracts admiring glances from all that pass. It's small wonder it has more listed buildings than any other British university.

To see where the students hang out, explore some of the West End's quirky, funky shopping streets and arcades, like **the Hidden Lane and the Hive** (1081 Argyle St.; www.thehiddenlaneglasgow.com; hours vary, most businesses open Sat. noon-5pm, with some weekday hours) and **Ruthven Mews Arcade** (57 Ruthven Ln.; www.visitwestend.com/discover/the-lanes; 11am-5:30pm Mon.-Sat., noon-5pm Sun.). You'll find everything from antiques and vintage goods to jewelry and art.

3. Teuchter's Triangle

Argyle St.

Enjoy a delicious and laid-back seafood dinner at **Crabshakk** (1114 Argyle St.;

tel. 0141 334 6127; www.crabshakk.com; noon-midnight daily; entrées £9.95), before ending your night with a traditional music session at one of three famous pubs that make up Teuchter's Triangle: **Ben Nevis** (1147 Argyle St.; tel. 0141 576 5204; www.facebook.com/TheBenNevisBar; noon-midnight Mon.-Sat., 12:30pm-midnight Sun.) across the road, **Islay Inn** (1256 Argyle St.; tel. 0141 334 7774; www.islayinn.com; 11am-midnight daily), or **Park Bar** (1202 Argyle St.; tel. 0141 339 1715; www.parkbarglasgow.com; 11:45am-midnight daily). This is one of the best places in the city for whisky and folk music, a winning combination.

TRANSPORTATION

Air

Both **Glasgow** and **Edinburgh** are well connected with international flights from the United States, Canada, and Europe.

- **Edinburgh Airport** (EDI; www.edinburghairport.com) is located 13 km (8 mi) west of the city.
- **Glasgow Airport** (GLA; Paisley; www.glasgowairport.com), located 13 km (8 mi) west of the city, is the main airport where most visitors to Glasgow will arrive.

Train

A relatively good train system links the main towns and cities in Scotland. **ScotRail** (www.scotrail.co.uk) has tickets and details on timetables and connections. Glasgow is by far the best-connected city in Scotland, with several trains a day to most main towns and cities. Edinburgh is reasonably well connected and is less than an hour from Glasgow (about three trains an hour).

Probably the most enjoyable way to travel between London and Scotland is by train (approximately 4.5 hours to both Edinburgh and Glasgow; from £30 each way); ticket prices can be compared through Trainline (www.thetrainline.com). For a little more adventure (and to save on a night's accommodation), book a cabin on the **Caledonian Sleeper** (www.sleeper.scot) train that sets off from London Euston at night, arriving into Scotland in the morning (from around £130 each way).

- **Edinburgh Waverley** (Princes St.; www.networkrail.co.uk/stations/edinburgh-waverley) on Waverley Bridge, which overlooks Princes Street Gardens, is the city's main station and is the departure and arrival station for trains from Glasgow.
- **Glasgow Central** (Gordon St., www.scotrail.co.uk/plan-your-journey/stations-and-facilities/glc) and **Glasgow Queen Street** (North Hanover St., George Square; www.scotrail.co.uk/plan-your-journey/stations-and-facilities/glq) are both centrally located stations. From

top, Scottish whisky; bottom, University of Glasgow

Edinburgh, a train runs every few minutes into either Glasgow Queen Street or, less regularly, Glasgow Central. Journey time varies from 50 minutes to 1.25 hours, and tickets cost as little as £14 one-way.

- London and Paris (page 44)
- The North Coast 500 (page 256)

Public Transportation

Edinburgh

In Edinburgh, by far the most enjoyable way to explore the city is on foot, to discover the city's secret passageways and hidden corners; sights are close enough together that you likely won't need to utilize public transit to get from one place to another.

Glasgow

Glasgow is built on a series of drumlins (hills), so while it's definitely possible to walk between all of the places recommended on this route, you may find it helpful to utilize the excellent Subway and bus system. The circular **Subway** (www.spt.co.uk/travel-with-spt/subway) system, actually one of the oldest underground systems in the world, is an easy way to get around the city. Purchase tickets in a machine at the station; these need to be tapped in and out at card reader panels as you enter and leave stations (from just £1.55 one-way). A very good bus system reaches all of the spots that the Subway doesn't serve. The main bus company is **First Glasgow** (www.firstbus.co.uk/greater-glasgow). There are timetables on the FirstBus website (www.firstbus.co.uk) or, better, download the **FirstBus app.** You can pay onboard using your contactless debit card, or buy in advance through the app.

Getting Back

To return to Edinburgh, simply hop on the train back to Edinburgh Waverly. Alternatively, since Glasgow is also very well connected by air and train, you may be able to get back home, or to your next destination, from there.

AMSTERDAM, BRUSSELS, AND BRUGES

Why Go: The refined art and culture scenes of these three cities are warmed by the concept of gezelligheid—the Dutch version of hygge—perhaps best experienced sipping a tea or beer in a cozy, historic bar or café.

Number of Days: 5

Total Distance: 324 km (201 mi)

Seasons: Spring and summer

Start: Amsterdam

End: Bruges

The compactness of the Netherlands and Belgium means you can get a captivating glimpse into their cultures in a relatively short time. Most cities are only 1-2 hours away from each other, connected by an efficient train network, so it doesn't matter too much whether you fly into Brussels or Amsterdam. On this itinerary, you'll get a taste of the best of Amsterdam and Brussels—world-class cities known for their museums, impressive restaurant scenes, and lovely walkable neighborhoods—plus a day strolling Bruges's stunning medieval center.

TOP 3

Finding gezelligheid, a cozy sense of warmth and comfort, at an atmospheric Amsterdam **brown bar** (page 90).

Taking in Brussels' magnificent **Grand Place.** Lined with imposing 17th-century buildings, this square truly lives up to its name (page 91).

Gazing at picturesque, medieval Bruges from atop the **Belfry of Bruges** (page 95).

Amsterdam

Where to Stay: Grachtengordel neighborhood for canal views from your balcony

Arrive by: Plane to Schiphol Airport

DAY 1

1. Rijksmuseum

Museumstraat 1; tel. 020 674 7000; www.rijksmuseum.nl; 9am-5pm daily; €17.50

On your first day, stroll through Amsterdam Centrum and the infamous Red Light District toward Museumkwartier, where you can take in the Rijksmuseum, one of the premiere Dutch art institutions. The museum showcases the Middle Ages and Dutch Golden Age, with exquisite pieces like Rembrandt's masterpiece *The Night Watch* and Vermeer's *The Milkmaid,* plus Van Gogh's self-portrait.

2. Vondelpark

open 24/7

Afterward, get some fresh air with a wander through Vondelpark, Amsterdam's answer to Central Park. Built in the English garden style, with small ponds, tree-lined lawns, and bridges to stroll along, the park is full of picturesque, watery landscapes and several pedestrian-only paths that loop around lakes. Have a light lunch at a park-side café or brewery, like **Gollem's Proeflokaal** (Overtoom 160-162; tel. 020 612 9444; 11am-1am Sun.-Thurs., 11am-3pm Fri.-Sat.), a haven for beer lovers with 22 taps and more than 180 bottles available behind the counter.

3. Van Gogh Museum

Museumplein 6; tel. 020 570 5200; www.vangoghmuseum.nl; 9am-6pm daily; adults €19, children free

Head back toward Museumkwartier to visit one of Amsterdam's most popular museums, which holds the world's largest collection of Vincent Van Gogh's works. The paintings are ordered chronologically, with artwork and information spread across four floors. See *The Potato Eaters* among his early works, and *Irises* and *Almond Blossom* from his later years. In the Kurokawa Wing, which was added

Vondelpark

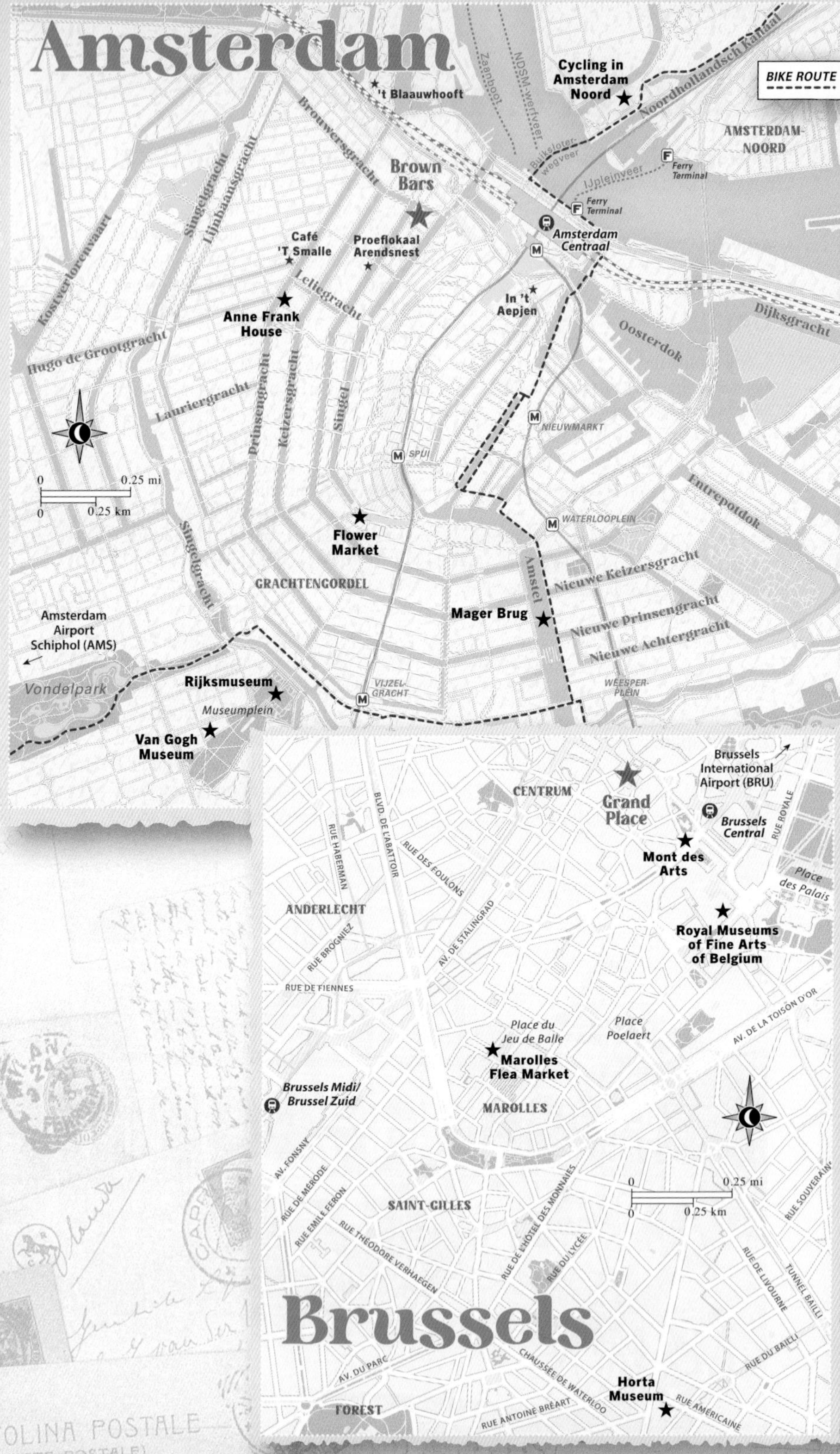

Amsterdam
BIKE ROUTE
Cycling in Amsterdam Noord
't Blaauwhooft
Brown Bars
Café 'T Smalle
Proeflokaal Arendsnest
Anne Frank House
In 't Aepjen
Amsterdam Centraal
Ferry Terminal
Ferry Terminal
AMSTERDAM-NOORD
Noordhollandsch Kanaal
Zaanboot
NDSM-werfveer
Buiksloterwegveer
IJpleinveer
Brouwersgracht
Leliegracht
Singelgracht
Lijnbaansgracht
Kostverlorenvaart
Hugo de Grootgracht
Lauriergracht
Prinsengracht
Keizersgracht
Singel
Oosterdok
Dijksgracht
NIEUWMARKT
SPUI
0 0.25 mi
0 0.25 km
Flower Market
WATERLOOPLEIN
Entrepotdok
GRACHTENGORDEL
Amstel
Nieuwe Keizersgracht
Nieuwe Prinsengracht
Nieuwe Achtergracht
Mager Brug
Amsterdam Airport Schiphol (AMS)
Vondelpark
Rijksmuseum
Museumplein
Van Gogh Museum
VIJZELGRACHT
WEESPERPLEIN
Brussels
CENTRUM
Grand Place
Brussels International Airport (BRU)
Brussels Central
Mont des Arts
Place des Palais
Royal Museums of Fine Arts of Belgium
RUE ROYALE
RUE HABERMAN
BLVD. DE L'ABATTOIR
RUE DES FOULONS
AV. DE STALINGRAD
ANDERLECHT
RUE BROGNIEZ
RUE DE FIENNES
Place du Jeu de Balle
Place Poelaert
AV. DE LA TOISON D'OR
Marolles Flea Market
MAROLLES
Brussels Midi/ Brussel Zuid
AV. FONSNY
RUE DE MERODE
RUE EMILE FERON
SAINT-GILLES
RUE THÉODORE VERHAEGEN
RUE DE L'HÔTEL DES MONNAIES
RUE DU LYCÉE
0 0.25 mi
0 0.25 km
RUE SOUVERAIN
RUE DE LIVOURNE
TUNNEL BAILLI
RUE DU BAILLI
AV. DU PARC
CHAUSSÉE DE WATERLOO
Horta Museum
RUE AMÉRICAINE
RUE ANTOINE BRÉART
FOREST

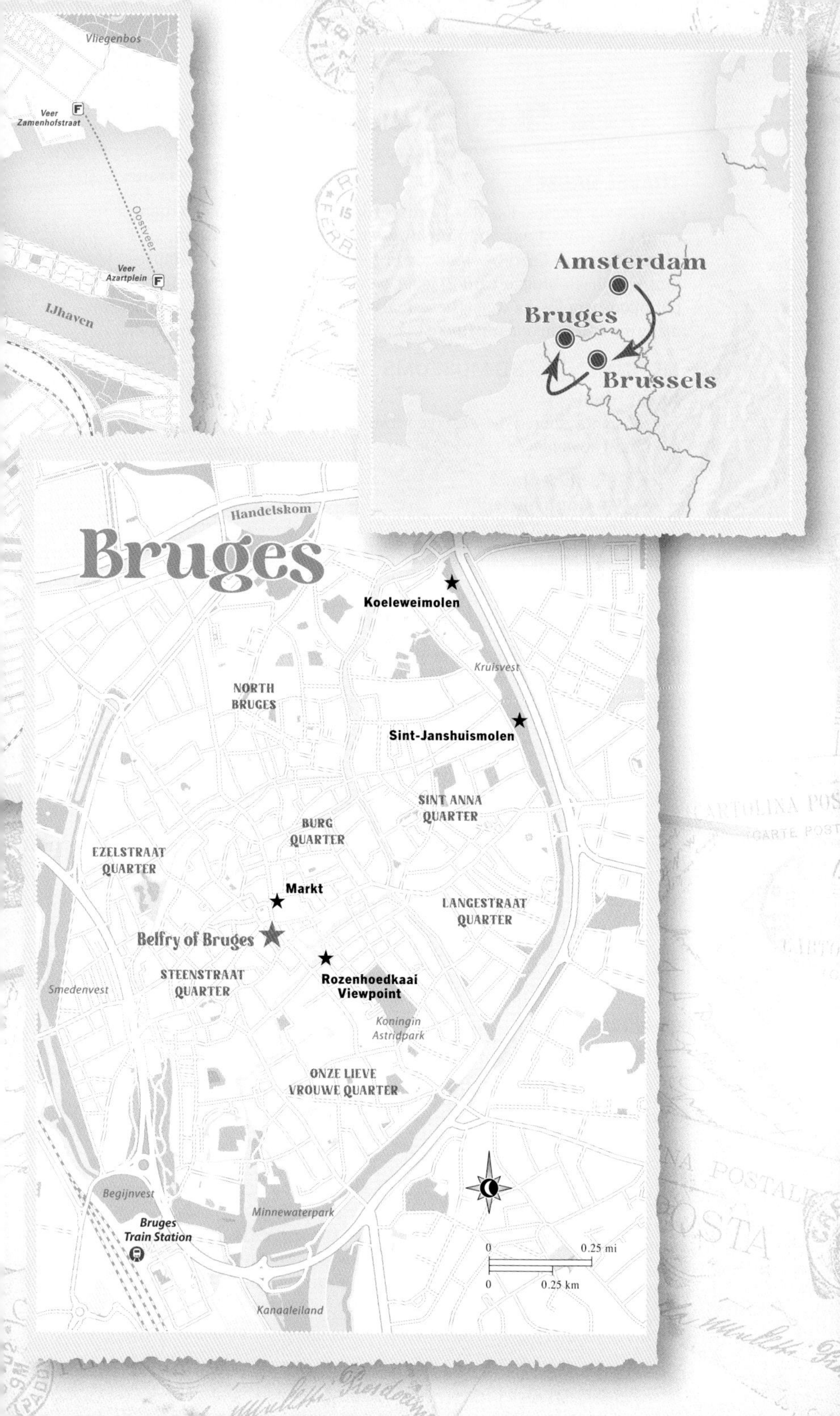
Vliegenbos
Veer Zamenhofstraat
Oostveer
Veer Azartplein
IJhaven
Amsterdam
Bruges
Brussels
Handelskom
Bruges
Koeleweimolen
Kruisvest
NORTH BRUGES
Sint-Janshuismolen
SINT ANNA QUARTER
BURG QUARTER
EZELSTRAAT QUARTER
Markt
LANGESTRAAT QUARTER
Belfry of Bruges
STEENSTRAAT QUARTER
Rozenhoedkaai Viewpoint
Smedenvest
Koningin Astridpark
ONZE LIEVE VROUWE QUARTER
Begijnvest
Bruges Train Station
Minnewaterpark
0
0.25 mi
0
0.25 km
Kanaaleiland

Key Reservations

TRAVEL PASSES

Sightseeing passes like the **iAmsterdam pass** (www.iamsterdam.com), **Museum Pass Belgium** (www.museumpassmusees.be), and **Musea Brugge Card** (www.discoverbruges.com/en/attractions-museums/pp/musea-brugge-card-2) focus on museums; some include transportation benefits as well. These make the most sense when visiting many museums in one trip (more than what is included in this itinerary).

MONUMENTS AND MUSEUMS

Amsterdam

These sights should be reserved two months in advance.

- **Rijksmuseum**
- **Van Gogh Museum**
- **Anne Frank House**

Brussels

- **Horta Museum**

Van Gogh Museum

RESTAURANTS

Advance bookings are generally smiled upon in Amsterdam and Brussels; to get the best seat at many cafés and restaurants, it's generally recommended to make a reservation at least a few hours beforehand.

in 1999, temporary exhibitions often showcase Japanese artists, illustrating the connection between those works and Van Gogh's. During high season (Apr.-Sept.), it's best to reserve your tickets well in advance online. Avoid the crowds by going at opening or in the late afternoon, after the tour groups have left.

4. Magere Brug

open 24/7; free

Head east until you find the Amstel River and enjoy a walk with views of the canal houses and the Magere Brug, Amsterdam's most famous bridge. First built in the 1600s, the current, pedestrian-only bridge dates back to 1969. Crossing the bridge provides a dreamy glimpse of Amsterdam's skyline north of the Amstel River. It's a favorite among couples and of filmmakers (you may recognize it from the James Bond movie *Diamonds Are Forever*). It's said that if you kiss someone on the bridge, or on a boat underneath it, you'll be in love forever.

5. Indonesian Food at Tujuh Maret

Utrechtsestraat 73; tel. 020 427 9865; https://tujuhmaret.nl; noon-10pm daily; from €22

From Magere Brug, it's a short walk to this restaurant serving rijsttafel, Dutch for "rice table." Though rooted in the Dutch colonization of Indonesia, this feast is a great way to sample Indonesian food if you're unsure where to start—Tujuh Maret offers five versions, including vegetarian. Reservations recommended.

6. Evening at a Brown Bar: In 't Aepjen

Zeedijk 15-1; tel. 020 626 8401; noon-1pm Sun.-Thurs., noon-3am Fri.-Sat.

End the evening at this historic brown bar in the heart of Amsterdam's Red Light District.

(clockwise from top) Anne Frank House; Rijksmuseum; Magere Brug

Regional Cuisine

Belgium is practically synonymous with beer and chocolate, but you may be surprised to find out that some of the best food in Amsterdam is not traditional Dutch, but comes from the complicated legacy of Dutch colonialism in Indonesia and Suriname.

INDONESIAN FOOD

The Dutch and other Europeans colonized in Indonesia in the 16th century to take advantage of the many spices produced there, including nutmeg and cloves. Mass migration of Indonesians to the Netherlands following Indonesian independence in 1945 means that it's easy to find Indonesian food all throughout the country. At **tokos,** cozy Indonesian takeaway restaurants, you'll find typical rames dishes, or rice with a protein (fish, tofu, chicken, egg, etc.) and one or two vegetable sides of your choice. One famous Indonesian-inspired dish is **rijsttafel,** Dutch for "rice table," in which 40-plus dishes are presented alongside tables of rice, a way for the Dutch to try the specialties of as many Indonesian dishes as possible.

SURINAMESE FOOD

Suriname was an English colony before it became Dutch, when the Dutch West India Company brought thousands of enslaved Africans to work the plantations, as well as contract workers of Chinese, Indian, and Indonesian (Javanese) origins. When Suriname ceased to be a colony, many Surinamese people had to emigrate to the Netherlands to keep their Dutch citizenship. The resulting fusion of cultures created a new and interesting cuisine: **telo terie** is small salted fish cooked and fried with spices; **bara** is a fried donut-esque bread made with mung bean flour that can be cut open to have a filling added; **moksi meti** is Chinese Surinamese-style sliced pork.

Though it once had a seedy reputation, In 't Aepjen is now a quiet establishment where Amsterdammers have a drink or read the newspaper while sipping on a coffee or beer. The interior is gezellig in the truest Dutch sense with candle-lit tables, old Delftware, jenever bottles from its past, bronze chandeliers, and a wood-beamed ceiling that shows the café's true age.

DAY 2

1. Anne Frank House

Westermarkt 20; tel. 020 556 7105; www.annefrank.org; 9:30am-4:30pm daily; adults €12.50, ages 10-17 €6.50, ages €1 (plus €1 booking fee)

The Diary of Anne Frank is one of the most iconic books about the Holocaust, and this museum is a testament to Anne Frank's legacy. For two years during World War II, Anne and her family stayed hidden

CHOCOLATE

Famous all the world over, Belgian chocolate is, for many, one of the highlights of a trip to Brussels and Bruges. Cocoa beans were first brought to Belgium in the 17th century from the South American colonies of Spain, which ruled Belgium at the time. But it wasn't until the Belgians brutally colonized the Congo that they gained access to large quantities of the beans; by the late 19th and early 20th centuries, Belgium had the upper hand in the cocoa and chocolate trade. Happily, today the best Belgian chocolatiers are now obsessed with transparent and ethical sourcing of their cocoa beans.

Many of Belgium's best-known chocolatiers have their roots in Brussels, and the **praline** was invented here by a pharmacist who hoped to disguise the terrible taste of some medicines with delicious chocolate. In Bruges, keep an eye out for the **Bruges's Swan** (het Brugsch Swaentje), a praline specific to the city that is made with a secret recipe of almonds, biscuits, and a spice mix used for beer brewing.

BEER

A visit to Belgium, where people have been brewing for more than 800 years, is the holy grail for many beer lovers. More than 1,500 types of beer are produced in Belgium, often divided between **abbey beers,** which refer to brews made using traditional brewing methods and recipes, and **Trappist beers,** which are still produced entirely by Trappist monks. Belgian beers tend to be heavier in alcohol than other European brews, so do pay attention to the ABV while you're imbibing.

Most bars have a solid selection of Belgian beers; ask your bartender for recommendations of local options that might be harder to find elsewhere, like **quadrupel,** a heavy and rich Belgian beer style with often fruity undertones and a yeasty flavor, or **gueuze,** a sour blend of lambics, with a significant amount of head, similar to champagne, traditionally produced in the Brussels region.

in a part of this home that was only accessible via a secret stairwell behind a bookshelf. The secret annex has been re-created with replicas to give visitors an idea of what life was like for the family at the time. Listen for nearby Westerkerk's 51 carillon bells, which ring every 15 minutes, a sound that Anne Frank famously described in her diary.

2. Flower Market

Singel between Muntplein and Koningsplein; www.holland.com/global/tourism/destinations/amsterdam/things-to-do/floating-flower-market.htm; 9am-5:30pm daily

For something lighter after the heavy subject matter of the museum, walk over to the world's only floating flower market. Although it's certainly touristy, there's something quite nice about picking out flowers along such a scenic canal-side

★ Find Your Favorite Brown Bar

As much as people associate the classic pub with the English, the Dutch have perfected the brown bar, a neighborhood bar where virtually every inch is covered in dark wood. Some say that the name (which, contrary to what you may think, has nothing to do with marijuana) comes from the walls, stained from years of smoking inside before it was prohibited, but you can decide for yourself.

Brown bars are often visited during the day as cafés, where older locals catch up on the news with friends over a cup of coffee. Some cafés have hardly changed for 100 years, besides an ever-rotating bar cat. At these cafés, you can truly experience the gezellig side of Amsterdam's nightlife with a glass of beer on tap. Be aware that many of these cafés do not accept foreign cards, so be sure to bring cash. **In 't Aepjen** (page 86) is a historic bar; here are a few more of the best in the city:

- Just a little outside the Red Light District, you'll find the always charming **'t Blaauwhooft** (Hendrik Jonkerplein 1; tel. 020 623 8721; http://blaauwhooft.nl; 11am-1pm daily), a neighborhood bar where it's easy to lose track of time and get lost in conversation.
- For a quiet beer in the Jordaan district, just west of the Grachtengordel, **Café 't Smalle** (Egelantiersgracht 12; tel. 020 623 9617; 10am-1am Sun.-Thurs., 10am-2am Fri.-Sat.) offers stunning canal views with a modern beer menu.
- For a proper education on Dutch craft beer, **Proeflokaal Arendsnest** (Herengracht 90; tel. 020 421 2057; www.arendsnest.nl; noon-midnight Sun.-Thurs., noon-2am Fri.-Sat.) offers a beautiful location along the scenic Herengracht canal.

spot. When buying tulip bulbs to take home, check to make sure that they can be legally imported into your home country. For a lunch, try nearby **Blue Amsterdam** (Winkelcentrum Kalverpassage, Singel 457; tel. 020 427 3901; www.blue-amsterdam.nl; 11am-6:30pm Sun.-Mon., 10am-6:30pm Tues.-Wed., 10am-8pm Thurs., 10am-6:30pm Fri.; €10), a rooftop restaurant with 360-degree views and reasonable prices.

3. Cycling in Amsterdam Noord

Spend the afternoon getting a taste of the city's famous bicycling culture in Amsterdam Noord, a less hectic experience than biking through the city center. Away from the crowds, you'll ride through a polder landscape, passing by grazing sheep.

Take the tram to Amsterdam Centraal station, where you can rent a bike from nearby vendors, then hop on the free Amsterdam Noord Ferry to IJPlein. Follow a road called **Meeuwenlaan** north until you turn right onto **Nieuwendammerdijk.** After this, you'll hit **Schellingwouderdijk,** which turns into **Durgerdammerdijk.** Make a left onto **Durgerdammergouw,** which leads to **Ransdorp,** where you'll make a left onto **Nieuwe Gouw** to cycle west toward **Zunderdorp.** Once you reach Zunderdorp, make a left onto **Zunderdorpergouw,** and continue heading south until this street turns into **Beemsterstraat.** Make a right onto Nieuwendammerdijk to head back toward the ferry via Meeuwenlaan, the way that you came. Staying on the path of this 20.3-km (12.6-mi) ride is easy: Just follow signs toward the multiple charming villages en route, which include (in order) Nieuwendam, Schellingwoude, Durgerdam, Ransdorp, and Zunderdorp.

4. Beer at Oedipus Brewing

Gedempt Hamerkanaal 85; tel. 020 244 1673; https://oedipus.com; 5pm-10pm Thurs., 2pm-11pm Fri.-Sat., 2pm-7:30pm Sun.

For a refreshment after all the cycling, make a stop at Oedipus Brewing before heading to the ferry. (From Meeuwenlaan, turn left onto Motorkade, which turns into Gedempt Hamerkanaal.) This trendy Dutch microbrewery produces some of the most delicious craft beers in Amsterdam and has a nice tasting room/terrace perfect for a casual post-ride sip.

5. Surinamese Dinner at New Draver

Tweede Oosterparkstraat 2-4; tel. 020 663 0230; www.newdraver.nl; 2pm-11pm daily; €12

Make your way to this long-time Creole Surinamese spot, well-known for its authenticity and great atmosphere. Try herie herie, a dish with Portuguese influences that includes cassava, banana, and potatoes. For an after-dinner cocktail on your last night in Amsterdam, you can't go wrong with **Bar Lempicka** (Sarphatistraat 23; tel. 020 622 0209; www.barlempicka.com; 9am-1am Sun.-Thurs., 9am-3am Fri.-Sat.), about a 15-minute walk north, and the lovely views of the Amstel from its terrace.

Brussels

Where to Stay: Brussels Centrum, although location is less important here thanks to the walkable center and efficient Metro

Arrive by: Train from Amsterdam Centraal to Brussels Midi (2 hours)

DAY 3

★ 1. Grand Place

open 24/7; free

Hop on the high-speed train to Brussels, where you can take in the grand view of the city from Grand Place (or Grote Markt in Dutch). A UNESCO World Heritage Site for its representation of 17th-century Belgian social and cultural life, the square has been a marketplace since the 12th century and increased in stature alongside Brussels' wealth and prosperity, reflected in the glittering gold inlays decorating the grand buildings, once guild houses for Brussels' industries, from haberdashery to baking. Today, these buildings are taken up largely by commercial shops and cafés, some of which have tables on the square for a drink. The building at #10 remains inhabited by the Belgian beer brewers guild, as it has for centuries.

A very short walk from Grand Place, be sure to visit the small bronze statue of a peeing young boy on top of a fountain that has become a symbol of the city (intersection of Rue du Chêne and Rue de

(top to bottom) Grand Place; Royal Museums of Fine Arts of Belgium; Mont des Arts; Marolles Flea Market

l'Étuve; www.brussels.be/manneken-pis; open 24/7; free). **Manneken Pis,** which means "Little Man Peeing" in the Brussels Flemish dialect, is a perfect example the self-deprecating humor of the Bruxellois (the French term for the residents) or Zinnekes (*little mutt* in Brusseleir dialect). Continuing the joke, the Little Man has two related statues: **Jeanneke Pis** (Impasse de la Fidélité 10-12), the female counterpart, and **Zinneke Pis** (Rue des Chartreux 35), Manneken Pis's pet.

2. Royal Museums of Fine Arts of Belgium

Rue de la Régence 3; tel. 02 508 32 11; www.fine-arts-museum.be; 10am-5pm Tues.-Fri., 11am-6pm Sat.-Sun.; €10 per exhibition

Spend the afternoon at one or a few of the institutions that make up the Royal Museums of Fine Arts of Belgium, located together in the center of Brussels. The **Old Masters Museum** focuses on paintings by the Flemish Primitives and from the Flemish Renaissance and the baroque period, with rooms dedicated to Pieter Bruegel the Elder and Peter Paul Rubens. The **Magritte Museum** holds 230 works by surrealist René Magritte, the most complete collection of his work in the world. Dedicated to impressionism and art nouveau, the **Fin-de-Siècle Museum** houses works from the end of the 19th century and early 20th century, ranging from ornate sculptures by Auguste Rodin to wild and symbolic paintings like *The Caress* by Fernand Khnopff.

3. Chocolate at Neuhaus

Galerie de la Reine 25-27; tel. 02 512 63 59; www.neuhauschocolates.com; 11am-7pm Mon.-Fri., noon-8pm Sat.-Sun.

Time for a sweet treat after all the museums. For a taste of Belgium's famous chocolate with a bit of history, visit the Neuhaus shop in the Royal Galleries nearby. There are locations all over Brussels, but this is the original location, where in 1857 Jean Neuhaus opened a pharmacy and covered his medicines in chocolate to make them go down easier. For more food,

WATCH

In Bruges (2008) is a cheeky film about two Irish hitmen who await their next orders while sightseeing in Bruges, starring Colin Farrell, Brendan Gleeson, and Ralph Fiennes.

READ

Anne Frank: The Diary of a Young Girl by Anne Frank: This heart-wrenching diary of a Jewish teen living in hiding during the Nazi occupation of Amsterdam has touched millions around the world. It's also available as an audiobook read by Selma Blair.

King Ottokar's Seuptre by Hergé: Filled with classic Belgian humor, this 1939 comic features the iconic Tintin, a Belgian reporter and adventurer who gets embroiled in a plot to steal a scepter from a king.

try **Wolf** (Wolvengracht 50; https://wolf.brussels; noon-10pm Sun.-Thurs., noon-11pm Fri.-Sat.; €10), a food court with an assortment of affordable options, from Syrian to authentic Italian pizza.

4. Mont des Arts

https://visit.brussels/site/en/place/Mont-des-Arts-Gardens; open 24/7; free

For sunset, it's hard to beat Mont des Arts ("Hill of Art" in French), Brussels' most beautiful lookout. The view, which overlooks the entire city, is now just as beautiful as the art found in museums in Brussels today.

Gist (Place de la Vieille Halle aux Blés 30; tel. 02 512 70 06; https://gistbeerand-co.business.site; 4pm-11pm Tues.-Sun.) is an inviting place to end your day. This hip Belgian beer bar feels very much like a neighborhood spot due to its friendly owners, who make everyone feel at home.

DAY 4

1. Marolles Flea Market

Place du Jeu de Balle; 6am-2pm daily; cash only

You'll want to rise early to browse the goods at Brussels' main flea market, which dates back to a secondhand clothing market in the 17th century. Laid out on the sidewalk in the center of the Marolles neighborhood, treasures mingle with junk galore, patrolled by both casual browsers and serious antique hunters. It's easy to spend a few hours here, marveling at finds from beautiful Louis XV furniture to delightful postcards. Most items don't have a price on them, so don't be afraid to ask—and to try your luck at haggling.

2. Frites at Broebbeleir Marolles

Place du Jeu de Balle 62; https://lesvignes-duliban.be; 11am-3pm and 5pm-10pm Mon.-Thurs., 11am-3pm and 5pm-11pm Fri., 11am-11pm Sat., 11am-10pm Sun.; €5

For lunch, delicious fries at Broebbeleir Marolles. Just across from the Marolles Flea Market, Broebbeleir serves up their organic frites alongside local Brussels-made beers and other fried Belgian foods in a beautiful former 19th-century fire station.

3. Brasserie Cantillon

Rue Gheude 56; tel. 02 521 49 28; www.cantillon.be; 10am-5pm Mon.-Tues., 10am-5pm Thurs.-Sat.

Fortified with fries, make the 15-minute walk to Brasserie Cantillon for a real beer experience (reserve ahead). Established in 1900, this family-run brewery is the last traditional brewery in Brussels, still brewing using original methods. Geuze beers are their specialty, and you can see (and taste) how it's done on one of their tours or tastings. You can also purchase rare bottles at the shop.

4. Horta Museum

Rue Américaine 27; tel. 02 543 04 90; www.hortamuseum.be; 2pm-5:30pm Tues.-Fri., 11am-5:30pm Sat.-Sun.; €10, students €5

Hop on a tram or make the half-hour walk southeast to the Horta Museum, one of

Belfry of Bruges

the most magnificent art nouveau sights in Brussels, the birthplace of this art and design style. The home and studio of the grandfather of art nouveau, Victor Horta, has been perfectly preserved, with its original furniture, stained glass windows, architectural fixtures, and even decorations, supplemented with period pieces. Every detail of the house, from the curvature of the banister that hides a heater to a swiveling urinal, is thought out to maximize beauty and functionality simultaneously—the philosophy behind art nouveau.

5. Mussels at Aux Vieux

Rue Saint-Boniface 35; tel. 02 503 31 11; www.auvieuxbruxelles.com; 6pm-11:30pm Mon.-Thurs., 6pm-midnight Fri.-Sat., 6pm-11pm Sun.; €27

Head back north on a tram to Aux Vieux for a taste of Brussels-style mussels. Despite its location on one of the city's hippest squares, the café feels like a time capsule from the past. It also has a lovely terrace.

6. Beer at Delirium Café

Impasse de la Fidélité 4; tel. 02 514 44 34; www.deliriumvillage.com; 3pm-11pm Mon.-Thurs., 2pm-11pm Fri.-Sun.

Located at the end of the alleyway home to Jeanneke Pis, the Delirium Café holds the world's record for the most beers available at a café (2,004). You'll of course find Delirium on tap, but the Trappist beer selection is also worth studying. The walk from Aux Vieux (20 minutes) takes you past a number of the sights you've seen over the past two days.

Bruges

Where to Stay: Steenstraat Quarter

Arrive by: Train from Brussels Central or Brussels Midi to Bruges Train Station (1 hour)

DAY 5

1. Markt

Markt 1; open 24/7; free

From Brussels, the train ride to Bruges takes just an hour. Get an early start and you can have breakfast at a café on the glittering central square of Bruges. Markt, the ancient heart of the city, is one of its most classic views, with the Belfry rising in the east. For a millennium, this square has been the city's main marketplace, and still today, on Wednesday mornings, the square transforms into a bustling local market with fruit, vegetables, flowers, and cheeses. Countless cafés in former guild houses vie for tourists' money. Sit down at **Grand Café Craenenburg** (Markt 16; tel. 050 33 34 02; www.craenenburg.be; 8am-10pm daily), housed in a 14th-century building that used to be a smokers room, and watch the growing bustle. Afterward, stop in Bruges's oldest bookshop, **De Reyghere Bookstore** (Markt 12-13; tel. 050 33 34 03; https://dereyghere.be; 9am-6pm daily), which has been in the same location on the square for more than 100 years.

★ 2. Belfry of Bruges

Markt 7; tel. 050 44 87 11; www.visitbruges.be/en/belfort-belfry; 9:30am-6pm daily; €12

On Markt's south side, the Belfry is an iconic symbol of Bruges (not to mention a key location in the cult classic film *In Bruges*), and this 13th-century tower is a must-see for lovers of history, cultural heritage, and a good photo. The Belfry housed various government functions, from treasury to outpost to archives, and the carillon, installed in the 16th century with 47 bells, is played by the Bruges carillon master a few days a week and still keeps time for the city. The steep and winding 366 steps up the Belfry's skinny 83-meter (272-foot) tower can leave you out of breath, but the view of the

left, chocolatier in the Steenstraat Quarter; right, Rozenhoedkaai Viewpoint

medieval city of Bruges from the top will take your breath away.

3. Chocolatier-Hopping in the Steenstraat Quarter

Head west on Steenstaat from Markt, and you'll hit your first chocolate shop on Simon Stevinplein: **The Chocolate Line** (Simon Stevinplein 19; tel. 050 34 10 90; www.thechocolate-line.be; 10:30am-6:30pm Sun.-Mon., 9:30am-6:30pm Tues.-Sat.; €10 small box) is beloved for its famous chocolate shooter and traditional Belgian pralines. From there, keep going south to Mariastraat, where you'll find **Pol Depla Chocolatier** (Mariastraat 20; tel. 050 33 49 53; www.poldepla.be; 10am-6pm daily; €10 small box), one of Bruges's premiere chocolatiers, and **The Chocolate Brothers** (Mariastraat 34; 10am-6pm daily; €7 small box, cash only), a surprisingly affordable shop with a popular crunchy milk chocolate praline. If you need sustenance along the way, try **Otomat** (Simon Stevinplein 12; tel. 050 66 21 21; https://otomat.be; 11am-10pm daily; €10-20), close to The Chocolate Line. This popular Belgian pizzeria uses Duvel's beer yeast in their dough.

4. Rozenhoedkaai Viewpoint

Rozenhoedkaai; open 24/7; free

To see the Bruges Belfry from another (and most iconic) angle, stroll over to the famous Rozenhoedkaai viewpoint along the Dijver canal. You can enjoy a view of passing boats and picturesque buildings in the medieval style lining the Kraanrei canal.

5. Lace at 'T Apostelientje

Balstraat 11; tel. 050 33 78 60; www.apostelientje.be; 1pm-5pm Tues.-Sat.

For a lesson on the Flemish tradition of lace in Bruges, walk east toward the Sint Anna Quarter. The Bruges style of lace-making is incredibly time-consuming, using up to 200 needles (known as bobbins) and 1,500 threads at once for more elaborate pieces. 'T Apostelientje is an antique shop specializing in Flemish lace. It is almost like a museum and has something for every budget. Balstraat itself is worth lingering on, as well, with its beautiful whitewashed former almshouses that look straight out of a fairy tale.

6. Sint-Janshuismolen and Koeleweimolen Windmills

Kruisvest 3 and 11; tel. 050 44 87 43; www.visitbruges.be/en/koeleweimolen-koelewei-mill-2; 9:30am-12:30pm and 1:30pm-5pm Tues.-Sun. Apr.-Sept.; adults €4, children free

If you haven't seen any windmills up to this point, you have another chance at the Bruges ramparts on the eastern end of the medieval city center. Nearly 25 windmills once stood here. Today Bruges has only four windmills, with just two of these open to the public in peak season. **Sint-Janshuismolen** was constructed in 1770 and stands in the place of an even earlier windmill. The **Koeleweimolen** was built in 1765 and still grinds grains into flour today. Both windmills hold small museums open during peak season that give you a glimpse into their history. Those without a fear of vertigo can climb the slightly terrifying stairs to see the windmills in action.

7. Le Trappiste

Kuipersstraat 33; tel. 0475 45 50 66; www.letrappistebrugge.com; 5pm-1am Thurs.-Tues.

Walk back toward the center of Bruges to toast the day—and your trip—with your choice of any number of beers at this well-known Belgian beer bar. Set in a stone cellar, Le Trappiste has 25 high-quality and occasionally rare beers on tap, not including their massive bottle list and private collection (including beers brewed by the owners).

TRANSPORTATION

Air

The Amsterdam and Brussels airports are easily accessible from overseas destinations and well-connected to the rest of Europe. The airport closest to Bruges, Oostende-Brugge International Airport, is not practical for most travelers.

- **Amsterdam Schiphol Airport** (AMS; Evert van de Beekstraat 202; www.schiphol.nl): About 20 km (12 mi) southwest of Amsterdam; 10-15 minutes by train to central Amsterdam (€4.50 one-way)
- **Brussels International Airport** (BRU; Leopoldlaan; www.brusselsairport.be): 15 km (9 mi) northeast of Brussels Centrum; 16-30 minutes by train to central Brussels (€9.10 one-way)

Train

Both the Netherlands and Belgium have good public transit within and between major cities, making the train the best way to travel in the region. The **Thalys** (www.thalys.com), a high-speed train that originates in Paris, connects Amsterdam and Brussels (2 hours; €29-100). Bruges and Brussels are also well connected by regular Intercity (IC) trains

Amsterdam Centraal train station

(1 hour; €14.30) run by **NMBS/SNCB** (www.belgiantrain.be).

- **Amsterdam Centraal** (Stationsplein 15; tel. 030 751 5155; www.ns.nl): Amsterdam's main train station is centrally located and easily accessible to the sights in this itinerary.
- **Brussels Central** (Carrefour de l'Europe): Located 500 meters (1,600 feet) from Grand Place, this most central station in Brussels is a good departure point for Bruges.
- **Brussels Midi/Brussels-Zuid** (Avenue Fonsny 47B): Located 2 km (1 mi) south of the city center, this station (one of four) is where high-speed trains from Amsterdam arrive. Trains to Bruges also depart from here.
- **Bruges Train Station** (Vrijdagmarkt 10; tel. 02 528 28 28; www.belgianrail.be): The main train station in Bruges is about 1 km (0.6 mi) southwest of the city center, just outside the oval of Bruges' widest canal.

Public Transportation

Some local bus systems, including the system in Brussels, are moving to a cashless model. Belgian and Dutch public transportation websites are often intended for residents and can be hard for visitors to figure out, so it may be best to purchase your ticket at transit hubs before boarding your bus. On the other hand, the dedicated bus app for each region—**De Lijn** (www.delijn.be) for northern Belgium or **GVB** (https://en.gvb.nl) for Amsterdam—is very useful, especially to check the bus schedule.

Amsterdam

The public transit agency in Amsterdam, **GVB** (https://en.gvb.nl), operates a network of buses, trams, and a Metro in the larger Amsterdam region, though not to other cities like Rotterdam or the Hague. Generally, trams are more tourist-friendly, as there's typically a kiosk manned by a person on board and announcements

CONNECT WITH

- London and Paris (page 44)
- Holland Junction Network (page 377)

often note nearby attractions. The day pass is a steal at €8 per 24 hours for adults. Public transit in the Netherlands requires checking out when you exit—if you forget to check out, you may invalidate your pass.

Brussels

STIB, or **MIVB** in Dutch (www.stib-mivb.be), is the main public transit agency in Brussels, responsible for buses, trams, and the Metro. The Metro in particular is very easy to navigate, with an easy-to-understand circular shape. A 24-hour pass costs €7.50, with unlimited transfers.

Bruges

De Lijn (headquartered at the Bruges Train Station, Stationsplein 5; www.delijn.be) runs buses in the Flanders region, but walking is the best way to see the city.

Walking

All the cities in this itinerary are very walkable, and aside from a few longer distances and the Amsterdam Noord cycling route, it's reasonable to reach the sights within each city on foot.

Getting Back

If you need to get back to Amsterdam from Bruges, it takes three hours by train. Transfer in Brussels to take the high-speed Thalys back to Amsterdam. If you want to fly home or to your next destination, it's an easy train ride back to Brussels, where there is a well-connected international airport. The closed airport to Bruges, Oostende-Brugge International Airport, only serves limited destinations.

BARCELONA AND MADRID

Why Go: From cosmopolitan, architecturally stunning Barcelona to Madrid, with its rich artistic history and legendary social scene, Spain's two biggest cities offer unique perspectives on Spanish life.

Number of Days: 5

Total Distance: 600 km (375 mi)

Seasons: Spring and fall

Start: Barcelona

End: Madrid

Digging into the world-class art, fascinating food culture, and quirky hidden gems of Barcelona and Madrid will give you incredible insight into Spanish life. Barcelona is bestowed with a laid-back ambiance, thanks to its location on the Mediterranean. Its infectious energy and fairytale-like Modernisme design have made it one of the world's top destinations. Madrid, rich in history and art and the seat of Spain's government, is seen by some as more serious. But wander around and you'll be surprised at what you find: lively tapas bars and outdoor terraces, century-old shops, and neighborhoods that feel like their own little villages.

TOP 3

Sampling classic Spanish bites and watching the world go by at Barcelona's **Mercat de la Boqueria** (page 101).

Being awed by the soaring towers of Gaudí's fantastical masterpiece, **La Sagrada Família,** which has become an emblem of Barcelona long before its scheduled completion date (page 106).

Immersing yourself in one of the world's most famous art galleries, the **Prado,** which houses a treasure trove of works by Spanish and European masters (page 112).

Barcelona

Where to Stay: Barri Gòtic (Gothic Quarter), touristy but historical; or Eixample, conveniently located in the heart of Barcelona's Modernista masterpieces

Arrive by: Plane to Barcelona-El Prat airport

DAY 1

1. Plaça de Catalunya and La Rambla

Head straight for Plaça de Catalunya, the vast central square where the Ciutat Vella (old town) meets the 19th-century gridded city. Get your bearings while watching the morning buzz from the terrace of **Café Zurich** (Plaça de Catalunya, 1-4; tel. 93/317-9153; 8am-11pm Mon.-Fri., 9am-midnight Sat., 9am-11pm Sun.). This historic establishment has served as a classic meeting point for more than a century.

Then, set off on a leisurely ramble down La Rambla, taking in the sights and sounds of the city's most famous street. This tree-lined boulevard is lined with stalls—from artists selling their visions of Barcelona to newspaper and souvenir kiosks flogging football shirts, fridge magnets, and postcards—and some of the city's key buildings, like the opera house and the Boqueria food market, where you'll be heading next.

★ 2. Mercat de la Boqueria

La Rambla, 91; tel. 93/318-2584; www.boqueria.barcelona; 8am-8:30pm Mon.-Sat.

A five-minute walk down La Rambla is the glorious Mercat de la Boqueria. This bustling fresh food market is a carnival of color, smell, and flavor, with more than 200 stalls selling everything from sheep's heads to live lobster (though tourists often outnumber local shoppers). The building you see today dates to the 19th century, with Modernista touches like the arches by the entrance added in the 20th century. If you want to sample the market's seasonal morsels, fresh from the stalls, grab a stool at the legendary **Bar Pinotxo** (tel. 93/317-1731; 6:30am-4pm).

La Rambla

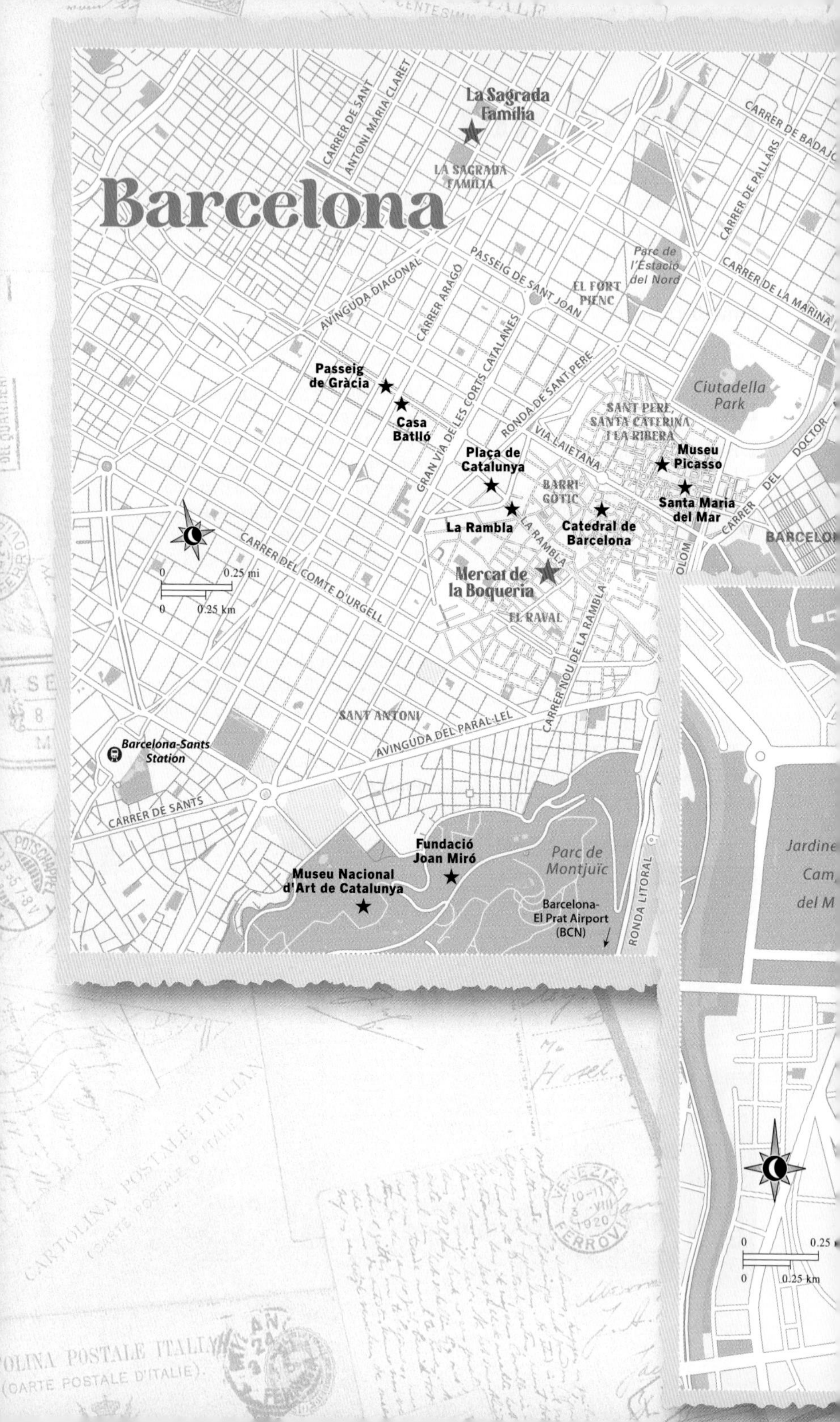
Barcelona
La Sagrada Família
LA SAGRADA FAMÍLIA
CARRER DE SANT
ANTONI MARIA CLARET
CARRER DE BADAJOZ
CARRER DE PALLARS
Parc de l'Estació del Nord
CARRER DE LA MARINA
EL FORT PIENC
PASSEIG DE SANT JOAN
AVINGUDA DIAGONAL
CARRER ARAGÓ
GRAN VIA DE LES CORTS CATALANES
RONDA DE SANT PERE
Ciutadella Park
Passeig de Gràcia
Casa Batlló
SANT PERE, SANTA CATERINA I LA RIBERA
VIA LAIETANA
Museu Picasso
Plaça de Catalunya
BARRI GÒTIC
Santa Maria del Mar
La Rambla
LA RAMBLA
Catedral de Barcelona
CARRER DEL DOCTOR
CARRER DEL COMTE D'URGELL
0 0.25 mi
0 0.25 km
Mercat de la Boqueria
EL RAVAL
CARRER NOU DE LA RAMBLA
SANT ANTONI
AVINGUDA DEL PARAL·LEL
Barcelona-Sants Station
CARRER DE SANTS
Fundació Joan Miró
Parc de Montjuïc
Museu Nacional d'Art de Catalunya
Barcelona-El Prat Airport (BCN)
RONDA LITORAL

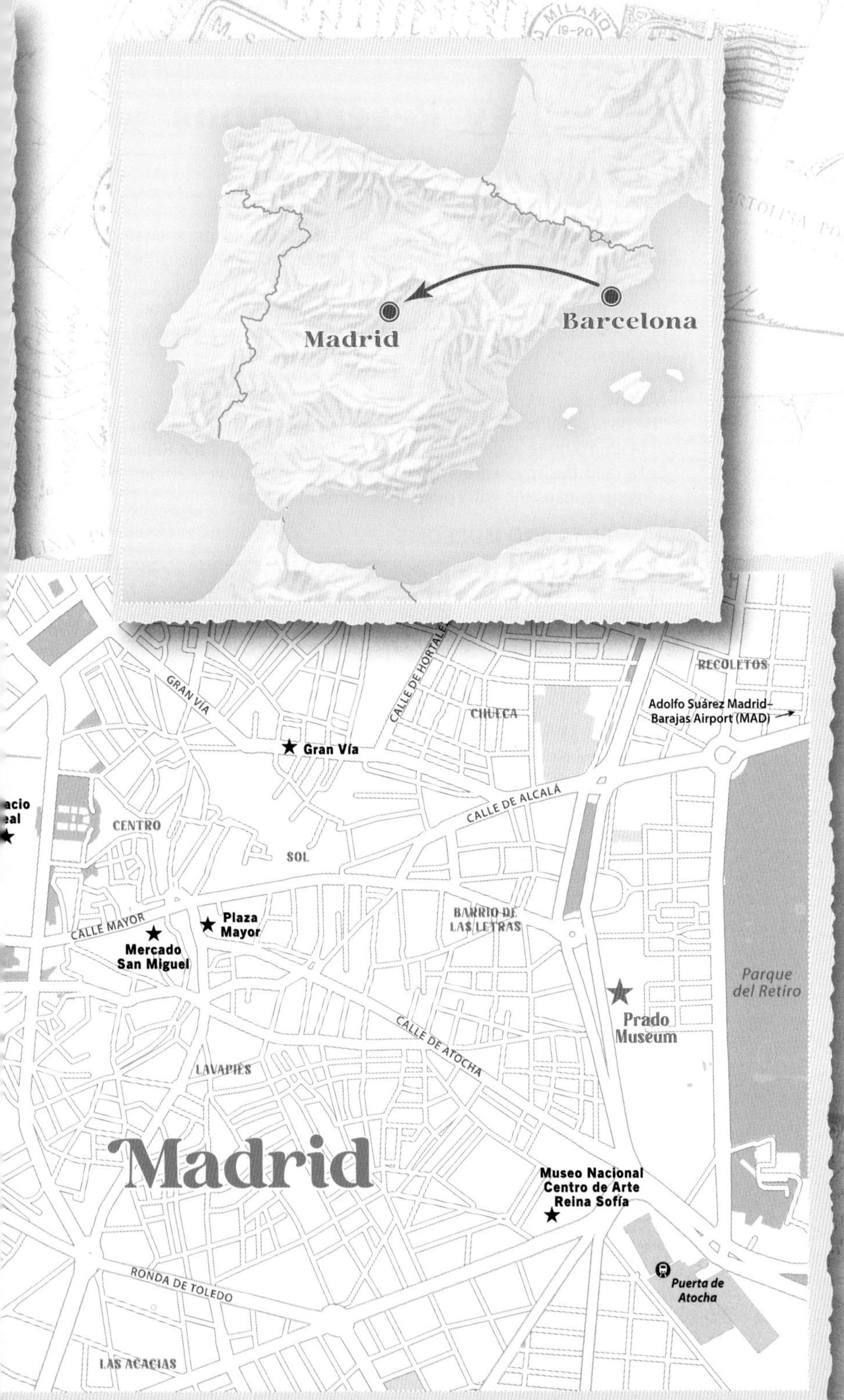

Madrid
Barcelona
GRAN VÍA
CALLE DE HORTALEZA
RECOLETOS
CHUECA
Adolfo Suárez Madrid–Barajas Airport (MAD)
Gran Vía
CALLE DE ALCALÁ
CENTRO
SOL
CALLE MAYOR
Plaza Mayor
Mercado San Miguel
BARRIO DE LAS LETRAS
Parque del Retiro
Prado Museum
CALLE DE ATOCHA
LAVAPIÉS
Madrid
Museo Nacional Centro de Arte Reina Sofía
RONDA DE TOLEDO
Puerta de Atocha
LAS ACACIAS

Key Reservations

TRAVEL PASSES

Barcelona

The Barcelona Card (www.barcelonacard.com) and its shorter time-period alternative, the Barcelona Card Express, are among the best-value cards for their wide range of freebies and discounts, with public transport included. The **Art Ticket** (www.articketbcn.org) provides access to six of Barcelona's top museums and cultural attractions.

Madrid

The **Paseo del Arte Card** (€32) can be used to visit the collections of Madrid's three major art galleries: the Prado Museum, the Reina Sofía, and the Thyssen-Bornemisza Museum; it gets you a 20-percent discount on the entry price of the three museums.

MONUMENTS AND MUSEUMS

Barcelona

- **Museu Picasso**
- **Sagrada Família**
- **Casa Batlló**
- **Park Güell**

Madrid

- **Prado Museum**
- **Museo Nacional Centro de Arte Reina Sofía**

Casa Batlló

Note that many of Barcelona's museums and cultural attractions are closed or have shorter hours on Mondays. Neighborhoods known for their nightlife (especially in Madrid) rise slowly in the morning. At 9am, expect closed shops and eerily empty streets.

3. Catedral de Barcelona

Pla de la Seu; www.catedralbcn.org; cathedral 8am-7:30pm Mon.-Sat., 8am-7:30pm Sun., cloister 8:30am-12:30pm and 5:15pm-7pm Mon.-Sat, 8:30am-1pm and 5:15pm-7pm Sun.; €7

Heading east from La Boqueria, dive into the **Barri Gòtic (Gothic Quarter),** a medieval warren tangle of streets hiding beautiful little squares and curiosities at every turn. You're making your way to Barcelona's cathedral, a huge island in the tiny warrens that make up the Gothic quarter, and one of the best examples of Gothic architecture in Spain. The richly decorated facade was added in the late 19th century; the rest of the structure was built between 1298 and 1448. The vast interior of the cathedral is divided into a central nave surrounded by 28 chapels. Take the elevator (€3) up to the cathedral's rooftop for spectacular views of the cathedral's spires and the heart of Gothic Barcelona.

For lunch, head to **Bar la Plata** (Carrer

left, Museu Picasso; right, Catedral de Barcelona

de la Mercè, 28; tel. 93/315-1009; www.barlaplata.com; 9am-3:15pm and 6:15pm-11pm Mon.-Sat.; €3), one of the most authentic old tapas bars in the Gothic quarter. Tables are scarce; this is a place to prop up the bar or spill out onto the street, like the locals.

4. Museu Picasso

Carrer Montcada, 15-23; tel. 93/256-3000; www.bcn.cat/museupicasso; 10am-5pm Mon., 9am-8:30pm (Thurs. until 9:30pm) Tues.-Sun.; adults €12, ages 18-25 and over 65 €7, free 6pm-9:30pm Thurs. and first Sun. of the month

After lunch, trace the roots of a genius at the Museu Picasso, the city's most visited art gallery. Although born in Málaga, Picasso spent a lot of his youth in Barcelona; you could say that it was here that he learned to be an artist. As such, the Picasso Museum is a key reference for his early works and inspirations, giving insight into the foundations of his illustrious career. Book tickets, audio guides, and tours online ahead of time to avoid the lines.

After your visit to the museum, walk two minutes to the magnificent Gothic basilica of **Santa Maria del Mar** (Plaça de Santa Maria, 1; tel. 93/310-2390; www.santamariadelmarbarcelona.org; 9am-8:30pm Mon.-Sat., 10am-8pm Sun.; cultural visits 1pm-5pm Mon.-Sat., 2pm-5pm Sun.; €10 during visiting hours, free at other times; mass 7:30pm daily, noon Sun.). It may not be Barcelona's most famous church, but it is arguably its most beautiful. Take some time to recharge at your hotel before dinner.

5. A Night Out in El Raval

West of Las Ramblas, El Raval is home to some of the city's oldest bars, bohemian enclaves that have been doing business since the early 19th century. Start with a predinner vermouth at **La Confitería** (Carrer de Sant Pau, 128; tel. 93/140-5435; www.confiteria.cat; 7pm-3am Mon.-Thurs., 6pm-3:30am Fri., 5pm-3:30am Sat., 5pm-3am Sun.), an atmospheric bar that was once confectioner's shop and has retained many of the original fittings. For dinner, try another, hipper take on tapas at **Bar Cañete** (Carrer de la Unió, 17; tel. 93/270-3458; www.barcanete.com; 1pm-midnight Mon.-Sat.; €15), then head to **Bar Marsella** (Carrer de Sant Pau, 65; tel. 93/442-7263; 6pm-2am Mon., 10am-2pm Tues.-Sun., 6pm-2am Tues.-Thurs., 6pm-2:30am Fri.-Sat., 6pm-2am Sun.), an El Raval staple since 1820. Ernest Hemingway used to sink an absinthe here, and it still specializes in the drink known as "the green fairy."

DAY 2

★ 1. La Sagrada Família

Carrer de Mallorca, 401; tel. 93/208-0414; www.sagradafamilia.org; 9am-6pm daily Nov.-Feb., 9am-7pm Mar. and Oct., 9am-8pm Apr.-Sept.; basic ticket €15, ticket plus audioguide €22, guided experience €24, top views €29

Start bright and early at Barcelona's most famous monument, the Basilica and Expiatory Church of the Holy Family, widely known as La Sagrada Família. Now 70 percent complete, the construction of Antoni Gaudí's ambitious design began in 1882 and is projected to be completed in 2026, on the centenary of Gaudí's death (he was struck by a tram in 1926, at the age of 73). The longest-running architectural project on earth is a firm fixture of the Barcelona skyline, its soaring spires and yellow cranes a sign of the work still to be done on this famously unfinished church.

Admire the ornately decorated Nativity Facade and the starker Passion Facade, and look heavenward at the soaring towers of Gaudí's fantastical masterpiece. Inside, marvel at the kaleidoscopic colors of the two-story-high stained-glass windows. The columns are reminiscent of trees; Gaudí felt that it was in a forest that man felt closest to God.

All tickets can and should be purchased online ahead of time.

2. Lunch on Passeig de Gràcia

Walk 20 minutes or take the metro (L5) from Sagrada Família to Diagonal to **Mordisco** (Passatge de la Concepció, 10; tel. 93/487-9656; www.mordisco.com; €12), set in a leafy conservatory on a cute little street just off the Passeig de Gràcia, Barcelona's answer to the Champs-Elyseés. With a kitchen open all day, it's a favorite among locals for

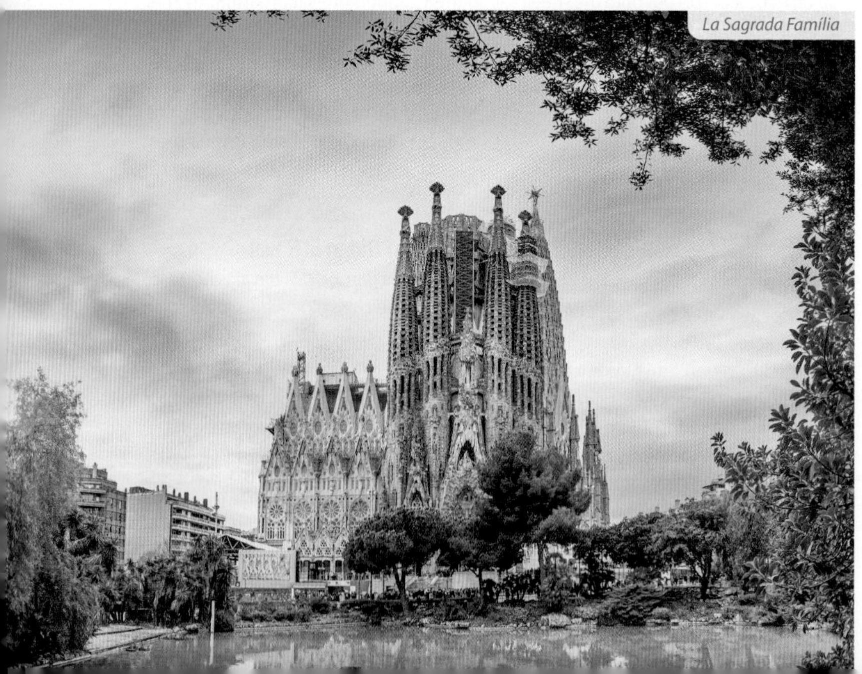

La Sagrada Família

NAME CHECK: Antoni Gaudí

Antoni Gaudí i Cornet was born on June 25, 1852, in Reus, Catalonia. In 1870, he moved to Barcelona to study architecture; he was a mediocre student who only occasionally displayed flashes of the genius to come. When he graduated from the School of Architecture in 1878, the school's director, Elies Rogent, said, "I do not know if we have awarded this degree to a madman or to a genius; only time will tell." He went on to become one of the most creative and imaginative architects of his era, and was central to **Catalan Modernism** (also known as Modernista or Modernisme), an architectural, artistic, and literary movement toward the end of the 19th century that sought to find a cultural expression of Catalan identity.

In addition to **La Sagrada Família** (page 106), widely considered to be Gaudí's greatest masterpiece, and **Casa Batlló** (page 107), his best-known residential work, Barcelona is blessed by several other buildings created by the singular artist.

- **Casa Vicens** (Carrer de les Carolines, 20; www.casavicens.org; 10am-8pm daily; €16, children under 16 free): In 1883, Gaudí was commissioned to create his first residential building, this summer house in Gràcia. It shows several motifs that the architect would use again and again, such as intricate wrought-iron work, a focus on curves and nature, and a new technique called trencadís, which used broken ceramic pieces to make colorful mosaics.
- **La Pedrera** (Casa Milà; Passeig de Gràcia, 92; tel. 93/214-2584; www.lapedrera.com; 9am-8:30pm daily; €25): Gaudí's last private home design, with its curved stone facade, wrought-iron balconies and doors, and artisanal creative touches in murals, doorknobs, and furniture, was unlike anything seen before. Locals gave it the scornful nickname La Pedrera ("the Quarry") for its similarity to a big pile of stone.
- **Park Güell** (Carrer de Larrard; www.parkguell.cat; 8:30am-6:15pm Oct. 28-Mar. 24, 8am-8:30pm Mar. 25-Apr. 29, 8am-9:30pm Apr. 30-Aug. 26, 8am-8:30pm Aug. 27-Oct. 27; advance ticket online €7.50, on-site ticket €8.50): With its much-photographed dragon sculpture and mosaic benches overlooking the Mediterranean, Park Güell is one of the most emblematic Gaudí sights in Barcelona. The complex was built as a high-class housing estate set on Carmel Hill in the north of Gràcia.

its fresh, seasonal produce and creative dishes. After lunch, wander down the city's most elegant boulevard, a parade of fin-de-siècle wealth and high-end shops. It's the central artery of L'Eixample ("Expansion"), built in the 19th century to ease crowding in the booming Barri Gòtic. The new bourgeoisie flooded into the area, commissioning fantastical new buildings, and Modernisme flourished.

3. Casa Batlló

Passeig de Gràcia, 43; tel. 93/216-0306; www.casabatllo.es; 9am-9pm daily; €24.50

After a 10-minute walk down Passeig de Gràcia, you'll reach Casa Batlló. Built as an apartment block in 1877 by Emilio Sala Cortés (one of Gaudí's architecture professors), this building was bought in 1903 by textile magnate Josep Batlló y Casanovas, who employed Antoni Gaudí to fully renovate the house. Batlló had originally planned to completely demolish the building, but Gaudí persuaded him to keep the structure and completely re-create its design. Gaudí changed the exterior and the internal layout of the building, adding characteristic touches such as his broken mosaics, ceramics, and curved designs (he believed that there are no straight lines in nature so there should be none in the building). This spectacular residence culminates in a polychromatic tiled roof resembling a dragon's scaly back.

Several ticket options, including the Casa Batlló + FastPass (€29.50 online, €33.50 from ticket office), allow visitors to skip the line. It is worth buying tickets via the official Casa Battló website for a discount.

4. A Night Out in L'Eixample

Eixample is home to some of Barcelona's most expensive restaurants, but there are also plenty of accessible, interesting places to visit. Start out at **Monvinic** (Carrer de la Diputació, 249; tel. 93/272-6187; www.monvinic.com; 7pm-10:30pm Mon., 1:30pm-3:30pm and 8pm-10:30pm Tues.-Fri., 7pm-10:30pm Sat.), a sleek and spacious bar and shop that's like a temple for wine buffs; have a glass of cava, Catalonia's sparkling wine.

For dinner, you can check out one of Eixample's fancier restaurants, like the tasting menu at **Disfrutar** (Carrer de Villarroel, 163; tel. 93/348-6896; www.disfrutarbarcelona.com; 1:30pm-2:30pm and 8pm-9:30pm Mon.-Fri.; €120), which should be booked well in advance, or have more vermouth and tapas at **Senyor Vermut** (Carrer de Provença, 85; tel. 93/532-8865; 6pm-11pm Tues.-Wed., noon-4pm and 6pm-11pm Thurs., noon-11pm Fri.-Sat., noon-4pm Sun.; €5). After dinner, try stylish, wood-clad cocktail bar **Dry Martini** (Carrer d'Aribau, 162-166; tel. 93/217-5072; www.drymartiniorg.com; 1pm-2:30am Mon.-Thurs., 1pm-3am Fri., 6:30pm-3am Sat., 6:30pm-2:30am Sun.), or on one of the neighborhood's many hotel rooftop terraces, such as the Sky Bar at the **Axel Hotel Barcelona** (Carrer d'Aribau, 33; tel. 93/323-9393; www.axelhotels.com).

DAY 3

1. Museu Nacional d'Art de Catalunya

Palau Nacional, Parc de Montjuïc; tel. 93/622-0376; www.museunacional.cat; 10am-6pm Tues.-Sat. and 10am-3pm Sun. Oct.-Apr., 10am-8pm Tues.-Sat. and 10am-3pm Sun. May-Sept.; €12

Grab a pastry from classic old bakery **Mauri** (Carrer de Provença, 241; tel. 93/215-1020; www.pasteleriasmauri.com; 8am-10pm daily) in the Exiample. Mauri has been serving locals freshly made bread, cakes, and desserts since 1929. Then take the metro to Espanya and climb up Montjuïc (the hill south of Barcelona—there are escalators if you don't want to face the stairs) to the Paulau Nacional, home of the fantastic Museu Nacional d'Art de Catalunya, which houses a thousand years of the region's art. At the top, be sure to stop and take in the panorama of the city from the terrace—many come just for the views and don't enter the museum at all.

But the museum is definitely worth a look, particularly the collection of Romanesque art from the 11th-13th centuries. The building itself, built for the 1929 International Exhibition, is well worth a visit; expansive and light-filled, its grandeur and its domes make it seem much older than it is.

2. Fundació Joan Miró

Parc de Montjuïc; tel. 93/443-9470; www.fmirobcn.org; 10am-6pm Tues.-Wed. and Fri. Nov.-Mar., 10am-8pm Tues.-Wed. and Fri. Apr.-Oct., 10am-9pm Thurs., 10am-8pm Sat., 10am-3pm Sun. year-round; adults €12, under 15 free

Walk past the Olympic Stadium, home to Barcelona's triumphant 1992 summer Olympics, to the Fundació Joan Miró. Born in Barcelona in 1893, Miró was one of the 20th century's most famous

Local Drinking

VERMOUTH

Vermouth, a fortified white wine flavored with botanicals, has always been a popular drink in Spain, but while it was long considered strictly for grandmas, it has experienced something of a renaissance in recent years.

Traditionally vermouth was meant to stimulate the appetite and aid digestion, and in Spain it is usually enjoyed before lunch from around noon, a time known as la hora de vermut (vermouth hour). Spaniards typically drink sweet, red vermouth with a tapa—be it olives or potato chips, or something a little more elaborate. Many of the city's old tavernas serve the drink from the barrel, with an olive and an orange slice garnish. Order vermouth with soda water if you want to dilute it.

CAVA

Cava is a Spanish sparkling wine made using the same methods as champagne. Grapes (usually macabeu, xarello, and parellada) are fermented and mixed with sugar and yeast, then bottled, sealed, and kept in cellars for around nine months for a second fermentation.

About 95 percent of all cava is produced in the Penedès region of Catalonia, centered around the village of Sant Sadurní d'Anoia, 60 km (37 mi) west of Barcelona, and there are several traditional cava bars in Barcelona where you can try local bubbly.

surrealist painters, known for his use of vivid primary colors and distorted shapes in paintings, ceramics, sculpture, and murals. This museum, which opened in 1975, was created by the painter himself, and he endowed it with much of his personal collection. The museum offers visitors a tour through Miró's career, from his early paintings, depicting his family summer home in Mont-roig, through his huge canvas paintings to his ceramics and bronze sculptures.

3. Afternoon on the Beach

Take a 10-minute ride on the **cable car** (Teleferico del Puerto; access points at Av. Miramar and Passeig de Joan de Borbó, 88; €11 one way, €16.50 round-trip) down to the port and enjoy a laid-back lunch at a chiringuito or paella at one of the

top, Barceloneta; bottom, Ciutadella Park

restaurants along the seafront, such as **Can Majo** (Carrer de l'Almirall Aixada, 23; tel. 93/221-5455; www.canmajo.es; 1pm-3:30pm and 8pm-11:30pm Tues.-Sat., 1pm-3:30pm Sun.; €20). Pair your lunchtime paella with a glass of crisp white wine, as the locals do.

Walk off your lunch along the seafront promenade or spend the afternoon on **Barceloneta,** the famous city beach. Don't miss a glass of cava in **Can Paixano** (Carrer de la Reina Cristina, 7; tel. 93/310-0839; www.canpaixano.com; 9am-10:30pm Mon.-Sat.), a hugely popular local cava bar just off the waterfront.

4. Sunset in Ciutadella Park

Passeig de Picasso, 21

As the sun is setting, head over to the famous Ciutadella Park, originally the site of a great citadel, built by Philip V after he took Barcelona during the War of the Spanish Succession. (The citadel, which was intended to prevent locals from rising up against the central powers in Madrid, was detested by locals and finally demolished in 1869.)

The 28-hectare (70-acre) park as we know it today is a popular leisure spot, constructed for the 1888 Universal Exhibition; the Arc de Triomf was built as the main access gate to the exhibition. Architect Josep Fontsère designed the park, and his young apprentice Antoni Gaudí assisted with the construction of the huge fountain, the Cascada. At golden hour, you're likely to find locals and tourists alike wandering, sitting on the grass, and watching buskers and other street performers.

Madrid

Where to Stay: Sol and Centro neighborhoods, within easy walking distance to all the main sights

Arrive by: Train from Barcelona-Sants to Puerta de Atocha (2.5-3 hours)

DAY 4

1. Plaza Mayor

After an early morning train from Barcelona Sants station to Madrid, start your first day in Spain's capital city with a classic local experience: dunking some fresh churros into a cup of thick hot chocolate at **Chocolatería San Ginés** (Pasadizo de San Gines, 5; tel. 91/365-6546; https://chocolateriasangines.com; open 24 hours). Then walk one minute to the heart of the city, Plaza Mayor. Madrid's grand central square has been the scene of many important events throughout its over 400-year history, from markets and bullfights to public trials and executions during the Spanish Inquisition. Today, Plaza Mayor and its winding side streets reveal Madrid life in all its forms, from early-morning delivery men and menu-touting waiters to locals rushing to work and tourists snapping photographs.

2. Palacio Real

Calle de Bailén; tel. 91/454-8700, www.patrimonionacional.es; 10am-6pm Mon.-Sun winter, 10am-8pm Mon.-Sun. summer; €10, €14 with kitchen tour

A five-minute walk away, visit the Palacio Real. Madrid's Royal Palace is gigantic; it has more than 3,000 rooms, making it the largest palace by floor area in Europe to this day. Tour the palace to get a good taste of the lavish lifestyles of Spanish monarchs through the ages. Today, while it is the official residence of Spain's royal family, King Felipe and Queen Letizia choose to live in the more modest, 300-room Zarzuela Palace, on the outskirts of the city, using the Royal Palace for state occasions only.

Next door to the palace, stroll around the tranquil Sabatini Gardens (Calle de Bailén, 2; 8am-9pm daily). They are laid out in a neoclassical style, with box hedges,

(top to bottom) Plaza Mayor; Palacio Real; vermouth at Mercado San Miguel; Prado Museum

little mazes, and fountains. The northern end of the central rectangular lake is a popular spot for photographs of the palace—the huge building reflected in the waters is a memorable sight.

3. Vermouth at Mercado San Miguel

Plaza de San Miguel; tel. 91/542-4936; www.mercadodesanmiguel.es; 10am-midnight Sun.-Wed., 10am-2am Thurs.-Sat.

A 10-minute walk back toward Sol, stop at Mercado San Miguel for a bite to eat. This wrought-iron-covered food market, built in 1916, can be touristy, but it's well worth a visit. You'll find everything from olives and jamón Ibérico (Iberian cured ham) to tapas, oysters, and a huge range of wines, cider, and cocktails; you could spend hours eating and drinking here. It can get very busy, so head there for a pre-lunch vermouth or else embrace the crowds and get ready to swoop when you spot a free table. **La Hora de Vermut** is a great place in the market to stop for a pre-lunch vermouth.

★ 4. Prado Museum

Paseo del Prado; tel. 91/330-2800; www.museodelprado.es; 10am-8pm Mon.-Sat., 10am-7pm Sun.; €15

From the market, it's a 20-minute walk to the Prado Museum, one of the world's most renowned art galleries. The Prado Museum holds three floors of treasures spanning the 12th-early 20th centuries based on the former Spanish Royal Collection. It is the place to see works of some of Spain's greatest painters as well as masterpieces from farther afield.

The Italian Painting Collection includes works from Renaissance artists including Raphael, Caravaggio, Titian, and Tintoretto. The Early Netherlandish and Flemish Painting Collection includes Bosch's "Garden of Earthly Delights" and nearly 90 works by Rubens. If you are on a tight schedule, dedicate your time to the Spanish Painting Collection; don't miss Diego Velázquez's "Las Meninas," which shook up European art and is one of the museum's most famous paintings.

WATCH

Mujeres al borde de un ataque de nervios / Women on the Verge of a Nervous Breakdown: Set in Madrid, director Pedro Almodóvar's earliest international hit (1988) is a riot of melodrama, color, and comedy.

READ

The Shadow of the Wind by Carlos Ruiz Zafón: This worldwide bestseller is set in Barcelona just after the Spanish Civil War, following Daniel Sempere and his journey into the Cemetery of Forgotten Books and the mystery that lies within.

LISTEN

"El Meu Avi" by José Guardiola: The most famous of the habaneras, or sailor songs born from Barcelona's seagoing heritage, this song tells the story of a ship called *El Català,* which sunk during the War on Cuba.

"Vuelvo a Madrid" by Ismael Serrano: This Spanish singer-songwriter has written several songs about Madrid, and this is one of the most evocative.

Plan to spend up to three hours taking everything in, and avoid the lines by buying tickets online in advance. The middle of the day is when the museum tends to be at its quietest.

5. Las Letras

Weave into the literary neighborhood of Las Letras, which has attracted writers and artists since the time of Spain's most famous novelist, Miguel de Cervantes. It's also known as "Huertas" for the **Calle de Las Huertas,** the area's most famous street, which drops steeply down through the barrio and is home to some excellent restaurants and bars. Check out some old Ernest Hemingway haunts, like **Cervecería Alemana** (Plaza Santa Ana, 6; tel. 91/429-7033; www.cerveceriaalemana.com; 11am-12:30am Sun.-Mon., 11am-12:30am Wed.-Thurs., 11am-2am Fri.-Sat.), on the pretty Plaza Santa Ana, a 15-minute walk from the Prado Museum.

6. Night Out in Malasaña

End your day in Malasaña, a 15-minute walk north, for a dose of Madrid's legendary nightlife. This has long been a rebellious barrio; here, locals rose up against occupying French troops on May 2, 1808, and La Movida Madrileña—Madrid's countercultural scene—flourished after the death of Francisco Franco. Today, it's an indie-cool neighborhood, with a host of hip bars like **Café de la Luz** (Calle de la Puebla, 8; tel. 91/523-1199; 10am-2am Mon.-Thurs., 10am-2:30am Fri.-Sat., 10am-1am Sun.) that sit alongside some classic old bars, like **Casa Camacho** (Calle de San Andrés, 4; tel. 91/531-3598; noon-2am Mon.-Fri., noon-2:30am Sat.), which has been going for well over a century. In summer, the action spills out onto the streets, especially around the **Plaza del Dos de Mayo,** the central, terrace-lined square.

DAY 5

1. Museo Nacional Centro de Arte Reina Sofía

Calle de Santa Isabel, 52; tel. 91/774-1000; www.museoreinasofia.es; 10am-9pm Wed.-Sat., 10am-7pm Sun., 10am-9pm Mon.; €10; under 18, students 25 and under, over 65, and disabled people free with ID

The Reina Sofía, Spain's national museum of 20th-century art, is home to a vast collection of Spanish and international art from the late 19th century to the present day. The permanent exhibition includes Works by Dalí, Miró, and Juan Gris, but many visitors start on the second floor (Collection 1) at the nucleus of the Reina Sofía—Pablo Picasso's ***Guernica.***

Picasso's depiction of the bombing of the Basque town of Guernica during the Spanish Civil War is regarded as one of

top, Museo Nacional Centro de Arte Reina Sofía; bottom, Retiro Park

the world's most powerful portrayals of warfare; it's a stinging indictment of the war that ripped the country apart from 1936 to 1939. The huge black, white, and gray mural shows the agony, violence, and horrific results of the bombing of Guernica on April 26, 1937, by German and Italian allies of Nationalist leader General Francisco Franco.

A three-hour visit is enough to take in the key works of this museum without rushing.

2. Retiro Park

Plaza de la Independencia, 7; tel. 91/400-8740; 6am-10pm daily Oct.-Mar., 6am-midnight daily Apr.-Sept.

To contemplate the art you've just taken in, walk 15 minutes to Retiro Park, Madrid's loveliest green space where Madrileños young and old come to relax, play sports, sunbathe, and enjoy a family day out. Originally laid out by Philip IV in the 17th century, the park was used exclusively by royalty until it was opened to the public in 1868. Grab a bite to eat at a lakeside kiosk, rent a row boat, or simply enjoy the peace with a picnic under the trees.

3. Gran Vía

Walk up the cinematic Gran Vía, taking in the early-20th-century architecture of Madrid's most famous streets, including its iconic Schweppes sign. Stop for a drink on the ninth-floor terrace of **El Corte Inglés** department store (a 20-minute walk from Retiro Park; Plaza del Callao, 2; tel. 91/379-8000; www.elcorteingles.es; 10am-10pm Mon.-Sat., 11am-9pm Sun.) and enjoy the panoramic views from its terrace.

4. Flamenco at Las Carboneras

Plaza del Conde de Miranda, 1; tel. 91/542-8677; www.tablaolascarboneras.com; €36

At night, catch a stunning flamenco performance at Las Carboneras. Even better, take a flamenco tour before the show to learn about the history of this dance. One of the most enduring symbols of Spain, flamenco actually has a multiethnic provenance, with gypsy, Sephardic Jewish, and Muslim influences combining in this traditional form of dance, music, and singing. While it is mainly associated with Andalusia, in southern Spain, Madrid is one of the best places to see a flamenco show; many of the top dancers live in the capital and dance in some of its most famous tablaos (flamenco shows).

This tablao was founded by three flamenco dancers and features twice-nightly shows in an intimate atmosphere. Performers, including some of Spain's top flamenco dancers, rotate on a weekly basis.

5. Tapas at Calle de Cava Baja

For dinner on this last night, explore Calle de Cava Baja, just a two-minute walk away. This street is lined with tapas bars, including some of the city's most famous, visited by everyone from the Prime Minister to people on their very first trip to Madrid. Some tapas bars are standing-room-only—order at the bar and pack in, balancing your drink and food on the bar or little ledges around the edge. Others have seats, and still others have restaurant areas, usually at the back. **Taberna Tempranillo** (Calle Cava Baja, 38; tel. 91/364-1532; 1pm-4pm and 8pm-midnight Mon.-Sun.; €12) is a good place to start.

TRANSPORTATION

Barcelona and Madrid both have excellent public transport networks, and within each city, a combination of walking and using the metro is the best way to get around.

Air

Most international travelers arrive in Spain by air, and Barcelona and Madrid host the country's two largest airports.

- **Barcelona-El Prat Airport** (BCN; www.aena.es): 12 km (7.5 mi) southwest of the city center; 27 minutes to Passeig de Gràcia station by train (€4.10 one-way).

- **Adolfo Suárez Madrid–Barajas Airport** (MAD; www.aeropuertomadrid-barajas.com/eng): 12 km (7.5 mi) northeast of Madrid's city center; 30 minutes by airport express bus (line 203) to Atocha train station (€5, cash only).

Train

Spain's national rail network is operated by **RENFE** (www.renfe.com), with rail links to most cities in Europe. While flying is the quickest way to travel between Madrid and Barcelona, the most comfortable and easiest way to travel is by train. The high-speed Tren de Alta Velocidad Española **(AVE)** train can zip between Barcelona Sants train station and Madrid's Atocha train station in 2.5-3 hours, but prices are steep—around €100 each way is the norm.

- **Barcelona-Sants Station:** Barcelona's main train station is located due west of the city center, connected by metro Line 3 run to Liceu on Las Ramblas, and Catalunya on Plaça de Catalunya.
- **Puerta de Atocha:** Madrid's main railway station is located southeast of the center, connected to Metro Line 1.

Public Transportation

Public transportation in both Madrid and Barcelona is excellent and affordable. Both cities have metros (underground subways) and bus routes that run until around 1am and connect the main neighborhoods and sights; night buses run when the metro is closed (usually between around 1am-6am).

Barcelona

Barcelona's metro is split between two different companies, **Transports Metropolitans de Barcelona** (TMB; www.tmb.cat) and **Ferrocarrils de la Generalitat de Catalunya** (FGC; www.fgc.cat), which share the running of its eight color-coded lines. Single tickets (€2.20) can be purchased on all public transport (metro, bus, and tram), but if you're spending a few days in the city, consider buying a tarjeta, a discount ticket that can be used multiple times and can be bought at metro, train, and tram stations (but not on buses). The T-10 (€10.20) is valid for 10 separate journeys and can be shared between passengers.

Madrid

Metro Madrid (www.metromadrid.es) operates the city's metro. A single metro ticket costs €1.50-€2. Riders must possess a Tarjeta Multi Card (€2.50; available at all metro stations) to ride the metro. Although you will usually get everywhere you need to go much easier on the metro, buses are especially useful during the night, when the metro does not run. Madrid's bus network is operated by the **Empresa Municipal de Transportes** (EMT; www.emtmadrid.es) and travels throughout the city from 6:30am to 11:30pm.

Getting Back

Head to Madrid's airport for your flight home, or catch a train back to Barcelona. It's also possible to take a short flight between Madrid and Barcelona (1 hour 20 minutes; from €40).

- London and Paris (page 44)
- Sevilla, Córdoba, and Granada (page 117)
- Bordeaux and the Pyrenees (page 279)
- The Canary Islands (page 568)
- The Douro Line (page 663)

SEVILLA, CÓRDOBA, AND GRANADA

Why Go: Famed worldwide for its flamenco and tapas, Andalusia holds layers of history and culture, from prehistoric civilization to the Roman era and Muslim rule—all of which can be seen in this trio of cities.

Number of Days: 7

Total Distance: 342 km (213 mi)

Seasons: Spring and fall

Start: Sevilla

End: Granada

If Madrid is the political capital and Barcelona the economic hub, Andalusia is the spiritual beating heart of Spain. Feel its pulse on this exploration of three great cities—Sevilla, Córdoba, and Granada—that encapsulate the best of Andalusian heritage. In Sevilla, explore a city that first rose to prominence under Roman rule before becoming the capital of Muslim Spain. Often overlooked, Córdoba is the only city in the world able to lay claim to four UNESCO World Heritage Sites. Head up from the Spanish plains into the foothills of the Sierra Nevada to the poetic city of Granada, home to the Alhambra, one of the greatest examples of Moorish art and architecture in the world. Along the way, enjoy a flamenco show and some of Spain's most mouthwatering tapas.

TOP 3

★ Attending an evening **flamenco performance**, which plunges you into the experience of Andalusia like nothing else (pages 122 and 138).

★ Marveling at the **Mezquita-Cathedral of Córdoba**, a wonderfully preserved mosque that was converted to a cathedral, with impressive architecture that encapsulates the spiritual heart of Andalusia (page 130).

Taking a contemplative walk through the **Alhambra's Gardens of the Generalife**, an unmissable stroll back in time to an era when the Moors ruled the region (page 137).

Sevilla

Where to Stay: Barrio de Santa Cruz, the former Jewish neighborhood of Casco Antiguo, or the old city, is the most central and within walking distance of most monuments. Nearby Barrio Alfalfa, just north of Barrio Santa Cruz, is a great option as well, with its indie shops and boutique hotels.

Arrive by: Plane to Sevilla Airport or train from Madrid's Puerta de Atocha station, to Sevilla's Santa Justa station (2.5-3 hours)

DAY 1

1. Real Alcazar Palace

Patio de Banderas; tel. 91/230-2200 or 61/064-9410; www.alcazarsevilla.org; 9:30am-6pm Mon.-Sun. Oct. 29-Mar. 31, 9:30am-8pm Mon.-Sun. Apr. 1-Oct. 28; €13.50

The Real Alcazar Palace is a vast compound of competing architectural styles showing 1,000 years of Andalusian evolution. It was founded by the Caliph of Córdoba, Abudrrahman III al-Nasr, in 913, and the Abbadies and Almohades dynasties continued to build onto the palace, cementing its seat of power for the region. It is one of the more ornate and diverse examples of Moorish architecture in Andalusia. After the Reconquista, the Castillians, notably Isabella and Ferdinand, kept the palace as a royal residence. Over the years, various schools of architecture and design have further added to the palace, from the Mudéjar Palace of Pedro I in the 14th century to the to the baroque halls that Charles V built in the mid-18th century. The ponds, pavilions, fountains, and waterways make this an enchanting, quiet corner of Sevilla.

Afterward, have lunch at a local favorite, **Pelayo Bar de Tapas** (Calle de Placentines, 25; tel. 95/422-7000; www.pelayobar.com; noon-midnight daily; €20). Have a glass or two of tinto de verano accompanied by tapas such as gambas pilpil, jamon de serrano, and queso Manchego.

Real Alcazar Palace

Córdoba
Sevilla
Granada
Tangier

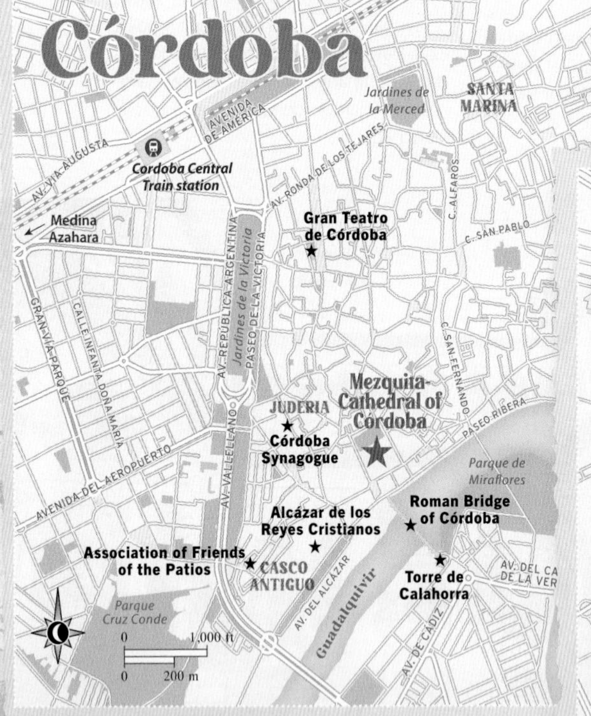

Córdoba
Jardines de la Merced
SANTA MARINA
AVENIDA DE AMÉRICA
AV. VIA AUGUSTA
Cordoba Central Train station
AV. RONDA DE LOS TEJARES
C. ALFAROS
Medina Azahara
Gran Teatro de Córdoba
C. SAN PABLO
AV. REPÚBLICA ARGENTINA
Jardines de la Victoria
PASEO DE LA VICTORIA
GRAN VÍA PARQUE
CALLE INFANTA DOÑA MARÍA
C. SAN FERNANDO
Mezquita-Cathedral of Córdoba
JUDERIA
Córdoba Synagogue
PASEO RIBERA
Parque de Miraflores
AVENIDA DEL AEROPUERTO
AV. VALLELLANO
Alcázar de los Reyes Cristianos
Roman Bridge of Córdoba
Association of Friends of the Patios
CASCO ANTIGUO
Torre de Calahorra
AV. DEL CA DE LA VER
AV. DEL ALCAZAR
Guadalquivir
AV. DE CÁDIZ
Parque Cruz Conde
0
1,000 ft
0
200 m

AV. DE LA CONSTITUCIÓN
CALLE ANCHA DE CAPUCHIN
Granada Train Station
C. SANTA BÁRBARA
C. SAN JUAN DE DIOS
C. RECTOR LÓPEZ ARGUETA
Granada
CALLE PEDRO ANTONIO DE ALARCÓN
C. HORNO DE HAZA
C. ALHÓNDIGA
C. SÓCRATES
C. OBISPO HURTADO
C. SANTA TERESA
C. BUENSUCESO
CALLE MESO

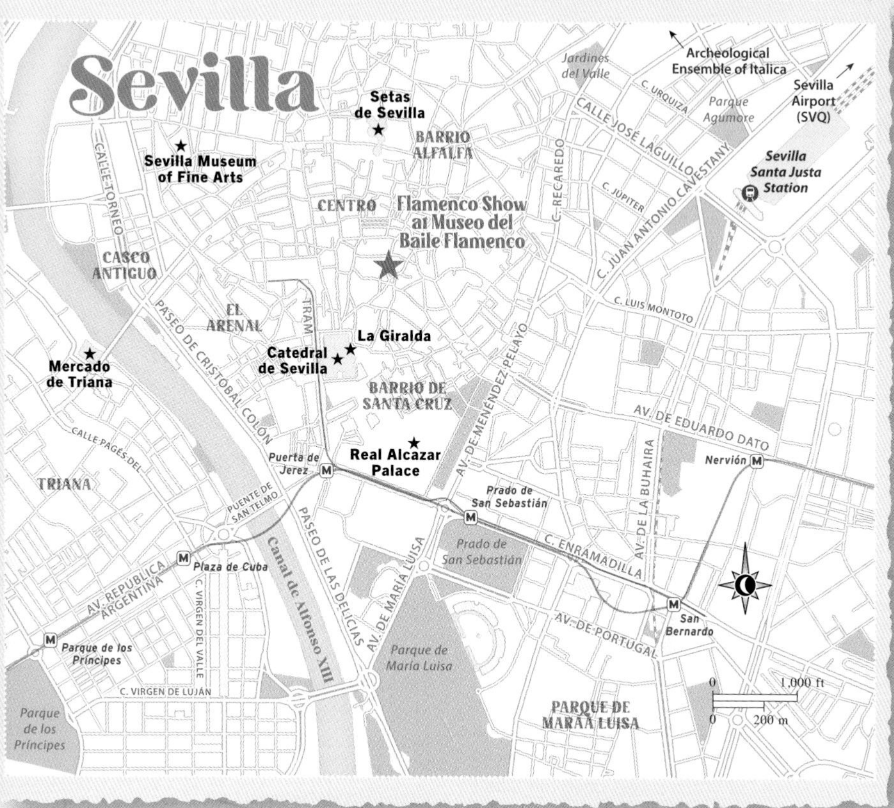

Sevilla
Setas de Sevilla
Sevilla Museum of Fine Arts
BARRIO ALFALFA
CENTRO
Flamenco Show at Museo del Baile Flamenco
CASCO ANTIGUO
EL ARENAL
La Giralda
Catedral de Sevilla
Mercado de Triana
BARRIO DE SANTA CRUZ
Real Alcazar Palace
Puerta de Jerez
TRIANA
Prado de San Sebastián
Plaza de Cuba
Canal de Alfonso XIII
Parque de los Príncipes
Parque de María Luisa
PARQUE DE MARAA LUISA
Nervión
San Bernardo
Jardines del Valle
Archeological Ensemble of Italica
Parque Agumore
Sevilla Airport (SVQ)
Sevilla Santa Justa Station
CALLE TORNEO
PASEO DE CRISTOBAL COLÓN
TRAM
CALLE PAGÉS DEL
PUENTE DE SAN TELMO
AV. REPUBLICA ARGENTINA
C. VIRGEN DEL VALLE
C. VIRGEN DE LUJÁN
PASEO DE LAS DELICIAS
AV. DE MARÍA LUISA
AV. DE MENÉNDEZ PELAYO
C. RECAREDO
C. URQUIZA
CALLE JOSÉ LAGUILLO
C. JÚPITER
C. JUAN ANTONIO CAVESTANY
C. LUIS MONTOTO
AV. DE EDUARDO DATO
AV. DE LA BUHAIRA
C. ENRAMADILLA
AV. DE PORTUGAL
0 1,000 ft
0 200 m

ALBAICÍN
Albaicín
0 1,000 ft
0 200 m
San Salvador Church
Flamenco in Sacromonte
Sacromonte
Plaza de San Nicolás
Great Mosque of Granada
C. DE SAN ANTONIO
CARRETERA DE MURCIA
CUESTA ALHACABA
C. SANTA ISABEL LA REAL
CUESTA DEL CHAPIZ
C. ZENETE
C. ELVIRA
Rio Darro
PASEO DEL PADRE MANJÓN
C. SAN JUAN DE LOS REYES
C. CARCEL BAJA
Carrera del Darro
Nasrid Palaces
El Partal
Generalife
Alcazaba
CENTRO
Catedral de Granada
LA ALHAMBRA
Palace of Charles V
C. REYES CATÓLICOS
REALEJO
Alhambra
La Alcaicería

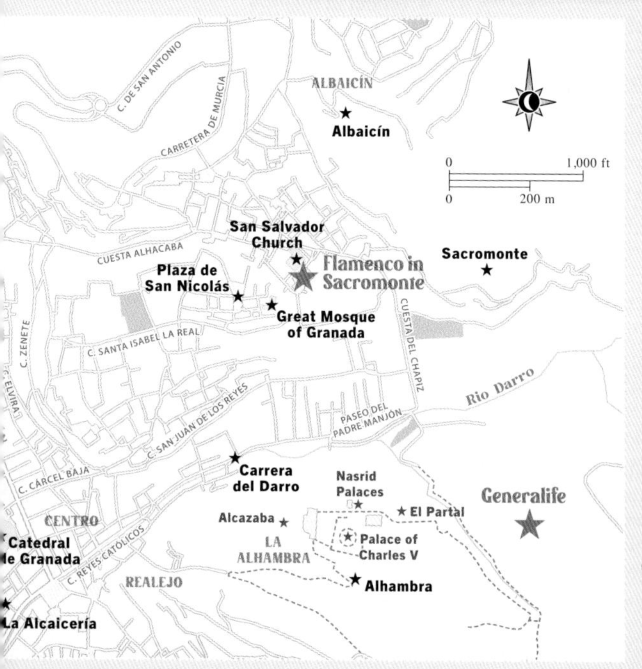

Key Reservations

Reservations are highly recommended for hotels and all major sights, some of which will often be fully booked months in advance. The **Alhambra** in Granada is so popular that it is best to plan your trip around your reservation there. The various festivals that happen throughout the year create surges of demand, while occasionally a big football (soccer) match might make for a really congested weekend. For this route, it really pays to look at the festivals and events calendar and plan accordingly.

2. Sevilla Cathedral and La Giralda

Catedral and Giralda; tel. 95/421-4971; www.catedraldesevilla.es; 10:45am-7:30pm Mon.-Sat., 2:30-7:30pm Sun.; online ticket €11, in-person €12

Dominating the skyline of Barrio Santa Cruz is the unmissable masterpiece of the Sevilla Cathedral, the world's largest Gothic cathedral, constructed in the 15th century. Built over a former mosque, the Giralda belltower is all that remains of the 12th-century Muslim minaret. At nearly 97 m (320 ft), this was once the tallest monument in the world; climb the many stairs to the top of belltower and enjoy the views over Sevilla. Another reminder of the cathedral's Islamic heritage is the midha, an octagonal fountain in the Courtyard of Orange Trees at the entrance of the cathedral. The Muslim faithful would ritually wash themselves in this fountain before performing prayer. In the cathedral, stop by the South Transept to view the Tomb of Christopher Columbus as well as the intricate altarpiece of the main chapel. Book tickets online to beat the line, and spend a few euros one of three guided tours (the Roof Tour, the Stained Glass Tour, or the Magna Tour) of the cathedral's interior.

★ 3. Flamenco Show at Museo del Baile Flamenco

Calle Manuel Rojas Marcos, 3; tel. 95/434-0311; https://museodelbaileflamenco.com; 5pm, 7pm, and 8:45pm daily; €25

There is, perhaps, nothing more associated with Andalusia than the art of flamenco. Flamenco music and dancing are by turns sensual and passionate, tragic and solemn. In Sevilla, Cristina Hoyos, the world's most decorated flamenco dancer, opened a museum that not only takes the uninitiated through the art of flamenco, but also hosts nightly hour-long shows. There are two types of performances available: the "Dreams" show takes place on the outdoor patio, while the more intimate "Poems" show happens in a 5th-century exposed-stone Roman centenary vault.

4. Dinner at Abantal

Calle Alcalde José de la Bandera; tel. 95/454-0000; www.abantalrestaurante.es; 2pm-4pm and 8:30pm-10:30pm Tues.-Sat.; from €100

The Michelin-starred Abantal is a foodie must. Chef Julio Fdez Quintero and his team have put together a creative menu featuring many of the traditional flavor profiles found in the regional cuisine. Arabic heritage is a clear highlight, as is the attention to texture, color, and local provenance. Individualized menus are created, taking into account any allergies or intolerances that guests have. Pair dishes with local wines for a dinner experience you will talk about for years to come.

DAY 2

1. Setas de Sevilla

Place de la Encarnación; tel. 60/663-5214; www.setasdesevilla.com; 9:30am-midnight daily; €10

(clockwise from top) Sevilla Cathedral and La Giralda; Setas de Sevilla; flamenco dancer

Flamenco 101

Flamenco music is wide and varied. At different times it can be soulful and somber, lively and playful, or passionate and erotic. This emotional range is conveyed through different styles, or palos. In each palo, the basic performers remain the same: guitarist, singer, and dancer, though the number of dancers, singers, and even guitarists can vary according to the musical arrangement of the palo. Here are a few different palos you'll hear:

- **Alegría:** These are happy, 12-beat palos. Often thought of as originating in Cadiz, this is the type of tune that really shows off the dancer's quick footwork.
- **Bulería:** Another light, quick, 12-beat palo, this is usually played toward the end of a performance with the musicians, dancers, and singers aligned toward the audience in a half-circle. Here the guitarists show off their virtuoso fast hands accompanied by impossibly fast, rhythmic clapping.
- **Fandango:** The palo with the most influence from the Moors, this distinct 3/4 rhythm can be both slow or fast, serious or playful. Of all the palos, this has perhaps the widest emotional range with the most known fandangos hailing from nearby Huelva.
- **Seguirilla:** Flamenco aficionados consider the seguirilla to be the soul of all flamenco. It is known as one of the oldest palos, if not the oldest. These are emotional, tragic, and intense palos that are somber and slow, much like their soléa counterparts.
- **Soleá:** Like the seguirilla, this is a slow, soulful performance. The basic 12-beat rhythm is echoed in many of the other flamenco palos.
- **Tango:** The tango in flamenco has little resemblance to the Argentinian tango, though like its Argentinian cousin, it is joyful, sensual, and erotic. Typically, tangos have a fast 4-beat rhythm, though the tempo may occasionally slow down for the dancer. Nearly every city in Andalusia claims its own specific style of tango.

Now that you have spent a day getting up close and personal with Sevilla, head to the Setas of Sevilla, or the "Mushrooms of Sevilla." From atop this wooden fungi-shaped monument, thought to be the largest wood structure in the world, you see across all of Sevilla. The intricate structure, the brainchild of German-born architect Jürgen Mayer, makes for an incredible photo op. Get there early to beat the crowds and the heat.

2. Mercado de Triana

Calle San Jorge, 6; tel. 67/407-4099; www.mercadodetrianasevilla.com; 9am-5pm Mon.-Sat., noon-5pm Sun.; free

left, Sevilla Museum of Fine Arts; right, Mercado de Triana

Follow up your tour of the mushrooms and maybe shop for a few of the edible fungi at Sevilla's oldest, most entertaining market, Mercado de Triana. Consider taking a one-hour tour of the market with a local for lunch. **Taller Andaluz de Cocina** (https://tallerandaluzdecocina.com) offers small-group tours starting from €12, though the real treat is the €50 market tasting with more than 15 different local specialties to try, from seasonal fruits and artisanal cheeses to Sevillian olives and charcuterie. You can also pick up snacks yourself, cross the Puente de Triana bridge, and have a relaxing picnic lunch in the **Jardines de Rafael Montesinos** park.

3. Sevilla Museum of Fine Arts

Pl. del Museo, 9; tel. 95/478-6498; www.museosdeandalucia.es; 9am-9pm Tues.-Sat., 9am-3pm Sun.; €1.5

Founded in 1835 by royal decree in a 17th-century former convent, the Museo de Bellas Artes in Sevilla houses many of Andalusia's masterworks. Behind the Prado in Madrid, this is the most important art collection in all of Spain. Spend a cool afternoon perusing the permanent collection, including paintings by Velázquez, Goya, and El Greco.

4. Tapas Dinner at La Brunilda

Calle Galera, 5; tel. 95/422-0481; www.labrunildatapas.com; 1:30pm-4:30pm and 8:30pm-11:30pm daily; €15

Head to this tiny, unassuming little bar for a light tapas dinner. Run by a husband-and-wife team, with a menu featuring seafood favorites and a wine list with some of Spain's finest vintages. Try the buñuelos de bacalao (codfish donuts) and lomo de salmón con salsa de chili dulce (salmon loin with sweet chili sauce).

DAY 3

1. Archeological Ensemble of Italica

Avenida de Extramadura, 2; tel. 69/934-1142; www.italicasevilla.org; 9pm-3pm Tues.-Sat. (or later, depending on season), 9am-3pm Sun.; €1.5

Regional Cuisine

TAPAS 101

While in Andalusia, or anywhere else in Spain, you will undoubtedly come across the culinary world of tapas more than once. Tapas are small dishes that can be served cold (such as slices of aged cheese or Iberian ham) or hot (like fried chorizo in garlic or baked clams). The menus and ordering system can be confusing as different regions, cities, and even bars have their own sort of tapas culture.

For the tourist, it is important to know a few words in Spanish. As a tapa only comes with a drink, you will want to know that draft beer generally comes in three sizes: caña, tubo, and jarra (small, medium, and large), and a bottle is a botella. Wine comes by the chato (glass) with your choice of vino tinto or vino blanco (red or white). Two of the more popular types of reds come from Rioja and Ribero del Duero.

In some bars and cafés, with each drink order, a tapa will automatically come free. In these establishments, there is no choosing. You just get what you get. In others, you may have to pay a nominal amount (€1-3) for a small tapa, though you will be able to choose which tapa you want. Simply learn to say, for example, "Una caña y una tapa de queso, por favor! Gracias!"

COMMON TAPAS DISHES

- **Queso:** semi-hard cheese, usually cured in olive oil
- **Jamón Ibérico:** Iberian ham
- **Aceitunas:** olives, usually stuffed with anchovies or red pepper
- **Bacalao:** salted cod
- **Boquerones:** cured white anchovies
- **Ensaladilla Rusa:** potato salad, often with tuna and vegetables
- **Patatas Bravas:** fried potato cubes, usually served with a spicy tomato sauce
- **Tortilla Española:** a type of frittata with fried potatoes and onions

ANDALUSIAN SPECIALTIES

- **Rabo del Torro:** literally "bull tail," this oxtail stew is a classic traditional dish (throughout Andalusia)
- **Cazón en Adobo:** marinated, fried fish cubes (Sevilla)
- **Patatas a lo Pobre:** slow fried potatoes in garlic, pepper, and often chorizo (Granada)
- **Flamenquitos:** deep-fried pork rolls (Córdoba)

Built around 206 CE, this former Roman economic hub proved important over the years, particularly as it was the birthplace of two Roman Emperors: Trajan and Adriano. Today, the well-excavated site provides over 52 hectares (124 acres) of space to wander through the public buildings, homes, streets, and plazas that made up Italica, to say nothing of the large semicircular amphitheater. Guided tours (typically 4 hours; €35) are available and most include transportation—Italica is about a 30-minute drive from central Sevilla.

ADDING ON Tangier

Located just 14 km (8 mi) from Andalusia across the Strait of Gibraltar, Tangier, Morocco, is rich with same Islamic heritage that informed so much of the history and culture of Andalusia. Tangier is part of Africa, but it has also been tied over the centuries to various Mediterranean empires, from the Carthaginians and Romans to the Portuguese and even the British. Though it is possible to enjoy Tangier as a day trip, it really is best to stay overnight. Once the day-trippers clear out, Tangier really comes alive and you'll get much more of a local experience.

- From the ferry terminal, walk up through Dar Bab al Baroud to the old **Kasbah** (fortress) atop the hill. The ancient fortifications that were once in charge of the city's defenses are still largely intact hundreds of years after their erection.
- There are several museums in the Kasbah. Try the **Museum of Moroccan Art and Antiquities** (Pl. du Mechouar; tel. 0539/932 097; 9am-4pm Wed.-Mon.; 10Dh), which displays the rich history of Tangier through various relics from the Stone Age to the early 20th century.
- From there, head down to Tangier's famed **medina,** and stroll down Rue as-Siaghin, the former Jewish gold market.
- You will end up in a small square called the **Zoco Chico,** also known as the Petit Socco (Little Market). If Tangier had a heart, this would be it. No trip to Tangier would be complete without a stop for coffee at **Café Central,** a hot spot in the Tangier International Zone days.
- Walk down to the **American Legation** (8 Rue d'Amerique; tel. 0539/935 317; http://legation.org; 10am-5pm Mon.-Fri., 10am-3pm Sat., closed Sun. and holidays; 20Dh), the only US National Monument outside the United States.

GETTING THERE

The ferry to Tangier departs from **Tarifa,** Spain (1 hour; 8+ ferries daily; €50 round-trip). Avoid the ferries leaving from Algeciras as those ferries take longer and drop you off an hour outside of Tangier proper. The Tarifa ferry drops you off at the bottom of the old medina, about a 15-minute walk from the Kasbah.

Tarifa is easily reached from **Sevilla:** The 309 bus, operated by Transpores Comes (www.tgcomes.es; 3 daily; 3 hours; €15-25), departs from the **Prado de San Sebastián.**

2. Lunch at Sal Gorda

Calle Alcaicería de la Loza, 23; tel. 95/538-5972; 1pm-4:30pm and 8pm-11:30pm daily

Back in the center of Sevilla, dive into this brightly colored Sevillian bar for some fun fusion tapas, introducing some far East flavors, including edamame and kimchi, alongside traditional dishes, like a cool ajoblanco soup. The craft beer selection is refreshing.

3. Barrio Santa Cruz

The historic neighborhood of Barrio Santa Cruz was once the Jewish mellah, or neighborhood, of Sevilla, though its history goes all the way back to the Romans in the first century. The characteristic medieval winding streets and patchwork of little public squares, the footprint largely dating from Roman times, once served a real purpose: to confuse invading armies who breached the city walls. These days, the confusion is felt mostly by travelers. A late afternoon stroll through the barrio as the temperature begins to cool is just the thing to transport you back in time. **Calle Mateos Cago,** at the Sevilla Cathedral, makes a good starting point for exploration. For a nibble and a fun time with a bit of music and a mix of locals and other travelers, head to the **Mariscal Café Español** (C. Mariscal, 3; open 24 hours daily; €20).

Córdoba

Where to Stay: San Basilio, Santa Marina, and Juderia are neighborhoods in the old city and central enough for exploration on foot.

Arrive by: Train from Sevilla-Santa Justa station to Córdoba-Central (45 minutes)

DAY 4

1. Alcázar de los Reyes Cristianos

Campo Santo de los Mártires; tel. 95/742-0151; https://alcazardelosreyescristianos.cordoba.es; 8:15am-6pm Tues.-Fri., 9:30am-6pm Sat., 8:15am-2:45pm Sun. winter, 8:45am-3:15pm Tues.-Sun. summer; €2

Christian nobility, namely Isabella and Ferdinand, only lived here for about eight years in the early years of this 14th-century palace, dubbed the Palace of the Christian Kings. The Alcázar was constructed over the ruins of the former Islamic palace. It is a large, defensive fortress, a landmark of the military architecture of the Reconquista with obvious Mudéjar-stylings. There are collected Roman mosaics from the 2nd and 3rd centuries, taken from a house of a wealthy Roman landowner, and Gothic towers offering panoramic views of Córdoba. Also of note is the Roman-Moorish bath system, much like the traditional Moroccan hammams found all over Morocco today. It was in this palace that Christopher Columbus first discussed exploring a new passage to India with Isabella and Ferdinand; a sculpture in the gardens marks this first-ever meeting.

2. Association of Friends of the Patios

Calle D San Basilio, 44; www.amigosdelospatioscordobeses.es; 10am-2pm daily; free

If you are not so lucky as to visit Córdoba in May during the Festival of the Patios, be sure to step into this year-round patio celebration to get a feel for the love and care that go into the annual festival. This is a private home that is opened just for visitors to experience a more intimate side of Córdoba. For garden lovers, this is a must-see.

3. Rabo del Torro at Bodega San Basilio

Calle Enmedio, 12; tel. 95/729-7832; 1pm-4pm and 8pm-11:30pm Mon. and Wed.-Sat., 1:30pm-4pm Sun.; €14

If you were ever going to have bull tail (el

NAME CHECK: Isabella I of Castille and Ferdinand II of Aragon

The marriage of Isabella and Ferdinand was largely responsible for the **Reconquista,** the reunification of Spain, following the invasion of the Iberian Peninsula by Moroccan forces in 711 CE and the subsequent eight centuries of Moorish rule under various Islamic empires, from the Almoravids to the Nasrids. For this, they were the first rulers of Spain to be called queen and king, and ushered in Spain's Golden Age.

Toward the end of the Reconquista, the **Spanish Inquisition** of 1478 formed under their leadership. Under the laws of Spanish Inquisition, all non-Catholics were either forcefully converted to Catholicism or expelled from Spain, often violently. The Inquisition wasn't abolished until nearly 400 years later, in 1834. The year 1492 was a big year for Isabella and Ferdinand; not only did they complete the Reconquista by conquering Granada, but they also financed the voyage of Christopher Columbus to the New World. This arrangement would solidify Spain's naval dominance, and the new trade routes and gold from the Americas would be a source of wealth for centuries to come as Spain quickly grew into a colonial force.

These days, Isabella and Ferdinand are most associated with places they had taken over: the **Alcázar of Córdoba** and the **Alcázar of Sevilla,** though you will find sculptures of them throughout the region, and many streets and boulevards carry their names. They are also entombed in the **Royal Chapel of Granada,** which is adjacent to the Cathedral of Granada.

rabo del torro), this local bodega may just be the joint. Located in San Basillio, this still has the feel of a working-class Córdoba classic, with many locals crowding in for a quick lunch bite or to gather with friends at night.

4. Synagogue of Córdoba

Calle Judíos, 20; tel. 95/701-5334; www.turismodecordoba.org/synagogue; 9am-9pm Tues.-Sat., 9am-3pm Sun.; €0.30

One of the finest examples of medieval Jewish Muejar architecture in all of Spain, this small synagogue has been through a lot since it was reconstructed in 1314-1315. Though not much is known specifically about its Sephardic roots, it is thought that this synagogue may have been a private building or perhaps have belonged to a trade guild. When the Jews and Muslims were expelled from Spain during the Reconquista in 1492, the synagogue was converted into hospital for those suffering from rabies; later it was used as a community center, and then as a chapel for a shoemakers' guild and their patron saints, Crispin-Crispian. In 1885 it was declared a national monument. Today, though no longer strictly a place of worship, it is open to the public for a very nominal entry fee. Visitors will see highly decorative stucco panels, Hebrew inscriptions, and Almohad-inspired architecture likely taken from the Synagogue of Santa María la Blanca in Toledo. Then, take a stroll through the labyrinthine former Jewish Quarter (Juderia) of Córdoba and get a feel for what life was like a thousand years ago for the Sephardic Jews who once were numerous here.

5. Concert at the Gran Teatro de Córdoba

Avenida del Gran Capitán, 3; tel. 95/748-0644; https://teatrocordoba.es; prices vary by performance

(top to bottom) Mezquita-Cathedral of Córdoba; Roman Bridge of Córdoba; Medina Azahara

Check out the event calendar with the Gran Teatro de Córdoba to see what performances are available. Typically, there are weekly performances by classical and flamenco guitarists, as well as nationally famous flamenco groups and other local artists with modern takes on traditional Andalusian music and dance. As part of the annual Guitar Festival in 2015, Bob Dylan even performed here. The 19th-century theater itself is something to behold, with an Italian-inspired horseshoe design, sculpted balconies, and lush red curtains.

For dinner, a stop at **Casa Mazal Restaurante Sefardi** (Calle Tomás Conde, 3; tel. 95/724-6304; www.casamazal.es; 12:30pm-4pm and 7:30pm-11pm Thurs.-Tues.; €45), which has a fresh seasonal menu that highlights Judeo-Spanish dishes.

DAY 5

★ 1. Mezquita-Cathedral of Córdoba

Calle del Cardinal Herrero, 1; tel. 95/747-0512; https://mezquita-catedraldecordoba.es; 10am-7pm Mon.-Thurs., 10am-6:30pm Fri.-Sat., 8:30am-11:30am and 3pm-6pm Sun. (hours vary by season); €11

A true monument to world heritage, the Mezquita-Cathedral of Córdoba encapsulates much of the rich history of this region. In fact, the oldest parts of this mosque turned cathedral are actually the Visigoth Basilica of Saint Vincent of Saragossa dating from the 6th century in a Roman-Paleo-Christian tradition. For 1500 years, this very spot has been the spiritual center of Córdoba. Under Abd al-Rahman I, when the Moors controlled the Iberian Peninsula, the great mosque underwent its original construction in the summer of 786 CE. Its outdoor courtyard garden, the oldest continuously planted Islamic garden in the world, and series of decorative double-tiered archways set the tone for the centuries and various expansions to come under al-Rahman's successors. In 1236, when Córdoba was

Córdoba Patio Festival

One of the very few festivals to be named a UNESCO World Heritage Site, the Córdoba Patio Festival is a riot of flowers and color done up only as the Córdovans could imagine. The festival takes places every year during the first two weeks of May, as it has since the very first patio festival in 1918. Over these two weeks, dozens of historic private homes open their doors to visitors to enjoy their gardens and floral display. Against the whitewashed background of these houses, beneath bright blue Andalusian skies, these arrangements pop in a festival of colors.

taken by the Reconquista, the mosque was converted to a cathedral, though it wasn't until the 16th century that the ornate, downright gaudy, Renaissance cathedral was constructed within the mosque and the minaret fully converted to a belltower.

2. Roman Bridge of Córdoba

Avenida de Alcazar; free

It's not every day you can walk across a 2,000-year-old bridge. Originally constructed in the 1st century BCE, this Roman bridge was the only bridge crossing the river until the 20th century. It has been restored and repaired over the years, with most of the current bridge still held up by the 8th century reconstruction under the Umayyid Caliphate.

3. Torre de Calahorra

Puente Romano; tel. 95/729-3929; www.torrecalahorra.es; 10am-7pm Thurs.-Tues., 10am-2pm and 4:30-8:30pm Wed.; €4.50

Across the old Roman Bridge is the Tower of Calahorra, used to control passage on the bridge. Over the years, it has served various functions: a prison for Cordovan nobility, a military barracks, and even a 19th-century all-girls' school. In 1931 it was declared a national monument and is now home to the Living Museum of Andalusia (Museo Vivo de al-Andalus). Of the more important aspects of this small museum is how it highlights positive collaboration of the three Abrahamic religions—Judaism, Christianity, and Islam—in this region of the world. After visiting, make your way back to the other side of the river for lunch at **Restaurante Damasco** (Calle Romero, 4; tel. 63/150-3436; noon-5:30pm and 7:30-11:30pm Wed.-Mon.; €15), which is located in one of the historic old houses of Córdoba and serves classic Mediterranean cuisine.

4. Medina Azahara

Carreterra Palma del Río, km 5.5; tel. 95/710-3637; www.museosdeandalucia.es; 9am-7pm Tues.-Sat., 9am-3pm Sun. (hours vary by season); €1.5

Once the grand Islamic capital of Andalusia, the 1,000-year-old ruins of Medina Azahara—or Medinat al-Zahra, the "Shining City"—make for an exploration of one of the great eras of Córdoba. From here, the first caliph of Córdoba, Abd al-Rahman III, once ruled and built this palatial complex in the model of the Umayyad Palace in Damascus. From the patios and courtyards, gardens, mosque, and royal residence, exploring this once shining city puts you in touch with the wealth and power that once flowered from this otherwise quiet Andalusian city. It's located outside of central Córdoba, so it can be a little tricky to access—you may want to opt for a guided tour. The two-hour night tour from **Art en Córdoba** (www.artencordoba.com; €14) starts at 9pm and includes shuttle bus service from downtown Córdoba.

5. Dinner at Bar Miguelito

Calle Acera Pintada, 8; tel. 95/729-0338; www.barmiguelito.es; 11am-midnight Thurs.-Tues.; €12

Pop into this local for a light dinner and cool beverage. The expansive terrace and influx of locals promise a fun evening. Though this spot specializes in fried foods, particularly fish, the grilled calamari is a treat.

Granada

Where to Stay: The Albaicín Quarter makes for romantic stay and can be a great budget option, while the trendiest boutique hotels are along the Carrero del Darro on the north side of the Alhambra near Plaza Santa Ana.

Arrive by: High speed train from Córdoba Central train station to the Granada train station (1.5 hours)

DAY 6

1. Albaicín Quarter

Albaicín Quarter; open 24/7; free

Narrow cobblestone roads open to charming plazas while the traditional homes often have doors ajar, allowing you to peek at their quaint courtyards to glimpse what life is like in this former Muslim quarter of Granada. While the

Albaicín Quarter

WATCH

Blood Wedding by Federico García Lorca: The most famous play by Granada's foremost poet and playwright, this passionate tale of a vendetta, involving a long family feud that threatens to ruin a wedding, is set in rural Spain.

READ

Tales of the Alhambra by Washington Irving: In 1828, American writer and politician Washington Irving set off across the Spanish plains from Madrid to discover the abandoned, mysterious Moorish palace known as the Alhambra. For months, Irving stayed there, making sketches, scribbling notes, and collecting the stories and myths of this enchanted corner of Andalusia.

Collected Works of **Federico García-Lorca:** One of Spain's most celebrated playwrights and poets, Granada-born García-Lorca was part of the avant-garde "Generation 27," which also included Salvador Dalí and Luis Buñuel.

LISTEN

"Entre dos Aguas" by Paco de Lucía, a classic flamenco standard. After this, listen to as much flamenco music as you can!

unmissable Alhambra fortress and palace occupy the uppermost, most militarily strategic point, the actual city abuts the fortress to take advantage of the protection it afforded. The hillside placement of the Albaicín neighborhood offers commanding views over to the Alhambra and the rest of Granada below, especially at bustling **Mirador de San Nicolás.** Though the views from the plaza are wonderful anytime, try to get here shortly after sunrise for great light and less crowds. Sunsets are also magical, though usually with more people about taking their own sunset photos.

While strolling through this neighborhood, keep an eye out for remnants of this once thriving Muslim city. The streets here can be a bit steep with uneven footing, so be sure to wear a good pair of walking shoes.

2. Great Mosque of Granada

Plaza de San Nicolás; tel. 95/820-2526; www.mezquitadegranada.com; 11am-2pm and 5pm-8:30pm daily; free

Just off the plaza is the Great Mosque of Granada (Mezquita de Granada). Opened in 2003, this is the first new mosque constructed in Granada since the 1400s. The architecture adheres to the principles of Islamic architecture as it existed in Andalusia during the period of the Moorish Dynasties, complete with a traditional courtyard, an intricate cedar wood paneled ceiling made of 2,400 individual pieces, and a mihrab with obvious design cues taken from the historic Mosque of Córdoba.

Afterward, get lunch at **El Picoteo** (Calle Agua del Albayzín; tel. 95/829-2380; www.casatorcuato.com; 12:30pm-4pm and 8pm-11:30pm Thurs.-Sat.; €8), a chill locale to people-watch and enjoy some local tapas with an icy cold jarra of Sangria.

3. San Salvador Church

Plaza del Abad, 2; tel. 95/827-8644; www.archidiocesisgranada.es; 9am-5pm Tues.-Sun., 6:30-7:30pm Mon.; free

The original "Great Mosque of Granada" constructed here in the 13th century was once considered one of the most beautiful mosques in the entire world. After the Reconquista, the mosque was converted into a Parrish and consecrated for Christian worship while working to indoctrinate the local Muslim population; however, shortly after, the mosque was largely torn down with a new church built in its place in the 16th century. Interestingly, there are still several inscriptions in Arabic running throughout the church.

4. Carrera del Darro

Carrero del Darro; open 24 hours; free

The most emblematic street in Granada, this pedestrian-friendly thoroughfare is the sort of walk you dream of when thinking of Europe and Andalusia. A cobblestone lane winds alongside the trickle of the Darro River. Stone footbridges cross the river, and above towers the Alhambra. From the Albaicín, walk down to the **Plaza de los Tristes** and continue downhill from there onto the Carrero del Darro. The main walk to the **Plaza de Santa Ana** is only 650 m (about half a mi). At the Plaza de Santa Ana, there are often buskers, flamenco dancers, and other street performers. Here, you could also pop into the **11th-century Arab Baths** (El Bañuelo; Carrera del Darro, 31; 9:30am-2:30pm and 5pm-8:30pm daily; €5) for a quick look. Information is sparse, so a visit is best for those with an interest in Arab art and architecture.

Wind down with dinner at **La Mancha Chica Chaoen** (Cam. Nuevo de San Nicolás, 1; €15). This cozy, husband-and-wife-team restaurant is as authentically Moroccan as it gets. Make sure to order a mint tea no matter the time of year.

top, San Salvador Church; bottom, Cathedral of Granada

DAY 7 MORNING

1. Cathedral of Granada

Gran Vía de Colón, 5; tel. 95/822-2959; https://catedraldegranada.com; 10am-6:15pm Mon.-Sat., 3pm-6:15pm Sun.; €5

The lavish Renaissance Cathedral of Granada is a one of the monumental attractions of Granada, and conveniently unmissable right in the center of town. Like many cathedrals dotted around Andalusia, this cathedral was built atop the ruins of a mosque. Work on the cathedral began in 1518, but it would be more than 150 years before the cathedral was finished. Most impressive is the stained-glass domed chapel.

2. La Alcaicería

Reyes Católicos, 12; open 24 hours; free

At first glance, the small, narrow streets of the La Alcaicería district seem kitschy and full of cheap souvenirs, but spend a little time exploring and you'll quickly pick up on the fact that this little district has more in common with the souks of Marrakesh than it does Granada. Delicate hand-spun and painted pottery from Fez and sturdy Moroccan leather bags are piled high in the bazaars. A walk through here and you will undoubtably hear a peppering of Arabic and be ushered back to the Granada that was, before the Reconquista. Have lunch nearby; try **Cafeteria Alhambra** (Plaza de Bib-Rambla, 27; tel. 95/852-3929; www.cafeteria-alhambra.com; 8am-2pm and 4pm-9pm daily; €12).

TOP EXPERIENCE

Alhambra, Granada

Address: Calle Real de la Alhambra

Contact: tel. 95/802-7971; www.alhambra-patronato.es

Hours and Price: 8am-sunset daily (closing time varies seasonally); €15

DAY 7 AFTERNOON

The Alhambra is the jewel of Andalusia. When you first ascend to this ancient palace, a masterful work of Islamic design, you may feel like the Spanish baroque novelist and playwright Lopa de Vega: "I do not know what to call this land upon which I stand. If what is beneath my feet is paradise, then what is the Alhambra? Heaven?" Spend at least half a day touring the exquisite remains of this heavenly palace and gardens. The Alhambra is a vast complex, so get organized to make the most of your time.

1. Nasrid Palaces

Within the Nasrid Palace, you will find three primary buildings: The Mexuar, the Palace of Comares, and the Palace of the Lions. Each of these buildings is a masterful work of Islamic art and architecture, combining hand-chiseled-and-set colorful mosaic work that runs along the bottom half of the walls, while above, delicate stucco work—replete with knotted kufic and cursive Arabic inscriptions intricately woven into the design—continue to the ceiling where they meet the geometrically complex, and intricately carved, kaleidoscopic cedarwood ceilings. The Mexuar is the oldest of these buildings, a great hall once used as a courtroom for the king's ministers. The Comares Palace, once the official palace of the sultan, also has the reflective pool within the Courtyard of the Myrtles, the Hall of Ambassadors, the Hall of the Boat, as well as the Comares Tower.

The Palace of the Lions, however, is one of the most cherished works of Islamic art and architecture in the world. Four halls are arranged around the courtyard of the famed fountain guarded by its statues of lions. To the west is the Hall of Muqarnas, named for its ornamented vaulting, while the Hall of Kings opens to a series of rooms, each with its own ornate ceilings. To the south is the Hall

left, Nasrid Palaces, Palace of the Lions; right, Palace of Charles V

Visiting the Alhambra

As the Alhambra is the most visited site in all of Spain, tickets are often sold out weeks, sometimes months, in advance. You really need to organize your stay in Granada around the tickets you find available—advance planning is mandatory.

PLANNING TIPS

- There are multiple types of tickets available. To visit the entire complex, purchase the **General Daytime** tickets, which provide access to the entire Alhambra complex from 8am to closing for the day of your ticket, no matter what time you arrive.
- When you are purchasing your tickets and select the date of your visit, you will see a reservation time slot for the **Nasrid Palaces.** On the day of your visit, you will only have access to the Nasrid Palace within the Alhambra complex at the time and day of your reservation. Choose your time wisely! Typically, afternoons have smaller crowds.
- When making reservations, you must **purchase tickets for everyone in your group** ages 3 and up, even though minors under the age of 12 are free. Children ages 2 and under will be given a ticket upon entry.
- When you visit, remember to **bring your passport!** ID is needed to enter the Alhambra.

of the Two Sisters, originally known as the hall of the "Great Dome" for its elaborate muqarnas dome, which features over 5,000 prismatic pieces that give a feathery weight to this great mass. Past the great dome you'll find the Eye of the House of Aisha, or Lindaraja, a small room with intricate stucco work, mosaics, and carved wood. Named for the 12 mythical white lions that hold the central fountain, the Palace of Lions is also home to some impressive use of 13th-century water technology. The lions spurt water from their mouths, feeding the four small channels of water, each channel representing a river of heaven, where the water runs through the palace and cools each of the rooms.

Note: You must select a specific time slot to visit the Nasrid Palace when buying your tickets to the Alhambra.

2. Palace of Charles V

A ruler has never lived in this Renaissance-styled palace. Commissioned by Charles V, the grandson of Isabella and Ferdinand, construction begin in 1527, but the building was never completed and, in fact, was without a roof until 1967. The exterior of the palace gives little clue to the large, round courtyard found within, a ringing example of Renaissance architecture. The lower level is home to the **Alhambra Museum,** which features some smaller fragments of some of the ornate carvings and marble work. The Vase of the Gazelles, one of the few intact vases from the Alhambra during the Islamic rule, is a true standout. On the upper floor, the **Fine Arts Museum of Granada** houses various paintings and sculptures from Spanish artists from the 16th-20th centuries.

3. Alcazaba

Located on the southwesternmost tip of the Alhambra, the Alcazaba is the military fortress and the oldest part of the Alhambra. Here you can walk through what remains of the soldiers' barracks, public bath, and communal kitchen. Below grounds, there are the ruins of silos and dungeons, though the most interesting parts of the Alcazaba are the two towers: Tower of Homage (Torre del Homenaje) and Tower of the Candle (Torre de la Vega). From the Tower of the Candle, commanding views over Granada, the Alhambra, the Sierra Nevada Mountains, and the rolling Spanish countryside are worth the short climb up.

top, Alcazaba; bottom, Generalife

4. El Partal

This section of the Alhambra is perhaps the quietest and least visited. The Partal Palace, though likely the oldest palace in the complex, is also one of the most damaged, with the decorative ceiling having been dismantled and taken to Germany over a century ago. Around the palace you can find gardens and ponds, as well as the Partal Dwellings, four houses that are known for their plasterwork and mural paintings, which many scholars believe are the only known examples of Nasrid painting in the entirety of the Alhambra.

★ 5. Generalife

When the weather was too warm or the sultan wanted a bit of quiet, he retreated to the Generalife, the summer palace. Most likely constructed toward the end of the 13th century, the palace was intentionally set to disappear against the backdrop of the extraordinary garden, one of the oldest examples of its kind. There are numerous palace arcades and, if you squint, you can still see some of the magic of it. The Royal Chamber is best preserved and includes an impressive muqarnas vaulted ceiling, as well as views out to the Albaicín. However, it is the **gardens** that take precedence here. Though influenced over the years by various schools of gardening, the original layout is Moorish in origin, with a stress on the importance of water. While walking up the stairs to the Generalife, you will see rivulets of water streaming down though small channels. This same water seemingly defies gravity as it moves back up and around the gardens. In fact, this water is brought from the river, which lies nearly 1 km (about half a mi) downhill. The secret is with the Nasrid technology, the first of its kind, that used a combination of dams and waterwheels to lift the water uphill.

Ending your visit to the Alhambra here around sunset provides some contemplative quiet time in the gardens where you can hear the water trickle down, not to mention stunning lighting for pictures over the Alhambra and Granada.

★ 6. Flamenco in Sacromonte

Camino del Sacromonte, 89; tel. 95/812-1183; www.marialacanastera.com; open nightly until late; €62

Cap off your time in Granada with a night of flamenco. It is thought that flamenco began in the zambras, or "caves," of Sacromonte, where Arabs once lived, though the gypsies took over the neighborhood after the Reconquista. Today, Flamenco lives on in these caves. There are numerous different caves with different performers. The Zambra María la Canastra is the oldest flamenco establishment in Granada, and María's descendants continue her performances to this day. Since this part of Sacromonte is a bit more remote, far on the northern edge of the city, it is convenient to enjoy "dinner and a show." Many of the venues can arrange shuttle service to and from your accommodation.

TRANSPORTATION

Air

Sevilla Airport (SVQ; www.aena.es/es/sevilla.html) is about 15 km (9 mi) from Casco Antiguo (35 minutes by bus line EA, €4; 15 minutes by taxi, €23-31), but flights from outside Europe usually require at least one stop. Another option is flying into Madrid's Adolfo Suárez Madrid–Barajas Airport (MAD; www.aeropuertomadrid-barajas.com/eng), 12 km (7.5 mil) northeast of Madrid's city center; 30 minutes by airport express bus (line 203) to Atocha train station (€5, cash only), then taking a train to Seville (2.5-3 hours).

- Barcelona and Madrid (page 99)

Train

Spain is well-connected by the national rail service, RENFE (www.renfe.com). In Sevilla, trains arrive to the **Sevilla Santa Justa** train station (Calle Joaquin Morales y Torres), a short 2 km (1 mi) east of Sevilla's old city center. From **Madrid,** trains depart from Puerta de Atocha station multiple times a day (2.5-3 hours; from €65).

Trains from Sevilla arrive at the **Córdoba Central** train station (Gta. Tres Culturas; 45 minutes; €7-20), located just a few blocks north of Córdoba's historic city center. High speed trains from Córdoba Central arrive at the **Granada train station** (Avenida de Andaluces;1.5 hours; €25-40), which rests right on the western edge of the old city.

Getting Back

The direct AVANT train connects Granada and Seville, including a stop in Córdoba (3 daily departures; 2.5 hours; from €47.20). To get back to Madrid, the AVE (Alta Velocidad Española) high-speed train connects from Granada with the capital city (3 daily departures; 3 hours; €30-80).

For frequent flyers, Granada is served by the **Federico García Lorca Granada Airport** (Ctra. de Málaga, Chauchina; tel. 91/321-1000; www.aena.es). This smaller airport has limited connections with travels hubs throughout Europe.

ROME, FLORENCE, AND VENICE

Why Go: Encompassing three of Italy's most famous cities, this trip is a good introduction to the country for first-timers.

Number of Days: 7

Total Distance: 526 km (327 mi)

Seasons: Spring and fall

Start: Rome

End: Venice

Rome is a convenient starting point for a three-city tour of Italy. Most transatlantic flights land directly in the Italian capital and tickets are less expensive than to Florence or Venice, which may require connecting flights. The 526 km (327 mi) that separate the cities are covered by high-speed trains, which make it quick and easy to travel between destinations. A Rome-to-Florence-to-Venice itinerary also allows you to travel from most populated to least populated and from oldest to newest, which can facilitate appreciation and understanding of the cities.

Seeing everything is impossible, and visiting one museum after another will leave you exhausted and unable to enjoy anything. You're better off taking it slow and balancing your days with a mix of sights and everyday activities, like lingering in piazze, searching for the best gelato, and partaking in aperitivo (happy hour).

TOP 3

On a visit to the Vatican, gazing up at Michelangelo's **Sistine Chapel**—the greatest fresco ever painted (page 148).

Climbing to the top of Florence's **Duomo**; Brunelleschi's iconic and innovative dome has become a symbol of the city (page 152).

★ Watching boats sail up and down Venice's Grand Canal from **Punta della Dogana** (page 158).

Rome

Where to Stay: Aventino or Monti neighborhoods, which are close to all the ancient sights
Arrive by: Plane to Fiumicino Airport

DAY 1

1. Campo De' Fiori Market

Walking is the best cure for jet lag, so after you drop off your bags at the hotel, head out for lunch and a stroll. Zigzag along pedestrian streets toward Campo De' Fiori, a lively square that's filled with market stalls selling flowers, vegetables, and knickknacks during the day.

2. Pizza at Il Forno

Campo De' Fiori 22; tel. 06/6880-6662; www.pantheonroma.com; 7:30am-2:30pm and 4:45pm-8pm Mon.-Sat., closed Sat. afternoons Jul.-Aug.; €5

Head to the northwestern corner of the square to Il Forno, where you can watch long strips of pizza being prepared and pulled from the ovens to help you make your selection. The most popular are the white, red, and zucchini, and you pay by the kilogram.

3. Piazza Navona

Piazza Navona is not a typical square—in fact, it's not a square at all. The piazza has its oblong shape because it was once an ancient Roman track. At the center is the most intricate of the plaza's three fountains, Bernini's Fontana dei Quattro Fiumi (Fountain of Four Rivers), installed in 1651. Musicians play near the fountains, and street painters work on colorful canvases, making for good browsing. At the first sign of a yawn, enter a bar and order an espresso.

4. Pantheon

Piazza della Rotonda; tel. 06/6830-0230; Mon.-Sat. 9am-7:15pm and Sun. 9am-5:45pm; free

Just a few hundred meters from Piazza Navona is the Pantheon, Rome's largest temple and the best-preserved ancient Roman building in the world. Its immense portico columns still influence architects today. A striking feature

Pantheon

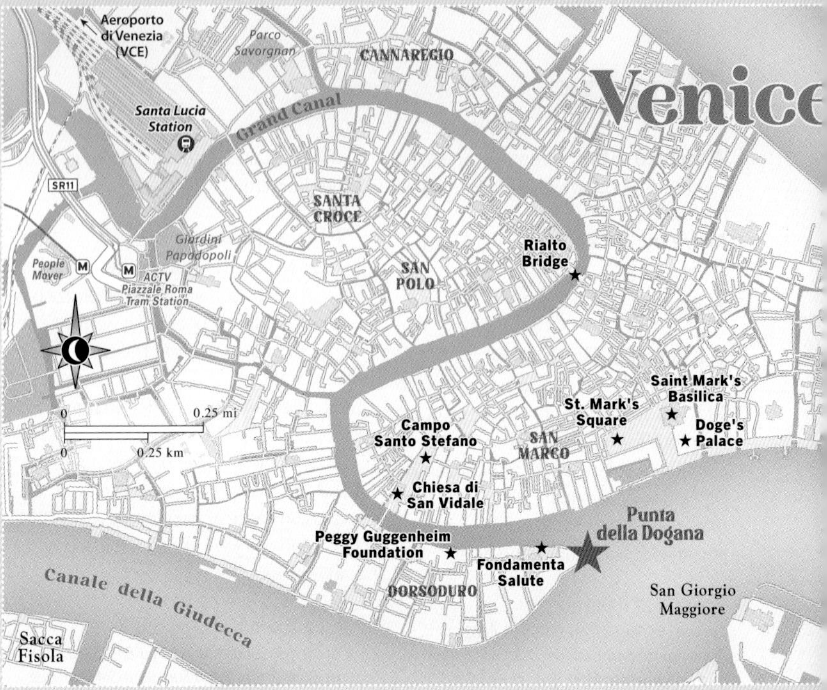

Venice

Aeroporto di Venezia (VCE)
Parco Savorgnan
CANNAREGIO
Santa Lucia Station
Grand Canal
SR11
SANTA CROCE
Giardini Papadopoli
People Mover
ACTV Piazzale Roma Tram Station
SAN POLO
Rialto Bridge
Saint Mark's Basilica
St. Mark's Square
Doge's Palace
Campo Santo Stefano
SAN MARCO
Chiesa di San Vidale
Peggy Guggenheim Foundation
Punta della Dogana
Fondamenta Salute
DORSODURO
Canale della Giudecca
San Giorgio Maggiore
Sacca Fisola
0 0.25 mi
0 0.25 km

Rome

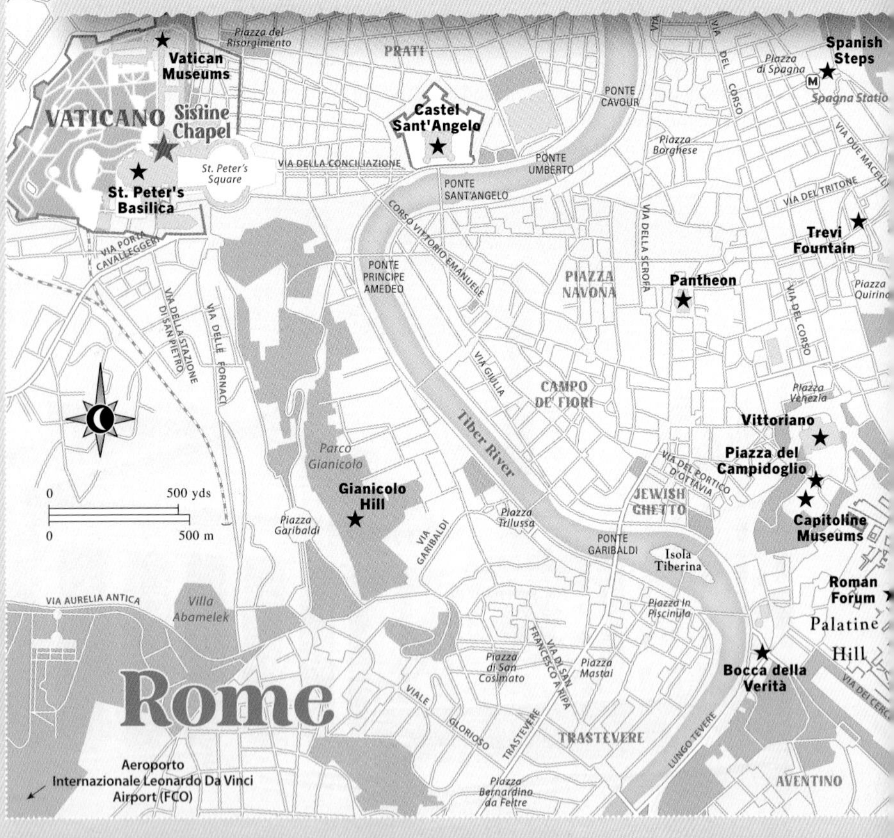

Piazza del Risorgimento
Vatican Museums
PRATI
VATICANO
Sistine Chapel
Castel Sant'Angelo
PONTE CAVOUR
Spanish Steps
Piazza di Spagna
Spagna Station
VIA DEL CORSO
VIA DUE MACELLI
St. Peter's Square
VIA DELLA CONCILIAZIONE
St. Peter's Basilica
Piazza Borghese
PONTE UMBERTO
PONTE SANT'ANGELO
VIA DEL TRITONE
Trevi Fountain
VIA PORTA CAVALLEGGERI
CORSO VITTORIO EMANUELE
PONTE PRINCIPE AMEDEO
PIAZZA NAVONA
VIA DELLA SCROFA
Pantheon
Piazza Quirinale
VIA DELLA STAZIONE DI SAN PIETRO
VIA DELLE FORNACI
VIA GIULIA
CAMPO DE' FIORI
Piazza Venezia
Vittoriano
Piazza del Campidoglio
Tiber River
VIA DEL PORTICO D'OTTAVIA
Parco Gianicolo
JEWISH GHETTO
Gianicolo Hill
Capitoline Museums
0 500 yds
0 500 m
Piazza Garibaldi
Piazza Trilussa
VIA GARIBALDI
PONTE GARIBALDI
Isola Tiberina
Roman Forum
VIA AURELIA ANTICA
Villa Abamelek
Piazza in Piscinula
Palatine Hill
Piazza di San Cosimato
VIA DI SAN FRANCESCO A RIPA
Piazza Mastai
Bocca della Verità
VIA DEI CERCHI
VIALE GLORIOSO
TRASTEVERE
LUNGO TEVERE
AVENTINO
Aeroporto Internazionale Leonardo Da Vinci Airport (FCO)
Piazza Bernardino da Feltre

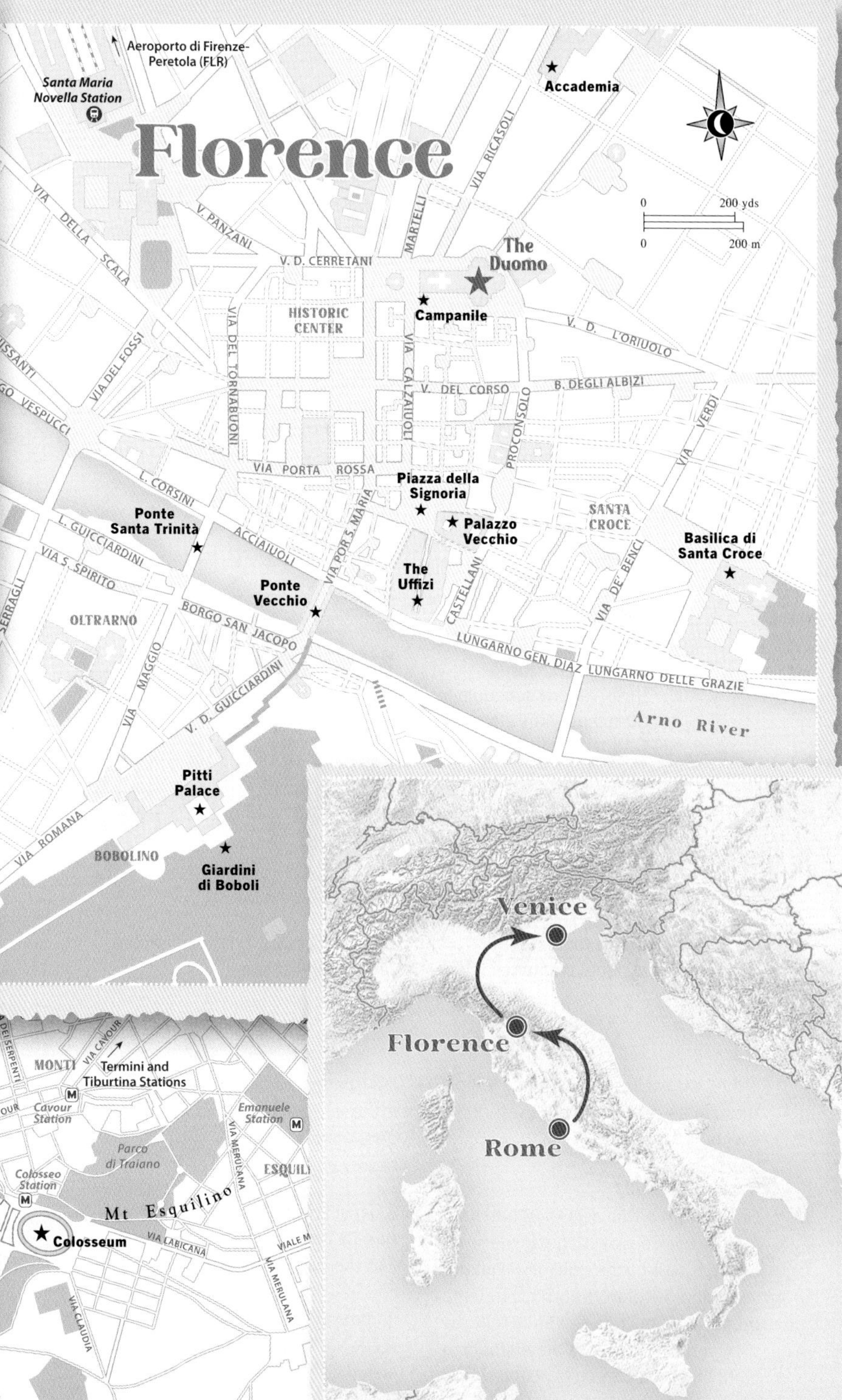

Florence
Aeroporto di Firenze-Peretola (FLR)
Santa Maria Novella Station
Accademia
VIA RICASOLI
0 200 yds
0 200 m
VIA DELLA SCALA
V. PANZANI
MARTELLI
V. D. CERRETANI
The Duomo
Campanile
HISTORIC CENTER
VIA DEL TORNABUONI
VIA CALZAIUOLI
V. D. L'ORIUOLO
V. DEL CORSO
B. DEGLI ALBIZI
PROCONSOLO
VIA VERDI
VIA DEL FOSSI
RIGO VESPUCCI
VIA PORTA ROSSA
L. CORSINI
Piazza della Signoria
Palazzo Vecchio
SANTA CROCE
Ponte Santa Trinità
ACCIAIUOLI
VIA POR S. MARIA
L. GUICCIARDINI
VIA S. SPIRITO
The Uffizi
Basilica di Santa Croce
VIA DE' BENCI
CASTELLANI
Ponte Vecchio
SERRAGLI
OLTRARNO
BORGO SAN JACOPO
LUNGARNO GEN. DIAZ
LUNGARNO DELLE GRAZIE
VIA MAGGIO
V. D. GUICCIARDINI
Arno River
Pitti Palace
VIA ROMANA
BOBOLINO
Giardini di Boboli
Venice
Florence
Rome
MONTI
VIA CAVOUR
Termini and Tiburtina Stations
Cavour Station
Emanuele Station
Parco di Traiano
VIA MERULANA
Colosseo Station
Mt Esquilino
Colosseum
VIA LABICANA
VIALE M
VIA CLAUDIA
Mt Celio

Key Reservations

TRAVEL PASSES

Local travel cards like **RomaPass** (www.romapass.it), **Firenzecard** (www.firenzecard.it), and **Venezia Unica** (www.veneziaunica.it) help get the most out of your journey without wasting precious hours in line.

MONUMENTS AND MUSEUMS

Most monuments and museums offer convenient online prebooking services that can save you the frustration of waiting in line. There's a small fee and reservations should be made a couple of weeks in advance to ensure a spot. Note that during COVID outbreaks, advance reservations are not only recommended, but required, at a number of sights. Be sure to book in advance for the following sights:

Rome

- **Pantheon**
- **Colosseum**
- **Vatican Museums**

Florence

- Climbing the **cupola** of Florence's **Duomo** (reservations schedule for 30-minute time slots)
- **Galleria dell'Accademia**
- The **Uffizi**

Venice

- **Doge's Palace**
- **St. Mark's Basilica**

The Vatican

RESTAURANTS

Reservations for restaurants aren't usually necessary, but to guarantee a seat at popular eateries, it's wise to arrive early or late.

is the beam of light entering the temple through an oculus in the largest dome ever built in antiquity.

5. Spanish Steps

Going north on Via del Corso, turn right (east) on Via Condotti to get to the Spanish Steps, passing through the glamorous shopping neighborhood of Tridente on the way. Built by the French in the 17th century, the steps are a stunning combination of terraces, curves, and balustrades that are especially beautiful in the spring and summer when they are decorated with flowers. Have dinner at a nearby trattoria.

6. Trevi Fountain

Piazza di Trevi; 24/7; free

End the day sitting in front of the Trevi Fountain, located south of Tridente. Rome's largest fountain sets a dramatic scene: Oceanus, god of the sea, occupies the central niche and stands in a

(clockwise from top) Spanish Steps; Roman Forum; Colosseum

shell-shaped chariot guiding two horses. Water gushes from the center and flows over jagged travertine rocks into an immense pool around which hundreds of visitors gather. The later you arrive, the more likely you'll score a seat. Legend (and Gregory Peck) has it that tossing a coin into the water with your back turned ensures a return trip to Rome.

DAY 2

1. Colosseum

Piazza del Colosseo; tel. 06/774-0091; www.coopculture.it; 8:30am-7:15pm daily summer and 8:30am-4:30pm winter; €16 combined with Palatine Hill and Forum, valid 24 hours, €22 with access to underground or third tier, valid 48 hours

The Colosseo, ancient Rome's largest amphitheater, cannot be missed. It's nearly as impressive today as it must have been in 80 CE when it was inaugurated before a crowd of 50,000 eager spectators, after taking only eight years to build. Spend an hour exploring the interior with the audio guide (€6).

top, Capitoline Museums; bottom, Bocca della Verità

2. Roman Forum

Via dei Fori Imperiali; tel. 06/3996-7700; 8:30am-7:15pm daily summer, 8:30am-4:30pm winter; €16 combined with Colosseum and Palatine Hill

Then, head next door to the Roman Forum. This narrow strip of land beneath the Palatine and Capitoline Hills was once the epicenter of the Roman Empire. Today its temples, government buildings, triumphal arches, shops, and monuments are in various states of decay, but walking along the Via Sacra path still feels like a monumental step into history. Afterward, head into the nearby **Monti** neighborhood for lunch—there are dozens of tempting options along Via Urbana.

3. Capitoline Museums

Piazza del Campidoglio 1; tel. 06/3996-7800; www.museicapitolini.org; 9:30am-7:30pm daily; €12 or RomaPass, audio guide €4, video guide €6

To see more artifacts, climb the Capitoline Hill and visit the **Musei Capitolini.** Founded in 1471, the oldest publicly owned museum in the world holds a mix of ancient and Renaissance art including Bernini's marble version of Medusa and a bronze statue of Rome's legendary twin founders, Romulus and Remus. What's more, Michelangelo designed the **Piazza del Campidoglio,** the square outside, and there's a great view of the city from the adjacent **Vittoriano** monument (free).

4. Bocca della Verità

Piazza della Bocca della Verità 18; tel. 06/678-7759; 9:30am-6pm daily; free

A short walk away, the church of Santa Maria in Cosmedin is famous for its bocca della verità or "mouth of truth," an ancient drain cover with a face carved into it, said to bite off the hands of falsehood tellers. There's usually a long line of tourists in the portico, waiting to test the legend. While there, stop inside the church to see the colorful mosaic flooring.

Gelato
THE ART OF ITALIAN ICE CREAM

Gelato is just milk, sugar, and natural fruit or cacao flavors, but when those ingredients are fresh and combined with care, something special happens. Here are a few basic guidelines for finding the best:

- **Avoid unnatural colors and showy displays.** Overly bright colors and gravity-defying mounds are often a sign of artificial flavoring and preservatives.
- **Sample the classics.** Start with fundamental flavors like chocolate (cioccolato), cream (crema), and hazelnut (nocciola).
- **Taste test.** Clerks readily provide small samples. Just ask, "Posso provare?" (May I try?)
- **Go cone-less.** Between cone or cup, purists advocate the latter on the grounds of taste.
- **Get the scoop(s).** Gelato sizes usually translate into two, three, and four scoops. Each scoop can be a different flavor. There's only one size of cone, while cups come in multiple dimensions.
- **Say yes to whipped cream.** At the end of every order the clerk will ask an important one-word question: "Panna?" Whipped cream and gelato go wonderfully together, so say, "Sì"! It's also free. The best gelateria prepare fresh panna daily.

One final tip: Unless you exert some authority inside a crowded gelateria, you may never place an order. Determine who is the last person in line when you walk in and make sure you are served after them. "Scusi, ero primo" (excuse me, I was ahead) can be very useful.

WHERE TO TRY IT

- **Rome:** At **Frigidarium** (Via del Governo Vecchio 112; tel. 334/995-1184; 10:30am-midnight daily; €3-5), lovers of pistachio and chocolate will enjoy the Mozart flavor topped with panna (whipped cream).
- **Florence:** At **Vivoli** (Via dell'Isola delle Stinche 7r; tel. 055/292-334; 9:30am-11pm Tues.-Sun.; €3-5), they've been scooping quality gelato since the 1930s. Try the crema de' Medici (cream-flavor) in a cone or a cup.
- **Venice: Da Nico** (Fondamenta Zattere al Ponte Lungo 922; tel. 041/522-5293; 6:30am-10pm Fri.-Wed.; €4-8) is famous for its hazelnut and cacao-flavored giandiotto gelato, invented in Venice and served here for over 80 years.

MAKE IT Active

Any trip will to Rome, Florence, and Venice will likely involve a lot of walking. But for a bit more recreation outdoors, swap out a few hours for one of these excellent active experiences.

ROME

Cycling Via Appia Antica: One of the most scenic trails in Rome and great for biking, Via Appia Antica (also known as the Appian Way) rolls past pine trees and ancient monuments. You can rent bikes from the Appia Antica Park Office (3.5 km/2 mi from Rome's historic center) and ride the ancient road from there to the town of Ciampino (11.5 km/6.5 mi one-way; 2 hours).

FLORENCE

Lungarno Bike Path: Both sides of the Arno River are equipped with bike paths, but the one on the northern bank west of the city is the longest and most panoramic. Starting at Ponte Vecchio, you can pedal all the way to Parco dei Renai (12 km/7 mi round-trip; 1-1.5 hours). Rent bikes from the shops near the Florence train station.

VENICE

Kayaking the canals: For a unique Venice experience, take a kayak tour through the canals with **Venice Kayak** (Certosa Marina, Certosa Island; tel. 041/523-6720; www.venicekayak.com; half-day tour €110) or **Venice by Water** (Cannaregio, Calle Brazzo 3346; tel. 389/985-1866; www.venicebywater.com; one hour tour €50).

5. Dinner in the Jewish Ghetto

Roman kosher is a unique combination of Italian and Jewish culinary traditions. To try them, walk along the Tiber River to the Jewish Ghetto for a taste of deep-fried artichokes prepared Jewish style at **Nonna Betta** (Via del Portico d'Ottavia 16; tel. 06/6880-6263; www.nonnabetta.it; noon-5pm and 6pm-10:30pm Wed.-Mon.; €9-13) or any of the kosher restaurants lining Via del Portico D'Ottavia.

DAY 3

★ 1. Vatican Museums and Sistine Chapel

Viale Vaticano; tel. 06/6988-4676; www.museivaticani.va; 10am-8pm (last entry 6pm) Mon.-Thurs., 10am-10pm (last entry 8pm) Fri.-Sat.; €17, audio guide €7

Ride Metro A to Ottaviano and follow the pilgrims to Vatican City. Remember to dress appropriately, with shoulders and knees covered, and arrive early to the Vatican Museums. Inside you can choose from several itineraries and could easily spend an entire day here. If you arrive on Sunday morning you can join the faithful in the square below and receive the pope's blessing. Most visitors beeline to the Sistine Chapel, but there are plenty of underrated sections of the museum such as the first-floor antiquities collection near the entrance.

The Sistine Chapel, the greatest fresco in the world, is the climax of any visit to the Vatican Museums. It took Michelangelo four years to complete the Biblical scenes depicted on the 12,000-square-foot (1,115-square-meter) ceiling. The

left, Trastevere; right, view from Gianicolo Hill

Creation of Adam and *Temptation* are portrayed upon the central spine of the vault; *The Last Judgment,* commissioned later, covers the entire altar wall. The chapel also includes three paintings by Sandro Botticelli. There's no time limit for visiting the chapel, so spend as long as you like gazing at the masterpieces.

2. St. Peter's Basilica

Piazza San Pietro; tel. 06/6988-3731; 7am-7pm daily; free

Once you've gotten your fill of the treasures of the Vatican Museums, enter St. Peter's Basilica. The gargantuan interior leaves no doubt that this is the largest church in the world, containing 11 chapels and 45 altars, all built of the finest materials. Light a candle and descend into the crypt to pay homage to past popes, then climb your way to the top of Michelangelo's **cupola** (€10 for elevator, €8 on foot). On foot, the climb is 551 steps, and even riding the elevator is followed by a climb of 320 steps. You'll need some stamina to reach the highest point in the city—and one of its best views.

3. Castel Sant'Angelo

Lungotevere Castello 50; tel. 06/681-9111; www.castelsantangelo.com; 9am-7:30pm daily; €15 or RomaPass

The nearby streets of **Borgo Pio** and **Borgo Vittorio** have catered to pilgrims since the Middle Ages and are lined with eateries and souvenir shops. Follow either of these parallel roads to Castel Sant'Angelo. There's a good view from atop the ancient mausoleum (built for Emperor Hadrian), which was expanded and modified over the centuries into a castle, prison, and papal safehouse. Today it houses a museum of artworks and artifacts that reflect its complex history, and a convenient rooftop bar that serves cold beer and excellent views.

4. Gianicolo Hill

For a final view, climb to the top of Gianicolo Hill, about a 30-minute walk from Castel Sant'Angelo. At the top is a long terrace with one of the best views of the city—you can see the Pantheon, Vittoriano monument, and the historic center, all places you've been.

5. Wandering and Dinner in Trastevere

Descend into Trastevere, which literally means "across the Tiber." With a high concentration of trattoria-style restaurants and cocktail bars, this neighborhood is popular with locals, university students, and visitors. The heart of the neighborhood is Piazza di Santa Maria in Trastevere, but explore the labyrinthine side streets to find that perfect little spot, like **Trattoria da Enzo** (Via dei Vascellari 29; tel. 06/581-2260; 12:30pm-3pm and 7:30pm-11pm Mon.-Sat.; €10-12), for dinner on your final night in Rome.

Florence

Where to Stay: Around the Duomo

Arrive by: Train from Termini or Tiburtina stations in Rome to Santa Maria Novella station in Florence (1.5 hours)

DAY 4

1. Lunch on Florentine Classics

Depart Rome midmorning so you can enjoy lunch in Florence. After you've checked-in, find a small trattoria like **Trattoria Mario** (Via Rosina 2r; tel. 055/218-550; www.trattoriamario.com; 12:30pm-3:30pm Mon.-Sat.; €10-12, cash only), and discover the difference between Florentine and Roman gastronomy. Order pappa al pomodoro or T-bone fiorentina steak from Chianina cattle raised along the Tuscan coast.

2. The Uffizi

Piazzale degli Uffizi; tel. 055/294-883; www.uffizi.it; 8:15am-6:50pm Tues.-Sun.; €20, €38 combined ticket with Palazzo Pitti and Boboli Gardens, or Firenzecard

After lunch, take your time wandering the rooms of the Uffizi, which boasts one of the greatest art collections in the world. Gaze upon Botticelli's Birth of Venus and works by Caravaggio. At the end of the second-floor galleries, step out on the terrace of the museum café overlooking Piazza della Signoria for a coffee break. The Uffizi is considerably smaller than the Vatican Museums, and you can see it all in a couple of hours.

3. Pitti Palace

Piazza Pitti 1; tel. 055/294-883; www.uffizi.it/palazzo-pitti; 8:30am-6:50pm Tues.-Sun.; €16, €38 combo ticket with Uffizi, or Firenzecard

Stroll over to the other side of the Arno river (or Oltrarno, as the area is called) to visit the Pitti Palace. This is the largest palace in Florence, and it can easily take a half day to explore its two art galleries, several museums, and 11-acre garden. For now, peek into any of the galleries and exhibits that interest you, then take a stroll through the **Giardini di Boboli,** a tranquil escape from the city.

4. Sunset Over Ponte Vecchio

Make your way back to the river and the 14th-century Ponte Vecchio. Picturesque workshops (once butchers, now jewelry shops) line both sides of the bridge, which is filled with pedestrians, who seem in no hurry to get to the other side, both day and night. But at sunset, viewing the bridge, rather than crossing it, is the attraction. The streets running along the Arno, as well as neighboring bridges, provide the best vantage points. Locals and visitors gather on the **Ponte**

top, Ponte Vecchio; bottom, the Duomo

NAME CHECK: Michelangelo

Sculpture, painting, urban planning, and architecture: Michelangelo Buonarroti (1475-1564) could do it all. He was recognized as a genius nearly from the moment he picked up a chisel, and spent his long life executing high-profile commissions for cardinals, popes, and princes. What he produced has captivated viewers for half a millennium and inspired generations of artists. The majority of his works are in Rome and Florence, where he was born and eventually died.

- **Piazza del Campidoglio, Rome:** Pope Paul II commissioned Michelangelo to renovate this piazza and give what was then a dilapidated part of Rome a new splendor.
- **The Vatican, Rome:** The Sistine Chapel is arguably Michelangelo's magnum opus. In St. Peter's you can see one of his earliest sculptures, the Pietà. The artist was also appointed the Vatican's chief architect in 1564 and spent most of his time planning the dome.
- **Galleria dell'Accademia, Florence:** This gallery contains one of Michelangelo's best-known masterpieces, the statue of David, as well as some sensual uncompleted statues.
- **Basilica di Santa Croce, Florence:** The artist's final resting place (alongside none other than Machiavelli and Galileo Galilei) is inside this Gothic basilica with frescoes by Giotto.
- **The Uffizi, Florence:** This museum houses Michelangelo's first painting, *Tondo Doni,* a colorful portrayal of the Holy Family.

Santa Trinità, 150 yards downriver, to admire the way the setting sun gradually transforms the Ponte Vecchio. Afterward, disappear into the side streets of Oltrarno for dinner. Try **Trattoria Casalinga** (Via Michelozzi 9r; tel. 055/281-624; https://trattorialacasalinga.it; 12:30pm-2:30pm and 7pm-10pm daily, Sun. lunch only; €13-15) for dozens of Tuscan possibilities.

DAY 5

★ 1. The Duomo

Piazza del Duomo; 7:30am-6pm daily; https://duomo.firenze.it/en/discover/cathedral; church free, dome (by reservation only) €20

Grab an espresso and get ready to visit what many consider the finest church in Italy. Work began on Santa Maria del Fiore, better known as the Duomo, in 1296, and took nearly 600 years to complete. Its Filippo Brunelleschi-designed cupola, or dome, can be seen from nearly everywhere in the city, and inside the Duomo appears even bigger; the austere, harmonious, and geometrical nave is 45 m (148 ft) high and almost two football fields long.

Climbing the cupola is one of the most popular activities in Florence; there are 463 steep steps to the top of the dome, but they culminate in a 360-degree view of the city. Next door is the **campanile** (bell tower; €15), another beautiful and unique feature of the Florentine skyline. Also called Giotto's Tower in reference to the artist who initiated work on it in 1337, it's one of the only towers in Italy not connected to a church, partly due to the independent nature of Florence during the Renaissance. Getting to the top is easier than ascending the cupola, and there are several intermediary platforms for visitors to rest and admire the increasingly better **views of the Duomo** and city. There's often a line of tourists ready to climb its 414 steps.

2. Palazzo Vecchio

tel. 055/276-8325; museum 9am-7pm Fri.-Wed., 9am-2pm Thurs. Oct.-Mar., 9am-11pm Fri.-Wed., 9am-2pm Thurs. Apr.-Sept., tower 10am-5pm Fri.-Wed. and 10am-2pm Thurs. Oct.-Mar., 9am-9pm Fri.-Wed. and 9am-2pm Thurs. Apr.-Sept.; €12.50 for single sight, €15.50 combined ticket option, or Firenzecard

Just a few blocks south is **Piazza della Signoria,** the political center of the city, where Palazzo Vecchio stands imposingly with its high walls and 94-m (308-ft) tower. This is where magistrates, nobles, dignitaries, and citizens gathered to discuss and decide countless matters that shaped the city. Even if you don't intend the visit the palazzo, it's worth a peek inside the courtyard and the Roman remains underground, both of which are free. The lower floors include residential quarters and reception halls, and from here you can set off on another bell tower ascent, with an excellent view of the Duomo.

3. Tripe Sandwiches at Mercato Centrale

Piazza del Mercato Centrale; tel. 055/239-9798; 10am-10pm daily; €12-14

For lunch, make your way to Mercato Central, Florence's largest and most animated covered food market and a good place to learn about local culinary traditions. Head to **Narbone** on the ground floor for a lunch of tripe sandwiches, a Florentine favorite.

4. Accademia

Via Ricasoli 58-60; tel. 055/098-7100; www.galleriaaccademiafirenze.it; 9am-6pm Tues.-Sun.; €8 or Firenzecard, €4 online reservation fee

From Mercato Centrale, walk east to the Accademia, the world's oldest art school and home of Michelangelo's masterpiece, David. The portrayal of David's struggle against Goliath was a common theme among Renaissance artists, but Michelangelo's take is unique: In his version, David is not brandishing the severed head of the giant, nor is he celebrating his deed. Instead, he sizes up his nemesis

left, Basilica di Santa Croce; right, statue of David at the Accademia

Espresso 101

For many Italians, the day begins with the ritual of coffee in the morning. Fall into the Italian rhythm by taking part in this essential custom on your trip.

COFFEE CULTURE

Italians regularly crowd into coffee bars for their morning fix, and often end their lunches with a cup. Most locals drink at the counter, where there's hardly ever a wait. Here's a quick rundown of what to order:

- **Caffè:** Espresso, served black, has become so popular that when you order a caffè (coffee) you automatically receive an espresso. The espresso is served in a ceramic cup, unless "al vetro" is requested—in which case it will be poured into a shot glass. Order it corto (short) if you want it slightly stronger, or lungo (long) if you want it slightly weaker.
- **Caffè Macchiato:** Espresso with a dash of steamed milk. (Macchiato means stained; the milk "stains" the espresso.)
- **Latte Macchiato:** The opposite of caffè macchiato—a glass of milk stained with a little coffee.
- **Cappuccino:** Served in a larger cup and creamier than a caffè macchiato. A cappuccino is almost always ordered in the morning and often accompanied by a pastry.
- **Marocchino:** A cross between a caffè macchiato and miniature cappuccino, topped with cacao and served in a glass or ceramic cup.
- **Caffè Freddo:** Italians don't stop drinking coffee in summer, but they often order iced espresso when temperatures rise. It's served black, with milk, or topped with whipped cream.

WHERE TO TRY IT

- **Rome:** **Caffè Sant'Eustachio** (Piazza Sant'Eustachio 82; tel. 06/6880-2048; 7:30am-midnight daily), located east of Piazza Navona, has been serving a blend of locally ground beans since 1938.
- **Florence:** At **Ditta Artigianale** (Via dei Neri 32r; 8:30am-7pm daily), between Basilica di Santa Croce and Palazzo Vecchio, they choose their beans carefully and control every step in the blending process, resulting in one of the best espressos in the city.
- **Venice:** **Pasticceria Rizzardini** (San Polo, Campiello Meloni 1415; tel. 041/522-3835; 7am-8pm Wed.-Mon.) has an extensive pastry selection, including burranei, a classic Venetian butter cookie. Once you've picked a pastry, you can order a coffee at the metal counter.

as he holds the stone he is about to sling. The rest of the worthwhile collection of medieval paintings, half-completed sculptures, and Florentine art from the 12th-15th centuries, is often overlooked. You'll need reservations, as the number of visitors allowed in at a time is capped.

5. Basilica di Santa Croce

Piazza Basilica di Santa Croce 16; tel. 055/246-6105; www.santacroceopera.it; 9:30am-5pm Mon.-Sat., 2pm-5pm Sun.; €8 or Firenzecard

After seeing David, head southeast to the Santa Croce neighborhood. The tombs inside Basilica di Santa Croce are the resting places of a number of historic figures, including Michelangelo, Machiavelli, and Galileo Galilei. It's designed in a Latin cross plan with three naves, a number of side chapels, and a vast wooden ceiling, with frescoes by Renaissance artists who set the early standards of Western art.

6. Wine at Coquinarius

Via delle Oche 11r; tel. 055/230-2153; www.coquinarius.it; 12:30pm-3pm and 5:30pm-10:30pm daily

Tuscany, the region of which Florence is the heart, produces some of Italy's best wines, and you can discover just how good it is at restaurants and bars around the city. But if you're really serious about wine, visit an enoteca like Coquinarius, just around the corner from the Duomo. It's a cheery spot with appetizers that can substitute for dinner.

Venice

Where to Stay: Dorsoduro or Cannaregio, more intimate and less busy neighborhoods than San Marco

Arrive by: Train from Santa Maria Novella station in Florence to Santa Lucia station in Venice (2 hours)

DAY 6

1. St. Mark's Square

Take the train to Venice, and after you've settled into your hotel, follow the yellow signs to St. Mark's Square, the largest square in the city and the administrative and religious heart of Venice, bordered by some of its most famous buildings: St. Mark's Basilica, Doge's Palace, the **campanile** bell tower (www.basilicasanmarco.it; €10), and **Torre dell'Orologio** astronomical clock tower (tel. 848/082-000 or 041/4273-0892 from abroad; https://torreorologio.visitmuve.it; €12, €7 with Museum Pass or St. Mark's Square Pass). The piazza is animated with competing quartets playing on outdoor stages at elegant cafés, tour groups waiting to enter the Doge's Palace, and fearless seagulls searching for their next meal.

2. Coffee on the Square

The cafés of San Marco are nearly as famous as the square itself and have shared in the history of the city. They're extremely elegant, and each café provides outdoor seating where you can admire the monuments and listen to musicians playing classical music.

St. Mark's Square

(top to bottom) café tables in San Marco; Doge's Palace; St. Mark's Basilica; Campo Santo Stefano

Location and history come with a price tag, though. A cup of coffee, a couple of drinks, some snacks, and a dessert could add up to a three-digit bill. Either you don't care and count it as a once-in-a-lifetime experience or go inside and drink at the bar where there's as much atmosphere at a fraction of the cost. **Caffè Florian** (Piazza San Marco 57; tel. 041/520-5641; 9am-midnight daily) once attracted Venice's nobles, politicians, and intellectuals, and **Caffè Quadri** (Piazza San Marco 121; tel. 041/522-2105; 10:30am-midnight daily) is beautiful, with affordable offerings, unless you choose to sit at an outdoor table.

3. Doge's Palace

Piazza San Marco 1; tel. 041/271-5911; www.palazzoducale.visitmuve.it; 8:30am-7pm Apr.-Oct., 8:30am-5:30pm Nov.-Mar.; St. Mark's Square Pass €25 or Museum Pass €35, audio guide €5

Understanding Venice requires visiting the Palazzo Ducale, where the doge—the ruler of Venice when it was a Republic (AD 697-1797)—resided and the Venetian senate met to make decisions that maintained the city's power throughout the Mediterranean. The most visited monument in Venice, it's an immense U-shaped complex with stunning facades and sumptuous interiors. If you want a behind-the-scenes look at the palace, reserve the Secret Itineraries tour (reservations required; €28, or €15 with the Rolling Venice card). This 75-minute walk through lesser-known parts of the palazzo will take you across the **Bridge of Sighs,** where prisoners were once led to the gallows.

4. St. Mark's Basilica

Piazza San Marco 328; tel. 041/270-8311; 9:30am-5pm www.basilicasanmarco.it; Mon.-Sat., 2pm-4:30pm Sun.; free

Next door is St. Mark's Basilica. Founded in 832, the basilica was influenced by Greek, Byzantine, and Islamic art and architecture; the five domes are reminiscent of a mosque, and the floor plan is a Greek cross. Inside, golden mosaics embellish over 3,716 square m (40,000

Regional Cuisine

ROME

- **Roman pizza:** Roman pizza is thin, prepared in long trays, and served by the kilo at hundreds of pizzeria al taglio (takeaway pizza shops). Varieties range from bianca (white) and margherita (tomato and mozzarella) to other more creative alternatives.
- **Deep-fried artichokes:** The artichoke holds a central place in Roman cuisine, and if you want to taste this Jewish contribution to Roman cooking, head to the Ghetto, where you can decide if you prefer artichokes alla romana (stewed) or alla guidia (deep-fried).
- **Cacio e pepe:** Every town and region in Italy has its own particular pasta shapes and sauces. In Rome, this pasta seasoned with a creamy mix of sharp cacio goat cheese and pepper, reigns supreme.

FLORENCE

- **Pappa al pomodoro:** This vegetarian, tomato-based stew, reminiscent of gazpacho, is perfect in summer.
- **Bistecca alla fiorentina:** This thick T-bone steak cut from local Chianina beef is the most popular main course in Florence, grilled for three minutes on either side and served close to rare, alone on a plate.
- **Tripe sandwiches:** Tripe is Florence's favorite fast-food ingredient, and eateries around the city have been preparing tripe sandwiches for decades, with salt and pepper the only traditional condiments.

VENICE

- **Cicchetti:** A gastronomic highlight of any Venetian vacation, this finger food consists of an assortment sliced bread topped with creamed fish, sauteed vegetables, cheese, and many other enticing ingredients. Best enjoyed in a traditional bacari, or Venetian bar, with a glass of prosecco.
- **Burranei:** These unevenly shaped butter cookies, coated with powdered sugar, are found in bakeries and pastry shops throughout Venice.
- **Venetian risotto:** Rice plays a major role in the Venetian diet and is usually served with risi bisi (peas) or sparasi (asparagus) in early spring and summer.

square ft) of the cavernous church; hop on a free **tour** to understand the meaning behind the mosaics.

5. Campo Santo Stefano

From St. Mark's Basilica, navigate your way on foot to Campo Santo Stefano, the largest of the San Marco neighborhood's campi—irregularly-shaped squares that provide space for locals to commune and children to play. Enjoy the evening eating and drinking in this lively square. At the **Chiesa di San Vidale,** classical concerts are held every evening and the repertoire nearly always includes Vivaldi.

DAY 7

1. Rialto Bridge and Markets

The early morning hours (before 8am) are your best chance to avoid the crush of tourists throughout the city. This (or late evenings) is the best time to cross the Rialto Bridge, which is the grandest—and most crowded—of the four bridges spanning the Grand Canal. Cross over from the San

Marco side and appreciate the bridge's harmonious stonework and twin archways. The bridge divided into three lanes, the outermost of which provides good views of the canal. Like the Ponte Vecchio in Florence, it's flanked with shops and is a magnet for commercial activity.

The San Polo side is the busier of the two, and where the city's main markets are located. You can escape the crush of visitors by exploring the alcoves parallel to the main street, Ruga dei Oresi, or by heading north to the nearby Campo Cesare. Farther along and facing the Grand Canal are the fish market and produce market. Having a look at the goods is the perfect preview for lunch or dinner.

2. Lunch at a Bacari Bar

Head to any of the traditional bacari bars (traditional Venetian bars that sell wine by the glass or pitcher) nearby. **Osteria Bancogirco** (San Polo, Campo San Giacometto 122; tel. 041/523-2061; 9am-midnight Tues.-Sun.), with its view of the Grand Canal, stands out. A locally produced sparkling **prosecco** wine is a fine accompaniment to any meal.

★ 3. View from the Punta della Dogana

Campo della Salute 2; tel. 041/200-1057; www.palazzograssi.it; Wed.-Mon. 10am-7pm; €15 with Palazzo Grassi

Hop on a vaporetto and cruise down the Grand Canal to Dorsoduro, alighting at Salute at the eastern end of the neighborhood. Punta della Dogana is a renovated customhouse and warehouse with a dozen spacious exhibit rooms. At the end of the complex are a bar, museum shop, and stairs leading to a lookout tower. The **Fondamenta Salute** embankment leads to the easternmost tip of the Dorsoduro and one of the best views of the city.

4. Peggy Guggenheim Collection

Fondamenta Venier 704 or 701; tel. 041/240-5411; www.guggenheim-venice.it; 10am-6pm Fri.-Mon.; adults €16, over 65 €14, students 11-26 €9, ages 0-9 free

Leave historic Venice behind and fast-forward a few centuries at this unique gallery, which is filled with 20th-century masterpieces from Chagall, Dalí, and more. You can enjoy another view of the canal from the terrace at the front of the building.

5. Cicchetti at Al Bottegon

Fondamenta Nani 992; tel. 041/523-0034; 8:30am-8:30pm Mon.-Sat.; €6-12

You can't leave Venice without sampling cicchetti, the city's unique take on appetizers. Al Bottegon, located along the Rio

WATCH

Roman Holiday: The Spanish Steps, and many other iconic Roman scenes, play key roles in this delightful romp around the city starring Audrey Hepburn and Gregory Peck.

READ

A Room with a View by E. M. Forster: This novel (also adapted into a successful film) is memorably set in Florence, with pivotal scenes in the Basilica di Santa Croce and Piazza della Signoria.

LISTEN

"Me So' Mbriacato" by Mannarino: This Rome-born singer-songwriter takes his inspiration from the street musicians you'll find busking throughout Rome, Florence, and Venice.

Learn Italian with Lucrezia: Pick up the musical Italian language on the go by plugging into this delightful podcast, in which an Italian teacher will give you tips on essential vocabulary and phrases.

The Bittersweet Life: Learn about Italian art, history, and culture on this podcast from two expats who have each spent many years in Rome.

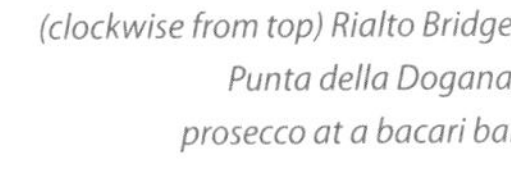

(clockwise from top) Rialto Bridge; Punta della Dogana; prosecco at a bacari bar

TO TAKE Home

PAPER

Paper production has a long history in Florence, although the marble variety for which the city is famous originated in Turkey. **Il Papiro** (Piazza del Duomo 24r; tel. 055/281-628; 10am-7pm daily)—Florence's primary paper purveyor, with six outposts in the city—is filled with cards, journals, and other marbled paper items.

LEATHER GOODS

Leatherwork in Florence also goes back centuries. The **San Lorenzo street market** (Piazza San Lorenzo and Via dell'Ariento; 8am-8pm daily), adjacent to Mercato Central, is lined with stands selling every type of leather product. A few tips for the quality conscious: If the label is sewn on, it's a good sign; indoor shops are where the best leather products are found; and whatever sounds too cheap probably is.

VENETIAN MASKS

One of the most iconic things to take home with you from your trip, masks are everywhere in Venice, but **Ca' Mancana** (Calle de le Botteghe 3172; tel. 041/520-3229; 10am-8pm daily) sells its own handmade versions, created with traditional papier-mâché techniques. When Stanley Kubrick wanted masks for *Eyes Wide Shut,* he came here.

GLASS ART

On the island of **Murano** in the Venice lagoon, you can see demonstrations of the famed art of glassblowing and perhaps pick up a delicate piece of glass art to take home with you. If you can't make it out to Murano, stop by **FGB** (S. Maria del Giglio 2514; tel. 041/523-6556; 10am-6:30daily) and **EMI Art Glass** (Calle della Mandola 3803; tel. 041/523-1326; 9am-7:30pm Mon.-Sat.), two excellent glass shops in the San Marco neighborhood of Venice.

de S. Trovaso canal, is one of Dorsoduro's best cicchetti bars; you can spend your last evening sampling the addictive finger foods at this friendly and wonderfully worn bacaro.

TRANSPORTATION

You don't need a car for this trip: Travel between cities is easy to do by train, and walking and public transportation are the best ways to get around within each city.

Air

All three cities have major airports, though travelers outside Europe are most likely to arrive at Rome's **Aeroporto Internazionale Leonardo Da Vinci Airport** (FCO; Via dell'Aeroporto 320; tel. 06/65951; www.adr.it), 26 km (16 mi) west of the Colosseum. Venice's **Aeroporto di Venezia** (VCE; Via Galileo Galilei 30; tel. 041/260-6111; www.veniceairport.it), 13 km (8 mi) northeast of Venice, across the Venetian Lagoon, also receives some flights from outside Europe, including

CONNECT WITH

- Zagreb, Ljubljana, and Trieste (page 205)
- Tuscany and Umbria (page 289)
- Alta Via 1: Dolomite High Route (page 439)
- Naples, Capri, and the Amalfi Coast (page 536)

North America. Florence's airport, **Aeroporto di Firenze-Peretola** (Aeroporto Amerigo Vespucci; FLR; Via del Termine 11; tel. 055/30615; www.aeroporto.firenze.it), 5 km (3 mi) west of Florence, is the smallest, with no direct flights from anywhere outside Europe.

Train

Traveling between Rome, Florence, and Venice by trains operated by **Italo** (www.italo.it) or **Trenitalia** (www.trenitalia.it) is fast, easy, and convenient.

- **Termini Station, Rome** (www.romatermini.com): The hub of Rome's rail network, 10 minutes east of the city center.
- **Tiburtina Station, Rome:** High-speed train station, 2 km (1.2 mi) east of Termini.
- **Santa Maria Novella Station, Florence:** Florence's central train station, 10 minutes from the Piazza del Duomo (1.5 hours from Rome; from €35.90 one-way).
- **Santa Lucia Station, Venice:** Located in the northwestern sestiere (neighborhood) of Cannaregio; 25-minute, 2-km (1-mi) walk to St. Mark's Square, or take a vaporetto or water taxi (2 hours from Florence; from €39 one-way).

Public Transportation

Rome

Rome's **subway** system is made up of two lines, Metro A and Metro B, which intersect at Termini train station. To supplement the metro, six **trams** and hundreds of **bus** lines operate throughout Rome day and night. There are a variety of travel passes available from ATAC (www.atac.roma.it). Single tickets can be purchased at automated kiosks within subway stations as well as most tabacchi (tobacco shops).

Florence

Much of Florence's center is pedestrianized, and distances between monuments are short. If your accommodation is located in the Historic Center or Oltrarno, you won't need public transportation.

Venice

There are three principle modes of water transportation in Venice: vaporetto, traghetto, and water taxi. But for the purposes of this itinerary, you're most likely to find yourself aboard a **vaporetto,** the aquatic equivalent of buses. Twenty-four vaporetto lines are operated by ACTV (tel. 041/2424; https://actv.avmspa.it); each neighborhood has a handful of vaporetto stations. Tickets can be purchased at larger stations or some newsstands; you can choose from a range of tickets, from single tickets to seven-day passes.

Getting Back

Many visitors fly home or to their next destination from the Venice airport. To get back to Rome, it takes a little over 3.5 hours from Venice by train (approx. 50 daily departures; from €49 one-way). Trains departing from Venice stop in Florence.

BERLIN, WARSAW, AND KRAKOW

Why Go: Prussian palaces, rich Holocaust history, meticulously rebuilt city centers, and a buzzy contemporary culture in these three cities create one of the most varied and emotionally resonant scenes in all of Europe.

Number of Days: 7

Total Distance: 782 km (486 mi)

Seasons: Summer

Start: Berlin

End: Krakow

Strike out for one of Europe's most emotionally charged regions on this route, which takes you to the heights of the architectural wonders of the Prussian Empire and a young, vibrant contemporary art scene, and to the lowest of lows and of the darkest of days in Nazi-ruled Germany, where you must grapple with the specter of the Holocaust. Confront the Cold War at what remains of the Berlin Wall; discover the birth of Warsaw, a figurative Phoenix that has risen from the ashes of destruction; and take a sobering stroll through the Auschwitz-Berkenau death camp outside of the wonderfully preserved medieval city of Krakow.

TOP 3

Admiring the transformation of the Berlin Wall into a vibrant art space in the **East Side Gallery** (page 174).

Listening to Chopin in Warsaw, his birthplace (page 176).

Confronting the horrors of our past in the **Auschwitz concentration camp** (page 182).

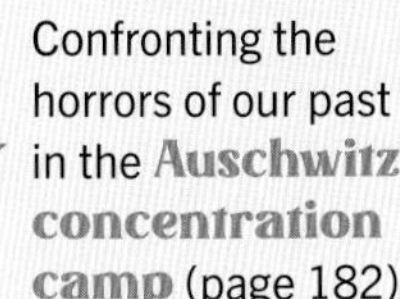

Warsaw
Park Traugutta
WYBRZEŻE KOŚCIUSZKOWSKIE
Multimedia Fountain Park
POLIN Museum of the History of Polish Jews
Old Town Market Square
Chopin Concert
Royal Castle
Saint Anne's Cathedral
Chocolate Café E. Wedel
Presidential Palace
CENTRAL WARSAW
Ogród Krasińskich
Ogród Saski
Park Kazimierzowski
Park Praski
Polish Museum of Vodka
Vistula River
JAGIELLOŃSKA
ALEJA "SOLIDARNOŚCI"
STEFANA OKRZEI
TARGOWA
OKOPOWA
BONIFRATERSKA
GEN. W. ANDERSA
ALEJA JANA PAWŁA II
DZIELNA
NOWOLIPKI
NOWOLIPIE
ELEKTORALNA
ŻELAZNA
WRONIA
MARSZAŁKOWSKA
ŚWIĘTOKRZYSKA
ALEJE JEROZOLIMSKIE
Museum of Fryderyk Chopin in Warsaw
Warsaw Rising Museum
Warsaw Central Railway Station
Warsaw Chopin Airport (WAW)
0
0.5 mi
0.5 km
Berlin
Oranienburger Tor
Oranienburger Straße
Krausnickpark
Weinmeisterstraße
Berlin Hbf
LUISENSTRASSE
FRIEDRICHSTRASSE
0
1,000 ft
200 m
MITTE'S SCHEUNENVIERTEL
Monbijoupark
Hackescher Markt
REINHARDTSTRASSE
Spree
GOVERNMENT DISTRICT
Bode Museum
Old National Gallery
Pergamon Museum
Bundestag
Friedrichstraße
Neues Museum
BODESTRASSE
BURGSTRASSE
UNIVERSITÄTSSTRASSE
REICHSTAGUFER
Altes Museum
Berlin Cathedral
Lustgarten
Former Location of Berlin Wall
DOROTHEENSTRASSE
PLATZ DER REPUBLIK
UNTER DEN LINDEN
MITTELSTRASSE
Museumsinsel
MITTE
B5
Museum Island
Charlottenburg Palace
STR DES 17. JUNI
Brandenburger Tor
Unter den Linden
Brandenburg Gate
SCHLOSSPLATZ
OBERWALLSTRASSE
BREMER WEG
BEHRENSTRASSE
FRANZÖSISCHE STR
Tiergarten
Memorial to the Murdered Jews of Europe
EBERTSTRASSE
AHORNSTEIG
JÄGERSTRASSE
Spreekanal
FRIEDRICHSGRACHT
MAUERSTRASSE
WILHELMSTRASSE
GLINKASTRASSE
TAUBENSTRASSE
Hausvogteiplatz
MOHRENSTRASSE
Kurstrassenpark
Kaiser Wilhelm Memorial Church
Mohrenstraße
KRONENSTRASSE
TIERGARTENSTRASSE
VOSSSTRASSE
Stadtmitte
CHARLOTTENSTRASSE
MARKGRAFENSTRASSE
LEIPZIGERSTRASSE
Spittelmarkt
SEYDELSTRASSE
POTSDAMER PLATZ
Potsdamer Platz
POTSDAMER STR
LEIPZIGERSTRASSE
KRAUSENSTRASSE
B1
SCHÜTZENSTRASSE
Checkpoint Charlie
ZIMMERSTRASSE
Tilla-Durieux Park
Berlin Brandenburg Airport
RUDI-DUTSCHKE-STR
KOCHSTRASSE
Kochstraße/ Checkpoint Charlie
Waldeckpark

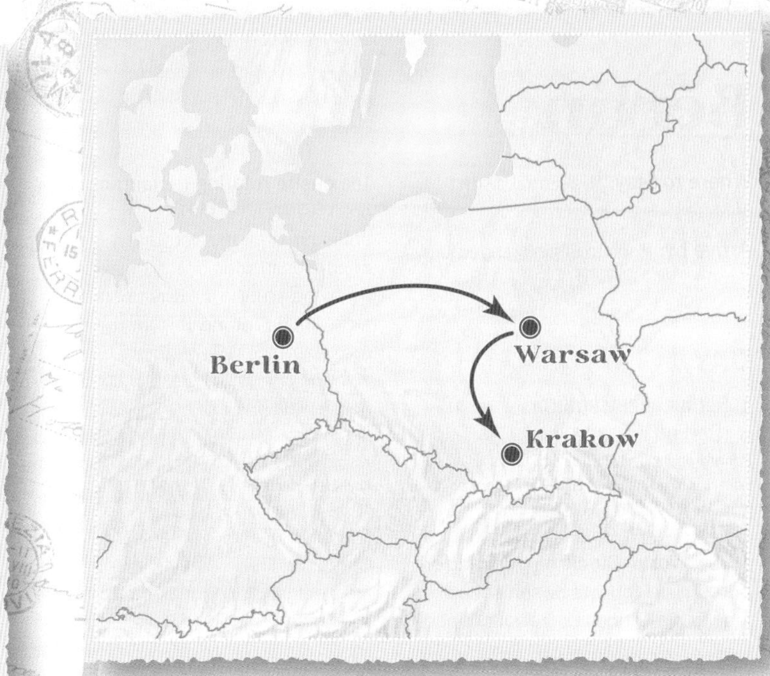
Berlin
Warsaw
Krakow

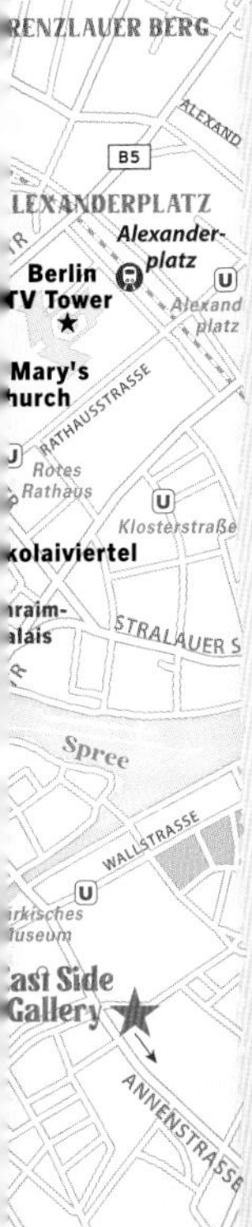
PRENZLAUER BERG
ALEXAND
B5
ALEXANDERPLATZ
Alexander-
platz
Berlin
TV Tower
Alexand
platz
Mary's
hurch
RATHAUSSTRASSE
Rotes
Rathaus
Klosterstraße
kolaiviertel
raim-
alais
STRALAUER S
Spree
WALLSTRASSE
rkisches
useum
ast Side
Gallery
ANNENSTRASSE

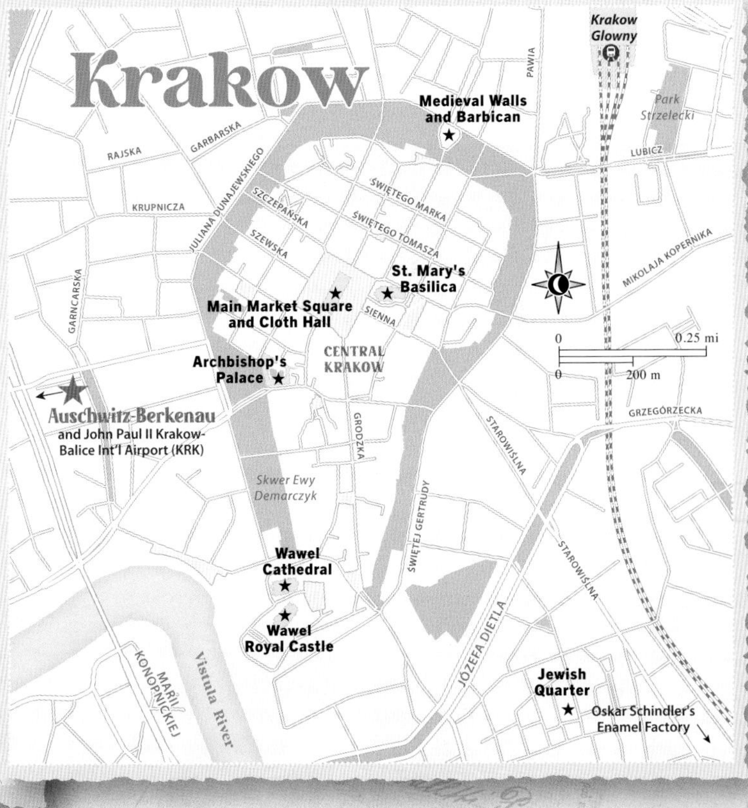
Krakow
Krakow
Glowny
PAWIA
Medieval Walls
and Barbican
Park
Strzelecki
LUBICZ
GARBARSKA
RAJSKA
JULIANA DUNAJEWSKIEGO
KRUPNICZA
SZCZEPAŃSKA
ŚWIĘTEGO MARKA
ŚWIĘTEGO TOMASZA
SZEWSKA
St. Mary's
Basilica
MIKOLAJA KOPERNIKA
GARNCARSKA
Main Market Square
and Cloth Hall
SIENNA
0
0.25 mi
0
200 m
CENTRAL
KRAKOW
Archbishop's
Palace
Auschwitz-Berkenau
and John Paul II Krakow-
Balice Int'l Airport (KRK)
GRODZKA
STAROWIŚLNA
GRZEGÓRZECKA
Skwer Ewy
Demarczyk
ŚWIĘTEJ GERTRUDY
STAROWIŚLNA
Wawel
Cathedral
Wawel
Royal Castle
JÓZEFA DIETLA
MARII
KONOPNICKIEJ
Vistula River
Jewish
Quarter
Oskar Schindler's
Enamel Factory

Berlin

Where to Stay: The central district of Mitte

Arrive by: Plane to Berlin Branderburg Airport "Willy Brandt"

DAY 1

1. Berliner Fernsehturm (Berlin TV Tower)

Panoramastraße 1A; https://tv-turm.de; 9am-11pm daily Apr.-Oct., 10am-10pm daily Nov.-Mar.; €24.50

Check the time on your first day in Berlin at the **World Clock** on **Alexanderplatz.** Here you will be thrust back in time to the German Democratic Republic as it rebuilt this historic town center after World War II. From the plaza, take the elevator up nearly 207 m (700 ft) to the observation deck of the **Berlin TV Tower** for incredible views over the sprawling city. Admission discounts are available using the Berlin Welcome Card. The **onsite rotating restaurant** offers breakfast Monday through Friday and a buffet breakfast the first Sunday of every month for an additional €6, making this the highest spot in the Berlin for the day's most important meal! From the bird's-eye view of the TV Tower, get acquainted with the city you'll be exploring for the next few days.

2. St. Mary's Church

Karl-Liebknecht-Str. 8; tel. 30 24759510; 10am-4pm daily; free

The stark beauty of the soaring neo-Gothic St. Mary's Church makes it an architectural standout along the esplanade toward the Spree River.

3. Nikolaiviertel District

The medieval Nikolaiviertel, or Nicholas' Quarter, has largely been rebuilt over the centuries. The famed Rococo **Ephraim-Palais** (Poststraße 16; tel. 30 24002162; www.stadtmuseum.de/

Berlin TV Tower

Key Reservations

TRAVEL PASSES

The **Berlin Welcome Card** (www.berlin-welcomecard.de) conveniently combines a pass for public transportation with some free and discounted museum admissions and other benefits.

MONUMENTS AND MUSEUMS

Most monuments and museums offer online prebooking services that can save you the frustration of waiting in line. There's a small fee and reservations should be made a couple of weeks in advance to ensure a spot. Be sure to book in advance for the following sights and activities:

Berlin

- **Berlin TV Tower**

Warsaw

- **Chopin Concert**
- **Presidential Palace**
- **Polish Museum of Vodka**
- **POLIN Museum of the History of Polish Jews**

Krakow

- **Auschwitz-Berkenau**
- **Wawel Castle** tour
- **Jewish Quarter** walking tour

RESTAURANTS

- **Rotisserie Weinrün**
- **Schnitzelei Mitte**

Krakow Jewish Quarter

ephraim-palais), originally built for the financier of King Frederick II of Prussia, is an architectural highlight here.

Have a lunch of authentic German cuisine at **Mutter Hoppe** (Rathausstraße 21; https://mutterhoppe.de; 11:30am-midnight daily; €20) along the way. Go for the lentil soup, pork knuckle, and mulled wine, or just stick to a heaping plate of bratwurst and sauerkraut.

4. Museum Island

Spree Island; www.smb.museum; 10am-6pm Tues.-Sun. for all museums; €5-12

The entire northern tip of the Spree Island, dubbed "Museum Island," is a work of architectural wonder. Since 1999, this museum complex has enjoyed favor as the only architectural and cultural ensemble in the UNESCO World Heritage catalog. There are five museums here, each of which is outstanding in its own right for its collection, place in history, and architectural gift to the streets of Berlin. Built successively by five different architects over the course of 100 years, 1830-1930, by the order of the Prussian monarchy, each of these museums could be the crown jewel of pretty much any other city in the world. In general, it is

MAKE IT Active

Berlin is one of the most **bike-friendly cities** in all of Europe, particularly when the sun is out. Here you'll find a relatively flat landscape and considerate drivers, resulting in one of the highest rates of bicycle commuting in the world. It may be surprising to know that three out of every four Berliners owns a bike. There are more than 630 km (400 mi) of bike paths zigzagging throughout the city.

Keep an eye out for entire fahrradstrassen (bicycle streets), where bicycles have the priority and vehicles are limited to 30 kmh (20mph). The 160-km (100-mi) **Berliner Mauerweg** (Berlin Wall Trail) is a popular route that traces the former German Democratic Republic border fortifications surrounding West Berlin.

Grab a bike via **Call A Bike** (www.callabike.de/en/cities-berlin). With your phone, you can unlock bikes throughout the city and get rolling in no time.

best to pick one or two museums to explore for the afternoon and leave the others for another visit.

- **Altes Museum** (Bodestraße 1-3), the first public museum in Prussia, holds a collection of Greek and Roman sculptures.
- **Bode Museum** (Am Kupfergraben) houses an extensive collection of treasures and sculptures of the Byzantine and late Antique age.
- **Neues Museum** (Bodestraße 1-3) houses the Egyptian Museum as well as the Museum of Prehistory and Early History, though everyone really comes for the bust of Nefertiti.
- **Old National Gallery** (Bodestraße 1-3) features a staggering collection of Romantic, Impressionist, and Early Modern artworks.
- **Pergamon Museum** (Bodestraße 1-3) is the most visited museum because of its excellent collection of antiquities, including complete reconstructions of the Pergamon Altar and Ishtar Gate of ancient Babylon.

There are several different admission tickets sold for the museums. You can visit any single museum for €5-12, while a one-day pass will give you access to five museums for €19, or you could opt to get a three-day museum pass (€29) that gives you access to even more museums and sites. For this route, opt for either the €19 pass or get the **bundled pass** with the **Berlin Welcome Card.**

5. Berliner Dom (Berlin Cathedral)

Am Lustgarten; www.berlinerdom.de; 11am-8pm Mon.-Thurs., 11am-7pm Fri., 11am-8pm Sat., noon-8pm Sun.; €7

The unmissable, towering dome of the neo-Renaissance Berlin Cathedral, the common name for the Supreme Parish and Collegiate Church, dominates the skyline here. The crypts of this place of worship are some of the most formidable dynastic burial grounds in Europe, housing 90 burials from Prussian and German rulers from the 16th century to the 20th century, though the Hohenzollern crypt is closed until 2024 for renovation. The cathedral has a vibrant music lineup (check the website) with choral singing by the English Choir Berlin one Saturday every month. Breathtaking views across

(clockwise from top) St. Mary's Church; Museum Island; Berlin Cathedral

(top to bottom) Checkpoint Charlie; Holocaust Memorial; Tiergarten; Brandenburg Gate

Mitte, the Spree, and the rest of Museum Island can be had from a climb up the stairs to the dome.

Afterward, dine at **Rotisserie Weingrün** (Gertraudenstr. 10-12; tel. 30 20621900; www.rotisserie-weingruen.de; 5pm-11pm Tues.-Sat.; €40), about as fancy as German cuisine gets for dinner. This lively joint is a neighborhood staple with ample outdoor seating. Stick to the roast duck with sides of roasted vegetables and potato gratin, and don't forget to explore the wine menu. Reservations are recommended.

If you are looking for a nightcap, **Lokal Tante Ollis** (Wollankstraße 21; 6pm-2am Wed.-Sun.; €5) is a truly authentic Berliner local bar.

DAY 2

1. Checkpoint Charlie

Friedrichstraße; open 24 hours; free

This is the most famous crossing that existed between East and West Germany during the Cold War (1961-1989). It has become an iconic symbol of Berlin's reunification and one of the most visited sites in the city. For nearly 40 years, this was the primary crossing point between the two sides, and over those years, the military guards who once manned this post, saw many daring escapes by Germans fleeing from the East. Many of these escapes are celebrated in the nearby **Checkpoint Charlie Museum** (Haus am Checkpoint Charlie; Friedrichstraße 43-45; tel. 0302512075; www.mauermuseum.de; €14.50).

2. Holocaust Memorial (Memorial to the Murdered Jews of Europe)

Cora-Berliner-Straße 1; tel. 30 2639430; www.stiftung-denkmal.de; 10am-6pm Tues.-Sun.; free

The striking abstract design of architect Peter Eisenman and engineer Buro Happold, with 19,000 square m (200,000 square ft) full of concrete slabs (stelae), conveys a funereal atmosphere. This is a place for contemplation as you make your way around row upon row of concrete blocks, each stelae signifying the

German Cuisine:

FROM BRATWURST TO SCHNITZEL

Traditional German cuisine is a hearty, meat-and-potatoes sort of affair meant for cold, long, dark winters and roaring fires to melt the snow off your boots and thaw your fingers. Once you are satiated, the sweets come out to brighten the mood. Here are a few traditional dishes to enjoy, coupled with a crisp German lager.

- **Wurst:** This is German for "sausage," and with more than 1,500 types of sausage to try throughout Germany, you will be hard-pressed to find your best (or your worst!) wurst. Around Berlin, one of the most popular is currywurst, which, as the name implies, is a sausage seasoned with curry spices.
- **Bratwurst:** Typically made with veal and pork and seasoned with caraway, coriander, ginger, and nutmeg, this is the most popular street food in Germany.
- **Hasenpfeffer:** An incredibly rich rabbit stew. The rabbit is braised with wine and onions, while the sauce is a wine reduction thickened with rabbit blood. It's usually served with root vegetables as well as a potato side.
- **Kochklopse:** Meatballs in a creamy white sauce are zested with capers and lemon juice.
- **Pretzels:** Made to resemble arms folded in prayer, the large pretzels served in bars around Germany make a delicious snack. They're typically served with salt, though you can find varieties with cheese, cinnamon, sugar, and other toppings.
- **Sauerbraten:** German's national dish is this pot roast—sometimes made with horse meat, though typically beef these days—that is not unlike French boeuf bourguignon. The meat is marinated in vinegar, spices, and wine for several days before roasting and serving with potato dumplings and red cabbage.
- **Sauerkraut:** Spiced and pickled cabbage is a staple of every German household and traditional restaurants throughout the country.
- **Schnitzel:** A slice of meat—generally beef, pork, or veal—that is breaded and fried.
- **Shweinshaxe:** A slow-roasted pork knuckle dish where the meat is tender but the outside skin is delicate and crispy. This is very popular in Bavaria, served with potatoes and cabbage.
- **Spargel:** Asparagus in any form is "spargel." Spargel season is around mid-April, when there are festivals celebrating this tasty grass all around the country and it's on the menu of seemingly every restaurant in Germany. There are a variety of preparations to try, from a simple garlic and melted butter or coupled with a schnitzel.
- **Black Forest Cake:** Named for the region it hails from, this spongy chocolate cake is done up with layers alternating with whipped cream, and usually served with a tart cherry sauce.
- **Apfelstrudel:** Delicate layers of dough stuffed with apples and spices will give your grandma's apple pie a run for its money.

Holocaust History

A visit to modern-day Berlin, Warsaw, and Krakow entails confronting one of the darkest periods in human history. Also known as the Shoah, the Holocaust was the genocide of European Jews, homosexuals, and other groups at the hands of Nazi Germany from 1941 to 1945. Over these years of systematic murders, more than six million Jews were killed, about two thirds of Europe's entire Jewish population.

Today's Berlin reflects a country unflinchingly reckoning with its past. Laws against hate speech, antisemitism, and disseminating Nazi propaganda are strictly enforced on the streets, and some of the most popular visitor attractions to Berlin grapple with this horrific, brutal past. To learn more about the Holocaust, read *Night* by Elie Wiesel, a masterwork about Wiesel's survival as a teenager in the Nazi extermination camps. The following sights also provide an opportunity to learn about and confront this history.

- Holocaust Memorial, Berlin (page 170)
- POLIN Museum of the History of Polish Jews, Warsaw (page 176)
- Oskar Schindler's Enamel Factory, Krakow (page 180)
- Auschwitz-Berkenau, outside Krakow (page 182)

endurance of the Jewish people. The Information Center on the eastern edge, beneath the expanse of stelae, provides an intimate look at those who lost their lives during the Holocaust, including a room that tells the story of 15 families and various other letters and memorabilia, while in the Room of Names, all known victims of the Holocaust are read aloud as an act of remembrance.

3. Brandenburg Gate

Pariser Platz; open 24 hours; free

Undoubtedly Berlin's most famous historic landmark, the Brandenburg Gate (Brandenburger Tor) was once the symbol for a divided nation. Inspired by the Propylaea in the Acropolis in Athens, Greece, this 18th-century behemoth of a neoclassic gate reaches 26 m (85 ft) in height in the middle of the busy Pariser Platz, near the **Reichstag Building.** Throughout the Cold War, it was the most prominent of blocked gates along the Berlin Wall, serving as a symbol for the division of that era. These days, it is a symbol of unity, bringing together the two halves of Berlin and, thus, the world.

4. Tiergarten

Berlin's oldest, largest garden, formerly a royal hunting ground, features many walking paths, play parks, and statues, as well as the **Berlin Zoological Garden** (Hardenbergpl. 8; www.zoo-berlin.de; 9am-6:30pm daily; €20), which makes for an attractive outing, particularly for those traveling with children. A pleasant walk

(3.7 km/2.3 mi; 45 minutes-1 hour) connects the Brandenburg Gate at the eastern edge of the park with Gedächtniskirche at the western edge. Take advantage of Berlin's wonderful delivery service and order a picnic lunch from **Picnic Berlin** (tel. 17 78973522; https://picnic-berlin.com; noon-8pm daily; €20). Your picnic lunch will be delivered right to you at your new favorite spot in the park.

5. Gedächtniskirche

Breitscheidplatz; tel. 30 2185023; https://gedaechtniskirche-berlin.de; 9am-7pm daily; free

The destroyed Gedächtniskirche, also known as the **Kaiser Wilhelm Memorial Church,** stands now in the midst of the daily Berliner traffic as an antiwar monument. In the Hall of Remembrance, historic photos of this 19th-century church and broken pieces of the elaborate mosaic on display serve to set the scene of what once was. Egon Eiermann, one of the most prominent architects of post-World War II Germany, designed the bell tower and new octagonal church, where every Saturday evening at 6pm music can be heard.

6. Charlottenburg Palace

Spandauer Damm 10-22; tel. 3319694200; www.spsg.de; 10am-4:30pm Tues.-Sun.; €17

Hop on a bus to Charlottenburg Palace. Begun in 1695, the baroque palace gardens were designed borrowing inspiration from the Palace of Versailles in France to create an artfully choreographed escape from the urban sprawl of Berlin. Stroll the same paths where Sophia Charlotte, the first queen of Prussia, once philosophized with Gottfried Wilhelm Leibniz. The gardens are dotted with palaces, with the Charlottenburg Palace, of course, being the must-visit. The neo-classical **New Pavilion,** the summer retreat of King Frederick William III near the Spree, features a wonderful collection of early 19th-century paintings, including works by Karl Blechen, Caspar David Friedrich, and Eduard Gaertner. One should not forget to pay their respects at the **Mausoleum Charlottenburg,** the temple where you can admire Christian Daniel Rauch's masterwork tomb sculpture that stands as a monument to Queen Luise, who tragically died young.

left, East Side Gallery; right, Charlottenburg Palace

7. Dinner at Schnitzelei Mitte

Chaussestr 8; tel. 03032519422; https://schnitzelei.de 4pm-midnight Mon.-Sat., noon-midnight Sun.

Head back to the center and have dinner at Schnitzelei Mitte, which offers a creative twist on German classics, such as the vegan oyster mushroom schnitzel, and some wonderful outdoor dining. Reserve ahead to ensure your spot.

DAY 3

★ 1. East Side Gallery

Mühlenstraße 79; open 24 hours; free

Take in the views from the iconic brick wonder that is the double-decker Oberbaum Bridge on the short walk from U Schlesisches Tor station to East Berlin. Afterward, stroll along the East Side Gallery, the world's largest open-air art gallery. About 1.3 km (almost 1 mi) of the Berlin Wall, the longest section still in existence, was quickly transformed into a place for artistic expression. Follow the wall down the Spree River and see how 118 artists from 21 countries interpreted the monumental collapse of the Berlin Wall, the reunification of East and West Berlin, and the fall of the oppressive communist region. Dmitri Vrubel's *Fraternal Kiss* and Birgit Kinders's *Trabant Breaking through the Wall* are two of the more notable works found on the wall.

Spend some time here before heading to Berlin Hbf (Central Station) to catch your afternoon train to Warsaw, where you'll arrive about six hours later.

Warsaw

Where to Stay: In or near the Old Town, Śródmieście

Arrive by: Train from Berlin Hbf (Central Station) to Warsaw Central (6 hours)

Old Town Market Square

DAY 4

1. Old Town Market Square

Stare Miesto; free

The rebuilding of Warsaw following World War II comes to full focus in this square. Approximately 90 percent of the Old Town was reduced to rubble during the war, but the subsequent rebuilding of these many detailed period structures has earned the Old Town of Warsaw a place in the pantheon of UNESCO World Heritage Sites.

2. Royal Castle

Plac Zamkowy 4; tel. 223555170; www.zamek-krolewski.pl; 10am-6pm Tues. and Thurs.-Sun.; 30zl

Perhaps the most quintessentially Polish street in all of Warsaw, the wide boulevard of **Krakowskie Przedmieście** begins at the Royal Castle (Zamek Króewski) in the Old Town. This reconstructed 14th-century castle is the former home of the monarchy. You will want to reserve tickets at least a day or two before your visit. Art lovers should make sure to give leave 30 minutes or more for the Masterpieces Gallery with works by Rembrandt.

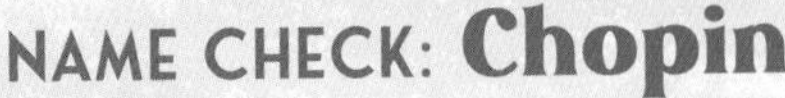

NAME CHECK: Chopin

Born in the outskirts of Warsaw and raised in the city, prodigal musician Fryderyk Franciszek Chopin (1810-1849) spent his formative years strolling the Old Town, shopping at the market, and studying music theory, composition, and thorough bass at the Warsaw Conservatory, where he wrote his earliest musical compositions.

Chopin premiered his first ever published work, Rondo in C Minor, Op 1, a solo piano piece, on June 10, 1825. This piece began Chopin's swift rise to international recognition and success. After he left Poland in 1830, he never returned, becoming part of Poland's Great Emigration following the failure of the November Uprising against the ruling Russian Empire. Considered the brightest composer and pianist of his generation, Chopin tragically died young from complications due to tuberculosis in Paris, France.

PLACES AND MONUMENTS

Chopin is memorialized throughout Poland, his name adorning countless shops, streets, T-shirts, mugs, and even the international airport. He is particularly venerated in Warsaw.

- The **Chopin Museum** showcases his life and work (page 176).
- Listening to Chopin's music performed at **concerts** organized by Time for Chopin is a must in Warsaw (page 176).
- Designed by Wacław Szymankowski, the often-photographed **Chopin sculpture** in Łazienki Park south of Warsaw's Old Town depicts the composer near a willow tree.
- In the western side of the Planty, a greenbelt surrounding Krakow's Old Town, a **Chopin Monument** (Franciszkańska 3) takes the form of a fountain that conjures piano hammers.

3. Saint Anne's Cathedral

Krakowskie Przedmieście 68; tel. 572551254; https://swanna.waw.pl; 10am-6pm Tues.-Sun.; free

Saint Anne's Cathedral (Kościół Akademicki św. Anny) features a dazzling 18th-century neoclassical facade that has made it through the centuries unscathed. The functioning church itself dates back to the 15th century and still has service and organ performances throughout the week. Climb the 147 stairs to the bell tower for the best view over Warsaw.

4. Chocolate Café E. Wedel

Krakowskie Przedmieście 45; tel. 228284288; https://wedelpijalnie.pl; 10am-10pm Sun.-Thurs., 10am-11pm Fri.-Sat.; 18zl

Nothing says "welcome to Warsaw" quite like a frothy cup of hot chocolate by Poland's most famous chocolatier. Settle into Warsaw's splendid Old Town vibe here.

5. Presidential Palace

Krakowskie Przedmieście 48/50; tel. 223555170; www.president.pl; 10am-6pm daily; free, reservations required

Construction on the Presidential Palace (Pałac Prezydencki) began in 1643 as an aristocratic residence and was completed in 1818. This neoclassical landmark has served as the backdrop for countless historic events. Since 1994, it has been the official residence of the Polish president. For a free guided tour, email wycieczki@prezydent.pl.

On the walk to your next stop (the Chopin Museum), stop for lunch at **STOR Café** (Tamka 33; tel. 222905190; www.stor.cafe; 8:30am-9pm Mon.-Fri., 9:30am-9pm Sat.-Sun.), a local third-wave coffee haven with outdoor seating.

6. Chopin Museum

Pałac Gnińskich, Okólnik 1; tel. 224416251; https://muzeum.nifc.pl; 11am-7pm Tues.-Sun.; 23zl, reservations required

The Chopin Museum (Muzeum Fryderyka Chopina w Warszawie) is a treat for music lovers and shouldn't be missed. Tickets should be purchased online ahead of time, though the morning of your visit or the day before should be fine. Chopin's music plays in rooms where you can view his original musical manuscripts and letters, as well as the last piano he ever played.

★ 7. Chopin Concert

Old Gallery, 8 Castle Square; https://timeforchopin.eu; concerts begin at 6pm; 75zl

It would be disrespectful to venture to Warsaw and fail to hear the music of its most favorite son, Fryderyk Chopin. **Time for Chopin** organizes nightly concerts where master pianists perform in an intimate salon, Chopin's preferred type of venue. Head out to a performance after stopping at your hotel to rest and freshen up.

After an evening of Chopin, dine at the gloriously ornate restaurant **U Fukiera** (Rynek Starego Miasta 27, tel. 228311013; www.ufukiera.pl; noon-11pm Sun.-Wed., noon-11:45pm Thurs.-Sat; 50zl). Owned by Magdalena Gessler, a celebrity chef known locally as a "Magda," this refurbished tenement building just off the Old Town's market square is the perfect place to dig into some pierogi and potato pancakes.

Chopin Museum

DAY 5

1. Warsaw Rising Museum

Grzybowska 79; tel. 225397905; www.1944.pl; 9am-6pm Mon. and Wed.-Fri., 10am-6pm Sat.-Sun.; 20zl

Start your day of museums on the western side of the city, at the Warsaw Rising Museum. In 1944, Warsaw rose up against the occupation of Nazi forces. This interactive museum details the uprising; it's incredibly moving, though at times it's difficult to watch, with graphic photos and unflinching footage that documents the starvation and subsequent death of many of Warsaw's citizens.

2. POLIN Museum of the History of Polish Jews

Mordechaja Anielewicza 6; tel. 224710301; www.polin.pl; 10am-6pm Sun.-Thurs., 10am-3pm Fri., 10am-8pm Sat.; 30zl

Take a deep dive into the brilliant, 1,000-year-long history of the Jews of Poland in the POLIN Museum of the History of Polish Jews (POLIN Muzeum Historii Żydów Polskich). This modern, elaborate museum with lots of interactive exhibits also has a lot of online content, so you can experience part of the museum before leaving the house. From the Warsaw Rising Museum, it's about a 20-minute tram and bus ride to get here.

If you're hungry, stop in the museum restaurant, **Warsze,** for traditional Jewish food.

top, Royal Castle; bottom, Old Town Market Square

3. Polish Museum of Vodka

Koneser Square 1; tel. 224193150; https://muzeumpolskiejwodki.pl; noon-8pm Sun., Tues.-Thurs., noon-9pm Fri.-Sat.; 49zl

Walk (20 minutes) or take a bus (10 minutes) to this vodka museum. Sure, you could come and take notes on the history and process of the distinguished Polish vodka that is registered as an EU product with Protected Geographical Indication and is as much part of the national spirit as it is a spirit. Or... you could come for the vodka tasting at the end of the hour-long tour.

4. Dumplings at Pyzy Flaki Gorące

Brzeska 29/31; tel. 606294499; http://pyzyflaki-gorace.pl; noon-10pm Mon.-Sat., noon-9pm Sun.; 24zl

For dinner, cross the river to this low-key spot with sweet and savory dumplings to please every palate. Don't hesitate to share an order of herring as a starter, dig into a minced meat dumpling topped with bacon and mushroom gravy, and round it out with a plum-filled potato dumpling topped with sweet cream and fresh berries.

5. Multimedia Fountain Park

Skwer 1 Dywizji Pancernej; tel. 228493286; http://park-fontann.pl; open 24 hours; free

Jump on a tram to get back over the river and trip the light fantastic. In this park, images and animations are displayed on the fountains jetting out of the 227 digitally controlled nozzles of one of Warsaw's most contemporary open-air art installations. The main season lasts May-September, though wintertime shows are also coming into vogue as the locals bundle up for an LED-infused extravaganza.

Krakow

Where to Stay: The Old Town, Stare Miasto

Arrive by: Train from Warsaw Central to Krakow Glowny station (3 hours)

Market Square

DAY 6

1. Medieval Walls and Barbican

30-547 Pijarski St; 10:30am-6pm daily Apr.-Oct.; 8zl

Wake up early in Warsaw to cat the 6am train to Krakow, arriving around 9am, giving you a full day in the city to explore.

There are a scant 200 m (650 ft) left of the 13th-century medieval walls of Krakow. These formidable walls once measured 3 m (10 ft) thick and housed 39 watchtowers overseeing the eight gates to the city. The entire wall was surrounded by a 6-m-wide (20-ft) moat. This sets the scene for medieval Krakow, one of the first ever entries on the UNESCO World Heritage list.

2. Main Market Square and Cloth Hall

At over 40,000 square m (400,000 square ft), the medieval town square at the center of Old Town Krakow is Europe's largest. From this picturesque

WATCH

Schindler's List: Based on the Thomas Keneally novel *Schindler's Ark,* this film takes place in Krakow and details the real-life story of Oskar Schindler, a German member of the Nazi party, and his role is saving hundreds of Jewish people in Poland.

All These Sleepless Nights is an evocative portrait of Warsaw's vibrant club scene. The story of three young friends won Marczak the Best Director award at the 2016 Sundance Film Festival.

READ

Ludwika: Polish Woman's Struggle to Survive in Nazi Germany by Christopher Fischer: A young Polish woman is forced to flee her family and work for an SS officer in Germany. It's a story of survival set against the backdrop of one of humankind's darkest moments.

LISTEN

Complete Works by Fryderyk Chopin (1810-1849): Download the complete oeuvre of Poland's greatest composer and pianist for a listen on the plane.

Those Who Were There: Voices from the Holocaust: This podcast (https://mjhnyc.org/those-who-were-there-podcast-series) draws on first-hand testimonies of survivors of the Holocaust.

13th-century plaza, there is access to several of Krakow's finest sites. In the middle of the plaza, the splendor of the Renaissance-style rebuild of the Cloth Hall (Sukiennice), once an important center for trade and commerce, is on full display. This has become a symbol of Krakow and the scene of cultural and historic significance over the centuries.

3. St. Mary's Basilica

Plac Mariacki 5; tel. 124220521; www.mariacki.com; 10zl

This basilica abutting the square is a towering brick structure featuring some wonderfully authentic Gothic architecture throughout. You can't miss the famed trumpeter poking out from its tallest tower every hour, on the hour, where he blasts a trumpet call, the Hejnał Mariacki (St. Mary's Trumpet Call), across the square. A climb up the 272 steps to the tower for the views and to meet the trumpet player (one of seven working in teams of two on a 24-hour shift) should not be missed.

4. Archbishop's Palace

Franciszkańska 3; 9am-dusk; free

For 30 years, Cardinal Karol Wojtyla, who became Pope John II, addressed his followers from the Papal Window, a tradition Pope Francis continued. A brilliant mosaic portrait of the former Pope by Magdalena Czeska now adorns the window, a place of continued pilgrimage for Catholics worldwide. Located south of the town square, the courtyard is open to the public and houses a statue of John Paul II.

Chopin fans can make the short walk to the monument to the composer located in the nearby greenway. Afterward, head to **Czarna Kaczka** (Poselska 22; tel. 500195149; http://czarnakaczka.pl; 1pm-10pm Sun.-Thurs., 1pm-11pm Fri.-Sat.), "The Black Duck," for heaping servings of goulash.

5. Jewish Quarter Walking Tour

It's about a 20-minute walk to the Kaszimierz (the Jewish Quarter of Krakow) from Old Town. By the mid-16th century, this area was the center of Jewish life around the world. In Poland, Jews had found unrivaled freedom and autonomy where their community could flourish. In many ways, this is still an important center as millions of Jews flock to Kaszimierz to connect with their heritage. Free walking tours by **Walkative** (https://freewalkingtour.com/tours/jewish-krakow; 10:30am and 2:30pm daily) start at the Old Synagogue (Szeroka 24). Best to reserve ahead of time, and do tip your guide!

6. Oskar Schindler's Enamel Factory

Lipowa 4; tel. 122571017; 10am-7pm Tues.-Sun., open until 8pm in summer, 10am-2pm Mon., closed first Tues. of the month; 28zl

Located about a 20-minute walk across the river from the Kaszimierz, this museum takes you through the incredible, heartbreaking story of Oskar Schindler (also depicted in Steven Spielberg's Oscar-winning film *Schindler's List.*) in the very factory where he saved so many lives from the horrors of the Holocaust. It's a must-visit for any traveler to Krakow.

End the day back in the Kaszimierz with a meal of locally sourced Polish food at **Pierwszy Stopien** (Krakowska 17; tel. 577767670; http://pierwszystopien.pl; 1pm-10pm Mon.-Sat., 12pm-9pm Sun.; 70zl). This garden-themed restaurant serves up picturesque plates of some of Poland's finest cuisine, from grilled goat cheese to cod sirloin and goose dumplings. Vegans and vegetarians alike will be right at home here, as well, with baked beetroot salads, and millet and lentil vegan burgers.

Wawel Cathedral

DAY 7

1. Wawel Cathedral

Wawel 3; tel. 124299515; www.katedra-wawelska.pl; 9am-4:30pm Mon.-Sat., 12:30-4pm Sun.; 22zl

The most important building in Poland, this is the place where Polish kings and queens have been crowned and buried since the consecration of the cathedral in 1364. Inside, find a wealth of intimate Polish history and 18 elaborately decorated and gilded chapels. Do yourself a favor and visit with an audio guide. Though somewhat cramped, the bell tower, home of the 11-tone Sigismund bell, can be visited, and the crypts below will tickle every historian's fancy. Entry includes the Cathedral Museum.

2. Wawel Royal Castle

Wawel 5; tel. 124225155; https://wawel.krakow.pl; 9:30am-1pm Mon., 9am-5pm Tues.-Sun.; free

Holding court from atop its perch on the hillside of Old Town, the nearby Wawel Castle is a remarkable achievement of 14th-century architecture, with updates throughout the ages creating an elegant amalgamation of medieval, Gothic, Romanesque, baroque, and even Italian Renaissance. A walk around the castle grounds is free, though if you want to see the state rooms and the crown jewels, you will need to book a guided tour at least a few weeks in advance.

(clockwise from top) Wawel Royal Castle; Jewish Quarter; St. Mary's Basilica

3. All Aboard for Lunch at Barka Arkadia

Bulwar Czerwieński 172; tel. 604299000; https://barkaarkadia.pl; 11am-9pm daily; 60zl

It is hard not to love a repurposed barge boat restaurant, particularly one that does burgers as well as this one. There are also tasty traditional Polish dishes on offer, but sometimes cozy pub food does the trick.

★ 4. Auschwitz-Berkenau

Ofiar Faszyzmu 12, Brzezinka; tel. 338448099; www.auschwitz.org; from 8am daily, closing hour varies from 2pm in winter to 7pm in summer; free, guided educator tour from 85zl

To visit the former concentration camps of Auschwitz on your own, you will need to make this reservation weeks, if not months, in advance. As a UNESCO World Heritage Site that is part memorial, part museum to the horrors of the extermination camps of World War II, Auschwitz is the busiest tourist destination in Poland. Individual tours are often limited to the morning hours or the late afternoon. Plan to leave Krakow at least an hour and a half before your scheduled tour time. The easiest connection is from the bus station just north of Old Town (14zl each way). Buses drop off and pick up at the main entrance. A guided educator tour is highly recommended here, as you will likely get much more from the experience.

5. Dinner at Amerylis

Józefa Dietla 60; tel. 124333306; www.amarylisrestaurant.pl; 4pm-10pm Tues.-Sun.; 140zl

Back in Krakow, cap off your trip at this award-winning restaurant in the wonderfully brick-lined basement of the chic Queen Boutique Hotel. Continental European fare combined with traditional Polish cuisine yield some surprising flavor notes.

TRANSPORTATION

Air

The **Berlin Brandenburg Airport "Willy Brandt"** (BER; Willy-Brandt-Platz, 12529 Schönefeld; tel. 30 609160910; https://ber.berlin-airport.de/en.html) is a new airport, but has been beset by challenges from its opening on October 31, 2020. Expect longer-than-normal lines, and if flying out of Berlin, allow at least three hours before your departing flight. From the airport, the FEX, RE7, and RB14 **airport express trains** connect with the city center. The **S-Bahn** (the local tram service) is slower but runs nonstop on weekends and late nights. The S9 tram connects with Alexanderplatz in the heart of Mitte.

The **Warsaw Chopin Airport** (WAW; tel. 22 650 42 20; www.lotnisko-chopina.pl) is located about 12 km (7.5 mi) southwest of the city center. Bus 175 into the city takes about 30 minutes.

The **John Paul II Krakow-Balice International Airport** (KRK; tel. 12 295 58 00; https://krakowairport.pl) is a short 30-minute train ride from downtown Krakow.

Train

Deutche Bahn (https://reiseauskunft.bahn.de) runs direct trains between **Berlin Hbf** (Central Station) and **Warszawa Centralna** (Warsaw Central; 6 hours; from €30). All other trains from Berlin either leave from Berlin Gesundbrunnen, or you may have to change trains in Frankfurt. Warsaw Central station is connected to Old Town Warsaw via the 160 bus, with departures every 20 minutes. Alternatively, if you are traveling light and want to stretch your legs, it is a 25-minute walk or so from train station to Old Town.

PKP Intercity (www.intercity.pl) runs direct trains from the **Warszawa Centralna** station to the **Krakow Glowny** station (3 hours; €10). In Krakow, the 3 tram takes you from the station directly to the Old Town with departures every 15 minutes. Alternatively, if you are traveling light and want to stretch your legs, it is a 20-minute, 2.5-km (1-mi) walk from the train station to Old Town.

Berliner U-Bahn

Public Transportation

Berlin

Berlin is well-served city-wide by the **U-Bahn,** which goes underground and serves the center of town, and the **S-Bahn,** which runs aboveground in the suburbs. The U-Bahn runs 4am-1am on weekdays and 24 hours on the weekend, with connections running every 3-5 minutes during rush hour and every 15 minutes at night.

The 72-hour **Berlin Welcome Card** (www.berlin-welcomecard.de; €39), which includes Berlin and Potsdam, will cover your connections with the airport. Another version of the welcome card offers museum entrance for the five museums on Museum Island for an additional €16, which is a good value for museumgoers.

Warsaw

In Warsaw, the extensive bus system and tram network operated by **Warzawski Public Transport** (www.wtp.waw.pl) are well-connected throughout the city. Single fares are 7zl and last for 90 minutes, though most travelers should opt for the three-day pass (36zl).

Krakow

In Krakow, **MPK** (www.mpk.krakow.pl) runs buses and trams throughout the city, although, except for Auschwitz, all the main sights are walkable. The **KrakowCard,** available at various spots around the city, including train and bus stations, covers two or three days (164zl-184) of unlimited public transportation rides and 38 sights, such as the Medieval Walls and Barbican, St. Mary's Basilica, and Schindler's Enamel Factory.

Getting Back

Budget carrier Ryan Air (www.ryanair.com) operates direct flights from the Krakow Airport to Berlin (Mon. and Fri.; 1.5 hours; €25). There are few connections from the Krakow airport outside of continental Europe, though most major carriers have a presence here. Your flight home will likely have one stop over in a European hub.

There are daily trains connecting with Berlin from the Krakow Glowny station (2 per day; 7 hours; €20). The 10pm overnight train is an 11-hour ride, though it's a popular choice for backpackers.

CONNECT WITH

- Copenhagen to Berlin by Bike (page 389)
- Vilnius, Riga, and Tallinn (page 688)

PRAGUE, VIENNA, AND BUDAPEST

Why Go: Combining the fairy-tale atmosphere of Prague's Old Town Square and Vienna's palaces with classic coffeehouses, ruin bars, and thermal baths, this trip showcases the grandeur and street-level ambience of these Eastern European capitals.

Number of Days: 7

Total Distance: 600 km (375 mi)

Seasons: Spring to fall

Start: Prague

End: Budapest

Prague, Vienna, and Budapest offer travelers a rich tapestry of history and culture. Before World War I, all three cities resided within the Austro-Hungarian Empire, and traces of the crumbled Habsburg dynasty still linger in the decadent palaces and wide boulevards lined with extravagant buildings. Central Europe echoes the "World of Yesterday," with its gilded opera houses, grand hotels, and the wood-paneled cafés perfumed with percolating coffee and freshly baked cakes. Against this historic backdrop, modern (futuristic, even) innovations, from cryptocurrency-friendly cafés to eye-catching public art installations, are a delightful contrast.

TOP 3

★ Getting away from the crowds at the **Vyšehrad Complex,** which offers stunning views, an impressive basilica, a cemetery full of local legends, and even a beer garden (page 192).

★ Experiencing the former Austrian Empire's opulent grandeur at **Schönbrunn Palace.** The former summer residence of the Habsburg dynasty is now a museum in Vienna (page 194).

★ Enjoying stunning architecture while you soak in healing waters at one of **Budapest's thermal baths** (page 200).

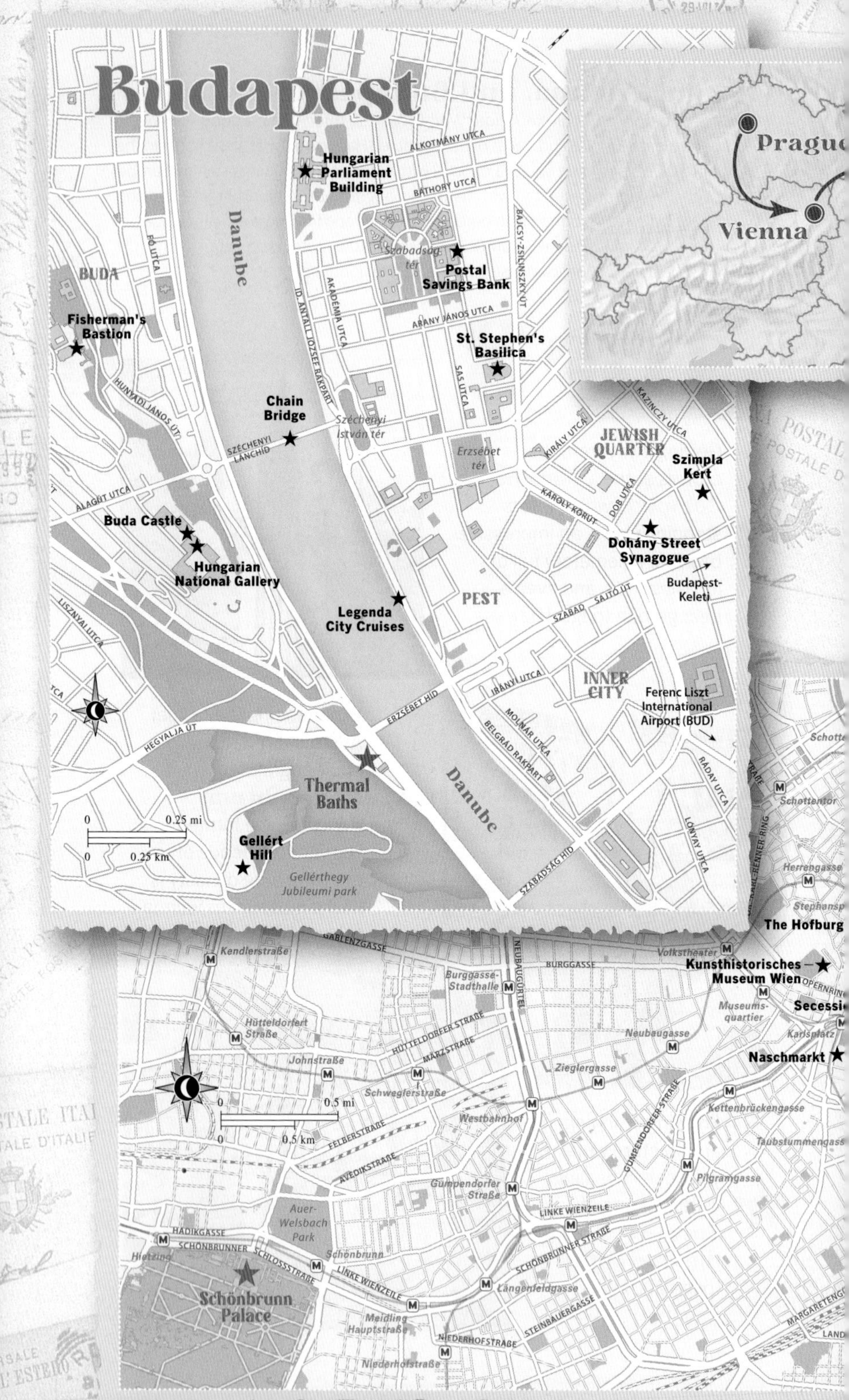

Budapest
Hungarian Parliament Building
Postal Savings Bank
St. Stephen's Basilica
Fisherman's Bastion
Chain Bridge
Buda Castle
Hungarian National Gallery
Legenda City Cruises
Jewish Quarter
Szimpla Kert
Dohány Street Synagogue
Budapest-Keleti
Pest
Buda
Inner City
Ferenc Liszt International Airport (BUD)
Thermal Baths
Gellért Hill
Gellérthegy Jubileumi park
Danube
Széchenyi István tér
Szabadság tér
Erzsébet tér
Széchenyi Lánchíd
Erzsébet híd
Szabadság híd
Alkotmány utca
Báthory utca
Bajcsy-Zsilinszky út
Fő utca
Id. Antall József rakpart
Akadémia utca
Arany János utca
Sas utca
Hunyadi János út
Alagút utca
Király utca
Kazinczy utca
Károly körút
Dob utca
Szabad sajtó út
Irányi utca
Molnár utca
Belgrád rakpart
Ráday utca
Lónyay utca
Lisznyai utca
Hegyalja út
0 0.25 mi
0 0.25 km
Prague
Vienna
The Hofburg
Kunsthistorisches Museum Wien
Secessi
Naschmarkt
Schönbrunn Palace
Kendlerstraße
Burggasse-Stadthalle
Hütteldorfer Straße
Johnstraße
Schweglerstraße
Westbahnhof
Neubaugasse
Zieglergasse
Gumpendorfer Straße
Kettenbrückengasse
Taubstummengass
Pilgramgasse
Museumsquartier
Karlsplatz
Volkstheater
Schottentor
Herrengasse
Stephansp
Auer-Welsbach Park
Schönbrunn
Hietzing
Längenfeldgasse
Meidling Hauptstraße
Niederhofstraße
Gablenzgasse
Burggasse
Neubaugürtel
Hütteldorfer Straße
Märzstraße
Felberstraße
Avedikstraße
Linke Wienzeile
Schönbrunner Straße
Hadikgasse
Schönbrunner Schlossstraße
Steinbauergasse
Gumpendorfer Straße
Opernring
0 0.5 mi
0 0.5 km

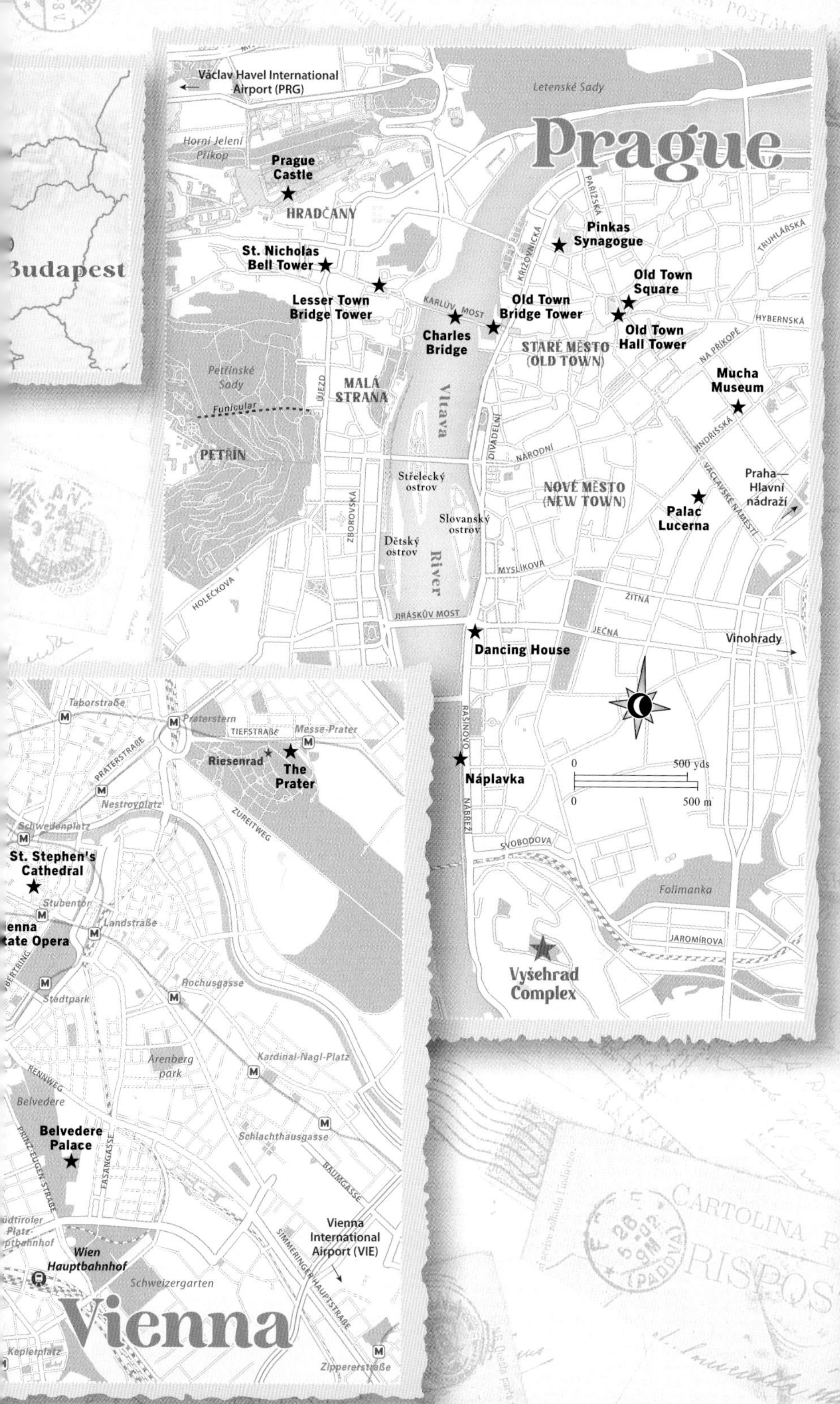

Prague
Václav Havel International Airport (PRG)
Letenské Sady
Horní Jelení Příkop
Prague Castle
HRADČANY
St. Nicholas Bell Tower
Lesser Town Bridge Tower
Charles Bridge
Old Town Bridge Tower
Pinkas Synagogue
Old Town Square
Old Town Hall Tower
STARÉ MĚSTO (OLD TOWN)
Mucha Museum
Petřínské Sady
Funicular
PETŘÍN
MALÁ STRANA
Vltava River
Střelecký ostrov
Slovanský ostrov
Dětský ostrov
NOVÉ MĚSTO (NEW TOWN)
Palac Lucerna
Praha—Hlavní nádraží
Vinohrady
Dancing House
Náplavka
Folimanka
Vyšehrad Complex
0
500 yds
500 m
PAŘÍŽSKÁ
KŘIŽOVNICKÁ
KARLŮV MOST
TRUHLÁŘSKÁ
HYBERNSKÁ
NA PŘÍKOPĚ
JINDŘIŠSKÁ
VÁCLAVSKÉ NÁMĚSTÍ
ÚJEZD
DIVADELNÍ
NÁRODNÍ
ZBOROVSKÁ
HOLEČKOVA
MYSLÍKOVA
ŽITNÁ
JEČNÁ
JIRÁSKŮV MOST
RAŠÍNOVO NÁBŘEŽÍ
SVOBODOVA
JAROMÍROVA
Budapest
Vienna
Taborstraße
Praterstern
TIEFSTRAßE
Messe-Prater
Riesenrad
The Prater
PRATERSTRAßE
Nestroyplatz
ZUREITWEG
Schwedenplatz
St. Stephen's Cathedral
Stubentor
Landstraße
Vienna State Opera
Rochusgasse
Stadtpark
Arenberg park
Kardinal-Nagl-Platz
RENNWEG
Belvedere
Belvedere Palace
PRINZ-EUGEN-STRAßE
FASANGASSE
Schlachthausgasse
BAUMGASSE
Südtiroler Platz-Hauptbahnhof
Wien Hauptbahnhof
Vienna International Airport (VIE)
SIMMERINGER HAUPTSTRAßE
Schweizergarten
Keplerplatz
Zippererstraße
CARTOLINA

Prague

Where to Stay: Malá Strana, Old Town, or New Town

Arrive by: Plane to Vaclav Havel International Airport (PRG)

DAY 1

1. Old Town Square

If you've ever seen a postcard of Prague, there's a good chance it was taken in Old Town Square. The architectural blend of church spires, Gothic towers, and pastel buildings draw a steady stream of tour groups with their camera lenses aimed at the sky.

Head straight to the **Old Town Hall Tower** (Staroměstské náměstí 1; tel. 775 400 052; www.staromestskaradnicepraha.cz; tower open 9am-9pm Tues.-Sun., 11am-9pm Mon. July-Sept., 10am-8pm Tues.-Sun., 11am-8pm Mon. Oct.-June; 250 CZK) for 360-degree views from above the 15th-century Astronomical Clock.

2. Pinkas Synagogue and Holocaust Memorial

Široká 3; tel. 222 749 211; www.jewishmuseum.cz; 9am-4:30pm daily Nov.-Mar., 9am-6pm daily Apr.-Oct.; entry covered by Jewish Museum ticket (350 CZK)

Walk five minutes to Pinkas Synagogue. The second-oldest synagogue in Prague, built in 1535, now functions as a somber memorial to nearly 80,000 victims of the holocaust. The synagogue's interior walls are covered in handwritten names, and there is a hall of drawings made by children who were held at the Jewish ghetto of Terezín while en route to the concentration camps at Treblinka or Auschwitz.

After this sobering but important sight, walk 10 minutes to **U Dvou Koček** (Uhelný trh 10; tel. 224 229 982; www.udvoukocek.cz; 11am-11pm daily; entrées 100-300 CZK). Choose from the daily lunch menu of soups and specials at this classic Czech pub.

Old Town Square

Key Reservations

In general, it's a good idea to purchase tickets for museums in advance, as you can save a lot of time skipping the lines when you arrive. Usually, you can do this before you set out in the morning—just ask your hotel to print out the ticket before you go.

PRAGUE

- Book English-language tours for the **Prague Castle** in advance.
- Visitors may be surprised to find that local **nightlife** requires reservations. For a seat in a popular pub or a table at a wine or cocktail bar, call ahead with a name, time, and number in your party, or check the venue's website for an online reservation system.
- Make reservations at the restaurants **U Dvou Koček, Martin's Bistro, U modré kachničky,** and **Eska,** and at wine bar **Veltlin.**

VIENNA

- Reserve a table at **Figlmüller.**

BUDAPEST

- Book your ticket for the **Hungarian Parliament** before going. Spots are limited and fill up quickly in high season.

Prague Castle

(top to bottom) Palac Lucerna; Mucha Museum; St. Nicholas Bell Tower

3. Palac Lucerna

Štěpánská 61; tel. 224 224 537; www.lucerna.cz; free; passage open 24 hours

Prague's city center is filled with covered passageways that connect the cafés, shops, and venues housed in the buildings that surround them. Palac Lucerna (Lantern Palace), a seven-minute walk from U Dvou Koček, was the first of these shopping and culture centers built in the Czech Republic. Today, one of the biggest draws for visitors is the highly photographable David Černý sculpture hanging from its domed ceiling, which contrasts with the proud statue of St. Wenceslas on the square outside.

In Palac Lucerna, have a drink at **Kavárna Lucerna** (Vodičkova 36; www.restaurace-monarchie.cz; tel. 224 215 495; 10am-midnight daily) for a glimpse of old-world glamour, or take the paternoster elevator to the **Střecha Lucerny** rooftop bar (Palác Lucerna; tel. 604 707 686; https://strechalucerny.cz; May-Oct.; 100 CZK entry).

4. Mucha Museum

Panská 7; tel. 224 216 415; www.mucha.cz; 10am-6pm daily; 300 CZK

While the art nouveau movement is generally associated with Paris, one of its original innovators is an undeniably local hero, Alfons Mucha. This three-room museum offers an easy introduction to one of the most revered Czech artists, whose work contributed to the beauty of the Municipal House and St. Vitus Cathedral. The museum is a five-minute walk from Palac Lucerna.

5. Night Out in Vinohrady

Head back to Wenceslas Square and get on the metro at the Můstek stop. Take the green Metro line A three stops to Jiřího z Poděbrad square in Vinohrady and have a Czech microbrew at **Beer Geek Bar** (Vinohradská 62; tel. 776-827-068; www.beergeek.cz; 3pm-2am daily). Beer Geek Bar was one of the earliest purveyors of microbrew culture in Prague. The 32 rotating taps still draw an international crowd of locals and travelers.

A NOTE ABOUT CURRENCY

The EU is generally great to travel in since you usually have a single currency, but in the case of Prague, Vienna, and Budapest, we're sorry to say that only **Austria** is in the Eurozone. The Czech Republic uses the **Czech Koruna** (also called the Crown), and Hungary the **Hungarian Forint.**

After your drink, walk five minutes to **Martin's Bistro** (Velehradská 4; tel. 774 100 378; 11:30am-10pm Mon.-Sat., 10am-4pm Sun.; entrées 150-300 CZK) for dinner from a seasonal, fresh-from-the-farmers-market menu.

DAY 2

1. St. Nicholas Bell Tower

Malostranské náměstí 556/29; tel. 725 847 927; www.prague.eu/en/object/places/175/st-nicholas-bell-tower-svatomikulasska-mestska-zvonice; 10am-6pm daily Oct.-June, 9am-9pm July-Aug., 10am-7pm Sept.; 150 CZK

Start your second day in Prague at the St. Nicholas Bell Tower. The six floors or platforms of this belfry, spread across 215 steps, take you through a decade-by-decade tour of Czech history. Climb the stairs from the bedrooms of 18th-century watchmen, through a shadowy bell tower, all the way up to re-created holographic conversations of the top floor, which was used as a Communist spy center in the 1980s. There are also 360-degree views on both the outdoor gallery level and covered windows of the top floor.

2. Lesser Town Bridge Tower

Karlův most; www.prague.eu; daily 10am-6pm Oct.-June, 9am-9pm July-Aug., 10am-7pm Sept.; 150 CZK each or 225 CZK combined ticket

From the tower, walk three minutes to the Charles Bridge—but don't cross it yet. Instead, spend 30 minutes climbing the Lesser Town Bridge Tower for a bird's-eye view of the afternoon crowds. The **Old Town Bridge Tower,** the shorter tower on the other side of the bridge, can also be climbed.

Just a few steps away, **Roesel - Beer & Food** (Mostecká 20; tel. 777 119 368 or 212 241 552; roesel-beer-cake.business.site; 10am-10pm daily; entrées 75-200 CZK), a friendly local café, is a good place to grab a coffee or beer and a bite to eat at.

3. Prague Castle

Pražský hrad; tel. 224 372 423 or 224 371 111; www.hrad.cz

After a light lunch, head to Prague Castle. It's a 15-minute walk, or you can hop on tram 22. The name Prague Castle is a bit misleading: The "castle" is not one building of turrets and royal residences, but actually refers to a massive fortified area of government buildings, churches, museums, and manicured gardens. This roughly 70,000-square-meter area (more than 6 hectares/17 acres) holds the Guinness World Record for the largest castle complex in the world.

A must-see within the castle grounds is **St. Vitus Cathedral** (Pražský hrad-III. nádvoří; tel. 224 372 423; www.katedral-asvatehovita.cz; 10am-6pm Mon.-Sat., noon-6pm Sun. Apr.-Oct., 9am-4pm Mon.-Sat., noon-4pm Sun. Nov.-Mar.; limited free access, full access with Circuit A 350 CZK or B 250 CZK). The cathedral is the dominant figure of the Prague skyline and is what most people associate with

(top to bottom) Old Town Hall Tower; Basilica of Sts. Peter and Paul in the Vyšehrad Complex; Lesser Town Bridge Tower; Charles Bridge

the historic castle grounds, although it wasn't entirely completed until the 20th century. Prepare to be awed while taking in the Gothic towers, intricate rose window, and stained glass.

4. Charles Bridge

Karlův most; free

Exit the Prague Castle by heading west through the South Gardens, stopping for a few panoramic photos. Head to **U modré kachničky** (Nebovidská 6; tel. 602 353 559 or 257 320 308; www.umodrekachnicky.cz; noon-4pm and 6:30pm-11:30pm daily; entrées 500-600 CZK) for a multicourse dinner (book in advance).

After dinner, walk 10 minutes to the Charles Bridge to enjoy the moonlight with fewer tourists. The famous bridge dates back to 1357, and baroque statues along the edges of the bridge up the landmark's visual appeal.

DAY 3

★ 1. Vyšehrad Complex

V Pevnosti 159/5b; tel. 261 225 304; www.praha-vysehrad.cz; free

Start your third day in Prague at the Vyšehrad Complex, which is quieter than Prague Castle but filled with comparable levels of history and beauty. The grounds include a maze of green spaces dotted with statues, alongside some of the city's oldest historic monuments. Wander the edges of the park complex for stunning city-wide viewpoints from an alternate angle to those of Old Town or Malá Strana.

In the complex, head to the **Basilica of Sts. Peter and Paul** (Štulcova; tel. 224 911 353; www.kkvys.cz; 90 CZK). The tall neo-Gothic towers of the basilica mirror the Prague Castle's St. Vitus Cathedral across the river, and the interior contains gorgeous art nouveau-style depictions of saints along its columns, as well as flowered ceilings and stained-glass windows.

Next to the basilica you'll find the **Vyšehrad Cemetery,** home to some of Prague's most famous names, such as composer Antonín Dvořák and art nou-

left, Vyšehrad Complex; right, Dancing House

veau painter Alfons Mucha. The final resting places are artfully decorated with intricate headstones and designed for visitors.

There is no need to be bashful about day drinking in this beer-loving capital. Grab a cold beverage and a snack at the laid-back **Hospůdka Na Hradbách** (V Pevnosti 2; tel. 734 112 214; 2pm-midnight Mon.-Fri., noon-midnight Sat.-Sun.) beer garden inside the Vyšehrad Complex, five minutes east of the basilica.

2. Dancing House

Jiraskovo Namesti 6; observation deck 9am-midnight

A 15-minute walk along the **Náplavka Boardwalk,** a cobblestone walkway below street level along the Vltava River, will take you to the Dancing House. The modern collaboration between two 20th-century architects, Canadian-American Frank Gehry and Croatian-Czech Vlado Milunić, was inspired by the shape of famous dancing couple Fred Astaire and Ginger Rogers. Its tension and intertwined embrace between the materials also represents the mid-1990s state of the Czech Republic, blending respect for the past while charging optimistically into the future, navigating cultural influences of East and West.

Take the elevator to the top-floor **Glass Bar** (www.galerietancicidum.cz/glass-bar-en) and order any beverage for access to the 360-degree viewing platform for a last look at Prague. Afterward, head to the train station for the five-hour trip to Vienna.

Vienna

Where to Stay: Historic Center or the Hofburg area

Arrive by: Train from Prague's Hlavní nádraží to Vienna's Wien Hauptbahnhof (4 hours)

DAY 4

1. Kunsthistorisches Museum Wien

Maria-Theresien-Platz; tel. 01/525-240; www.khm.at; 10am-6pm Fri.-Wed., 10am-9pm Thurs. June-Aug., closed Mon. Sept.-May; €16

If you only visit one museum in Vienna on your trip, make it the Kunsthistorisches Museum, the largest art history museum in the country. The museum houses pieces that span chronologically from the ancient Egyptians to the masters of the Renaissance and baroque periods. Arrive when the museum opens at 10am to avoid the crowds; you can easily spend all day here unless you prioritize a specific section you're interested in.

If you need refueling, there is a café and restaurant in the Kunsthistorisches Museum Cupola Hall (www.genussim-museum.at; 10am-5:30pm Tues.-Sun.).

2. The Hofburg

Michaelerkuppel; http://hofburg-wien.at

Afterward, walk to the nearby Hofburg for some fresh air. This palatial complex, home to the Habsburgs from 1273 to 1918, was the epicenter of life for the European royals. It now offers numerous museums, libraries, and more—and it serves as the residence of the Austrian president. The grand courtyards are open for free to the public.

3. Café Hawelka

Dorotheergasse 6; tel. 01/512-8230; www.hawelka.at; 9am-7pm Sun.-Wed., 9am-11pm Thurs.-Sat.

Take a coffee break at Café Hawelka, perhaps the most iconic of the Viennese cafés. It has catered to an artistic clientele, counting Andy Warhol and Arthur Miller among its former regulars.

4. St. Stephen's Cathedral

Stephansplatz 3; tel. 01/51552-3054; www.stephanskirche.at; 6am-10pm Mon.-Sat., 7am-10pm Sun.; €6 individual entry to North Tower, catacombs, or cathedral, €5 South Tower

Next, walk 10 minutes St. Stephen's Cathedral, Vienna's most famous landmark. You can spot its Gothic spires from as far as the hills surrounding the city. Look inside—the cathedral is full of quirky details, such as stone basilisks, dragons, eagles, lions, toads, and salamanders—or take the elevator or the stairs up to one of the towers for panoramic views.

For dinner, try some Austrian specialties at **Figlmüller** (Wollzeile 5; tel. 01/512-6177; www.figlmueller.at; 11am-10pm daily; mains €10-20.50) around the corner. This traditional Beisl (a typical Viennese tavern) serves some of the biggest Schnitzels in the city.

5. Vienna State Opera (Staatsoper)

Opernring 2; tel. 01/514-442-250; www.wiener-staatsoper.at; English language tours 1-3 times a day, see website for times; tours €10

Vienna is a city known for classical music, and the Vienna State Opera, a cathedral to classical music, makes for a fine evening out. (Get tickets in advance.) There are shows virtually every night at this prestigious opera house, and each night brings a different opera or ballet production.

DAY 5

★ 1. Schönbrunn Palace

Schönbrunner Schloßstraße; tel. 01/811-13-239; www.schoenbrunn.at; 9:30am-5pm daily; €18-22

Take the metro to Schönbrunn Palace—arrive early to beat the crowds. This palace is the centerpiece of Habsburg

(clockwise from top) St. Stephen's Cathedral; Kunsthistorisches Museum; Vienna State Opera

grandeur, where the imperial family spent their summers. The palace is home to 1,441 rooms—only 40 of which can be visited—most in the rococo style. Some are clad with porcelain, others are inspired by ancient Chinese art, and still others feature original Indian and embedded Persian miniatures.

After you've explored the opulent palace, head out into surrounding gardens, which feature lush vegetation, secret nooks, and amazing views over the palace. Hike up the hill to the **Gloriette,** a triumphal arch flanked by arcaded wings on the hill opposite the palace.

2. Naschmarkt

Wienzeile; 6am-7:30pm Mon.-Fri.; 6am-6pm Sat.

Take the metro back to the city center to see Naschmarkt, the city's large open-air market. There are at least 120 market stalls, where you'll find fresh vegetables, dried fruit, cheese, cold cuts, and much more. Head into one of the trendy restaurants for a hearty meal and then take some time to wander, but don't forget to look up at Otto Wagner's Majolica Wienzeile—a beautiful apartment block with tiles depicting roses and floral motifs.

top, Schönbrunn Palace; bottom, Naschmarkt

3. Secession

Friedrichstraße 12; tel. 01/587-5307; www.secession.at; 2pm-6pm Tues.-Sun.; €9.50

Visit the Secession building nearby. Stop and admire the golden dome before popping inside to admire Klimt's stunning ***Beethoven Frieze.*** You only need about an hour to explore this small museum.

4. Belvedere Palace

Prinz Eugen-straße 27; tel. 01/795-570; www.belvedere.at; 10am-6pm daily; €16 for Unteres Belvedere

Hop on tram D and get off at the Schloss Belvedere for a visit to the Belvedere Palace. This palace was the summer residence for Prince Eugene of Savoy, the general of the Imperial Army, who beat back the Turks at the beginning of the 18th century. It is one of the most spectacular examples of baroque architecture you can explore.

The Belvedere includes the main palace building, and state and ceremonial rooms that serve as spaces for fine art, including the highlight: Gustav Klimt's famous piece ***The Kiss.*** The surrounding gardens are beautiful, too.

5. The Prater

Prater; tel. 01/728-0516; www.prater.at; open 24 hours; free

Take the S-Bahn to the Praterstern station for an evening at the Prater, Vienna's largest park. The Prater is all about fun, whether that means hopping on one of the rides or having a beer at **Schweizerhaus,** a breezy biergarten. Ride the **Riesenrad,** Vienna's historic Ferris wheel, for sunset vistas.

Hop on the U1—or walk—to Schwedenplatz for the riverside bars at the Danube Canal, like the **Strandbar Herrmann** (Herrmannpark; tel. 07/20-229-996; www.strandbarherrmann.at; 2pm-1am Mon.-Fri., 10am-1am Sat.-Sun. weather permitting).

Viennese Coffeehouses

Even more essential than a visit to the Hofburg is a trip to an authentic Kaffeehaus. These classic coffeehouses capture the Viennese spirit, each with its own character and style. Some are more opulent than others, but they will usually have cozy booths and marble tables, newspapers, coat stands by the door, and elegantly dressed waiters. And don't expect service with a smile—the waiters' grumpy demeanor (or perhaps grumpy by American standards) is part of the coffeehouse experience.

Some of the best coffeehouses to try include:

CAFÉ HAWELKA

Dorotheergasse 6; tel. 01/512-8230; www.hawelka.at; 9am-7pm Sun.-Wed., 9am-11pm Thurs.-Sat.

Hawelka might be the most iconic café in Vienna. It's dark and a bit moody, with faded upholstered booths, wooden coat stands, and local art on the wall. Go after 8pm when freshly made Buchteln, baked dumplings filled with jam (Josephine's family recipe) are available, fresh out of the oven. They have a street-side terrace if you prefer to sit outside.

CAFÉ BRÄUNERHOF

Stallburggasse 2; tel. 01/512-3893; 8am-7:30pm Mon.-Fri., 8am-6:30pm Sat., 10am-6:30pm Sun.

A street away from the Hofburg, Bräunerhof still retains its timeless local charm. Come here to enjoy old-world ambience with a classic Viennese coffee like an Einspänner, a black coffee topped with cream.

CAFÉ SPERL

Gumpendorferstraße 11; tel. 01/586-4158; www.cafesperl.at; 7am-10pm Mon.-Sat., 10am-8pm Sun.

Sperl, which opened in 1880, has hardly changed—and without turning into a caricature of itself. You may want to try the house cake, the Sperl Schnitte, a rich chocolate wafer.

Budapest

Where to Stay: Jewish Quarter or Inner City

Arrive by: Train from Vienna's Wien Hauptbahnhof to Budapest Keleti (2.5-3 hours)

DAY 6

1. Chain Bridge

After taking the train from Vienna to Budapest in the morning, start your day at one of the city's most spectacular bridges, the Chain Bridge, with amazing views over the Danube. It's Budapest's oldest permanent stone bridge, a suspension bridge featuring two vaulted, classical-style pillars connected by large iron chains. Make sure you stop to look at the stone lions, created by sculptor János Marschalkó, that flank the entrances to the bridge.

2. Fisherman's Bastion

Szentháromság tér; 9am-7pm Mar.-Apr., 9am-8pm May-Oct.; HUF 1,000

Walk 10 minutes and climb the stairs up to Fisherman's Bastion. Glimmering white above the Danube, the romantic Fisherman's Bastion overlooks the Hungarian Parliament Building and the rooftops of Pest. It was built as a spectacular viewing platform between 1890 and 1905, and it's still one of Budapest's most beautiful structures.

Grab something to eat at **Ruszwurm** (Szentháromság utca 7; tel. 06/1-375-5284; www.ruszwurm.hu; 10am-7pm Mon.-Fri., 10am-6pm Sat.-Sun.; HUF 450-850), the oldest café and confectionary in Budapest. It's a one-minute walk from Fisherman's Bastion.

3. Buda Castle

Next, walk 15 minutes to Buda Castle, a symbol of the city. Perched on top of the hill overlooking the Danube, the castle's neo-baroque facade spreads out in columns under a copper-green dome. Inside, the spartan walls offer a stark contrast to the Habsburg opulence you'd

Chain Bridge

left, Fisherman's Bastion; right, Danube Cruise

find in Vienna, as the interior was severely damaged in the war. Later, the interior was gutted and "modernized" under the Communist regime of the 1950s.

You'll want to spend a couple of hours at the **Hungarian National Gallery** (Szent György tér 2; tel. 06/20-439-7331; www.mng.hu; 10am-6pm Tues.-Sun.; HUF 2,800 permanent exhibition, audio guides HUF 800) in the Royal Palace. The gallery chronicles Hungarian art from the Middle Ages to the avant-garde in the period following 1945. Highlights include late-Gothic winged altarpieces, the realism of Mihály Munkácsy, and the explosive colors from Hungarian Expressionists.

4. St. Stephen's Basilica

Szent István tér; www.bazilika.biz; 9am-5pm Mon.-Fri., 9am-1pm Sat., 1pm-5pm Sun.; HUF 200 recommended donation

Head back over the Danube to visit St. Stephen's Basilica, an impressive neoclassical cathedral. It took half a century to build this basilica, partly because its iconic dome collapsed halfway through construction. You can scale over 300 stairs (or take an elevator) to the **viewing platform** (10am-4:30pm daily Nov.-Mar., 10am-5:30pm Apr.-May and Oct., 10am-6:30pm June-Sept.; HUF 600) outside the dome for 360-degree views of Budapest's most famous sites.

5. Legenda Danube Cruise

Dock 7 Jane Haining rakpart; tel. 06/1-317-2203; www.legenda.hu; HUF 4,200

Walk down to the river and get yourself on a Danube cruise organized by Legenda, which offers a classic 70-minute sightseeing trip with a glass of sparkling wine, beer, or soft drink included. Audio guides are available, or you can just sit and relax.

6. Szimpla Kert

Kazinczy utca 14; tel. 06/20-261-8669; www.szimpla.hu; noon-4am Mon.-Sat., 9am-5am Sun.

End the night at Budapest's most famous ruin bar. A phenomenon unique to Budapest, ruin bars are set inside crumbling,

TOP EXPERIENCE

★ Thermal Baths

It's no accident Budapest has earned the nickname "City of Spas"; below the city there are more than 100 geothermal springs, each with its own mineral profile. Budapest's thermal baths are a perfect antidote for its wild nightlife and are a must-do on any visit to the city.

There is a bath in Budapest for everyone's taste, whether you want to bathe in a historic monument or go where the locals go.

SZÉCHENYI BATHS

Állatkerti körút 11; tel. 06/1-363-3210; www.szechenyibath.hu; 6am-7pm daily; HUF 6,200 on weekends, HUF 5,900 on weekdays

The Széchenyi Baths is Budapest's largest and most famous thermal bath complex. Go for the stunning columned outdoor pools. Stay because you find out there are even more pools indoors. This bath is well known for its wild Sparties (spa parties) on Saturday nights.

LUKÁCS

Frankel Leó út 25-29; tel. 06/1-326-1695; http://en.lukacsfurdo.hu; 6am-10pm daily; HUF 3,900 on weekends, HUF 3,500 on weekdays, HUF 800 Sauna World supplement

Laid-back Lukács is popular with locals for its understated turn-of-the-century elegance, pump room, and the healing properties of the water. In the winter, Lukács takes over as host for the Saturday night Sparties.

RÓMAI OPEN-AIR BATHS

Rozgonyi Piroska utca 2; tel. 06/1-388-9740; http://en.romaistrand.hu; 9am-8pm daily June-Sept.; HUF 2,800 on weekends, HUF 2,500 on weekdays

Open-air and seasonal, the Római Open-Air Baths are popular with kids thanks to the jungle of waterslides there.

GELLÉRT THERMAL BATHS

Kelenhegyi út 4; tel. 06/1-466-6166; www.gellertbath.hu; 6am-8pm daily; HUF 6,200 on weekends, HUF 5,900 on weekdays

The Gellért Thermal Baths are an art nouveau architectural treasure.

RUDAS

Döbrentei tér 9; tel. 06/1-356-1322; http://en.rudasfurdo.hu; Turkish bath 6am-10pm daily, wellness center 8am-10pm daily; HUF 3,800 Turkish bath, HUF 6,900 combined ticket for Turkish bath, wellness center, and swimming pool on weekends and HUF 5,500 on weekdays

If you go to the Rudas on weekdays, the bath is single-sex, and although you won't need a swimsuit, you will be given a loin cloth you need to wear. (The bath is now trying to cut down on full nudity.) Women's day is Tuesday, and men's are Monday, Wednesday, Thursday all day, and Friday morning.

DANDÁR

Dandár utca 5-7; tel. 06/1-215-7084; http://en.dandarfurdo.hu; 6am-9pm Mon.-Fri., 8am-9pm Sat.-Sun.; HUF 2,100 thermal bath, HUF 2,600 wellness center and thermal bath

For a simple thermal bath experience, the Dandár is a great budget option.

semi-abandoned buildings filled with eclectic furniture and local art. Szimpla Kert is a nocturnal wonderland with fairy lights, old computer monitors, and creaking furniture painted in a kaleidoscope of colors. You can even sit in a Trabant car in the courtyard.

DAY 7

1. Postal Savings Bank

Hold utca

Today has an architectural theme to it. Head first to Postal Savings Bank. It is not open to the public but is worth passing by. Designed by Ödön Lechner and completed in 1901, this striking example of Hungarian art nouveau is an architectural symphony of Hungarian folk ornamentation. If you want to see the rooftop from above, go into the Hotel President across the street to the rooftop café—it's worth it for the view.

2. Hungarian Parliament Building

Kossúth tér 1-3; tel. 06/1-441-4904; http://latogatokozpont.parlament.hu; 8am-6pm daily Apr.-Oct., 8am-4pm daily Nov.-Mar., tours 10am-4pm daily; HUF 6,700 non-EU citizens including guide

Stroll over to the Hungarian Parliament Building, a short walk away. Facing the Danube, in carved blocks of white Hungarian marble and topped with neo-Gothic spires on a wine-hued rooftop crowned with a dome, the Hungarian Parliament Building is an architectural wonder. Completed in 1902, its 691 rooms exist in a labyrinth of gilded corridors and grand staircases. Take one of the English-language tours to see inside this amazing building.

3. Dohány Street Synagogue

Dohány utca 2; tel. 06/1-413-5585; www.jewishtourhungary.com; 10am-6pm Sun.-Thurs. and 10am-4pm Fri. Mar.-Oct., 10am-4pm Sun.-Thurs. and 10am-2pm Fri. Nov.-Feb.; HUF 4,500 (with guide)

Hop on the metro at Kossuth Lajos tér and get off at Astoria to see the Grand Synagogue, more colloquially known as the Dohány Street Synagogue. This is Europe's largest synagogue. The architecture deviates from traditional synagogues; the architects were inspired by Christian basilicas. It includes a stunning rose window and a cluster of stars made out of stained glass.

Grab a bite to eat at the **Karavan** (Kazinczy utca 18; tel. 06/30-934-8013; 11:30am-11pm Sun.-Wed., 11:30am-1am Thurs.-Sat. Mar.-Sept.), a street food court that serves up a range of snacks from its numerous food trucks. The area might look familiar—it's right next door to Szimpla Kert.

4. Gellért Hill

Walk 20 minutes across Elizabeth Bridge or take the bus Gellért Hill, a green, rocky outcrop on the banks of the Danube. A statue of the hill's namesake, St. Gellért, towers above a human-made waterfall, surrounded by columns opposite Elizabeth Bridge.

Take the stairs going past the waterfall and the statue of the saint, and then follow a labyrinth of paths up to the Citadel, a dramatic structure that crowns the top of the hill. The city views from here are amazing. Continue down the hill to reach the Gellért Thermal Baths.

Hungarian Parliament Building

top, Gellért Thermal Baths; bottom, Budapest riverside

5. Gellért Thermal Baths

Kelenhegyi út 4; tel. 06/1-466-6166; www.gellertbath.hu; 6am-8pm daily; HUF 6,200 on weekends, HUF 5,900 on weekdays

On the southern slopes of Gellért Hill, the Gellért Thermal Baths capture the grandeur of Budapest's golden age at the turn of the 20th century. Unwind with a soak, and maybe even splurge on a massage.

Relaxed and refreshed, have dinner and drinks at **Hadik** (Bartók Béla út 36; tel. 06/1-279-0290; www.hadik.eu; 11am-8pm daily; HUF 1,890-3,290), a former literary hangout in the early 1900s that's now a trendy bistro. The bistro is a 10-minute walk from the baths.

TRANSPORTATION

Air

All three cities have international airports, but Vienna is your best bet for a direct flight from outside Europe.

- **Vaclav Havel International Airport, Prague** (PRG; Aviatická; www.prg.aero): Prague's international airport is 17 km (about 10.5 mi) east of the city center, with buses connecting to the Prague metro for trips to the city center. There are few direct flights to Prague from outside Europe.
- **Vienna International Airport, Vienna** (VIE; tel. 01/700-722-233; www.viennaairport.com): Vienna's international airport is 16 km (10 mi) southwest of the city center, with the City Airport Train providing a direct connection to the city center. There are direct flights from Chicago and the New York area (Newark).
- **Ferenc Liszt International Airport, Budapest** (BUD; tel. 06/1-296-7000; www.bud.hu): Budapest's international airport, sometimes known by its former name of Ferihegy Airport, is located in the southeastern suburbs, with the 100E bus connecting with the city center. Flights from outside Europe will require at least one connection.

Train

Getting between Prague, Vienna, and Budapest, the easiest way is to go by train or by bus. Each city has direct connections. The main rail companies running in Central Europe are **ÖBB Railjet** (www.oebb.at), **MÁV** (www.mavcsoport.hu), **České Dráhy** (www.cd.cz), **RegioJet** (www.regiojet.com) and **Deutsche Bahn** (www.bahn.de). You can check timetables for all continental European connections on Deutsche Bahn's website.

- **Praha—Hlavní nádraží, Prague** (Wilsonova 8): Often written as Praha hl. n in Czech, Prague's main train station is located in the center of New Town.
- **Wien Hauptbahnhof, Vienna** (Am Hauptbahnhof 1): Trains from Prague (multiple departures daily; 4 hours during the day, 8-10 hours overnight; 238-1,200 CZK) arrive at Vienna's main

top, Prague underground; bottom, tram in Budapest

train station, located close to the city center, near Belvedere Palace.

- **Keleti (Eastern) Train Station, Budapest** (Kerepesi út 2-4): Trains from Vienna (multiple departures daily; 2.5-3 hours; €13-30) arrive at Budapest's main train station, which is located on the eastern side of the Danube and connected to the metro.

Bus

Long-distance buses operated by companies like **Flixbus** (www.flixbus.com) operate between the three cities.

Public Transportation

One thing Central European cities have in common is excellent **public transport.** Each city has a well-connected subway service, a vast network of tram lines, and of course, buses. Each of the three cities' public transit systems is operated by one managing entity, so you can use the same passes on multiple forms of transit, such as bus and metro. All three cities have passes that are sold in chunks of time, so you can get a pass for 24 hours, 48 hours, etc. In Budapest and Vienna, it's also possible to purchase single-ride tickets.

You can also get around each city by **bike,** as all three have bike-sharing systems. Budapest and Vienna are bike friendly cities, with designated bicycle lanes and paths all across the city. Prague is not quite as bike-friendly inside the city, and drivers are not always known for giving way or stopping for crosswalks, but there are numerous cycling paths once you get into the countryside.

Getting Back

Fly out of Budapest's **Ferenc Liszt International Airport** (BUD; tel. 06/1-296-7000; www.bud.hu) to get home. To get back to Prague, trains by Regiojet and MÁV depart from Budapest (6.5-7 hours; €16-39/5,500-12,675 HUF).

WATCH

The Third Man: This iconic film noir starring Orson Welles was filmed on location in 1940s post-war Vienna. If there is one movie you watch before going to Vienna, make it this one—then you can follow in its footsteps.

READ

The Book of Laughter and Forgetting by Milan Kundera: Kundera's first major international success weaves together politics, philosophy, surrealism, and banality through rumination on the challenges of life in communist Czechoslovakia.

The Door by Magda Szabó: Visceral, moving, and beautiful, this character-based novel based in Budapest tells the story of a writer and her mysterious cleaning lady.

LISTEN

All three cities are known for their famous composers of **classical music.** Prague has names like Antonín Dvořák and Bedřich Smetana; Vienna was home to Mozart, Beethoven, Strauss, Schubert, and more; and Budapest has Franz Liszt and Béla Bartók.

CONNECT WITH

- Berlin, Warsaw, and Krakow (page 162)
- Zagreb, Ljubljana, and Trieste (page 205)

ZAGREB, LJUBLJANA, AND TRIESTE

Why Go: This truly off-the-beaten path itinerary takes you to three less-visited European cities that surprise with their elegant café lifestyle, beautiful architecture, and diverse mixture of cultural influences.

Number of Days: 5

Total Distance: 234 km (145 mi)

Seasons: Spring and early summer

Start: Zagreb

End: Trieste

Most people who seek out Zagreb, Ljubljana, and Trieste are either seeking out the road less traveled, or are on their way to somewhere else. But to skip over these unique, elegant European cities would be mistake. Uniquely situated between east and west, these cities have seen changing rulers and the rise and fall of empires, from the Romans to the Germans to the Serbians, and this complicated history lends complexity to the architecture, food, and culture. What's more, both Trieste and Zagreb were once stops on the Orient Express, and that old-world sophistication remains in beautiful Art Nouveau buildings, locals sipping coffee in cafés, and a lack of hurry that encourages unsuspecting visitors to stay longer than they planned.

TOP 3

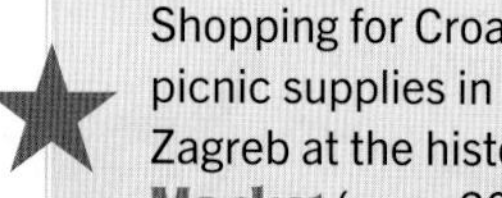

★ Shopping for Croatia-grown picnic supplies in the heart of Zagreb at the historic **Dolac Market** (page 207).

★ Learning how urban planning can transform a city in **Plečnik's Ljubljana.** The impact of one architect, Jože Plečnik, is visible all over the Slovenian capital (page 213).

★ Sipping a capo in b (mini cappuccino) at one of many elegant **cafés in Trieste.** Many visitors are surprised to learn the city is considered Italy's coffee capital (page 219).

Zagreb

Where to Stay: Lower Town

Arrive by: Plane to Zagreb Airport

DAY 1

The Croatian capital can be divided into dozens of neighborhoods; most important for the traveler are **Upper Town (Gornji Grad),** home to the old town and many of the city's most charming attractions, and **Lower Town (Donji Grad),** where much of the shopping, socializing, and business is carried out, interconnected by the world's shortest **funicular.** You'll spend the bulk of today in Lower Town.

1. Coffee and Strolling on Zagreb's Squares

Start your morning the way the locals do, with a coffee on pretty **Flower Square (Cvjetni trg),** nicknamed for its lovely flower stands (the square's official name is Preradović's Square, or Preradovićev trg). Sunny days seem to bring all of Zagreb to the cafés here.

Wander north to **Ban Jelačić Square (Trg bana Jelačićica),** Zagreb's main square and another central meeting point in the city since at least the 17th century. It's surrounded by over-the-top Neoclassical architecture and Successionist buildings, influenced by the highly decorative Austrian Succession and Art Nouveau movements. Here you'll find more cafés frequented by Zagreb's elite, politicians, and writers, as well as frequent concerts, political rallies, parades, and several markets, depending on the day.

★ 2. Picnic Shopping at Dolac Market

Dolac 9; tel. 01 642 2501; www.trznice-zg.hr; morning-2pm daily

From here, follow the row of fresh flower stands topped with red umbrellas north to Dolac Market, and join the pre-noon crowd bargaining for fresh produce to get some ingredients for a picnic. This has been the city's main market since 1930, and if you're looking for the heart and soul of Zagreb, you'll find it here. Old men drink tiny glasses of brandy at the old cafés along the market's edges and watch the crowd bargaining with vendors for fresh produce, herbs, eggs, and homemade cheeses. This is a great spot to savor the best of the Croatian harvest, hailing from the fertile hills of Istria, and to search for souvenirs, from embroidered tablecloths to quirky elixirs and health remedies.

If you aren't sure what to buy, try a fresh burek (flaky filled pastry) from one of the bread shops to eat right away, and pick up some local olives or a jar of domestic honey seasoned with lavender or rosemary for the trip home. After you're through

top, Zagreb's squares; bottom, Dolac Market

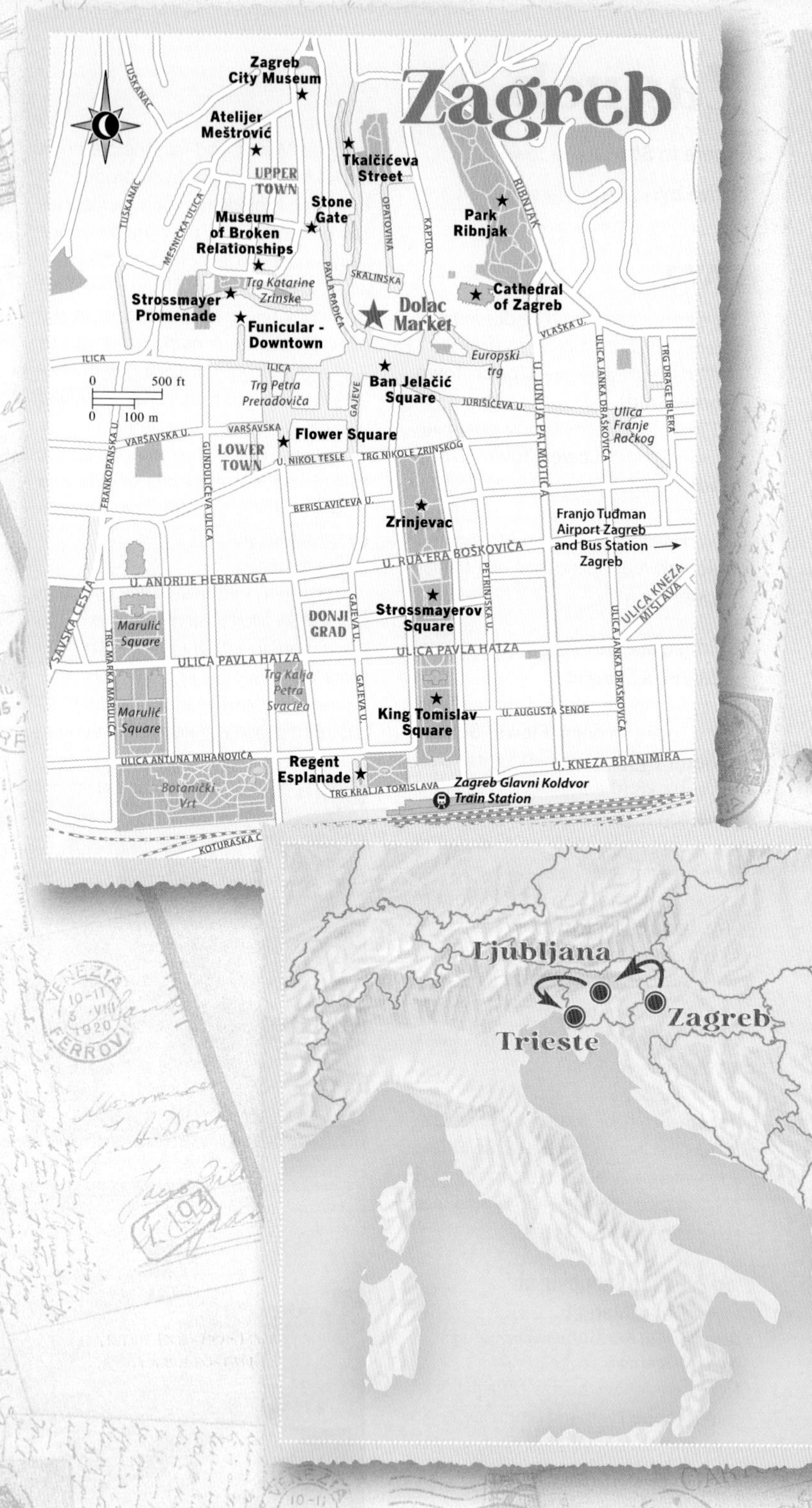
Zagreb
Zagreb City Museum
Atelijer Meštrović
Tkalčićeva Street
UPPER TOWN
Stone Gate
Museum of Broken Relationships
Park Ribnjak
Trg Katarine Zrinske
Strossmayer Promenade
Funicular - Downtown
Dolac Market
Cathedral of Zagreb
Europski trg
Ban Jelačić Square
Trg Petra Preradoviča
Ulica Franje Račkog
Flower Square
LOWER TOWN
Zrinjevac
Franjo Tuđman Airport Zagreb and Bus Station Zagreb
Strossmayerov Square
DONJI GRAD
Marulić Square
Marulić Square
Trg Kalja Petra Svaciča
King Tomislav Square
Regent Esplanade
Zagreb Glavni Koldvor Train Station
Botanički Vrt
0 500 ft
0 100 m
TUSKANAC
MESNIČKA ULICA
OPATOVINA
KAPTOL
RIBNJAK
SKALINSKA
PAVLA RADIĆA
VLAŠKA U.
ILICA
GAJEVE
JURIŠIĆEVA U.
U. JUNIJA PALMOTIĆA
ULICA JANKA DRAŠKOVIĆA
TRG DRAGE IBLERA
VARŠAVSKA U.
U. NIKOL TESLE
TRG NIKOLE ZRINSKOG
FRANKOPANSKA U.
GUNDULIĆEVA ULICA
BERISLAVIĆEVA U.
U. RUĐERA BOŠKOVIĆA
U. ANDRIJE HEBRANGA
PETRINJSKA U.
ULICA KNEZA MISLAVA
SAVSKA CESTA
TRG MARKA MARULIĆA
ULICA PAVLA HATZA
GAJEVA U.
U. AUGUSTA ŠENOE
ULICA ANTUNA MIHANOVIĆA
U. KNEZA BRANIMIRA
TRG KRALJA TOMISLAVA
KOTURAŠKA C.
Ljubljana
Trieste
Zagreb

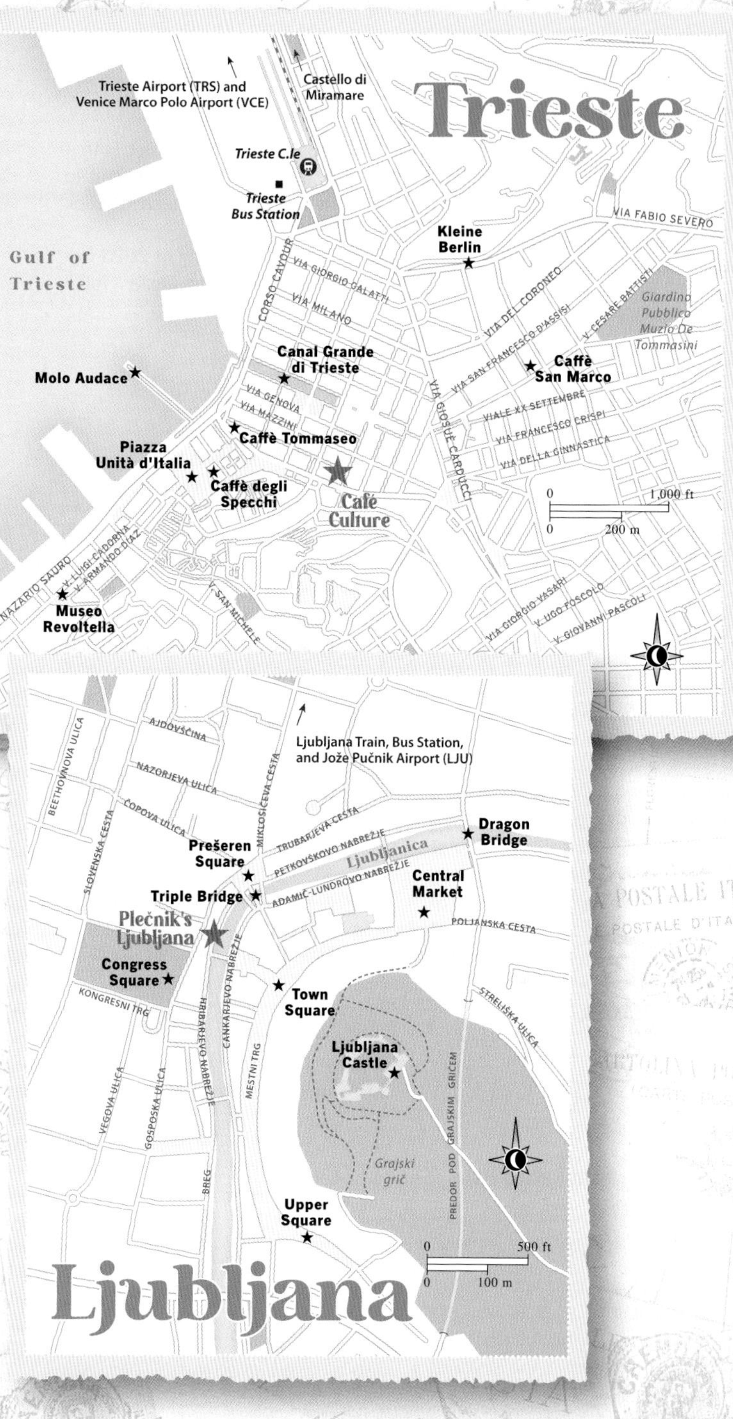
Trieste
Trieste Airport (TRS) and
Venice Marco Polo Airport (VCE)
Castello di
Miramare
Trieste C.le
Trieste
Bus Station
Gulf of
Trieste
VIA FABIO SEVERO
Kleine
Berlin
CORSO CAVOUR
VIA GIORGIO GALATTI
VIA MILANO
VIA DEL CORONEO
V. CESARE BATTISTI
VIA SAN FRANCESCO D'ASSISI
Giardino
Pubblico
Muzio De
Tommasini
Canal Grande
di Trieste
Caffè
San Marco
Molo Audace
VIA GENOVA
VIA MAZZINI
VIA GIOSUÈ CARDUCCI
VIALE XX SETTEMBRE
VIA FRANCESCO CRISPI
VIA DELLA GINNASTICA
Caffè Tommaseo
Piazza
Unità d'Italia
Caffè degli
Specchi
Café
Culture
0
1,000 ft
0
200 m
V. LUIGI CADORNA
V. ARMANDO DIAZ
RIVA NAZARIO SAURO
V. SAN MICHELE
Museo
Revoltella
VIA GIORGIO VASARI
V. UGO FOSCOLO
V. GIOVANNI PASCOLI
Ljubljana Train, Bus Station,
and Jože Pučnik Airport (LJU)
AJDOVŠČINA
BEETHOVNOVA ULICA
NAZORJEVA ULICA
MIKLOŠIČEVA CESTA
ČOPOVA ULICA
SLOVENSKA CESTA
TRUBARJEVA CESTA
Dragon
Bridge
Prešeren
Square
PETKOVŠKOVO NABREŽJE
Ljubljanica
ADAMIČ-LUNDROVO NABREŽJE
Triple Bridge
Central
Market
Plečnik's
Ljubljana
POLJANSKA CESTA
Congress
Square
CANKARJEVO NABREŽJE
KONGRESNI TRG
Town
Square
STRELIŠKA ULICA
HRIBARJEVO NABREŽJE
MESTNI TRG
Ljubljana
Castle
VEGOVA ULICA
GOSPOSKA ULICA
PREDOR POD GRAJSKIM GRIČEM
Grajski
grič
BREG
Upper
Square
0
500 ft
0
100 m
Ljubljana

Key Reservations

One of the virtues of traveling to some of Europe's less-visited cities is that you won't have much competition from other tourists. Still, if you want to learn about the period of Nazi Occupation in Trieste, you'll need to book ahead to visit the former air-raid tunnels of **Kleine Berlin.**

Croatia instituted the **euro** as its currency at the beginning of 2023 (replacing the kuna), making a trip combining these cities even easier: You'll only need euros when visiting all three.

haggling, walk northeast past the grand, neo-Gothic **Cathedral of Zagreb** (Kaptol 31; tel. 01 481 4727; 10am-5pm Mon.-Sat., 1pm-5pm Sun. and religious holidays; free) to have your picnic on the lovely green slopes of **Park Ribnjak,** which dates to the 19th century.

3. Shopping on Tkalčićeva Street

Walk west to historic Tkalčićeva Street. Often referred to simply as Tkalča by the locals, this pedestrian zone serves as another of the city's social hubs. It takes only 10 minutes to journey between Dolac market and the end of the street, but it's a must-do to get a real sense of Zagreb, and you're sure to be tempted by the many bars and restaurants set in petite, colorful buildings straight out of a Brothers Grimm tale. Stop into one of the many cafés for coffee and dessert and do a little window-shopping, then snag a table at tiny **La Struk** (Skalinska Ulica 5; tel. 01 483 7701; 11am-10am Mon.-Sat., 11:30am-10pm Sun.; €3-10) serving sweet and savory strukli (a regional delicacy of pulled dough stuffed with fillings).

4. Sampling Rakija at Rakhia Bar

Tkalčićeva 45; tel. 098 964 0587; noon-2am daily; €4-7

Something of a Croatian national spirit, rakija is a brandy made with various fruits and sometimes nuts. You can try over two dozen varieties of the drink at Rakhia Bar, located at the heart of Tkalčićeva Street, which is also a great street for bar-hopping.

DAY 2

1. Museums of Upper Town

Start at what was once the eastern entrance to the old town, the 13th-century **Stone Gate (Kamenita vrata).** The gate has survived renovations, fires, and various motions by the city to tear it down. It's a quiet, reverent way to enter the old part of town, and clearly marks your departure from modernity.

From here, climb north for a wonderful selection of museums to choose from: The **Zagreb City Museum** (Opatička 20; tel. 01 485 1361; www.mgz.hr; 10am-7pm Tues.-Sat., 10am-2pm Sun., closed holidays; €4) is the best place to learn about the history of the capital and the country; at the **Meštrović Studio** (Meštrović Atelier, Mletačka 8; tel. 01 485 1123; www.mestrovic.hr; 10am-6pm Mon.-Fri., 10am-2pm Sat.-Sun., closed holidays; €4)**,** you can view over 300 works by Croatia's most famous sculptor, Ivan Meštrović; or visit the one-of-a-kind **Museum of Broken Relationships** (Sv. Ćirila i Metoda 2; tel. 01 485 1021; www.brokenships.com; 9am-10:30pm June-Sept., 9am-9pm Oct.-May, closed holidays; €5), where objects signifying the end of a relationship are displayed, from toys and postcards to fuzzy handcuffs and three volumes of Proust.

2. Strossmayer Promenade

Take a break from all the museum-viewing with a stroll on the Strossmayer Promenade, which has magnificent city

(clockwise from top) Tkalčićeva Street; Cathedral of Zagreb; Strossmayer Promenade

views along the old medieval city walls. It's a great place to get your fill of Upper Town's picturesque streets and take photos of the city's stunning, red-roofed skyline. Then, grab lunch at **Pod Starim Krovovima** (Basaričekova 9; tel. 01 485 1342; 8am-11pm Mon.-Sat.; €3-5), which claims to be the oldest café in Zagreb.

3. The Green Horseshoe

Take the adorably short **funicular** (Tomićeva ulica; tel. 01 483 3912; every 10 minutes 6:30am-10pm daily; €0.50 one-way), spanning just 66 m (216 ft), to the Lower Town, where you'll spend the afternoon walking through Zagreb's "green horseshoe," a string of parks, squares, and museums in the shape of a "U" designed by 19th-century urban planner Milan Lenuci. Start at **Zrinjevac Square,** possibly Zagreb's prettiest, lined by giant trees with crackled white and gray bark and surrounded by some of the city's loveliest architecture, then walk through **Tomsilav** and **Strossmayerov Squares,** filled with fountains, pavilions, and green paths great for strolling.

4. Dinner at Zinfandel's

Mihanovićeva 1; tel. 01 4566 644; www.zinfandels.hr; 6am-11pm Mon.-Sat., 6:30am-11pm Sun.; €20-27

You'll end up at the grand **Regent Esplanade** hotel (www.regenthotels.com), built for Orient Express passengers in 1925—hence its proximity to the main train station, **Glavni Kolodvor.** The pink-stone, red-roofed station is straight out of a Wes Anderson film and certainly lives up to the romantic history of the famed train route, as does the hotel, with its marble and mirrored art nouveau lobby. Inside the Regent Esplanade at Zinfandel's, you'll be wowed by the elegant, pink-tinted dining room and excellent European cuisine that is beautifully presented, a great way to soak up the old-world feel of this refined city.

Ljubljana

Where to Stay: Old Town or around Prešeren Square

Arrive by: Train from Zagreb Glavni Koldvor to Ljubljana Train Station (2 hours)

Dragon Bridge

DAY 3

1. Congress Square

Start your tour of Slovenia's capital city in Jože Plečnik-designed Congress Square, a large square and park in the middle of Ljubljana. The great architect's touch—heavily influenced by the symmetrical elegance of classical architecture—is evident in the landscape design and many of the monuments.

2. Triple Bridge

Head north of Congress Square to **Prešeren Square** (Prešernov Trg), which leads to the landmark Triple Bridge (Tromostovje). In a signature Plečnik move, the architect solved traffic problems on what was formerly a congested single bridge by adding two parallel pedestrian bridges to make crossing the bridge into

NAME CHECK: Jože Plečnik

It's rare for a city to have been almost entirely designed and renovated by one man, but damage from an 1895 earthquake gave Jože Plečnik, Slovenia's most famous architect, the chance to transform the city in the 1920s and '30s.

Born in Ljubljana in 1872, Plečnik studied with the famous Viennese architect Otto Wagner in the 1890s, then worked in Vienna and Prague before returning in 1921to Ljubljana, where he went to work renovating churches and the municipal cemetery and building new bridges, waterfronts, buildings, monuments, and parks. Jože Plečnik died in the city in 1957, but the impression he left here is so strong that UNESCO has recognized Plečnik's Ljubljana as a World Heritage Site.

★ PLEČNIK'S LJUBLJANA

Viewing some of Plečnik's works leads you through an architectural history of the city and the vision of the architect who was a genius in human-centered design.

- **Trnovo Bridge** (Karunova ulica 1): Plečnik designed its pyramids to mimic the nearby trees and the spires of the Church of St. John the Baptist to the south.
- **Križanke Theater** (Trg francoske revolucije 1): Plečnik designed this outdoor theater when he was in his 80s. One of the complex's courtyards is extremely well-lit, because, Plečnik said, the communists needed enlightening. He also placed columns decorated with the hammer and sickle directly opposite a statue of Christ in the main courtyard.
- **Vegova Street:** This beautiful street was planned by the architect. It leads past **Congress Square** (page 212), which was also touched by Plečnik's skilled hand.
- **Slovenian Philharmonic Hall** (Kongresni trg 10; tel. 01/241-0800; www.filharmonija.si): Plečnik changed the back facade and added on to the neo-Renaissance structure.
- **Triple Bridge:** This bridge may be Plečnik's most iconic creation. He added the two pedestrian bridges alongside the motor bridge, along with some handsome street lamps (page 212).
- **Central Market:** Even buying bread did not escape Plečnik's elegant, symmetrical touch, and the market is filled with his signature columns (page 214).

WATCH

Nora: This biopic from the perspective of Nora Barnacle, the wife and muse of James Joyce, takes place largely in Trieste, where she and the writer lived during a formative period in Joyce's artistic development.

READ

The 8:55 to Baghdad: From London to Iraq on the Trail of Agatha Christie and the Orient Express by Andrew Ames: Agatha Christie traveled extensively in Slovenia and Croatia, and took inspiration from the true story of the Orient Express breaking down in the rural Croatia in winter for her book *Murder on the Orient Express.* This book includes a section in which the author tracks down Slovenian and Croatian locals who met Christie on her travels, and its musings on the countries are not to be missed.

LISTEN

"The Whistleblowers" by Laibach: This name of this uncharacterizable band—formed in the 1980s in former Yugoslavia—comes from the German word for Ljubljana, an ironic comment on the German occupation. This song picks up on the band's subversive spirit, inspired by whistleblowers Edward Snowden and Chelsea Manning.

the more medieval neighborhood across the river more efficient—preserving history while also beautifying it and making it more functional.

3. Central Market

Adamič-Lundrovo nabrežje 6; tel. 01 300 1200; 7am-4pm Mon.-Fri., 7am-2pm Sat.

The Triple Bridge funnels right into the **Town Square,** the center of **Old Town,** where the baroque and medieval buildings have a fairy-tale quality. Another of Plečnik's works, nearby Central Market is filled with colorful stands of fruits and vegetables. It's a great place to pick up sausages, homemade sauerkraut, and Slovenian cakes from friendly local vendors.

4. Dragon Bridge

At the at the corner of the square which houses the Central Market, Dragon Bridge is a wonderful example of art nouveau architecture and the first bridge to be paved with asphalt in Slovenia. The triple-hinged arched bridge is an important symbol of Ljubljana: Its menacing green dragon statues are a nod to Greek myth, which holds that the hero who stole the Golden Fleece, Jason, slayed a dragon that lived in the Ljubljanica River.

5. Ljubljana Castle

tel. 01 432 7216; www.ljubljanskigrad.si; 9am-8pm daily Apr.-May and Oct., 10am-7pm daily Dec., 10am-6pm Jan.-Mar. and Nov., 9am-9pm daily June-Sept.; €7.50

Head up the glass **funicular** (lower station is at Krek Square, opposite the Central Market; 10am-8pm daily Jan.-Mar. and Nov., 9am-9pm daily Apr.-May and Oct., 9am-11pm daily June-Sept., 10am-10pm daily Dec.; €4 return ticket, less with castle admission), or take the pleasant 20-minute trek up **Študentovska pot** to Ljubljana Castle.

The hill where Ljubljana Castle sits has been home to forts since at least the first century CE, first occupied by the Celts, then the Illyrians, and later the Romans. The medieval stone fortress today consists mainly of buildings from the 16th and 17th centuries, peeking above the treetops over the city. The highlights of the castle are the 15th-century **St. George's Chapel (Kapela sv. Jurija),** decorated with 60 colorful coats of arms

top, Ljubljana Castle; bottom, Congress Square

Slow It Down

Though it's true you can see most of the highlights of Zagreb, Ljubljana, and Trieste in a day, you can get much more out of these destinations if you slow down to their old-world speed, and take time to explore the beautiful countrysides around them as well. The relatively compact countries of Croatia and Slovenia pack a lot into a little space, and below are a few places to visit if you choose to allot more days to this special region.

Though a car is not necessary to travel between the cities on this route, it might come in handy if you want a bit more flexibility to visit the Croatian and Slovenian countrysides, where public transit is infrequent.

THE ZUMBERAK

West of Zagreb, just off the route to Slovenia, the Žumberak are filled with densely forested hills and the weekend homes of city-dwellers, and since the early 19th century, **Samobor** has served as the entry point to the mountains. With charming streets and local specialties including kremšnita (cream cake), this is a great place to get a sense of traditional Croatia and maybe go on a hike or two.

Samobor is just over 20 km (12 mi) west of Zagreb, a 30-minute drive; the Žumberak start about 30 km (18 mi) west of the capital.

SLOVENIA'S KARST REGION

Slovenia's Karst Region is littered with caves, none more famous than the **Postojna Cave** (Jamska cesta 30; tel. 05 700 0100; www.postojnska-jama.eu; visits every hour 9am-5pm daily May-June and Sept., every hour 9am-6pm daily July-Aug., 10am, 11am, noon, 2pm, 3pm, and 4pm daily Apr. and Oct., 10am, noon, and 3pm daily Jan.-Mar. and Nov.-Dec.; €27.90), a 23-km (14-mi) network of underground rock formations that are millions of years old. It's not far from the spectacular **Predjama Castle** (tel. 05 700 0100; www.postojnska-jama.eu; 10am-4pm daily Nov.-Mar., 10am-4pm daily Oct. and Apr., 9am-6pm daily May-June and Sept., 9am-7pm daily July-Aug.; €14.90), a towering white structure carved into the rock face on a hill—with a history that lives up to the fairy-tale appearance.

These two top tourist destinations are right on the road between Ljubljana and Trieste, 45 km (28 mi; 45 minutes) south of Slovenia's capital.

COASTAL ISTRIA

Just over the border from Trieste, the seaside villages of Coastal Istria—often called Slovenian Istria after its famous Croatian neighbor to the south—are wonderful to explore, filled with winding cobblestone streets that will satisfy those in search of a pretty view. A medieval walled Venetian town dating to Greek times, **Piran** is the prettiest city on the coast, with Venetian architecture, and a view of the lights of Trieste from the waterfront. Slow down here with a trip to **Mesečev Zaliv Beach,** sometimes called Moon Bay, and enjoy fresh seafood and sunsets over the Adriatic.

Piran is 120 km (1.5 hours) southwest of Ljubljana, and only 39 km (24 mi; 40 minutes) from Trieste, across the Italian border to the north.

top, town of Samobor; bottom, Postojna Cave

from the 18th century, and the 19th-century **Lookout Tower,** where you can get a super view of Ljubljana's rooftops and the Julian Alps in the distance. Eat a late lunch with a view at the castle café or one of two restaurants.

6. Wine-Tasting and Dinner

After your tour of the castle, head back down to the Old Town, stopping at **Upper Square (Gornji trg)** to see the city's oldest houses. Then relax with a bit of wine-tasting at **Wine Bar Suklje** (Breg 10; tel. 68 19 40 99; www.winebar.suklje.com; 9am-midnight Mon.-Thurs., 9am-1am Fri.-Sat., 9am-11pm Sun.; €4-8); many of Slovenia's 40,000 registered wineries are small operations, so it's likely you've never had the chance to try them. Finish your day with dinner at the lovely **Julija** restaurant (Stari trg 9; tel. 01 425 6463; www.julijarestaurant.com; noon-10pm daily; €19), where cozy shabby-chic décor inside or gingham tablecloth topped tables outside are lovely for savoring a meal of like scallops with lemon crème and gnocchi with truffles.

Trieste

Where to Stay: City Center

Arrive by: Bus from Ljubljana Bus Station to Trieste Autostazione (1.5 hours)

DAY 4

1. Piazza Unità d'Italia

Bordered by the Adriatic Sea on one side and a mountainous hinterland on the other, from where the famous bora wind originates, Trieste, on the Italy side of the Italy-Slovenia border, is compact by necessity, neatly organized along elegant Austro-Hungarian era boulevards. Arrive around midday, and head to the elegant and dramatic Piazza Unità d'Italia, which faces the sea. Bordered by impossibly grand Renaissance-inspired municipal buildings and palazzos, this square acts as a kind of living room for locals, who take their daily constitutionals here. Tourists sit at outdoor cafés admiring the imposing town hall and **Fountain of the Four Continents** in the center of the square—so called because at the

Piazza Unità d'Italia

★ Café Culture

Sipping coffee in a worldly café is an important local ritual in all of the cities on this route, but in Trieste, it's been elevated to an artform. Coffee has a long tradition here; the city was declared a free port under Austro-Hungarian rule in the 18th century, and it quickly became the main supplier of coffee for Viennese cafés up north. Trieste is home to similarly sumptuous cafés, many of which have hardly changed for over a century. These grand shrines to java don't just serve great coffee; they provide an elegant atmosphere that inspired poets, politicians, revolutionaries, and thousands of more ordinary drinkers. Today, you can soak it all up on sunny terraces or inside ornate rooms where locals gather daily for their favorite fix.

Whichever café you choose, keep in mind ordering is a little different in Trieste. For an espresso, ask for a **nero;** a cappuccino is called a **caffelatte;** and the most popular drink in town is a **capo in b,** a mini cappuccino served in a glass.

- **Caffè San Marco** (Via Cesare Battisti 18) is a time machine. It was founded in 1914 and that's what it looks like inside. Everything is original, from the bronze coffee leaves on the ceiling to the Viennese-style furnishings to the vintage copper espresso machines. There's a small bookstore and cast-iron tables where you can play chess and sip whatever you like for as long as you like.
- **Caffè Tommaseo** (Piazza Nicolò Tommaseo 4) began the caffeine rush in Trieste. It opened in 1830 and is the oldest café in the city. The atmosphere is old-world, with elegant antique mirrors and dark mahogany furniture that are literally from another era. Just find a seat in one of the cozy rooms and a uniformed waiter will be right with you.
- **Caffè degli Specchi** (Piazza Unità d'Italia 7) has a big advantage: It's located on the most beautiful square in the city. Although the interior is nice, here you'll want to sit outside and enjoy the view.

(top to bottom) Canal Grande di Trieste; Museo Revoltella; cicchetti at Al Ciketo; Castello di Miramare

time it was built, there were only four known continents. It's always lively and is worth a return visit at nightfall, when couples gather to watch the sunset.

If you're hungry after people-watching, have lunch at **Marise Osteria** (Via Felice Venezian 11; noon-2:30pm and 7pm-10:30pm Fri.-Wed.; €12-14), a family-run restaurant with a dozen tables. Food in Trieste has little to do with traditional Italian cuisine; menus have been influenced by centuries of Austro-Hungarian reign, and dishes like jota soup (sauerkraut, beans, potatoes, and sausage), goulash, and cevapcici (minced meat sausage) are local favorites.

2. Kleine Berlin

Via Fabio Severo; tel. 339 253 9712; www.cat.ts.it; €5

Next, get a sense of a pivotal period in Trieste's history, when the city was occupied by Germany at the end of World War II. The threat of air raids led the Nazis to build underground galleries to shelter soldiers and civilians. Little has changed underground since that time in these bunkers, and volunteers show small groups around the network of tunnels that provided protection when bombs were falling overhead (reservations required), and detailed videos and photographs bring this dark period in the city's history to life.

Though Italian Fascism never reached the extremes of German Nazism, and no concentration camps were built, after Italy surrendered to the allies, the Germans converted a large factory on the southern outskirts of Trieste into a transit camp that included a crematorium, today known as the **Risiera di San Sabba** (Via Giovanni Palatucci 5; tel. 040 826 202; www.risierasansabba.it; 9am-7pm daily; free). A lot of suffering took place here, and a visit isn't for everyone, but this is a concrete reminder of the horror men are capable of inflicting upon one another and always worth remembering. Entrance to this national monument is free and phones should remain on silent mode; it's a 10-minute drive (5 km/3 mi) south of the city center.

3. Strolling the Canal Grande di Trieste

Head back to the city center. Despite frequent comparisons to its nearby sister city, Trieste is no Venice, but it does have its own grand canal, where ships once docked and deposited merchandise from around the world when the city was the most important port in the Austro-Hungarian empire. Walking from the church of Sant'Antonio Nuovo, which marks the end of the canal, to the seafront, you'll pass small squares, bridges, and a statue of James Joyce, who lived in the city for 16 years. There also cafés and bars where university students gather for aperitivo (happy hour).

4. Sunset at Molo Audace

A stroll on this walkway that shoots out over 200 m (656 ft) into the Gulf of Trieste provides unrivaled views of the city and the hillsides beyond, and is another great sunset spot.

5. Dinner at Odio Il Brodo Trieste

Largo Santorio Santorio 5; tel. 040 260 7179; https://odioilbrodo.com; 11:30am-2:45pm and 6pm-9:30pm Tues.-Sat.; €8-14

As you make your way toward dinner, you'll walk some of the historic center's narrow streets and pass an ancient Roman archway, the **Arco di Riccardo,** along with a multitude of bars, clubs, and artisanal shops where bags, sculptures, and jewelry are still produced by hand. Have dinner at this gastronomic start-up in a neighborhood full of tempting culinary options. Odio il Brodo Trieste has made a name for itself by offering quality sandwiches and spectacular fries made with fresh ingredients.

DAY 5

Now that you've explored the center, visit the city's best museum, then head up the coast to explore an extravagant seaside castle.

1. Museo Revoltella

Via Armando Diaz 27; tel. 040 675 4350; www.museorevoltella.it; 9am-7pm Wed.-Mon.; €7 or €16 with exhibition

Museo Revoltella is Trieste's modern art—and best—museum, and feels like two museums in one. Part of the collection, which includes 19th- and 20th-century paintings by local and national artists, is housed within an ornate palace donated by a wealthy baron, while the other part is displayed in a modern gallery. The names on the walls aren't world famous (Lucio Fontana, Arnaldo Pomodoro, Ruggero Rovan), but they do illustrate the independent nature of artists in the city and how they evolved under Viennese influence.

2. Cicchetti at Al Ciketo

Via S. Sebastiano 6; tel. 040 246 0257; 10am-midnight daily; €7-10

Cicchetti are small bite size appetizers (€1-2) that are usually eaten standing up or seated on stools, and are often served with prosecco (€3.5)—a common ritual in Trieste's neighbor to the west, Venice. The street outside Al Ciketo is usually crowded, a good sign: Inside you can choose from creamed cod, cold cuts, grilled vegetables served on thin slices of fresh bread, and a long list of local wines.

Arco di Riccardo

3. Castello di Miramare

V.le Miramare; tel. 040 224 143; 9am-7pm daily; €10

Extravagant Castello Miramare is the incarnation of the cultural ferment that took place in Trieste during the 19th century. The flamboyant residence, the brainchild of Archduke Maximilian of Hapsburg, was built on a promontory just north of the city, easily reached by a quick 10-minute train ride. It's a mix of Gothic, medieval, Renaissance, Central European, and Mediterranean styles. Inside original furnishings decorate the apartments where the archduke and his family spent their summers and formal reception areas meant to impress visitors. Equally impressive are the gardens and terraces, ideal for a seaside walk.

4. Dinner at Buffet da Pepi

Via della Cassa di Risparmio, 3; tel. 040 366 858; www.buffetdapepi.it; 8:30am-10pm Mon.-Sat., 10am-4pm Sun.; plates from €9.50

When you are served a steaming plate of boiled meats with plenty of mustard at Buffet da Pepi, you might once again wonder if you're truly in Italy. The sliced meats here, served with plenty of sauerkraut, have roots in Austro-Hungarian cuisine, and Triestine buffet-style dining that emerged to feed dockworkers a quick, filling meal so they could get back to their jobs. A hot sausage washed down with a cold European-style beer in the steamy, classic dining room of Buffet da Pepi is the perfect way to end your Trieste trip.

TRANSPORTATION

Zagreb boasts the largest airport of the cities on this itinerary, though all three cities are well-connected to the rest of Europe by train and bus.

Air

Zagreb's airport receives flights from across Europe, as does Ljubljana's, though the latter offers fewer options. Trieste also has a small airport, but you may have more luck flying into Venice Airport, which is under two hours away and has more arrivals and departures.

- **Franjo Tuđman Airport Zagreb** (ZAG; www.zagreb-airport.hr): 17

Zagreb's funicular

• Rome, Florence, and Venice (page 139)
• The Magistrala Coastal Road (page 331)

km (10.5 mi) from the city center; 30 minutes to Zagreb's main bus station by Croatia Airlines bus (€5).

- **Jože Pučnik Airport** (Ljubljana) (LJU; www.lju-airport.si): 23 km (14 mi) northwest of central Ljubljana; 40 minutes to the city center by airport shuttle (€8).
- **Trieste Airport** (TRS; https://triesteairport.it/en/airport): 40 km (25 mi) northwest of Trieste; 35 minutes to the city by train (from €2).
- **Venice Marco Polo Airport** (VCE; www.veneziaairport.it/en): 148 km (92 mi) from Trieste; 2 hours from the city by bus (from €10).

Train

Given this route's proximity to European countries such as Austria and Hungary, traveling by train can be a great option if you're adding these cities onto another European itinerary.

- **Zagreb Glavni Kolovdor:** Zagreb's train station is conveniently located in the Lower Town.
- **Ljubljana Train Station:** Trains from Zagreb (2.5 hours; from €9 one-way) arrive at the main train station, conveniently located near the city center, a 10- to 15-minute trek north from the main sights.
- **Trieste Centrale:** The train station is located a 10-minute walk north of the city center.

Bus

Though trains do travel to all the cities covered here, sometimes the bus can be more reliable—and even quicker.

- **Bus Station Zagreb:** The city has a large and busy bus station with lots of connections, located east of Glavni Kolovdor.
- **Ljubljana Bus Station:** The bus station has both international and local connections and is located adjacent to the train station, a 10- to 15-minute walk north of the city center.
- **Trieste Autostazione:** Trieste's bus station is conveniently located near the train station, a 10-minute walk north of the city center. Buses from Ljubljana arrive here (1.5 hours; from €3 one-way).

Public Transportation

The centers of Zagreb, Ljubljana, and Trieste are very walkable. Besides a ride on Zagreb's **funicular,** the world shortest, to travel between the Upper and Lower Towns, or perhaps a ride on Trieste's efficient public transportation network to get to Castello di Miramare north of the city, these cities are all compact enough to get around **on foot.**

Getting Back

Return to Zagreb by bus (4 hours; €20); or, since you're so close to Venice, consider taking a bus to that city and its well-connected airport before heading to your next destination (2 hours; €10).

ROAD TRIPS

ROAD TRIPS
THE NORTH COAST 500
Inverness
CAUSEWAY COAST
Derry
Belfast
UNITED KINGDOM
North Sea
Irish Sea
IRELAND
ICELAND'S RING ROAD
Ísafjörður
Húsavík
Akureyri
Egilsstaðir
Grundarfjörður
ICELAND
Borgarnes
REYKJAVÍK
Keflavík
Selfoss
Höfn
NETHERLANDS
BELGIUM
English Channel
FRANCE
ATLANTIC OCEAN
Bay of Biscay
BORDEAUX AND THE PYRENEES
Bordeaux
Cauterets
AND.
PORTUGAL
SPAIN
Mediterranean Se
MOROCCO
ALGERIA
60°
10°
0°
50°
40°

FINLAND
NORWAY
RUSSIA
SWEDEN
DENMARK
Baltic Sea
POLAND
GERMANY
LOFOTEN
Svolvær
Å
Norwegian Sea
SWEDEN
NORWAY
UKRAINE
CZECHIA
Würzburg
ROMANTISCHE STRASSE
Füssen
SLOVAKIA
MOLDOVA
ROMANIA
AUSTRIA
HUNGARY
SWITZ.
TRANSYLVANIA
Bucharest
SLO.
CROATIA
Black Sea
BOSNIA & HERZEGOVINA
SERBIA
ITALY
Adriatic Sea
Zadar
BULGARIA
Florence
Orvieto
Dubrovnik
MONTENEGRO
KOS.
NORTH MACEDONIA
TUSCANY AND UMBRIA
THE MAGISTRALA COASTAL ROAD
ALBANIA
Aegean Sea
TURKEY
GREECE
TUNISIA
MALTA

ICELAND'S RING ROAD

Why Go: The most popular way to tour Iceland, a road trip on the scenic Ring Road, which circles the entirety of Iceland, takes in some of the country's most well-known attractions and also reveals some unexpected gems.

Number of Days: 9

Total Distance: 1,332 km (828 mi)

Seasons: Summer

Start/End: Reykjavík

Iceland is revered for its breathtaking landscapes, which insist not just on being seen, but being experienced. Here, you can witness a rainbow materialize over a thundering waterfall, then soak away your worries in a geothermal pool. In summer, the days seem endless—the sun shines for nearly 24 hours around the solstice—the ideal time to embark on an epic drive around the Ring Road.

Paved for most of its 1,332-km (828-mi) length, the Ring Road (Route 1) encircles the island and is the most accessible route around the country. On this trip, you'll encounter breathtaking landscapes ranging from towering mountains to barren lava fields to glaciers looming in the distance. For scenery and adventure, Iceland is unmatched.

TOP 3

★ Visiting **Gullfoss** along the Golden Circle route. If you see one waterfall in Iceland, let it be this spectacular example (page 235).

★ Standing in awe of **Jökulsárlón,** an icy, otherworldly glacial lake (page 238).

★ **Whale-watching in Húsavik,** a tiny town that has earned its reputation as as the whale-watching capital of the island (page 239).

ICELAND'S RING ROAD

Greenland Sea
Grímsey
Raufarhöfn
Kópasker
Norwegian Sea
85
Bajjaflói
Whale-Watching in Húsavík
Eyjafjörður
85
Bakkafjörður
Húsavík
Ásbyrgi
Vopnafjörður
82
845
Vopnafjörður
Laugar
87
Reykjahlíð
917
Akureyri
Goðafoss
Lake Mývatn
Mývatn Nature Baths
1
85
Lake Mývatn
Egilsstaðir
Lagarfljót
1
95
955
Fáskrúðsfjörður
Stöðvarfjörður
Hálslón
1
Kvíslavatn
Vatnajökull
Höfn
1
Jökulsárlón
Langisjór
Vatnajökull National Park
1
Overnight Stop
Route
0
25 mi
0
25 km

Keflavík International Airport to Reykjavík

1. Blue Lagoon

Svartsengi; tel. 354/420-8800; www.bluelagoon.com; 8am-9pm daily Aug. 19-May 30, 7am-11pm May 31-June 27, and 7am-midnight June 28-Aug. 18, must be booked in advance

After landing at Keflavík International Airport in the morning or afternoon, pick up your rental car and head south. Make your first stop in Iceland a relaxing soak at the Blue Lagoon. Built on an 800-year-old lava field, the Blue Lagoon draws visitors from around the world to soak in its gloriously milky-blue waters amid a dreamlike atmosphere. The water is geothermally heated, and the bottom is covered with white silica mud. It's common to see visitors cover their faces with the mud—it's great for your skin, and all guests receive a free silica mud mask with standard admission.

You must book a time slot on the Blue Lagoon's website several weeks ahead of your arrival. This is a popular activity, so make your reservation soon after you book your flights.

Driving Directions: From Keflavík International Airport, it's a 25-minute (21.5-km/13.4-mi) drive east on Route 41 and then south on Route 43.

2. Sightseeing in Reykjavík

Revived, you're ready to explore Iceland's vibrant capital city, starting at **Hallgrímskirkja** (Hallgrímstorgi 1; tel. 354/510-1000; www.hallgrimskirkja.is; 10am-5pm daily; free), Reykjavík's landmark church. The modern concrete building's basalt-style columns reach 73 m (240 ft) high, and the church is home to

Blue Lagoon

Key Reservations

- Reserve a time slot at the **Blue Lagoon.**
- A **Glacier Lagoon boat tour** at Jökulsárlón should be arranged in advance.
- It is highly recommended to book **accommodations** in advance, as options are limited in many parts of the island.
- In the busy summer tourist season, book your **rental car** in advance, as some dealers sell out early.

Jökulsárlón

a gorgeous organ and beautiful stained glass windows. The highlight for many is a visit to the top of the tower (1,000ISK), which has spectacular views of the city.

Walk down the main street, **Laugavegur,** popping into the many shops and cafés, then stroll around **Tjörnin,** a small pond rich with birdlife, situated next to **Reykjavík City Hall** (Tjarnagata 11; tel. 354/411-1111; https://visitreykjavik.is; 8:30am-4:30pm daily). The scenic strip of colorful houses surrounding the pond begs to be photographed. For dinner, head to trendy **Fiskmarkaðurinn** (Aðalstræti 12; tel. 354/578-8877; www.fiskmarkadurinn.is; 5:30pm-10:30pm daily; entrées from 4,900ISK) for the freshest catch of the day.

Driving Directions: From the Blue Lagoon, it's a 50-minute (49-km/30-mi) drive to Reykjavík. Head north on Route 43, and then east on Route 41. Route 41 becomes Route 40; turn onto Route 49 west to get to Reykjavík city center.

THE ICELANDIC HOT DOG

Hot dogs are wildly popular among Icelanders. Called **pylsur,** Icelandic hot dogs are done up in a traditional bun with chopped onions, mustard, ketchup, crispy fried onions, and pickled mayonnaise. They're delicious. Here are a couple places to try them when you're in Reykjavík:

- **Bæjarins Beztu Pylsur** (Tryggvatagata 1; tel. 354/511-1566; www.bbp.is; 10am-1am Sun.-Thurs., 10am-4:30am Fri.-Sat.; 450ISK): Perhaps the quintessential place to try an Icelandic hot dog, this tiny shack has long been delighting tourists and locals alike.

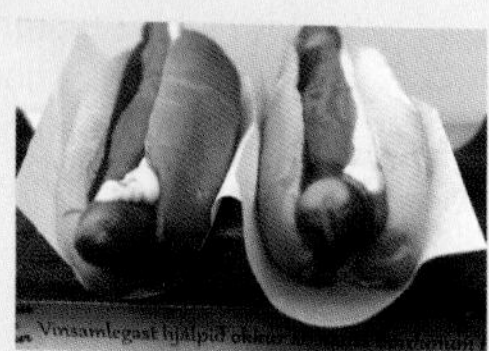

- **Lobster Hut** (tel. 354/691-3007; 11:30am-8pm daily; from 1,600ISK): Check Facebook for the location of this food truck that specializes in all things lobster, including lobster hot dogs.

DAY 2

Reykjavík to the Golden Circle and Selfoss

1. Þingvellir National Park

Route 36, 47 km/30 mi (45 minutes) northwest of Reykjavík; free, parking 750ISK

The **Golden Circle** encompasses the three most visited sights in South Iceland: Þingvellir National Park, Geysir, and Gullfoss. Your first stop is Þingvellir National Park, a geological wonder and also the birthplace of democracy in Iceland—it's said that a group of settlers met as a democratic legislature here close to a millennium ago. The park is home to the Mid-Atlantic Ridge fault line, which means visitors can literally plant one foot on Europe's side and the other in North America. Outside of Reykjavík, Þingvellir is the most visited site in Iceland.

Start at the **Þingvellir Interpretive Center** (tel. 354/482-2660; www.thingvellir.is; 9am-8pm daily June-Aug., 9am-5pm Sept.-Apr.; free) for a great overview of the national park's history and geographical significance, and to pick up maps for hiking trails.

One highlight of the park's stony, moss-covered landscape is **Almannagjá** (All Man's Gorge), which is the tallest cliff face in the national park and the original backdrop to Iceland's first parliament. This impressive rock structure is considered the edge of the North American plate. Another must-see is **Lögberg** (Law Rock). During Iceland's Commonwealth period (930-1262), members of the Alþing (parliament) gave speeches and held events at the rock.

Driving Directions: Take Route 49 east, which turns into Route 1 (the Ring Road). Take Route 1 to Route 36 and drive east to Þingvellir National Park. The drive takes 50 minutes (48 km/30 mi).

2. Geysir and Strokkur

Get back in the car and drive 50 minutes

left, Geysir; right, Gullfoss

to your next stop, Geysir, the country's most famous example of natural geothermal energy—it's actually the source of the word "geyser." Visitors to the site today unfortunately aren't going to see the dormant Geysir erupt—it hasn't blown since 2005. Thankfully, Geysir's nearby cousin, **Strokkur** (Churn), erupts every seven minutes or so. Crowds gather to watch the frequent eruptions, and the churning, gurgling pool of hot water turning out a rush of pressure from the clay-like earth is an impressive sight.

Have lunch in the cafeteria at **Geysir Center** (Biskupstungnabraut; tel. 354/519-6020; 9am-10pm daily June 1-Aug. 31 and 9am-6pm Sept. 1-May 31), a large visitor's center where you can also shop for souvenirs.

Driving Directions: Take Route 36 east, which turns into Route 365 and leads to a roundabout to Route 37. Continue east to reach Geysir (total drive 50 minutes; 60 km/37 mi).

★ 3. Gullfoss

After lunch, head to nearby Gullfoss (Golden Falls), Iceland's most famous and most photographed waterfall. There are three levels of water at the falls, ranging from 11 to 21 m (36-69 ft), meeting at a 70-m (230-ft) gorge. If you get too close, expect to get soaked. Because of Iceland's changing weather, you have a good chance to see a rainbow over the falls, making for a perfect snapshot of your visit. Take some time to walk around, enjoying not only the wonder of the falls but also the beautiful surrounding landscape.

Driving Directions: Drive northeast on Route 35 for 10 minutes (10 km/6 mi).

4. Overnight in Selfoss

After a long day of sightseeing, drive to Selfoss, the largest town in South Iceland and a service hub where you'll find plenty of places to fill up your gas tank, get a bite to eat, or rest your head in one of several nice hotels or guesthouses.

Driving Directions: Selfoss is a one-hour (72-km/45-mi) drive from Gullfoss. Take Route 35 southwest to Route 1.

Selfoss to Vík

1. Seljalandsfoss

After having breakfast at your hotel, set off on today's drive, which is full of waterfalls. From Selfoss, drive along the spectacular south coast on Route 1. Stop at beautiful Seljalandsfoss, a highlight for many visitors to the South Coast. You'll delight in the spray from the 40-m (131-ft) falls, but what makes this waterfall unique is a path that lets you walk behind it for a memorable view.

Driving Directions: Take Route 1 east for 1 hour (70 km/43 mi). Turn left on Þórsmerkurvegur (Route 249) for the Seljalandsfoss parking lot.

2. Skógafoss

Up next, head to Skógafoss in the village of **Skógar.** Skógafoss is another epic waterfall, one of the biggest in the country. It looms 25 m (82 ft) high and has a drop-off of 60 m (197 ft). According to Viking lore, a local settler buried a treasure chest in a cave behind the waterfall. It was said that locals discovered the chest years later, but it quickly disappeared before they could grasp it. It's common to see rainbows over the falls here too.

Driving Directions: Take Route 1 east for 30 minutes (30 km/19 mi). Turn left on Skógar, then left again on Skógafoss to reach the parking lot.

3. Reynisfjara Black-Sand Beach

Your next stop is Reynisfjara beach near the village of Vík. This is probably the most famous of Iceland's black-sand strands, which get their hue from the island's intense volcanic activity: The sediment was once boiling hot lava. The juxtaposition of the white waves crashing on the stark black sand and pebbles is beautiful. From the beach, you can see **Reynisdrangar,** a cluster of striking basalt sea stacks that jut out from a sandy beach. It's fun to climb on the stacks and take photos, then roam the black-sand

left, Reynisfjara black-sand beach; right, Seljalandsfoss

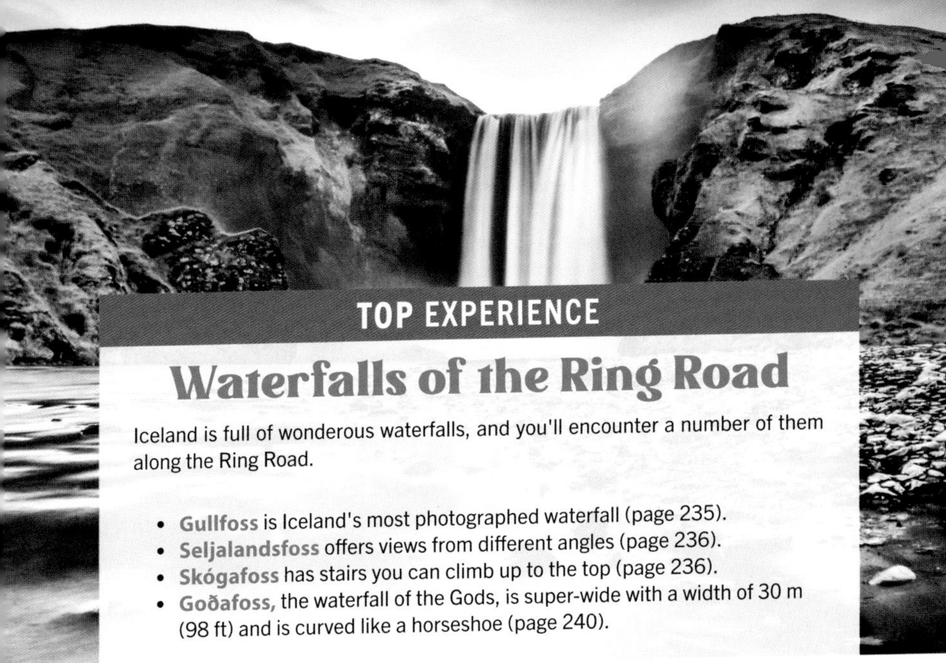

TOP EXPERIENCE

Waterfalls of the Ring Road

Iceland is full of wonderous waterfalls, and you'll encounter a number of them along the Ring Road.

- **Gullfoss** is Iceland's most photographed waterfall (page 235).
- **Seljalandsfoss** offers views from different angles (page 236).
- **Skógafoss** has stairs you can climb up to the top (page 236).
- **Goðafoss,** the waterfall of the Gods, is super-wide with a width of 30 m (98 ft) and is curved like a horseshoe (page 240).

beach, picking up stones and admiring the rock formations.

Driving Directions: Drive east on Route 1 for 30 minutes (34 km/21 mi), then turn toward the coast on Reynishverfisvegur (Route 215) to reach the parking lot.

4. Refuel in Vík

Backtrack to Route 1 and head east to the tiny town of Vík (home to fewer than 400 people), where you'll spend the night. Be sure to stop at **Skool Beans** (Klettsvegur; tel. 354/830-0079; www.skoolbeans.com; 9am-5pm Tues.-Fri., 10am-5pm Sat.-Sun.) for a late-afternoon pick-me-up; delicious coffee, hot chocolate, and snacks are served out of this bright yellow school bus. For dinner, have a hearty meal at **Strondin Pub** (Austurvegi 18; tel. 354/790-1442; www.strondin.is; noon-11pm daily; entrées from 2,790ISK), a cozy gastropub in the heart of Vík that's a great place to stop for homecooked comfort food.

Driving Directions: Take Route 215 north, then Route 1 east to Vík (15 minutes; 10 km/6 mi).

DAY 4

Vík to Höfn

1. Vatnajökull National Park

Get ready to see some icebergs today, as you drive the Ring Road to Vatnajökull National Park. **Skaftafell**—which used to be its own national park and is now the southern part of Vatnajökull National Park—is the home of Europe's largest ice cap. This is one of East Iceland's most beautiful places, where visitors are treated to views of striking white glaciers against a backdrop of green fields and black-sand beaches.

Stop by **Skaftafellsoffa** (Skaftafells vegur; tel. 354/478-1627; www.vatna jokulsthjodgardur.is; 10am-6pm daily Jan.-Feb., 9am-6pm daily Mar.-May, 8am-7pm daily June-Aug., 9am-6pm daily Sept.-Oct., 10am-6pm daily Nov.-Dec.), the national park office, for information about the many footpaths and hiking trails in the region. Plan to spend the morning here hiking and taking in some of the park's many vistas and waterfalls.

Driving Directions: Drive east along Route 1 for two hours (140 km/86 mi).

★ 2. Boat Tour on Jökulsárlón

Continue on Route 1 for about an hour to Jökulsárlón (Glacier Lagoon), a spectacular sight that begs to be photographed. Chunks of ice are scattered about this lagoon—the deepest lake in Iceland—and walls of ice jut from the sea, while icebergs of various sizes float on the water. Huge blocks of ice constantly break off the Breiðamerkurjökull glacier into the lagoon and then slowly move toward a river mouth and the Atlantic Ocean.

Take a 40-minute boat tour of the lagoon, which you should book in advance, with **Glacier Lagoon** (Jökulsárlón Ehf; tel. 354/478-2222; www.icelagoon.is; 10am-5pm daily in May, 9am-7pm daily June-Sept., 10am-5pm daily in Oct.; 5,800ISK). During the excursion, you sail among the huge icebergs, get to taste the 1,000-year-old ice, and, if you're lucky, see seals bobbing in the lagoon.

Driving Directions: Take Route 1 east for an hour (58 km/36 mi) to Jökulsárlón.

3. Overnight in Höfn

Get back on Route 1 and drive to the sleepy town of Höfn, where you'll spend the night. Have dinner at **Pakkhús Restaurant** (Hafnarbraut 4; tel. 354/478-1200; www.pakkhus.is; langoustine entrées from 5,900ISK, other entrées from 2,900ISK).

Driving Directions: Take Route 1 east, then Route 99 south (1 hour; 80 km/40 mi).

DAY 5

Höfn to Lake Mývatn

1. Pit Stop at Petra's Stone Collection

Fjarðarbraut 21, Stöðvarfjörður; tel. 354/475-8834; www.steinapetra.is; 9am-6pm daily May 1-Sept. 30, closed Oct. 1-Apr 30. and Feb.-Apr.; 1,500ISK, free for children 13 and under

About 2.5 hours into your drive, make a stop at Petra's Stone Collection, right off the Ring Road in **Stöðvarfjörður.** This stunning private collection includes more than 1,000 cut and polished stones and is a good place to break up your drive. The owner started amassing stones in 1976, and the collection includes lava, crystals, basalt, pearls, granite, opals, and amethysts.

Driving Directions: Take Route 1 north for 2.5 hours (180 km/112 mi) to reach Stöðvarfjörður.

2. Lunch in Fáskrúðsfjörður

Continue to nearby Fáskrúðsfjörður, nestled on a long fjord of the same name and one of the most unique towns in the country. This small village of fewer than 500 people is the most "French" part of Iceland: The village was originally a base for more than 5,000 French fishermen who came every year to fish, and some settled here in the late 19th century. The history remains in some of the architecture and in the streets themselves, marked in both Icelandic and French. After spending some time exploring, stop for lunch at **Café Sumarlína** (Búðavegur 59; tel. 354/475-1575; www.sumarlina.is; 11am-10pm daily; entrées from 2,650ISK).

top, Lagarfljót; bottom, Petra's Stone Collection

Driving Directions: Take Route 1 north for 25 minutes (28 km/17 mi). Fáskrúðsfjörður is on Route 955.

3. Lagarfljót

Up next, visit the town of **Egilsstaðir** to stretch your legs at Lagarfljót, a long and narrow lake with a legend. Scotland has the Loch Ness monster, and Iceland has **Lagarfljótsormur,** a huge worm-like monster said to call this freshwater, glacier-fed lake home. Take a few minutes to see if you can spot this humped, slithering monster before getting back in the car.

Driving Directions: Drive north on Route 1 for 45 minutes (50 km/31 mi).

4. Lake Mývatn

Drive another two hours northwest toward Lake Mývatn. Just before reaching the lake, you'll pass the sulfurous, multicolored Námaskarð pass, striking for its otherworldly atmosphere of yellow and brown colors of the clay and gray mud pools.

After all that driving, you deserve a relaxing soak at the **Mývatn Nature Baths** (tel. 354/464-4411; www.myvatnnaturebaths.is; 9am-midnight daily May 15-Sept. 30, noon-10pm daily Oct. 1-May 14; Jan. 1-Apr. 30 4,500ISK, May 1-Sept. 30 5,300ISK, Oct. 1-Dec. 31 4,500ISK). This lagoon is far less crowded than the Blue Lagoon, and a dip in the mineral-rich waters is beneficial for skin problems such as eczema and psoriasis, as well as respiratory issues. The views of the landscape are beautiful, with the volcanic crater of Hverfjall and the edge of Lake Mývatn in the background.

Fuel up at the lagoon's café, or choose one of several restaurants and hotels around scenic Lake Mývatn.

Driving Directions: Drive northeast along the Ring Road for just over two hours (177 km/110 mi).

DAY 6

Detour to Húsavík

★ 1. Whale-Watching

Today you'll drive to Húsavík. A worthwhile detour off the Ring Road, this placid seaside town has become Iceland's unofficial whale-watching capital. The main whale-watching season runs from the middle of May to the end of October, but the high season is June and July, when you have the best chance to see as many as 12 species of whales, with the most common being minke and humpback whales. If you're lucky, you'll also spot fin whales, orcas, and blue whales. You can always count on sighting dolphins, as they love to hang out close to the bay.

Take a morning whale-watching tour with **Gentle Giants** (tel. 354/464-1500; www.gentlegiants.is; 3-hour tour adults 10,400ISK, ages 7-15 4,400ISK, 6 and under free) to get a glimpse of these giant mammals.

Afterward, stroll along the **harbor** and have a seafood lunch at **Naustið** (Naustagarður 2; tel. 354/464-1520; noon-10pm daily; entrées from 2,800ISK).

Driving Directions: Take Route 1 along the west side of Lake Mývatn to Route 845, and Route 85 north to Húsavík (50 minutes; 62 km/38 mi).

2. Ásbyrgi

From Húsavík, make an excursion to Ásbyrgi (Shelter of the Gods), a horseshoe-shaped gorge full of interesting rock formations, lush grass, well-maintained walking paths, thriving birdlife, and several bodies of water, including rivers and waterfalls. Follow the 1-km (0.6-mi) **footpath** starting from the parking lot; it takes 30-60 minutes, depending on how often you pause to soak in the natural beauty. At the bottom of the canyon you'll see small lakes, thick trees, and interesting rock formations.

Driving Directions: Drive east along Route 85 to the Ásbyrgi turnoff (50 minutes; 62 km/39 mi).

top, Húsavík; bottom, whale-watching

3. Overnight in Húsavík

Head back to Húsavík to have a hearty dinner of fish and lamb dishes at **Gamlí Baukur** (Hafnarstett 9; tel. 354/464-2442; www.gamlibaukur.is; 9am-9pm daily; entrées from 2,700ISK), and spend the night in town.

Driving Directions: Take Route 85 west to Húsavík (50 minutes; 62 km/39 mi).

DAY 7

Húsavík to Siglufjörður

1. Goðafoss

Rejoin the Ring Road and get ready to see the "Waterfall of the Gods": Goðafoss, one of the most beautiful waterfalls on the island. In a country full of spectacular waterfalls, what sets Goðafoss apart is its sheer width. White water surges over the rim, thundering down and crashing into rocks and water. It's quite a show. Plan to spend some time here, walking along the perimeter, snapping photos, and taking in the beauty.

Driving Directions: Take Route 85 south to Route 845. Head south to rejoin Route 1 and continue south to Goðafoss (40 minutes; 47 km/29 mi).

2. Akureyri

Get back in the car and continue along the Ring Road until you reach Akureyri. As northern Iceland's biggest city, Akureyri has a thriving art scene and restaurants that rival Reykjavík's.

Be sure to visit the **Akureyri Botanical Gardens** (Eyrarlandsholt; tel. 354/462-7487; www.lystigardur.akureyri.is; 8am-10pm Mon.-Fri., 9am-10pm Sat.-Sun. June-Sept.; free), one of the northernmost botanical gardens in the world. The gorgeous grounds boast native and international species alike. You'll also find walking paths, bridges, and a fountain.

Make your way to the city center (a few minutes' drive or a 10-minute walk from the Botanical Garden) to check out the exquisite **Akureyrarkirkja** church (Eyrarlandsvegur; tel. 354/462-7700; www.akureyrarkirkja.is; 10am-4pm Mon.-Sat., 4pm-7pm Sun. June 15-Aug. 15; free) and perhaps visit some art museums and galleries. Have lunch at **Berlín Akureyri** (Skipagata 4; tel. 354/772-5061; entrées from 1,350ISK), where you'll find breakfast classics like bacon, eggs, and pancakes.

Driving Directions: Drive west on Route 1 for 1.5 hours (83 km/52 mi) to reach Akureyri.

3. Overnight in Siglufjörður

From Akureyri, set off along the western side of **Tröllaskagi** (Troll Peninsula). You'll be following **Eyjafjörður,** Iceland's longest fjord, with breathtaking views of mountains and jagged cliffs. After just over an hour, you'll reach the pretty town of Siglufjörður.

Check out the **harbor** area and visit the fascinating **Herring Era Museum** (Snorragata 10; tel. 354/467-1604; www.sild.is; 10am-6pm daily June-Aug., 1pm-5pm daily May and Sept., by appointment rest of the year; 1,800ISK), dedicated to the fishing industry that was this town's livelihood for generations; or maybe the **Folk Music Center** (Norðurgata 1; tel. 354/467-2300; www.folkmusik.is; noon-6pm daily June-Aug., by request rest of year; 800ISK), showcasing a collection of classic Icelandic folk songs along with interesting instruments, photographs, and film clips.

Have dinner at the **Kaffi Rauðka** (Gránugata 19; tel. 354/467-1550; www.kaffiraudka.is; 11am-10pm daily; from 800ISK), where you can have a delicious pizza sitting in the restaurant's outdoor seating area if the weather's nice, before bedding down for the night.

Driving Directions: Drive north from Akureyri for one hour (78 km/48 mi) to reach Siglufjörður. Take Route 1 north to Route 82, which turns into Route 76.

DAY 8

Siglufjörður to Grundarfjörður

1. Skagafjörður Heritage Museum

tel. 354/453-6173; www.glaumbaer.is; 10am-4pm Mon.-Fri. Apr 1.-May 19, 9am-6pm daily May 20-Sept. 20, 10am-4pm daily Sept. 21-Oct. 20, open by request rest of year; adults 1,700ISK, under 17 free

Today's long journey to the Snæfellsnes Peninsula will take nearly the entire day. Make a pit stop about a third of the way through your drive in Skagafjörður, a region known for its Icelandic horses, and visit the Skagafjörður Heritage Museum, where you can learn about the turf houses Icelanders used to call home. The museum is mostly made up of 13 buildings that

MAKE IT Active

From scaling soaring mountaintops to diving into some of the clearest water in the world, Iceland is world-class destination for outdoor recreation.

HIKING

Iceland is undeniably a hiker's paradise, and these are just a few of the hikes you can enjoy while on your Ring Road trip. Near Reykjavík, the 8-km (5-mi) hike to the summit of **Mount Esja** is a favorite hiking destination (25 minutes; 22 km/14 mi north of Reykjavík, accessible from Route 1). Þingvellir National Park is also lovely for the casual hiker; try the short hike to the **Öxarárfoss** waterfall (4.5 km/2.7 mi). Finally, **Rauðhóll** (2.3 km/1.4 mi) is a leisurely hike within Snæfellsjökull National Park that takes hikers around a vast, jagged lava field giving unobstructed views of Snæfellsjökull Glacier looming in the distance.

DIVING

For those who aren't afraid of taking a dip in some chilly water, the **Silfra fissure** in Þingvellir National Park is a popular site for diving and snorkeling. The crystal-clear water reveals an underwater world with jagged canyon walls, plant life, and fish. **Dive Iceland** (Ásbúðartröð 17, Hafnarfjör›ur; tel. 354/699-3000; www.dive.is) offers a Silfra diving tour for 31,490ISK.

GLACIER TREKING

An experienced tour operator offers guests the unique opportunity to hike on a glacier, rather than just view the magnificent icecaps from afar. **Icelandic Mountain Guides** (tel. 354/587-9999; www.mountainguides.is) offers a 2.5-hour guided walking tour on the Svínafellsjökull glacier tongue in Skaftafell for 9,300ISK.

ZIPLINING

In the town of Vík in southern Iceland, **True Adventure** (Suðurvíkurvegur 5; tel. 354/698-8890; www.trueadventure.is; 14,900ISK) offers a fun one-hour zipline tour through in the region. You'll be surrounded by sweeping valleys and waterfalls as you zip through the air.

view of Mount Esja

make up part of what used to be the Glaumbær farm; the farm's roots date back to the 11th century, but the last residents departed the area in the mid-20th century. Each building had its own function, ranging from a kitchen to a sleeping room.

Driving Directions: Drive west and south on Route 76 out of Siglufjörður, and then take Route 75 west to Skagafjörður (1.5 hours; 107 km/66 mi).

2. Grundarfjörður

After a long drive through northwestern Iceland, you'll eventually reach your turnoff: a detour around Route 54, a semi-elliptical road circling the beautiful Snæfellsnes Peninsula. One of the peninsula's most arresting sights is Kirkjufell, near the town of **Grundarfjörður.** Popular with photographers in Iceland thanks to its unique shape, when viewed from the south, the mountain looks very thin, coming to a point at the top, resembling a fin. To stretch your legs upon arriving in Grundarfjörður, explore the picturesque beaches around the mountain and take pictures of it from every angle.

You'll stay in this tiny town for the evening, taking a relaxing soak and mingling with the locals at **Grundarfjörður Swimming Pool** (Borgarbraut 19; tel. 354/430-8564; 7am-9pm Mon.-Fri., 10am-6pm Sat.-Sun.; 900ISK), then heading to **Kirkjufell Hotel** (Nesvegur 8; tel. 354/438-6893; www.kirkjufellhotel.is; rooms from 19,000ISK) for the night; the in-house **restaurant** (breakfast 7am-10am, dinner 5pm-9pm daily; entrées from 2,800ISK) has a reputation for excellent seafood.

Driving Directions: Drive west for four hours (285 km/177 mi). Start Route 1, then Route 59, and finally Route 54.

DAY 9

Grundarfjörður to Snæfellsjökull National Park and Borgarnes

1. Snæfellsjökull National Park

On the morning of the last full day of your Ring Road trip, you'll drive to Snæfellsjökull National Park. Perhaps the most beautiful park in Iceland, Snæfellsjökull National Park's eponymous **glacier** became world famous after author Jules Verne described it as the starting point in his novel *Journey to the Center of the Earth*. Though it's not possible to explore the glacier unless on a guided tour, its ice-capped glory provides a gorgeous backdrop for your drive as you round the tip of the Snæfellsnes Peninsula.

Some of the more picturesque landmarks, the park's southern cliffs—**Dritvík Cove** and **Lóndrangar Cliffs,** as well as **Hellnar** and **Arnarstapi Cliffs**—are known for their rich bird life. These sites are all within minutes of each other, so plan to spend the entire morning driving short distances, wandering footpaths, and enjoying the vistas of this beautiful national park, with Snæfellsjökull glacier looming in the background.

Driving Directions: Drive on Route 54 to Route 574 around Snæfellsjökull National Park. From Grundarfjörður, the most direct route is to take the northern stretch of Route 54 to Route 574 and approach the park from the north (1 hour; 52 km/32 mi).

WATCH

101 Reykjavík: Based on the 2007 novel by Hallgrímur Helgason, this fun tale follows an unemployed twentysomething whose life takes an unexpected turn when a former girlfriend announces she's pregnant.

READ

Independent People by Halldór Laxness: Laxness remains Iceland's sole recipient of the Nobel Prize for Literature for this 1946 novel. The tale follows the life of a Bjartur, a sheep farmer, as he grapples with life, loss, and the sacrifices he made to achieve independence.

LISTEN

"It's Oh So Quiet" by Björk: Icelanders tend to be quite proud of Björk, for her work both an artist and an environmentalist.

"Hoppípolla" by Sigur Rós: These indie favorites have been recording since 1994.

"Little Talks" by Of Monsters and Men: This song by the Icelandic band took the world by storm in 2011.

2. Borgarnes

On your way back to Reykjavík, stop at the lovely town of Borgarnes. Have a pizza lunch at **La Colina** (Hrafnaklettur 1b; tel. 354/437-0110; 5pm-9pm Mon.-Fri., noon-9pm Sat.-Sun.; entrées from 2,100ISK) and visit the **Settlement Center** museum (Brákarbraut 13-15; tel. 354/437-1600; www.landnam.is/eng; 10am-9pm daily; adults 2,500ISK, students/seniors 1,900ISK, under 14 free), where you can learn about the sagas, Iceland's rich literary and historical tales. Interactive displays and replica dwellings show what the earliest days of Icelanders during the settlement were like, from food to fashion.

Driving Directions: Drive east on Route 54 for 1.5 hours (134 km/83 mi).

3. Return to Reykjavík

Get back on the Ring Road and drive to Reykjavík to spend a low-key evening in the city after your long journey and before you head home. Spend time visiting the city's bustling **Grandi** harbor area, taking in the glass-paneled, architecturally significant **Harpa** concert hall (Austurbakki 2; tel. 354/528-5000; www.harpa.is; 9am-10pm daily) and the dramatically situated waterfront ***Sun Voyager (Sæbraut)*** sculpture, which resembles a Viking ship.

Driving Directions: Take Route 1 south for one hour. Route 49 heads west into Reykjavík (76 km/47 mi from Borgarnes).

TRANSPORTATION

Air

Keflavík International Airport (KEF; tel. 354/425-6000; www.kefairport.is) is about 50 minutes west of Reykjavík by car. There are many car rental companies with offices at the airport, including Hertz, Avis, and Budget.

Road Trip Tips

Car Rental

If you are planning a summer ring road trip, a **2WD** car will be adequate, though having a **4WD** vehicle wouldn't hurt. In the winter, you will want a car with **studded tires** for potentially icy roads. In the busy summer tourist season, it is recommended to **arrange your rental in advance** because some dealers sell out early. In Iceland, you will find a number of international rental car agencies including **Hertz, Avis,** and **Budget,** as well as local rental agencies. Note that although this is arguably the best way to see Iceland, it's not a cheap trip: Car rental prices are very expensive, and gas prices are sky high compared to many other counties (approximately $6.50 per gallon). A rental for a small car starts at 18,000ISK per day.

Deciding what kind of **insurance** to get is extremely important (sand and ash insurance, for instance). Collision damage waiver insurance is included in the price of the rental, and it is recommended to get additional **gravel protection insurance.** When collecting your car, you should **take photos of existing damage** to the vehicle, and make sure you understand your rental agreement and insurance policy. Check all the lights and tires, and make sure there's a **spare tire. Paper maps** are preferable to GPS devices.

Traveling around Iceland by **campervan** is a popular option in season, but note that travelers must stay at **campsites,** where you will have access to facilities like toilets, showers, and cooking areas, so this makes sense only during the summer months when campsites are open.

Getting Gas

Gas stations are located around the ring road, but there are pockets where they become scarce, namely between **Vík** in the south and **Mývatn** in the north. It's a good idea to fill your tank when you have the opportunity.

Unmanned gas stations are common in rural areas. You must have a **4-digit PIN** for your credit card to fill up at these gas stations. If you don't have a card with a PIN, contact your bank ahead of your visit.

Driving Laws

There are a few rules travelers should be aware of when driving the Ring Road.

- **Off-road driving is strictly prohibited** and there are hefty fines from authorities.
- All passengers in a vehicle must **wear a seat belt.**
- **Talking on a mobile phone** while driving is prohibited.
- **Driving under the influence** is illegal and fines start at 80,000ISK.
- Drivers must **use headlights at all times,** even in bright daylight.

Speed Limits

Speeding **fines** are high, and can be collected through the rental car company, which will have an imprint of your credit card. Fines can range from 30,000ISK to 200,000ISK. There are **speed cameras** along the Ring Road. The speed limits are:

- 90kmh (56mph) on paved roads (like the Ring Road)
- 80kmh (50mph) on gravel roads
- 50kmh (31mph) or less in residential areas

Road Conditions

Road conditions in Iceland can change quite quickly, as the weather is unpredictable. As a rule, always check road conditions before you head out on a trip. The best way to get information about road conditions and the weather is to call **1777** (or tel. 354/522-1100). The line is open 8am-4pm in the summer and 6:30am-10pm in the winter.

The Ring Road is paved for most of its length, but there are stretches in East Iceland with an unpaved gravel surface. **F roads** are unpaved tracks that may only be driven in vehicles with four-wheel drive. You can check on road conditions at **www.road.is.**

CAUSEWAY COAST

Why Go: This road trip along the coast of Northern Ireland has it all: haunted ruins, a famous distillery, and stunning sea views. You'll learn more about Northern Ireland's history in the region's two biggest cities, where the road trip starts and ends.

Number of Days: 2

Total Distance: 241 km (150 mi)

Seasons: Summer

Start: Belfast

End: Derry

Northern Ireland is its own region of the United Kingdom, with a distinct atmosphere and character. People in this region can be reserved, even a bit guarded, given the long, sad history of the Troubles. Focus on the natural beauty, however, and you'll create memories to savor for years to come.

Counties Antrim and Derry have most of Northern Ireland's most famous sights—the Carrick-a-Rede Rope Bridge, Giant's Causeway, the Derry City walls—but the biggest attraction is the coast itself. To drive the Causeway Coast, most visitors start in Belfast, drive north past the Glens, pass through Ballycastle, and wind up in Derry City after a two- or three-day tour. Take your time and savor all the historic ruins, natural wonders, and small towns along the way.

TOP 3

★ Learning about Belfast's political history on an eye-opening **Black Taxi Tour** (page 250).

★ Swaying on the **Carrick-a-Rede Rope Bridge,** a 20-m (65-ft) suspension bridge that hangs 24 m (80 ft) above a sea gorge (page 252).

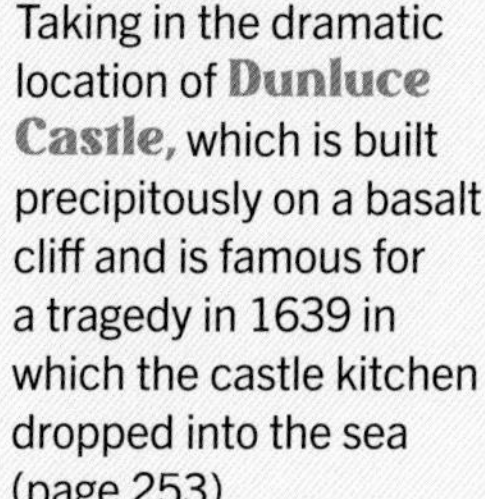

★ Taking in the dramatic location of **Dunluce Castle,** which is built precipitously on a basalt cliff and is famous for a tragedy in 1639 in which the castle kitchen dropped into the sea (page 253).

CAUSEWAY COAST

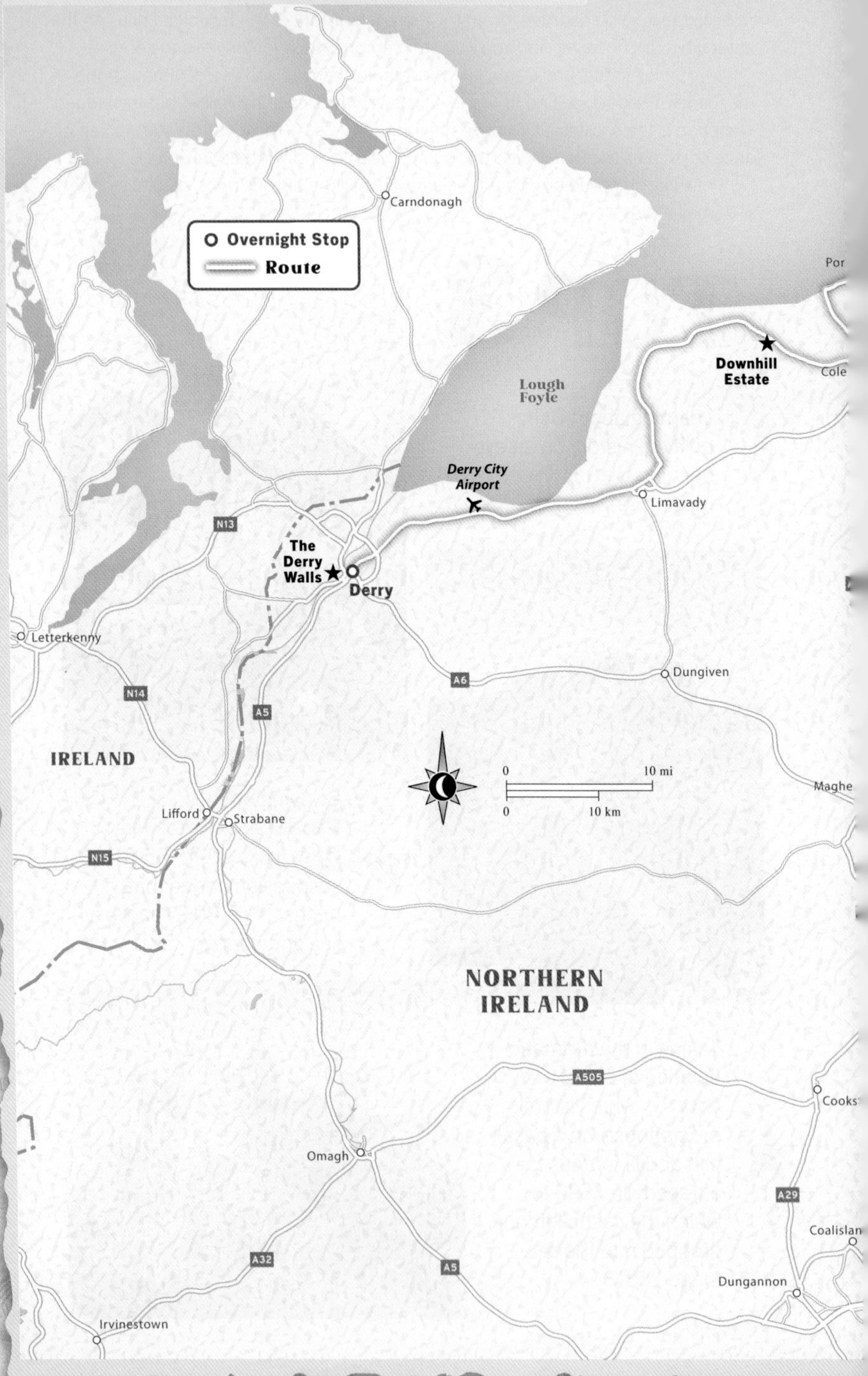
Carndonagh
Overnight Stop
Route
Lough Foyle
Downhill Estate
Derry City Airport
Limavady
N13
The Derry Walls
Derry
Letterkenny
Dungiven
A6
N14
A5
IRELAND
0
10 mi
0
10 km
Lifford
Strabane
N15
NORTHERN IRELAND
A505
Omagh
A29
A32
A5
Dungannon
Irvinestown
Por
Cole
Maghe
Cooks
Coalislan

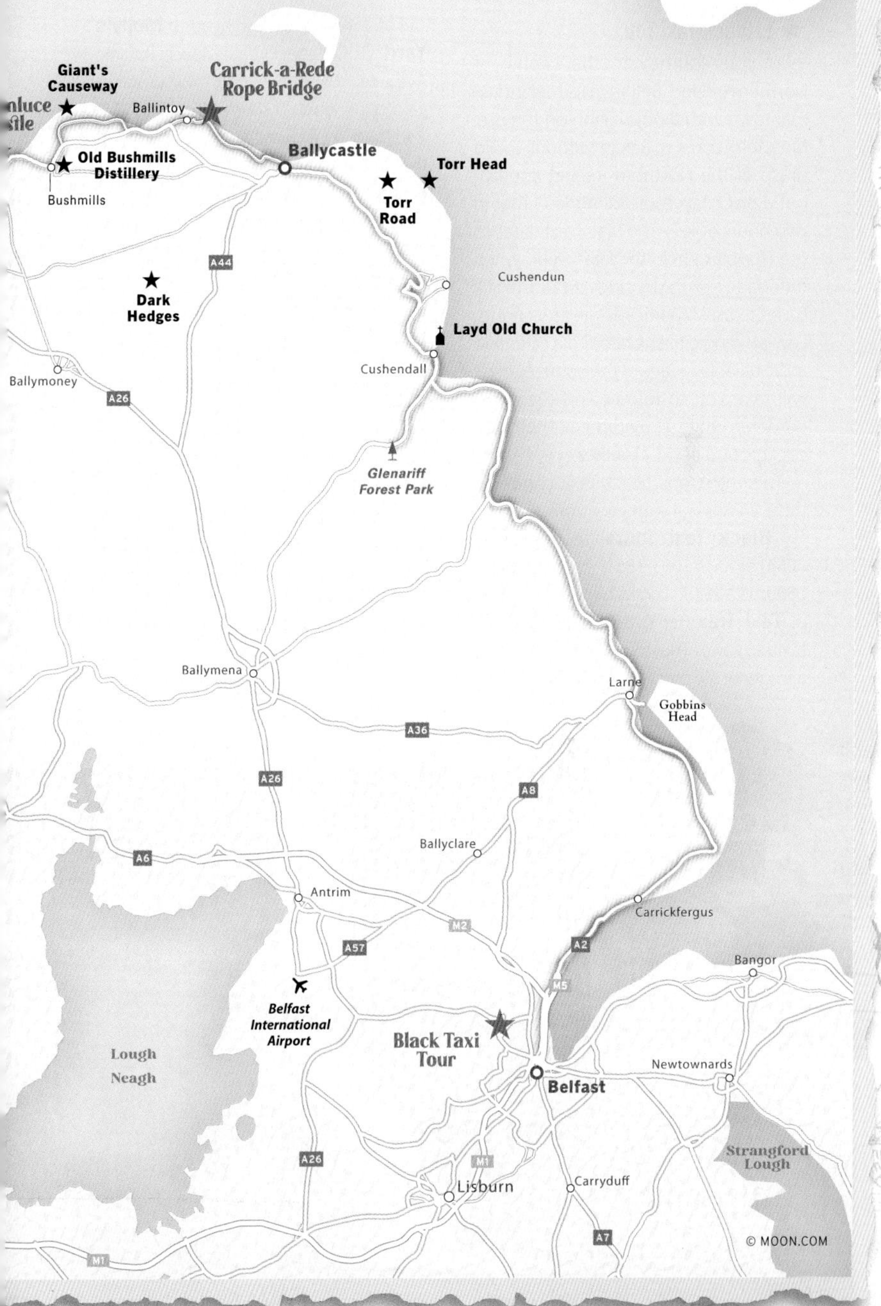

UNITED KINGDOM
Giant's Causeway
Carrick-a-Rede Rope Bridge
Ballintoy
Old Bushmills Distillery
Bushmills
Ballycastle
Torr Head
Torr Road
Dark Hedges
A44
Cushendun
Layd Old Church
Cushendall
Ballymoney
A26
Glenariff Forest Park
Ballymena
Larne
Gobbins Head
A36
A26
A8
Ballyclare
A6
Antrim
M2
Carrickfergus
A2
A57
M5
Bangor
Belfast International Airport
Black Taxi Tour
Lough Neagh
Newtownards
Belfast
Strangford Lough
A26
M1
Lisburn
Carryduff
A7
M1
© MOON.COM

DAY 1

Belfast to Ballycastle

★ 1. Black Taxi Tour

Start your journey in the capital of Northern Ireland, Belfast, a former industrial town with a population on the rise. Most folks come to Belfast without a solid grasp of the Northern Ireland conflict, but a Black Taxi tour will remedy that in two hours or less. The black taxi dates to the Troubles era in the late 1960s, when renegades on both sides would hijack buses to use as barricades in street fights. Law-abiding citizens needed a safer and more reliable means of transport. A driver will take you to murals and memorial gardens while providing a thorough background of the Troubles.

There isn't one "Black Taxi" company; there are several with very similar names. Try **Black Taxi Tours** (tel. 028/9064-2264 or 078/1003-3831, freephone tel. 0800/052-3914; www.belfasttours.com) or **Taxi Trax** (tel. 028/9031-5777; www.taxitrax.com). The tour lasts 1.5-2 hours and generally costs £18 per person.

For a meal in Belfast, head to **Molly's Yard** (1 College Green Mews, Botanic Ave.; tel. 028/9032-2600; www.mollysyard.co.uk; noon-9:30pm Mon.-Sat.; £13-23), long considered the best eatery in the city. The menu here is modern Irish. Reservations are essential.

Driving Directions: Belfast city center is 29 km (18 mi) east of Belfast International Airport, a 30-minute drive on the A57 and M2.

2. Glenariff Forest Park

tel. 028/2175-8232, 10am-dusk all year, cars £4.50

It's time to hit the road! As you set off north from Belfast on the A2, the beautiful **Glens of Antrim** will be on your left. One of the few glens you can actually traipse through is Glenariff Forest Park—which also happens to be the prettiest of them all. Stop here and choose a walking trail; there are plenty of trails (from 30 minutes to 3 hours' duration), delineated on a map at the entrance and clearly

left, stop along a Black Taxi Tour; right, Glenariff Forest Park

Key Reservations

- It's a good idea to reserve all accommodations in advance.
- Make reservations for dinner at **Molly's Yard** in Belfast.

marked throughout. The gem of the park is the substantial **Ess-na-Larach waterfall.** Eyeing it from the wooden "Rainbow Bridge" spanning the Glenariff River will give you the distinct feeling you've entered an enchanted forest.

Driving Directions: Glenariff Forest Park is a 1.5-hour drive (80 km/50 mi) from Belfast on the A2 coastal road.

3. Layd Old Church

1 km/0.6 mi outside Cushendall; always open; free

Your next stop, lovely church ruins overlooking a babbling brook rushing toward the North Channel, is one of the most romantic sights in the north. Once you've admired an exquisite 19th-century high cross, follow the unpaved path to the right of the ruins for a short coastal walk. Layd Old Church is signposted from the town of **Cushendall,** the Glens' largest town where you'll find some food and accommodation options.

Driving Directions: Layde Old Church is a 15-minute drive (13 km/8 mi) from Glenariff Forest Park.

4. Torr Head

The 18-km (11-mi) scenic route from the town of Cushendun to Ballycastle, **Torr Road,** takes you through some of the most blissfully unspoiled bucolic countryside in Northern Ireland, made even more stunning by panoramic sea views. At Torr Head, signposted a short distance off the main road, you'll spot a coast guard building abandoned in the 1920s (to reach it, you can hike up a rocky path from the small car park) and an ice house (used for packing fish) left to ruin around the same time. The hill holds a couple of passage tombs as well. This is Ireland's closest point to Scotland, which is 19 km (12 mi) away.

Driving Directions: Torr Head is a 25-minute drive (16 km/10 mi) from Layde Old Church on Torr Road.

5. Ballycastle

Your final stop for the day is Ballycastle, a town with a lovely Blue Flag beach and a wonderfully friendly vibe. The town is best known for its annual **Ould Lammas Fair,** which takes place over the last weekend in August and features plenty of market stalls and street entertainment, as well as two local delicacies: **dulse,** a dried seaweed, and **yellow man,** hard toffee made from a top-secret recipe.

House of McDonnell, Ballycastle

Torr Head

Northern Ireland Walks

With approximately 900 km (560 mi) of trails, the **Ulster Way** is the island's longest walking route, winding through all six Northern counties as well as central Donegal. Trekking all of it would take about five weeks, though most travelers walk the **Causeway Coast Way** (www.causewaycoastway.com) between the Giant's Causeway and the Glens of Antrim (from Portrush to Ballycastle, or vice versa), a little over 25 40 km (25 mi). There are plenty of accommodations along this route, but be sure to book well advance even in shoulder season. The Ulster Way begins in the suburbs of northern **Belfast,** by far the least attractive part of the route, before you come to the most popular segment in northern Antrim.

The tourist board is now marketing the longer coastal itinerary between Belfast and **Derry** as the **Causeway Coastal Route** (www.causewaycoastalroute.com), which is 190 km (120 mi) in total but offers numerous diversions—to the Glens of Antrim or the **Dark Hedges** for instance. Check out the website for a map and suggested itineraries. An alternative for day-trippers is the 2.5-hour guided cliff walk at **The Gobbins.**

As with all signposted walking routes, there are detailed guides with maps available at the local tourist office and bookstore. Websites like the **Ramblers Association** (www.ramblers.org.uk) and **Walking-World** (www.walkingworld.com) are helpful planning resources.

For live music in town, head to **House of McDonnell** (71 Castle St., west of the diamond; tel. 028/2076-2975), the locals' favorite watering hole. Fridays are trad (traditional music) and Saturdays are folk. **O'Connor's** (5-7 Ann St.; tel. 028/2076-2123; www.oconnorsbar.ie; 11:30am-9pm daily; £8-16) has a seafood pub menu and traditional music on Thursday.

Driving Directions: Ballycastle is a 20-minute drive (13 km/8 mi) from Torr Head on Torr Road and A2.

DAY 2

Ballycastle to Derry

★ 1. Carrick-a-Rede Rope Bridge

Signposted off the B15; tel. 028/2073-1582; 10am-5:15pm daily early Mar.-May and Sept.-Oct., 10am-6:15pm daily June-Aug.; £9

Before departing Ballycastle, have breakfast at **Ursa Minor Bakehouse** (45 Ann St.; tel. 079/5519-2389; www.ursaminorbakehouse.com; 9am-4pm Tues.-Sat.; £4-9), a slightly hipster vegetarian bakery-café that boasts some of the best java in the North. Afterward, your first stop for the day is one of the most exhilarating experiences in the north: a walk across the 20-m (65-ft) Carrick-a-Rede Rope Bridge, suspended 24 m (80 ft) above a dramatic sea gorge and swaying in the blustery winds. Beginning in 1755, local fishermen used to reassemble the bridge every spring to catch salmon on the far side of this little island, and today it's one of the National Trust's most popular attractions. There's nothing on the wee island on the far side (which is called Carrick-a-Rede) but pretty ocean views; most folks take their time snapping photos and watching the birds.

Driving Directions: The Carrick-a-Rede Rope Bridge is a 10-minute drive (10 km/6 mi) from Ballycastle on the B15.

2. Giant's Causeway

Up next: the Giant's Causeway. According to legend, this UNESCO World Heritage Site was a footbridge between Ireland and Scotland, destroyed by the warrior Fionn mac Cumhaill to prevent the giant Finn Gall from following him back to Ireland. Under an undulating series of cliffs are towering walls and a seaward staircase fashioned by nature out of gray basalt, some 37,000 hexagonal columns in all.

Walkers and cyclists get free entry, but the admission charge is £12.50 per person to park in the official lot. This includes a guided walk and admission to the exhibition in the **visitors center** (3.2 km/2 mi north of Bushmills on the B146; tel. 028/2073-1855; www.giants-causewaycentre.com; 10am-6pm daily July-Aug., 10am-5pm daily Mar.-June and Sept.-Oct., 10am-4:30pm daily Nov.-Feb.).

If hunger strikes, stop by **The Nook** (48 Causeway Rd.; tel. 028/2073-2993; 10:30am-8:30pm daily; lunch £6-10, dinner £8-14), a fantastic 19th-century schoolhouse-turned-restaurant just beside the Giant's Causeway entrance.

Driving Directions: Giant's Causeway is a 20-minute drive (13 km/8 mi) from Ballintoy along the A2 and Causeway Road.

3. Dark Hedges

At Bushmills, make a detour off the coastal roads to the Dark Hedges, better known as the Kingsroad on the popular HBO series *Game of Thrones*. The Dark Hedges, a tunnel formed of gnarled old beech trees, are shiveringly picturesque. The owner of nearby **Gracehill House** planted more than 150 of them in the late 18th century to create a pretty avenue, though today only 90 or so beeches remain. The Dark Hedges have their own ghost, an unidentified "gray lady" who vanishes as she passes the last tree on the avenue.

Driving Directions: The Dark Hedges are a 15-minute drive (16 km/10 mi) from Bushmills along Castlecat Road.

4. Old Bushmills Distillery

Distillery Rd., signposted on the B66; tel. 028/2073-1521; www.bushmills.com; 9:30am-5:30pm Mon.-Sat. and noon-5:30pm Sun. Apr.-Oct., 10:30am-3:30pm Mon.-Fri. and 1:30pm-3:30pm Sat.-Sun. Nov.-Mar., £9

The famous Old Bushmills Distillery has been licensed to distill since 1608 (making this the oldest licensed distillery on the planet), and on the tour you'll learn everything you ever wanted to know about the making of uisce beatha (water of life). Naturally, a shot or two is included in the price of admission.

Be sure to stop by (or stay in) the **Bushmills Inn** (9 Dunluce Rd.; tel. 028/2073-3000; www.bushmillsinn.com; lodging £110-190 pp, singles charged at double rate; restaurant noon-6pm and 7pm-9:30pm Mon.-Sat., noon-9pm Sun.; lunch £10-14, dinner £15-28), a gorgeously authentic 17th-century hotel where you'll still find gas lamps burning in the downstairs sitting rooms.

Driving Directions: Bushmills is a 7-minute drive (5 km/3 mi) from Giant's Causeway.

★ 5. Dunluce Castle

87 Dunluce Rd., signposted off the A2; tel. 028/2073-1938; 10am-5:30pm daily Apr.-Sept., 10am-4:30pm daily Oct.-Mar.; £5

Get back in the car and head to Dunluce Castle. If there were an award for a castle ruin with the most dramatic situation, Dunluce would surely win the distinction. The castle perches precipitously on a cliff over a cave (called Mermaid's Cave, reachable by a steep path down from the castle), and the basalt rock beneath is slowly crumbling away: In 1639 part of the castle tumbled into the sea during a reception, taking most of the servants along with it.

WATCH

Derry Girls (2018-2022): This TV show follows a group of teenagers living in Derry in the '90s. The main characters' hilarious hijinks are set against the reality of the Troubles.

READ

Seamus Heaney is Ireland's most famous contemporary poet, having translated *Beowulf* into English and produced an oeuvre worthy of the 1995 Nobel Prize in Literature. He was a native of Northern Ireland.

Say Nothing: A True Story of Murder and Memory in Northern Ireland by Patrick Radden Keefe: Learn more about the Troubles in this gripping—though at times disturbing—bestselling book.

LISTEN

Sean Ó Riada was one of the musicians behind the mid-20th century resurgence of the Irish folk music tradition. He composed music for **"Mná na hÉireann,"** an 18th-century poem, which has been performed and sung by many artists. Kate Bush also has her own version of the song/poem.

The earliest extant structures (towers and walls) date from the mid-13th century, though archaeological excavations indicate the land was inhabited as early as the 9th century. Dunluce was home to the McQuillans, the ruling family of north Antrim in the 16th century and was later owned by Scottish rogue Sorley Boy McDonnell (whose brother married a McQuillan).

Driving Directions: Dunluce Castle is a five-minute drive (8 km/2 mi) from Bushmills along the A2.

6. Downhill Estate

Hezlett Farm, 107 Sea Rd., Castlerock, signposted from the A2; tel. 028/7084-8728; www.nationaltrust.org.uk; dawn-dusk year-round; £6.85

Blink once and you might miss your next stop: Downhill is a tiny place, only on the map for the 18th-century clifftop estate of Bishop Hervey, now a huge and extremely eerie ruin. Beneath that cliff is a pristine beach popular with surfers.

The grand estate of the infamous Bishop of Derry and fourth Earl of Bristol, Frederick Augustus Hervey, has lain in ruin since World War II. More entrepreneur and playboy than holy man, he invented and grew wealthy on Hervey's Bristol Cream (ask for it instead of Bailey's while you're in the North) and built this rambling mansion in 1774. These ruins are among the very creepiest in all Ireland, especially if visited on a sunless day. Much of the original 160-hectare (395-acre) Downhill Estate now makes up **Downhill Forest** (10am-dusk daily; free), which slopes eastward to the little resort town of Castlerock.

Driving Directions: Downhill Estate is a 25-minute drive (26 km/16 mi) from Dunluce Castle along the A2.

7. Derry

After about 45 minutes on the A2 from Downhill, you'll arrive in Derry, your destination for the night and the end of your road trip. Vibrant Derry, known to British loyalists as Londonderry, is the island's fourth-largest city. Have delicious Lebanese food, at **Cedar** (32 Carlisle Rd.; tel. 028/7137-3868; http://cedarlebanese.webs.com; 5:30pm-9:30pm Wed.-Sat.; £5-15), and relax in the evening.

In the morning, take a leisurely walk along the **Derry city walls** (always open, free), a highlight of any trip here. Constructed between 1614 and 1619, Derry's ramparts are the only intact city walls in all Ireland, sturdy enough at 9 m (30 ft) thick and up to 8 m (26 ft) high. The four original gates were rebuilt in the 18th and 19th centuries, along with three new entrances. Make the circuit around the walls to observe the city within and without; the circumference is about 2 km (1.25 mi), and staircases are located at many points along the inner walls. You can view many of the **peace murals** (part of Derry's more recent history) from the southwestern section of the city wall, including *The Death of Innocence,* but take the time to exit the old city and view them from the street.

To learn more about the city's 20th-century Catholic struggle for civil rights, take a walking tour or visit the **Museum of Free Derry** (55-61 Glenfada Park, off Rossville St.; tel. 028/7136-0880; www.museumoffreederry.org; 9:30am-4:30pm Mon.-Thu., 9:30am-3pm Fri., 1pm-4pm Sat.-Sun.; £6).

TRANSPORTATION

Air

Most travelers will fly into **Belfast International Airport** (29 km/18 mi west of Belfast on the A57 and M2; tel. 028/9448-4848; www.belfastairport.com). To get to the city center, it's a 30-minute drive on the A57 and M2.

Train

Northern Ireland's train operator is **Northern Ireland Railways** (tel. 028/9089-9411; www.translink.co.uk). **Belfast Lanyon Place,** also known as Central Station (E. Bridge St.; tel. 028/9066-6630), is less than a kilometer (0.6 mi) east of the city center.

Bus

Northern Ireland is served by **Ulsterbus** (tel. 028/9066-6630; www.translink.co.uk). The main bus station in Belfast is **Europa Bus Centre** (adjacent to Europa Hotel, entrance on Glengall St. off Great Victoria St.; tel. 028/9066-6630) in the city center.

Car Rental

Remember, we drive on the **left** here! In Northern Ireland, signs list distances in miles rather than kilometers.

You'll find numerous rental companies at airports here: **Europcar** (www.europcar.ie), **Avis** (www.avis.ie), **Budget** (www.budget.ie), **Hertz** (www.hertz.ie), and **Enterprise** (www.enterprise.ie).

Note that rental cars with automatic transmission are in high demand and cost a good deal more than cars with manual transmission, so you'll pay less and have more cars to choose from if you can drive a stick. Choose the smallest car available that still works for your number of passengers and amount of luggage, as local roads can be *very* narrow.

Getting Back

You can fly out of Derry at **Derry City Airport** (Airport Rd., Eglinton, 11 km/7 mi northeast of Derry; tel. 028/7181-0784; www.cityofderryairport.com). The **Airporter** shuttle runs six times daily between the airport and Derry's Quayside Shopping Centre.

The fastest way to drive back to Belfast is via the A6 (1 hour 20 minutes, 113 km/70 mi).

CONNECT WITH

- Edinburgh and Glasgow (page 65)
- Dublin and the Wicklow Way (page 354)

THE NORTH COAST 500

Why Go: The North Coast 500 is an epic driving route that encircles much of Scotland's northwest Highlands, revealing some of the country's most stunning scenery en route, from tiny communities to ruined castles, paradisial beaches, and lunar-like landscapes.

Number of Days: 7

Total Distance: 830 km (516 mi)

Seasons: Spring and summer

Start/End: Inverness

The northern Scottish Highlands is a place of extreme, empty beauty. Vast landscapes give way to deep glens and wide straths, which are covered in purple heather in spring and summer, turn golden in autumn, and are blanketed by snow in winter. Isolated white sand beaches could be in the tropics were it not for the whirring winds, and often the only clue to human habitation is the occasional lonesome bothy or cottage. The North Coast 500 driving route, through the upper reaches of the Highlands, attracts tens of thousands of visitors each year to this part of Scotland.

TOP 3

★ Visiting **Badbea,** a windswept abandoned settlement that serves as a stark reminder of the impact of the Highland Clearances (page 261).

★ Driving the thrilling **Drumbeg Road.** This diversion from the North Coast 500 route takes in breathtaking vistas from Scotland's western coast (page 264).

★ **Kayaking on Loch Ness** offers a chance to avoid the tour buses and enjoy a unique vantage point on Scotland's enormous loch (page 267).

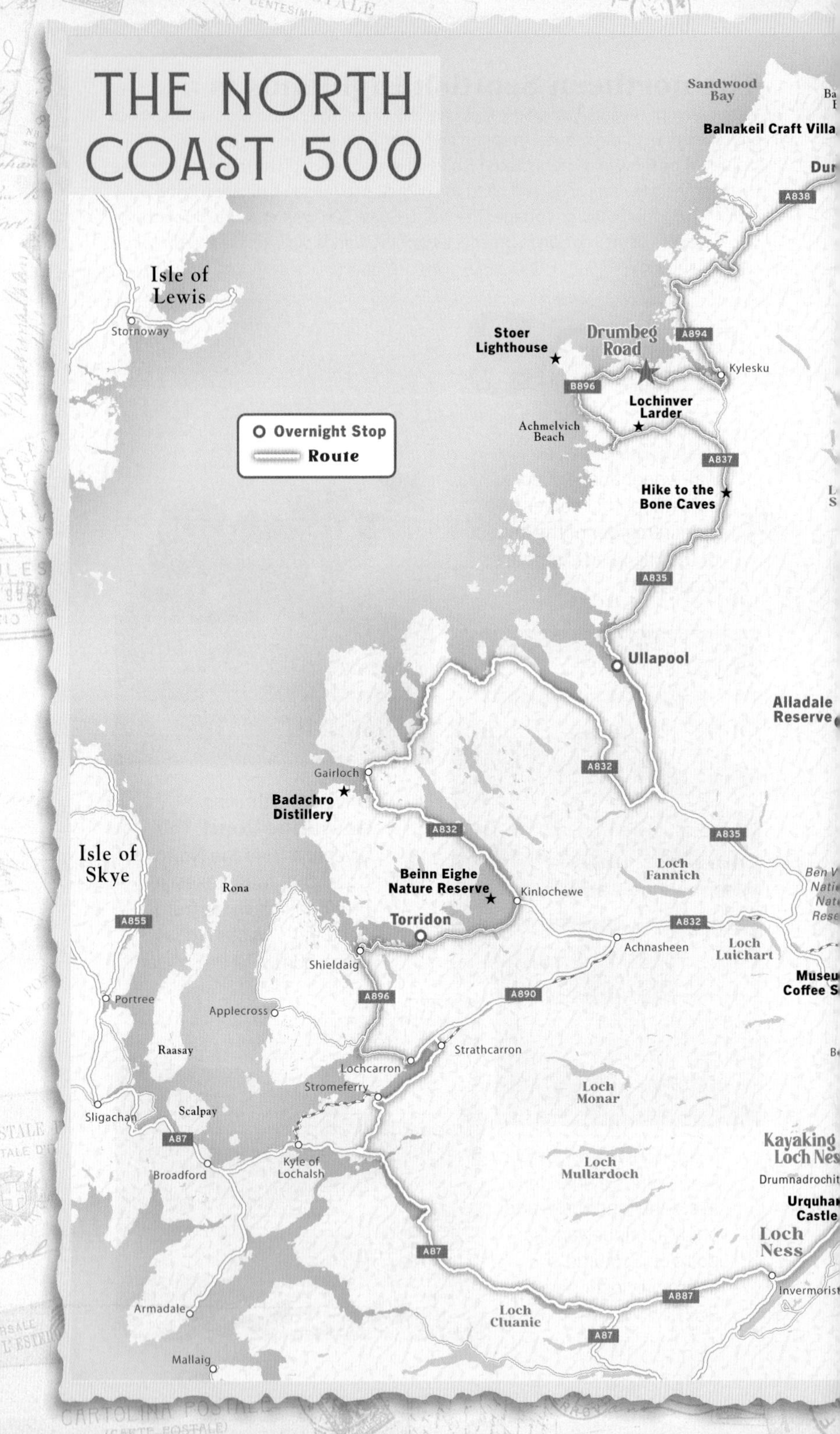
THE NORTH COAST 500
Overnight Stop
Route
Sandwood Bay
Balnakeil Craft Villa
A838
Isle of Lewis
Stornoway
Stoer Lighthouse
Drumbeg Road
A894
Kylesku
B896
Lochinver Larder
Achmelvich Beach
A837
Hike to the Bone Caves
A835
Ullapool
Alladale Reserve
A832
Gairloch
Badachro Distillery
A832
A835
Loch Fannich
Isle of Skye
Rona
Beinn Eighe Nature Reserve
Kinlochewe
A855
Torridon
A832
Achnasheen
Loch Luichart
Shieldaig
A896
A890
Portree
Applecross
Raasay
Strathcarron
Lochcarron
Loch Monar
Stromeferry
Sligachan
Scalpay
A87
Kyle of Lochalsh
Broadford
Loch Mullardoch
Drumnadrochit
Loch Ness
A87
A887
Invermorist
Armadale
Loch Cluanie
A87
Mallaig

Dunnet Head
John O'Groats Sign
Farr Beach
A838
A836
Thurso
Dunnet Bay Distillery
A99
A9
Loch Loyal
Forsinard Flows National Nature Reserve
Wick
Old Pulteney Whisky Distillery
Loch Naver
A99
A9
River Bothy
Badbea
A9
Duke of Sutherland Monument
Brora
Golspie
Bonar Bridge
Tain
0
10 mi
0
10 km
A9
Alness
Cromarty Firth
Culbrin Forest
A96
Elgin
Inverness Airport
Nairn
Moray Firth
Inverness
Cawdor Castle
A96
A941
Keith
Inverness Train Station
Culloden Battlefield
Dufftown
Huntly
A95
Grantown on Spey
Carr Bridge
A96
Cairngorms National Park
COTLAND
Aviemore
Abernethy National Nature Reserve
© MOON.COM

DAY 1

Inverness to Alladale Reserve

1. Inverness Museum and Art Gallery

Castle Wynd; tel. 01463 237 114; www.highlifehighland.com/inverness-museum-and-art-gallery; 10am-5pm Tues.-Sat. Apr.-Oct., noon-4pm Tues.-Thurs., 11am-4pm Fri.-Sat. Nov.-Easter; free

Before hopping in the car, walk along the river toward Inverness Castle and have a look in the Inverness Museum and Art Gallery. Don't let the ugly exterior put you off (there are proposals to update the 1970s façade). It's a fascinating walk through Highland culture and history. Exhibits cover everything from the geological development of Scotland to the beginnings of clan culture and the plight of the Jacobites.

Driving Directions: Inverness is 14 km (9 mi) west of Inverness Airport, a 20-minute drive on the A96.

2. Alladale Reserve

Ardgay; tel. 01863 755 338; https://alladale.com; from £2,750 per week (sleeping up to 12)

It's time to set off on your North Coast 500 journey, heading north on a scenic stretch of the A9. Just after crossing the Cromarty Firth, turn off the road on a detour to the Alladale Reserve. This huge tract of land in the process of rewilding will one day resemble Scotland as it should be, covered in native trees that will hopefully encourage the return of native wildlife. There are all kinds of outdoor activities here, including guided mountain hikes, trout fishing, clay pigeon shooting, and archery.

This is also where you'll find your accommodations for the night. Three catered cottages come with delicious meals delivered to your doorstep. The main lodge can either be booked exclusively for large groups or as individual rooms. The fourth property, which is self-catered, is possibly one of the most remote places you could find to stay in Scotland, the perfect place to disconnect from real life and discover a world of nature and adventure.

Driving Directions: Alladale Reserve is just over an hour (665 km/43 mi) from Inverness, turning off the A9 onto the B9176 after about 30 minutes.

DAY 2

Alladale Reserve to Wick

1. Duke of Sutherland Monument

Golspie

In your rental car, head back to the North Coast 500 route. Shortly after returning to the A9, you'll pass a very conspicuous and rather controversial statue: the Duke of Sutherland Monument. George Granville Leveson-Gower, the first Duke of Sutherland, was one of the callous landowners who oversaw some of the most brutal of all the Highland Clearances, in which communities were forced from their land to make way for more profitable sheep farming. Looming over the village of Golspie, from its position on top of Ben Bhraggie hill, atop a huge plinth, the monument is a reminder that in these parts it was often the powerful

WATCH

Brave: This 2012 animated Pixar film, set in the Scottish Highlands in medieval times, tells the story of a rebellious princess.

READ

Rob Roy by Sir Walter Scott: Sir Walter Scott is celebrated for having introduced literary tourism to Scotland with his depictions and romanticism of Highland clans and the landscape they called home. He is also largely responsible for the romantic view we have of Highland culture, particularly through his novel *Rob Roy,* which tells of the plight of the Jacobites.

LISTEN

Bagpipes are a traditional instrument, long associated with the Highland clans. For a classic bagpipe tune, find "Scotland the Brave" played by The Pipes & Drums of the Royal Tank Regiment, featured on various compilations of Scottish music.

few who benefited from the land.

Though he is much maligned, many people choose to **hike** up here (park in the Highlands Wildcat Trail car park, pay the donation, then follow signs for Ben Bhraggie), a round-trip of around two hours with good paths underfoot (4.7 km/2.9 mi).

Driving Directions: Take the B9176 back to the A9 and head north. The monument is about an hour (56 km/35 mi) from Alladale Reserve.

★ 2. Badbea

A9, near Ousdale

Continuing north on the A9, you'll see brown signs for the cleared village of Badbea. Pull into the signposted car park and you can follow a footpath to the former settlement, on the steep cliffs above Berriedale (1 hour round-trip; 2 km/1.25 mi). Today, most of the houses are little more than a drystone wall.

Families began to arrive in Badbea in the late 18th century; many of them had been evicted from their homes nearby in Ousdale when the landowner decided he would rather use his fertile straths for sheep-farming. A plaque en route to the abandoned township reads that it was first settled by "12 families whose homes in Sutherland had been destroyed during

Old Pulteney Whisky Distillery

Duke of Sutherland Monument

History and Literature

East of Inverness are two major sights related to history and literature. Visit them before starting your North Coast road trip or after—or do one of each.

CULLODEN BATTLEFIELD

Culloden Moor, Inverness; tel. 01463 796 090; www.nts.org.uk/visit/places/culloden; visitor center adult £11, entry to the battlefield free

For a history lesson, a visit to Culloden, scene of one of the most brutal battles on Scottish soil, is unforgettable. On this battlefield, 1,600 men and boys (1,500 of whom were Jacobites) were brutally slaughtered in an hour, bringing to a crashing end the Jacobite dream of ridding Scotland of the rule of King George II and sending its leader, Bonnie Prince Charlie, running for the hills. If you are at all unfamiliar with the lead-up to the battle or the significance of the Jacobite cause, then paying to enter the visitor center is a must. From Inverness, the battlefield is a 10-km (6-mi) drive east along the B9006, which takes about 15 minutes.

CAWDOR CASTLE

Nairn; tel. 01667 404 401; www.cawdorcastle.com; adults £11.50

This well-preserved 14th-century castle is inextricably bound to King of Scots Macbeth, due, seemingly, to poetic license. Shakespeare's Thane of Cawdor, Macbeth, never lived here—he died some 200 years before the current castle was built. Nonetheless, this medieval fortress, which is still lived in by the Cawdor family, draws fans of the play and doesn't disappoint, with its 11 rooms filled with exquisite furnishings.

the Highland Clearances." It's a moving experience standing here, looking out at the gray angry north sea and imaging what life would have been like here.

Driving Directions: Drive north on the A9 for 30 minutes (37 km/24 mi) to reach the car park.

3. Lunch at The River Bothy

Ivy Cottage, Berriedale; tel 01593 751 569; 10am-2pm daily mid-Mar.-Dec.; toasted sandwiches £8.50, coffee from £2.20

After the sobering walk around the former Highland settlement, warm your spirits with a lunch at the River Bothy. This delightful café-cum-shop serves huge slices of cake, yummy toasted sandwiches, tea and coffee, plus some bigger meals such as burgers loaded with fixings.

Driving Directions: The café is a four-minute (5-km/3-mi) drive along the A9 from the Badbea car park.

4. Overnight in Wick

Head to the town of Wick, where you'll spend the night. **Mackays Hotel** (Union Street, Wick; tel. 01955 602 323; www.mackayshotel.co.uk; £125 d) has comfortable rooms and a delicious in-house restaurant in a 19th-century building.

While in town, head to the **Old Pulteney Whisky Distillery** (Huddart Street, Wick; tel. 01955 602 371; www.oldpulteney.com; 10am-4pm Mon.-Fri.; tours £10, master classes £20) for a tour and a sample. The whisky here is known as Maritime Malt thanks to the area's seafaring past.

Driving Directions: Wick is 35 minutes (40 km/26 mi) from the River Bothy north on the A9 and A99.

DAY 3

Wick to Thurso

1. John o' Groats Sign

Wick; open 24/7

It's time to head north. After about 30 minutes of driving, stop in John o'Groats for breakfast at **Stacks Coffee House & Bistro** (3 Craft Centre, John o'Groats; tel. 01955 611 582; www.stacksbistro.co.uk; 10am-4pm Wed.-Sun.; flatbreads £4.95) and for an obligatory photo at the John o'Groats signpost. Not having your photo taken at this famous white sign, which shows how far you are from New York, Land's End, Edinburgh, Orkney, and Shetland, is a bit like visiting London and not taking a picture in front of Big Ben.

Driving Directions: Head north on the A99 for 25 minutes (27 km/17 mi).

2. Dunnet Head

Brough, Thurso

Your next stop is the true northernmost spot in the UK: Dunnet Head. Take a brisk stroll down to **Dunnet Head Lighthouse,** located on the tip of a thumb-shaped peninsula that rises into the Pentland Firth like a hitchhiker hailing a ride. It's a breeding spot for seabirds; look for razorbills, puffins, kittiwakes, fulmars, and guillemots. On a clear day you can make out several of the offshore islands. Dunnet Bay, a gorgeous crescent beach with big dunes, right by the village of Dunnet, is also a lovely spot.

Driving Directions: The town of Dunnet is 15 minutes from John o' Groats, a 25-minute drive (17 km/11 mi) along the A836.

3. Dunnet Bay Distillery

Dunnet; tel. 01847 851 287; www.dunnetbay-distillers.co.uk; £20 per boat shed (seats 2)

Next, head into town and try some gin at Dunnet Bay Distillery. This small batch distillery, opened in 2014 by couple Claire and Martin, has steadily been making a name for itself in the busy gin market. Using local botanicals, the Rock Rose Gin cleverly taps into all the local seasons; it's so fresh and zesty that you don't even feel the need to add ice.

4. Overnight in Thurso

Head to the family-run **Manor House** (6 Janet Street, Thurso; tel. 07379 881 307; www.manorhousethurso.co.uk; £114 d) in Thurso, where a cozy bed and delicious meal await you for the night.

Driving Directions: Manor House is a 15-minute drive (14 km/9 mi) from Dunnet west along the A836.

DAY 4

Thurso to Durness

1. Farr Beach

Clachan, Bettyhill

Begin your day by heading to Farr Beach, a sandy strand that's protected by dunes and treasured by locals. Park by the Strathnaver Museum to reach the beach, which is about a 10-minute walk away. Start with a stroll through **Farr Church,** where you can see the Farr Stone—a Pictish slab that stands just to the west, serving as an impressive gravestone. From the back of the churchyard turn right, past a couple of houses and the Farr Bay Inn on the right, and then follow the sign to the left through two kissing gates, which lead to the sand dunes behind the beach. A clear path will bring you to one sand dune, which is like a huge slide down to the beach. With acres of golden sand, this is a really lovely beach that feels like a local treasure.

Coast Coffee, Tea and Treats (SwordlyMill, Swordly, Bettyhill; tel. 07843 682 343; facebook.com/COAST-coffetea-and-treats_nc500-463716250870926; 10am-4pm daily) is a great place to get your caffeine fix after walking on the sand.

Driving Directions: Take the A836 west for 45 minutes (48 km/30 mi) to reach Farr Beach.

2. Balnakeil Craft Village

1.6 km (1 mi) west of Durness; 10am-6pm daily Apr.-Oct.

Keep heading west to the town of Durness, where you can check into your lodging at **Mackay's Rooms** (Durness; tel. 01971 511 202; www.visitdurness.com; £149 d; bunkhouse beds £22 per night), followed by a trip to Balnakeil Craft Village. This little arts hub is home to several art studios and craft shops, and you can see skills such as wood turning and stained glass making in action. The **Plastic Lab** can offer tips on becoming plastic-free, and **Durness Deep Time** is an exhibition where you can learn about the archaeology and geology of the area and book guided walks with a geologist.

Driving Directions: The town of Durness is a little over an hour (68 km/42 mi) from Farr Beach; drive west on the A838 and A836.

3. Balnakeil Beach

Near Durness

Watch the sunset from Balnakeil Beach, regularly ranked among the best beaches in Scotland. Walk to the far end of the beach, around the large grassy rock, for some tranquility.

DAY 5

Durness to Ullapool

★ 1. The Drumbeg Road

B869, from Kylesku to Lochinver

Not long after you've crossed the Kylesku Bridge, you'll see a right turn signposted toward **Drumbeg.** You don't have to go this way—you can continue along the A894 toward Inchnadamph—but for confident and experienced drivers, this route is a must. The road is narrow and climbs and descends seemingly at will, often leaving little space between you and the cliff edge, but the views are immense, and the excitement is high. Though there are lots of passing places, as it is largely single-track, you'll have to keep your wits about you as there are plenty of blind corners.

Highlights of the route include **Stoer Lighthouse** (Lairg; www.stoerlighthouse.co.uk); the pretty village of Drumbeg, which has a local store and a great viewpoint; and **Achmelvich Beach** (which itself requires another short detour). Once you come to the end of the B869, turn left and this road will bring you back to the main North Coast 500 route.

Driving Directions: You'll reach the start of the Drumbed Road (B869) after a one-hour drive (60 km/37 mi) southeast from Durness. The Drumbeg Road is 35 km (22 mi) long and will take around 1 hour 10 minutes, not including stops.

2. Lunch at Lochinver Larder

Main Street, Lochinver; tel. 01571 844 356; www.lochinverlarder.com; pies £5.95

Be sure to stop at the Lochinver Larder as a reward for your intrepid driving. This place is known for miles around for their tasty pies and lovely loch views.

3. Hike to the Bone Caves

Lairg; www.walkhighlands.co.uk/ullapool/bonecaves.shtml

Follow this up with a hike (1.5-2 hours; 4.5 km/2.75 mi) to the limestone Bone Caves, where a treasure trove of animal remains from the glacial period were found. From the Allt nan Uamh Car Park, go through the gate and follow the path past the building. The rough but clear path will take you above a waterfall before gradually ascending upstream. You'll soon see the caves on a steep cliff and when you reach a junction by a large boulder, take the path to the right. The final section is up a steep and narrow path that will take you to several cave openings. Explore with care and consideration—inside they may be slippery. When you're ready to leave, take the downhill path that continues across the steep slope, bearing left as you go, until you return to the car park.

Driving Directions: From Lochinver Larder, the Allt nan Uamh Car Park is a 20-minute (24 km/15 mi) drive east and south along A837.

4. Overnight in Ullapool

End your night in Ullapool, with a pint and some traditional music at the **Ceilidh Place** (14 West Argyle Street, Ullapool; tel. 01854 612 245; www.theceilidhplace.com; £100 d), where you'll also be sleeping for the night. This sophisticated, small hotel, a destination in its own right, hosts regular gig nights.

Driving Directions: From Allt nan Uamh Car Park, drive 30 minutes (34 km/21 mi) south on the A837 and A835 to reach Ullapool.

DAY 6

Ullapool to Torridon

1. Badachro Distillery

Aird Hill, Badachro; tel. 01445 741 282; www.badachrodistillery.com; 1-hour tour 2pm Mon., Wed.-Fri.; £20 per person

Continue your North Coast 500 road trip with a 1.5-hour drive out of Ullapool. After you pass Gairloch, a single-track road will bring you to the small hamlet of Badachro, home to this fledging distillery that makes craft gins and also whisky—its first single malt was released in 2020. Tours run weekdays (except Tues.) but even if there are no tours available you can pop in for a chat, a taste, and a look in the small shop.

Driving Directions: Badachro is 1.5 hours (100 km/62 mi) from Ullapool.

Beinn Eighe Nature Reserve

2. Beinn Eighe Nature Reserve

Kinlochewe, IV22 2PA; www.nature.scot; open 24/7, visitor center 10am-5pm Mar.-Oct.; free

Next, enjoy some time outdoors at this nature reserve, which is Britain's oldest. Its nucleus is the Beinn Eighe ridge—an assembly of crooked, craggy peaks and slopes that lie between Loch Macree and Glen Torridon. The natural setting attracts eagles, pine marten, crossbills, divers, and red deer, and there are lots of walking and cycling trails to follow.

TO TAKE Home

In the Highlands, unique souvenirs often take the form of textiles.

- **Tartan:** Woolen cloth woven in a pattern of checks or crossed lines that is usually associated with a particular Scottish clan or region. Tartan scarves make an easy-to-pack gift.
- **Tweed:** A rough woolen cloth, renowned for its hardiness; originating from Scotland, it is typically woven of spun wool of different colors, giving it a speckled finish.
- **Kilts:** Knee-length pleated skirts of tartan, traditionally worn by Highlanders.

For playful gifts, **Nessie hats** and **plush Highland cattle** are ubiquitous.

Driving Directions: Drive west for 30 minutes (29 km/18 mi) on the B8056 and A832.

3. Overnight in Torridon

You'll spend the night at **The Torridon Hotel & Inn** (By Achnasheen, Wester Ross; tel. 01445 791 242; www.thetorridon.com; £320 d), which overlooks Upper Loch Torridon. The fine-dining restaurant on site features four- and seven-course menus.

Driving Directions: The Torridon is 25 minutes (23 km/14 mi) from the Beinn Eighe Nature Reserve.

DAY 7

Torridon to Loch Ness

1. Museum Coffee Shop

Strathpeffer IV14 9HA; tel. 07557 505 264; 10am-5pm Tues.-Sun. spring and summer, 10am-4pm Thurs.-Sun. winter

Make your first pit stop of the day at the Museum Coffee Shop in Strathpeffer. This former train station is a reminder of Strathpeffer's affluent past, when Victorians would arrive in droves to soak in its healing waters. The original building remains as the Highland Museum of Childhood, and this café is a delight, serving teas, coffees, sandwiches, and standard cafeteria staples.

Driving Directions: Museum Coffee Shop is a little over an hour (80 km/50 mi) from Torridon; drive east on the A896, A832, and A835.

2. Urquhart Castle

A82, Drumnadrochit; tel. 01456 450 551; www.historicenvironment.scot/visit-a-place/places/urquhart-castle; 9:30am-6pm Apr.-Sept., 9:30am-5pm Oct., 9:30am-4:30pm Nov.-Mar.; adults £9, children £5.40

Next, head straight for **Drumnadrochit** on the shores of Loch Ness, where you can get your bucket list photo amid the ruins of Urquhart Castle. This ruined castle on the bonnie banks of Loch Ness has endured 1,500 years of history, from lavish royal banquets to countless sieges. You can wander the grounds freely, nip in and out of the ruined segments, including the miserable-looking prison cell, and head down to a little pebble beach in front of the castle that looks out over Loch Ness. For the best views, climb the five-story Grant Tower and see if you can spot unusual ripples—large unidentified objects have shown up on sonar here. There's also a decent café and a large shop in the visitor center.

Driving Directions: Urquhart Castle is a 45-minute drive (47 km/29 mi) south from Museum Coffee Shop.

★ 3. Kayaking on Loch Ness

To get out on the waters of Loch Ness, book a guided canoe or kayak tour with an activity provider like **In Your Element** (Fort Augustus; tel. 0333 600 6008; https://iye.scot; adults £22, children £15 per hour), or you can rent a kayak from **Loch Ness Shores** campsite (Monument Park, Lower Foyers; tel. 01456 486 333; https://lochnessshores.com) for a solo paddle from £10 per hour. The southern end of the loch is safest, and even with the murmur of cars on the A82 in the distance, it can still feel very peaceful with miles of blue water in front of you and green banks of trees on either side.

4. Dinner at Dores Inn

Dores; tel. 01463 751 203; www.thedoresinn.co.uk; noon-5pm lunch menu, 5pm-8:45pm evening menu; entrées £4.95

Drive north along the famous loch and around to the southern shore of the loch, where you can have dinner at the homey Dores Inn. Sit by the fire as you fill up on home-cooked food or take in the views of Loch Ness from one of the window seats. From here, you're less than 20 minutes from Inverness, where your journey began.

TRANSPORTATION

Air

Inverness Airport (www.hial.co.uk/inverness-airport) lies 14 km (9 mi) east of the city, a 20-minute drive on the A96.

Train

Inverness Train Station is located on Academy Street in the city center. **ScotRail** (www.scotrail.co.uk) has trains into Inverness from all major Scottish cities, including Edinburgh and Glasgow.

Inverness Train Station is also the starting point for the **Kyle Line** (www.scotrail.co.uk/scotland-by-rail/great-scenic-rail-journeys/kyle-line-lochalsh-inverness), which includes several stops along the North Coast 500.

Bus

Just a block away from the train station, **Inverness Bus Station** (Margaret St.) is accessed from Academy Street and offers all manner of connections.

Car Rental

Car rentals are available all of Scotland's major airports. Inverness Airport has a number of operators, including **Arnold Clark** (www.arnoldclarkrental.com/airport-car-hire/inverness-airport) and **Avis** (www.avis.co.uk). There are also car rental offices at the Inverness train station. A lot of cars are manual transmission, but you can request an automatic, which tends to be more expensive.

Road Rules and Safety

Scotland is in the UK, so cars drive on the **left** side of the road.

Many caravans and motorhomes travel the North Coast 500; pay attention to road signs that discourage caravans. Use the passing places where safe to do so, not only to let cars coming from the opposite direction pass, but also to let cars overtake you if you're going slower. Winter brings snow and ice, so you'll need to take extra care. Try to stick to the main roads and give yourself extra time. Some sections of road may become impassable in winter.

- Edinburgh and Glasgow (page 65)

LOFOTEN

Why Go: This archipelago in northern Norway rewards visitors with dramatic vistas, mountain hikes, and stays in historic fishing cabins.

Number of Days: 5

Total Distance: 210 km (130 mi)

Seasons: Summer and early fall

Start: Svolvær

End: Å

The Lofoten archipelago–often referred to as the Lofoten isles or just Lofoten—stretches east to west across the islands of Austvågøy, Gimsøy, Vestvågøy, Flakstadøy, and Moskenesøy. In addition, there are some smaller islands that are considered part of Lofoten, such as Henningsvær, Værøy, and Skrova.

Lofoten is a region with spectacular landscapes, consisting of pristine waters, jagged mountaintops, and white sand beaches. As you explore the wondrous natural surroundings, you will also come across charming fishing villages and cozy fishermen's cabins, usually painted red or yellow. Towns and villages are small, and even Svolvær, the largest town, has fewer than 5,000 inhabitants. So, prepare yourself to slow down and enjoy long drives and quiet days.

TOP 3

Surfing with Arctic Surfers, a once-in-a-lifetime experience (page 274).

Hiking up **Reinebringen** for an unforgettable view (page 277).

Reaching **the end of the road at Å,** a picturesque fishing village and museum (page 277).

LOFOTEN

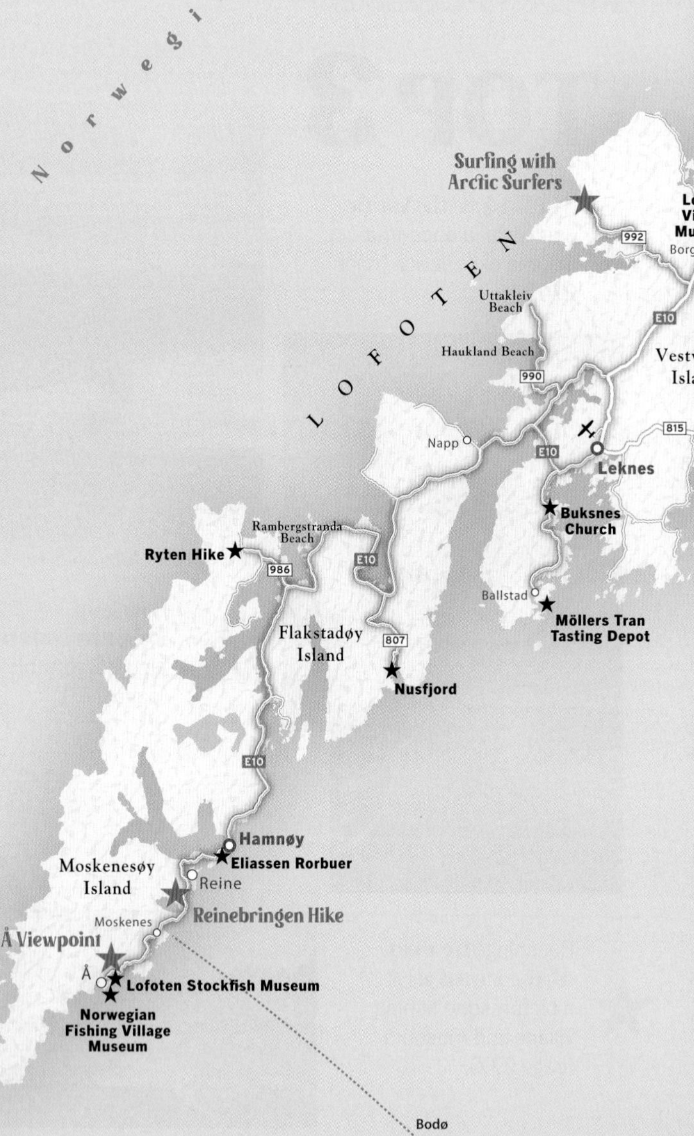

Norwegian Sea
LOFOTEN
Surfing with Arctic Surfers
992
Borg
Uttakleiv Beach
E10
Haukland Beach
990
815
Napp
E10
Leknes
Buksnes Church
Ballstad
Möllers Tran Tasting Depot
Rambergstranda Beach
Ryten Hike
986
E10
Flakstadøy Island
807
Nusfjord
E10
Hamnøy
Eliassen Rorbuer
Moskenesøy Island
Reine
Reinebringen Hike
Moskenes
Å Viewpoint
Å
Lofoten Stockfish Museum
Norwegian Fishing Village Museum
Bodø

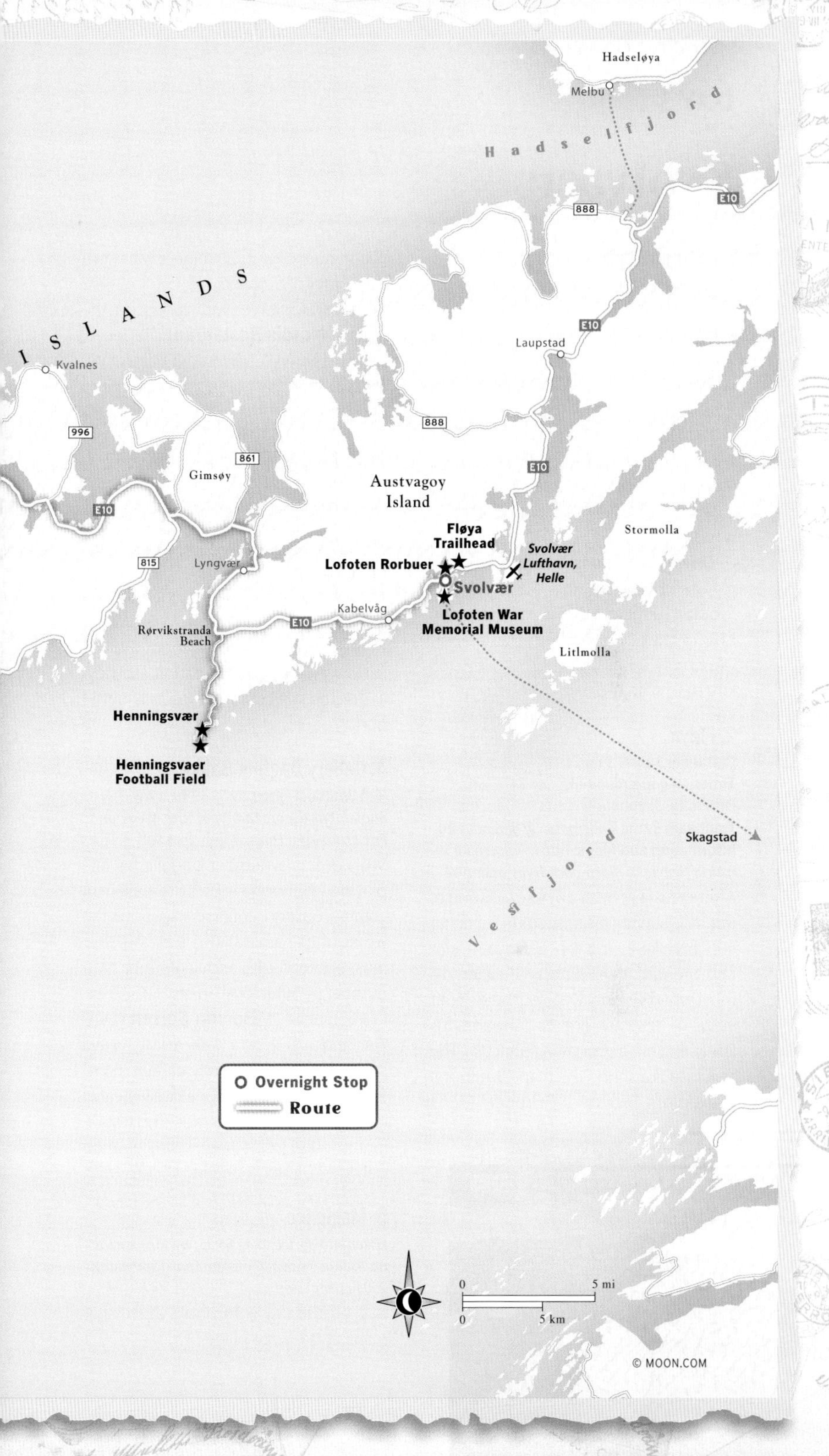

Hadseløya
Melbu
Hadselfjord
888
E10
ISLANDS
Kvalnes
Laupstad
996
888
861
Gimsøy
E10
Austvagoy
Island
E10
Fløya
Trailhead
Stormolla
Svolvær
Lufthavn,
Helle
Lofoten Rorbuer
815
Lyngvær
Svolvær
Kabelvåg
Lofoten War
Memorial Museum
Rørvikstranda
Beach
E10
Litlmolla
Henningsvær
Henningsvaer
Football Field
Skagstad
Vestfjord
Overnight Stop
Route
0
5 mi
0
5 km
© MOON.COM

Svolvær

1. Lofoten Rorbuer

Jektveien 10; tel. 91 59 54 50; www.lofoten-rorbuer.no; 1,200 Kr

This road trip starts on the island of Austvågøy in Svolvær, the largest town in the Lofoten archipelago. Wake up at Lofoten Rorbuer, a hotel situated in one of the oldest dock houses in Svolvær, dating back to 1828. The building served as a fisherman's cabin and storage unit before it became the quaint accommodation it is today.

Driving Directions: Svolvær is a 5-10-minute drive from the closest airport, Svolvær Lufthavn Helle, 6 km (4 mi) on E10. To reach Svolvær from Harstad-Narvik Airport Evenes, drive 2.5 hours (165 km/103 mi) on E10.

2. Fløya

Distance: *3 km (1.9 mi)*
Time: *3-4 hours round-trip*
Difficulty: *Strenuous*
Trailhead: *By the kindergaten in Blåtindveien*
Information and Maps: *https://lofoten.info/hiking-highlights/floya-and-devils-gate-hike*

After breakfast, head out to enjoy one of the mountain hikes this region is known for. The hike to the top of Fløya mountain, though demanding, is considered a must when visiting Svolvær. The summit views of the town and its surroundings stretching out below are spectacular. The trailhead is a short (less than 10-minute) walk from Lofoten Rorbuer, or a five-minute drive or 20-minute walk from the center of Svolvær.

Fløya

Afterward, refuel with lunch on the patio at **Nordis Restaurant** (Torget 15; tel. 41 29 20 00; www.nordisrestaurant.no/svolvar), which serves a varied menu of hearty fare.

3. Lofoten War Memorial Museum

Fiskergata 3; tel. 91 73 03 28; www.museumnord.no/vare-museer/lofoten-krigsminnemuseum; 10am-4pm Mon.-Fri. and 11am-3pm Sat.-Sun. June-Sept.; adults 100 Kr, children 50 Kr

This museum holds Norway's largest collection of memorabilia from World War II. Here, you can learn more about the war in Norway, the Nazi occupation, and how it affected the country, especially in the north.

4. Gallery Dagfinn Bakke

Rich Withs gate 4; tel. 99 59 69 49; www.dagfinnbakke.no; 11am-3pm Tues.-Weds. and Fri., 11am-7pm Thurs., 11am-2pm Sat.

Svolvær has a number of galleries displaying the works of artists based in Lofoten. Gallery Dagfinn Bakke shows the works of its namesake, as well as paintings, photographs, and sculptures by a number of other local artists.

For dinner, try **Børsen Spiseri** (Gunnar Bergs vei 2; tel. 76 06 99 31; www.svinoya.no/en/restaurant; seatings 6pm-9pm daily; 295-425 Kr) for a lovely meal of local food in a historic setting: This restaurant is found inside one of the commercial docks of Svolvær, dating back to 1828.

5. Magic Ice

Fiskergata 36; tel. 45 41 85 35; www.magicice.no/listings/svolvaer-lofoten; 6pm-10pm daily; 250 Kr per person

Cap off the day with drinks at this bar made entirely out of ice.

Key Reservations

If you want to surf with **Arctic Surfers** (rather than watch the wave riders from the shore), book a lesson or experience with them ahead of time.

DAY 2

Henningsvær

Henningsvær is a village scattered across several islands south of E10, the main road connecting the Lofoten islands.

Driving Directions: Henningsvær is 25 km (15.5 mi) southwest of Svolvær on E10 and 816/Henningsværveien. The drive takes approximately half an hour, but the road is narrow and busy in summer, so allow some extra time.

1. Henningsvær Football Field

Løktveien 25

The drive from Svolvær to Henningsvær is quite scenic, and it might seem odd to end it at a football (soccer) field, but you'll know why once you see it. The field's location, taking up the majority of one of the islands that make up Henningsvær, is dramatic: just a few feet from the edge of the green are cliffs and the ocean.

Pick up some lunch at **Henningsvær Lysstøperi & Kafe** (Gammelveien 2; tel. 90 55 18 77; www.henningsvarlys.no; hours vary; 25-119 Kr), a colorful and cozy café.

2. Rørvikstranda Beach

Kabelvåg

If you fancy a swim or just want to stretch your legs on the way back to E10, stop by this jewel of a beach and its turquoise waters. It's located right near the junction of E10 and 816/Hennigsværveien, about 15 minutes north of the stadium.

Vestvågøy

Vestvågøy is one of the major islands in the Lofoten archipelago. Leknes, its administrative center, is the second largest city in Lofoten, and Ballstad at the southern end of the island is the other main town for visitors.

Driving Directions: From Rørvikstranda, Leknes is about an hour's drive (53 km/33 mi).

3. Lofotr Viking Museum

Vikingveien 539, Bøstad; tel. 76 08 49 00; www.lofotr.no/nb; 11am-4pm Tues.-Sat.; adults 225 Kr, children 150 Kr

On the way to Leknes, stop by one of the major attractions in the area. This outdoor museum allows you to meet and interact with Viking reenactors to get a glimpse of what life was like here from the 9th to the early 11th centuries. The chieftain's house is built in a spot where it is believed there once actually was a chieftain's house, based on some artifacts found there.

4. Buksnes Church

Buksnesveien 450, Gravdal; hours vary; free

Buksnes Church is a beautiful, large wooden church found just by the road

Tørrfisk

Tørrfisk, also known as Lofoten stockfish in English, is considered a Norwegian delicacy. In short, tørrfisk is wild-caught cod from around the Lofoten islands that has been hung to dry and mature. When visiting Lofoten you will notice that many of the villages have a very strong (and not great) smell, coming from the codfish drying in the breeze along the ocean. Lofoten stockfish has received the European Union's Protected Geographical Indication status, similar to champagne and roquefort cheese.

WHERE TO TRY IT

You'll be able to try tørrfisk in many of the restaurants along the road trip, such as **Makalaus.** To learn more about Lofoten stockfish and how important it has been for the local culture and trade, make sure to visit the **Lofoten Stockfish Museum** in Å (page 277).

in Gravdal, south of Leknes. The 1905 building is red, with white and green details and a large front tower, and it is a popular spot for visitors to stop and snap photos. You don't need to go inside: The highlight of this church is its exterior and setting, perched on a hill overlooking the Lofoten landscape.

Head back into Leknes for the night. Have dinner at **Makalaus** (Storgata 27, Leknes; tel. 92 50 96 80; www.makalaus.as; 11am-9pm Mon.-Thurs., 11am-midnight Fri., 11am-1am Sat.; 185-225 Kr), which serves stockfish and pepper steak in a relaxed space.

DAY 3

Vestvågøy

This day focuses on the north side of Vestvågøy island, where the most beautiful beaches in Lofoten are located.

★ 1. Surfing with Arctic Surfers

Unstadveien 105; www.unstadarcticsurf.com; 10am-6pm daily; surfboard rentals from 300 Kr per hour

The Arctic Surfers on Unstad Beach (about 30 minutes north of Leknes) are famous for braving all kinds of temperatures. If you want to try the waves yourself for a once-in-a-lifetime experience, you're in luck. Here, you can rent surfboards of various sizes or take surf lessons from highly trained professionals. During their three-hour beginner lesson, you will learn surf theory and water safety, as well as the basics of surfing. After the lesson, take advantage of the on-site sauna.

2. Haukland Beach

Uttakleivveien; www.hauklandbeach.no

This beach might just have the bluest water in the Lofoten isles and is often included on lists of the most beautiful beaches in the country. If you haven't gotten enough of the water after your surf lesson, this beach is great for swimming. Have lunch at the small café, open only in high season.

3. Uttakleiv Beach

End of Uttakleivveien

From Haukland Beach you can drive through the tunnel, under Mannen mountain, and get to one of the most popular photo spots in Lofoten. This sandy beach is scattered with rocks and rocky terrain, shaped by the ocean through the centuries. This makes for a beautiful sight as the waves roll in and pour back out, and lots of photographers gather toward the south end of the beach to snap a shot of the water.

4. Möllers Tran Tasting Depot

Hattvikveien, Ballstad; https://hattvikalodge.no/activity/mollers-cod-liver-oil; hours vary; free

For a complete change of pace, head to the tasting depot of Norway's most famous producer of tran, or cod liver oil, located in Ballstad, 15 minutes south of Leknes. Tran was believed to be a source of health for centuries in Norway, and a tablespoon of it used to be served to school children every morning as the school bell rang. At the tasting depot, run by **Hattvika Lodge** (Hattvikveien 14, Ballstad; https://hattvikalodge.no), you can sample various versions of tran (don't be fooled by the fancy flavors, though—it tastes exactly as it sounds).

Appetite whetted? You can have dinner at Hattvika Lodge before heading back to Leknes.

DAY 4

Flakstadøy

Flakstadøy is the next island you reach after Vestvågøy. The highlight is the beautiful fishing village of Nusfjord.

1. Nusfjord, Flakstadøy

The trip out to Nusfjord is a beautiful drive past lakes and mountains, through the "inner" parts of the island. One of the oldest fishing communities in Norway, Nusfjord is iconic Lofoten, appearing in many photos of the region. The (mainly) yellow-painted wooden buildings of this charming village are all nestled on the docks, and a half-hour (or longer if you linger) stroll around the docks and village is quite relaxing. This is still an active spot for fishing, and you'll find plenty of fish hanging out to dry on the docks. There is a small hill right by the houses, and from the top of it (2-3 minutes' walk) are views out over the ocean.

Driving Directions: From Leknes, take E10 west over to Flakstadøy and south down the west coast of the eastern arm of the island. Right where the road starts turning northwest, leave the E10 and turn south onto the smaller Route Fv807. Nusfjord is more rural, and getting there will require leaving the E10 and taking the smaller Route Fv807. The drive takes 30 minutes, but allow for more time on the narrow road.

2. Rambergstranda

E10 190, Ramberg

After seeing Nusfjord, head back to E10 and continue tracing the island's coast. Stop at Ramberstranda beach for another common photo subject: The red hut at the viewpoint.

Driving Directions: Ramberstranda is about a 20-minute drive from Nusfjord, on Route Fv807 and E10.

Northern Moskenesøy

Moskenesøy is the last of the islands that are connected by the road in Lofoten. The E10 main road crosses onto it farther south, but a smaller road (Fv808) near Ramberg on Flakstadøy leads to the northern part of the island. The landscape of Moskenesøy is perhaps the most dramatic in Lofoten, with jagged peaks and steep mountainsides.

3. Ryten Hike

Distance: *3.5 km (2.2 mi)*
Time: *2 hours (one-way)*
Difficulty: *Moderate*
Trailhead: *Fv806 7 (parking at Fredvang School is encouraged)*
Information and Maps: *https://ut.no/turforslag/1112155862/ryten-og-kvalvika*

This trail follows along a ridge to the top of Ryten mountain (543 m/1,780 ft above sea level). There are spectacular views throughout the hike, and at the top, you'll find a rock formation that is popular in photos. Here, you can pretend to be "hanging" in thin air, with nothing below you. It's just an illusion and is completely safe. Just angle the camera so the ground is out of the image. This is perhaps the most well-known hiking spot in Lofoten. Afterward, you can hike down to Kvalvika Beach (you will have seen the junction on the way up) if you want to add a few more hours to your time here.

Driving Directions: From Ramberg, take E10 south and then west for a few minutes until you come to the smaller Route Fv808, which crosses onto Moskenesøy. Where Fv808 turns south, continue straight onto Fv806. The Fredvang School parking lot is off Fv808, just before the Fv806 junction. The drive from Ramberg takes about 10 minutes.

Hamnøy

4. Eliassen Rorbuer

Hamnøy; tel. 45 81 48 45; https://rorbuer.no; 2,500 Kr

After the hike, head to your lodging for the evening. Eliassen Rorbuer (10 minutes northeast of Reine on E10) is the oldest fisherman's cabin resort in the Lofoten archipelago and is considered by many to be the original resort of this kind. The accommodations are in traditional rorbuer (fishermen's cabins); some are located right on the docks, while others are a little inland on the tiny island. Even if you don't stay here, the cabins are a charming sight.

Driving Directions: To reach Eliassen Rorbuer, drive along E10 from Ramburg for about 20 minutes and turn right when you reach one of the two roads coming off E10 to Hamnøy.

Hamnøy

DAY 5

Reine

Reine is the administrative center of Moskenesøy.

Driving Directions: Reine is about 10 minutes southwest of Hamnøy on E10.

★ 1. Reinebringen Hike

Distance: *2.7 km (1.7 mi)*
Time: *2.5 hours*
Difficulty: *Strenuous (not recommended for children)*
Trailhead: *Center of Reine*
Information and Maps: *www.facebook.com/reinebringen*

Reinebringen is one of the most popular hikes in Norway, offering spectacular views of the town of Reine and the jagged mountain ranges of Moskenesøy. At 448 m (1,470 ft) above sea level, this is not the highest of hikes, but it is still considered relatively difficult due to the steep Sherpa steps you climb for the majority of the hike. From the center of Reine (start anywhere) follow the main road, E10, until you get to the old main road heading south. Follow this on the outside of the tunnel (E10 goes through the tunnel) until you get to the Sherpa steps. From here, the steps go straight up the mountainside almost all the way up. At the very end, there are a lot of loose rocks, so step carefully as you reach the top. Check the Reinebringen Facebook page for up-to-date information on whether the hike is accessible or not during your visit, and as always, ask locals.

After the hike, have a nourishing lunch at **Tapperiet Bistro** (Reineveien 164, Reine; tel. 90 19 73 35; www.tapperiet.com; noon-11pm daily).

Å on Moskenesøy is not only the last letter of the Norwegian alphabet, but it is also the last town you get to along E10—literally the end of the road. In addition to being a landmark, the town is practically a living museum dedicated to the fishing history of Lofoten.

Driving Directions: Å is located at the end of the E10 main road. The drive to Å from Reine takes about 15 minutes.

2. Lofoten Stockfish Museum

Moskenesveien 1270; tel. 76 09 12 11; daily mid-June-mid-Aug.; 100 Kr

You will have noticed cod hanging up to dry all around Lofoten by the time you reach Å. Lofoten stockfish (dried fish) is actually a protected brand in the EU, and the Lofoten Stockfish Museum is dedicated to sharing how the process of drying fish happens. In addition to learning about this process, you can try a selection of stockfish snacks.

3. The Norwegian Fishing Village Museum

Å Vegen 21; tel. 76 09 14 88; www.museum-nord.no/vare-museer/norsk-fiskevaersmuseum; 11am-6pm daily June-Aug., 11am-3pm Mon.-Fri. Sept.-May; adults 100 Kr, children 70 Kr

Here is another museum dedicated to the lifestyle and culture of the Lofoten archipelago. The Norwegian Fishing Village Museum is one of the best kept and most complete traditional fishing villages in Norway. Here you can walk around the village and see several buildings, like the bakery from the 1800s, with its working oven from 1878 (make sure to get one of their cinnamon buns), and the old post office.

★ 4. Å Viewpoint

End E10

This is the culmination of your road trip. As you drive through the E10 tunnel in Å, you will reach the literal end of the road. There is a large parking lot here

WATCH

Twin: A crime drama series that premiered in 2019, *Twin* follows a man who takes over the identity of his twin brother. The show takes place in Lofoten, and the unfolding drama is set against striking landscape of the archipelago.

READ

A Descent into the Maelström by Edgar Allen Poe: This short story is set in Lofoten. The main character describes getting caught in the Moskstraumen, a unique tidal whirlpool phenomenon that occurs off the island of Moskenesøya.

LISTEN

Sami Musicians: The Sami are the Indigenous people of Norway, and notable Sami musicians include Spellemann prize winner Marja Mortensson, Mari Boine, and Frode Fjellheim, who wrote for the *Frozen* soundtrack.

(just outside the tunnel). Park and follow the pathway starting by the parking lot for about five minutes. When you get to the point where the land ends, enjoy the view of the wide ocean stretching out in front of you. Here, you are standing at the end of the Lofoten isles.

Afterward, head back to Eliassen Rorbuer for another night before returning to Svolvær and your next destination.

TRANSPORTATION

Getting There

Travelers to Svolvær usually arrive by plane or boat. Those arriving by boat will travel from ports all along the Norwegian coast via **Hurtigruten** (tel. 81 00 30 30; www.hurtigruten.no; three weekly departures). Hurtigruten starts in Bergen and stops in Ålesund, Trondheim, and Bodø among other smaller places before docking in Svolvær.

The local airport is **Svolvær Lufthavn Helle** (Helle; tel. 67 03 39 50; https://avinor.no/svolvaer), with some flights arriving into **Harstad-Narvik Airport Evenes** (tel. 67 03 41 00; https://avinor.no/flyplass/harstad), a 2.5-hour drive away along E10.

Car Rental

The best way to explore Lofoten is by car. There are plenty of car rentals available at both airports. At Svolvær you will find major rental agencies **Avis** (tel. 76 07 11 40; www.avis.no), **Europcar** (tel. 95 45 06 20; www.europcar.no), **Hertz** (tel. 95 13 85 00; www.hertz.no), and **Sixt** (tel. 76 70 60 00; www.sixt.no), in addition to the smaller **Rent A Car Lofoten** (tel. 47 64 35 60; www.rentacar-lofoten.com). At Harstad-Narvik Airport, you will find **Avis** (tel. 76 98 21 33; www.avis.no), **Budget** (tel. 76 98 21 33; www.budget.no), **Europcar** (tel. 76 98 21 20; www.europcar.no), **Hertz** (tel. 41 58 22 28; www.hertz.no), and **Sixt** (tel. 76 98 23 00; www.sixt.no).

Getting Back

From Å, it takes a total of 2.5 hours to drive back to Svolvær.

- Copenhagen to Oslo (page 519)
- The Bergen Line (page 675)

BORDEAUX AND THE PYRENEES

Why Go: This trip showcases the fantastic variety France has to offer, while at the same time teaching about the country's singular soul.

Number of Days: 4

Total Distance: 282 km (175 mi)

Seasons: Late spring to early fall

Start: Bordeaux

End: Cauterets

What more iconic image of the French countryside is there than venerable chateaus and rolling vineyards as far as the eye can see? For within it is captured the heady mixture of respecting nature and bending it to civilization's will that so epitomizes the country's character and joie de vivre. The area surrounding Bordeaux personifies this. Then, add to that the 18th-century elegance and layered history of the city of Bordeaux itself, the possibility of extending your trip south to Lourdes, Western Europe's "miracle central," then farther into the wild beauty of the Pyrenees mountains, and you've a trip that goes way beyond preconceptions, demonstrating the depth this country has to offer.

The region is well accommodated for tourists, with plenty of excellent hotels and restaurants to suit all budgets, good transport between all locations, and convenient links to and from the region.

TOP 3

★ Strolling the elegant, 18th-century **city center of Bordeaux,** the largest urban UNESCO World Heritage Site in the world (page 281).

Sampling **Bordeaux wine** among grapevines revered by oenophiles for centuries on a tour of the region's vineyards (page 283).

Joining in the candlelit procession to the sanctuary of **Notre-Dame de Lourdes,** feeling the spiritual power that has been luring faithful here since the 19th century (page 285).

Bordeaux

★ 1. Bordeaux City Center

A town of unparalleled 18th-century elegance, the center of Bordeaux is the single largest urban UNESCO World Heritage Site on Earth.

After arriving by fast TGV train from Paris, checking into your hotel, and maybe grabbing a bite to eat, head to the **Place de la Bourse** to start your exploration. From this striking, symmetrical square (with its dominant, deliberately reflective water feature, the **Miroir d'eau**), head south to fairytale **Porte Cailhau,** the 15th-century turreted gate leading into Bordeaux's old town. It's just a short walk from there to Rue Saint-Eloi and its iconic **Grosse Cloche**—literally "big bell." This appropriately named eight-ton behemoth was once employed as the city's early warning system in case of attack and fire. From there, cut west to the **Cathedrale Saint-Andre** (Pl. Pey Berland; tel. 05 56 44 67 29; www.cathedrale-bordeaux.fr; 10am-1pm and 3pm-7:30pm Tues.-Sun., 3pm-7:30pm Mon.; free), the city's main church. Consecrated in 1096, it is a splendid Gothic construction around a Romanesque core—well worth stepping inside to tour.

2. Musée d'Aquitaine

20 Cr Pasteur; tel. 05 56 01 51 00; www.musee-aquitaine-bordeaux.fr; 11am-6pm Tues.-Sun.; adults €5, reduced €3

One of the largest French history museums outside Paris, the Musée d'Aquitaine is dedicated to the fascinating story and famous personages of the surrounding region, and in some cases beyond—the city's coastal position means it's long been very outward-facing, so there's lots of global archaeology in the museum's exhibitions. The museum is housed in a beautiful neoclassical building from the 18th century, and it's a great opportunity to dig under the surface of Bordeaux. A tour here can last up to two hours.

left, Porte Cailhau; right, Place de la Bourse

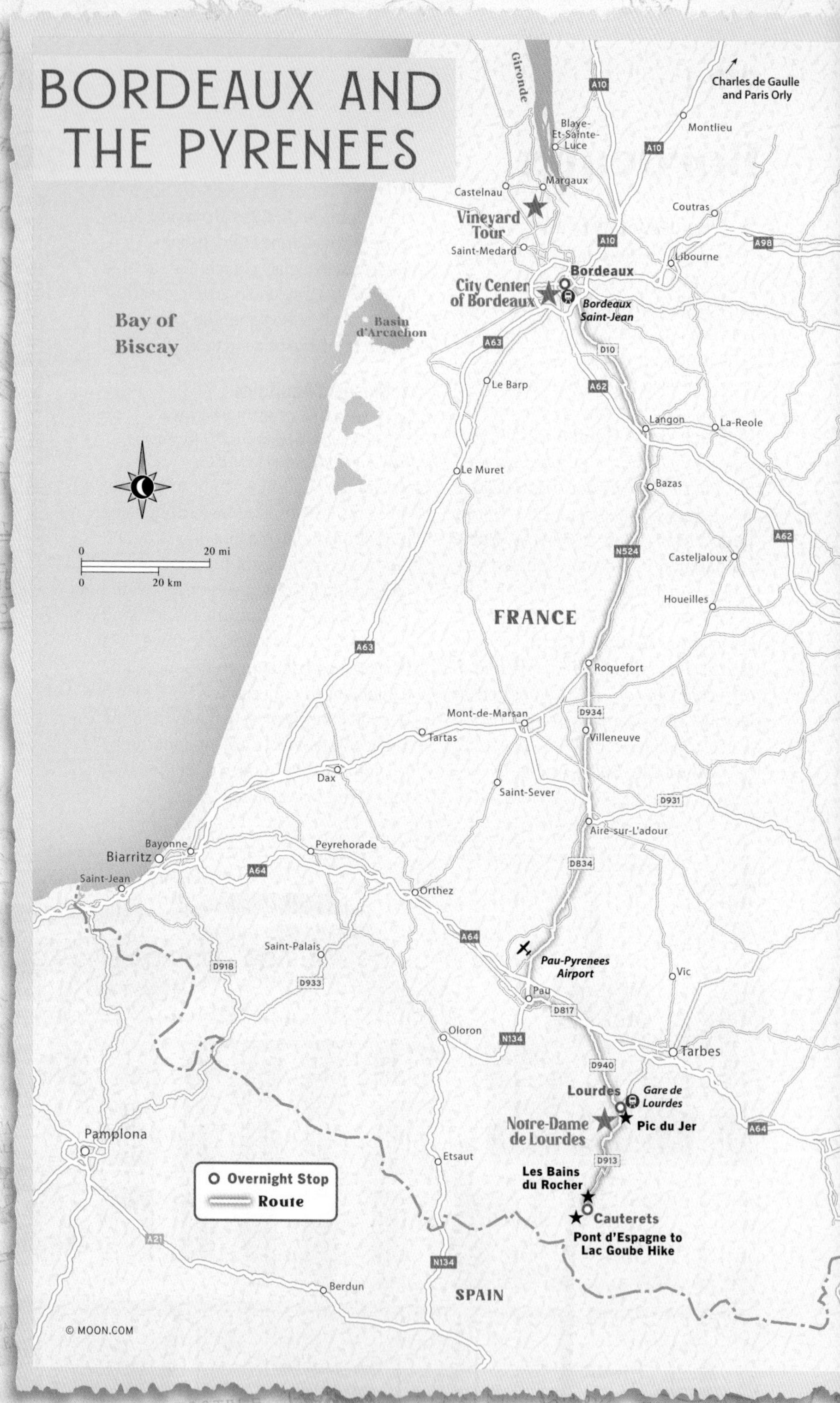

BORDEAUX AND THE PYRENEES
Gironde
A10
Charles de Gaulle and Paris Orly
Blaye-Et-Sainte-Luce
Montlieu
Castelnau
Margaux
Vineyard Tour
Coutras
Saint-Medard
A98
Libourne
Bordeaux
City Center of Bordeaux
Bordeaux Saint-Jean
Bay of Biscay
Basin d'Arcachon
A63
D10
Le Barp
A62
Langon
La-Reole
Le Muret
Bazas
N524
0
20 mi
20 km
Casteljaloux
Houeilles
FRANCE
Roquefort
Mont-de-Marsan
D934
Tartas
Villeneuve
Dax
Saint-Sever
D931
Aire-sur-L'adour
Bayonne
Peyrehorade
Biarritz
A64
D834
Saint-Jean
Orthez
Saint-Palais
Pau-Pyrenees Airport
D918
D933
Vic
Pau
D817
Oloron
N134
Tarbes
D940
Lourdes
Gare de Lourdes
Notre-Dame de Lourdes
Pic du Jer
Pamplona
Etsaut
D913
Overnight Stop
Route
Les Bains du Rocher
Cauterets
Pont d'Espagne to Lac Goube Hike
A21
Berdun
SPAIN
© MOON.COM

Key Reservations

- Be sure to book a **wine tour** with A La Française, an essential part of any Bordeaux trip.
- You'll benefit from booking ahead at most **restaurants,** especially popular spots like La Tupina.
- The further ahead you book your **transportation,** including TGV tickets and rental car, the cheaper they are likely to be.

3. Bordelais Cuisine in La Tupina

6 Rue Porte de la Monnaie; tel. 05 56 91 56 37; https://latupina.com; noon-2pm and 7pm-10pm daily; mains from €25

Loosen your belt and get ready to enjoy a most lavish meal and the best of Bordelais cuisine in this rustic restaurant, a 15-minute walk from the museum. All the kitchen's ingredients, from radishes to raw meat, are laid out for customers to see, both uncooked and as they are fried, roasted, or broiled right there over an open woodfire flame. Make sure to book ahead.

DAY 2

Bordeaux Wine Country

★ 1. Vineyard Tour and Tasting

After getting a canelé—Bordeaux's most famous sweet snack, a small, frilled pastry usually flavored with rum and vanilla—from **La Toque Cuivrée** (41 Pl. Gambetta; tel. 05 57 83 61 67; www.la-toque-cuivree.fr; 8am-8pm daily; canelés from €0.40), it's time for a trip out to the vineyards and wineries that have made the city famous.

Though it's possible to visit the wineries in your own rental vehicle, you'll enjoy a far more in-depth, safer, and more relaxing experience on a chauffeured guided tour. There are plenty to choose from, with the **A La Française** tours run by Bordovino (www.alafrancaise.fr/bordeaux; from €49 per person) among the most professional and the best.

These tours tend to include visits to at least two chateaus (depending on the day these might include the buildings at the heart of the Ferrand, Pressac, Grand Mayne, or Soutard estates), and a drive out through the vineyards, which are most impressive in early fall, just before the grape harvest, when the air smells like the inside of a wine barrel. You'll gain insight into the region's history,

vineyard in St. Emilion

Wine Land

Bordeaux wine can be said to convey the essence of France, distilled and then bottled to mature. The drink that made its name is as much a product of Bordeaux's coastal outward-looking location as it is of the hinterland where grapes are grown. There's plenty of history to learn, venerable old estates to tour, and of course lots of wine to drink, all of which make **guided tours** well worth your time.

HISTORY

The first wines in the region were produced by the Romans in the 1st century CE, but it was not until the marriage of Eleanor of Aquitaine to the English king Henry Plantagenet that the industry really took off, as it led to a massive increase in English demand for claret, a popular dark-pink wine from the region. A second golden era came about in the 18th century, thanks to Dutch traders who drained some of the city's surrounding marshland, thus opening up further room for viticulture. And as if all this foreign influence wasn't enough, when a vine disease decimated Bordeaux's vineyards in the late 19th century, the industry was only saved by grafting native vines onto pest-resistant rootstock from California. No wonder these reds have such a cosmopolitan palate!

REGIONS AND VARIETALS

For the novice wine enthusiast, it is true that Bordeaux can be intimidating. There are just so many different wines to try! However, it helps to know that there are effectively four main categories.

- **Cabinet Sauvignon blends:** These originated in the area in the 1700s and hail from the Garonne river's "left bank," otherwise known as the **Medoc.** These wines tend to have higher tannins and acidity, and so they keep well and develop into eye-wateringly priced vintages.
- **Merlot blends:** These originated from the "right bank," characterized by fruitier, more velvety flavors.
- **Sweet whites:** Among these, the most famous is easily **Sauternes,** so-called because it comes from the Sauternais region. It's known for its golden color and rich honey taste.
- **Dry whites:** These wines make up just 10 percent of the region's produce but are nevertheless extremely popular and refined.

but more appealing still are the various wines you will have a chance to taste, the snacks they will be paired with, and the tasting notes that accompany them so that you might enjoy them more. What these wines will be depends on which tour you choose, so it helps to do a little homework (i.e., drinking) before you go. **Medoc,** known for Cabernet Sauvignon and grand crus, and **St. Emilion,** for Merlot and family producers, are the most popular labels.

2. Dinner at Le Chien de Pavlove

45 Rue de la Devise; tel. 05 56 48 26 71; www.lechiendepavlov.com; 12:15pm-2:30pm and

7:30pm-10:30pm Wed.-Sat., 7:30pm-10:30pm Tues.; mains from €15

By now you're probably feeling up to your neck in tradition, so, back in Bordeaux, give yourself dinner off with lighter, more modern regional flavors at Le Chien de Pavlove. The tasting menu is a veritable culinary odyssey, not to mention being a great value, while the interior is both trendy and cozy. It's worth booking ahead, especially on weekends.

DAY 3

Bordeaux to Lourdes

Pick up your rental car for the drive down the A62 and A65 to Lourdes, France's most famous and popular pilgrimage destination. This is a motorway drive, mostly between French forest and farmland, which grows more exciting the closer you get to your destination, as the foothills of the Pyrenees begin and off in the distance you start to make out a jagged line of true mountain peaks.

1. Picnic Fare from Halles et Marchés Lourdes

11 Pl. du Champ Commun; www.facebook.com/halles.marches.lourdes; 6:30am-2pm Mon.-Sat.

It should be around lunchtime when you arrive, so the first thing to do in Lourdes should be getting something to eat. Selecting a picnic lunch of cheese, dried sausage, and rotisserie chicken from the central covered food market, heaving with produce from local farmers, is easily your best bet for an authentic meal.

Driving Directions: Lourdes is 252 km (157 mi) from Bordeaux, a drive of just over 2.5 hours. To get there, find the A631 heading south of the city along the Garonne River, which turns into the A630. After just under 1 km, exit onto the A62 heading south. You'll be on this road for over 40 km (25 mi) before turning south on the A65/E7. You'll be on this road for most of your drive, over 150 km (93 mi), and then head southeast when you hit the A64. After about 23 km (14 mi), get on the D940 for about 20 km (12 mi) until it turns into the D914, and you'll see Lourdes in the distance.

2. Picnic at the Pic du Jer

59 Avenue Francis Lagardère; tel. 05 62 94 00 41; www.picdujer.com; 9:30am-5pm daily; adults €12.50 round-trip, ages 6-17 €10 round-trip, under 6 free

Constructed all the way back in 1900, the **funicular railway** in the south of Lourdes takes you up to the magnificent summit of the Pic du Jer in style; from there you can look back over the town and the Pyrenean foothills that surround it, or to the Pyrenees proper—a stunning crenulation of real mountain peaks that define the horizon to the south. Find a perch and enjoy your market haul.

★ 3. Candlelit Procession to Notre-Dame de Lourdes

Start at Grotte des apparitions; 9pm daily; free

A relatively unassuming town in the Pyrenean foothills for much of its history, Lourdes shot to prominence in the mid-18th century following a number of appearances of the Virgin Mary to peasant girl Bernadette Soubirous. The site then became famous as a location of healing miracles, and a vast industry was established to cater to the steady flow of year-round pilgrims. Even if you're not Catholic, the town is fascinating to visit, offering a front-row seat to the still-vibrant religious culture of modern Europe.

Perhaps the best way to do this is by taking the nightly candlelit procession from the **Grotte des Apparitions**—the shallow cave overlooked by a statue of the Virgin Mary where Bernadette Soubirous had her visions and is now the

(top to bottom) Pic du Jer; candlelit procession at Sanctuaire Notre-Dame de Lourdes; Pont d'Espagne; Sanctuaire Notre-Dame de Lourdes

main sanctuary of the town—out to the vast esplanade in front of **Notre-Dame de Lourdes,** the church built in honor of these visitations. It starts at 9pm and, despite covering less than half a kilometer (0.3 mi), takes around an hour. Remember, this is a deeply religious ceremony, so you should come dressed with shoulders and knees covered. This is easily the best way to first encounter the holy sanctuary, among the prayers and songs and high intentions of the international faithful.

DAY 4

Lourdes to Cauterets

1. Sanctuaire Notre-Dame de Lourdes

1 Avenue Mgr Théas; tel. 05 62 42 78 78; www.lourdes-france.org; 6am-12am; free

After the magic of the previous night's procession, it's worth revisiting Lourdes's church complex to explore at your own speed. Head to the grotto and spend a moment in front of the statue of the Virgin, drink the waters (as Bernadette was herself instructed to do), and light a candle on your way out. Lourdes is relatively modern as most places of religious worship on the continent go, having been built in the late 19th century following Saint Bernadette's visitations in an admittedly impressive but still relatively fresh looking neo-Gothic style. The whole area is also explicitly designed with high numbers of tourists and pilgrims in mind, so it can sometimes feel something like a Christian Disneyland. The grotto itself transcends the hubbub: It is located under an ancient rock face, and a deep sense of spirituality pervades the whole site.

2. Cauterets

Your next stretch in the car heads into the proper Pyrenees, driving from village

WATCH

Lourdes: This French documentary by Thierry Demaizière and Alban Teurlai was filmed over eight months at the famous Pyrenean pilgrimage site. It follows a number of people making their journey to the healing waters and offers a lasting impression of what the town means for so many believers around the world.

READ

The Billionaire's Vinegar: The Mystery of the World's Most Expensive Bottle of Wine by Benjamin Wallace: A global story with a bottle from Bordeaux at its heart. This tale about a Château Lafite, which supposedly once belonged to Thomas Jefferson and sold at auction for $156,000, is the best introduction to the murky world of the wine industry. Expertly told, it's an excellent primer before any vineyard tour or tasting.

LISTEN

"Mon Dieu que je suis à mon aise" ("My God I'm at My Ease") by Nadau: Nadau formed in the 1970s to celebrate the traditional music of Gascony, the region of southeastern France covered by this route. Listen to the live version of this song, recorded in 2010, to get a sense of how beloved the band is in France: The crowd sings along to every word.

to village between lushly beautiful and ever-growing hills and mountains all the way to the delightful spa town of Cauterets. For the moment, though, you're just passing through, so store your luggage at a hotel in town, and then continue the farther 8 km (5 mi) into the mountains and the Pont d'Espagne.

Driving Directions: Cauterets is 30 km (18.5 mi) from Lourdes, a 30-minute drive. Get on the D821 heading south for 17 km (10.5 mi), then take the D921 (1 km/1.6 mi) to the D920 (10.5 km/6.5 mi).

3. Pont d'Espagne to Lac Goube Hike

Pont d'Espagne, Puntas; tel. 05 62 92 52 19; www.cauterets.com/grand-site-pont-despagne; open 24 hours daily; free

Now that you're truly in the Pyrenees, the best way to experience them is on a hike. A 2.5- to 3-hour there-and-back ramble takes you from the Pont d'Espagne, a magnificent 19th-century bridge alongside a spectacular waterfall, to this staggering punchbowl of a mountain lake, surrounded by turquoise slopes and jagged peaks. The way is part of the well-marked GR10 walking route—look for the red and white way-markers—though of course you should come equipped with a map, plus warm-weather gear, no matter the season.

Driving Directions: The parking lot for Pont d'Espagne is 7 km (4 mi) from Cauterets, a 15-minute drive on the D920.

4. Spa Time at Les Bains du Rocher

Avenue du Dr Domer; tel. 05 62 92 14 20; www.bains-rocher.fr; 2pm-7:30pm Mon.-Thurs., 10am-12:45pm and 2pm-8pm Fri.-Sun.; 2-hour pass €19

Dotted with copious natural hot springs, the town of Cauterets has been host to spas since the mid-19th century, attracting famous visitors from Victor Hugo to George Sand. There remain several to choose from, with Les Bains du Rocher among the best. Relax after your walk in the heated outdoor pool (even better in the winter when the surrounding mountains can be covered in snow), or explore the inside of the refined modern complex, with its neoclassical stylings, numerous jacuzzies, jets, plunge pools, and more.

5. Dinner at L'Assiette Gourmande

7 Rue Richelieu; tel. 06 07 60 89 48; www.facebook.com/LAssiette-gourmande-394453054336704; 7pm-11pm Fri.-Wed.; mains from €20

After a long day, you've earned a slap-up meal, and Cauterets is a great place to provide one. L'Assiette Gourmande is perhaps the best of a whole host of restaurants specializing in hearty mountain cuisine: the kind where a whole plethora of meats can meet a whole plethora of cheeses, often on the same plate, sometimes with a side of butter-roasted potatoes. It's a satisfying end your jaunt through the southwest corner of France.

TRANSPORTATION

Air

France's largest airports are in Paris: **Charles de Gaulle** (Roissy-en-France; www.parisaeroport.fr/roissy-charles-de-gaulle) and **Paris Orly** (Orly; www.parisaeroport.fr/orly). To reach Bordeaux from Paris, take the high-speed TGV train (2-2.5 hours).

Bordeaux also has a smaller airport, **Bordeaux-Mérignac Airport** (www.bordeaux.aeroport.fr), located a 20-minute drive (10 km/6 mi) from the city center.

Train

France's rail network and its famous high-speed TGVs make travel time from one side of the country to the other overland very nearly the same as flights.

- **Paris Montparnasse:** Trains from Paris to Bordeaux originate at this major train station located south of Luxembourg Gardens.
- **Bordeaux St. Jean Station:** Bordeaux's main train station is located 2.3 km (1.4 mi) south of the city center.
- **Gare de Lourdes:** Lourdes's main train station is conveniently located in the city's compact downtown.

Car Rental

Rental car prices start at around €60 a day. All the usual providers (Hertz, Avis, Europcar, etc.) have outlets at Bordeaux's St. Jean train station and airport.

Most of the driving on the trip is between Bordeaux and Lourdes on the motorway and is relatively straightforward. Even leaving Lourdes for the mountains, the roads are wide and well-maintained and won't prove a challenge to any relatively confident driver. Pulling away from the main route in the Pyrenees may require something of a head for heights, even though a decent amount of social spending keeps the roads in good condition, and there's usually space for two vehicles to pass without trouble. If you can, try to avoid night driving on the smaller mountain roads.

Getting Back

To get home from Cauterets, fly out of **Pau-Pyrenees Airport** (Uzein; www.pau.aeroport.fr), a 1-hour 20-minute drive from Cauterets (95 km/59 mi). From Cauterets, the drive back to the start of the route in Bordeaux takes about three hours (300 km/186 mi).

CONNECT WITH

- London and Paris (page 44)
- Barcelona and Madrid (page 99)
- Camino de Santiago (page 459)

TUSCANY AND UMBRIA

Why Go: A drive through Tuscany and Umbria gives you one of the best possible tastes of Italian culture, beauty, nature, and people.

Number of Days: 6

Total Distance: 265 km (165 mi)

Seasons: Spring

Start: Florence

End: Orvieto

The secret has been out on Tuscany for centuries. Merchants, students, artists, and travelers have long come here to trade, to learn, and to experience a remarkable mix of art, history, and cuisine that still exists today. Venture beyond Florence, the region's capital, and anyone with the instinct to explore and a driver's license can discover UNESCO-rated landscapes and hill towns where culture radiates from ancient stones and local dishes vary from one post code to the next.

Farther south, Umbria is Tuscany's little brother, less visited by the masses but no less intriguing, with a high spiritual quotient—this is the birthplace of Saint Francis, after all.

Together, Umbria and Tuscany offer lessons about Italy's past and insights into its present.

TOP 3

★ Climbing to the top of a medieval tower, centuries-old ramparts, or a 4,000-foot-tall mountain for **breathtaking views** of the Italian countryside (page 295).

★ Discovering how **local wine** is made and tasting it straight from the source (page 300).

★ Exploring **Basilica di San Francesco,** where art history was made (page 301).

DAY 1

Florence

Whether arriving from Pisa, Rome, or elsewhere, plan to wake up in Florence, Tuscany's capital, on the day you embark on your Tuscany and Umbria road trip. For ideas of what to see and do in Florence, see page 150.

San Gimignano

The roads headed south out of Florence are soon surrounded by Tuscany's quintessential landscape. In a little over an hour, you'll catch your first glimpse of San Gimignano. This renown hill town with an impressive medieval skyline is no mirage. In the Middle Ages, San Gimignano was a crossroads along the Via Francigena trail, which brought a steady stream of pilgrims and merchants to town. Locals grew wealthy producing and trading in saffron, which was highly valued at the time.

Driving Directions: From Florence, head south on Via Senese to the Raccordo Autostradale Firenze-Siena. You'll exit at Poggibonsi Nord and follow Strada Regionale 429 to SP1, where San Gimignano (53 km/33 mi; 1 hour) will eventually come into view. The slower scenic option is on the SP80 and SP79 provincial roads. There are three large parking lots to the north and south of San Gimignano from which the historic center can be easily reached on foot.

1. Rocca di Montestaffoli

Via della Rocca; open 24 hours; free

Small brown signs indicate the way from the center of town up to the Rocca di Montestaffoli. Of all the vantage points this town offers, this is perhaps the most satisfying one to reach, built by Florentines after they captured the town in 1353. The pentagon-shaped fortress housed troops to keep an eye on comings and goings. The walls are still in good shape, and

left, Monteriggioni; right, San Gimignano

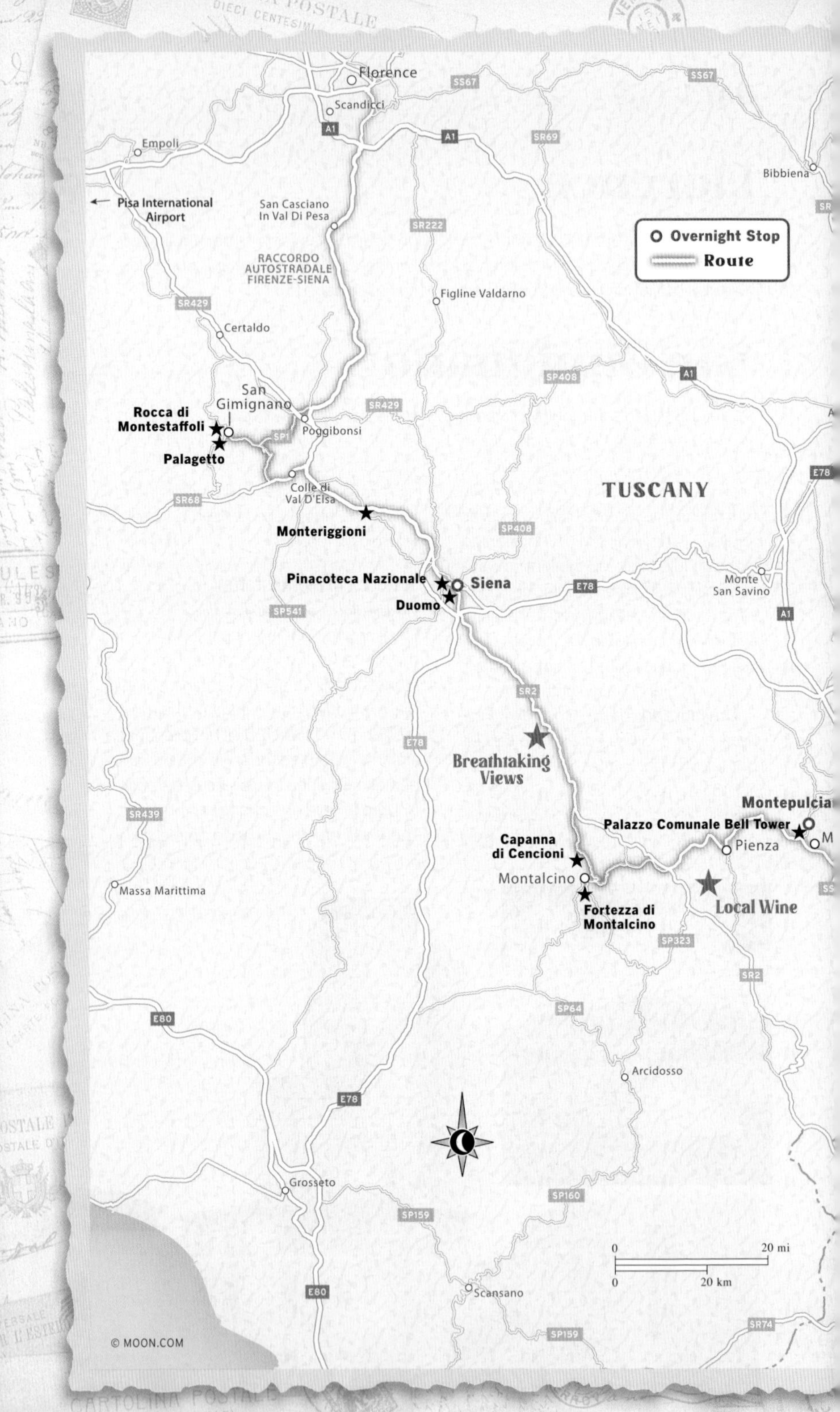

Florence
Scandicci
Empoli
Pisa International Airport
San Casciano In Val Di Pesa
RACCORDO AUTOSTRADALE FIRENZE-SIENA
Bibbiena
Overnight Stop
Route
Figline Valdarno
Certaldo
San Gimignano
Rocca di Montestaffoli
Palagetto
Poggibonsi
Colle di Val D'Elsa
Monteriggioni
TUSCANY
Pinacoteca Nazionale
Siena
Duomo
Monte San Savino
Breathtaking Views
Montepulcia
Palazzo Comunale Bell Tower
Pienza
Capanna di Cencioni
Montalcino
Fortezza di Montalcino
Local Wine
Massa Marittima
Arcidosso
Grosseto
Scansano
0
20 mi
0
20 km
SS67
A1
SR69
SR222
SR429
SP408
SR429
SP1
SR68
E78
SP541
SR2
E78
SR439
SP323
SP64
E80
E78
SP160
SP159
E80
SR74
© MOON.COM

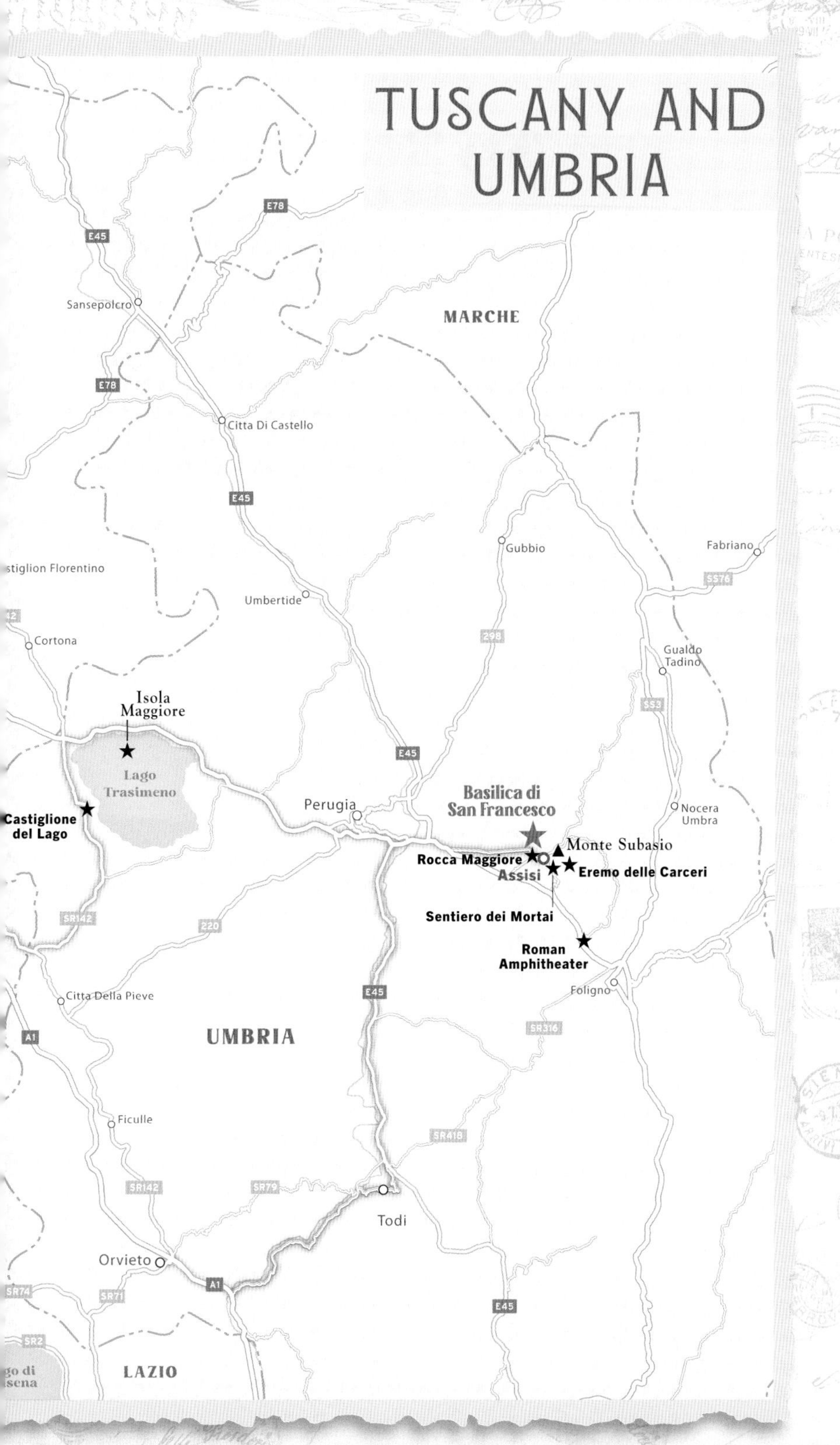

TUSCANY AND UMBRIA
MARCHE
E78
E45
Sansepolcro
E78
Citta Di Castello
E45
Gubbio
Fabriano
SS76
stiglion Florentino
Umbertide
Cortona
298
Gualdo Tadino
Isola Maggiore
SS3
E45
Lago Trasimeno
Castiglione del Lago
Perugia
Basilica di San Francesco
Monte Subasio
Nocera Umbra
Rocca Maggiore
Assisi
Eremo delle Carceri
Sentiero dei Mortai
SR142
220
Roman Amphitheater
Foligno
Citta Della Pieve
E45
A1
UMBRIA
SR316
Ficulle
SR418
SR142
SR79
Todi
Orvieto
A1
SR71
SR74
E45
SR2
LAZIO

Key Reservations

Siena

Tuscany is famous internationally and attracts millions of tourists every year. Many **accommodations** are booked well in advance and some only accept multiday or week-long stays during the summer. **Activities** like biking, horseback riding, and guided wine tours are also very popular and can fill up fast. That said, Tuscany is a place of experiences rather than sights, and most museums and other monuments don't require reservations. Still, it's usually better to arrive early or late when crowds are generally thinner.

The one exception may be Siena, the largest town visited on this road trip, where the **Opa Si Pass** (€17) is your ticket to seven sights and is available online or at the Duomo ticket office (Piazza del Duomo; tel. 05/7753-4511; www.operaduomo.siena.it; 9am-6pm daily) in the square outside.

you can climb a tower for your first 360-degree look at Tuscan countryside. Near the entrance, the **San Gimignano Wine Experience** (www.sangimignanomuseovernaccia.com; 11:30am-7:30pm daily) organizes tastings of the town's famous white wine, Vernaccia.

To fill up after your climb, follow the charming Via Piandornella to **Le Vecchie Mura** (Via Piandornella 15; tel. 05/7794-0270; €9-12). Ask for "una tavola fuori, per favore" (an outdoor table, please) to dine on thick pici pasta served with white ragu or wild boar on the lovely terrace overlooking the valley.

2. Ring Walls

Satisfied, walk off lunch by strolling San Gimignano's 13th-century **ring walls,** topped with a pedestrian path, Passeggiate delle Mura, that circumnavigates the city. There are a half-dozen historic gates along the way, including Porta delle Fonti, which leads to the medieval well where villagers once washed their clothes. The entire 2-km (1.2-mi) circuit takes 30-40 minutes to complete.

3. Monteriggioni

Monteriggioni, a tiny hamlet off the SR2 regional road between San Gimignano and Siena, is the first of many tempting Tuscan detours. Few Middle Age strongholds are so well-preserved—this one held out against multiple Florentine sieges over the centuries. It did eventually fall in 1554, and Siena was conquered the very next year. Behind the walls are a small church, a museum dedicated to the Templars, and a clutch of eateries. If you haven't sampled Tuscan gelato yet, order a cone or cup at **La Bottega del Castello** (Piazza Roma 11; tel. 057/730-4898; 10am-7:45pm daily; €3-5) and browse the artisanal shops selling local delicacies, leather goods, and other souvenirs.

Driving Directions: Backtrack on the SP1 back to the Raccordo Autostradale Firenze-Siena, exiting at Monteriggioni (26 km/16 mi; 33 minutes).

★ Tuscany and Umbria's Best Views

Tuscany is synonymous with gorgeous countryside. People have been living on and cultivating this land for thousands of years, and not much has been left to chance. It's a unique combination of nature and civilization that is a wonder to gaze upon and makes driving a pleasure. Once you arrive at your destination there are always ramparts to circumnavigate, turrets to climb, and towers to mount. Getting to the top in Tuscany and Umbria means getting a bird's-eye view of a landscape that has enchanted poets and travelers for centuries.

- **Rocca di Montestaffoli, San Gimignano:** A Florentine stronghold overlooking town (page 291).
- **Torre del Mangia, Siena:** The highest spot in Siena once used to spot marauding enemies (page 296).
- **Fortezza di Montalcino, Montalcino:** A pristine fortress with ramparts you can walk around (page 298).
- **Belvedere walkway, Pienza:** A romantic look out point with benches and a bar (page 298).
- **Bell tower, Palazzo Comunale, Montepulciano:** A grand municipal tower with a 360-degree views of Tuscany (page 299).
- **Monte Bivio, Sentiero dei Mortai, Assisi:** A mountaintop trail with endless Umbrian vistas (page 304).

Siena

Though Siena is smaller and less renown than illustrious Florence, it's still a must on any Tuscany itinerary. The city rose to prominence under the Lombards and began booming in the Middle Ages through trade, which allowed the church and wealthy families to build the monuments that attract millions of travelers today.

Driving Directions: Return to the Raccordo Autostradale Firenze-Siena. As you near Siena, the road becomes the Viale Giovanni Paolo II, and then the SR2. The entire drive (21 km/13 mi) should take just over 20 minutes.

4. Piazza del Campo

Wherever you enter Siena, you're inevitably drawn to Piazza del Campo. The main square has been a natural gathering place for centuries and the land was purchased by the town in the Middle Ages to host a market and local celebrations. Since then it has been refined and perfected; old buildings were demolished and new ones built in conformity to the guidelines set by city elders. The result is a stunning seashell-shaped piazza on a delicate incline that hosts city's famous saddleless horse race, **Palio delle Contrade,** in early July and again in mid-August. It's a grueling three-lap race cheered on by an avid public who pack every available inch of the square. If your visit happens to coincide with the Palio, arrive early and stand near

(top to bottom) Duomo, Siena; Pinacoteca Nazionale; Montalcino; Fortezza di Montalcino

the fountain for the best view of the action.

Palazzo Pubblico (Piazza del Campo 1; tel. 05/7729-2111; 10am-6pm; €9), at the bottom of the sloping square, was constructed in the 12th century by Gothic architects. The palace is Siena's town hall and has been since the 12th century. Part of the palace is now a museum, and visitors can explore magnificent rooms where Siena's leaders gathered. Inside, you'll also find the entrance to the **Torre del Mangia,** which rises 102 m (334 ft) above the city and offers distant views of Tuscan countryside. The tower took 23 years to build and has been a symbol of the city ever since. All that separates you from the top are 300 steep steps.

After dark, Siena's ancient streets fill with locals heading to their favorite restaurants. Many of these, including **Grotta di Santa Caterina da Bagoga** (Via della Galluzza 26; tel. 05/7728-2208; noon-3pm and 7pm-11pm Tues.-Sat., noon-3pm Sun.; €10-12), set up tables on the cobblestones outside. Opt for the typical menu (€40), featuring six hearty courses of Sienese classics, like pici pasta, which resembles thick spaghetti; hearty vegetable ribbolita stews; and grilled meats.

DAY 2

Siena

1. Duomo

Piazza del Duomo; tel. 05/7728-6300; www.operaduomo.siena.it; 10:30am-5pm Mon.-Sat., 1:30-5pm Sun.; €5

Siena's Duomo is hard to miss. It's the largest building in Siena and would have been Tuscany's biggest cathedral had the plague not halted construction. The intricate facade is decorated with statues, gargoyles, mosaics, and sculptures that mesmerize the eye, while the sides are covered in alternating stripes of white and green marble.

There's a lot to see inside, including the

TO TAKE Home

Souvenirs of the gastronomic variety are perhaps the best things you can bring home from your Tuscany and Umbria trip.

Siena

In Siena, head to **Antica Drogheria Manganelli** (Via di Città 71-73; tel. 05/7728-0002; 9:30am-7:30pm daily). Inside you'll discover what a supermarket looked like 100 years ago. This one opened in 1879 and carries everything you need to faithfully re-create a Tuscan dinner back home. Shelves are lined with quality grappa, exotic sweets, and select cold cuts. Pasta is handmade by small producers in the area, and some of the vinegar is over 80 years old.

Piccolomini library with frescoes by Raffaello (he's the one wearing red pants and holding a candle), the baptistry sculpted by Donatello, an ancient underground crypt, and the Museo dell'Opera that explains how the cathedral was built.

The panoramic **Porta Cielo** (10:30am-6pm daily; €20) route up the inside of the cathedral provides an overhead view of the central apse and the city outside. It's a guided tour that leaves every 30 minutes with a maximum of 18 participants. You can also hire a guide (info@guidesiena.com; €150 for 3 hours), use interactive touch-screen tablets (€7), or listen to the audio stations (€2) located at different points within the church.

2. Ospedale di Santa Maria

Piazza Duomo 1; tel. 05/7729-2615; 10am-7pm daily summer, 10am-5pm Mon.-Fri., 10am-7pm Sat.-Sun. winter; €9, guided tours €5

Ospedale di Santa Maria was the first hospital in the city where pilgrims would go for first aid and where anyone with a disease could find relief. It was operational until recently and now houses a labyrinthine museum and magnificent frescoes illustrating medieval medical treatments.

Have lunch nearby at the rustic **Hosteria il Carroccio** (Via di Casato di Sotto 32; tel. 05/774-1165; 12:15pm-2:45pm and 7:15pm-9:45pm Thurs.-Tues.; €8-12).

3. Pinacoteca Nazionale

Via San Pietro 29; www.pinacotecanazionale.siena.it; 8:15am-7:15pm Tues.-Sat., 9am-1pm Sun.; €4

Palazzo Buonsignori houses the Pinacoteca Nazionale, a premier collection of Sienese artwork, most from the 13th-17th centuries. There's an unrivaled number of gold-painted canvases, many of which were donated by local churches and convents. Ambrogio, Pietro Lorenzetti, Sassetta, and Beccafumi may not be as famous as their Florentine counterparts but that doesn't make them any less talented. The sculpture room in the second-story loggia has great views of the city.

Cravings for cheese and cured meats can strike at any moment in Siena. When they do, **Grattacielo** or **Skyskraper** (Via dei Pontani 8; tel. 334/631-1458; 11:30am-3pm and 7:30pm-10pm daily; €6-9) has a cutting board ready. The osteria also prepares one traditional dish each night.

Montalcino

Leaving Siena, today you'll dive deeper into the Tuscan countryside, stopping first in Montalcino, surrounded by hillsides covered in vines and dotted with local wineries. Montalcino lies on a steep hill overlooking a wide plain, which has made it a vital possession over the centuries for any power who wanted to control the area.

Driving Directions: Drive south on the SR2 until you reach the Strada Provinciale del Brunello. You'll make a right on Via Traversi Monti/SP14, which leads to Montalcino (42 km/26 mi; 50 minutes).

1. Fortezza di Montalcino

Via Ricasoli 54; tel. 05/7784-9211; 9am-8pm daily; €4

Montalcino was fortified by Etruscans, Romans, and the Republic of Siena, who began constructing Fortezza di Montalcino in 1361. They built this pentagonal fortress to last and it has. Today, you can walk around the ramparts to get a panoramic view of the Val d'Orcia valley, which is a UNESCO World Heritage Site. Entry to the fortress is through the **Enoteca La Fortezza** (www.enotecalafortezza.com; 9am-8pm daily; €5) wine bar in the courtyard that offers wine tastings and Tuscan finger food.

Piazza Pio II

Pienza

Head west toward Pienza, formerly known as Corsignano. It used to be that there wasn't a whole lot to be excited about if Corsignano was your hometown, until native son Pope Pius II commissioned Bernado Rossellino to transform the medieval village into an ideal town.

Driving Directions: Return to the SR2 via Via Traversi Monti/SP14, getting off fairly quickly on the Strada Provinciale 146, which leads to Pienza (24 km/15 mi; 30 minutes).

2. Piazza Pio II and Palazzo Piccolomini

Based entirely on principles of Renaissance urban planning, Piazza Pio II and Palazzo Piccolomini presented a kind of public space that influenced architectural thinking for centuries. Long stone benches line the palazzo and provide good vantage points from which to take in the details of this remarkable square.

3. Belvedere Walkway

Via del Casello

Next, climb to the Belvedere walkway on the southern edge of town. "Belvedere" literally means "beautiful view," and this paved brick pathway is more a romantic place to stop and look out on the countryside than to do any serious walking. Still, if you're getting hungry, stop at down-to-earth **Trattoria Latte di Luna** (Via San Carlo 2; tel. 05/7874-8606; noon-2pm and 7-9pm Wed.-Mon.; €8-12) for traditional handmade pici pasta and ragù that's been simmering all day.

Montepulciano

Montepulciano is an enchanting wine town with Etruscan and Roman roots. Grapes have played a vital role in the town's development since the Middle Ages. Florence and Siena fought for control of the area, and when the Medici eventually triumphed in the 16th century, they began an aesthetic overhaul that transformed Piazza Grande into a Renaissance masterpiece. Today, the imposing ring walls and narrow streets are filled with wine bars and rustic cantinas where Montepulciano DOC can be savored.

Driving Directions: Head west from Pienza on the SP146, getting off on Via della Circonvallazione Vincenzo Cozzani in Bivio di San Biagio, which turns into Viale i Maggio (15 km/9 mi; 20 minutes).

4. Palazzo Comunale

Piazza Grande 1; tel. 05/787-121; €5

The town's Palazzo Comunale was built in the 13th century and given a facade lift in the 15th by the pioneering Renaissance architect Michelozzi. If it looks remarkably similar to Palazzo della Signoria in Florence, that's because Cosimo di Medici wanted it that way. The inner courtyard has an elegant double loggia and ornate well, but the most impressive feature is the view from the imposing **bell tower.** On a clear day you can see all the way to the Sibillini Mountains in Le Marche and the Gran Sasso in Abruzzo. It's particularly steep, so use the hand rails and avoid selfies until you reach the top.

To finish off your day with some food and a few glasses of wine, you don't have to go far. On the Piazza Grande, **Contucci** (Piazza Grande 13; tel. 05/7875-7006; www.contucci.it; 10am-6:30pm daily, 11am-7pm enoteca daily; free) goes back a thousand years and is the oldest winemaker in Montepulciano. Forty-one generations of the same family have harvested grapes here, and their cantina is devoted to the history of Vino Nobile, the locally produced wine.

DAY 4

Lake Trasimeno

Getting from Montepulciano to Assisi requires circumnavigating Lago di Trasimeno, but fortunately, the lake is a pleasant first stop in Umbria.

Driving Directions: Take the SP17 to the SP326 to the SR454 (24 km/15 mi; 30 minutes).

1. Palazzo della Corgna

Piazza Antonio Gramsci; tel. 075 951099; www.palazzodellacorgna.it; 10am-5pm Fri.-Mon.; €9

Palazzo della Corgna is the main attraction in the small lake town of **Castiglione del Lago** on the western shore. The former Renaissance residence is full of colorful frescoes. Down an olive tree-lined path nearby is the awkwardly shaped **Rocca Forte,** which dominated the area in the Middle Ages. You can walk along the battlements and climb up the towers for unobstructed views of the lake.

The historic center of Castiglione consists of a pedestrian main street with a scattering of shops and restaurants. You can tell you're in Umbria from the food at **L'Angolo del Buongustaio** (Via Vittorio Emanuele 40; tel. 329/316-8456; www.angolodelbuongustaio.com; 10am-3pm and 6-10pm Wed.-Sun.; €8.50-15). It smells like cured meat and cheese inside, and the generous tasting plates are mandatory. Firsts include hearty bean soups

★ Tuscan Wine Sampler

Driving along Tuscan roads, it won't take long before you spot rows and rows of vines lining the hillsides. They've been making wine in these parts for thousands of years, and the mix of nutrients, altitude, weather, and tradition make Tuscan wines great. The grapes in the area primarily sangiovese.

You can sample the results of local vineyards at eateries and wine bars (enoteca, vineria, cantina) or you can visit the source. There are dozens of wineries along the way that are open to the public and offer the opportunity to take short tours to learn about the production process and sample the results. You can drop in on most wineries unannounced and sample production. There's no pressure to buy, but if you do many wineries can ship cases directly to your door back home. Winery owners and staff are happy to show you around and many organize tours, which should be planned in advance.

Here are three worth visiting, but there are many other wineries in between that can form the stops on a Tuscan wine tour.

PALAGETTO

Via di Racciano 10, San Gimignano; tel. 05/7794-3090; tastings@palagetto.it

A 10-minute walk south of San Gimignano on the SP47 provincial road, Palagetto is a good place to educate a palate. Tours last around an hour and there are a variety of tasting options (€10-16), depending on the number of glasses of white and red wine you intend to drink. They also organize light lunches (€27) that include four glasses of wine, a platter of Tuscan cold cuts, and a pasta dish. Tastings should be reserved a day or two in advance.

and thick fondues, which would be unthinkable on a Tuscan menu.

2. Isola Maggiore

Ferry: Viale G. Garibaldi 24; 8:35am-6:55pm daily; 30 minutes; €9.10 round trip

After lunch, take a ferry to Isola Maggiore (main island). It may sound big, but it's actually pretty small, with only 15 full-time residents. The tiny island's claim to fame is as a place where Saint Francis paused to meditate. Follow the Lungolago path around the island or head up through the olive groves to the 13th-century church overlooking the lake.

Assisi

Assisi stands out from a distance. The town lies on the slope of Monte Subasio and is the famed birth and resting place of Saint Francis. The center is surrounded by a medieval wall with entrances at eight fortified gates. Porta Nuova (New Gate) leads to the main square and parallel main streets leading to the Basilica.

If you have a spiritual side you've come to the right place. Assisi has two basilicas, a cathedral, and nine houses of worship. The saint of saints attracts a crowd: More than six million pilgrims visit Assisi every year, giving rise to stores selling postcards and the Tau cross worn by San Francesco.

Driving Directions: There are two ways of getting from Castiglione to Assisi (72 km/45 mi; 1 hour). The southern route (SP306 and SR 220) passes through Um-

CAPANNA DI CENCIONI

Loc. Capanna 333, Montalcino; tel. 05/7784-8298; www.capannamontalcino.com; 9:30am-12:30pm and 2pm-6pm Mon.-Sat.; €15

At this picturesque winery a few kilometers north of Montalcino, Giuseppe Cencioni and his two sons lead informative tours from vine to fermenting room to the cellar where Brunello is aged in enormous Slovenian oak casks. Tours, which include a tasting, last 90 minutes and are available by reservation only. Cost varies according to what you're drinking, but the Introductory level (€15 for glasses of rosso di montalcino, brunello di montalcino and sant'antimo) is a good place to start.

MANVI

Via Villa Bianca 13, Montepulciano; tel. 392/746-4727; 10am-5pm daily; €15-60

There are a lot of boutique vineyards scattered around Montepulciano, but only a handful of hectares that manage to produce great wine. Manvi is one of them, but it's the husband-and-wife team from India who own this winery that makes coming here so special. You'll get a warm welcome, whether you know about wine or not, and see firsthand how their full-bodied Vino Nobile is produced, aged, and bottled. Call a few weeks in advance to arrange a simple tasting (€15 pp for 4 glasses), a tasting and tour of the vines and cellar (€20 pp), or a tasting and four-course lunch (€60 pp).

brian farm country while the northern alternative is a two-lane highway.

★ 3. Basilica di San Francesco

Piazza Inferiore di San Francesco 2; tel. 075/819-9001; www.sanfrancescoassisi.org; Basilica Inferiore 6am-6:50pm daily, Basilica Superiore 8:30am-6:50pm daily; free, audio guide available

The iconic Basilica of San Francesco is two churches, one built on top of the other. The lower church was begun in 1228 to honor San Francesco. Its dimensions are intimate, and it was intended to serve the growing number of pilgrims venerating the soon-to-be saint. The upper church (1230) is grander in style. Both were finely frescoed by the greatest artist of the day, **Giotto,** who created a new way of portraying the world on the basilica walls. His brush strokes and color added new depth to landscapes and figures that had previously been static and flat.

Giotto painted the series of 28 frescoes inside the upper church over five years starting in 1290; they illustrate the life of San Francesco. The most dramatic panel portrays him renouncing his father's wealth and stripping himself before God. The lower church also contains biblically themed frescoes by Lorenzetti and Martini, while the saint's body is housed in a crypt below.

4. Rocca Maggiore

Via della Rocca; tel. 075/813-8680; 10am-7pm daily; €8

Situated on a hillside north of town, the medieval castle of Rocca Maggiore (1174) has seen its share of battles. It was demolished and restored more than twice over the centuries and looks

SLOW IT DOWN: Agriturismo

"Agriturismo" is tough to translate. Literally a combination of "agriculture" and "tourism," in practice it's a charming accommodation on a working farm. Agriturismi are located outside of towns in open countryside throughout Tuscany and Umbria, providing plenty of contact with nature. Many have pools and all produce their own fresh ingredients (honey, oil, cheese, cakes, jams, and juices), which are on offer at breakfast and dinner.

Every road trip needs a slow day, and besides, you're in Tuscany now, and nothing should move too fast. Stop at an agriturismo, and you may find yourself rethinking your road trip, deciding to park yourself in one place, hike iconic hillsides, and taste locally grown ingredients underneath the Tuscan sky. Here are some of the best places to do it.

AGRITURISMO TERRE DI NANO

Località Villa Nano, Monticchiello di Pienza; tel. 05/7875-5263; www.terredinano.com; €145-185

The spirit of Tuscany is condensed into this agriturismo located on the rolling hills between Pienza and Montepulciano. Organize a cooking class with your friendly hosts, spend the afternoon playing bocce and relaxing by the pool, or rent a scooter and discover where all the winding roads outside the estate lead.

IL SEGRETO DI PIETRAFITTA

Località Cortenanno 56/57, San Gimignano; tel. 05/7794-0016; www.ilsegretodipietrafitta.com; €110-150

The sign outside Pietrafitta welcomes guests to paradise, and it's no exaggeration. This renovated farmhouse is a 25-minute walk from San Gimignano. The staff are exceptionally helpful, breakfast is spectacular, and both the pool and restaurant provide stunning countryside views.

IL PODERE SANTE MARIE

Località Santa Maria 298, Montalcino; tel. 05/7784-7081; www.santemarie.it; €80

A lot of vineyards offer accommodation, but none are as simple and authentic as Il Podere Sante Marie. This small, three-room agriturismo on the outskirts of Montalcino with 2.5 hectares of vines provides a hands-on wine experience. The best thing about this place is the owner, Marino, who passionately shares his wine knowledge with guests.

MONASTERO GIUSEPPE

Via S. Apolinaire 1, Assisi; tel. 075/81-2332; www.msgiuseppe.it; €55 d

If you've ever wondered what it would be like to be a monk, stay at this monastery in Assisi. It's a busy day that starts early and is more than just marathon prayer sessions. The extensive grounds overlooking the valley are ideal for contemplation and self-care.

like a castle should. Inside are exhibits demonstrating daily life in the Middle Ages. It's a steep climb that takes around 20 minutes on foot. There are a couple different routes to get there from the center, and it's possible to find tranquility by heading up these cobbled back streets. They're all good, so try taking one up and another down.

Close to the central square, **La Piazzetta dell'Erba** (Via San Gabriele dell'Addolorato 15a; tel. 075/815-352; 12:30pm-3:30pm and 7:30pm-10:30pm Tues.-Sun.; €12-13) is a dinner choice that combines tradition and innovation. The spaghetti with oil, garlic, chili, and herbs looks mundane on paper, but every mouthful is a pleasure.

DAY 5

Hiking Around Assisi

1. Roman Amphitheater

Via Anfiteatro Romano; free

Today you'll be following in the footsteps of Saint Francis to the countryside around Assisi, so make sure you've got the right walking shoes and supplies for a picnic. **Alimentari e frutta** (Via S. Paolo 6; tel. 07/581-2277; 7:30am-2pm and 4pm-8:30pm Mon.-Sat., 9am-1:30pm and 4pm-7pm Sun.) is a cross between a mini-market and deli with all the ingredients you'll need. Just point to the cold cuts and cheeses inside the vintage glass case and the veteran owners will fix you something to enjoy after your walk.

Best known for its associations with the Christian saint, Assisi was also a Roman town (Asisium), and like all Roman towns had an amphitheater. Today the outlines are still visible and located in one of the most charming and least visited parts of Assisi. It's a 15-minute walk through beautiful side streets east of Piazza del Comune. Follow Via Santa Maria delle Rose and turn left at the San Rufino church. Head up the hill, and take the last right to find it.

2. Eremo delle Carceri

Via Ermo delle Carceri 1a; tel. 075/812-301; www.assisiofm.it; 7:30am-6pm daily; free

Eremo delle Carceri is the mountain hermitage built on the site where Saint Francis convened with nature. It grew over the years into a cozy stone sanctuary where pilgrims have been coming for centuries. It includes a modest chapel and monastery where four monks live and share the teachings of the saint. You can also see the grotto where Saint Francis prayed and attend mass, which is held five times a day. Morning and afternoon tours in English recounting the saint's life last 20 minutes and must be reserved in advance.

From the amphitheater, the retreat is reached by way of Via Eremo delle Carceri. It's a 70- to 90-minute uphill hike along a paved mountain road. Walk on the inside to be safe and avoid the occasional car.

Eremo delle Carceri

(top to bottom) Parco del Monte Subasio; Todi; Orvieto; Orvieto Duomo

3. Parco del Monte Subasio

tel. 075/815-5290; www.montesubasio.it; free

Parco del Monte Subasio covers acres of mountainous area east of Assisi where San Francesco walked and meditated. There are 14 trails managed by **CAI** (Italian Alpine Club; www.cai.it), marked with red and white stripes on rocks and trees. **Sentiero dei Mortai** (no. 50) is the panoramic high trail that starts on the edge of town and continues from the sanctuary all the way to the town Spello to the south. The route is 15 km (9 mi) one-way and will takes 6.5 hours to complete at a decent clip. There are stupendous long-distance views, and you can take a taxi or bus from Spello on the way back.

4. Dinner at Trattoria degli Umbri

Piazza del Comune 40; tel. 07/581-2455; noon-2:45pm and 7:15pm-9:45pm Fri.-Wed.

This down-to-earth trattoria is just what you need after a long day. It's clean, it's rustic, and the menu isn't overly complicated. There are lots of vegetarian options, along with pasta, soup, and steaks, and desserts like their panna cotta are all homemade.

DAY 6

Todi

On the last full day of your road trip, head to the pristine hill town of Todi for one of the most rewarding climbs in Umbria. Remnants of ancient Etruscan, Roman, and medieval walls surround this idyllic village with one of the best-preserved historic centers in the region. The narrow streets leading off the main square are an invitation for travelers to enter old shops that look out onto the surrounding countryside.

Driving Directions: From Assisi, make your way back to the SS75 via the SS444, Via di Messo, and Via di Montesubasio, and head northwest to the E45. Exit to

WATCH

Stanley Tucci: Searching for Italy: An entertaining primer on Italian food culture, this gourmet travel show dedicates season 1 episode 5 entirely to Tuscany; season 2 episode 3 covers Umbria.

READ

A Vineyard in Tuscany: A Wine-Lover's Dream by Ferenc Maté: Author Maté's memoir recounts the search for the perfect plot of land to grow grapes, and the detours and mishaps along the way. The setting is a vineyard outside of Montalcino where Maté and his family still live and produce top-notch Brunello.

LISTEN

"L'Estate Addosso" by Jovanotti: The artist known as Jovanotti has been on the music Italian scene for more than 30 years, recording memorable, funky pop ditties that have grown more profound over the years. All 15 of his studio albums are worth a listen but this song from *Lorenzo 2015 CC* is a solid introduction to the singer, who lives in Cortona.

the SS79bis, which will take you to Todi (61 km/38 mi; 45 minutes).

1. Piazza del Popolo

The cathedral and civic buildings surrounding Piazza del Popolo are the expression of Middle Age and Renaissance harmony. Construction of the **Palazzo dei Priori** began in 1134. The former town hall is adorned with an oddly shaped tower and a bronze eagle which is the town's mascot. **Palazzo del Popolo** was built a century later and is one of the oldest civic buildings in Italy. It houses the **Pinacoteca and Etruscan Museum** (tel. 075/894-4148; 10am-1pm and 3pm-6pm Fri.-Sun.; €7).

Fuel up at **Vineria San Fortunato** (Piazza Umberto I; tel. 07/5372-1180; noon-3:30pm and 6pm-1am Tues.-Sun.; €13-14), a shop that sells wine and serves food, and you can sit on a lovely, shaded deck with a church view.

Orvieto

Orvieto was founded on a high, easily defended plateau by the Etruscans. The steep natural defenses, however, weren't enough to keep the Romans at bay and they sacked the town in 265 BCE. It wasn't until the Middle Ages that Orvieto was bustling again and took on the characteristics that can be seen today.

Driving Directions: Take SS79bis to SS448 until it hits SS205. Turn onto SR71 from a roundabout and you'll eventually approach Orvieto (38 km/24 mi; 45 minutes).

2. Duomo

Piazza del Duomo; 8am-7:15pm daily; free

Orvieto's Duomo is stunning, one of the greatest churches built during the Middle Ages. It was commissioned by Pope Niccolo IV in 1290 and the final stone wasn't laid until four centuries later. It was worth the wait: The bright golden mosaics that cover the facade illustrate stories from the Old Testament, and the side walls are surprisingly different but no less hypnotic. Inside is yet another surprise and one of the greatest earth-colored palates ever created.

3. Pozzo di San Patrizio

Viale Sangallo; tel. 07/6334-3768; 9am-5pm daily; €5

Located near the end of Corso Cavour in a panoramic spot along the town's gardens, Pozzo di San Patrizio is one of the most unusual sights in Orvieto. "Pozzo" means well, and this one is a cylindrical masterpiece built with two intertwining staircases that prevent underground traffic jams.

Pozzo di San Patrizio isn't the only hole in Orvieto. Over the centuries, hundreds of caves were dug into the soft tufa stone on which the town sits. New discoveries are still being made. **Orvieto Underground** (tel. 07/6334-4891; www.orvietounderground.it; 11am-12:15pm and 4pm-5:15pm daily; €5.50) gives geologists and lovers of the macabre an unforgettable 45-minute tour through the hidden parts of the town.

After all that subterranean exploring, get a pick-me-up at **Caffe Bar Montanucci** (Corso Cavour 21; tel. 07/6334-1261; 6:30am-midnight daily), the oldest cafeteria in Orvieto (though it looks pretty new these days). Go for a slow sip in the little courtyard out back; it's a great place to contemplate your journey and the bits of Umbria and Tuscany that will stick with you.

Pozzo di San Patrizio

- Rome, Florence, and Venice (page 139)
- Cinque Terre (page 423)

TRANSPORTATION

Air

The closest international airport is **Aeroporto Di Pisa-San Giusto** (Piazzale d'Ascanio 1; tel. 050/849-111; www.pisa-airport.com), located a little over an hour from San Gimignano (74 km/46 mi) along single-lane roads like the SP11 and SP26 that get prettier the farther you go.

Arriving from Rome's **Fiumicino** airport is another option. Italy's capital is 290 km (180 mi) from San Gimignano, and it takes just over three hours to get there on the A1 highway. There's also an airport in Florence, but it's small and has few intercontinental flights.

Train

Hill towns aren't adapted to trains and the closest stations are usually miles away. Getting to San Gimignano from Pisa requires a transfer in Empoli and a bus ride from Poggibonsi. There are hourly departures from Pisa Centrale and a one-way adult ticket costs €8.70. There are few train alternatives after that but the towns are linked by local bus service.

Getting Back

Orvieto is located near the A1 highway that runs down the Italian peninsula and connects Rome to Florence. It's a 2.5-hour (250-km/155-mi) drive back to Pisa, 2 hours (165 km/ 100 mi) to Florence, and 1.5 hours (120 km/75 mi) to Rome. Orvieto has a convenient train station with regional and high-speed service that connects to all three cities.

ROMANTISCHE STRASSE

Why Go: Driving Germany's Romantic Road is a dreamy trip filled with fairy-tale castles, cozy Bavarian lodgings, delicious local wines, and medieval charm.

Number of Days: 4

Total Distance: 339 km (211 mi)

Seasons: Spring and fall

Start: Würzburg

End: Füssen

The rolling hillside around Würzburg quickly gives way to the towering snowcapped peaks of the Alps and medieval towns cozily nestled in their valleys, while majestic castles loom large atop strategic hillsides. For many, this is the quintessential road trip through central Europe, where it isn't difficult to squint and feel as though you've been transported to a simpler, more rustic time. Cobblestone streets, timbered Gothic buildings, baroque churches, and more are scattered through Bavaria. This well-paced route makes sure to squeeze in all the highlights, from medieval Rothenburg to the King Ludwig II's medieval fantasia, the Neuschwanstein Castle, while still allowing time for cultural highlights and a couple of tucked-away gems.

TOP 3

Taking a trip back to medieval Rothenburg on the **Nightwatchman Tour** (page 311).

Shopping in Rothenburg's **Kathë Wohlfahrt Christmas market,** which runs all year long (page 312).

Stepping into a fairy tale at medieval **Neuschwanstein Castle** (page 317).

DAY 1

Würzburg

1. Würzburg Residence

Residenzpl. 2; tel. 931355170; www.residenz-wuerzburg.de; 9am-6pm daily Apr.-Oct., 10am-4:30pm daily Nov.-Mar.; €8

The lavish Würzburg residence sets a high bar. The palatial rooms immediately call to mind the great rooms of Versailles in their learned decadence. Balthasar Neumann's suite of rooms, which include a staircase, vestibule, White Hall, and Imperial Room, are considered some of the finest in all of palace architecture. From this palace, we get the "Würzburg rococo" style. In total, 40 rooms are open to the public, each with treasures to be admired. Don't forget to take a stroll through the court gardens, a masterwork of Bohemian-born gardener Johann Prokop Meyer.

Driving Directions: Würzburg is a 1-hour drive from Frankfurt International Airport, 122 km (76 mi) on the A3 freeway (autobahn).

2. Wine Tasting and Tour at Staatlicher Hofkeller

Residenzpl. 3; tel. 9313050923; www.hofkeller.de; 10am-6pm Mon.-Fri., 10am-4pm Sat.; €8

For over 1,300 years, the vineyard of Würzburger Stein has been producing wines, once serving the world's elite. In fact, its 1540 vintage is thought to be the oldest wine ever tasted. Duck into the endless cellars and taste your way through local history and to one of today's finest Silvaner white wines in the region.

Afterward, have lunch at **Restaurant & Weinhaus Stachel** (Gressengasse 1; tel. 93152770; www.weinhaus-stachel.de; 11:30am-midnight Tues.-Sat.; €20). This 500-year-old tavern provides the quintessential backdrop to plop you right into medieval Germany. Enjoy a generous plate of Blaue Zipfel, a blue-tip sausage. Reservations recommended, though not always necessary.

3. Alte Mainbrücke

Alte Mainbrücke; open 24 hours daily; free

Built over the 15th and 16th centuries, this pedestrian-only bridge was once the sole link over the powerful Main River that flows beneath. Dotting the bridge are statues of 12 saints, reminiscent of the Charles Bridge in Prague. Today, it is a friendly meeting spot for locals, particularly on warm summer evenings, when a shared bottle of crisp, dry Spätlesen is ubiquitous and the views over Würzburg unbeatable.

top, Würzburg residence; bottom, Alte Mainbrücke

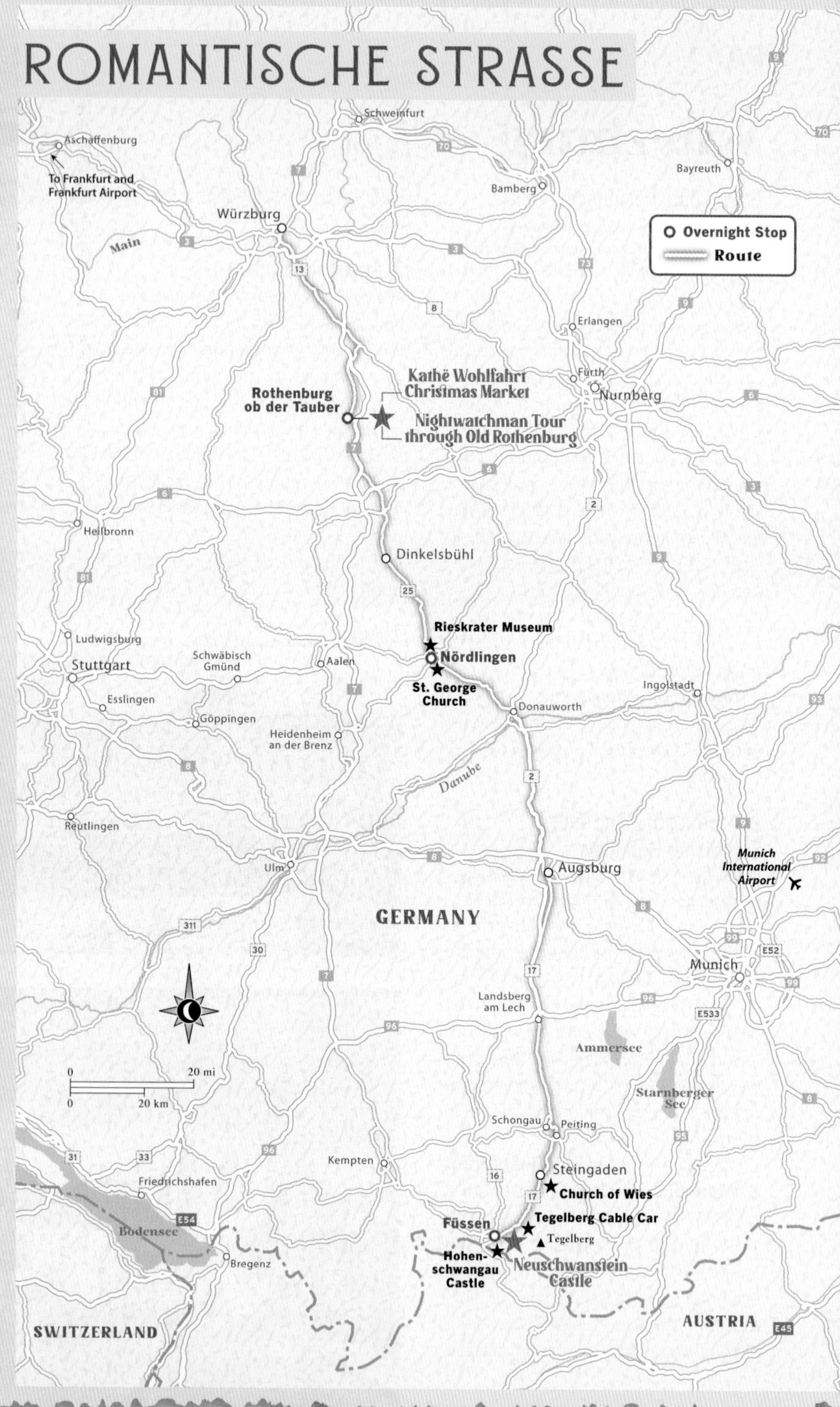

ROMANTISCHE STRASSE
Overnight Stop
Route
Schweinfurt
Aschaffenburg
To Frankfurt and Frankfurt Airport
Bayreuth
Bamberg
Würzburg
Main
Erlangen
Fürth
Nurnberg
Kathë Wohlfahrt Christmas Market
Rothenburg ob der Tauber
Nightwatchman Tour through Old Rothenburg
Heilbronn
Dinkelsbühl
Rieskrater Museum
Nördlingen
St. George Church
Ludwigsburg
Schwäbisch Gmünd
Stuttgart
Aalen
Esslingen
Göppingen
Heidenheim an der Brenz
Ingolstadt
Donauworth
Danube
Reutlingen
Ulm
Augsburg
Munich International Airport
GERMANY
Munich
Landsberg am Lech
Ammersee
Starnberger See
0
20 mi
0
20 km
Schongau
Peiting
Kempten
Steingaden
Church of Wies
Friedrichshafen
Füssen
Tegelberg Cable Car
Tegelberg
Bodensee
Bregenz
Hohen-schwangau Castle
Neuschwanstein Castle
SWITZERLAND
AUSTRIA
CARTOLINA POSTALE
(CARTE POSTALE)

Key Reservations

Summer and the winter holiday season are both extremely busy—though beautiful—seasons along the Romantische Strasse. If you are traveling during these high seasons, you will want to have all your accommodations booked in advance. No matter when you are traveling, you will want to pre-arrange for your rental car and to prebook these attractions:

- **Neuschwanstein Castle**
- **Hohenschwangau Castle**

Neuschwanstein Castle

4. Marienberg Fortress

Marienberg; tel. 9313551750; www.schloesser.bayern.de/deutsch/schloss/objekte/wu_fest.htm; 9am-6pm Tues.-Sun.; €8

Nearly destroyed during World War II, this 1,000-year-old fortress has undergone an extensive rebuild. Highlights include Saint Mary's Church, which dates from 706, as well as the expansive Prince's Garden. The adjacent **Museum für Franken** (https://museum-franken.de; €6.6) has a collection of art and sculpture for those who are inclined and have a bit more time.

Rothenburg ob der Tauber

★ 5. Night Watchman Tour through Old Rothenburg

Marktplatz, Rothenburg ob der Tauber; tel. 9861938633; www.nightwatchman.de; 8pm nightly Apr. 1-Dec. 30; €9

After the last tour buses leave for the evening, the fairy-tale charm of Rothenburg ob der Tauber truly comes alive. There is perhaps nothing more romantic than walking these medieval cobblestone streets in the warm glow of the evening lights, laughter echoing out into the night from friends cheering in a local tavern. This is the scene on the Nightwatchman Tour, where you stroll with the nightwatchman on patrol as in times of yore. Take this moment to feel transported and try to catch the sunset from Criminal's Tower on the westside of the city.

Before the tour, cozy into **Zur Hoell** (Burggasse 8; tel. 98614229; 5pm-11pm Mon.-Sat.; €20), a historic medieval restaurant featuring generous portions of succulent regional cuisine. Order the roast goose with red cabbage served with a potato dumpling, but do leave room for the apple strudel. Reservations recommended; cash-only.

Driving Directions: From Würzburg, you could opt for a shortcut to Rothenburg via the A7 (65 km/41 mi; 45 minutes) or follow the traditional Romantic Road on a meandering tour through the countryside where you can discover vineyards, castles, and more (104 km/65 mi; 2 hours).

Frankenweins

For more than 1,200 years, the Franken region of Germany has played host to vineyards fed by the Main River. More than 80 percent of the grapes grown here are of the white variety, with the Silvaner grape in particular being able to thrive here. This grape enjoys the limestone and keuper soil. They may not be known internationally very well, but locally these Frankenweins have quite the reputation!

The finest wines are bottled in a special, flat-sided ellipsoid bottle called a bocksbeutel. Look out for these easily identifiable bocksbeutel bottles as a sign of regional quality. Local favorites are the **Silvaner** (an easy drinking, dry white) and **Bacchus** (a sweeter white).

Würzburg is the center of the Frankenwein region. From the city center, drive in any direction and within 10 minutes you will find a vineyard. With all the ornate medieval castles and towers serving as backdrop to these sprawling vineyards, you couldn't ask for a more picturesque setting for a wine-tasting flight. As in many wine-centric cultures, a springtime gaiety explodes when the "new wine" (or Federweißen) is released, usually some time in March, making this a particularly festive time of year to visit.

DAY 2

Rothenburg ob der Tauber

1. Rothenburg Town Square

Marktplatz; open 24 hours daily; free

The Rothenburg central market is a bustling town square that can be overwhelmed by midday with travelers in coach buses descending on the city, so it is best to strike out in the morning. Try to arrive at the square near the hour so you can see the animated figures on each side of the **town clock** reenacting the Meistertrunk, an apocryphal local legend.

★ 2. Kathë Wohlfahrt Christmas Market

Herrngasse 2; tel. 8004090150; www.kaethe-wohlfahrt.com/christkindlmarkt-rothenburg; 10am-5pm daily; free

It doesn't take long to see why Rothenburg emits such a festive Christmas charm year-round. Kathë Wohlfahrt is a must-stop shop for Christmas lovers, no matter the time of year. Perhaps no single purveyor of holiday goods has done

MAKE IT Active

Cyclists looking to **bike** the entire Romantische Strasse are in for a treat. There are several well-marked bike paths away from the busy main road, though the **D9** is what you will likely stick to as it covers the entire route. Surprisingly, even though this route meanders through the foothills of the Alps, there are no really steep climbs. The beginning of the route is largely flat, while the middle is mixed. The end of the route features a relatively big climb to Füssen, by far the most challenging part of the route, though also the most picturesque.

Download the official cycling guide from the Romantische Strasse organization (www.romantic-road-shop.com), which recommends 10 days to do the entire route, though experienced cyclists can easily merge some of the shorter sections. Towns along this route, such as Würzburg, are served by **Next Bike** (www.nextbike.de), making it easy to get around on two wheels.

quite so much in the last few decades to influence what is considered quintessential "Christmas" decoration more than Kathë Wohlfahrt.

Originally started in 1964, this humble little store began as a way to resell German music boxes to American officers stationed at the military base in Stuttgart. The music boxes were a huge success. In 1977, they moved their headquarters to Rothenburg and quickly began marketing traditional German Christmas ornaments, decorations, and keepsakes. In 1991, they began manufacturing their own Christmas decorations and gifts, always adhering to the same principles of using natural materials and keeping that Germanic holiday zeitgeist alive.

Dinkelsbühl

3. St. George's Cathedral

Marktpl. 1; tel. 98512245; https://st-georg-dinkelsbuehl.de; free, tower access €2

After the short drive from Rothenburg, take an afternoon pause in the second of today's walled medieval cities, Dinkelsbühl. As in Rothenburg, the charm of the city lies in strolling the cobblestone roads, and St. George's Cathedral is the one truly must-see building here. This imposing cathedral is known by pilgrims for its ornate altars. In the afternoons, it is possible to climb up to the tower for views over the town.

St. George's Cathedral

The Story of the Meistertrunk

In 1631, in the midst of the terrible 30 Years' War, a brutal war between Catholics and Protestants throughout Europe, the medieval town of Rothenburg was besieged by Count Tilly and his large Catholic force. Count Tilly ordered the town of Rothenburg to be razed, and the mayor and councilmen to all be executed.

To broker a peace deal, the town offered Count Tilly and his army wine from the local vineyards. They presented the count with an ornate flagon of wine that was 3.25 liters (nearly a full gallon) large. The count took a sip and, pleased by the wine, offered a deal. He would spare the city if anyone could finish the flagon in one go. However, there was a catch. If this person failed, they would be put to death. In the count's mind, the choice was clear: It would be either death by wine or death by the sword.

Georg Nusch, the town's major, was the first to rise to the challenge. He held the flagon and, as the story goes, finished the giant flagon of wine in one go, thus not only sparing his life, but also saving the town.

This story of how Georg Nusch saved the town is now known as the "Meistertrunk." You can witness this reenacted every hour, on the hour, by little animatronic figures on the clock in the town square.

If you have a hankering for a pint and some schnitzel, lunch at **Weib's Brauhaus** (U. Schmiedgasse 13; tel. 9851579490; www.weibsbrauhaus.de; 11am-1pm and 5-10pm daily; €25) is just the ticket.

Driving Directions: Follow the traditional Romantic Road (B25) from Rothenburg to Dinkelsbühl (44 km/27 mi; 45 minutes).

Nördlingen

4. Rieskrater Museum

Eugene-Shoemaker-Platz 1; tel. 908184710; www.rieskrater-museum.de; 10am-4:30pm daily; adults €5, family ticket €11, single adult with child €6, students €2, under 6 free

Begin your exploration of Nördlingen with a bang of the cosmic variety. Nördlingen, the last of the three completely intact walled medieval cities along the Romantic Road, was built completely within the crater of a meteor that is estimated to have been 1 km (about half a mile) across; it struck about 15 million years ago and left a crater 25 km (16 mi) in diameter.

Driving Directions: Continue along the traditional Romantic Road (B25) from Dinkelsbühl to Nördlingen (32 km/20 mi; 30 minutes).

5. St. George's Church

Marktpl. 10; tel. 90814035; www.kirchengemeinde-noerdlingen.de/st.-georg-als-bauwerk; 9:30-5pm daily; free, Daniel's Tower €3

Amazingly, this church built in the 15th and 16th centuries has managed to remain unscathed from the traditional problems that have plagued most of Germany's great churches over the years: Reformation, fire, and World War II. The Gothic structure itself is sufficiently imposing, but the real draw is the long climb up the rickety stairs to Daniel's Tower for views out over Nördlingen and to make out the ring of the crater that town lies within.

Have dinner at **Wengers-Brettl** (Löpsinger Str. 27; tel. 908188282; http://cms.wengers-brettl.de; 5pm-midnight Mon.-Sat.; €20), where the very woodsy, hunting-lodge vibe works well with a plate of schweine (pork) medallions. But you are really coming here for the gugelhupf, a German chocolate cake topped with deliciously warm cherries.

DAY 3

Augsburg

1. Augsburg Cathedral

Frauentorstraße 1; tel. 82131668511; www.bistum-augsburg.de; 7am-6pm daily; free

Take a stroll around Augsburg after arriving to catch some of the morning bustle, and make sure to stop in the Augsburg Cathedral. Originally built in the 11th century, with additions made in the 15th century, this cathedral is particularly notable for its five intact stained-glass windows dating from 1100, the oldest figurative stained-glass windows in the world.

Driving Directions: Leave Nördlingen on the traditional Romantic Road (B25). After passing through Donauworth, the

left, Fuggerei; right, Augsburg Town Hall

road changes from B25 to B2; continue on to Augsburg (75 km/47 mi; 1 hour).

2. Augsburg Town Hall

Rathausplatz 2; tel. 8213240; www.augsburg.de; 9am-6:30pm Mon.-Fri.; free

Built largely during the German Renaissance between 1615 and 1620, the Augsburg Town Hall is a must-see for the imposing Golden Hall, named for its gold-gilded wood ceiling. The ceremonial hall is highlighted by wall frescoes, six portals, and of course the incredible Renaissance coffered ceilings complete with their allegorical paintings. The centerpiece showcases the triumphal march of the goddess Sapientia (Wisdom), while another painting shows the town hall under construction.

3. Fuggerei

Jakoberstraße 26; tel. 8213198810; www.fugger.de; 8am-8pm daily Apr.-Sep., 9am-6pm daily Oct.-Mar.; €6.50

The world's oldest continuing social housing, the Fuggerei, still houses 140 families whose rent—€0.88 a year and three daily prayers for the Fugger family, whose wealth built the Fuggeri—most would consider a good deal. This city-within-a-city boasts its own school, church, and museum, as well as the 140 family apartments.

A lunch of Bavarian classics is on offer at **Berghof** (Bergstraße 12; tel. 821998432; www.berghofaugsburg.de; noon-2pm and 5pm-11pm daily; €15), with its seasonal menu and tall, frothy pints of kellerbier.

Steingaden

4. Church of Wies

Wies 12; tel. 8862932930; www.wieskirche.de; hours vary, open daily, closed during services; free

Hoc loco habitat fortuna, hic quiescit cor ("Happiness abides in this place, here the heart finds peace"). Find your own slice of peace in this splendid rococo church, both a world-famous pilgrimage site and a UNESCO World Heritage Site. Built in the 18th century, it is a quintessential example of the architecture and decor of the age—and of Bavaria as a whole. Do call ahead to ensure the church will be open for your visit time.

Driving Directions: After Augsburg, the route continues on the B17, which passes by the Church of Wies along the way (88 km/55 mi; 1.5 hours).

Füssen

5. Dinner with a Sunset View at Haus Hopfensee

Höhenstraße 14; tel. 83626752; www.haus-hopfensee.de; 11:30am-9pm Mon.-Sat.; €18

After arriving in Füssen, stop in for a Bavarian dinner at Haus Hopfensee with plenty of choices for dumplings, strudels, and the like, though you are really coming here for the kind service and incredible terrace views over the lake and to the Alps and surrounding countryside. There is perhaps no better sunset view around.

Driving Directions: Continue on the B17 to Füssen (25 km/15 mi; 30 minutes).

Füssen

WATCH

Chitty Chitty Bang Bang: This classic road trip musical comedy starring Dick Van Dyke and a derelict, though fantastic, car includes key scenes filmed in Rothenburg.

READ

The Swan King: Ludwig II of Bavaria by Christopher McIntosh: The subject of this biography is one of the most enigmatic figures of the 19th century, and the man responsible for constructing the iconic Neuschwanstein Castle.

LISTEN

The **Germany Experience Podcast** (www.thegermanyexperience.de): With episodes tackling all sorts of questions, from how to be a good dinner guest in Germany to making German candy, this pod has anything you could want about Germany with a rotating guest list.

Bavarian Folk Music: Make sure to tune in at a local beer garden (biergarten) at least once while in Bavaria.

DAY 4

Schwangau: Ludwig's Castles

Driving Directions: From Füssen, both the Neuschwanstein and Hohenschwangau castles are a short drive (4 km/2 mi; 10 minutes) east on Parkstrasse. There are several parking lots around the Hohenschwangau castle.

TOP EXPERIENCE

★ 1. Neuschwanstein Castle

Neuschwansteinstraße 20, Schwangau; tel. 08362930830; www.neuschwanstein.de; 9am-6pm Apr.-mid-Oct., 10am-4pm mid-Oct.-Mar.; guided tour €15 (required for entry)

The inspiration behind the famous Walt Disney logo, the romantic fantasy of King Ludwig II of Bavaria is a definite must-visit, even if the obligatory guided tour is a bit rushed and a tad disappointing in the end; only 15 of the castle's 200 rooms were ever finished, and the tour only allows you to visit a handful of these rooms. That said, you aren't going to come all the way here and *not* step inside the castle, are you? Interior photography is strictly prohibited, unless you ask for permission at least 10 days in advance. The breathtaking exterior of the castle, its charming location atop a forested Bavarian hill backdropped by snowy alpine peaks, seemingly sparkles in the morning sun. To get to the castle, it is a bit of an uphill walk from the village of Hohenschwangau, though to complete the fantasy, consider hopping into a horse-drawn carriage to make your grand arrival.

2. Hohenschwangau Castle

Alpseestraße 30, Schwangau; tel. 8362930830; www.hohenschwangau.de; 9am-5pm daily Apr.-mid-Oct., 9am-4pm daily mid-Oct.-Mar.; guided tour €21 (required for entry)

Before creating his fantasy escape, Ludwig was born and raised in the Hohenschwangau Castle, a much more interesting castle

TO TAKE Home

From Würzburg to Füssen, your route will be lined with shops selling local wares. Some shops, particularly those in tourist hubs, sell goods of dubious quality. Oftentimes, the best products will be found in stores that specialize in that product. Here are some favorite gifts and mementos from this region.

- **Bavarian beer steins:** A traditional Bavarian beer stein is an intricate work of art made in various materials, from glass to porcelain. The best, and most expensive, will be hand-painted and elaborately decorated, sometimes with reliefs in metalwork.
- **Ceramics:** Like the locally famous beer steins, the ceramics of Bavaria feature intricate, hand-painted motifs.
- **Chocolates:** If anyone you know is a chocoholic, there isn't a sweeter gift than a carefully wrapped box of Bavarian chocolates.
- **Christmas ornaments:** The world-famous Kathë Wohlfahrt is the place to pick up various German-themed Christmas ornaments and stocking stuffers for the coming holiday season.
- **Wine:** A bottle or two of the fine regional Slivaner wine in the traditional bocksbeutel bottle makes for a great addition to any wine cellar.
- **Wood carvings:** This region is known for its intricate woodwork. Though larger pieces are available and can be shipped back home, most travelers opt for small figurines, often of the nativity scene.

for the history-minded. First mentioned in historical records in the 12th century, the castle was partially destroyed in the 16th century before being rebuilt under the behest of King Maximillian II, the father of Ludwig, in the neo-Gothic style popular at the time. Unlike his son, Maximillian was able to finish his castle and Ludwig lived here, using it primarily as a summer residence, as his castle was being constructed nearby. Through the guided tour, you will learn more about the family and the history of the castle, as well as period-specific furniture.

3. Tegelberg Cable Car

Tegelbergstraße 33, Schwangau; tel. 836298360; www.tegelbergbahn.de; 9am-5pm daily, weather dependent; €13.50 each way

For the most impressive views over Neuschwanstein castle, take the Tegelburg Cable Car to the top of the mountain. The cable car makes its way up the mountain in a swift 10-minute ride, climbing over 1,700 m (5,500 ft). Make sure you have your camera charged and at the ready! There is perhaps no better view over the Neuschwanstein Castle than from here.

Sip on a well-earned pint or a cozy coffee at the top of the Tegelburg mountain. In colder weather, large glass windows at **Panoramarestaurant Tegelburg** (Tegelbergstraße 33, Schwangau; tel. 8362930431; www.panorama-gaststaette.de; 9am-4:30pm daily; €25) provide views over the mountains, while in warmer weather, a large terrace affords views over the awe-inspiring nature of this corner of Bavaria.

The downhill hike from the Tegelberg Cable Car station at the top of the mountain back down to the bottom cable car station in town is a great hike, easily accessible to most. The trailhead is well-marked and, as is the case throughout Germany and the Alps in general, the trail is well-maintained. Expect to spend 2-3 hours on the descent.

Driving Directions: After visiting the castles, from Hohenschwangau head to Tegelberg (3 km/1.5 mi; 5 minutes). Take Colomanstraße road north to Pöllatweg for about 2 km (1.2 mi). Take a right onto Tegelbergstraße and follow this about 1 km (0.9 mi) to Tegelberg. There are several parking lots here as well.

4. Back to Füssen

Head down the mountains, hop back in your car, and follow the road back to Füssen. Spend the rest of the day wandering the town's quant cobblestone streets. **Bread Market Square** is a great place to begin a walking tour. The surrounding 13th-century buildings have all been immaculately preserved. The remains of the city's old gate and fortifications add to the romanticism of Füssen, though the real gem is the deliciously ornate mid-18th-century rococo **Church of the Holy Spirit** (Heilig-Geist-Spitalkirche; Spitalgasse 2; 9am-5pm; free). The unmissable decorative painted facade gives way to a light baroque interior. The **Franciscan Monastery** (Franziskanerpl. 1; tel. 836291530; www.franziskaner-fuessen.de; free) on the southern hill gives out to impressive views over the town.

Wrap up your last evening in Bavaria in the lively, chestnut-tree-lined beer garden at **Hotel Hirsch** (Kaiser-Maximilian-Platz 7; tel. 836293980; www.hotelfuessen.de/biergarten.html; 11am-11pm; €25). When the weather is nice, with the nightly live music playing the background, not to mention the barbecue, this beer garden strikes just the right notes to round out your Bavarian experience.

TRANSPORTATION

Air

Frankfurt International Airport (tel. 696900; www.frankfurt-airport.com/de.html) is Germany's largest international airport and the closest to the northern end of the Romantic Road. From the airport, the A3 freeway (autobahn) is a straightforward drive to Würzburg (122 km/76 mi; 1 hour).

Train

Trains to Würzburg stop at **Würzburg Hauptbahnhf** (Bahnhofplatz 4; tel. 586020930; www.bahnhof.de; 7am-10pm daily), about a 15-minute walk to Würzburg Residence.

Car Rental

Frankfurt International Airport offers all the major car rental services, including Alamo, Budget, Hertz, Sixt, and more. You can also rent a car near the train station or elsewhere in town.

Getting Back

You can arrange to drop your car off in Munich and fly out from the **Munich International Airport** (Nordallee 25; tel. 8997500; www.munich-airport.de), as Munich is the closest large city to Füssen (150 km/93 mi via A96; 2 hours). Or, circle back to Frankfurt Airport (422 km/262 mi; 4 hours) or Würzburg (308 km/190 mi; 3 hours) via the A7 autoroute.

CONNECT WITH

- Prague, Vienna, and Budapest (page 184)
- Paris to Bucharest (page 600)
- The Alps (page 648)

TRANSYLVANIA

Why Go: Learn the truth behind the legend of Dracula in the mysterious, misty forests of Old Europe on this driving loop north of Bucharest, complete with castles, fairy-tale villages, and thrilling mountain drives.

Number of Days: 4

Total Distance: 591 km (367 mi)

Seasons: Summer

Start/End: Bucharest

This classic Romanian road trip plunges you into the Transylvanian countryside, where Disneyesque castles peak through storied forests and colorful medieval towns give way to the incredible snow-capped wonder of the Carpathian Mountains. A quick jaunt up the national freeway brings you to mountain passes with incredible views, with plenty of places to pull over and stare at castles hulking on sheer rock faces. Uncover the Gothic history of the world's most famous vampire, Count Dracula, while wandering enchanting villages, cobbled walkways, and lush green forests. The route loops north from Bucharest and back, making it easy to rent a car at the airport.

TOP 3

★ Touring the classic **Bran Castle,** enjoying the fairy-tale architecture, and unraveling its connections to the infamous Count Dracula (page 323).

★ Testing your mettle along the many switchbacks of the **Transfăgărășan Road** (page 328).

Soaking up the warm thermal waters of Romania's largest spa at **Therme Bucuresti** (page 330).

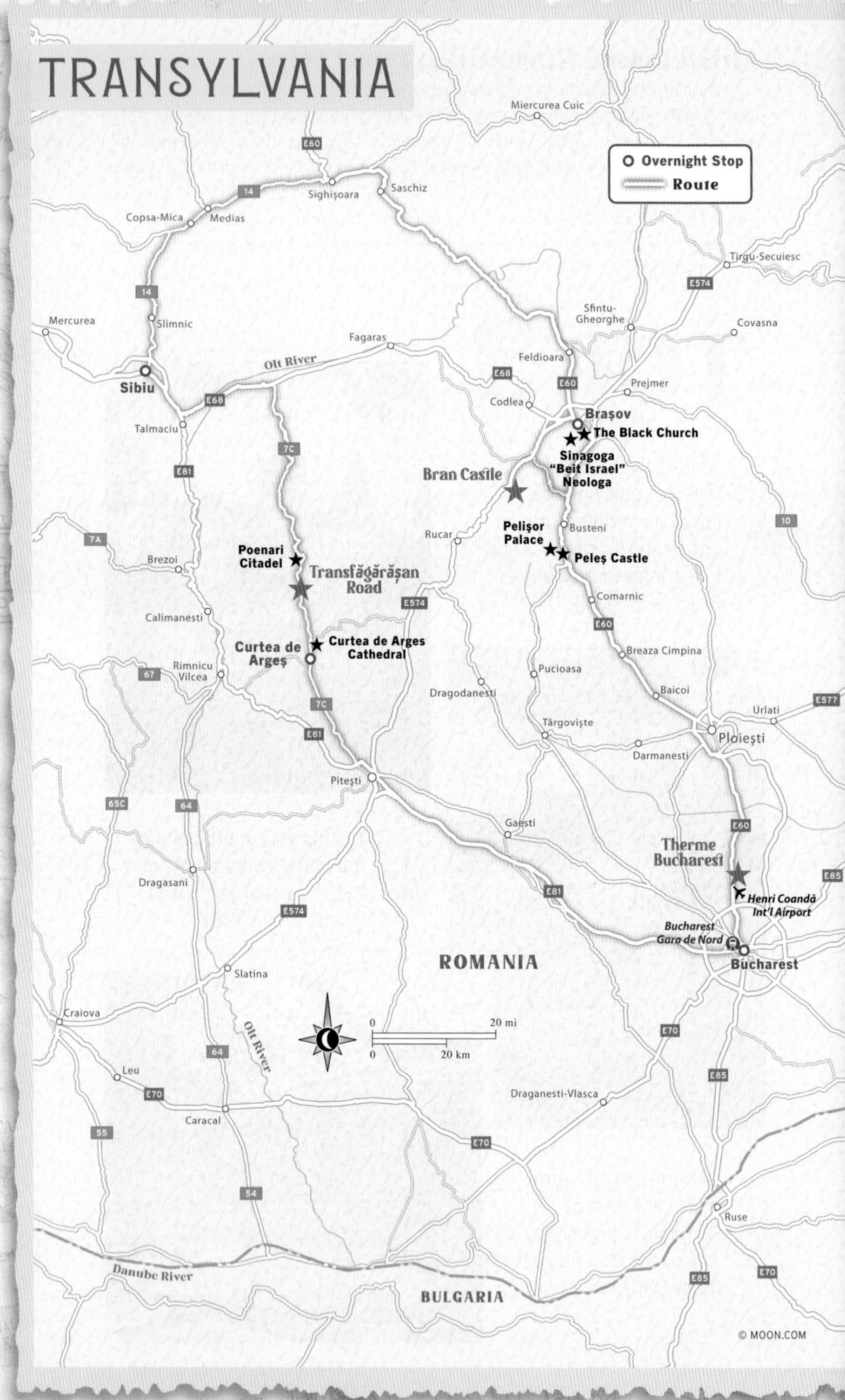

TRANSYLVANIA
Overnight Stop
Route
Miercurea Cuic
Sighișoara
Saschiz
Copsa-Mica
Medias
Tirgu-Secuiesc
Sfintu-Gheorghe
Covasna
Mercurea
Slimnic
Fagaras
Feldioara
Olt River
Sibiu
Prejmer
Codlea
Brașov
The Black Church
Talmaciu
Sinagoga "Beit Israel" Neologa
Bran Castle
Pelișor Palace
Busteni
Peleș Castle
Rucar
Poenari Citadel
Brezoi
Transfăgărășan Road
Comarnic
Calimanesti
Curtea de Arges Cathedral
Curtea de Argeș
Breaza Cimpina
Rimnicu Vilcea
Pucioasa
Dragodanesti
Baicoi
Urlati
Târgoviște
Ploiești
Darmanesti
Pitești
Gaesti
Therme Bucharest
Dragasani
Henri Coandă Int'l Airport
Bucharest Gara de Nord
Bucharest
ROMANIA
Slatina
Craiova
Olt River
0
20 mi
0
20 km
Leu
Draganesti-Vlasca
Caracal
Ruse
Danube River
BULGARIA
© MOON.COM

DAY 1

Bucharest's Airport to Brasov

1. Peleş Castle

Aleea Peleşului 2, Sinaia; tel. 244 310 918; https://en.peles.ro; 10am-4:15pm Wed., 9:15am-4:15pm Thurs.-Sun.; adults 40 Lei, seniors 65 and up 20 Lei, children and students 10 Lei

Your first stop after picking up your rental car at Henri Coanda Airport, just north of Bucharest, is the picturesque mountain ski town of **Sinaia.** Though technically in the region of Wallachia, it's a perfect stop en route to Transylvania. By far the biggest draw here is the neo-Renaissance Peleş Castle. Built in the 19th century as the summer home of King Carol I, who loved the scenery around Sinaia as much as locals and visitors do today, the palace offers 40-minute guided tours that take you through some of its 170 rooms, with decor inspirations that vary widely, from Gothic to Moorish to Florentine.

After your tour, check out the less-frequented 45-minute tour of **Pelişor Palace** (9:15am-4:15pm Wed.-Sun.; adults 20 Lei, seniors 65 and up 10 Lei, children and students 5 Lei) before you hop back on the road. Just up the hill from Peleş, this smaller palace was built in the art nouveau style for King Carol's nephew.

Driving Directions: From Henri Coanda Airport head north on DN1/E60 for 109 km (68 mi; 1.5 hours).

★ 2. Bran Castle

Bran; 40 268 237 700; www.bran-castle.com; noon-4pm Mon., 9am-4pm Tues.-Sun., last admission 4pm; adults 45 Lei, seniors 65 and up 35 Lei

Plan on getting to Bran around lunchtime. This small village of red-roofed houses is known around the world for

left, Bran Castle; right, Peleş Castle

Vlad the Impaler, Bram Stoker, and Count Dracula

Many people think of only one thing when they hear the word "Transylvania," and that's the legend of Count Dracula, the quintessential vampire imagined by Irish author Bram Stoker in his 1897 novel. Those familiar with the story may know that many suppose the real-life, 15th-century ruler of Wallachia, Vlad the Impaler, to be the inspiration for the book. But things get more complicated from there, especially when you learn that Vlad the Impaler never lived in Bran Castle, the fortress now referred to around the world as "Dracula's Castle."

VLAD THE IMPALER

Vlad III was born as the second son of Vlad Dracul, who became ruler of the region of Wallachia in 1436. After Vlad III, also known as Vlad Dracula, assumed the role of leader, constant invasions and territorial disputes meant that Wallachia was in constant conflict, and Vlad III became known for his extraordinary cruel war tactics. In particular, he seemed to have a penchant for impaling his enemies, from Saxon villagers residing in Transylvania to the envoys of an Ottoman sultan demanding tribute. These gruesome acts earned Vlad his nickname, but today, many historians regard him simply as a ruler of his time and an important figure in the history of Romania.

BRAM STOKER'S DRACULA

Scholars agree that Stoker was aware of Vlad Dracula while writing and researching his best-known novel. There's also a general consensus on a direct connection between Vlad III and the name of Stoker's vampire, but only in that the author picked it because of the ruler's ruthless and cruel reputation.

BRAN CASTLE

Though today most scholars agree neither Vlad the Impaler nor Bram Stoker ever set foot in Bran Castle, for years local lore had it that Vlad had once been imprisoned there. It was the communists in the 1970s who chose to overstate the connections between this castle and Vlad the Impaler in the hopes of boosting tourism to the area. They took advantage of extensive renovations ordered by Romania's beloved Queen Marie, who resided in the castle starting in the 1920s. The ploy worked: Today, the castle is by far Romania's most visited site. Dubious associations with vampires aside, the immaculately preserved and dramatically situated Bran Castle is well worth a visit.

one thing: the notorious Bran Castle, often called Dracula's Castle, which you will see towering on your left when you arrive in town. But first, lunch. You can't avoid a bit of kitsch in Dracula's hometown, so dig into some Vampire Fangs (rolled chicken breasts with spicy confit) at **Restaurant Casa Din Bran** (General Mosoiu 15, Bran; tel. 741 236 557; www.casadinbran.ro; 11am-3pm Sun.-Sat., bar 11am-midnight Mon.-Sat.; 70-110 Lei).

From the restaurant, it's a short five-minute walk up to the iconic Bran Castle. For centuries, this 14th-century castle was an important guardian of the trade route between Transylvania and Wallachia

Brasov

against raids from the Ottoman Empire. Later, when the territory around Bran was ceded from Hungary to Romania, it became a royal residence, and has subsequently shifted hands many times in disputes between the former communist regime and royal heirs.

Though connections to Dracula are dubious, it's certainly true that the dramatic fortress looks the part. Precariously perched high on a hill overlooking the village, with stone walls and numerous red-roofed towers, Bran Castle is truly straight out of a fairy tale. You'll enter through the main gate, Poarta Castel. Within the castle grounds, don't miss out on touring the grotesquely fascinating medieval torture instruments (10 Lei), while the Time Tunnel (20 Lei) is an incredible feat of modern engineering, with a multimedia exhibit tracing the history of Bran Castle from the myth of Dracula to the famed warmth of Queen Marie. Purchase tickets online to skip the lines.

Driving Directions: From Sinaia, continue north on DN1/E60. After Azuga turn left on DN73A, and then at Rasnov turn left onto DN73/E574 and drive 10 km (6 mi) to Bran (1 hour).

3. Brasov

It's time to head to Brasov, one of Romania's most charming, historic, and economically important cities, where you'll have dinner and spend the night. With a stunning mix of medieval architecture and contemporary living, Brasov is an architectural delight, a warren of cobblestone roads lining the bright facades of squat, medieval buildings tucked into verdant mountain forests. It's a stunning backdrop for photos or for a bit of people-watching at a local café. This is old-world Europe at its heart.

First, check into **Casa Rozelor** (Str. Michael Weiss 20; tel. 268 475 212; www.casarozelor.ro; 296-469 Lei). Friendly service and tasteful decor by designer and artist Mihai Alexandru combines modern comfort with period furniture and original art.

You're probably getting hungry after all the travel and sightseeing. For dinner, strike out to the cozy wine cave at **Albert Bistro**

(38 Republicii Street; tel. 722 886 054; www.casa-albert.ro; reservation recommended; 20-60 Lei) and have a hearty mountain meal paired with a Romanian vintage.

Driving Directions: From Bran, head northeast to Rasnov on DN73/E574 and drive 30 km (19 mi) straight to Brasov (30 minutes).

DAY 2

Brasov to Sibiu

1. The Black Church

Curtea Johannes Honterus 2; tel. 268 511 824; https://bisericaneagra.ro; usually 10am-5pm, hours vary, closed Mon. in winter; adults 15 Lei, seniors 65 and up and children 7 and up 10 Lei

In the morning, grab a flat white or coffee and a light breakfast at a nearby café before taking a stroll through the **historic city center** of Brasov. Constructed beginning in the 14th century, the Black Church is a monumental Gothic church and the icon of Brasov, and it's impossible to miss. Arguments for the church's name vary, from the theory that the stones got their dark hue from a 17th-century fire to the thought that they may have been darkened by modern pollution. Highlights of the church's collection on display include one of Europe's richest collection of Ottoman rugs. Coffee lovers will want to slip out back to the café on the church grounds for a heavenly cup of espresso.

top, Scholar's Stairs; bottom, Sighisoara Clock Tower

2. Sinagoga "Beit Israel" Neologa

Strada Poarta Schei 29; tel. 268 511 867; hours vary, ask to have opened on arrival; 7 Lei

The beautiful Sinagoga "Beit Israel" Neologa is easily missed, but worth seeking out. The synagogue was built in a distinctly Moorish style at the turn of the 20th century, following the plans of the Hungarian architect Lipót (Leopold) Baumhorn, and there is a memorial dedicated to the Holocaust near the orchard in the courtyard.

En route to the synagogue, you'll pass through the smallest street in the city, the **Strada Sforii** or "Rope Street." This narrow thoroughfare, the third smallest in Europe, is a cute and unmissable addition to your stroll through Brasov.

3. Sighisoara

Pack up and get ready to venture to the northernmost point on your road trip, Sighisoara. Prepare to have your breath taken away: Sighisoara is an incredibly well-preserved medieval town. Highlights include the 14th-century **Clock**

MAKE IT Active

There is nothing like coupling a great road trip with a wonderful forest hike. Throughout the Transylvanian Forest, there are a number of places to park the car and explore on foot or bike, on well-signed (and not-so-well-signed) trails; in winter, though some roads are closed, the intrepid are rewarded with excellent skiing; and for something totally different, the mountains of Romania are some of the best places in Europe to see brown bears.

BEAR WATCHING IN BRASOV

Bear Watching in Romania (tel. 773 823 466; http://bearwatching.ro; mid-Mar.-late Oct.; from 396 Lei) offers excursions from Brasov to witness Europe's largest population of brown bears in the wild. You will need at least a half day to head out into the forests. Photographers will want to choose the Bear Watching in the Land of Volcanoes excursion for some amazing hides 80 km (50mi) away, near Lake St. Anna. All excursions include short, guided hikes and instruction from a certified forest ranger.

SKIING AND MOUNTAIN BIKING IN SINAIA

Winter travelers will want to spend a day skiing the slopes at **Sinaia Mountain Resort** (www.sinaiago.ro), while summer travelers can head up into the forest for a day of mountain biking. Whatever the season, the views will be well-earned. This resort was the first established by the monarchy in the beginning of the 20th century and is considered the cradle of Romanian mountain sports.

HIKING ALONG THE TRANSFĂGĂRĂȘAN ROAD

At the **Complex Vila Balea** scattered around this cabin-like assembly of buildings hiding in the forest, there are a number of well-marked trails leading up into the mountains. The views from above over the mountains and Transfăgărășan road are well worth the climb.

Tower and the **Scholar's Stairs,** a covered, 19th-century staircase meant to protect students moving between the church and the school at the top of the hill. Today a restaurant, **Casa Dracula,** the childhood home of Vlad "The Impaler" Dracula, is also located here.

Break from walking the old town of Sighisoara for a big lunch at **Casa Georgius Krauss** (Bastionului Street no.11; tel. 744 540 262; www.casakrauss.ro/en/restaurant-1; 60 Lei). You could do worse than indulging in the Transylvanian stew.

Driving Directions: From Prejmer, the route backtracks toward Braslov before diverging north on the E574/E60 to Sighisoara (2 hours).

4. Overnight in Sibiu

You will want to pull into Sibiu before nightfall. An idyllic hilltop town with roots to the 12th century, crisscrossed with cobbled alleys made for strolling, it's a wonderful place to spend the night. Check into the **ART Hotel** (Centumvirilor St. Nr. 2; tel. 369 409 360; www.arthotel.ro; from 222 Lei), just off the main plaza in the old downtown.

For dinner, pick up a light bite at **Kuliarnium** (tel. 721 50 60 70; www.kulinarium.ro; noon-10pm daily; 30 Lei). This chic restaurant in a historic building in the oldest part of town wins points for its homey design, with whitewashed brick walls and wooden tables, as well as its international, contemporary twists on local dishes.

Driving Directions: From Prejmer, follow the DN14 for 94 km (58 mi) to Sibiu (1.5 hours).

DAY 3

Sibiu to Curtea de Arges

★ 1. The Transfăgărășan Road

You'll spend the day on one of the most beautiful routes in the world, the Transfăgărășan Road. This former military road crosses the southern pass through the Carpathian Mountains, twisting between the historic regions of Wallachia and Transylvania. Known as Ceausescu, the road was built in the 1970s by the dictator at the time as a way to move troops if the USSR invaded. In the valleys, you'll find grazing sheep in rolling green fields with the peaks of the highest mountains in the country, Moldoveanu and Negoiu, towering overhead. Note that in inclement weather, particularly in winter, the road can be closed. It's best to check the morning before heading out of Sibiu to make sure the pass is open. Give yourself plenty of time for pulling over to take photos, and rerouting, if necessary.

Transfăgărășan Road

Driving Directions: From Sibiu, follow the DN1/E68 for about 44 km (27 mi) before turning onto the Transfăgărășan/DN7C (1 hour).

2. Lunch at Complex Vila Balea

Transfăgărășan DN7C at km 103; tel. 722 999 303; https://complex-balea.ro; from 210 Lei

To steel your nerves after the twisty, turny road, enjoy the rustic cabin charm of Complex Vila Balea, buried in the quiet of the Transylvanian Forest. The **on-site restaurant** is one of the best in the region. Wild trout, caught in nearby Lake Vidraru, is usually on the menu, as are a host of smoked meats (made in their own home-built smoker!), as well as homemade syrups and jams. Time and energy allowing, there are several signed hikes from Vila Balea allowing you to explore the Transylvanian Forest on foot. If you want to stay the night, couples should splurge on the duplex in the Lespezi House (300 Lei).

Driving Directions: From the beginning of the Transfăgărășan/DN7C, it's 46 km (28.5 mi) to Vila Balea (1.5 hours).

3. Poenari Castle

Transfăgărășan, Arefu; tel. 248 212 561; 10am-6pm Wed.-Sun.; 10 Lei

Continuing south on the Transfăgărășan, you will cross over the **Lake Vidraru Dam.** At 165 m (102 ft)—the fifth tallest dam in Europe—coupled with its position nestled in the soaring mountain range, it makes for a stunning exit from the steepest of the mountain passes.

READ

I Am an Old Communist Hag by Dan Lungu: In this novel, a Romanian woman receives a visit from her daughter, who has been living in America for 10 years. The funny and heartwarming plot brilliantly illustrates Romania's complicated relationship with communism.

Along the Enchanted Way by William Blacker: With beautiful descriptions of the Romanian countryside, this story of a traveler in a land very different from his own will set the scene perfectly for your Transylvanian road trip.

LISTEN

"Se Serge Mandra Pe Frunte" by Maria Tanase: Known as the Edith Piaf of Romania, Tanase became a sensation of Romanian folk music in the 1930s with evocative, emotional songs. The upbeat rhythm will get you in the festive Romanian spirit of the countryside.

"Asfalt Tango" by Fanfare Ciocărlia: Dubbed the "Fastest Brass Band in the World," Fanfare Ciocărlia has the kind of sharp trumpets and rocking trombones that scream for the open roads. Just keep an eye out on the speedometer.

Vlad the Impaler is the (Partial) Inspiration for Count Dracula: Listen to this episode from *History Unplugged* to sink your fangs into the chilling story of Vlad Tepes, the ruler who impaled tens of thousands in the 1400s.

From here, it's just another 10 minutes or so to Poenari Castle, the breathtaking ruin that was Vlad Dracula's true home. You'll need to huff up 1,480 stairs to see the unmatched views that inspired Vlad the Impaler to choose this location as his preferred stronghold. The years have not been kind to the castle, but even in its dilapidated state, it's not hard to squint and transport yourself to medieval Romania. Keep an eye out for bears strolling through the surrounding forests.

Driving Directions: Poenari Castle is 45 km (28 mi) south of Vila Balea on the Transfăgărășan/DN7C (1 hour).

4. Curtea de Arges Cathedral

Bulevardul Basarabilor 1, Curtea de Arges; tel. 248 721 735; 8am-6pm daily; 4 Lei

South of Poenari Castle, this small town is one of the oldest in Romania and was once the capital of Wallachia. Be sure to admire the delicate beauty of the Curtea de Arges Cathedral, a Byzantine architectural wonder with arabesque flares. Legend has it that in the 14th century, Prince Neagoe Basarab was held hostage in Constantinople. While there, he designed an extraordinary mosque for the sultan. To show his thanks, the sultan allowed the prince to return with surplus materials from the mosque to build the cathedral. The cathedral itself is on the grounds of the local monastery.

And don't overlook the nearby **St. Nicholas Church.** The exterior of this church might be uninspiring, but the interior frescoes—all 130 of them dating from 1364—are anything but.

Afterward, have dinner at **Curtea Veche** (Bdul. Basarabilor nr. 121; tel. 745 994 345; 8am-11pm daily, reservation recommended; 20-60 Lei). The focus here is all on local produce and proteins, with ample attention paid to some of Romania's finest vintage wines and spirits. If you haven't had the fiery plum brandy known as Țuică yet, this is the spot. Head to your hotel for the evening.

Driving Directions: From Poenari Castle, continue 27 km (16 mi) south from Poenari Castle on the Transfăgărășan/DN7C (30 minutes).

DAY 4

Back to Bucharest

★ 1. Therme Bucuresti

Bucharest; https://therme.ro; 10am-9pm daily; experiences from 54 Lei

Leave yourself at least three hours to enjoy the regenerative waters of Therme Bucuresti, whether you want to have a well-being ritual in the saunas, relax in the exotic garden, or have a little fun in the water park, there is something for everyone at this massive wellness complex, less than 10 minutes from Henri Coandă International Airport.

Driving Directions: From Curtea de Arges, continue south for 32 km (20 mi) on the Transfăgărășan/DN7C to Bascov, where you'll get on the DN7/E81. You'll be on the E81 for about 110 km (68 mi), before turning north to drive for on the DNCB (the ring road that circles Bucharest) for about 16 km (10 mi), before turning north on the DN1/E60 for about 8 km (5 mi; 2 hours). The bath complex is right off the motorway. To get to the airport from Therme Bucuresti, you'll hop back on the DN1/E60 and head south for just over 2 km (1.2 mi).

Therme Bucuresti

TRANSPORTATION

Air

The **Henri Coanda International Airport,** commonly known as the **Otopeni Airport** (Calea Bucurestilor nr. 224 E; Bucharest; tel. 212 041 000; www.bucharestairports.ro), is well-connected to the rest of Europe by both standard and budget airlines. Bucharest is 16.5 km (10.3 mi) south of the airport.

Train

Most travelers coming by rail will arrive at Bucharest's primary train station, **Gara de Nord** (www.cfrcalatori.ro), which connects with trains from most major European destinations. This train station is located conveniently in the middle of downtown Bucharest and is well-connected by taxi, buses, and local trains throughout the city and the rest of the country.

Car Rental

It is best to arrange car rentals ahead of time. You can take your pick of car-rental agencies at Henri Coanda International Airport, including Avis, Eurocar, Hertz, and others. There are a few agencies at Gara du Nord train station.

CONNECT WITH

- Prague, Vienna, and Budapest (page 184)
- Paris to Bucharest (page 600)

THE MAGISTRALA COASTAL ROAD

Why Go: The magnificent Magistrala coastal road that hugs Dalmatia's coast is Croatia's quintessential road trip.

Number of Days: 9

Total Distance: 420 km (265 mi)

Seasons: Early summer and early fall

Start: Zadar

End: Herceg Novi, Montenegro

The Adriatic Highway, known in Croatia as the Jadranska Magistrala and marked D8 on Croatian road signs, connects the entire Adriatic Coast, from Rieka in Croatia to Herceg Novi in Montenegro. This gorgeous route is particularly beautiful south of Zadar, where this road trip begins, and dramatic views of the Dalmatian Islands are often sandwiched between scrubby white Mediterranean cliffs and bright blue seas. Despite the summer traffic, and maybe because of this route's many ups and downs and blind corners, it's considered one of the most beautiful drives in the world.

TOP 3

★ Taking a **boat tour** on the Krka River, carving a path through a limestone gorge, and seeing the waterfalls of **Krka National Park,** which flow down into the bright blue river (page 337).

★ Exploring the winding streets of **Diocletian's Palace.** Split's wonderfully preserved Roman monument is still vibrant today, filled with bustling shops, cafés, and restaurants (page 341).

Walking along Dubrovnik's **city walls:** There's no better way to get an eyeful of the white city (page 345).

DAY 1

Zadar

1. Land Gate

Start your trip in Zadar, one of Croatia's largest cities, filled with Roman and Venetian architecture, but with half of the crowds of Split and Dubrovnik.

Make a triumphant entrance into the historic center of Zadar through the Land Gate, the southeastern access point to the city. The gate was fashioned from a Roman triumphal arch into a Renaissance grand entrance topped with the Lion of Venice.

Driving Directions: Zadar Airport is about a 10-minute drive east of town. Croatia's busiest airport in Zagreb is a three-hour drive away. (If you want to get a taste of the Magistrala along the way, cutting over to the coastal route from about Senj will add 1.5 hours to the drive.) Once you arrive, there's a parking lot five minutes' walk south of the Land Gate (€0.30 hour).

2. Square of Five Wells

You're now within the city walls. Turn right toward the historic Square of Five Wells—the eponymous wells of this square were once Zadar's main source of drinking water. These days the square is a local gathering place, with frequent concerts and performances in summer.

Overlooking the square is the **Captain's Tower** (10am-1pm and 5pm-8pm Mon.-Fri., 10am-1pm Sat. summer; €1), built by the Venetians to defend the city against the Turks. Climb the tower for a view of Zadar.

3. Duke's Palace

Poljana Sime Budinica 3; tel. 023/627-765; www.knezeva.hr; 9am-midnight daily summer, 10am-8pm daily winter; €11

To learn more about Zadar, visit the magnificent Duke's Palace, just a one-minute walk away. This creamy stone-walled 13th-century structure was built as the residence of municipal officials and was later the site of council meetings. The small exhibition inside uses historically accurate rooms from different time periods to chronicle the history of Zadar.

left, Square of Five Wells; right, Land Gate

Otočac
Plitvice Lakes Naitonal Park
Bihać
Rab
Rab
Sjeverni Velebit National Park
E71
E65
D25
Park Prirode Velebit
Pag
Novalja
Gospić
D1
E761
D25
CROATIA
Pag
Nacionalni Park Una
D106
Paklenica National Park
Seline
Nin
D27
Galevac Beach
Obrovac
D8
D1
Zadar
Zadar Airport
D27
Ugljan
Krka National Park
Knin
Benkovac
D56
E65
Boat Tour of Krka National Park
Vrlika
Biograd na Moru
D8
Skradin
Skradinski Buk Waterfall
D1
Kornati Islands
Šibenik
Diocletian's Palace
Sinj
D58
Trilj
Kaštela
Solin
E65
D8
Trogir
Čiovo Island
Split
Omiš
Šolta
Supetar
Brač
Stari Grad
Hvar
Hvar
Vis
Vis
Komiža
Vela Luka
Korčula
Adriatic Sea
Lasto
0
20 mi
0
20 km
© MOON.COM

THE MAGISTRALA COASTAL ROAD
Banja Luka
BOSNIA AND HERZEGOVINA
SERBIA
E73
E761
Zenica
Sarajevo
E761
E73
E73
Overnight Stop
Route
Pljevlja
Mostar
Vrgorac
E73
E762
D8
E65
Ploče
Metković
Opuzen
Pelješac Peninsula
Mljet National Park
Mljet
MONTENEGRO
City Walls
Nikšić
D8
Dubrovnik
Lokrum
Dubrovnik Airport
D8
E762
Herceg Novi
Our Lady of the Rocks
Podgorica
E65
Kotor
Cetinje
Gulf of Kotor
Blue Grotto
Budva

Key Reservations

- Make reservations for dinner at **Pet Bunara** in Zadar.
- You must reserve a ticket to **Krka National Park** in advance online.
- Reserve all **accommodations** in advance in high season, especially in popular **Dubrovnik.**

Krka National Park

For lunch, have a truffle pizza or pasta at **4Kantuna** (Varoska 1; tel. 091/313-5382; www.restaurant4kantuna.com; 11am-10pm daily in season, call for off-season hours; €11), a two-minute walk from the Duke's Palace.

4. Forum

Next, walk five minutes to the Forum. Dating from the 1st century BCE, the Forum was the hub of everyday life in Zadar during Roman times. Today, it looks a bit more like a graveyard for old Roman columns. This is a place to get up close and personal with Roman history; you can even sit on the columns for a photo op before going to explore some of the grand buildings that line the square.

End the day with dinner at chic **Dva Ribara** (Blaža Jurjeva 1; tel. 023/213-445; 10am-11pm daily; €13), which serves meat and fish entrées.

DAY 2

Paklenica National Park

Paklenica National Park is the best place to trek through the craggy karst landscape of Northern Dalmatia. The park has more than 150 km (93 mi) of hiking trails, and the landscape ranges from jagged rocks and canyons to karst caves and shady paths. There's even a series of underground bunkers, built to hide the political elites of former Yugoslavia in an emergency.

Driving Directions: Paklenica National Park is a little over an hours' drive north-east (54 km/34 mi) from Zadar.

Paklenica National Park

1. Hike to Forest Hut Lugarnica

Distance: *4 km (2.5 mi) one-way*
Time: *1.5 hours one-way*
Difficulty: *Easy*
Trailhead: *Velika Paklenica parking lot*
Information and Maps: *Starigrad Paklenica Tourist office (www.np-paklenica.hr)*

The trail to the forest hut is quite easy,

and on the way there are lots of craggy rock outcroppings to explore. You will pass mountain climbers scaling the rocky faces at the trailhead, and pass the Yugoslavia-era **bunkers** if you'd like to pop in. The hike will pay off when you reach your destination, the **Forest Hut Lugarnica** (10:30am-4:30pm daily May-Oct.; €4), a superb stop for lunch. The restaurant's location is beautiful, next to a rushing stream (watch small children carefully). Sausages, bean stew, and beer are offered, along with sodas, coffees, and doughnuts.

Zadar

2. Ugljan

Back in Zadar after an active morning, hop on the next boat to Ugljan, the nearest island in the Zadar Archipelago. Ugljan is so close to Zadar it's almost a part of the city, and the relatively undeveloped shores fill up on weekends. Ferries from Zadar to the port in **Preko** (30 minutes) run about every 1.5 hours during the week (less on weekends) and cost around €3.

Once on Ugljan, grab a water taxi in the Preko harbor to the smaller islet of **Galevac,** which has Ugljan's best beach (less than 5 minutes; €3). Spend a relaxing afternoon swimming and lounging on the sand.

3. Riva

In the evening, head to Zadar's Riva, or seafront promenade. Starting at the southwestern corner of the peninsula, the 0.8-km (0.5-mile) long Riva is bordered by sandy, tree-lined parks and cafés. Time your walk so that you reach the **Sea Organ** 30-45 minutes before sunset. This work by local architect Nikola Bašić looks like a set of giant steps, and waves force interesting, organic sounds out of the openings between the stairs. It's the perfect spot to watch the sun go down. Nearby, the **Greeting to the Sun,** also by Bašić, is a 22-m (72-ft) circle that soaks up sunlight in its solar panels during the day and emits a glowing amalgam of colors once it gets dark.

Afterward, have a special dinner of local fare at **Pet Bunara** (Stratico 1; tel. 023/224-010; www.petbunara.com; 11am-11pm daily, reservations recommended; €15).

DAY 3

Krka National Park

Located northeast of Šibenik (where you're headed for the night), Krka National Park is lovely inland detour. This park is filled with bright blue water, waterfalls, an island monastery, and plenty of places for hiking and swimming.

Driving Directions: From Zadar, it's about 1.5 hours if you take the coastal road past Pirovac, and then cut inland on D59 to E65 for Skradin.

★ 1. Boat Tour

A boat tour is the best way to experience this beautiful national park. You'll catch the boat from the town of **Skradin.** There are several different boat tours available (Mar.-Nov., 2-4 hours; from €9). Most tours include a stop on the island of **Visovac,** home to a 16th-century Franciscan monastery, and some tours include a visit to **Roški Slap Waterfall,** where you can swim in the water in front of the waterfall. Stop at the **Krka National Park office** in Šibenik for more information, or book a package tour through one of the travel agencies in Šibenik.

2. Skradinski Buk Trail

Distance: *1.9 km (1.1 mi) one-way*
Time: *1 hour one-way*
Difficulty: *Easy*
Trailhead: *At the Skradin park entrance*
Information and Maps: *Available at either park entrance*

If you've still got the energy after your boat tour, this pleasant and easy hike crosses over wooden bridges and passes beautiful lakes. It includes an excellent viewpoint of the **Skradinski Buk Waterfall.** These beautiful falls empty into a lovely pool of water, which unfortunately is now closed to swimming. But there are lots of cafés and seating locations nearby, where you can relax and admire the falls.

Šibenik

Drive to Šibenik and check into your hotel. Many Croatians will wrinkle their noses if you mention Šibenik, as there are no resorts or real beaches to speak of. But the old town center is totally charming and almost perfectly preserved, without the made-for-travelers feel that many other historic cities have. The town is also a good jumping-off point for the Kornati Islands and packed with character-filled apartments where you can live like a local during your stay.

Driving Directions: Šibenik is less than 30 minutes (20 km/46 mi) from Skradin along the D56 and D33.

3. Dinner at Pelegrini

Jurja Dalmatinca 1; tel. 022/213-701; www.pelegrini.hr; 11am-midnight daily; €27

For dinner, go for a splurge at Michelin-starred Pelegrini. In good weather you can dine at the few outdoor tables overlooking the water or in the open-air courtyard just beyond the restaurant.

DAY 4

Šibenik

1. Day Tour of the Kornati Islands

If you've ever wondered what it would be like to live on a deserted island, you can find out in the wild Kornati archipelago, declared a national park in 1980. These islands are some of the most stunning landscapes in Croatia. They are immensely popular with yachters but are not otherwise very accessible. Organized tours of the islands set off from **Murter** (40 minutes north of Šibenik; 33 km/20 mi) and are usually for a full day. Most excursions include a tour, a swim, and lunch for around €33 per person. Another option is to rent a boat with a driver for the day from **Eseker Tours** (Majnova bb, Murter; tel. 022/435-669; www.esekertours.hr).

Kornati Islands

2. St. Jacob's Cathedral

Trg Republike Hrvatske; tel. 022/214-899; 9:30am-8pm Mon.-Sat. and 1pm-8pm Sun. July-Aug., 9am-6:30pm Mon.-Sat. and 1pm-6pm Sun. Sept.-May; free

Back in town, be sure to stop at the 15th-century St. Jacob's Cathedral,

NAME CHECK: Juraj Dalmatinac

Dalmatia's most famous stonemason and architect, Juraj Dalmatinac, put his stamp on churches and buildings throughout Dalmatia. He was born here around 1400 and studied his trade in Venice, where he had an atelier and contributed to carvings on the Doge's Palace. In Italy he was known as Giorgio da Sebenico (George of Šibenik); he returned to Dalmatia with his first big commission, Šibenik's **St. Jacob's Cathedral.** He settled down here, building a house in town, but due to a lack of funding, the cathedral project often stalled. As a result, he spent the time working on other projects up and down the coast. Known as the main artist of the Adriatic Renaissance, he died in 1473 with the Šibenik cathedral still unfinished.

Dalmatinac's signature touch can be found up and down the Dalmatian Coast:

- **Pag Town:** North of Zadar, the rocky island of Pag attracts tourists coming to enjoy its famed cheese, lamb, and lace, and those looking for an all-night party. In 1450 the architect created an urban plan for Pag, and his impact is visible all across the town.
- **Cathedral of St. Domnius, Split:** The Altar of St. Anastasius in the Split cathedral is evidence of Dalmatinac's status as a master stonemason (page 341).
- **Minčeta Fortress, Dubrovnik:** Dalmatinac helped in the building of this fortress in the 15th century. It's located on the northern corner of the **city walls** (page 345).

which glows over Šibenik's old-town waterfront. Now a UNESCO World Heritage Site, the church was built by local architect and famed Croatian son Juraj Dalmatinac (among others, since it took over 100 years to complete). The inside is luxurious, but the most interesting features are on the Gothic and Renaissance facade: The building is encircled by 71 stone heads—according to legend, the faces of those townspeople who didn't pony up for the construction.

For dinner, try **Konoba Dalmatino** (Fra Nikole Ružića 1; tel. 091/542-4808; generally 11am-10pm daily summer, call for off-season hours; €10), nestled in a narrow old-town alleyway.

DAY 5

Šibenik

1. Janjetina at Torcida

Donje Polje 42, Šibenik; tel. 022/565-748; 8am-11pm daily; €11

Before continuing on the drive, make a quick detour for an early lunch of janjetina, or spit-roasted lamb. The best lamb is found in ramshackle roadside establishments on the way to the beach, like **Torcida,** a 15-minute (12-km/7-mi) drive southeast of Šibenik. In the middle of nowhere, way up the hill from the coast, this is a cinder-block structure with

(top to bottom) Trogir; St. Lawrence's Cathedral detail; Čiovo Island; Diocletian's Palace

granite-tile floors, and about a dozen spits spinning a dozen lambs out back.

Trogir

Trogir is a postcard-perfect, prosperous fishing village squeezed onto a tiny island between the mainland and the larger island of Čiovo. It gets very crowded in summer. Upon arrival, you'll pass through the big, 17th-century **City Gate** (Gradska vrata). The figure on the top is the town's Saint John (Sveti Ivan), a local 12th-century bishop who locals claim was blessed with miracle-working powers.

Driving Directions: Trogir is 1 hour (60 km/37 mi) from Šibenik along the D8 Magistrala coastal road.

2. St. Lawrence's Cathedral

Trg Ivana Pavla II; tel. 021/881-426; 9am-7pm Mon.-Sat., mass Sun. summer, 9am-noon daily winter, hours not always observed; free

First, do a bit of sightseeing in town. Head to Trogir's nicest square, **John Paul II Square (Trg Ivana Pavla II),** where you'll find the must-see St. Lawrence's Cathedral, built between the early 13th and 15th centuries. The church's most stunning feature is the western portal, which features reliefs by the 13th-century stone carver Radovan. If the adjacent **Venetian bell tower** (built much later, 14th-16th centuries) is open, you can climb the almost 50 m (164 ft) to the top for about €1 and get some nice views.

3. Čiovo Island

Next, spend a couple hours in the sun. The best beaches around Trogir are on Čiovo Island, just across the bridge south of the old town. There are a few convenient, but usually crowded, beaches to the left after the bridge, or you can keep driving until the road turns to gravel to find a less-crowded beach for some quiet lounging.

You can have an early dinner in town—try **Vanjaka** (Radovanov Trg 9; tel. 021/882-527; www.restaurant-vanjaka.com; 8am-11:30pm; €12) for an upmarket take on local specialties—but it's best to head to **Split,** where you'll spend the night, while it's still light out. It can be dangerous to drive the Magistrala in the dark.

Driving Directions: Split is a 30-minute drive (30 km/18 mi) from Trogir along the D8 Magistrala coastal road.

Split

Croatia's second-largest city, Split is big and busy, traffic-clogged, and even a bit seedy in certain sections. But it's also loud and fun, filled with tons of historic monuments and buildings. Split is can't-miss, one of the most authentic cities on the Dalmatian coast, retaining its character even in the high season when thousands of tourists flood the city.

★ 1. Diocletian's Palace

Up first today is Diocletian's Palace, one of Croatia's most iconic sights. Built at the dawn of the 4th century, it's less a palace than a giant stone complex, which housed not only Roman Emperor Diocletian in his retirement, but also a military garrison. Today, the palace is in daily use—at least two hotels and dozens of apartments are located within its walls. The palace is part of the modern city of Split, so entrance is free, though some areas do charge a fee.

Enter Diocletian's Palace the same way the emperor would have: through the magnificent **Golden Gate.** Then, head to the **Peristyle,** a massive square dominated by the **Cathedral of St. Domnius** (Kraj Sv. Duje 2; 8am-8pm daily June-Sept., 8am-noon and 5pm-7pm daily May and Oct., 8am-noon daily Nov.-Apr.; €3). Pop into the grand cathedral, which was once Diocletian's mausoleum. It's also worth visiting the **palace cellars** (Ul. Iza Vestibula 3; tel. 021/360-171; 8am-10pm daily; €1), underground chambers that reconstruct what the palace was once like above, as the basement exactly mirrored the original ground floor, prior to all the renovations.

If hunger strikes, fuel up with a traditional baked good at **Slastičarna Tradicija** (Bosanska 2; tel. 021/361-070; 8am-11pm Mon.-Sat.; €4).

2. Riva

Continue south to the Riva seafront promenade, Split's center of social activity. This is a great place to have a coffee on a sunny day. In the evening, people meet up here for drinks and lively conversation. For lunch, stroll 10 minutes west to **Pizzeria Bokamorra** (Trumbićeva obala 1; tel. 099/417-7191; noon-1am daily; €11), where you can fill up on unique pizzas such as the fig and honey.

3. Ivan Meštrović Gallery

Šetalište Ivana Meštrovića 46; tel. 021/340-800; www.mestrovic.hr; 9am-7pm Tues.-Sun. May-Sept., 9am-4pm Tues.-Sat. and 10am-3pm Sun. Oct.-Apr.; €5

You'll now find yourself on the Marjan Peninsula. This is where Ivan Meštrović, Croatia's most famous sculptor, built this huge palace as his family home between 1931 and 1939. Today the mammoth house displays some 190 sculptures and over 500 drawings by the artist.

Near the gallery, a five-minute walk west, you'll find the **Kaštelet** (Šetalište Ivana Meštrovića 46; tel. 021/340-800; www.mestrovic.hr; 9am-7pm daily May-Sept., call to arrange a visit off-season; €5), originally built as the 16th-century summer home of a local noble family. It was restored by Meštrović in 1939 to be used as a gallery for 28 wooden reliefs depicting the life of Christ, and it still serves that purpose today. It's a moving display no matter your spiritual inclinations.

The museums are worth a visit, even if you've never heard of Meštrović, for the beautiful location, the views, and the artwork.

4. Park Šuma Marjan

Obala Hrvatskog narodnog preporoda 25; www.marjan-parksuma.hr; open 24 hours

As the day begins to wind down, climb to **Telegrin,** the highest point in sprawling Park Šuma Marjan, which covers the majority of the peninsula in green. If you're in the mood for the beach, **Kasjuni Beach** and its pebbled shores near the western tip of the Marjan Peninsula makes for a lovely summer afternoon.

Walk 30-45 minutes back to Diocletian's Palace (or grab a quick cab if you're tired of walking) for a special dinner at **Villa Spiza** (Kružićeva 3; tel. 091/152-1249; 9am-midnight Mon.-Sat.; €9-15).

DAY 7

Omiš

On your way to Dubrovnik, where you'll end the day, make a stop in Omiš, a pretty town at the mouth of the Cetina river gorge. It's most famous for having been a pirate stronghold against mighty Venice in the 13th century. The city is quite stunning: Craggy rocks give way to narrow streets and old stone houses, and finally to the crystal blue waters of the Adriatic.

Driving Directions: Omiš is a 30-minute drive (25 km/18 mi) from Split along the D8 Magistrala coastal road.

1. Mirabela

Peovo; 9am-10pm daily in summer; €4, cash only

In Omiš, get to know the town's pirate legacy at this Romanesque fortress built in the 13th century. In a 16th-century battle against the Turks, the locals successfully defended the city by confusing them with their shouts and echoes so that the Turks overestimated the number of defenders and fled. Mirabela is the most accessible of the pirate forts around Omiš—just follow the many stairs behind the parish church to climb the tower for a nice view.

2. Velika Strand

Gradska plaza bb

If you want to relax for a bit under the sun, head to this long beach that some describe as sand and other as very small pebbles. Velika Strand offers plenty of amenities including bars, sunbed rentals, beach volleyball, and more. It's only a four-minute walk west of town and is usually clean and easy to access.

For a treat in Omiš, don't miss **Nina-ICE** (Ribarska 2; tel. 095/883-0718; 3pm-10pm daily; €3), where the ice cream is made to order.

Dubrovnik

It's a long drive to Dubrovnik, but the beautiful scenery along the coast means you'll never get bored. This stretch of the D8 passes through Bosnia-Herzegovina, so make sure to keep your passport handy.

Driving Directions: Dubrovnik is a three-hour drive (190 km/119 mi) from Omiš along the D8 Magistrala coastal road.

3. Stradun

To get a feel for Dubrovnik, park your car and head to the Stradun. Also called by its more official name, **Placa** (which you'll see on street signs), the Stradun is the main thoroughfare of Dubrovnik, the beating pulse of the town even in the dead of winter. The street divides the city

MAKE IT Active

The **Cetina Gorge** is full of stunning karst rock formations, dotted with deep green scraggly forest, and cut through by bright blue water. You'll find some of the gorge's prettiest scenery just upstream from Omiš.

One of the best ways to see the gorge is on a rafting trip. The waters are usually pretty mild, unless there has been a lot of rain recently. The blue-green waters are lovely, and there are plenty of spots to get out and take a dip. Try **Active Holidays** (Knezova kačića bb; tel. 021/861-829; www.activeholidays-croatia.com) or **Rafting Pinta** (Duce, Rogac 1/10; tel. 021/734-016; www.rafting-pinta.com) to book a trip, which typically lasts 3-4 hours. Active Holidays also offers canoeing trips on the river. Rafting and boating trips start at around €47 for half a day.

into the southern side, Ragusa, inhabited by the Illyrians in the 4th century, and Dubrava, on the north, settled several centuries later by the Slavs. In 1438, Onofrio della Cava, creator of Dubrovnik's water system, designed a fountain for each end of Dubrovnik's main street, still called **Onofrio's Fountains.** The Large Onofrio's Fountain on the western edge of the Stradun is a huge domed structure, from which clean water flows from a series of carved gargoyle heads, and it's still in use today.

Though it's impossible to miss the Stradun, it's easy to overlook its beauty when you're moving along in a river of travelers. Stop for a coffee at one of the cafés to soak in the atmosphere. For dinner, try **Restaurant Forty-Four** (Ul. Miha Pracata 6; tel. 095/862-2411; 11am-11pm daily; €15), a great find in the old city off the Stradun.

left, Stradun; right, Omiš

top, Franciscan monastery; bottom, Lokrum

DAY 8

Dubrovnik

Dubrovnik, Croatia's most famous city, hosts masses of tourists, and it's easy to see why when you first spot the dramatic walled city on a cliff, with grand architecture, sunny cream stone, and red-tiled roofs contrasting with the blue Adriatic Sea.

★ 1. City Walls

Placa utica 32, entrance inside the Pile Gate to the left; www.wallsofdubrovnik.com; 8am-6:30pm Apr.-May and Aug.-Sept., 8am-7:30pm June-July, 8am-5:30pm Oct., 10am-3pm Nov.-March; €27 or Dubrovnik Card (includes entry to Fort Lovrijenac)

Start your day at the **Pile Gate** entrance of the city walls, located on the western edge of the Stradun. Walking the entirety of the walls, which extend for about 2 km (1 mi), will take you 1-1.5 hours, depending on your pace and the size of the crowds—this is the best way to start your tour of the Old Town. Built and tweaked from the mid-15th century until the great earthquake in 1667, the walls feature several gates and rounded defensive fortresses. The views from the walls that face the sea, contrasting with the red-tiled roofs of the city, are phenomenal.

2. Sponza Palace

On the opposite, eastern side of the Stradun, stop for a quick look at the Sponza Palace. Built in 1520 as a customs house, this elegant Gothic and Renaissance stone palace is today home to the **Memorial Room of the Defenders of Dubrovnik** (9am-9pm daily summer, 10am-3pm daily winter; free), displaying photos of those who died during the 1991-1992 siege of Dubrovnik.

3. Franciscan Monastery

Placa 2; tel. 020/321-410; 9am-6pm daily summer, 9am-5pm daily winter; €4

After lunch, head to the Franciscan monastery, one of the highlights of old Dubrovnik. Built in the 13th century, it's among the city's most popular attractions. A sprawling complex beginning near the Pile Gate, the facade of the monastery runs along the Stradun. The cloisters, which date from the 14th century, and the monastery's courtyard are perhaps the most beautiful features of the complex. In the alley near the monastery is the **Old Pharmacy,** a 700-year-old pharmacy that is supposedly the oldest continuously operating pharmacy in Europe and the third oldest in the world.

Have lunch at nearby **Buffet Škola** (Antuninska 1; tel. 020/321-096; 8am-2am daily summer, call for winter hours; €5), famous for its sandwiches on fresh-baked bread.

4. Lokrum

Boats leave the old town port, Stara Luka, on the hour 10am-3pm summer, last boat leaves the island at 4pm; around €27 round-trip, includes all island attractions

From the old town's harbor, catch a ferry to Lokrum, a forested island 1 km (0.6 mi) off the coast of the city. This is a great place for a swim—there's a nice little lake, **Mrtvo more,** at the southwest corner of the island, and beaches on the eastern side, or the southern side if you are up for a nudist beach. There are also walking paths that lead to a circular **Napoleonic fort (Napoleonsko utvrđenje).** Bring a good pair of walking shoes as the terrain is rocky.

When you get back, refresh with a cold beer on the tucked-away patio at **Dubrovnik Beer Factory** (Od Puča 8; 9am-1am daily) in the Old Town. For dinner with a view, seafood restaurant **Atlas Club Nautika** (Brsalje 3; tel. 020/442-526; www.nautikarestaurants.com; noon-midnight daily mid-Jan.-mid-Dec.; five-course meal €80) has two large terraces overlooking the sea.

Herceg Novi, Montenegro

A beautiful coastal town close to the border of Croatia, Herceg Novi is at the southern end of the Magistrala. Its ancient Stari Grad (Old Town) is a mix of architectural styles that reflect the many changes of power and influence throughout the centuries, shifting from Roman rule to Byzantine, Serb, Turkish, Venetian, Austro-Hungarian, and a few others thrown in for good measure.

Driving Directions: Herceg Novi is a one-hour drive (not including time spent at the border; 93 km/57 mi) from Dubrovnik along the D8 and E65. Wait times at the border crossing between Croatia and Montenegro can reach 2-3 hours in the summer.

1. Kanli Kula Fortress

Kanli Kula; tel. 031/323-072; 9am-7pm daily; €2

Towering above Belavista Square to the north is Kanli Kula Fortress, whose name means "bloody tower." Constructed by the Turks in the 16th century, it was originally built as a prison, and the prisoners' carvings can still be seen on the walls. Today it's a great viewpoint over the town and serves as a venue for outdoor summer performances. The nearby 17th-century clock tower **Sahat Kula** (Trg Herceg Stjepana), also built by the Turks, once served as the city's main gate.

2. Pet Danica Walkway

A great way to see the town and its surroundings is to walk along the Šetalište Pet Danica, a 6-km (3.7-mi) promenade that runs from the village of **Igalo** to the west to the village of **Meljine** in the east, following the path of an old railway line that connected the Montenegrin coast with Sarajevo. The walkway is named after five young girls, all named Danica, who fought and died in World War II. Today the promenade is lined with cafés, bars, and small beaches. Walking from one end to the other takes a little over an hour.

If you get hungry along the way or just want a break, stop at **Peter's Pie and Coffee** (Šetalište Pet Danica 18A; tel. 067/148-180; https://peterspie.com;

Herceg Novi

Crossing the Croatia-Montenegro Border

You'll be crossing the border into Montenegro at **Debelji Brijeg.**

PRACTICAL DETAILS

You will need your **passport,** and if you are driving, you will need border insurance, referred to as a **green card.** If you are renting your car in Dubrovnik, the agency can typically provide this for you in advance. If not, you can purchase the insurance at the border (office typically open 7am-7pm; €15 for 15 days). Occasionally border guards will wave you through or have you "pay them directly" if you are crossing at other hours. Some rental car companies require written permission for their cars to cross into another country. Read the fine print when making your reservation.

TIME-SAVING TIPS

Crossing the border between Croatia and Montenegro is usually easy, but can sometimes take very long due to heavy traffic (20 minutes-1 hour most of the year, 4 hours July-Aug.). The only time the border crossing is faster is at **dawn** (5am-7am)—the earlier the better. Night is usually just as busy as the day in either direction.

8am-5pm daily; €5), which offers a range of options for any time of day. Plenty of indoor and sea-view outdoor seating makes it the perfect spot to catch up on your messages while sipping coffee and enjoying the view.

3. Blue Grotto Tour

Montenegro Wild Boat, https://montenegrowildboat.com; 2-4 hours; from €220

Like its famous counterpart in Italy, the Montenegrin Blue Grotto gets its name from the effect that the light coming through the cave has on water, casting it a shade of ethereal turquoise blue. However, the Blue Grotto here is quite cave-like inside. (There is a Croatian Blue Grotto, with a ceiling "skylight" that makes it less cave-like. To access it, you need to take an excursion from Vis, an island off the coast of Split.) Because tourist boats can crowd the grotto in the summer, try to take a tour very early or late in the day to avoid the busiest times. Montenegro Wild Boat offers tours departing from the docks of several Herceg Novi hotels, with some time devoted to swimming in the grotto.

After the tour, have possibly the best seafood in Herceg Novi at waterside **Konoba Škver** (Šetalište Pet Danica; tel. 068/145-740; noon-10pm daily in summer, closed winter; €18). It's a great way to cap your trip down the Magistrana.

TRANSPORTATION

Air

- **Zadar Airport** (ZAD; tel. 023/313-311; www.zadar-airport.hr) is about a 10-minute drive east of town.
- **Franjo Tuđman Airport Zagreb** (www.zagreb-airport.hr/en) is Croatia's busiest airport, and it's a three-hour drive (300 km/186 mi) to Zadar.

ADDING ON Gulf of Kotor

Before heading back to Dubrovnik from Herceg Novi, consider visiting some sights on the Gulf of Kotor. The entire gulf is protected as a UNESCO World Heritage Site, and it's not hard to see why when you're driving through one of the most mountainous areas in Europe, lined by emerald-green waters, almost like a fjord.

Driving Directions: The famed town of Kotor is just over an hour's drive from Herceg Novi along the E65 that hugs the gulf.

KOTOR TOWN WALLS

Kotor; May-Sept.; €3

Nestled between the mountains in a magical fjord-like bay, the walled city of Kotor is steeped in history, though it's less polished than many of the popular towns along the Croatian coast. The city's churches and palaces have given it UNESCO World Heritage protected status; these buildings span Roman, Byzantine, Gothic, and Renaissance architectural styles and are amazingly preserved despite several earthquakes in the area.

When you arrive, spend 1.5-2 hours wandering the town walls, which were built and rebuilt from the 9th-19th centuries. Toward the southeast, the walls climb up a hill to the **San Giovanni fortress** (8am-8pm daily; €8), built in the 6th century by Byzantine Emperor Justinian I. On the opposite, northwestern wall, you'll find the **Kampana tower** (Trg od Oružja; 8am-4pm daily; €8), built in the 13th century to defend the juncture of the river and the Bay of Kotor.

Have a quick lunch at **Ladovina Kitchen and Wine Bar** (Njegoševa 209; tel. 063/422-472; www.ladovina.me; 8am-1am Mon.-Sat., 8am-midnight Sun.; €12), and then get cash from an ATM in town for your next stop.

OUR LADY OF THE ROCKS

9am-6pm daily; museum entry €1, taxi boat €5

Drive 15 minutes back the way you came to **Perast.** Park at the entrance to the town, walk down to the waterfront, and take a quick water taxi to Our Lady of the Rocks, one of Montenegro's top tourist attractions. Or if you didn't visit the Blue Grotto from Herceg Novi, you can take a combined tour from Perast.

The church, which looks like it's floating on the water, has a stone exterior topped by red-tiled roofs and blue domes. Dating from the 15th century, the church has a number of beautiful artifacts and paintings to complement its idyllic island position, but many might say it is the love stories surrounding the church that make it so special: Gold and silver plates abound in the church, donated by families hoping to keep their loved ones safe at sea.

WATCH

Game of Thrones: The hit fantasy show was filmed in several Croatian locations, but **Dubrovnik** is the place to go to feel like you're walking around King's Landing.

READ

Black Lamb and Grey Falcon by Rebecca West: This travel book chronicles the author's trip through the former Yugoslavia in the 1930s. She's been criticized for generalizing, but her detail on the local scenery, characters, and history as well as the underlying tension of the time makes for an absorbing read.

LISTEN

The dominant folk music tradition on the Dalmatian Coast is the **klapa,** an a cappella group of 4-10 men who sing rather sad songs. Check out **Oliver Dragojević** for a popular, modern take on the coastal sound.

Train

Croatian Railways (Hrvatske željeznice) (www.hznet.hr) trains are fairly reliable, fairly clean (if a little old at times), and usually cheaper than taking the bus. **Zadar's train station** (Ante Starčevića 4; tel. 052/212-555; www.hzpp.hr; ticket office 7:30am-9pm daily) is about a 15-minute walk southeast of the old town center.

Car Rental

Croatia is home to all the major rental agencies, such as **Hertz** (www.hertz.com), **Budget** (www.budget.com), **Alamo** (www.alamo.com), and **Europcar** (www.europcar.com). You may also want to check out the budget **Easy Car** (www.easycar.com) for a cheaper deal.

Note that some rental companies may have restrictions on taking cars into neighboring countries. In addition, dropping cars off outside Croatia might not be allowed, or might be subject to a large fee. Be sure to inquire about their policies when reserving.

The official speed limit on the Magistrala coastal road is 50 kph (about 31 mph).

Getting Back

Due to car rental policies, you will likely need to head back to Dubrovnik, or elsewhere in Croatia, to drop off your car and head home. **Dubrovnik Airport** (DBV; tel. 020/773-333; www.airport-dubrovnik.hr) is located about 20 km (12 mi) southeast of the city, in Čilipi. It's the third-busiest airport in Croatia, with plenty of flights during the busy summer months.

From Dubrovnik, Zadar is 355 km (220 mi) north, a four-hour drive, and Zagreb is 580 km (360 mi) north, about a seven-hour drive.

- Zagreb, Ljubljana, and Trieste (page 205)

OUTDOOR ADVENTURES

OUTDOOR
ADVENTURES
60°
10°
0°
50°
40°
UNITED
KINGDOM
North Sea
Keswick
Troutbeck
DUBLIN AND THE
WICKLOW WAY
Irish Sea
Dublin
ENGLAND'S
LAKE DISTRICT
IRELAND
HOLLAND
JUNCTION
NETWORK
English Channel
BELGIUM
ATLANTIC OCEAN
FRANCE
Bay of
Biscay
CAMINO DE
SANTIAGO
Santiago de
Compostela
Portomarín
AND.
SPAIN
PORTUGAL
Mediterranean
MOROCCO
ALGERIA
© MOON.COM

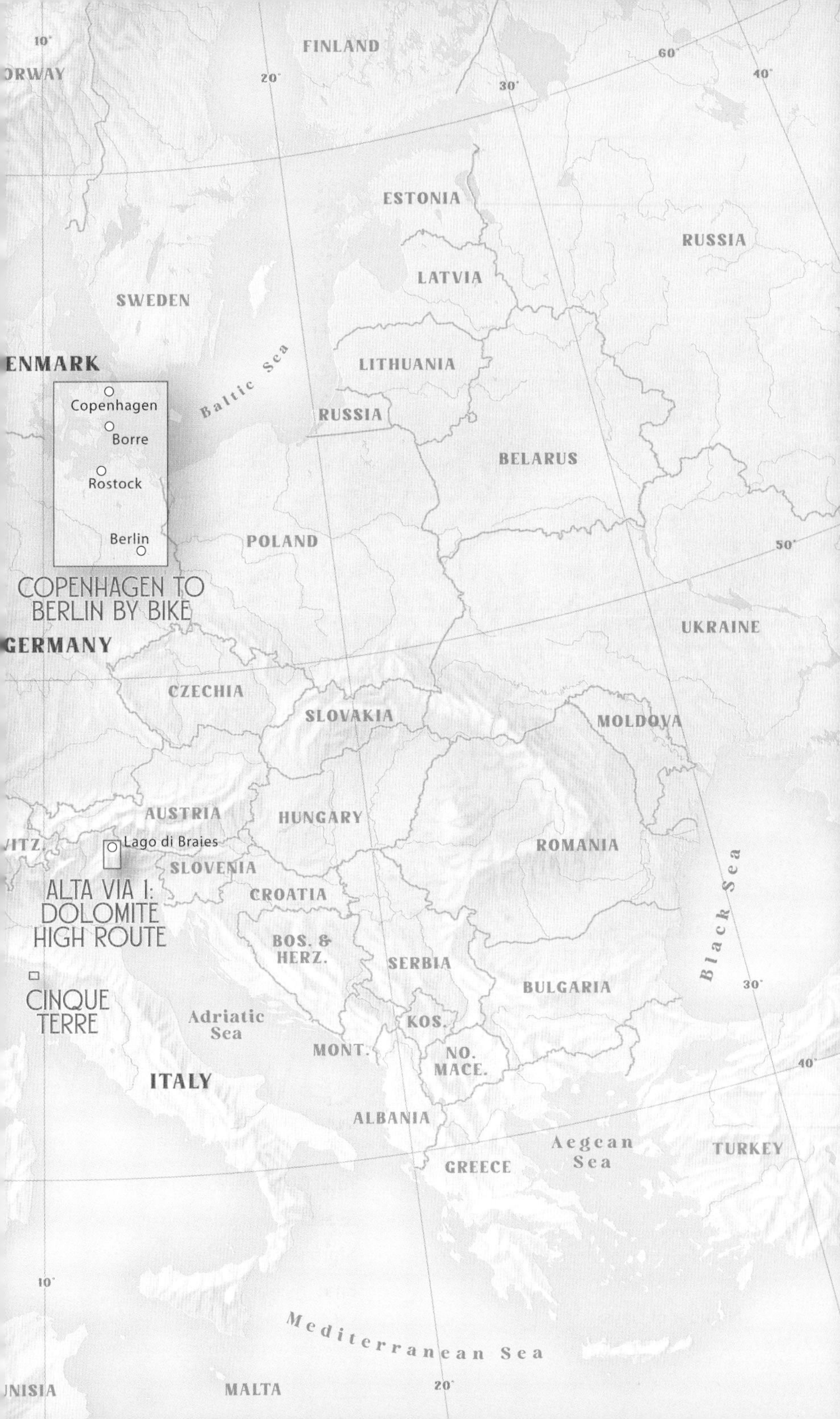

FINLAND
ORWAY
SWEDEN
ESTONIA
RUSSIA
LATVIA
LITHUANIA
ENMARK
Baltic Sea
Copenhagen
Borre
Rostock
Berlin
RUSSIA
BELARUS
POLAND
COPENHAGEN TO
BERLIN BY BIKE
GERMANY
UKRAINE
CZECHIA
SLOVAKIA
MOLDOVA
AUSTRIA
HUNGARY
ROMANIA
VITZ.
Lago di Braies
SLOVENIA
ALTA VIA I:
DOLOMITE
HIGH ROUTE
CROATIA
BOS. &
HERZ.
SERBIA
Black Sea
BULGARIA
CINQUE
TERRE
Adriatic
Sea
KOS.
MONT.
NO.
MACE.
ITALY
ALBANIA
Aegean
Sea
TURKEY
GREECE
Mediterranean Sea
UNISIA
MALTA
10°
20°
30°
40°
60°
50°

DUBLIN AND THE WICKLOW WAY

Why Go: Get to know Ireland on the country's most popular long-distance walking route, which starts south of Dublin and winds through dramatic mountains and placid green farmlands.

Number of Days: 5

Total Distance: 65 km (40 mi)

Seasons: Late spring and summer

Start: Dublin

End: Glenmalure

Your trip starts in Dublin, the fast-paced, cosmopolitan capital of the Irish Republic, but you'll soon trade noisy sidewalks for quiet walking trails. The 132-km (82-mi) Wicklow Way begins in the suburbs and winds south into Wicklow Mountains National Park, passing through the glacial valley of Glendalough and down the western flank of the monster-mountain Lugnaquilla in Glenmalure, and ending just over the Wicklow-Carlow border in Clonegal. This is a world of verdant hills and winding backroads—County Wicklow is aptly nicknamed the "Garden of Ireland." This itinerary details the most scenic stretch between Dublin and Glenmalure.

The route is dotted with hostels and plenty of B&Bs that cater especially to walkers. To plan your walk, the Wicklow Way walking trail website (www.wicklowway.com) has information on accommodations, meals, luggage transfer, and more.

TOP 3

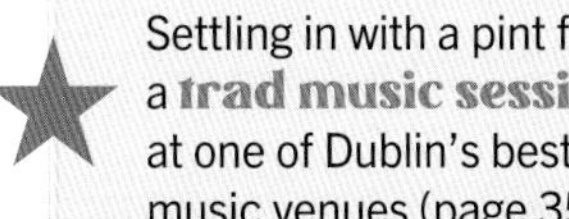

★ Settling in with a pint for a **trad music session** at one of Dublin's best live music venues (page 358).

★ Seeing **Glendalough** up close. This 6th-century monastic site was once one of Ireland's most important centers of learning (page 361).

★ Reveling in the quiet of **Glenmalure,** Ireland's longest glacial valley, an utterly remote locale with an appeal all its own (page 361).

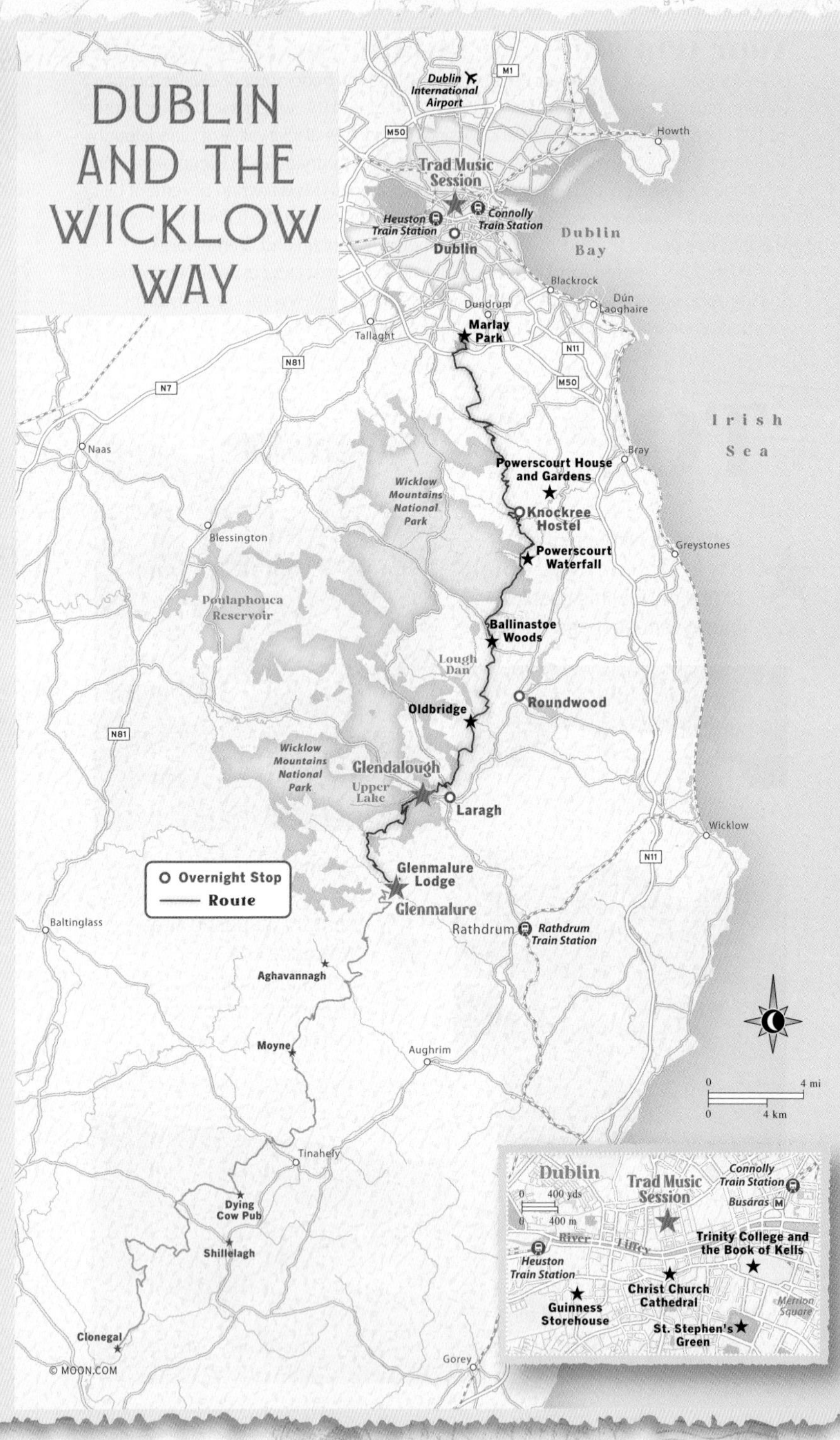
DUBLIN AND THE WICKLOW WAY
Dublin International Airport
M1
M50
Howth
Trad Music Session
Heuston Train Station
Connolly Train Station
Dublin
Dublin Bay
Blackrock
Dundrum
Dún Laoghaire
Tallaght
Marlay Park
N11
N81
N7
M50
Irish Sea
Naas
Bray
Powerscourt House and Gardens
Wicklow Mountains National Park
Knockree Hostel
Blessington
Greystones
Powerscourt Waterfall
Poulaphouca Reservoir
Ballinastoe Woods
Lough Dan
Roundwood
Oldbridge
N81
Wicklow Mountains National Park
Glendalough
Upper Lake
Laragh
Wicklow
N11
Overnight Stop
Route
Glenmalure Lodge
Glenmalure
Baltinglass
Rathdrum
Rathdrum Train Station
Aghavannagh
Moyne
Aughrim
0
4 mi
0
4 km
Tinahely
Dying Cow Pub
Shillelagh
Clonegal
© MOON.COM
Gorey
Dublin
0 400 yds
0 400 m
Trad Music Session
Connolly Train Station
Busáras
River Liffey
Heuston Train Station
Trinity College and the Book of Kells
Christ Church Cathedral
Guinness Storehouse
Merrion Square
St. Stephen's Green

Key Reservations

In general, expect plenty of company if you're walking the Wicklow Way in June, July, or August.

- Book popular attractions in Dublin, such as the **Book of Kells** and the **Guinness Storehouse,** online in advance.
- Let **Knockree Hostel** know at least four days in advance if you want a lunch or evening meal.

DAY 1

Dublin

Where to Stay: Near Trinity College

Arrive by: Plane to Dublin International Airport

1. St. Stephen's Green

At the bottom of Grafton St.; tel. 01/475-7816; https://ststephensgreenpark.ie; 7:30am-dusk Mon.-Sat., 9:30am-dusk Sun. and bank holidays, 9:30am-12:30pm Christmas Day; free

Before you start your long-distance walk, take a day to see the sights in Dublin. Head first to St. Stephen's Green, possibly Europe's largest city square, to get a feel for Dublin. The square's tranquil and immaculately kept 9 hectares (22 acres) are home to verdant walkways, duck ponds, and tidy flowerbeds, as well as memorials to Irish revolutionaries, writers, and other luminaries. Go for a leisurely stroll, or just pick a bench and watch Dublin go by.

2. Trinity College and the Book of Kells

College Green, at the eastern end of Dame St.; www.tcd.ie/visitors; combination campus and Book of Kells tour adults €29, family €65, under 12 free

Walk 10 minutes north on pedestrianized Grafton Street to reach Trinity College Dublin, Ireland's most prestigious university. Join the guided campus tour (tel. 01/608-1724; www.tcd.ie/visitors/trinitytrails; departs main gate every 40 minutes 10:15am-3pm daily mid-May-Sept.; €15) or take a few minutes to wander around the perimeter of the immaculate campus green, known as Parliament Square, which is lined with dignified Georgian buildings.

The highlight of the campus is the **Old Library,** which houses the Book of Kells (tel. 01/608-2308; www.tcd.ie/visitors/book-of-kells; 8:30am-5pm Mon.-Sat. and 9:30am-5am Sun. Apr.-Sept., 9:30am-5:30pm Mon.-Sat. and noon-4:30pm Sun. Oct.-Mar.; admission without campus tour adults €18.50, family €34, students with ID and ages over 60 €15, under 12 free). This is the best known of all Ireland's illuminated monastic manuscripts. A different two-page spread is on display each day—under thick glass, of course—and there's an engaging exhibition that puts the book into historical and religious context.

For lunch, head to **The Bank on College Green** (20-22 College Green; tel. 01/677-0677; www.bankoncollegegreen.com; 11am-12:30am Mon.-Wed., 11am-1:30am Thurs.-Sat., 11am-midnight Sun.; from €16), perhaps the most atmospheric of the fantastic eateries along Dame and South Great Georges Streets.

3. Christ Church Cathedral

Christchurch Place, west end of Lord Edward St.; tel. 01/677-8099; https://christchurchcathedral.ie; 10am-5pm Mon., Wed., Fri.-Sat., 10am-5:30pm Tues., Thurs., 12:30pm-3pm Sun.; €10

After lunch, walk 10 minutes east to the marvelous Christ Church Cathedral. The cathedral has its origins in the late 12th and early 13th centuries, though much of the building was rebuilt in the 1870s. The restoration preserved as much of the original edifice as possible and faithfully replicated the rest in the Romanesque and Early English Gothic styles. Inside, the cathedral offers a few surprises, such as the mummified cat-and-rat pair found in a pipe of the church organ and the massive arches on the north side of the aisle that lean at an unnerving angle.

4. Guinness Storehouse

St. James's Gate; tel. 01/408-4800; www.guinness-storehouse.com; 10am-7:45pm Mon.-Fri., 9:30am-8:45pm Sat., 9:30am-7:45pm Sun.; from €26

A pint of Guinness is a must on a visit to Ireland, and the Guinness Storehouse is one of the biggest tourist attractions in Dublin. Your ticket includes a self-guided tour and the best pint you'll ever taste in the upstairs, all-glass Gravity Bar with a panoramic city view. There's also an on-site restaurant that serves up some really good traditional meals, though you'll need to buy the admission ticket to dine there, too.

The walk from Christ Church Cathedral is doable (about 20 minutes), but you can also take a 10-minute bus ride.

TOP EXPERIENCE

★ 5. Trad Session

In the evening, find a pub, grab a pint, and get ready to enjoy a traditional, or trad, music session. The toursity Temple Bar neighborhood has plenty of options, and you can also seek out more low-key venues in other areas. Trad in Dublin is not necessarily "authentic"—there's an element of tourist-driven theatricality to it—but it certainly still makes for a good time.

One good pick is **The Stag's Head** (1 Dame Ct.; tel. 01/679-3687; www.stagshead.ie), an atmospheric Victorian bar. **O'Donoghue's** (15 Merrion Row; tel. 01/661-4303; www.odonoghues.ie) is a bit more touristy, but that's because it offers arguably the city's best trad.

DAY 2

Marlay Park to Knockree

Walking Distance and Time: 21 km (13 mi); 7 hours

1. Marlay Park

It's time to put on your hiking gear and begin your seven-day walk on the beautiful Wicklow Way. Marlay Park is the official start of the Wicklow Way. To get there, take the Ballinteer-bound #16 **Dublin Bus** (tel. 01/873-4222; www.dublinbus.ie; 3 hours 50 minutes) from O'Connell Street.

This first day of walking is strenuous, with a total ascent of about 600 m (1,968 ft). Along the way you'll go through **Kilmashogue Forest** and pass several mountains. The biggest climb is up to **Prince William's Seat,** where views stretch all the way out to the coast.

2. Powerscourt House and Gardens

Enniskerry; tel. 01/204-6000; www.powerscourt.com; 9:30am-5:30pm daily; adults €11.50, family €26, senior €9, student €8.50, ages 5-16 €5, under 5 free

While you could head straight to Knockree Hostel to finish your day of walking, it's worth a 4-km (2.5-mi) detour to Powerscourt House and Gardens in the town of Enniskerry. This gorgeous estate has

Traditional Music

Ireland's traditional music is a sound unto itself, by turns rollicking and otherworldly.

INSTRUMENTS

The Celts brought an exclusively oral tradition to this island about 2,000 years ago, and back then the **harp** was the primary instrument of the genre. Bards composed vocal and harp music for their patrons, the kings of Ireland. The **uilleann pipes,** comparable to Scotland's bagpipes, were played almost as far back, though they were an instrument of the "common" people rather than the highly revered bards. After the Flight of the Earls in 1607, this musical heritage was suppressed, along with so many other aspects of Irish culture.

You might be surprised to learn just how recently other essential instruments of "modern" folk music were introduced; the **fiddle** we recognize didn't appear in Ireland until the 1720s, and now it is the most iconic instrument of all. (The Irish fiddle is identical to a classical violin, which is pretty astounding, given how different the sound is!) The **bodhrán,** a goatskin drum struck by a wooden beater, was used during warfare and other nonmusical pursuits, only appearing in trad sessions starting in the 1960s. There was a flutelike instrument played in medieval Ireland, and the **Irish flute** is commonly heard in sessions today, though the modern tin whistle didn't show up until the early 19th century. Today guitarists sometimes join in, adding a flavor of international folk.

RECORDING AND REVIVAL

The old songs were gradually put to paper beginning in the 18th century. After a period of decline (apart from a recording project undertaken in the 1920s), the folk tradition saw a remarkable resurgence in the mid-20th century, thanks to **Sean Ó Riada** and many other dedicated musicians. Traditional music fostered close-knit immigrant communities in England, America, and Australia. Fortunately for us all, the Irish music revival continues to this day.

Powerscourt House and Gardens

the feel of a Florentine villa; only the temperature and Great Sugarloaf Mountain looming beyond remind you that the Mediterranean is a plane ride away. The house itself is home to shops, an interior design gallery, a garden pavilion, and a café overlooking the Italian garden.

3. Knockree Hostel

Lacken House, 7 km (4 mi) west of Enniskerry; tel. 01/286-4036 for info, tel. 01/830-4555 to book; www.anoige.ie; dorms €22-26

Your best bet for spending the night is Knockree Hostel, which has lovely pastoral and mountain views. If you want a lunch or evening meal here, you must pre-order at least four days in advance, or stock up on your own groceries.

DAY 3

Knockree to Roundwood

Walking Distance and Time: 18 km (11 mi); 6.5 hours

1. View of Powerscourt Waterfall

As you set off from Knockree, you'll cross Glencree River and walk through the Crone Woods. An uphill climb is rewarded with spectacular views over Powerscourt Waterfall, one of Ireland's tallest waterfalls at 121 m (397 ft). It's technically part of Powerscourt House and Gardens (not part of this walking route). The area around the base has a separate admission fee, but the views from above are free. The next part of the walk climbs the shoulder of **Djouce Mountain.**

2. Ballinastoe Woods

Next, the Wicklow Way follows a path through Ballinastoe Woods. The views of **Lough Tay,** a small nearby lake, are dazzling. Continue on to Roundwood.

3. Roundwood

The town of Roundwood is home to a handful of accommodations that cater to Wicklow Way walkers, as well as several cafés and pubs. Those who only have time to walk part of the Wicklow Way generally start here and walk south to Glendalough.

DAY 4

Roundwood to Glendalough

Walking Distance and Time: 12 km (7.5 mi); 4 hours

1. Oldbridge

This day is much easier that the first two. You'll first pass through Oldbridge, another town with accommodation options for Wicklow Way walkers. The walk then continues along **Paddock Hill** before reaching Glendalough.

2. Glendalough Town

The approach into Glendalough Valley is beautiful. If you can't wait, you can head into Glendalough today, though the Wicklow Way route winds through the

valley and its sites during tomorrow's stretch.

There are a handful of places to stay in Glendalough town, though if you continue along about 20 minutes to the nearby town of **Laragh,** you'll find more accommodation options, as well as cafés and places to stock up on groceries. One of the best picks is **Wicklow Heather** (on the main R756 road in Laragh; tel. 0404/45157; https://wicklowheather.ie; 8am-10pm daily; dinner €16-24, rooms from €90). Open for breakfast, lunch, and dinner, Wicklow Heather serves up a refreshingly eclectic menu (and good coffee) in a romantic, if slightly quirky, dining room.

DAY 5

Glendalough to Glenmalure

Walking Distance and Time: 14 km (8.7 km); 4.5 hours

1. Glendalough Visitor Centre and Tourist Office

Tel. 0404/45325; www.glendalough.ie; 9:30am-6pm daily mid-Mar.-mid-Oct., 9:30am-5pm mid-Oct.-mid-Mar.; €5

If you want to learn more about monastic sites, pop into the tourist office in Glendalough. The exhibit covers early Irish monasteries—the construction and function of round towers, manuscript illumination, everyday life, and so forth. There's also a collection of early grave slabs and a bullaun stone, a primitive crucible carved out of a larger rock.

★ 2. Glendalough

Tel. 0404/45352; www.glendalough.ie; free

Perhaps Ireland's most famous monastic site, Glendalough (Gleann dá loch, "Glen of the Two Lakes") is utterly enchanting. This is a lush, glacier-carved valley dotted in yellow gorse, with walking trails skirting two placid lakes and the substantial remains of a holy community founded by St. Kevin in the 6th century: a 10th- or 11th-century **round tower,** one of the tallest in the country at 30 m (98 ft), with a cap rebuilt from fallen stones in 1876; a weathered high cross; and the ruins of seven churches. By the 9th century Glendalough was second in size and prestige only to Clonmacnoise in County Offaly.

You can take in most of the monastic ruins (aside from **Temple na Skellig** on a ledge over the Upper Lake, accessible only by boat—though you can't hire one!) on a leisurely walk along the south shore of the Lower Lake. The old monastery grounds hold a small priest's house in the shadow of the round tower, the **Cathedral of Saints Peter and Paul** (dating from the 10th and 12th centuries), and the 12th-century St. Kevin's Church—this one is quite unusual, having its original stone roof. The miniature round tower in the west gable resembles a chimney, which is why it's better known as "Kevin's Kitchen."

A walk in any direction is glorious, though the path along the **Upper Lake** at sunrise or sunset offers the most breathtaking views of all (and you'll enjoy them in utter solitude). The official Wicklow Way route follows a climb to **Poulanass Waterfall** from the national park information office on the eastern shore of Upper Lake, and then skirts the eastern flank of **Spinc Mountain** on the way out.

★ 3. Glenmalure

Up next is the beautiful descent into Glenmalure Valley. Glenmalure, Ireland's longest glacial valley, features hills clad in evergreens and yellow gorse, nonexistent cell-phone service, horse-drawn caravans on shady backroads, and a mobile library in the parking lot of the Glenmalure Lodge. While you're here,

Completing the Wicklow Way

From Glenmalure, the Wicklow Way winds on for another 61 km (38 mi), which can be walked in three days. The last legs en route to the official end in Clonegal are quiet and scenic. Here are some of the highlights between Glenmalure and Clonegal.

GLENMALURE TO MOYNE

Walking Distance and Time: 21 km (13 mi); 7 hours

On this stretch of the Wicklow Way, you'll find the **Iron Bridge** in the town of **Aghavannagh.** Many people use this as a stopping (or starting) point to finish their walk.

MOYNE TO SHILLELAGH

Walking Distance and Time: 21 km (13 mi); 7 hours

The highlight on this stretch, between Tinahely and Shillelagh, is the **Dying Cow pub** (along the Wicklow Way; www.facebook.com/TheDyingCowPub). It's a must to stop here for a drink.

SHILLELAGH TO CLONEGAL

Walking Distance and Time: 19 km (12 mi); 6 hours

The official end (or start, if you choose to walk it in the other direction) of the Wicklow Way is the tiny village of Clonegal. Celebrate your journey with a pint at **Séan O'Dúinn** (High St.; 7pm-11:30pm Mon.-Thur., 7pm-12:30am Fri., 5pm-12:30am Sat., 5pm-11:30pm Sun.) or **Osborne's Pub** (Main St.; tel. 53 937 7359; 5:30pm-11:30pm Wed.-Fri., 4pm-11:30pm Sat., 2pm-11:30pm Sun.).

you might be forgiven for thinking you've entered a time warp (in the very best sense).

4. Glenmalure Lodge

11 km (7 mi) west of Rathdrum on a local road; tel. 0404/46188; www.glenmalurelodge.ie; noon-9pm; meals €10-20, B&B €45 pp; €50-60 s

Finish the day at the Glenmalure Lodge, which was established in 1801 and has a really cozy, amiable vibe. Enjoy a pint at one of the picnic tables out front and order a full Irish breakfast in the morning, between 8:30 and 10:30am. After breakfast, backtrack to the **Glendalough Visitor Centre**—the Glenmalure Valley's beauty deserves a second look—to catch the afternoon bus back to Dublin. Or, take a taxi to **Rathdrum** to board a train.

TRANSPORTATION

Air

Dublin International Airport (DUB; tel. 01/814-1111; www.dublinairport.com) is 12 km (7.5 mi) north of Dublin. **Dublin Bus** (tel. 01/873-4222) operates a frequent **Airlink** service from the airport to stations in Dublin. **Aircoach** (tel. 01/844-7118; www.aircoach.ie; departures from O'Connell St. every 15 minutes, every 30 minutes midnight-5am) and **Citylink** (tel. 01/626-6888; www.citylink.ie; daily, at least 14 per day) also offers bus services between Dublin and the airport. A **taxi** to or from the airport will run you €36-40.

WATCH

My Left Foot: This 1989 biopic stars Daniel Day-Lewis as Christy Brown, an Irish painter and author with cerebral palsy. The film was nominated for a handful of Academy Awards, and Dublin-born director Jim Sheridan has several other award-winning films to his name.

READ

The Green Road by Anne Enright: Enright's 2016 novel follows a family living in a small town on Ireland's west coast. Enright is one of Ireland's foremost fiction writers, having won the Booker Prize for her novel *The Gathering* in 2007.

Selected Poems: Rogha Dánta by Nuala Ní Dhomhnaill: Many of Ireland's finest poets are writing exclusively in Irish, and Ní Dhomhnaill is perhaps the most beloved among them. As you read, the original Irish is on the left page and the English translation on the right.

LISTEN

The Dubliners: This folk group got their start in the 1960s at O'Donoghue's pub in Dublin.

Train

Iarnrod Éireann, also known as **Irish Rail** (tel. 01/836-6222; www.irishrail.ie), operates from **Connolly Train Station** (1 km/0.6 mi north of Trinity College, across the River Liffey) and **Heuston Train Station** (west of the city center).

The **Rathdrum Train Station** is the closest to the end of this itinerary in Glenmalure.

Bus

Busáras (Store St.; tel. 01/836-6111) is the central bus depot located a 15-minute walk north of Trinity College across the River Liffey. From there, **Bus Éireann** (www.buseireann.ie) runs routes throughout Ireland.

St. Kevin's Bus Services (www.glendaloughbus.com) runs buses from Glendalough Visitor Centre to Dublin (twice daily; 1.5-2 hours; €13).

Getting Back

If you don't want to walk back to Glendalough, take a cab there from Glenmalure Lodge (15 minutes; about €25) to catch the **St. Kevin's bus** back to Dublin. Or take a cab to **Rathdrum** (15 minutes; about €25), where there is a train station with **Irish Rail** connections to Dublin (1.5 hours; €9-12).

For those going to the very end of the Wicklow Way, there is no bus service directly from Clonegal. Wexford Local Link provides service from both **Kildavin** (3 km/1.9 mi southwest of Clonegal on a local road; taxi €10-15) and the larger town of **Bunclody** (5 km south of Clonegal on the R746; taxi €15) to **Tullow.** From Tullow, **Bus Éireann** can take you back to Dublin (2 hours 20 minutes).

CONNECT WITH

- London and Paris (page 44)
- Edinburgh and Glasgow (page 65)
- Causeway Coast (page 246)

ENGLAND'S LAKE DISTRICT

Why Go: From lush green valleys to russet-colored fells and snow-crested peaks, the Lake District National Park has been drawing tourists for centuries to hike mountains, drift on serene lakes, and explore timeless villages.

Number of Days: 6

Total Distance: 322 km (200 mi), including trips to and from Lancaster where you can pick up a rental car

Seasons: Spring to early fall (avoid midsummer, when towns are busiest)

Start: Troutbeck

End: Keswick

Among the most beautiful areas in all of Europe, England's Lake District is a nature-lover's paradise of twisting country lanes, incomparable hikes, and staggering vistas. Well known to the English and countless visitors for generations, it has been home to many great artists, who've captured its landscape in poetry, prose, and painting, finding inspiration in its always changing weather and light.

This route is focused on walking, but does involve some driving to set you up for your hikes. The Lake District may look small on the map, but with its rugged topography, getting around it is slow going, so it's worth changing hotels a few times, always basing yourself close to the next day's action.

TOP 3

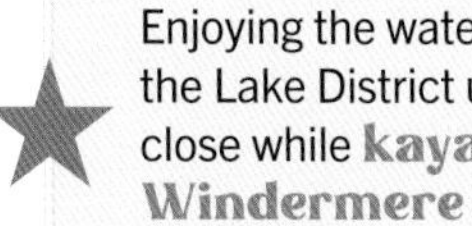

★ Enjoying the waters of the Lake District up close while **kayaking Windermere Lake** (page 368).

★ **Hiking Scafell Pike,** the tallest mountain in England, and having a well-deserved pint at the Wasdale Head pub at the walk's end (page 371).

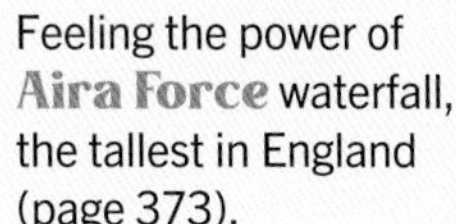

★ Feeling the power of **Aira Force** waterfall, the tallest in England (page 373).

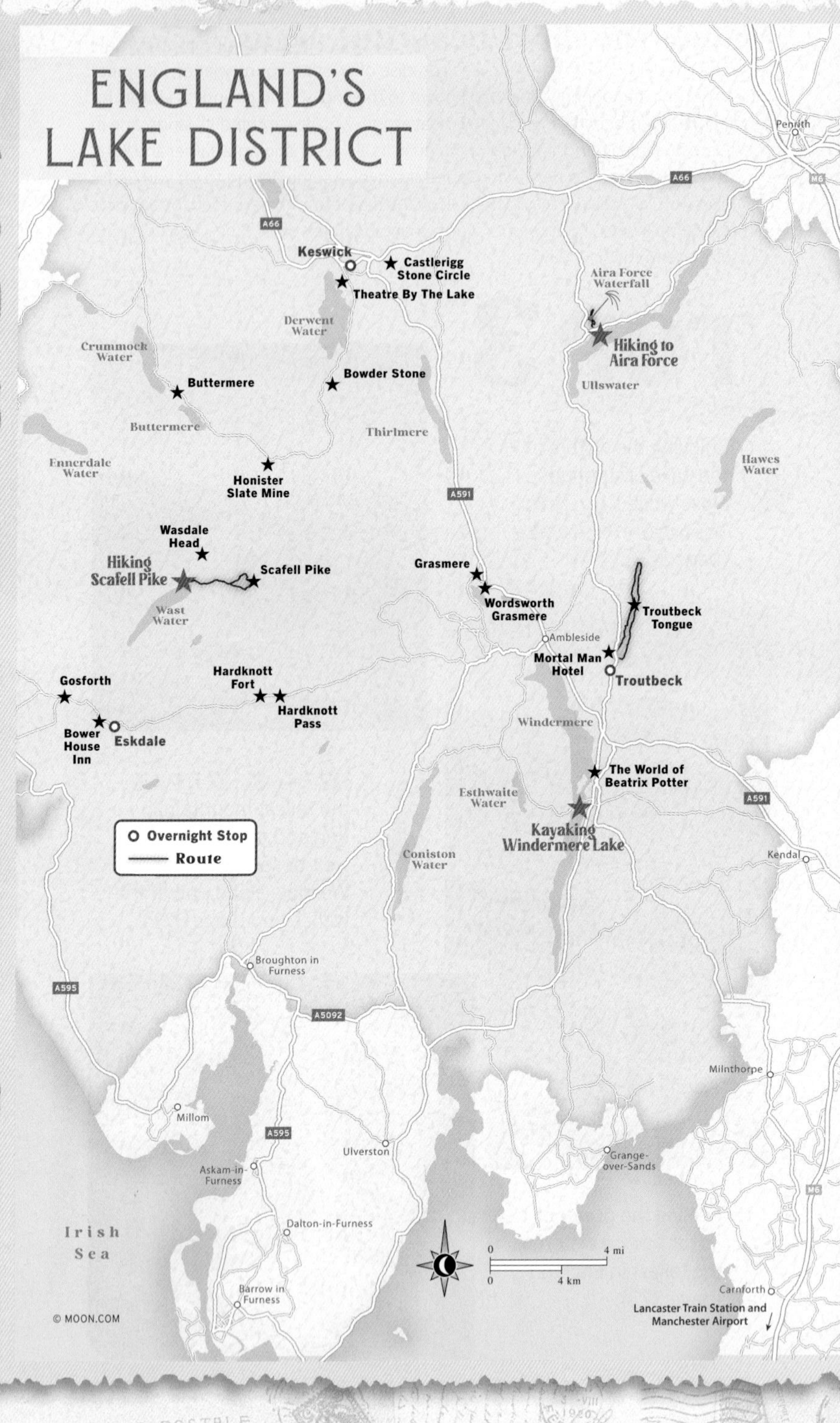

ENGLAND'S LAKE DISTRICT
Penrith
A66
M6
A66
Keswick
Castlerigg Stone Circle
Theatre By The Lake
Aira Force Waterfall
Derwent Water
Crummock Water
Hiking to Aira Force
Bowder Stone
Buttermere
Ullswater
Buttermere
Thirlmere
Ennerdale Water
Hawes Water
Honister Slate Mine
A591
Wasdale Head
Hiking Scafell Pike
Scafell Pike
Grasmere
Wordsworth Grasmere
Troutbeck Tongue
Wast Water
Ambleside
Mortal Man Hotel
Troutbeck
Gosforth
Hardknott Fort
Hardknott Pass
Bower House Inn
Eskdale
Windermere
The World of Beatrix Potter
Esthwaite Water
A591
Kayaking Windermere Lake
Overnight Stop
Route
Coniston Water
Kendal
Broughton in Furness
A595
A5092
Milnthorpe
Millom
A595
Ulverston
Grange-over-Sands
Askam-in-Furness
M6
Dalton-in-Furness
Irish Sea
0
4 mi
0
4 km
Barrow in Furness
Carnforth
© MOON.COM
Lancaster Train Station and Manchester Airport
CARTOLINA POSTALE

Key Reservations

During the high season (Mar.-Oct.), especially midsummer and any school holidays not in the winter, be prepared to book as far in advance as you can, particularly when it comes to **hotels,** and particularly on weekends. The same goes for **rental cars.**

The popular **Honister Slate Mine** should be booked well ahead to guarantee a fun experience.

Honister Slate Mine

DAY 1

Troutbeck

Arrive by: Train from London Euston Station to Lancaster

1. Troutbeck Tongue Circular

Walking Distance and Time: 12.4 km (7.7 mi) round-trip; 2 hours

Start/End: Mortal Man (Troutbeck, Windermere; tel. 015394 33193; www.themortalman.co.uk; from £90 d)

Pick up your rental car from Lancaster, from where it's a 44-minute, 51-km (32-mi) drive to the **Mortal Man,** a beautiful, freestanding pub in the hamlet of Troutbeck that has been around since 1689 and was once the meeting place of poets Wordsworth, Coleridge, and Hogarth.

After getting checked in, it's time to take a walk. A two-hour loop of just under 13 km (8 mi), the Troutbeck Tongue Circular is not too taxing. It's a great hike to take after your arrival to get you acquainted with the sights, smells, and other sensations the Lake District has to offer. It takes you up a steep, but relatively short, hill nestled in the midst of the Troutbeck valley. Views from its summit are impressive if not massively far reaching, for you remain mostly walled in by the surrounding higher fells. The pub staff are more than happy to consult on this and other first-day walking options, and if you order ahead, they can provide a packed lunch as well.

After your hike, Mortal Man's beer garden makes a splendid place to relax and rest, and its restaurant is just the ticket for refueling after a long day's travel.

Troutbeck Tongue Circular

Windermere

Walking Distance and Time: 11.25 km (7 mi) round-trip; just over 2 hours

At about 17 km (10.5 mi) long and one wide, Windemere lake is the largest in the region. The town of the same name, at the midpoint on its eastern shore, is among the Lake District's busiest and is a great base for waterborne fun. Leave on foot on the early side from the Mortal Man, from which it's a 5.5-km (3.4-mi) walk of just over an hour to Windermere town, along quiet country roads, the larger of which have sidewalks for pedestrians. (It's also possible to drive to Windermere: 6.4 km/4 miles; 10 minutes).

A quaint town in itself where old-fashioned stone and timber buildings abound, Windermere is well worth exploring on foot. As with most conurbations in the region, there's a profusion of shops selling hiking and camping equipment, making it a good place to gear up for the days ahead.

1. The World of Beatrix Potter

Crag Brow, Bowness-on-Windermere, Windermere; tel. 015394 88444; 10am-4:30pm daily; adults £8.20, ages 3-16 £4.20, under 3 free

If you have time—it should take roughly an hour—pop into the World of Beatrix Potter, an exhibition bursting with charm in which characters and scenes from the beloved children's book author, who lived and worked in the Lake District, are brought to life.

★ 2. Kayaking Windermere Lake

Windermere Outdoor Adventure Centre, Leigh Groves Bldg., Rayrigg Rd., Windermere; tel. 015394 47183; www.better.org.uk/leisure-centre/south-lakeland/windermere-outdoor-adventure-centre; closed Nov.-Mar., hours vary by season, check website for details; kayaks from £15 per hour

You can't truly claim to have experienced the Lake District unless you've gotten wet! The Windermere Outdoor Adventure Centre, a 20-minute walk north of the World of Beatrix Potter,

left, the World of Beatrix Potter; right, kayaking Windermere Lake

TO TAKE Home

In Windermere, there are a number of local galleries selling **paintings and high-quality photographs** of the surrounding lakes and fells.

offers a variety of lake-related activities, from kayaking to windsurfing to sailing, all heightened by the magnificence of Windemere's surrounding landscape.

With your appetite worked up after a morning spent splashing about on the lake, **Homeground Coffee + Kitchen** (Main Rd., Windermere; tel. 015394 44863; www.homegroundcafe.co.uk; 8:30am-5pm Mon.-Fri., 9am-5pm Sat.-Sun.; mains from £5) offers just the treat you deserve.

3. Windermere Lake Cruises

Windermere House, Glebe Road, Bowness on Windermere; tel. 015394 43360; www.windermere-lakecruises.co.uk; sailings 9am-5:30pm, see website for details; adults from £10.50, ages 5-15 £5.25, under 5 free

Take to the waters again in late afternoon, this time with more comfort and style, on the deck of one of several cruises departing from Windermere's Bowness jetty. These range from 45-minute tours of the central islands to full round-trips touring either the north or south of the lake, at 75 minutes and 90 minutes respectively. Each is accompanied by an informative commentary on your surrounds, and with the longer cruises, you can depart the ship for a spot of tea in the towns of Ambleside or Lakeside.

At the end of a long day, it's time to return to the Mortal Man to taste some more of their local ales and see what the chefs put on the specials board for dinner.

DAY 3

Troutbeck to Eskdale

There's not so much walking on this travel day, when you leave the Mortal Man and strike out across country, deeper into the Lake District toward the hamlet of Eskdale—but there is a thrilling drive on the Hardknott Pass, one of England's steepest roads.

1. Wordsworth Grasmere

Town End, Grasmere, Ambleside; tel. 015394 35544; https://wordsworth.org.uk; hours vary by season, check website for details; adults £12, ages 5-15 £5, under 5 free

Less than half an hour's drive from the Mortal Man in the charming village of Grasmere, you'll find the former home of one of England's greatest poets. William Wordsworth, much of whose best-known work was inspired by the Lake District, lived here 1799-1808, and his home has been restored to look much how it would have been then, and embellished with additional snippets from both the poet's work and his sister's evocative Grasmere journal, all dotted around the interior. The cottage is both a literary destination and a conduit to a deeper appreciation of the surrounding country, which is hard not to see through the Wordsworths' eyes when you leave.

Afterward, walk 0.8 km (half a mile; 10 minutes) to the center of Grasmere town to fuel up at **Baldry's** (Red Lion Square, Grasmere, Ambleside; tel. 015394 35301; https://baldrysgrasmere.com; 10am-4:30pm daily; egg on toast £5.25). Indulge in a second breakfast in the tea room, which offers some of the best home baking in the Lake District, served on fine china with even finer loose leaf teas.

Driving Directions: From the Mortal Man, head south on Holbeck Lane for 4

(top to bottom) Hardknott Pass; Wordsworth Grasmere; Scafell Pike; Wasdale Head Inn

km (2.5 miles), then turn right on the A591 for 9 km (5.7 mi). Total distance 13 km (8.2 mi), approximate driving time 22 minutes.

2. Hardknott Pass

Driving Hardknott Pass, which at points shares the title of the steepest road in England (tied with Rosedale Chimney Bank in North Yorkshire), you're really heading into the Lake District's heartland now, with stunning vistas every which way you look. There's an austere magnificence at the pass's highest point, where it's well worth pulling into one of the several lay-bys to take the air and a photograph or two.

Driving Directions: From Grasmere, turn back south on the A591 until you hit the A593, when you head west. After about just over 4.8 km (3 mi), you'll hit the turnoff for Hardknott Pass; the pass itself is 12 km (7.5 mi) up this road, a ride that will take about 30 minutes given the steep and twisty conditions. The road is liable to be shut because of snow and ice in winter, so check conditions before heading off—if it is closed, take the long way round to Eskdale via the A593 and Coniston (51 km/32 mi; 1 hour 10 minutes).

3. Hardknott Fort

Hardknott Pass, Holmrook; tel. 0370 333 1181; www.english-heritage.org.uk/visit/places/hardknott-roman-fort; open 24 hours; free

Shortly after the descent from the pass, pull into the small parking area and make your way on foot to Hardknott Fort, built in the 2nd century to watch over this very route and one of the most evocative Roman ruins in Europe. Today, it's not much more than a few concentric squares of decrepit walls, though it's impossible not to be transported back to a time when this was one of the very edges of the Roman Empire, manned by a garrison of soldiers all desperately far from home. The walk to the fort is very short and easy (0.8 km/0.5 mi; about 10 minutes), so long as you find a place in the parking area, on the right, roughly 200 m (656 ft) after the pass's most severe and steepest couple of hairpins as you're heading into Eskdale (keep an eye out for other parked cars). The lot does fill up in summer, though, so be prepared to hike farther if need be.

Driving Directions: The Roman fort is less than 1.6 km (1 mi) down the road from the pass, a 4-minute drive.

4. Bower House Inn

Eskdale, Holmrook; tel. 019467 23244; www.bowerhouseinn.com; rooms from £70

A coaching inn that dates all the way back to 1751, the Bower House Inn offers an excellent balance between traditional and modern. A crossroads for hikers of all stripes, it's also just a short drive from the trailhead of Scafell Pike, England's tallest mountain and your objective for tomorrow. Make sure to ask the hotel to prep you a packed lunch for the next day's hike, then sit down for a hearty evening meal (try the Cumberland sausage), and turn in for an early night.

Driving Directions: It's just 9.6 km (6 mi) from the fort to Bower House Inn; when the Hardknott Pass road hits Smithybrow Lane, turn right and you'll soon see the inn on the left. Total driving time about 20 minutes.

DAY 4

Scafell Pike

Get up early, as close to dawn as possible, and make the spectacular half-hour drive to the Scafell Pike trailhead. This journey takes you along the banks of **Wastwater,** a 4.8-km-long (3-mi) glacial lake, which happens also to be the deepest in England. Mountains rise to giddy heights on all sides, and on still days mirror on the lake's dark surface to make for one of the most jaw-dropping sights on the British isle.

1. Breakfast at Wasdale Head Inn

Wasdale Head, Gosforth; tel. 019467 26229; www.wasdale.com; rooms from £65; breakfast from £7

The Wasdale Head Inn has one of the most romantic aspects of any hotel in England. Standing entirely alone at the trailhead to Scafell Pike, with the word "inn" painted in huge black letters on its white, south-facing wall, it looks like a staging post at the edge of the world. What it really is, is a headquarters for British rock climbers, and an ideal place from which to launch your ascent of the nearby mountain. It's essential to book ahead for breakfast unless you're staying here—the grilled kipper is a particular treat!

Driving Directions: From Bower House Inn, follow Bowerhouse Bank northwest for about 3 km (2 mi) before turning right on the road to Wasdale. You'll be on this road for about 11 km (7 mi) until it ends at the Wasdale Head Inn. The entire drive should take about 30 minutes.

★ 2. Hiking Scafell Pike

Hiking Distance and Time: 8 km (5 mi) round-trip; 3-4 hours

To hike the tallest mountain in England, it should go without saying that you're going to need more than just this book to find your way to the top—a map, a compass, and a detailed guide to the walk are all essential. There are several routes to the top, though the most popular and easiest starts from Wasdale Head. "Easiest" is a relative term though; it's only 8 km (5 mi) there and back, but it's still a walk of 3-4 hours, which starts off at a particularly steep gradient (there's no shame in taking the first section slowly). About halfway up the route becomes less distinct, and you'll have to negotiate both rocks and scree, so keep your wits about you. This said, it's

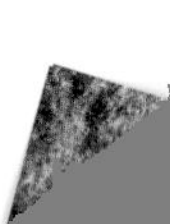

a very popular route, so there will usually be people around to ask for help or directions should you run into difficulties. Climbing Scafell Pike requires at least a moderate level of fitness, and you should be sure to take weather conditions into account before any ascent.

The summit is 978 m (3,210 ft) above sea level. This is it: the roof of the Lake District and England, with views out in all directions across a great undulating palate of earthen colors, often strafed by clouds and sunlight and columns of rain. It's also home to a large cairn, which doubles as Britain's highest war memorial, the land having been gifted shortly after World War I to Lord Leconfield, who subsequently dedicated it to the men of the region who had fallen in the fighting. It's a place of great beauty and contemplation, and a good location to shelter for a sandwich.

You've conquered a mountain, and upon returning to the Bower House Inn and washing off the day's activity, head down to the bar to relax and tell war stories, either around the wood fire on colder evenings, or in the charming beer garden in the summer. At dinner, take full advantage of the copious menu—some of the produce for which is grown on site. You've earned it!

Driving Directions: Follow the directions to Wasdale Head Inn in reverse to return to Bower House Inn.

DAY 5

The Keswick Loop

1. Buttermere Lake

It's time to make the 1.5-hour journey north toward the tiny settlement of Brackenthwaite, from which you can make a right onto the B5289, joining up with the scenic drive known as the Keswick Loop. This will take you first past the peaceful, isolated-feeling **Crummock Water,** especially impressive in spring, when its surrounding fields are covered in blue bells, then into the pleasant Buttermere Village, where you might want to stop for a coffee at the **Croft House Farm Café** (Buttermere, Cockermouth; tel. 017687 70235; www.crofthousefarmcafe.co.uk; 10am-5pm daily). Carry on past **Buttermere Lake,** another spot of outstanding natural beauty where there are plenty of opportunities to stop and go for an easy stroll.

Keswick Loop

Driving Directions: Follow Bowerhouse Bank to A595, then head north to A5086 and head northeast. Turn right at Mockerkin onto Fangs Brow, which leads to Brackenthwaite and B5289. Once you get onto the B5289, there are no significant turns leading off the "loop." As long as you keep to the main road it's almost impossible to get lost.

2. Honister Slate Mine

Honister Pass, Keswick; tel. 017687 77230; https://honister.com; 8:30am-5pm daily, check website for activity start times; £15-150

Next, it's up toward the **Honister Pass,**

climbing through towering, scree-dashed peaks. This takes you to the Honister Slate Mine, the last working slate mine in England. As well as being a spectacularly located home to a living slice of local history, the Honister Slate Mine has diversified its business model in recent years to become a mecca for adrenaline junkies, offering activities including climbing both in and outside of the mine, balancing across rope bridges, and learning the ins and outs of cliffside camping. For the less adventurous, there are also more straightforward tours of the mine, and a shop where you can pick up locally quarried slate as a souvenir. As well as being very popular, the mine is frequently taken over for local events, so make sure to book ahead.

3. Bowder Stone

After Honister Pass the B5289 starts looping left again, up to the north and through the village of **Rosthwaite,** which is surrounded by some excellent walking country, and then past the Bowder Stone—an unusual freestanding boulder, about 9 m (30 ft) high that can be mounted via wooden steps. The road then takes you down to the eastern shores of Derwentwater, the island-studded lake that **Keswick** sits on, and finally into the town itself, where there is a whole host of accommodations to suit a variety of budgets.

DAY 6

Keswick

1. Castlerigg Stone Circle

Castle Lane, Keswick; tel. 0370 333 1181; www.english-heritage.org.uk/visit/places/castlerigg-stone-circle; open 24 hours; free

The Lake District abounds in mysterious Paleolithic stone circles, the original purpose of which is unclear. Today, more than anything, they're monuments to dream over, often found at high points in the landscape, with panoramic views of the surrounding hills and evocative of the region's distant past. The one at Castlerigg, just outside Keswick, has been popular with tourists for centuries. It's free to enter (also a popular 2-hour, 4.8-km/3-mi round trip walk from the center of town).

Before heading out from Keswick, have a fortifying breakfast at local institution **Bryson's** bakery and tea rooms (42 Main St., Keswick; tel. 017687 72257; https://brysonsofkeswick.co.uk; 9am-5pm daily; full English breakfast £13).

Driving Directions: From central Keswick, take the A5271/A591 east for 1.5 km (about 1 mi), turning right on Eleventrees. The stone circle will be on your right after just under 1.5 km (about 1 mi), just past Castle Lane. The drive should take under 5 minutes.

★ 2. Hiking to Aira Force

Hiking Distance and Time: 4.8 km (3 mi); 1 hour

On the northern shore of region's second largest lake, Ullswater, is the car park at the trailhead to Aira Force, the tallest waterfall in England. There's a small National Trust **café** (Ullswater, Park Brow, Penrith; tel. 017684 82067; www.nationaltrust.org.uk/aira-force-and-ullswater; 10am-4:30pm Thurs.-Sun.; tea and scone £5.50) at this carpark for a snack or a sandwich to take on the walk ahead.

The walk in and out to see Aira Force is about an hour long, through magical shaded woodland. It is well sign-posted, with handrails and steps to aid less confident walkers—even so, there are some steep stretches, and it can become slippery in the rain. Aira Force waterfall itself is one of the true natural wonders of the Lake District—a powerful cascade of water 20 m (65 ft) in height, framed by a

left, hiking to Aira Force ; right, Castlerigg Stone Circle

couple of Victorian-era bridges that offer close-up views.

Driving Directions: From Castlerigg Stone Circle, continue on Eleventrees for about 0.8 km (0.5 mi) until it hits Burns/Old Coach Road. Turn left, then turn right on Old Coach road for just under 2 km (a little more than 1 mi); then turn right on the A66 for 8 km (5 mi). Turn right on the A5091; the trailhead to the waterfall will be on the left after another 8 km (5 mi). Total driving time 20 minutes; 19 km (12 mi).

3. Theatre By the Lake

Lakeside, Lake Rd., Keswick; tel. 017687 74411; www.theatrebythelake.com; season runs year-round, see website for details; from £10

Head back to your hotel at Keswick to freshen up, and prepare for a night of culture, because there's more to the Lake District than incredible scenery and Britain's best hikes. Keswick's Theatre By the Lake is a thoroughly cosmopolitan institution that has been staging excellent plays for residents and tourists since 1999. Shows often have a local flavor, and are almost universally appropriate for the whole family. There's also an on-site **restaurant,** serving until 7pm if you want to get in a meal before the show.

Driving Directions: Return to Keswick via the A5091 (8 km/5 mi), the A66 (13 km/8 mi). You'll hit a roundabout and take the first exit onto the A5271/A591 (0.8 km/0.5 mi); turn left again on Main Street and you'll be heading into downtown Keswick. Total driving time 22 minutes; 13 km (14.5 mi).

TRANSPORTATION

Air

- **Manchester Airport** (MAN; Manchester M90 1QX; tel. 0808 169 7030; www.manchesterairport.co.uk): The closest international airport to the Lake District is 142 km (88 mi) away by car, a 1-hour 30-minute drive. Manchester accepts regional flights from throughout Europe.

WATCH

Miss Potter: Beatrix Potter, the children's author, illustrator, and the creator of such classic characters as Peter Rabbit, Mrs. Tiggy-Winkle, and Jemima Puddle-Duck, is a large presence in the Lake District. This 2006 film starring Renée Zellweger, largely shot on location in the Lake District, tells the story of her personal struggles and accomplishments.

READ

Swallows and Amazons by Arthur Ransome: The apogee of charming children's adventure stories, set over the course of a summer on the lakes, this tale revolves around the outdoor antics of two families of children. One family calls themselves the Swallows, and the other the Amazons, and their adventures reveal a host of fascinating details about life in the Lake District when it was written (1929).

LISTEN

The Prelude by William Wordsworth: What better way to engage with the Romantic poets—who took so much of their inspiration from the landscape of the Lake District—than to listen to Wordsworth's autobiographical verse being read aloud. The BBC's audiobook version, read by Ian McKellen, will give the flavor of the piece as you drive from lake to lake.

Train

If you're traveling from London, there are multiple trains each day from **Euston Station** direct to Lancaster (4.5 hours; £45 one-way), where there are plenty of rental cars to facilitate the rest of your trip.

- **Lancaster Train Station:** Located just south of the Lake District, around 55 km (34 mi; 43 minutes) from the center of the national park by car.

Car

It's also always possible to drive a car directly from London, a trip of 453 km (282 mi) that takes over 5 hours.

Driving in the Lake District can be both a joy—thanks to the astonishing views around nearly every bend—and a little stressful for those unused to driving on the left and the narrow roads. There are even some where cars can only pass at certain points, so don't be surprised if you have to slip into reverse in order to let someone by. The important thing is to take things slow, and not to feel pressured by other speeding drivers. Also keep aware that there are a handful of very steep gradients on this route, which you will need to approach with confidence and in the lowest gear. Be kind to your car and switch it off to let the engine cool if you feel it's necessary after completing one of these steep climbs.

Below are a few rental car options, though it's a good idea to check out price comparison websites like www.rentalcars.com for more. If you're planning to rent from somewhere in the Lake District, it's best to reserve as early as possible as vehicle numbers are limited. Prices start at around £80 per day, though you may have to shop around to find deals at that cost.

- **Hertz Car Rental:** Caton Rd., Lancaster; tel. 01524 482482; www.hertz.co.uk; 9am-4pm Mon.-Fri.
- **Avis Car Hire:** Car Rental Village, Airport, Manchester; tel. 0344 544 6002; www.avis.co.uk; 8am-10pm Sun.-Fri., 8am-4pm Sat.

Public Transit and Taxis

There is a bus service in the Lake District, but it mainly serves to link the major towns, rather than trailheads. Thus you can catch buses between, say, Windermere and Keswick, but don't expect to be able to make it out across any of the passes or to Scafell Pike. On the upside, it's not expensive: A whole day pass is £3.70. This can be combined with a boat pass for £16, though boat travel on the lakes is more pleasant than practical. Another option is using local taxi firms, which tend to have knowledgeable drivers who are used to making long distance journeys and taking scenic routes if requested. Expect to pay around £3 per mile. It is essential to book ahead.

- **Merecab:** Brantfell Walk, Bowness-on-Windermere, Windermere; tel. 07985 100473; https://merecab.business.site
- **Lake District Taxis:** 91 Droomer Dr., Windermere; tel. 015394 45445; https://acetaxiwindermere.co.uk
- **Iains Taxis Keswick:** Lake District National Park, Flat 7 Leonards Place, Southey St., Keswick; tel. 017687 36333; www.facebook.com/iainstaxis

On Foot

The Lake District is a hikers paradise with a vast array of routes at all fitness levels and abilities. These run from easy lakeside rambles along well-tended, wheelchair-friendly paths to epic fortnight-long treks taking in numerous peaks and fells. In general, paths are relatively well trodden and signposted, either by actual signs or the piles of rocks known as cairns that are tended by other hikers, though it is always worth it to bring a physical map, as phone reception can be patchy between the hills.

Keep in mind that there are a number of real wilderness hikes in the region, which should not be attempted unless you are very well versed in hill-walking and are suitably prepared. This is particularly true in the winter months, where even relatively straightforward walks can be made treacherous by the weather and the fact that it gets dark in mid-afternoon. Even in high summer, though, you should keep an eye on the forecast and be prepared for conditions to change in the blink of an eye. It can be bright sunshine one moment and freezing hail the next, so waterproofs are essential.

CONNECT WITH

- London and Paris (page 44)
- Edinburgh and Glasgow (page 65)

HOLLAND JUNCTION NETWORK

Why Go: Perhaps nowhere else in Europe is it easier to see so much in so little time by bicycle. Take in classic Dutch landscapes of windmills and polders alongside sophisticated cities—all within easy rides of one another.

Number of Days: 3

Total Distance: 29 km (18 mi)

Seasons: Spring and summer

Start: The Hague

End: Rotterdam

The densely packed Holland Junction Network honeycombs the compact country of the Netherlands, even extending to Belgium and parts of France and Germany, and you'll be amazed how much you can see in just a 76-km (47-mi) ride. Feel the exhilaration of riding from quintessential Dutch scenes of picturesque towns and centuries-old windmills, to some of the most modern cityscapes the Netherlands can offer—all on your own steam. Pack light and do this tour completely self-supported (though you may find yourself wanting to send home some Delftware from its namesake city), or send your luggage ahead—the Netherlands are made to be biked, and they make doing so easy.

TOP 3

Snacking on Dutch apple pie at **Dudok,** a Hague institution (page 379).

Listening to the waves at **Scheveningen Beach and Pier** (page 381).

Feeling like you're upside-down viewing Rotterdam's **Cube Houses,** one of the Netherlands' most innovative examples of modern design (page 385).

DAY 1

The Hague

Where to Stay: Centrum, near the Binnenhof and Mauritshuis

Arrive by: Train from Amsterdam Central Train Station to Dan Hague Central Train Station (50 minutes)

1. Binnenhof

Lange Poten 4; tel. 070 318 2211; www.houseofrepresentatives.nl, www.prodemos.nl/binnenhof; 9am-5pm Mon.-Fri.; Tweede Kamer (Dutch Parliament) visit free, general tour with ProDemos €9.50

After arriving in the Hague, head straight to the Binnenhof, the oldest house of parliament in the world. Since the 13th century, a castle has stood on this exact spot; the only remaining part of that original building is the **Knight's Hall** (Ridderzaal), the castle-like structure that still stands at the heart of this government complex.

Although the capital of the Netherlands is in Amsterdam, the government meets in the Hague, and what happens here shapes politics both inside and outside the country: The Dutch royal family happily calls the city home, with multiple palaces within the city limits, and it holds many of the United Nations's most influential buildings.

It is possible to walk or cycle through the gates to admire the outside of the buildings, but to go inside, you'll need to book a **tour** in advance with ProDemos, House for Democracy and the Rule of Law, an organization that aims to inform citizens and encourage them to play an active role in their government.

★ 2. Apple Pie at Dudok

Hofweg 1A; tel. 070 890 0100; https://dudok.nl; 9:30am-11pm Sun.-Wed., 9:30am-midnight Thurs.-Sat.; €5

If you haven't yet had a piece of Dutch apple pie (deeper than the American version and often with a crumbly top), the most famous spot in the Hague to enjoy this dessert is Dudok, across from the Binnehof; wash it down with a fresh cup of coffee.

3. Mauritshuis

Plein 29; tel. 070 302 3456; www.mauritshuis.nl; 1pm-6pm Mon., 10am-6pm Tues.-Wed. and Fri.-Sun., 10am-8pm Thurs.; adults €15.50, children free

For a glimpse of *Girl with a Pearl Earring* by Johannes Vermeer, stop by the Mauritshuis, next to the Binnenhof. This world-class museum focuses on Dutch painters primarily out of the Golden Age, within a beautiful Dutch Classicist building that sits on the edge of the picturesque Hofvijver pond. The interior is straight out of a painting itself, with plush velvet, grand staircases, and elaborate period wallpapers.

4. The Passage

Passage 72; https://depassage.nl; noon-6pm Mon., 10am-6pm Tues.-Wed. and Fri.-Sat., 10am-9pm Thurs., noon-5pm Sun.

The Hague is known for being posh, and you'll certainly find your fill of exclusive

the Passage

HOLLAND JUNCTION NETWORK

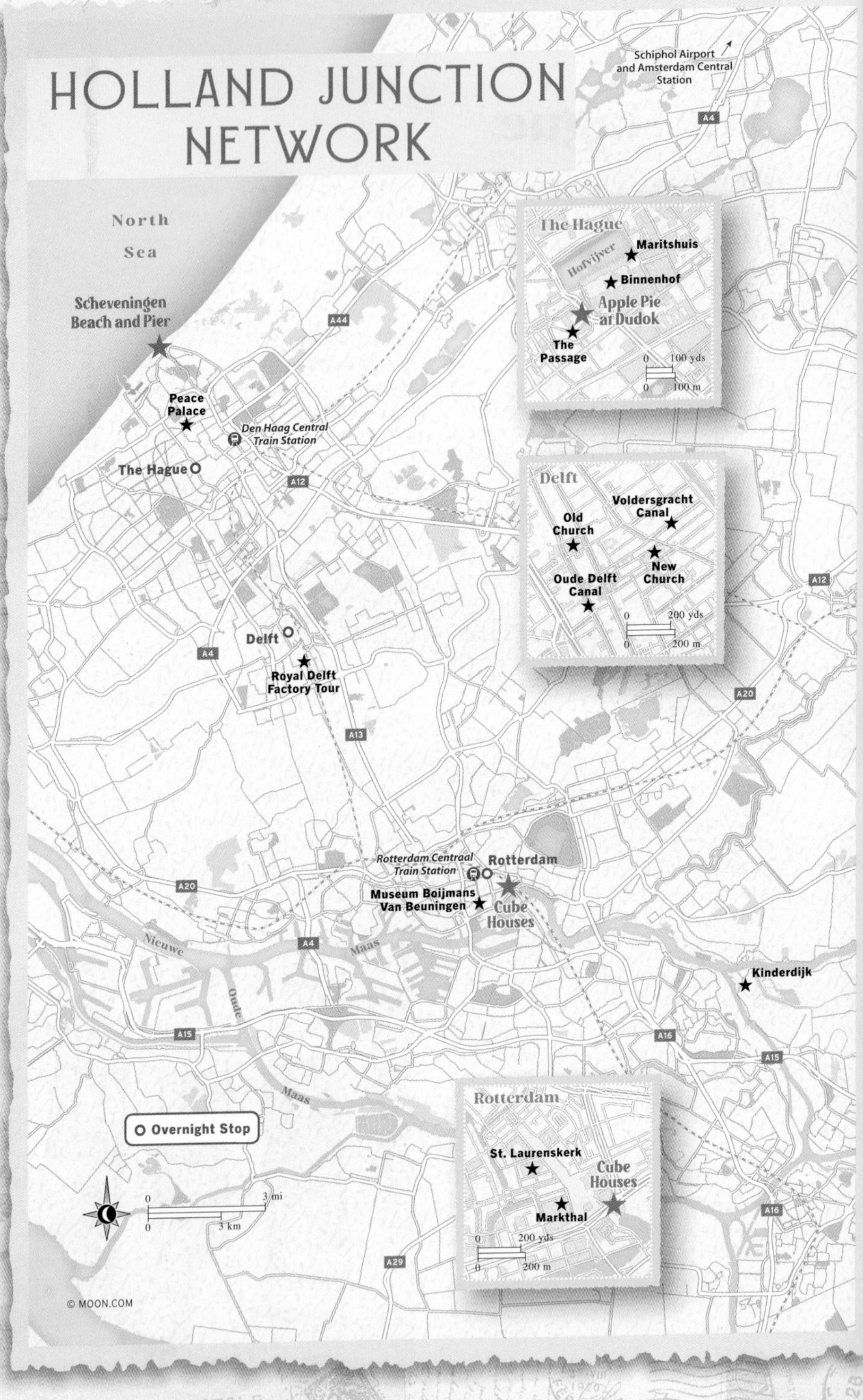

Key Reservations

Perhaps unsurprisingly, bikes are in high demand in the Netherlands, so it's a good idea to reserve your **bike rental** in advance. Most bike rentals will offer options for storage bags and baskets to carry your belongings, so if you pack light, you might just be able to do this route unsupported. Otherwise, consider booking a **cycling holiday tour package** (also recommended to book in advance). The tour providers will take care of your luggage and make sure you find your bags waiting for you whenever you get to your next accommodation.

bike rentals in Rotterdam

You'll benefit from making reservations at most sit-down **restaurants** on this itinerary.

streets for shopping high-end Dutch brands in the Passage, a beautiful 1882 arcade that is the oldest shopping center in the Netherlands. Be sure to look up to admire the glass dome in the center as you browse more than 20 stores and cafés.

5. Indonesian Food at Toko Frederick

Frederikstraat 225; tel. 070 360 3125; www.tokofrederik.nl; noon-9pm Mon.-Sat., 4pm-9pm Sun.; lunch €10, dinner €15

On your way to dinner, you'll pass **Noordeinde** (Noordeinde 68), the working palace of King Willem-Alexander; although it's not open to the public, you can admire it from outside.

The Hague's deep connection to Indonesia is rooted in the fact that the Indonesian colony was largely governed from the Hague, which brought many middle-class civil servants to the Hague in the postcolonial era. As a result, this is one of the best places in the Netherlands to sample Indonesian food. Although you'll find countless tokos throughout the city, a favorite has to be Toko Frederick, which has been serving up Indonesian specialties since 1984. It's best to reserve ahead.

DAY 2

The Hague

★ 1. Scheveningen Beach and Pier

Strandweg 150-154; tel. 06 10386859; www.pier.nl; pier 10am-10pm daily; free

Time to test out your bike! Before heading on to your next city, you have to stop at Scheveningen Beach. En route, you'll pass the impressive **Peace Palace** (Carnegieplein 2; tel. 070 302 42 42; www.vredespaleis.nl; 10am-5pm Tues.-Sun. Apr.-Oct., 11am-4pm Tues.-Sun. Nov.-Mar.; tour €11, visitors center free), home to the Permanent Court of Arbitration

Navigating the Holland Junction Network

The Holland Junction Network covers more than 35,000 km (almost 22,000 mi) in the Netherlands, Belgium, and parts of Germany and France, and growing. Originally composed of dozens of separate regional routes that were interconnected, this comprehensive series of interlocking routes, combined with the region's relatively flat topography and the fact that the Dutch own more bikes per capita than any other nation on earth (approximately 1.3 bicycles per person), make the Netherlands a true biker's paradise.

JUNCTIONS

Holland's network of cycling paths intersect at what the Dutch call knooppunt ("knot points"), or numbered junctions. In the Netherlands, all junctions have one or two digits. Some of the numbers are used more than once, but they are far enough apart that they shouldn't cause confusion. Junctions are well signed, both at each node point, and with signs leading up to them to let you know which junction you are approaching. Often, junction signs will also have arrows directing you to the nearest city or town, which helps with navigation.

PATHS

The paths themselves are mostly single-use bike paths in very good condition, especially in more rural areas. In cities and towns, it's more likely that you'll need to share the path with cars or pedestrians, though bike lanes are generally well signed and protected on roads that are shared with cars.

RESOURCES

There are tons of resources to help you to plan your route on the Holland Junction Network; a good one is Holland Cycling Route's **Online Cycle Route Planner** (www.hollandcyclingroutes.com/online-cycle-route-planner). To avoid constantly looking at your phone to check your next junction (it's actually forbidden to hold your phone while riding a bike in the Netherlands), write down or print out the list of junctions you'll be looking for on your ride, and tape it to your bike to refer to while cycling.

NOTE ON CYCLING DIRECTIONS

Distances in this route are approximate, and travel time assumes a speed of about 19 kph (12 mph). We haven't given directions to the first junction on each ride exactly, figuring that each cyclist will begin from a slightly different starting point. It may take a little city cycling to get to each junction, and it's always okay to dismount and walk your bike if you're less comfortable with more crowded city cycling.

and the International Court of Justice, two important organs of the United Nations.

Scheveningen's kitsch definitely stands at odds with the well-curated shopping streets of Noordeinde and the Passage, but it also lends an air of breeziness to this cosmopolitan city. The water isn't very warm, so most of the appeal comes from strolling along the boardwalk or enjoying activities along the pier, including bungee jumping and a Ferris wheel. In summer, the beach is lined with countless cafés, bars, and nightclubs, where you can listen to the waves and music from the cafés. Grab a seafood snack from one of the restaurants near the beach before getting on your bike to head to Delft.

Cycling Directions: Make your way toward **junction 28,** approximately 2 km (1.2 mi) east of the city center off Grote Marketstraat. Head left toward **junction 31** (300 m/984 ft), then west toward **junction 26** (2 km/1.2 mi) and north toward **junction 24** (2 km/1.2 mi). From there head west on LFKustroute-a, which will take you to the beach after about 3.5 km (2.1 mi). Total distance approximately 11 km (6.8 mi), and the ride should take just over half an hour.

Delft

Where to Stay: Delft city center

2. Delft Canals

Delft is one of the most iconic cities in the Netherlands, known for its well-preserved city center and beautiful Delftware pottery. The name Delft comes from an old Dutch word delven, which is related to digging a canal. Not surprisingly, Delft is full of pretty canals to explore, especially the **Oude Delft** canal and the tiny **Voldersgracht** canal. Take some time to check out the **New Church** (Markt 80; tel. 015 212 3025; http://oudeennieuwekerkdelft.nl; 11am-4pm Mon.-Fri., 10am-5pm Sat. Nov.-Jan., 10am-5pm Mon.-Sat. Feb.-Mar., 9am-6pm Mon.-Sat. Apr.-Oct.; New and Old Churches adults €5.50, children €4, New Church tower only adults €4.50, children €2.50, combination churches and New Church tower adults €8.50, children €3.50). Built in the 17th century, it's only "new" in comparison to the **Old Church** (HH Geestkerkhof 25), which was built in the 13th century. Then, get ready to learn more about the classic pottery this city is known for.

Cycling Directions: From Scheveningen Beach, return to **junction 24** via LFKustroute-b (approximately 3.5 km/1.9 mi), then head to **junction 26** (2 km/1.2 mi), **junction 31** (2 km/1.2 mi), **junction 28** (300 m/984 ft), **junction 44** (3 km/1.9 mi), **junction 68** (1 km/0.6 mi), **junction 45** (2 km/1.2 mi), **junction**

top, Delft canals; bottom, Delft

TO TAKE Home

Even if you don't consider yourself an aficionado of fancy vases or dishes, you'll likely recognize the striking blue-and-white-patterned ceramics that have made Delft famous. The base material for **Delftware** (also known as Delft Blauw, or Delft Blue) is typically marl, a clay from Germany and Belgium, which is coated with a tin glaze prior to a ceramic glaze. Designs range from ornate portraits of typically Dutch scenes, to flowers and flourishes that can be minimalistic or ornate.

Only two factories remain in Delft today. When buying Delftware, it's important to check the bottom carefully to find out if the item is authentic. All items produced within the Netherlands must be stamped and signed by the manufacturer. Many items produced abroad, including some of the cheaper items by the Royal Delft Factory, are not authentic; if a price seems too good to be true, it's probably because it is. These are generally mass-produced by a machine in a factory rather than hand-painted by artisans, which is why the real thing is so expensive.

Authentic Delftware can be found secondhand for as little as €5-10, but at reputable shops, there's no limit to what you might pay; depending on the size and complexity of design, nicer plates and vases can cost €100 or more. Be careful with packing your Delftware in your suitcase, as it's quite fragile! Many major manufacturers, including the Royal Delft factory, can ship your ceramics home for you.

50 (2 km/1.2 mi), and **junction 51** (800 m/2,625 ft). From here you'll need to take side streets to the center of Delft (just over 300 m/984 ft total). The entire ride is about 18 km (11 mi) and should take just under an hour.

3. Royal Delft Factory Tour

Rotterdamseweg 196; tel. 015 760 0800; www.royaldelft.com; 9am-5pm Mon.-Fri.; adults €14, teens €8.75, children free

This factory is the last remaining Delftware factory from the 16th century, and the tour provides more than just a quick overview of the process. It's a comprehensive look into the history of Delftware over the last 400 years and a peek at priceless pieces worthy of a museum. Visitors can also watch an artist creating some of this iconic Dutch pottery. The factory is about 20 minutes on foot or 5 minutes by bike outside the Delft historic city center.

Head back into the city center for dinner at **Thuis by Ladera** (Oosteinde 123; tel. 015 212 5950; www.facebook.com/thuisbyladera; 6pm-8pm Mon.-Fri.; €7.50), which prides itself on cooking up simple and delicious Dutch dinner specials—like those that you would find in a typical Dutch home—that won't break your budget. The small restaurant is decorated with cute Holland kitsch, perfect for immersing yourself in a bit of the Netherlands. Call to make a reservation—and remember to bring cash.

DAY 3

Rotterdam

Where to Stay: Rotterdam Centrum

★ 1. Cube Houses

Overblaak 70; tel. 010 414 2285; https://kubuswoning.nl; 10am-6pm daily; adults €3, children €1.50

Fuel up with breakfast at your Delft hotel for your ride to Rotterdam, often called Manhattan on the Maas thanks to its location on the Nieuwe Maas river and its cutting-edge architecture, exciting nightlife, and world-class museums.

The first thing you should do when you get here is make a beeline for the Cube Houses, Rotterdam's most famous landmark. They were designed by innovative Dutch architect Piet Blom in the 1970s, when Rotterdam was rapidly expanding. The 38 bright yellow and gray cube-shaped houses, tilted at a 45-degree angle, are connected by a central courtyard.

Today, two of the Cube Houses are open to the public, one of them as a hostel (Stayokay Hostel Rotterdam) and the other as a museum. For a few euros, you can explore the 1,080-sq-m (11,600-sq-ft) cube, including some of the original furnishings intended to make this unique house slightly more livable—conventional furniture would be at odds with the walls. It's best not to look down too much once inside the houses; vertigo from the shape of the windows can unnerve some visitors!

Cycling Directions: From Delft, make your way to **junction 52,** just under 400 m (1,312 ft) from the city center. Then, head south toward **junction 1** (1 km/0.6 mi), followed by **junction 57** (1 km/0.6 mi), **junction 58** (1.5 km/0.9 mi), **junction 64** (2 km/1.2 mi), **junction 80** (2 km/1.2 mi), **junction 3** (2 km/1.2 mi), **junction 2** (400 m/1,312 ft), **junction 12** (2 km/1.2 mi), **junction 87** (600 m/1,969 ft), **junction 36** (1 km/0.6 mi), **junction 75** (1 km/0.6 mi), and **junction 76** (400 m/1,312 ft). The entire ride is 16 km (10 mi) and will take just under an hour.

left, Markthal; right, Cube Houses

ADDING ON Kinderdijk

Rotterdam is a good jumping-off point for a visit to the famous windmill-strewn region of Kinderdijk. To get there by bike (total distance 15 km/9.3 mi; travel time about 50 minutes), start at **junction 69,** right in the middle of central Rotterdam; from there, head to **junction 60** (600 m/1,969 ft), **junction 61** (1 km/0.6 mi), **junction 62** (1.5 km/0.9 mi), **junction 73** (1.5 km/0.9 mi), **junction 25** (700 m/2,297 ft), **junction 63** (900 m/2,953 ft), **junction 64** (2.5 km/1.5 mi), **junction 21** (2.5 km/1.5 mi), and **junction 50** (1.5 km/0.9 mi).

You'll see the **ferry terminal** just east of junction 50; it's a quick, 15-minute hop across the water to Kinderdijk (€1.00 with a bike). For ideas on what to see and do in Kinderdijk, see **Rhine River Cruise** (page 503).

2. Markthal

Dominee Jan Scharpstraat 298; tel. 030 234 6468; www.markthal.nl; 10am-8pm Mon.-Thurs and Sat., 10am-9pm Fri., noon-6pm Sun.; €8

Another of Rotterdam's architectural marvels, the Markthal is hard to miss. This iconic food hall is the largest in the Netherlands, and it certainly impresses with its chic 21st-century mixed-use design. The ceiling of the hall notably has the world's largest mural—taking up more than 11,000 sq m (118,000 sq ft)—featuring digital images of fruits, vegetables, flowers, and insects, created by artists Arno Coenen and Iris Roskam. The hall has a multitude of options, with 70-plus food stalls, from Dutch croquettes to Turkish food.

Nearby, be sure to stop at 15th-century **St. Laurenskerk** (Grotekerkplein 27; tel. 010 413 1494; https://laurenskerkrotterdam.nl; 10am-5pm Tues.-Sat. Mar.-Oct., 11am-5pm Tues.-Sat. Nov.-Feb.; church only adults €3, children free, tower adults €6, tower children €3.50), one of the enduring symbols of Rotterdam and one of the only remnants of the beautiful medieval city that remained after World War II.

3. Museum Boijmans van Beuningen

Museumpark 18; tel. 010 441 9400; www.boijmans.nl; 11am-5pm Tues.-Sun.; adults €17.50, children €8.75

Spend the afternoon at Museum Boijmans van Beuningen, one of the most impressive art collections in the Netherlands outside Amsterdam. Visitors can enjoy works from European artists ranging in eras and styles, from van Eyck to van Gogh to Dalí. Whether you're more interested in modern art or the classics—including *The Tower of Babel* by Pieter Bruegel the Elder—the museum is one that art lovers shouldn't miss.

4. Kapsalon at Jaffa Shoarma

Witte de Withstraat 44; tel. 010 414 0326; noon-4am Sun.-Thurs., noon-6am Fri.-Sat.; €9

Rotterdam's most famous dish, kapsalon,

WATCH

Character: This 1997 movie set in 1920s Rotterdam won the Academy Award for Best Foreign Language Film. It tells the story of a young lawyer accused of murdering his own father, a powerful and cruel city official.

READ

Why the Dutch are Different: A Journey into the Hidden Heart of the Netherlands by Ben Coates: Wondering what exactly you might have done wrong when signaling a turn on your bike? This entertaining book that explores Dutch culture via its history and its people's common behaviors might be able to tell you.

LISTEN

Here in Holland: This cheerful, English-language podcast paints an honest picture of Dutch life—one that just might make you want to move here.

is served up at this popular, casual kebab shop; it's a late-night comfort food made with shawarma/doner kebab meat, fries, Gouda cheese, lettuce, garlic sauce, and hot sauce. Jaffa also sells staples such as falafels, shawarma wraps, and sandwiches for a quick bite.

TRANSPORTATION

Air

The largest airport in the Netherlands is Amsterdam's Schiphol Airport, well-connected both within Europe and overseas.

- **Schiphol Airport** (AMS; www.schiphol.nl): 20 km (12 mi) outside Amsterdam; 15 minutes by train to Amsterdam Central Station (€6.50 one-way).

Train

You'll likely find yourself getting to the Hague by train from Amsterdam (50 minutes; from €11 one-way), a convenient ride via the Netherlands' extremely efficient public transit network. The Netherlands' railway network is mainly operated by state-owned **NS** (www.ns.nl).

- **Amsterdam Central Station:** Amsterdam's main train station is conveniently located in the city center, with tons of connections within the Netherlands, to Belgium, and beyond.
- **Den Haag Central Train Station:** 1 km (0.6 mi) from the Hague city center, a 12-minute walk.
- **Rotterdam Centraal Train Station:** The main train station is a 2-km (1.2-mi) walk to the main attractions of Rotterdam, such as the Cube Houses.

Bike

Biking is an ideal means of transportation in the Netherlands, due to the country's small size and extensive bike networks, particularly on country roads where bikes have a separate bike path.

Rentals

Dutch bikes come in a few varieties. The cheapest is typically the footbrake bike, which requires pedaling backward to stop. Some basic bikes with no gears and a foot pedal are referred to as **omafiets,** or "grandma bikes," for their comfortable low entry. You can also rent a bike with hand brakes and limited gears. Those not as used to biking might want to consider renting an **electric bike.** A standard bike will start from around €6.50 a day (generally cheaper the longer you rent a bike for), including theft insurance, though you'll need to put down a refundable deposit of up to €150 when claiming your rental.

All bikes should come with **lights** on the front and back, which are required in the Netherlands. There will be options for **baskets** and **bike bags** at an extra cost to help you carry your belongings. Many bike rentals also offer seats to strap in young children. **Helmets** are typically rented separately, as they're surprisingly not required in the Netherlands.

There are tons of bike rental options throughout the country, often found at train stations or conveniently located in city centers. Most bike rental companies require you to drop off your bike at the same place you picked it up, so for this trip, you might consider renting your bike in Amsterdam, taking it on the train to the Hague (the Dutch make it easy and convenient to take your bike on a train), and then bringing it back to Amsterdam from Rotterdam via train.

Bike Holiday Tours and Luggage Forwarding

If carrying all of your belongings on your own back isn't an option for you, or if you want the flexibility to be able to pick up and drop off your rental bike at different destinations, a bike holiday tour may be right for you. They can also provide extra support with navigation and give you an orientation for cycling rules of the road. Most bike holiday tours will allow you to design a custom route, including the itinerary described here. A great place to start is **www.dutch-biketours.com.**

Rules of the Road

Bikers should always signal before turning, using their arm to denote the direction. Stoplights do apply to cyclists, and many busy roads with dedicated bike lanes might even have a special bike stoplight. A one-way road with a sign reading "Uitgezonderd," with a bike symbol, means that bikes are excepted from the rule that traffic is one-way.

It's prohibited to use a cell phone when riding a bicycle. Though it's not required to wear a helmet in the Netherlands, that doesn't mean it's not a good idea to do so!

Sharing the Road

Up to two bicycles maximum can ride side by side in a bike lane, unless this interferes with traffic, in which case you should ride single file. In general, the Dutch will appreciate it if you keep aware, alert, and courteous on the bike paths, and also keep up a decent speed. In most cases, cars are fairly aware of cyclists, but cyclists should stay as far to the right as possible where cyclists and cars share the road. Do not use your phone while cycling; pull over if you need to check it.

Pedestrian Areas

Once you get where you're going, it's probably best to lock up your bike and get around on foot. The Netherlands' compact city centers are often crowded with foot and car traffic, and city biking is something of an extreme sport. Many pedestrian squares are bike-free, and bikers can get fined for biking through them.

Locking up Your Bike

When you're not using your bike, you'll need to park it at a bike rack and use chains to properly lock the bike up. Typically, you'll be provided two locks as part of your rental, one with a key over the wheel and a secondary lock for the bike frame. Unfortunately, bike theft is a problem in major cities, and the city may tow your bike if you leave it somewhere it shouldn't be. Luckily, there are many designated bike parking spots throughout the city.

Getting Back

From Rotterdam, you can take the train back to the Hague (25 minutes; from €8) where you started, or Amsterdam (1 hour 15 minutes; from €12 one-way).

- Amsterdam, Brussels, and Bruges (page 81)
- Rhine River Cruise (page 503)

COPENHAGEN TO BERLIN BY BIKE

Why Go: A classic, easy-riding cycling route connects two hip European cities through rural countryside, quaint villages, tranquil forests, and incredible seascapes.

Number of Days: 9

Total Distance: 450 km (280 mi)

Seasons: Summer

Start: Copenhagen

End: Berlin

For cyclists, this route between Denmark and Germany's vibrant capital cities is culturally and geographically rich. From the trendy cafés and modern museums of Copenhagen, you head south through the Danish countryside. Breeze past sandy beaches and stunning cliff-lined coasts. Pass through picturesque fishing villages and pause to visit a palace or two. Ferry across the Baltic Sea and continue into storied northern Germany, through shady forests and rippling lakes to Berlin. This is a very friendly route for biking amateurs and enthusiasts, with plenty of stops, long flats, and nary a big climb in sight. Both of these countries are among the best in the world for bicyclists, so simply keep an eye out for the signs marking the way.

A note on cycling time estimates: These are based on an average speed of **17 kph (10.5 mph).**

TOP 3

Looking up at the dramatic white **cliffs of Møns Klint** from below (page 394).

Biking through the beautiful **Mecklenburg Lake District,** which is dotted with clearwater lakes and quaint villages (page 400).

Taking a celebratory selfie in front of historic **Brandenburg Gate** (page 402).

DAY 1

Copenhagen

After arriving in Copenhagen (likely via Copenhagen Airport), check into your accommodations in the Nyhavn or Kongens Nytorv neighborhood and relax before for your big ride. If you want to do a little sightseeing around Copenhagen, see **Copenhagen to Oslo** (page 519) for ideas.

DAY 2

Copenhagen to Køge

Cycling Distance and Time: 54 km (34 mi); 3.5 hours

Cycling Directions: After starting on cobblestone canals in central Copenhagen, you'll leave the city center and the rest of the day will be spent on world-famous bicycle roads that parallel Route 151 from Copenhagen to Køge. The route is fully marked by the **EuroVelo "Sun Route" Route 7** signs, as well as the **Danish National Bike Route, Route 9.** This is a very flat day in the saddle with no real climbs.

1. ARKEN Museum for Moderne Kunst

Skovvej 100, Ishøj; tel. 43 54 02 22; www.arken.dk; 10am-5pm Tues.-Sun., 10am-9pm Wed.; 120 Dkr

Depart central Copenhagen via one of the many famous cycling paths of this bike-friendly city. Once you reach the 20-km (12.4-mi) point, you will pass by the ARKEN Museum for Moderne Kunst, and modern art lovers will want to delve into this collection. Situated on a beautiful bay with a properly artsy café, this is the perfect place to relax, explore, and refuel.

2. Mosede Fort

Mosede Strandvej 87A, Greve; tel. 30 43 14 60; www.mosedefort.dk; 11am-4pm daily; 90 DKr

At 29 km (18 mi), the Mosede Fort sits along the rolling coast. A symbol and relic of Danish neutrality during World War I, the Mosede Fort offers exhibitions on the interactions between Denmark and the rest of Europe during this period of conflict. A great experience for history buffs, the exhibit also offers audio and text guidance in English.

top, bike bridge, Copenhagen; bottom, Køge Miniby

COPENHAGEN TO BERLIN BY BIKE

ARKEN Museum for Moderne Kunst
Copenhagen
Copenhagen Airport
Malmo
Mosede Fort
SWEDEN
Køge
Køge MiniBy
Soro
Odense
DENMARK
Rødvig
Præstø
Borre
Baltic Sea
Kalvehave Labyrintpark
GeoCenter Møns Klint
Bogø Havn
Stege
Cliffs of Møns Klint
Bogø Havn Ferry
Stubbekøbing Havn
Hesnæs Strand Beach
Nykobing
Marielyst
Gedser Havn
Kiel
GERMANY
Rostock
Bützow-Güstrow-Kanal
Güstrow
Güstrow Palace and Schlossgarten
Mecklenburg Lake District
Krakow am See
Nossentiner Heide National Park
Schwerin
Hamburg
Müritzeum
Waren
Müritz
Wesenberg Castle
Ravensbrück Concentration Camp Memorial
Fürstenberg
Lake Stechlin
Ziegeleipark Mildenberg
Zehdenick
Elbe River
Liebenwalde
Lehnitzschleuse & Memorial and Museum Sachsenhausen
Malzer Kanal
Overnight Stop
Oranienburg
Birkenwerder
Tegel Forest
Tegerler See
Berlin
Brandenburg Gate
Berlin International Airport
Potsdam

0 20 mi
0 20 km

Key Reservations

It is best to secure reservations for your accommodations along the way in the busier summer months.

3. Køge Miniby

Strandpromenaden 26, Køge; tel. 56 63 62 18; www.koegeminiby.dk; 10am-4pm daily; 60 DKr

Just south of the town of Køge, you can find Køge Miniby, a 1:10 scale replica of the town of Køge as it was in the year 1865. Take a step back in time but watch your step so you don't accidentally step on a townsperson! It's an unforgettable experience for those interested in seeing what historical Denmark looked like. A few hundred meters south of Køge Miniby will take you to the **Comwell Køge Strand Hotel** (Strandvejen 111, Køge; tel. 56 65 36 90; https://comwell.com; from 1,200 DKr), where you can get dinner and rest your head for the night.

DAY 3

Køge to Møn

Cycling Distance and Time: 122 km (76 mi); 7.5 hours

Cycling Directions: From Køge the bike route continues along the main road **Route 261** south out of town along the bike roads. Signs will point left at around 13 km (8 mi) and take you onto small country roads that wrap around the eastern shores to **Rødvig** and then onto **Præstø.** From Præstø the route wiggles through small quiet farm roads with an option to take the more direct Route 265 to the **Dronning Alexandrines Bridge.** Note: Route 265 is more heavily trafficked and without bike lanes or shoulders. Once across the bridge, continue straight following signs to **Stege** and then onward (now **Route 287**) to Møns Klint.

1. Præstø

Take a morning stroll along the sandy beach in Køge before getting ready to hop on the bike. The first half of today's route travels through pastoral fields and along the eastern coast of Denmark as you head south to the white cliffs of Møn. Situated right by the water, the small coastal town of Præstø makes a great stopping point for today's ride at **71 km (44 mi).** For lunch, enjoy fresh seafood, a juicy burger, or a crisp salad by the harbor at **Siv&Co** (Havnepladsen 2, Præstø; tel. 50171450; www.facebook.com/sivogco; 11am-9pm daily; 150 DKr).

cliffs of Møns Klint

Møn Is

Møn's locally produced ice cream, Møn Is, comes from cows that live on the island, and the ice cream is 100 percent organic. This means that your ice cream will be made from milk less than eight hours old, giving it a genuine, rich taste, whichever flavor you choose. Favorites include classic vanilla, pistachio, and coffee with salted caramel.

As you make your way across the island, you'll find plenty of chances to sample the ice cream, including at the **GeoCenter** (page 394). Wherever it's sold, you'll see the characteristic logo—an outline of the island turned into a blob of vanilla ice cream on a waffle. In the summer, visit the source: **Møn Is farm shop and dairy** (Hovgårdsvej 4, Stege; tel. 23 26 38 19; www.moen-is.dk; 11am-5pm June-Sept. and holidays, 11am-5pm Sat.-Sun. Oct.-May; from 22 Dkr for one scoop) is located in rural surroundings where you can enjoy the freshly made flavors and see the animals that provide the raw ingredients.

2. Kalvehave Labyrintpark

Hovvejen 12, Kalvehave; tel. 55 34 47 71; www.kalvehave-labyrintpark.dk; 10am-5pm daily; 100 DKr

For those who enjoy quirky and playful stops, Kalvehave Labyrintpark, about 5 km (3 mi) before Dronning Alexandrines Bridge, is a gem. Anyone who loves a good hedgerow or corn maze will have a blast. Let your inner child come out and enjoy this collection of mazes, puzzles, and mind games.

★ 3. Cliffs of Møns Klint and GeoCenter Møns Klint

Stengårdsvej 8, Borre; tel. 55 86 36 00; www.moensklint.dk; 11am-5pm daily; 150 DKr

The main feature of today's ride is the stunning white cliffs of the Møns Klint. Climbing from sea level to 143 m (470 ft) in the space of 1 km (0.6 mi), the melodramatic cliffs of Møns Klint seem to rise out of nowhere from the trees of western Møn. The chalk edifice topped by peaceful forests is one of the country's natural wonders and the pinnacle of the Møn UNESCO Biosphere Reserve. While much of the area is accessible by hiking and water activities such as kayaking, you can ride up to the GeoCenter along the road and hop off your bike for a view of a portion of the cliffs from a peaceful, pebbly beach (200-m/656-ft walk).

For the evening, **Liselund Ny Slot** (Langebjergvej 6, Borre; tel. 55 81 20 81; www.liselundslot.dk; from 1,200 DKr) is an old castle turned hotel that is a few kilometers north of the GeoCenter. With on-site dining and a collection of small traditional buildings throughout the property, this is a great place to spend some time wandering and exploring.

Slow It Down

Known for its white cliffs by the ocean that give the Cliffs of Dover a run for their money, Møn Klint is one of Denmark's cherished natural sites. Spend an additional evening here, particularly if you are a lover of oceanside activities (such as kayaking, fishing, and sailing), or if you are an avid hiker.

- **Bird- and Wildlife-Watching:** Unlike their British counterparts, these Danish cliffs are much less touristed and, thus, are home to all sorts of wildlife. Bird lovers will want to glimpse the indigenous ospreys, eagles, and peregrine falcons, while the entire family will be entertained if a curious seal pokes its head out of the water.
- **Water Sports:** **Camp Møns Klint** (https://campmoensklint.dk) is a local specialist that can arrange for sailing, kayaking, and fishing excursions for those looking to get out on the water. Though the waters of the Danish Sea are often tranquil, obvious considerations should be taken for the weather.
- **Hiking:** The paths around Møn Klint are all well-marked with distances and estimated time. The estimated time is based on a family hiking with younger kids. If you are with a group of adults, you can assume a shorter hike time. The most popular hike is along the cliffs. There are sturdy wooden boardwalks on the descent and ascent on both the north and south route. The climb covers 120 m (about 400 ft) of elevation change.

DAY 4

Møn, Denmark, to Rostock, Germany

Cycling Distance and Time: 94 km (59 mi); 5.5 hours

Cycling Directions: From eastern Møn retrace your route back to Stege, and then follow **Route 287** to **Bogø Havn** for the ferry to **Stubbekøbing Havn.** From here, head east out of town following the route signs to small country roads near the east coast of the island leading to **Marielyst.** Finally, follow signs to **Gedser Havn,** where you will find your second ferry of the day, this one to Rostock, Germany.

1. Bogø Havn Ferry

Grønsundvej 595, Bogø By; tel. 55 89 46 30; www.bogoe-stubbekoebing.dk/sejlplan; 15 minutes; 55 DKr one-way with a bike

Running roughly every hour from 9am each day, the Bogø Havn Ferry is a classic Danish ferry across a beautiful stretch of inlet connecting Bogø to Stubbekøbing to the south. If you arrive a little early, take a moment for a delicious baked good and coffee by the bay at **BogøBrød** (Grønsundvej 595, Bogø By; tel. 40 31 35 11; 9am-3pm Wed.-Sun., dinner until 8pm Thurs.-Sat.; 20 DKr).

(top to bottom) beach in Marielyst; Scandlines ferry from Gedser to Rostock, Germany; Rostock; Güstrow Palace and Schlossgarten

2. Hesnæs Strand Beach

500 m (0.25 mi) south of Hesnæs; open 24/7; free

Between Stubbekøbing and Marielyst, the route will trace the east coast of the island of Lolland. As you hit the coast, you'll come upon the Hesnæs Strand Beach, a beautiful stretch of sand with the small village of Hesnæs to its north.

3. Marielyst Town

Marielyst Town is 78 km (48 mi) into today's route and is an excellent place to stop for lunch. The town center has a variety of restaurants to choose from. For those looking for a nice café lunch, **Café Mynte** (Marielyst Strandvej, Væggerløse; www.instagram.com/cafemynte; 11am-11pm Wed.-Sat., 11am-5pm Sun.; 140 DKr) offers great smorgasbords full of cured meats, cheese, pickles, and veggies. For those looking for a more local pub feel, Larsens Plads (Marielyst Strandvej 57, Væggerløse; tel. 54 13 21 70; http://larsens-plads.dk; 11am-midnight Mon.-Sat., 11am-8pm Sun.; 160 DKr) has a homey interior with pub food on the menu. They also offer a big wooden deck outside with lots of picnic tables—perfect for dining outside on a warm summer day.

4. Scandlines Ferry from Gedser to Rostock, Germany

Jernbanevejen 1, Gedser, Denmark; tel. 33 15 15 15; www.scandlines.dk; 52 km/32 mi; 1:30am-10:30pm every 2 hours; 2 hours; 400 DKr (one adult with bike)

Willkommen in Deutschland! The ferry from Gedser to Rostock runs throughout the year, though it's weather dependent—be prepared for delays if facing inclement weather. The seas can be choppy here, as well. After arriving by ferry to the Rostock ferry port, it is 11 km (7 mi) to the center of Rostock along small roads for the first half, and then a separate cycling road that parallels the train tracks into the center of town. Once in Germany, you'll need to switch to paying in euros.

5. Rostock

Where to Stay: City Center

Once in Rostock, as you enter the center of town, you will pass by the Steintor, an imposing stone gate at the entrance of the city. Inside, you'll find **Neuer Markt,** a classic European cobbled square with restaurants and businesses. Check out the shops, pick out a restaurant for dinner later, and make a reservation, or take a seat and enjoy some people-watching by the fountain.

Rostock is known for its quintessential northern German architecture and cuisine, so take a spin around the small streets full of traditional buildings and treat yourself to your first real German food for dinner. **Blauer Esel** (Eselföterstraße 26; tel. 38 12526996; www.blauer-esel.de; 11:30am-10pm Mon.-Sat., 5pm-10pm Sun.; €30) provides a slightly modern spin on Germanic cuisine. If you're feeling low key, head down to the local brewery for a few pints and brats at **Braugasthaus Zum alten Fritz** (Warnowufer 65; tel. 38 1208780; www.alter-fritz.de; noon-midnight daily; €20).

DAY 5

Rostock to Güstrow

Cycling Distance and Time: 63 km (39 mi); 4 hours

Cycling Directions: Now in Germany the main signage you will be following is the **EuroVelo Route Number 7** signs. The route today is largely along the **Bützow-Güstrow Canal** and a series of cycling roads that parallel the main road, with a few small country roads between each of these smaller towns heading toward Güstrow.

1. Güstrow Palace and Schlossgarten

Franz-Parr-Platz 1, Güstrow; tel. 38 437520; www.mv-schloesser.de/guestrow; 11am-5pm Tues.-Sun.; €6.50

From Rostock, point your handlebars south toward the forests and lakes of northern Germany. Today's route will be full of small northern farm towns on your way to Güstrow. A towering Renaissance-era castle that sits on the south side of town, the Güstrow Palace is home to a variety of exhibits owned by royalty that have inhabited the palace over the years. Within is the Schlossgarten, a classic German design garden with squared-off features softened by a heart shape in the center.

2. Ernst Barlach Museen

Gertrudenpl. 1, Güstrow; tel. 38 43683001; www.ernst-barlach-stiftung.de/vorschaltseite; 10am-5pm Tues.-Sun.; €9

Arrive early to enjoy lunch in town and take time to explore Güstrow, home of the expressionist sculptor and printmaker Ernst Barlach. A top spot to visit is the Barlach Museum. Take in the works of this iconic artist, known for his sculptures that critiqued and criticized Germany's involvement in the first World War.

3. Kurhaus am Inselsee

Heidberg 1, Güstrow; tel. 38 438500; www.kurhaus-guestrow.de; €150

Four kilometers (2 mi) south of town on Inselsee Lake, you will find the Kurhaus am Inselsee hotel. This tranquil spot is home to extensive grounds with lake access, as well as kayak and stand-up paddleboard rentals. Enjoy sunset by the water and sit down for dinner at the in-house restaurant (€30). Kurhaus also has a spa that offers massages—a real treat after all the hard work your body has completed so far.

Güstrow Palace

DAY 6

Güstrow to Waren (Müritz)

Cycling Distance and Time: 77 km (48 mi); 4.5 hours

Cycling Directions: From Güstrow head south toward **Krakow am See,** then east toward **Waren.** Today's ride weaves through the peaceful forests of the Nossentiner Heide National Park and through small roads that connect the small lakeside towns of Güstrow and Waren. While many roads are lacking in cycling paths, the area is not typically heavily trafficked.

1. Nossentiner Heide National Park

Ziegenhorn 1; tel. 38 73873900; open 24 hours; free

At Nossentiner Heide National Park, enjoy the beautiful views of one of Germany's largest national parks. Half of today's route is spent inside the national park as you ride southwest along several lakes until you reach Waren.

2. Müritzeum

Zur Steinmole 1, Waren (Müritz); tel. 39 91633680; www.mueritzeum.de; 10am-7pm daily; €14

A portmanteau play on the old name for Waren (Müritz) and "museum," this natural museum highlights the local ecology, such as the fish, wildlife, and foliage, of the Nossentiner Heide National Park. Take a moment to learn about the forests and lakes you have been riding through all day. Then, head over to the lakeshore for a bite.

3. Tiefwaren Lake

A leisurely spa town, Waren is the perfect place to relax for an afternoon. Tiefwaren Lake stretches north from the city center, and the walking path around it is perfect for a sunset stroll. In Waren, there are a few options for eating and sleeping. **Heinos Fischerstuw** (Strandstraße 3, Waren/Müritz; tel. 39 91667970; www.heinos-fischerstuw.de; 11am-8pm daily; €20), as the name implies, is particularly known for its fish stew. **Spa Hotel Amsee** (Amsee 6, Waren; tel. 39 9167360; https://hotel-amsee.net; €200) is a hotel that also offers a spa, sauna, and massage services. It's situated near the lake 3.5 km (2.2 mi) north of downtown.

DAY 7

Waren to Fürstenberg (Havel)

Cycling Distance and Time: 96 km (60 mi); 5.5 hours

Cycling Directions: Leaving Waren from the south, you will hop on a cycling road separated from the main road through small-town neighborhoods that fade into shaded forest on a sleepy narrow country road. The day is largely made up of these small roads alternating with small farm

Mecklenburg Lake District

WATCH

***Run Lola Run*:** This award-winning 1998 experimental German thriller follows Lola (Franka Potente) as she races through Berlin in an attempt to procure 100,000 Deutschmarks to save her boyfriend's life.

READ

The Little Book of Hygge by Meik Wiking: Get insight into what makes Denmark the home of some of the world's happiest people in this book on hygge, a quintessentially Danish lifestyle concept that inadequately translates to "cozy."

LISTEN

Fra Højskolesangbogen: The Højskolesangbogen is *the* Danish song book, containing culturally significant Danish songs and in print since 1894. The book is only in Danish, but you can hear a selection of its songs on this album.

towns heading southeast to Fürstenberg. Continue to follow the **EuroVelo Route Number 7** signage.

★ 1. Mecklenburg Lake District

Continuing southwest toward Berlin, today's route flows between bogs, lakes, and forests of the Mecklenburg Lake District, which is incredibly photogenic any time of year. Often referred to as the land of a thousand lakes, this region is full of gorgeous nature preserves and small villages. For a good place to pause along the way, **Lake Stechlin** is one of the deepest, clearest lakes in the area and home to the endemic dwarfed fish. Resting on the banks makes for a picture-perfect picnic on a sunny day.

2. Wesenberg Castle

Tel. 39 83220621; 10am-6pm daily, hours vary by season; €5

At 64 km (about 40 mi), you will pass through the small lakeside town of Wesenberg, known for its castle. Originally built in the 13th century, the stone walls of the Wesenberg Castle have protected its citizens for centuries. These days, the castle features exhibitions on fishing and regional history, and is used as a forestry museum and tourist information office. There are 68 steps leading you up the Fangelturm to the lookout tower with views over the lake.

Afterward, head over to **Gaststätte Bodinka** (Kreuzstraße 1, Wesenberg; tel. 39 83220321; 11am-1:30pm and 4pm-10pm Mon.-Sat.; €15) for a traditional German lunch before heading out for the last portion of today's ride.

3. Ravensbrück Concentration Camp Memorial

Str. d. Nationen 1, Fürstenberg/Havel; tel. 33 0936080; www.ravensbrueck-sbg.de; 10am-6pm daily; free

On the north shore across from the town of Fürstenberg sits the remains of the Ravensbrück Concentration Camp, Germany's largest women's concentration camp. A hard reminder of the area's dark past from World War II, this site tells the tale of the horrors of the Holocaust, reminding the world of what happened here. Many of the exhibits around the museum and grounds include information that is translated into English.

4. Fürstenberg

Str. d. Nationen 1, Fürstenberg/Havel; tel. 33 0936080; www.ravensbrueck-sbg.de; 10am-6pm daily; free

Fürstenberg is a typical, quaint German village. It is hugged by three lakes, giving it a watery charm. There are several sleeping options here, including places to camp lakeside. About 500 m (1,640 ft) from the town center, the **Pension & Hotel Villa Ingeborg** (Steinförder Str. 20, Fürstenberg/Havel; tel. 33 093607990; www.hotel-villa-ingeborg.de; €220) occupies an outstanding vista. A large villa built in the early 1900s, the building was restored and refurbished into a hotel with modern amenities and old-time charm.

DAY 8

Fürstenberg to Oranienburg

Cycling Distance and Time: 76 km (48 mi); 4.5 hours

Cycling Directions: The day starts off heading south toward **Zehdenick** on small country roads before hopping onto the path along the **Malzer Kanal** into Oranienburg.

1. Ziegeleipark Mildenberg

Ziegelei 10, Zehdenick; tel. 33 07310410; www.ziegeleipark.de; 10am-6pm daily; €8

At 37 km (23 mi) on today's route, Ziegeleipark Mildenberg is an interactive museum on the grounds of a former brickworks factory. Take a moment to pop in for a look around at the history of brickwork technology.

2. Liebenwalde

At 55 km (34 mi), you will arrive at the small town of Liebenwalde on **Lake Wir.** This is a good moment to stretch your legs and have a little walk around. For lunch, tuck into the **Restaurant am See** (Lindenstraße 2f, Liebenwalde; tel. 33 054905936; www.

left, Memorial and Museum Sachsenhausen; right, Oranienburg

ankernundgastro-liebenwalde.de/wir-restaurant-am-see; 11am-8pm Wed.-Sun.; €20) for a traditional German schnitzel with a calming view over the lake.

3. Memorial and Museum Sachsenhausen

Str. d. Nationen 22, Oranienburg; tel. 33 01200200; www.sachsenhausen-sbg.de; 9am-6pm daily; free

The site of a former Nazi concentration camp and Soviet prison camp, the remains of Sachsenhausen Camps are located just north of central Oranienburg. Memorials of the camp sit alongside a few well-kept buildings, some of which have been turned into museum exhibits.

4. Oranienburg

Finish up your ride today in Oranienburg, a suburb of Berlin. From here, your ride becomes much more urban. Oranienburg is home to a few sites, and the general feeling of the town is much less sleepy than the villages of the past few days, though it doesn't have the urban cacophony of sprawling Berlin. If time allows, visit **Schloss Oranienburg** (Schloßpl. 1, Oranienburg; tel. 33 01537437; www.spsg.de/schloesser-gaerten/objekt/schlossmuseum-oranienburg; 10am-5:30pm daily; €6), a castle constructed in the 17th century. Beyond tours of the palace and grounds, there are also two museums on site. **Oranjehus Pension & Restaurant** (Clara-Zetkin-Straße 31, Oranienburg; tel. 33 018350972; www.oranjehus.de; €70) is a quaint B&B with warm interior, simple rooms, and a fantastic restaurant for dining in the evening.

DAY 9

Oranienburg to Berlin

Cycling Distance and Time: 50 km (31 mi); 3 hours

Cycling Directions: The first half of today stays relatively rural before hitting the urban adventure of central Berlin. The easy-to-follow cycle route heads directly south to **Birkenwerder** before hopping on the **Malzer Kanal Path** until it merges with the **Tegerler See** and heads east into central Berlin. For those looking to avoid city riding or shorten the trip, there is an **S-Bahn connection** between Oranienburg and Berlin (1 hour).

1. Tegel Forest

Berlin; open 24 hours; free

One of five forests surrounding Berlin, the Tegel Forest is about an hour (23 km/14 mi) south of Oranienburg on your way to Germany's capital. Here, you can enjoy an offroad cycling experience in forests that are untouched in parts, but do be aware of boar and deer. There are great spots for a picnic lunch in the forest and along the lake. For tree lovers, both Berlin's oldest tree, **Dickie Marie** (a giant oak estimated to be 800-900 years old), and tallest tree, the **Larch** at 43 m (141 ft), are well-signed and can be visited while in the forest.

★ 2. Brandenburg Gate

Pariser Platz, Berlin; open 24 hours; free

Congratulations, you've made it! The Brandenburg Gate is the symbol of Berlin. Inspired by the Propylaea in the Acropolis in Athens, Greece, this 18th-century behemoth of a neoclassic gate reaches 26 m (85 ft) in height in the middle of the busy Pariser Platz, near the Reichstag (parliament) building. Throughout the Cold War, it was the most prominent of blocked gates along the Berlin Wall, serving as a symbol for the division of

Brandenburg Gate

that era. These days, it is much more a symbol of unity, bringing together the two halves of Berlin and, thus, the world. Take a triumphant photo with your bike in front of it to mark the end of an epic cycling ride.

For Berlin itinerary ideas, see **Berlin, Warsaw, and Krakow** (page 162).

TRANSPORTATION

Air

- **Copenhagen Airport** (CPH, or Kastrup; Lufthavnsboulevarden 6; tel. 45 32 31 32 31; www.cph.dk) is the largest airport in the Nordic region with some direct flights to North America and many connections within Europe. Located about 10 km (6 mi) south of the city center, the airport can be reached via the Metro (15 minutes; 17-20 DKr). A taxis ride to the city center takes 20-30 minutes (from 300 DKr).
- **Berlin Brandenburg "Willy Brandt" Airport** (BER; Willy-Brandt-Platz, Schönefeld; tel. 30 609160910; https://ber.berlin-airport.de) has international flights and connections across Europe. The FEX, RE7 and RB14 airport express trains connect the airport with the city center, as does the slower S9 S-Bahn tram.

Bike

Rentals

One Way Bikeaway
Café Parforce, Dyrehavevej 1, Klampenborg; www.onewaybiketours.com; daily 10am-6pm
This outfitter offers convenient, high quality bike rentals with pick up just outside Copenhagen (right outside Klampenborg Station, 20-minute train ride from Copenhagen Central) and drop off in Berlin. Bikes are in stellar condition. For 10-days, expect to pay $250 on up, depending on bike selection and extras. If you are planning to start in Berlin, it's also possible to pick up in Berlin and drop off in Copenhagen. Inquire for details.

Tours

U-Tracks
www.utracks.com, starting from €2,200
This is one of the most dependable bike specialists operating in Europe. They have 24-gear bikes as well as 8-gear and E-Bikes available for rent. Their tours are self-guided (no tour guides), but they do take care of reservations, transfers, meals, and of course your gear. They offer an 11-day tour between Copenhagen and Berlin as well as other tours around Europe.

Experience Plus Tours
www.experienceplus.com; starting from €6,800
Those looking for a more cultural depth and a more bespoke experience should look to this tour outfitter specializing in small group, multi-day bike tours. There are typically two departures departing from Copenhagen in the summer for a 14-day bike tour. This is a bit more of a leisurely pace with a local bicycle guide with you on the roads and trails, helping you to get behind the scenes a bit more, and giving you more information as you go about local culture and customs.

Rob McManmon

tel. 405 213 9791; robmcmanmon@gmail.com; starting from $250

Rob will craft a self-guided tour you can follow to get to some real hidden gems by bike (and by foot!), with an emphasis on weaving beautiful nature and countryside with high quality stays and excellent suggestions for dining along the way. If you're comfortable biking by yourself and making your own reservations but would like someone to piece together a great tour for you, Rob is your guy.

Road Rules

Cycling in Denmark and Germany is not only easy, but it is something many residents do, whether for recreation or just to commute to work. Keep in mind a few basic rules:

- Always use a bike lane when available and keep to your right.
- Remember to use hand signals: extended right hand for right turns; left hand for left turns; upraised arm to stop.
- Walk bikes on sidewalks and when using pedestrian crossings.
- Look out for dedicated bike traffic lights, particularly in Berlin.
- Activate your bike lights at night. (It is a fineable offense to not use lights after sunset.)
- Give way to pedestrians at all stops, intersections, and traffic lights.
- Though helmets are not strictly mandatory by law, you should wear one anyway.
- It is a good idea to lock your bike up wherever you park.
- Don't drink and bike. This is a very serious offense (and quite dangerous!).

Ferry

Bogø to Stubbekøbing

Grønsundvej 595, Bogø By; tel. 55 89 46 30; www.bogoe-stubbekoebing.dk/sejlplan; 15 minutes; 55 DKr one-way with a bike

This local ferry service can generally accommodate walk-ons with bikes without issue. You could purchase tickets ahead of time, though this isn't strictly necessary.

Scandlines

www.scandlines.com

Scandlines operates the ferries crossing from Gedser to Rostock. Their hybrid ferries are cleaner than most other lines and deals can often be had if you book ahead of time.

Subway and Tram (Berlin)

Berlin is well served citywide by the **U-Bahn** (4am-1am weekdays, 24 hours on weekends), which goes underground and serves the center of town, and the **S-Bahn,** which runs aboveground in the suburbs, with a line that connects Oranienburg and Berlin, as well as the airport and central Berlin.

Getting Back

To get back to Copenhagen from Berlin via train (9.5 hours; €60-135), take a **Deutsche Bahn** intercity train (www.bahn.de) to Hamburg, where you'll transfer to a **Danish Railways** intercity train (www.dsb.dk) to Copenhagen. Both railways offer bicycle tickets, an extra charge for stowing your bike. There are also flights between Berlin and Copenhagen (1 hour 10 minutes). To get home or to your next destination, Berlin is well-connected by air and train.

- Berlin, Warsaw, and Krakow (page 162)
- Copenhagen to Oslo (page 519)

TOUR DU MONT BLANC

Why Go: Traverse the slopes of three countries—France, Italy, and Switzerland—on Europe's most iconic mountain hike.

Number of Days: 8

Total Distance: 92 km (57 mi)

Seasons: Summer

Start/End: Chamonix

Make no mistake, the Tour du Mont Blanc is no walk in the park. Known affectionately as the TMB, this long, sometimes grueling hike shepherds you through one of the world's most scenic mountain ranges. There are many different routes and variations that can accommodate different fitness levels, but for most people coming from overseas, the TMB begins in Chamonix and continues counterclockwise around Mont Blanc. Depending on your pace, the hike can take anywhere from 7-14 days.

This eight-day Tour du Mont Blanc route is an excellent choice if you are short on time or are new to long-distance hiking. You'll start in Les Houches, a village easily reached by train from Chamonix, where you will also end. You'll hike the most scenic parts of the trail and skip the not-quite-as-beautiful parts via transfers. You will hike 4-6 hours each day, with elevation gains from 500 m (1,640 ft) to 1,300 m (4,265 ft), so you will need to be reasonably fit.

TOP 3

★ Reaching the summit of the **Col de la Seigne** (2,516 m/8,255 ft) near the Italian border with breathtaking views over Mont Blanc (page 415).

★ Trekking through **Les Bovines** for epic views with every step (page 418).

Picnicking along the banks of **Lac Blanc,** with the alpine ridges and snowcapped peaks reflected in the crystal-clear still waters (page 422).

Key Reservations

Make sure to book your **accommodations** before arriving. Hotels, refuges, and lodges are often booked to capacity throughout the hiking season, making for a potentially dangerous situation if you are not prepared to sleep outdoors at altitude. You will want to make sure to have your accommodations secured on Day 1 before moving to Day 2, and have Day 2 secured before Day 3, etc. Note that the annual **Ultra-Trail du Mont Blanc** race is the last weekend of August and 10,000 or more trail runners will descend on the region, making accommodations even more scarce.

ORGANIZING YOUR TOUR DU MONT BLANC

This route is written to inspire you to plan and hike the Tour de Mont Blanc with additional research from other sources, such as the excellent *Tour du Mont Blanc* by Kingsley Jones. If organizing a trip yourself, be sure to allot plenty of time to arrange your accommodations. This can be a time-consuming process requiring multiple email threads, as there is no central booking system. You will also want to ensure that the distance from the previous accommodation is within your comfort level.

SELF-GUIDED TOURS

An alternative is to book a self-guided tour in which you'll still hike on your own, but a tour company takes care of the logistics for you. You can depend on a good company not only to book your accommodations while making sure everything is within your comfort level, but also to provide a GPS for the route, advise on current conditions, let you know about possible shortcuts and suggested stops for refreshments, and to be available in case of emergencies. Most companies will also offer the option of luggage transfer. This means is that you can hike with a light day pack, leaving the bulk of your clothes and other items in your suitcase where it will wait for you at the next stop.

Monkeys and Mountains Adventure Travel (https://monkeysand-mountains.com) and **Mont Blanc Treks** (https://montblanctreks.com) are two reputable companies to begin your search for the perfect partner to organize your self-guided tour.

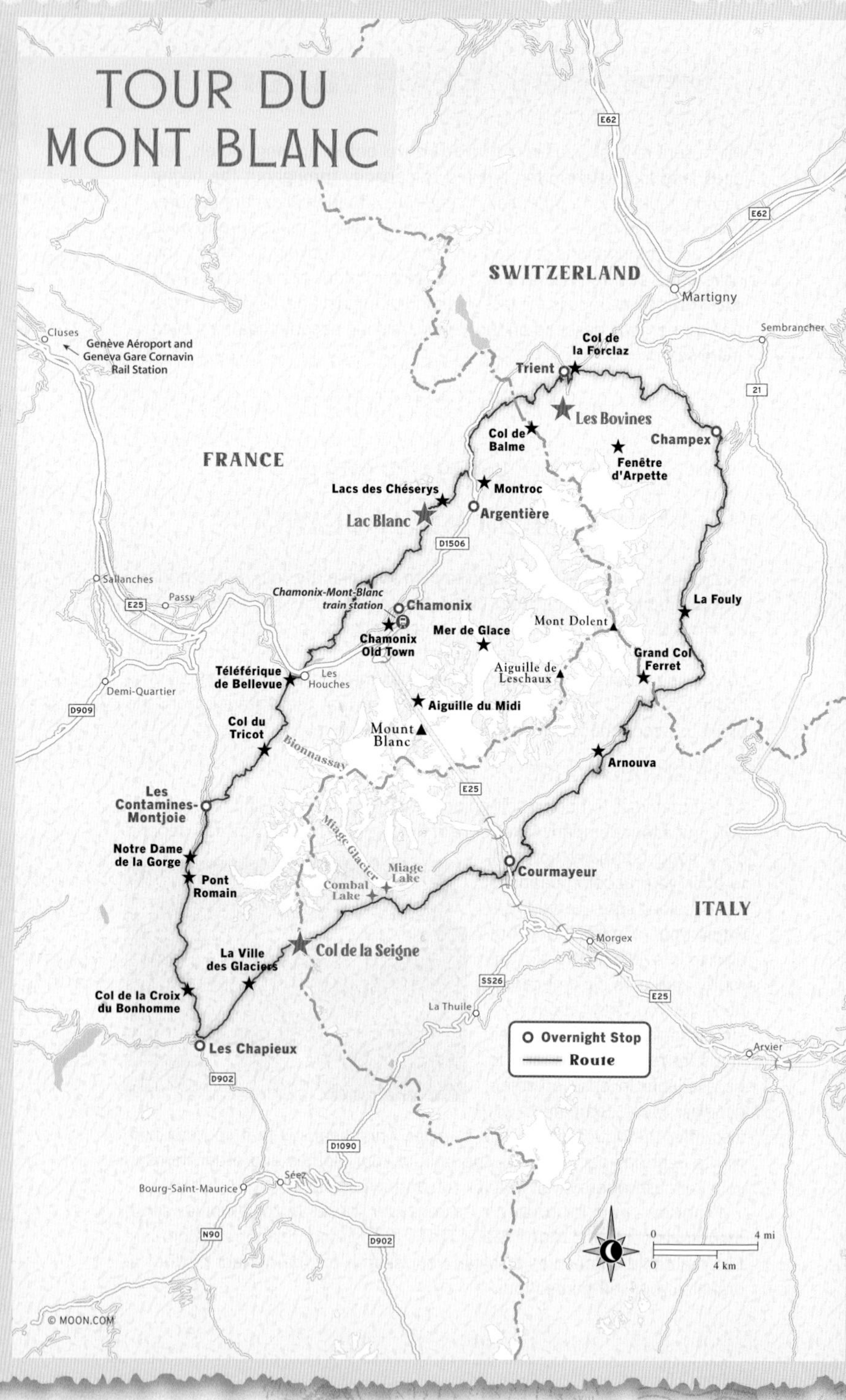

TOUR DU MONT BLANC
SWITZERLAND
FRANCE
ITALY
Martigny
Sembrancher
E62
21
Cluses
Genève Aéroport and Geneva Gare Cornavin Rail Station
Col de la Forclaz
Trient
Les Bovines
Col de Balme
Champex
Fenêtre d'Arpette
Lacs des Chéserys
Montroc
Argentière
Lac Blanc
D1506
Sallanches
Passy
E25
Chamonix-Mont-Blanc train station
Chamonix
Chamonix Old Town
Mer de Glace
Mont Dolent
La Fouly
Grand Col Ferret
Aiguille de Leschaux
Téléférique de Bellevue
Les Houches
Demi-Quartier
D909
Aiguille du Midi
Col du Tricot
Mount Blanc
Bionnassay
Arnouva
Les Contamines-Montjoie
Miage Glacier
Notre Dame de la Gorge
Pont Romain
Miage Lake
Combal Lake
Courmayeur
Col de la Seigne
La Ville des Glaciers
Morgex
SS26
E25
Col de la Croix du Bonhomme
La Thuile
Les Chapieux
Overnight Stop
Route
D902
Arvier
D1090
Bourg-Saint-Maurice
Séez
N90
D902
0
4 mi
0
4 km
© MOON.COM

Chamonix, France

Where to Stay: Central Chamonix

Arrive by: Bus or car transfer to Chamonix

1. L'Aiguille du Midi

Chamonix; www.montblancnaturalresort.com/en/aiguille-du-midi; 7am-5pm daily; access dependent upon weather, check website; €69

Europe's highest cable car whisks you away on a 20-minute ride to the peak of l'Aiguille du Midi, an impressive mountain at an elevation of 3,842 m (12,605 ft). Once you arrive at the top you will want to take a long view over Mont Blanc. From here, you will see the different possible routes leading to Mont Blanc and the breathtaking Mont Blanc du Tacul and Mont Maudit. **The Pipe,** a unique 32-m-long (105-ft) steel gallery, provides a circuit around the central pillar of the Aiguille du Midi with exhibitions and inspiring views along the way.

2. The Void

l'Aguille du Midi; 7am-5pm daily; free

Whether you like heights or the feeling of heights, or are outright terrified of heights, do yourself a favor and take a step into a glass box that dangles over 1,000 m (3,280 ft) in the air. In this skywalk, there is literally nothing below you. If you ever wanted to know what it was like to walk on air, this is about as close as it gets. Thrilling? Maybe. Terrifying? Most definitely.

Access the Void through the **Restaurant le 3842** (l'Aguille du Midi; tel. 450558223; www.restaurants-altitude.com/en/restaurants/le-3842; 11:30am-3pm daily; €25; reservations recommended), one of the highest restaurants in Europe. Enjoy a fine dining lunch while taking in the panoramic views over the Alps. The menu features fresh, locally sourced produce and proteins. If you want something less fancy, head for

left, the Void; right, L'Aiguille du Midi

What to Pack

There are different options for trekking the Tour du Mont Blanc, which may influence how much and what you pack. If you opt for luggage transfer services, your gear will be carried ahead to your next accommodation, which allows you to hike with just a daypack. If you are trekking with all of your luggage on you, you will want to pay good attention to the weight of your backpack. If you decide to camp, you will also have to factor in the weight of your tent.

PACKING LIST

- Quality pair of hiking shoes
- Comfortable pack
- Lightweight, waterproof outer shell
- Insulating layers for warm and cold weather
- Underwear, socks
- Wide-brimmed hat
- Gloves
- Sleeping gear (warm sleeping bag if camping; lighter survival blanket otherwise)
- Sunglasses
- Sunscreen
- Mobile phone with charger (and European plug adapter)
- Map and compass
- Flashlight
- Whistle
- Hiking poles
- Snacks and large water bottle or bladder
- A camera or device to take photos and videos
- Binoculars
- Toiletries
- First-aid kit (with kit for blisters)
- Medications
- Cash (euros and Swiss francs)

These are the basics you will need to make a successful trek along the Tour du Mont Blanc. Cash is important as many of the refuges and cafés along the more remote portions of the trail cannot take credit cards. If you are considering camping, keep in mind that camping regulations in France, Italy, and Switzerland are quite different from each other. In sum, in France you can free camp without issue. In Italy, you are only able to free camp at elevations above 2,500 m (8,202 ft). In Switzerland, there is no free camping, so you will have to use the licensed campgrounds.

the cafeteria and coffee shop for sandwiches and other light bites.

3. Mer de Glace

Chamonix; https://en.chamonix.com; hours vary, check website for details; €36

The Mer de Glace (or "Sea of Ice") is the largest glacier in France and the second largest in Europe at 7 km (4.3 mi) long and 200 m (656 ft) thick. To visit the Mer de Glace, you need to take a short train ride out of Chamonix on the **Montenvers line** (30 minutes; €36), an old funicular that brings you to the top station above the glacier. From here, it is a walk down to the ice grotto where you can literally walk through the glacier in a tunnel carved into the ice. Here you will learn about mountain life in the 19th century. The entire visit takes 2-3 hours.

4. Chamonix Old Town

At the heart of France's Haute-Savoie, Chamonix had the distinction of being the first ever host of a Winter Olympics back in 1924. The old-world ski lodge feel is most apparent in the Old Town, where cozy French bistros are tucked beneath chalet-style roofs. Even on a summer day, it feels as though a fresh snow could powder the cobblestone streets at any moment. There is a baroque church in the city center as well as a number of traditional-style chalets, rustic lodges, and Belle Epoque hotels. As this is France, you'll find plenty of cafés where you can linger and admire the views.

For dinner, head to **La Fine Bouche** (140 Pl. du Poilu; tel. 450211063; noon-1:45pm and 7pm-9pm Tues.-Sat., reservations strongly recommended; €35) for French classics, like onion soup and escargot slathered in garlic, butter, and parsley. Your hike begins in earnest tomorrow, so do not cut back on the cheese, potatoes, meats, and whatever else might give you the energy you'll need.

Travel Tip: If you will be connecting your hike of the TMB with other travels in Europe and have a large bag, ask your hotel in Chamonix if they can keep your large bag for you until you return. Many accommodations will happily do this if you are staying with them before and after your hike.

DAY 2

Les Houches to Les Contamines-Montjoie

Hiking Distance and Time: 11 km (6.84 mi) with 600 m (1,969 ft) ascent, 1,200 m (3,937 ft) descent; 5 hours

1. Les Houches

From Chamonix, hop on the local TER train (www.sncf-connect.com) to Les Houches (20 minutes; €10-20). If you wish to begin your hike in Chamonix, you can skip the train. The hike is 4.5 km (2.8 mi) with 797 m (2,615 ft) of ascent and takes about 1.5 hours.

While in Les Houches, this is a good opportunity to fill up on snacks and get any gear you might need. This quaint mountain town has the requisite cafés, as well as a small Carrefour grocery store for nibbles. There are also a few shops that specialize in mountain gear. Before you leave Les Houches, make sure to take a photo in the town square beneath the **start/finish arch** for the TMB.

2. Téléférique de Bellevue

77 Pl. de la Fruitière; tel. 450547093; www.ski-leshouches.com; 8am-5:30pm; €20

From Les Houches, take the Téléférique de Bellevue, a suspended cable car that will bring you up the mountain to **Bellevue** (1,780 m/5,840 ft). This is the

Les Houches

Summiting Mont Blanc

There are two primary routes to summit Mont Blanc, and both of them have very real dangers. One route, the **Three Mountains Route,** has a trail with avalanche hazards, while the **Normal Route** has a stretch of hike that has unpredictable rockslides. Nearly half of all mountaineering accidents happen on Mont Blanc, with nearly 50 percent occurring on the climb to the Goûter Hut, either because of falling rocks or unfavorable weather.

NECESSARY SKILLS

If you are considering summiting Mont Blanc, make sure you have the following skills and experience to reduce your risk of having a potentially fatal accident:

- Be able to endure hours of tough hiking at high altitudes.
- Be confident walking in crampons. Many fatal falls result from people tripping in new crampons.
- Know how to walk roped together with other climbers.
- Know how to get out of a crevasse.
- Be able to interpret mountain weather forecasts.
- Understand how to gauge snow and rock conditions.

GUIDES

Anyone without the proper skills would be safest hiring a professional guide. The **Compagnie des Guides de Chamonix** (www.chamonix-guides.com) is the official association of Chamonix's professional mountain guides. It's the best place to find certified guides. A guided hike to the summit will range from €900 to €1,500 for two people, in addition to other costs such as gear, accommodations, meals, and any transportation.

start of the "Normal Route" to summit Mont Blanc as well as the starting point for your own trek. You'll find the historic and wonderfully rustic **La Chalette** snack bar open should you need some fortification, such as a deliciously chilled bottle of Sylvanus Triple by Brasserie du Mont Blanc, before your trek begins.

The first stage of your hike takes you on the crossing beneath the glacier of **Bionnassay** through a quiet wood. There are some narrow sections of the trail here with handrails before a fairly steep descent to a suspension bridge. From here, it is a straight hike up to the next stage, Col du Tricot.

3. Col du Tricot

From the end of the Bionnassay glacier crossing, you turn uphill, though alpine pastures to Col du Tricot (2,120 m/6,955 ft). Be sure to take a little joy in the vast panorama of the Contamines-Montjoie valley at the top before you begin a zigzag descent to the valley floor. On the way down, the **Refuge de Miage** is a friendly place for a quick snack. Take a moment to enjoy the views out over the Dôme du Miage.

4. Les Contamines-Montjoie

From Col du Trictot, you descend a steep path through the rustic chalets of **Miage**

(1,559 m/5,942 ft). Next, you'll circle **Mont Truc** (1,811 m/5,942 ft) and then jump for joy as you reach the village of Les Contamines-Montjoie, the last stop on your first stage. This is the last major village you will cross for a few days, so be sure to stock up on food and other essentials.

In Les Contamines-Montjoie there are several places to consider bunking for the night. **Hôtel Gai Soleil** (288 Chemin des Loyers; tel. 450470294; www.gaisoleil.com; €125) is one of the most comfortable options, featuring individual rooms with private en suite bathrooms and the requisite on-site restaurant.

DAY 3

Les Contamines-Montjoie to Les Chapieux

Hiking Distance and Time: 13.5 km (8.39 mi) with 1,300 m (4,265 ft) ascent, 950 m (3,117 ft) descent; 5 hours

1. Notre Dame de la Gorge

Les Contamines-Montjoie

Discover the Notre Dame de la Gorge church nestled alongside the bubbling Le Bon Nant river. There has been a place of worship here for more than 700 years. The obviously baroque church was reconstructed by a stone mason in 1699. The painted facade provides a striking contrast to the alpine mountain forest surrounding it, while inside, the faithful pray for safe passage over the Bonhomme Pass.

Transfer: Today will be the most difficult day of your hike. If you arrange your TMB with a company that provides transfers, take advantage of the short transfer possible to begin the day at Notre Dame de la Gorge (3.7 km/2.3 mi) and save a bit of energy for the longer, more beautiful climb ahead.

2. Pont Naturel

From the Notre Dame de la Gorge, you continue down a steep stone path. This path is one of the few along the TMB put in place by the Romans. After about 1 km (0.5 mi), you will spot a sign that reads: Pont Naturel. This natural rock bridge that arches across the river has been carved out from a single piece of rock over the centuries by the swift-flowing waters.

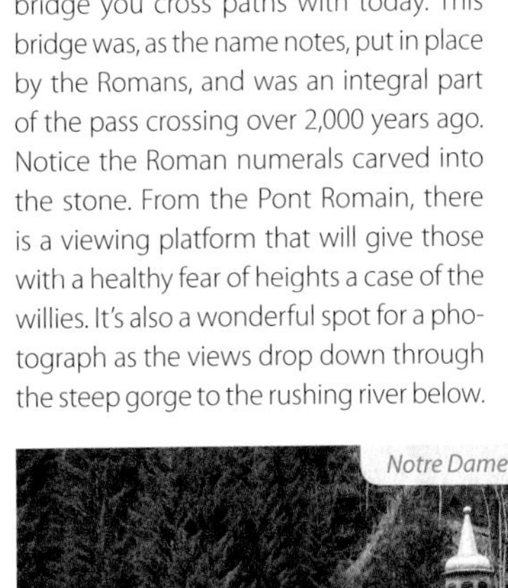

3. Pont Romain

Follow the trail from Pont Naturel. After about 100 m (320 ft), the trail bends and bring you to Pont Romain, the second old bridge you cross paths with today. This bridge was, as the name notes, put in place by the Romans, and was an integral part of the pass crossing over 2,000 years ago. Notice the Roman numerals carved into the stone. From the Pont Romain, there is a viewing platform that will give those with a healthy fear of heights a case of the willies. It's also a wonderful spot for a photograph as the views drop down through the steep gorge to the rushing river below.

Notre Dame de la Gorge

(top to bottom) Bonhomme Pass; Les Chapieux; La Ville des Glaciers; Col de la Seigne

4. Bonhomme Pass and Col de la Croix-du-Bonhomme

The trek through the Bonhomme Pass and to its ending point at Col de la Croix-du-Bonhomme is the most challenging uphill stretch of trekking on this route. From the Pont Romain, head uphill until you exit the tree line into the alpage (mountain pasture) of **La Rollaz.** This is one of the more picturesque passes you will cross, especially when the wildflowers are in bloom and grazing bovines lazily munch away on the alpine grass.

Cross through the alpage, sticking to the main trail before ascending at the opposite side, crossing a bridge, and continuing your ascent. The area ahead here is rocky and prone to occasional rockslides, so it is best to be quick. Here, the wider trail used by farmers and the Romans becomes a thinner single-file trail. You'll cross another wooden bridge and then up another rocky path until you reach the Col de la Croix-du-Bonhomme. This is the apex of your hike and you are rewarded with a brilliant panoramic view of **Mount Pourri** (3,779 m/12,398 ft). If you packed your lunch and the wind is calm, this is a great spot to break out your picnic lunch if you haven't already.

5. Les Chapieux

Descend down the trail into the hamlet of Les Chapieux (1,549 m/5,082 ft) for the night. The path here zigzags with some occasional rocky terrain. This is the southernmost point on the TMB. There are several small shops here for trail necessities. At the end of the town, there is a **war memorial** commemorating a local resistance that fended off an Italian advance into the valley during World War II. For the night, tuck into the rustic **Auberge de la Nova** (tel. June-Sept. 0982126435, Oct.-May 0664949835; https://refugelanova.com; €70-80), a mountain lodge that was used to house resistance fighters during World War II. In the evenings, the cozy stone-walled dining room fills with warm company.

Les Chapieux, France, to Courmayeur, Italy

Hiking Distance and Time: 13.5 km (8.39 mi) with 750 m (2,461 ft) ascent, 900 m (2,953 ft) descent; 5 hours

1. La Ville des Glaciers

From Les Chapieux, your path this morning takes you across a largely flat crossing for about 2.5 km (1.5 mi), traveling northeast across the **Barrage de Séloge** and across a bridge over the Ruisseau des Tufs before the real work begins to La Ville des Glaciers (1,800 m/5,906 ft). Though the name does not live up to the billing in this case (there is no village nor nearby glaciers), there is a wonderful farm where you can sample slices of the delicious local beaufort cheese. Be sure to get extra for lunch later today. Be prepared for a long, slow climb.

★ 2. Col de la Seigne

You could opt to head to the **Refuge des Mottets,** up a series of steep zigzags, for refreshments, or take a shortcut. The shortcut follows a TMB trail sign just after crossing the Ruisseau du Grand Praz. Take a right here and then your next right to rejoin the main route. You will cross a stream and then climb in the beautiful alpine pastures of the Col de la Seigne (2,516 m/8,255 ft). This is one of the best viewpoints of the Mont Blanc massif and a highlight of your tour.

Though the path here marks the **Franco-Italian border,** besides a large cairn and a border stone, there is nothing else denoting the change of countries (and no passport control). None of this will be on your mind at all as the vast scale of your first peek at the Italian face of Mont Blanc promises to be memorable.

3. Miage Glacier

You will then begin the descent into the Valle Veny, passing **Combal Lake** (Lago Combal), a glacier-fed shallow lake with picturesque reflections of the mountains—a boon for photographers. You will cross through the foot of the Miage Glacier. The glacier is the longest in Italy at an impressive 10 km (6.2 mi). It's also the largest debris-covered glacier in all of Europe. You'll arrive at **Miage Lake** (Lago del Miage), a popular tourist attraction with ice cliffs and a two-tone colored appearance created from the glacier sediment. You'll also find unique alpine flora in the area.

Transfer: From Miage Lake, it makes sense to take advantage of a short transfer to your next stop, Courmayeur (12 km/7.5 mi).

Combal Lake

4. Courmayeur

In Val Ferret (2,052 m/6,732 ft) the main village is Courmayeur. There are plenty of stores to stock up on essentials while the town itself maintains an alpine charm. Take the time to admire the views here at the foot of the Pre-de-Bar suspended glacier as well as Mont Dolent.

If you prefer private rooms, stay at the **Hôtel Edelweis** (Via Guglielmo Marconi, 42; tel. 0165 841590; www.albergoedelweiss.it; €125). You could dine here or head out for a night on the town at the **Ristorante la Terrazza** (Via Circonvallazione, 73; tel. 0165 843330; www.ristorantelaterrazza.com/courmayeur/sito-it-8.html; €30).

DAY 5

Courmayeur, Italy, to Champex, Switzerland

Hiking Distance and Time: 12.5 km (7.8 mi) with 850 m (2,789 ft) descent; 4.5 hours

1. Arnuova

Transfer: From Courmayeur, take the short transfer to the small village of Arnuova (13 km/8.1 mi) to begin today's hike. From Arnuova on the valley floor, it is a swift uphill ascent before a gradual downhill that takes you past an aid station, over a bridge, and onward to **Rifugio Elena** (Fraz. Lavachey; tel. 0165 844688; www.rifugioelena.it; June 15-Sept. 15). On the TMB, this is the very last of the Italian mountain huts. Pause here for the views across the Grandes Jorasses and the summit of Mont Dolent, where the borders of Italy, France, and Switzerland converge.

Grand Col Ferret

2. Grand Col Ferret

After Rifugio Elena, the path zigzags uphill to the east before turning north toward Grand Col Ferret, marking the **Italia-Swiss border.** This part of the trail is mostly a casual ascent, though with some occasional loose footing. Be sure to look over your shoulder before descending. As in all of the TMB, these crests are really highlights of your trek and offer stunning views. Here, in particular, let your eyes follow the Italian Val Ferret back toward the distant Col de la Seigne, marking the Franco-Italian border. Continuing on from Grand Col Ferret, there is an easy downhill walk to the **Gite Alpage de la Peule,** a retro-fitted farmhouse with dormitories, yurt, and, most importantly, refreshments.

3. La Fouly

From the Gite Alpage de la Peule, the TMB continues up an old shepherd's trail heading north. The trail here is a slight descent, narrowing before curving through the mountainside. You cross a valley and a few trickling streams before

Slow It Down

The TMB is the sort of trail that can be explored at different pacing for different sorts of travelers. Though this route is geared for those with moderate fitness and only a short time to travel, if you have more time and are comfortable with long walks, it is easy to augment this route, slow it down, and even cut back on your carbon footprint! Just skip the transfers. Instead of taking a transfer from Courmayeur to Arnuova in the morning, make this your walk for Day 5. Spend the night in Arnuova, and then the next day strike out to La Fouly, basically doing the walk listed in the route here. Finally, from La Fouly, break this stretch of the TMB into two days, stopping in Prez de Fort for the night before continuing onto Champex the next time. Like this, you would add a few days of trekking... and zero days using a vehicle!

continuing down through real pastoral country before crossing a bridge into the village of La Fouly. You can find an ATM, restaurants, and a few hotels and lodges here, as well as a tourist office. If you are not taking the transfer to Champex, La Fouly is the last real town you will pass through for a day or two.

Transfer: In La Fouly, there is a parking lot where you can meet up for your transfer to Champex (19 km/11.8 mi).

4. Champex

You'll take a bus to the village of Champex and its charming lake where you can go for a refreshing swim. Champex is the largest Swiss village you will pass through on the TMB. If you need supplies, it's best to grab them here for the next couple of days. There are a few shops, a bakery, and several restaurants to enjoy.

Various accommodations are on offer here. The more expensive options lie just on Lake Champex. One of the less expensive options in the area, though simpler, is **Gite Bon Abri** (Rte du Vallon 9; tel. 27 783 14 23; www.gite-bon-abri.com; €79) with dormitories that can be a bit noisy (creaky wood). If you are looking to splurge a bit, the **Hotel Splendide** (Rte de Signal, 22; tel. 277831145; €170) lives up to its name. The views here, not to mention the food, will make you feel like you have landed in the lap of luxury at this point on your journey on the TMB.

Champex to Trient

Hiking Distance and Time: 16 km (10 mi) with 700 m (2,297 ft) ascent, 800 m (2,625 ft) descent; 6 hours

★ 1. Les Bovines

You've been discovering the Swiss mountain pastures, and their cows that produce some of the most renowned cheeses from the Alps, so it should come as no surprise that the regular route is called the Bovine Route. It offers fantastic views of the Rhone Valley and the Valais Mountains.

Strike out from Champex following the trail northeast. At the forest junction, take a right following the signs for Gite Bon Abri. The forest path continues for about 500 m (0.25 mi) before crossing the quaint village of Champex d'en Bas. Turn left, cross a bridge, and continue for 1 km (0.5 mile) until the junction at Plan de l'Au. Here you will take a left and begin the trek through Les Bovines. Pastural and epically alpine, this section of the TMB is a real joy to trek.

Safety Note: As calm and tranquil as the cows usually are, every year a handful of hikers are gored. A common sign a cow is becoming aggressive is if it shakes its head back and forth.

While you're here, it would be impossible to skip the treats at the **Alpage de Bovine** (Le Fays 1, Martigny-Combe; tel. 79 679 23 11; 9am-5pm daily). These cakes are a sort of rite of passage for those trekking the TMB.

2. Col de la Forclaz

After the Alpage de Bovine, the path continues its descent through another forested path. There are a few sharp drops off to your right, but it is a pleasant, often shaded path. After about 2 km (1.2 mi), the trees begin to thin out as you reach the road at the Col de la Forclaz. After the gift shop, you will come to another junction from which you can follow the well-signed path to the right. From here, the path is a series of switchbacks downhill until you reach a footbridge and then Trient.

left, Les Bovines; right, Col de la Forclaz

The Arpette Window

Hiking Distance and Time: 14 km (8.7 mi) with 1,200 m (3,937 ft) ascent, 1,400 m (4,593 ft) descent; 8 hours

If you're seeking more of a challenge, rather than hiking Les Bovines, take the route to the Arpette Window (2,665 m/8,743 ft), which is more technical but offers one of the best views on the entire trip. There are sections of this route with loose scree and boulder fields, so footing will be occasionally difficult. Only take this route in good weather, when there's no snow later in the season, and if you are comfortable with this type of terrain.

Near the Champex tourist station, you'll come to the **La Breya Chairlift.** Follow the sign here for **Relais d'Arpette.** As you follow the path, a stream will be trickling away to your left. In a little more than 1.5 km (0.9 mi) you'll reach a junction. Take a right. Follow the path across the stream until you come to the junction with the **Col de Ecandies** path. Take another right. You'll begin a sharp ascent where you will undoubtedly hit large patches of scree and boulder fields. This is the most challenging part of the day's hike as the path continues uphill before reaching the apex. This climb takes a few hours. Your reward at the top is the **"Fenêtre d'Arpette,"** the window onto the Trient Glacier. Take in the views and enjoy the day's victory before beginning your descent.

The descent follows the path straight out, along the cliffs, and to some ruined buildings. The rest of the nearly 2 km (1.2 mi) of path is an easy walk to the Trient Glacier. You'll find the **Buvette de Trient** (Le Tissot 20, Trient; tel. 79 635 96 44; https://buvetteduglaciertrient.ch), where you can find a refreshment before continuing the last few kilometers to Trient. Just follow the path to the right at the junction to connect with the main TMB trail.

Either route you take this day ends at the village of **Trient** (1,280 m/4,199 ft).

WATCH

Alive: A Seven Day Solo Adventure on the Tour du Mont Blanc by Abbie Barnes: This YouTube video offers a two-hour deep dive into TMB, including footage of Abbie as she hikes in various weather conditions.

READ

Tour du Mont Blanc: The Most Iconic Long-Distance Circular Trail in the Alps by Kingsley Jones: This is a must-read if you are interested in the various routes possible for the TMB. The Cicerone guide by the late Kev Reynolds is another staple for those preparing for their hike.

LISTEN

The ***Hiiker Podcast:*** Season 1, Episode 3 of this podcast, covering trails around the world, focuses on the Tour du Mont Blanc.

The Tour du Mont Blanc episode on ***Trails Worth Hiking*** by Jeremy Pendrey: This podcast episode begins with a historic overview of the Tour du Mont Blanc and has great tips for families looking to attempt the hike.

3. Trient

After this challenging day on the TMB, you will be forgiven if you slump down into a comfy lounger and spend the rest of the day sipping on your beverage of choice. Stay at the **Hôtel la Grande Ourse** (Le Betty 30; tel. 277221754; www.la-grande-ourse.ch; €35), where there are a few private rooms mixed with the dormitories. Take a moment, if you haven't already, to get to know a few of your fellow hikers along the TMB. This area crosses with another hiking trail, the Haute Route, or High Route. You may meet a hiker or two who has done the TMB, maybe even multiple times, and is now tackling this secondary, though no less beautiful, trail through the Alps.

DAY 7

Trient, Switzerland, to Argentière, France

Hiking Distance and Time: 10 km (6.2 mi) with 900 m (2,953 ft) ascent, 750 m (2,460 ft) descent; 5.5 hours

1. Col de Balme

The Col de Balme (2,191 m/7,188 ft) marks the **Franco-Swiss border.** From here, you bid adieu to Switzerland and a big bonjour to France, and the penultimate leg of your epic trek through the alps. The hike up to the Col de Balme will get the day's biggest climb out of the way quickly.

In Trient, follow the trek south past the pink church and Le Peuty. Follow a series of switchbacks leading up from the

Trient Valley, which is a pleasant, forested climb. The path eases for 2 km (about 1 mi) before another series of steep switchbacks brings you to the Col de Balme. As with the many climbs on the TMB, you are rewarded with amazing views. Here you will enjoy a panoramic view of Mont Black, the Sea of Ice, and the vast glacier of Argenière.

2. Montroc

The good news is that it's all downhill from here, and if your legs are screaming at you, you can forgo the hiking on part of this section, opt for the **chairlift** (€16) you pass along this route.

From the Col de Balme, follow the signs for **Charamillon** and **Le Tour,** veering off the main track. This 2-km (1.2-mi) stretch zigzags a bit under the cable car and there are some loose stones. At both Le Tour and Montroc, just a farther 1 km (about 0.5 mi) down the path, there are a few gites and refuges to stop for refreshments if needed. Continue on the path. At **Tré la Champ,** follow the sign to descend into the village of Argentière.

3. Argentière

Just when you thought you couldn't get enough of quaint mountain villages, you descend on Argentière, where the cobblestone paths and rustic mountain architecture are just appetizers before the majestic, postcard-perfect mountain views. There are several options for sleeping and eating. At **Hôtel La Couronne** (285 Rue Charlet Straton; tel. 4 50 54 00 02; www.hotelcouronne.com; €85), you can look forward to private lodgings if you have been booking dormitories throughout your hike. For dinner, dig into some hearty French mountain cuisine at **La P'tite Verte** (89 Rue Charlet Straton; tel. 450 54 54 54; https://la-ptite-verte-restaurant-argentiere.eatbu.com; noon-2pm and 7pm-9:30pm Thurs.-Mon.).

DAY 8

Argentière to Chamonix

Hiking Distance and Time: 11 km (6.8 mi) with 950 m (3,117 ft) ascent, 650 m (2,133 ft) descent; 5 hours

1. Sentier Botanique

Strike out from Argentière, but not before you make sure you have your picnic fixings ready. You will want to picnic later on along the Lac Blanc. Follow the route you descended yesterday from Tré le Champ. At the car park, continue north going straight along the Sentier Botanique. The beginning of this route is challenging as you will climb a series of switchbacks that cut up above the cliffs of the **Aiguilles-Rouges** massif. Once at the top, the gradients ease up, leaving you to catch your breath for those breathtaking views.

2. Lacs des Chéserys

Not quite as well-known as its sister, Lac Blanc, Lacs des Chéserys is no less beautiful. After crossing the Aiguilles-Rouges

Lac Blanc

massif, the trail comes to a junction, **La Tête aux Vents,** where two of the primary trails through the Alps meet. From here, you'll follow the signs for Lac Blanc. Along this balcony ridge trail, you'll spot Lac Chésery about 500 m (0.25 mi) along the way. Be respectful of your fellow hikers if people are pushing through, but do keep your camera handy for some spectacular reflections of Mont Blanc in the still lake waters.

★ 3. Lac Blanc

In many ways, this is the culmination of your time along the TMB. The path continues from Lac Chésery where you come to a rocky section as you turn and see Lac Blanc for the first time. It is impossible not to feel a surge of adrenaline as you descend to the lake. Just watch your footing on the way down! This lake is quite popular along the TMB and it is highly unlikely you will find yourself with the entire lake to yourself. Explore the trails around the lake to find your quiet corner, pull out your picnic fixings, and take in the splendor. You will want to take a few pictures, but do yourself a favor and put the camera away for a little while just to take it all in. At this point, you truly deserve it!

4. Chamonix

After wringing out every possible moment along Lac Blanc, it's time to begin your final descent into Chamonix. It is an easy walk from Lac Blanc to **La Flégere,** where you can take the **gondola** down to Chamonix Les Praz. Depending on how you're feeling, you could walk the 3 km (1.75 mi) or take the next bus into Chamonix where your tour began.

TRANSPORTATION

Air

Geneva International Airport (GVA; www.gva.ch) is the closest airport to Chamonix. From the airport, you can arrange either a private or shared transfer (1 hour) or take a bus (1.5 hours; €10-40). **Alpy Bus** (www.alpybus.com), **Swiss Tours** (www.swisstours-office.ch), and **BlaBla Car Bus** (www.sncf-connect.com/blablacar-bus) operate bus services between Geneva Airport and Chamonix.

If you're arriving in Geneva after a long flight, try to book a flight that arrives early in the morning or even the day before so that you have time to acclimate in Chamonix and you're not jetlagged when you start hiking.

Train

Taking the train from Geneva Airport or central Geneva at **Geneva Gare Cornavin** (www.sbb.ch) to Chamonix requires a transfer and takes nearly twice as long as the bus (3 hours). From the city center, you can take the Léman Express and then transfer to the Mont Blanc Express at the Saint Gervais-les-Bains station for Chamonix.

The Mont Blanc Express arrives at the **Chamonix-Mont-Blanc train station** (Rue des Allobroges) in central Chamonix, a 10-minute walk to the cable car to L'Aiguille du Midi.

Bus

Buses from Geneva arrive at **Chamonix Sud bus station** (Av. De Courmayeur) at the southern end of central Chamonix, a five-minute walk to the cable car to L'Aiguille du Midi.

Getting Back

From Chamonix, take the bus back to Geneva to connect with your next destination via train or plane.

- The Rhone Valley (page 618)
- The Alps (page 648)

CINQUE TERRE

Why Go: In a country full of spectacular views, the Cinque Terre is a standout, with seaside trails, hypnotic sunsets, and the secret to the perfect pesto.

Number of Days: 3

Total Distance: 14 km (9 mi)

Seasons: Late spring and summer

Start/End: Riomaggiore

Though barely the size of Manhattan, Parco Nazionale delle Cinque Terre (www.parconazionale5terre.it), Italy's first national park, makes a huge impression. It's got the Mediterranean, mountains, five charming villages, and one hell of a coastline. It's the five (cinque) villages dotted along the mountainous coast—Riomaggiore, Manarola, Corniglia, Vernazza, and Monterosso al Mare—that give the area its name. They were founded more than 1,000 years ago by inhabitants who survived by carving (literally) a living from the surrounding hillsides and fishing. Many traditions faded after the railway line, inaugurated in 1870, brought the outside world in, but grapes and olives are still ubiquitous, and a few veteran fishermen still cast their nets.

Today people from all over the world come here to hike along old mule trails that boast panoramic views of the coast and sea. Beware, these are not laid-back strolls on a flat beach—they require solid shoes and a will to hike. If you've got that and a love of nature, you'll be rewarded with some of the most beautiful vistas you've ever seen.

TOP 3

★ Getting a seaside view of all five villages on a **sunset tour** with Cinque Terre dal Mare (page 429).

★ Discovering the extreme lengths **Azienda Agricola Cheo** have gone to produce wine (page 434).

Learning to prepare perfect pesto at **Nessun Dorma** (page 437).

Trail Tips

If you follow a few rules and a lot of common sense, you'll have an amazing time. Here are some tips.

- **Hike kindly:** Hiking isn't a solitary activity, and you'll meet a lot of people along the way. It's common to greet fellow hikers with "Buon giorno" and politely give way to people as they frequently pass. Also, respect plants, animals, cultures, and traditions. Hike marked paths only. Don't leave any trace of your passing.
- **Wear appropriate shoes:** You can recognize the tourists wearing flip-flops by the pain inscribed on their faces. Don't make the same mistake—invest in a solid pair of hiking books. It's actually forbidden to wear open-toed or smooth-soled shoes, and transgressors can be fined accordingly.
- **Be realistic:** Don't try hiking beyond your ability. Stick to the trails at your level.
- **Prepare:** Do your homework before hiking each trail and know what to expect. Get the latest trail conditions from the info points or download Pn5t plus, the free Cinque Terre app. Detailed paper maps facilitate exploration, but the next best thing is the official **Cinque Terre website** (www.parconazionale5terre.it), which should be consulted before and during the journey.
- **Mind the weather:** Mudslides are a real possibility, and even light rain can render trails unsafe. The civil protection agency issues yellow, orange, and red warnings according to the level of risk, and the latter two lead to trail closures. The latest trail info is available from each of the five tourist info points located inside the train stations.
- **Hydrate:** Pack a water bottle and remember to drink. You can top up at village fountains or any bar where they will happily provide a refill: "Aqua, per favore" ("Water, please").
- **Pay hiking fees:** There's a fee to hike some of the sections and the revenue is used to maintain the entire trail network. **Cinque Terre Cards** (www.parconazionale5terre.it) provide access to all trails.

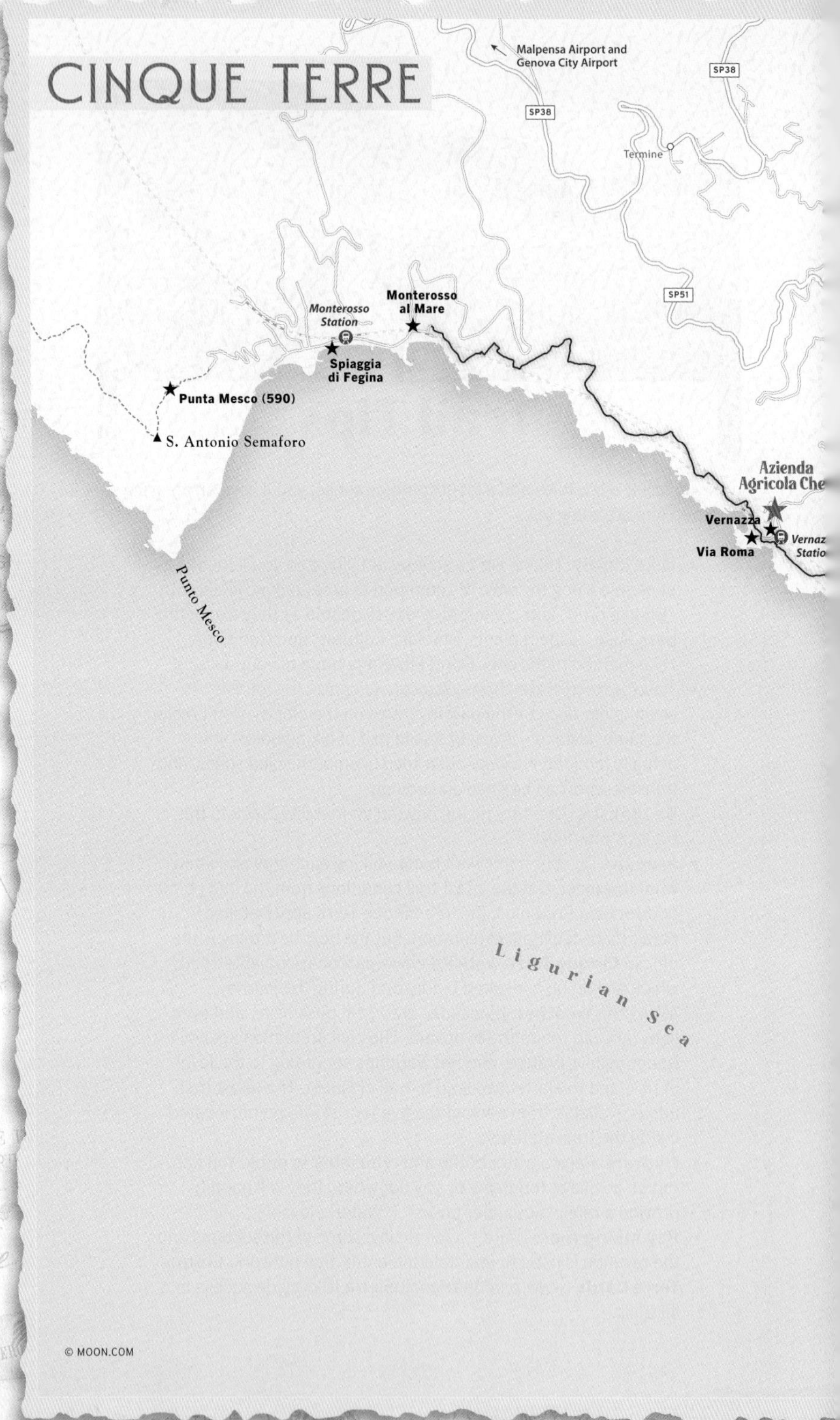

CINQUE TERRE
Malpensa Airport and Genova City Airport
SP38
SP38
Termine
SP51
Monterosso al Mare
Monterosso Station
Spiaggia di Fegina
Punta Mesco (590)
S. Antonio Semaforo
Punto Mesco
Azienda Agricola Che
Vernazza
Via Roma
Vernaz Statio
Ligurian Sea
© MOON.COM

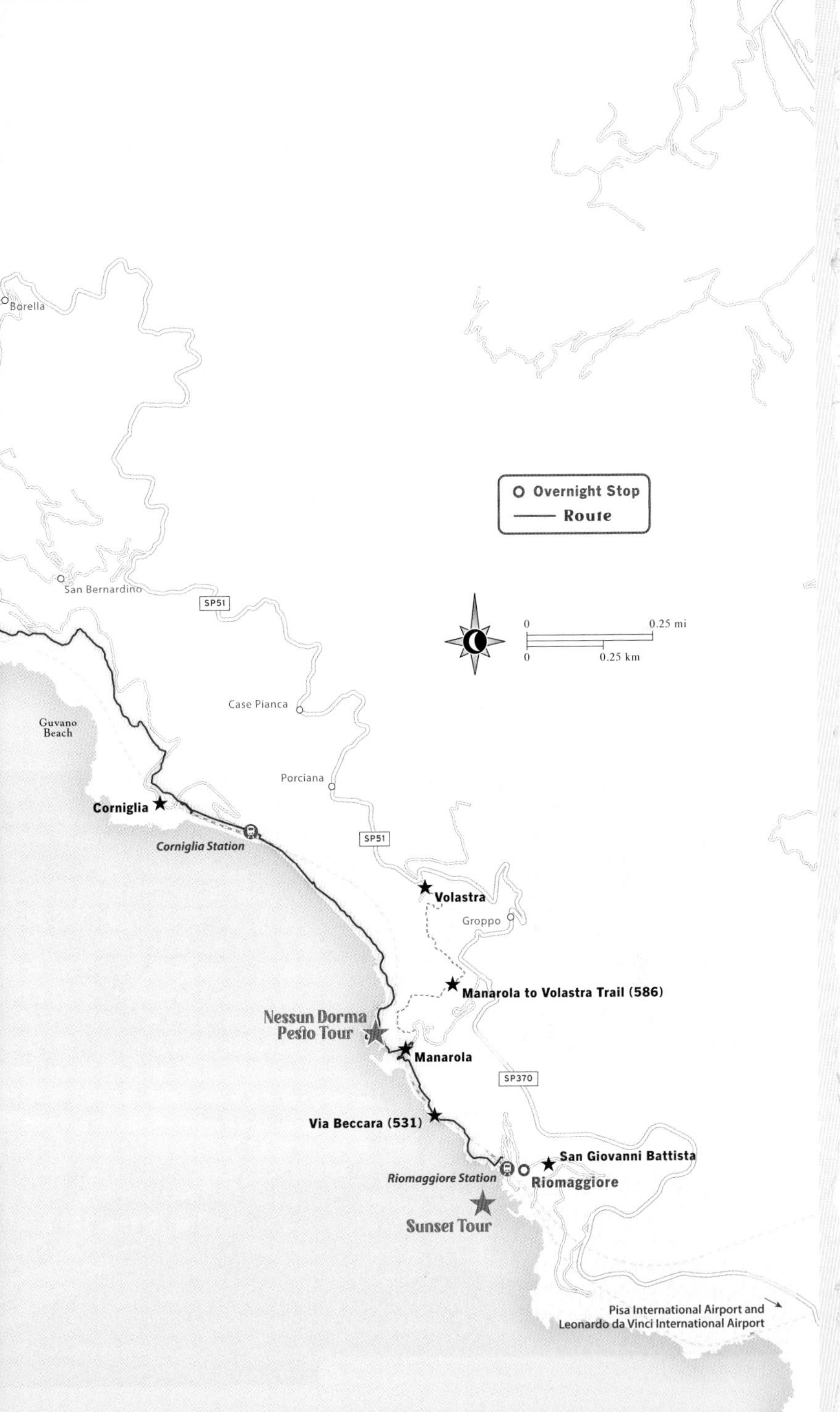
Borella
San Bernardino
SP51
Case Pianca
Porciana
SP51
Guvano Beach
Corniglia
Corniglia Station
Volastra
Groppo
Manarola to Volastra Trail (586)
Nessun Dorma Pesto Tour
Manarola
SP370
Via Beccara (531)
San Giovanni Battista
Riomaggiore Station
Riomaggiore
Sunset Tour
Pisa International Airport and
Leonardo da Vinci International Airport
Overnight Stop
Route
0
0.25 mi
0
0.25 km

Riomaggiore

Where to Stay: Riomaggiore (for the entire trip)

Arrive by: Train to Riomaggiore Station

1. Riomaggiore Town

It's hard to choose a favorite Cinque Terre town. They all have their charm and were all built with the same geographic constraints. Riomaggiore is the first, or the last, depending on your perspective, and makes a good base for this route.

Riomaggiore is a one-main-street town. **Via Colombo** is lined with small souvenir shops and bustling eateries. Start your stroll around the town with a protein-rich lunch from **Il Pescato Cucinato** (Via Colombo, 199; tel. 339/262-4815; 11:30am-9:30pm daily; €6-12). Their menu of street food features fresh squid, prawns, and vegetables, dipped in batter, lightly fried and served in small or large paper cones. If you prefer to sit while you chew, head to **Piazza Vignaoli.** Another good picnic spot is the medieval fortress, **Castello Riomaggiore,** with a trio of benches overlooking the port.

Via Colombo gets steeper the farther up you go, and near the top you'll see signs for **San Giovanni Battista** (Via Pecunia 47; free). This pretty church overlooks town, and from the square out front you get an eyeful of pastel buildings, rooftops, and the sea. The original church dates from the 14th century but it was rebuilt after it collapsed in 1870. The Gothic

left, Riomaggiore; right, Santuario di Nostra Signora di Montenero

Key Reservations

Accommodation is limited throughout the **Cinque Terre** (3,000 rooms), and reservations, especially during peak summer months, are recommended. Restaurants fill up fast and tables with sunset views are a limited commodity. Some, like **Nessun Dorma,** have reservation apps that facilitate the process. Most don't, so show up early (7pm or 7:30pm) or call ahead. Cooking **experiences** and kayak **tours** require a little advance planning as well.

The **Cinque Terre Card** (www.parconazionale5terre.it) is available online or from the **park info points.** You'll need it to walk some coastal trails; there are trekking-only options, but the convenient **Treno** option includes **unlimited train travel** (single or multiday) between each village and the towns of **Levanto** (north) and **La Spezia** (south), from which most travelers arrive.

rose window is the only original feature to have survived.

2. Sanctuary Trail (593V)

Distance: *1.5 km (0.9 mi) one-way*
Time: *40-50 minutes one-way*
Difficulty: *Strenuous*
Elevation: *335 m above sea level (1,099 ft)*
Trailhead: *Piazza Vignaoili/Via Antonio Gransci*

Looking up, it's hard to miss the hilltops above the Cinque Terre. That's where ancestors of today's inhabitants built their religious sanctuaries. The one in Riomaggiore is called **Santuario di Nostra Signora di Montenero** and is connected to town via a long set of stone stairs. They provide a good indicator of the difficulty to come, and if you have trouble climbing these you may want to consider alternatives to walking between the villages.

This is a short steep hike; a couple of roads need to be crossed, and small red and white stripes indicate the way. Like everything in the Cinque Terre, it's worth the climb and after 40-50 minutes you'll get your first glimpse of the Cinque Terre coastline, the Ligurian Sea, and (on clear days) the three islands in the Gulf of Poets. The sanctuary itself is usually closed but there are tables and benches to rest and admire the view. Take the same way back and get back to Riomaggiore within an hour.

Reward yourself with aperitivo (Italian happy hour) at **Ghemè** (Via Colombo 160; tel.339/374-5381; www.gheme5terre.com; 10am-8pm Wed.-Sun.; €7-10), sitting and sampling the area's dry white wine.

★ 3. Sunset Tour with Cinque Terre dal Mare

Via San Giacomo; tel. 366/509-9026; sunset tour 1 hour; €130 for 1-6 passengers

The Cinque Terre look a lot different from the sea than they do on land, and you can get an instant impression of the coastline from a boat. They can't be rented without a captain as the park includes a protected marine reserve, but leaving the sailing to locals means you can relax and enjoy the view. On this sunset tour, you'll get an eyeful of coastline and swim in a secluded cove.

Afterward, all that's left to do is eat. At **Osteria La Torpedine** (Via Antonio Gramsci 25; tel. 018/792-0692; 1pm-3pm and 7:30-11pm Tues.-Sun., 6pm-midnight Mon.; €9-12), the menu of local flavors includes stuffed mussels, stewed cuttlefish, and of course pesto served with trofie pasta, and tables are set up in a little courtyard off the main street.

Corniglia

Arrive by: Train from Riomaggiore Station to Corniglia Station (5 minutes)

1. Via Fieschi

Corniglia is the smallest of the Cinque Terre towns, and unlike the others it doesn't have direct access to the sea. Climb the long zigzag staircase from the station to town, where the action is concentrated along Via Fieschi. Keep going, and you'll reach a clifftop terrace with a great view and coin-operated binoculars for taking a magnified look.

Corniglia has two of the best **gelateria** in the Cinque Terre, both on Via Fieshi. Who says you can't have gelato for breakfast? **Alberto** (Via Fieschi 74; tel. 366/717-7602; 9:30am-8pm daily; €3-5) prepares basil flavored ice cream along with traditional flavors and granita, which is like Italian ice without the artificial flavors. **Gelateria Artigianale Corniglia** (Via Fieschi 43; tel. 333/803-5011; 9am-11pm daily; €2-5) is a cone's throw away and makes everything by hand using local fruit, honey, and even ricotta cheese.

You can stock up on fruit and drinks for the hike or have a panino (sandwich) made with local cheese and cold cuts at **A Butiega** (Via Fieschi, 142; 8:15am-7pm daily).

Via Fieschi

2. Sentiero Azzurro (592-3)

Distance: *3.5 km (2.2 mi)*
Time: *2 hours*
Difficulty: *Moderately strenuous*
Elevation: *209 m above sea level (686 ft)*
Trailhead: *Via Stazione/Via Fleschi (next to Lisa Market)*
Fee: *€7.50*

It doesn't take long to visit Corniglia, and once you have you can set out on the Sentiero Azzurro (Blue Trail), which is a favorite with travelers (and one of the busiest) and provides great scenery close to the seaside. The trail is one of the oldest and dates from the Middle Ages when going over land was the only way to move between towns. Today, it's a well-maintained path with sections in stone, dirt, and stairs. Vegetation is a mix of Mediterranean shrub, agave, and prickly pear. There are ancient bridges, small streams, and the kind of rock formations that excite amateur geologists.

It takes about two hours to reach Vernazza, and halfway along is the small hamlet of **Prevo,** where you can fill up your water bottle and order some caffeine. For more sustenance, make a lunch stop at **La Torre** (Loc. Preteccia 1; tel. 331/883-6610; noon-4pm and 6pm-8pm daily; €11-14), which is right off the Blue Trail at the entrance to Vernazza. Tables are set on two shaded terraces overlooking the town and the sea stretching out into the distance. This is the place to sample paccheri al sugo di pesce (pasta with fish sauce) and trofie al pesto.

Cinque Terre Sunsets

If you like sunsets, you've come to the right place. They're hard to miss in the Cinque Terre and there are plenty of great vantage points in each town to watch fading light transform sky and sea.

- **Riomaggiore:** If you can handle a short 30-minute hike to **Il Sole 180°** (Litoranea Cinqueterre, SP370; tel. 018/792-0201; 5pm-midnight daily; €6.50-8) you'll get an eyeful at this little bar-restaurant with an outdoor terrace overlooking the coast. If you want a front-row seat, reserve in advance.
- **Manarola:** Providing delicious food while light fades over the Ligurian Sea, **Trattoria dal Billy** (Via A. Rollandi 122, Manarola; tel. 018/792-0628; €8-14) serves up house-made pasta and thick, flavorful fish sauces. The restaurant is a short walk (down a long tunnel) from the Manarola train station. Trains stop running at midnight, so you can get a twilight view of town before heading back to Riomaggiore.
- **Corniglia:** Sunsets don't take much planning here and can be improvised without need of reservations or formalities. The terrace at the end of Via Solferino is a popular gathering spot with fellow travelers who happen to be at the right spot at the right hour. You can accompany the view with a spritz (€7) and cheese or cold cut platter from **Bar Terza Terra** (Via Fieschi 215; tel. 345/523-0369; noon-11pm Tues.-Sun.; €7-12) a few yards away. They don't mind if you bring glasses outside as long as you return them later.
- **Vernazza:** This colorful village is perched on a rocky spur that gradually alters shades with the onset of evening. The best place to watch the transformation is from the trail at the southern entrance of town. It may not be as comfortable as the other spots and requires standing, but it is one of the most photogenic (page 434).
- **Monterosso:** At the top of **Punta Mesco,** the entire Cinque Terre coastline is visible. There are always a few hikers who make the pilgrimage; many carry wine, and good cheer abounds well after the sun has set (page 435).

Through-Hiking the Cinque Terre

There are many ways to hike the Cinque Terre trails. You can hike the entire trail north to south or south to north. What changes is the steepness and the perspective upon the sea in relation to the movement of the sun. The **one-day hike** is a unique experience and no doubt the most challenging.

Below are the main segments of the hike that links all five towns of the Cinque Terre, listed from south to north. Distances and times given are all one-way; hiking fees, which are covered by the Cinque Terre Card, apply on segments between Corniglia and Monterosso, as well as the Via dell'Amore when it reopens.

RIOMAGGIORE TO MANAROLA

Trail: *531-506 (La Beccara)*
Distance: *1.9 km (1.2 mi)*
Time: *1 hour*
Difficulty: *Strenuous*
Elevation: *228 m above sea level (748 ft)*
Elevation Change: *203 m (666 ft) ascent, 209 m (686 ft) descent*
Trailhead: *Via S. Antonio/Salita Castello*

Don't judge a trail by its distance. This may look short on a map but there's a long steady up-and-down hike ahead of you. Along the way you'll pass vegetable gardens and cross a small bridge before ascending the long staircase past the cultivated terraces along the **Costa Corniolo ridge.** Many people stop at the top to view the Cinque Terre for the first time and understand what all the fuss is about. The descent follows an ancient staircase with many sections that are carved into the hillside.

Note that the popular **Via dell'Amore path** (hiking fee €7.50) that also connects Riomaggiore and Manarola was closed due to mudslides and is due to reopen by summer 2024.

MANAROLA TO CORNIGLIA

Trail: *506-586-587*
Distance: *6.7 km (4.2 mi)*
Time: *2 hours*
Difficulty: *Strenuous*
Elevation: *401 m above sea level (1,316 ft)*
Elevation Change: *399 m (1,309 ft) ascent, 333 m (1,093 ft) descent*
Trailhead: *Port of Manarola*

Since the closure of the panoramic **Blue Trail** (592-2) that runs at sea level between these towns, getting from one to the other has become more challenging. It is the hardest stage and requires switching trails twice. The first section is simply backtracking up the ancient stone steps to the 586 that is the easiest and most panoramic section that follows the ridgeline. It passes through the hamlet of **Volastra** where hikers gather at the bar and consult maps. It takes about 50 minutes to reach the 587, which heads steeply down natural staircasing to Corniglia.

CORNIGLIA TO VERNAZZA

Trail: *592-3 (hiking fee €7.50)*
Distance: *3.5 km (2.2 mi)*
Time: *2 hours*
Difficulty: *Moderate*
Elevation: *209 m above sea level (686 ft)*
Elevation Change: *140 m (459 ft) ascent, 218 m (715 ft) descent*
Trailhead: *Via Stazione*

This stage is only slightly less challenging than the previous and starts with a staircase with 33 railings and 377 uneven steps. Then, it's across a paved road and down a high stone-walled section that leads up and over the rugged hillside. Dense vegetation forms around the trail, making it occasionally secluded and tunnel-like. On a one-day through-hike starting around 8am, lunchtime should hit while you're on this segment and near **ITTITURISMO** (Strada Provinciale Corniglia-San Bernardino; tel. 392/587-3791; 11:30am-3:30pm and 7pm-10:30pm daily; €18-20). The owner is a fisherman, and whatever he catches is what they serve. His wife prepares hefty portions of pasta and mixed grilled fish in an informal outdoor garden with great views.

VERNAZZA TO MONTEROSSO

Trail: *592-4 (hiking fee €7.50)*
Distance: *3.6 km (2.2 mi)*
Time: *2 hours*
Difficulty: *Moderate*
Elevation: *174 m (571 ft)*
Elevation Change: *214 m (702 ft) ascent, 223 m (732 ft) descent*
Trailhead: *Church of St. Margaret of Antioch*

Getting out of town is as much fun as arriving and there are plenty of narrow alleys and porticoes in Vernazza to explore. These tight spaces are known as carruggio in local dialect, derived from the Latin quadrivium (crossroads), and make it possible to get momentarily lost. After that it's another stair ascent to a hard-packed dirt path with steep drops. Toward the end, the trail cuts through ancient lemon groves and terraced vineyards. Mediterranean brush often blocks the views and the trail is often flanked by high stone walls.

Perhaps the best reason to hike the Cinque Terre from south to north is diving into the warm Ligurian Sea at Monterosso's **Spiaggia di Fegina** at the end. You could also stay dry and finish the journey at the cliff where the **Capuchin convent** is located. From there you can look back and see nearly all the way back to where you started.

Vernazza

Arrive by: *Hiking the Sentiero Azzurro from Corniglia*

3. Via Roma

Vernazza is a photogenic village with a Gothic church and colorful houses overlooking a small port alive with activity. It's located near the highest point in the Cinque Terre and was founded over a thousand years ago. The architecture is distinct, and elaborately carved loggias and porticoes hint of economic prosperity the other towns never achieved. Via Roma is the main and busiest street in Vernazza. Its shops and restaurants are full most of the day and lead to the little port where boats are neatly lined against the concrete storm break that keeps the water calm.

★ 4. Wine Tour at Azienda Agricola Cheo

Via Brigate Partigiane 1; tel. 333/959-4759; www.cheo.it, 2:30pm-6:30pm Oct.-Apr.; €25-35 pp

It's time to take your wine IQ up a notch at Azienda Agricola Cheo. The owners will walk you around the winery and down into their cellar, all the while explaining what it takes to make wine in these parts. It's not easy. Steep hills make tending and harvesting grapes challenging. The solution required digging terraces into the hillsides so vines could be planted. Cheo's vineyard consists of 70 terraces growing bosco, albarola, and vermentino that vary in altitude, and each has a historic name. Tours last 1-2 hours and end with a sampling of Cheo's latest vintages.

left, Monterosso al Mare; right, Via Roma, Vernazza

Monterosso al Mare

Arrive by: Train from Vernazza Station to Monterosso Station (4 minutes)

5. Spiaggia di Fegina

Monterosso is the largest of the Cinque Terre and the one that gets the most crowded. Hop on the train to get there. The Monterosso train station is directly in front of the beach, Spiaggia di Fegina, with a boardwalk in between with benches looking out over the sea. Take just a moment here, though it's tempting to opt out of further activity, rent a lounge chair, and just relax on this long and sandy beach.

6. Kayaking with Carnassa

Beach Bar Stella Marina, Via Fegina 9/BIS; tel. 348/618-5603; www.carnassa.com

Chiara Maschio, who grew up near the Lago di Como and has spent the past five years in Monterosso, knows water and runs Carnassa, a small tour company that leads groups (max. 10) on 2-3-hour kayak tours around the coast (€65-80). There are tiny inlets and a waterfall to discover onboard single and double sit-on-top kayaks. These are easy to use, even if you've never paddled before. Tours include swimming and snorkeling breaks and all the equipment you'll need to have fun. To reserve, write to Chiara and let her know when you're coming.

7. Punta Mesco (590)

Distance: *2.5 km (1.6 mi) round-trip*
Time: *1.5 hours*
Difficulty: *Strenuous*
Elevation: *300 m above sea level (984 ft)*
Trailhead: *Via Fegina (near the beach)*

Monterosso isn't the end of the Cinque Terre. If you want to go the distance, you need to hike up to the Punta Mesco promontory. The trail starts at the end of the beachfront on Via Fegina and follows a paved road up to Hotel Suisse. After a half-dozen switchbacks you'll reach a turnoff with a steep set of stairs. That's where things get tough: This trail is rugged but there is a panoramic payoff along with ruins of an ancient hermitage and an abandoned military post. It takes about 45 minutes to reach the top and a lot less to return to town.

Back in Monterosso, have dinner at **L'Osteria** (Via Vittorio Emanuele 5; tel. 018/781-9224; noon-2pm and 7pm-9:30pm Tues.-Sun.; €10-13). Big portions of grilled fish and a selection of traditional pastas are a good way to refuel after an active day. Head back to Riomaggiore by train (21 minutes).

DAY 3

Manarola

Arrive by: Hiking Via Beccara from Riomaggiore

1. Via Beccara (531)

Distance: *2km (1.2 mi)*
Time: *45 minutes*
Difficulty: *Strenuous*
Elevation: *228 m above sea level (748 ft)*
Trailhead: *Via S. Antonio/Salito del Castello*

From Riomaggiore, there are two ways of getting to Manarola—arguably the prettiest of the Cinque Terre towns—but since the panoramic **Via dell'Amore** (Path of Love) was closed due to mudslides (scheduled to reopen in summer 2024) there has only been one: Via Beccara (531). It follows an inland route and is much more difficult, with a steep climb and descent. There's plenty of vegetation and the opportunity to spot wildlife

Regional Cuisine

Most of the dishes that Italy is famous for have very humble origins, and those in the Cinque Terre are no different. They call it **cucina povera,** or poor kitchen, but that doesn't mean it doesn't taste great; it just means ingredients are simple and nothing gets wasted.

Here, seafood is a central ingredient, and anchovies, sea bass, squid, cuttlefish, and octopus are fixtures of most menus. They're flavored with the oregano, thyme, and marjoram that grow on the hillsides and seasoned with olive oil. Vegetables grow in the gardens above each of the towns and produce the cabbage, potatoes, artichokes, leeks, and chard that are transformed into soups and savory pies.

- **Pesto:** Originated in Liguria, pesto ranks among the most renown pasta sauces. You can find it in a jar around the world, but it won't taste the same as it does here. Locals say it's about the basil, which has a different flavor here and is impossible to re-create anywhere else. Try it served with short trofie pasta, green beans, and potatoes, and you be the judge.
- **Stuffed mussels:** Locals like to stuff their mussels. It's done by combining fresh mussels with garlic, breadcrumbs, mortadella, eggs, grated cheese, and spices, which are placed in the shells and sautéed with tomatoes and olive oil. It's served as an appetizer or second course.
- **Zucchini flower pancakes:** When you can't afford to throw food away you find creative ways of preparing it. Frittelle di fiori di zucchino is a case in point and a delicious solution for making use of the seemingly discardable zucchini flower. It's chopped and combined with flour, water, and salt into a pancake-like mix that is then deep fried. It smells great, and after 60 seconds the round patties are drained and should be eaten while still warm. There's a fry shop in each Cinque Terre town that serves zucchini flowers and other calorie-intensive treats.
- **Cinque Terre and sciacchetrà wines:** Vineyards were in a serious decline in the middle of the 20th century, which was reversed by the creation of the Agricultural Cooperative in the early 1980s. They helped establish DOC (Controlled Designation of Origin) status for the area and the creation of the Cinque Terre and sciacchetrà wines. The first is dry and delicate, suitable for seafood, snacks, and sunset happy hours. It's made from a combination of bosco, alberola, and vermentino grapes, which grow well on the terraced hillsides. Sciacchetrà is a naturally sweet, fortified wine (14%) served with desserts and dry biscuits or on its own after dinner. It's produced from the pressing of fermented white grapes at the end of November.

overhead (herring gulls, peregrine falcons, buzzards) and on the ground (wild boar, badgers, foxes, and wall lizards). The trail is exposed with little shade along the way, and your skin will be better off if you get an early start. A viewing area at the top lets hikers rest and enjoy the view.

★ 2. Nessun Dorma Pesto Tour

Localita Punta Bonfiglio; tel. 340/888-4133; www.nessundormacinqueterre.com; noon-7:30pm Wed.-Mon.; €6-12

The pesto tour at Nessun Dorma starts at 10:30am, and you don't want to be late. This isn't your average cooking class, and it's not just because of the view. It's because of Simone and the passion he has for pesto and all the traditions that make the Cinque Terre special. The experience starts with an introduction to the famed sauce, and then you pick basil in a seaside garden, grind it in Carrara marble mortars, and add a few local ingredients to complete the magic. Lunch is the goal here and the best pesto wins a little prize. Aprons are provided and a wine tasting with a Ligurian sommelier is included.

Nessun Dorma has the best view of Manarola, so it's worth coming even if you don't want to get your hands green. There are lots of tables lining their terrace, but it's still useful to download their app and keep track of the wait. Once you are seated, order bruschette—focacce with fresh toppings—and a cheese or cured meat platter. It's all delicious and accompanied with local wine or Italian beer.

Volastra

Arrive by: Hiking from Manarola

3. Manarola to Volastra Trail (586)

Distance: *2.8 km (1.7 mi)*
Time: *1 hour*
Difficulty: *Strenuous*
Elevation gain: *500 m (1,640 ft)*
Trailhead: *Via Antonio Discovolo*

Getting to Volastra has never been easy and you need to be in top shape to get there. If your body is sending strange signals, this is not the hike for you. The 500-m (1,640-ft) elevation differential means views are good, but reaching them requires sweating. The trip up takes over an hour and cuts through dozens of vineyards. Many have been fenced off to prevent overeager hikers from nabbing grapes, so you're better off bringing your own snacks and especially water. Most of the trail is one long ascent up age-old stones.

The sleepy hamlet at the top is Volastra, where you'll find a sanctuary, several wineries, and fellow hikers studying the large map outside **Locanda Tiabuscion** (Via Nostra Signora della Salute; tel. 0187/185-8082; 9:30am-11pm daily). You can get a coffee there or fill up your water bottles at the fountain nearby.

If it's later in the day, go for aperitivo over at **Cantina Cappelini** (Via Montello 240, Volastra; tel. 351/519-2522; www.cantinacapellini.it), which comes with an incredible view and the wine to match. It happens every day at 7:30pm sharp. Don't worry about walking back. There's a bus stop nearby that will get you back to Manarola and the train station where you can connect back to Riomaggiore.

TRANSPORTATION

Air

- The closest international airports to the Cinque Terre are **Aeroporto Galileo Galilei/Pisa International Airport** (PSA; www.pisa-airport.com) and **Aeroporto Cristoforo Colombo/Genova City Airport** (GOA; www.airport.genova.it). Pisa receives more international traffic of the two.
- Rome's **Aeroporto Internazionale Leonardo Da Vinci Airport** (FCO;

WATCH

***Luca*:** This Pixar production is set in the Cinque Terre and shows off the landscape in beautifully detailed animations. The bonus content is equally compelling.

READ

Cinque Terre - Portofino, Hiking Map: This very detailed and easy-to-fold map indicates points of interest along dozens of trails and comes in handy before and during hikes.

LISTEN

The ***Untold Italy*** podcast provides a mix of insights and advice for anyone traveling to Italy. Episode 9 (https://untolditaly.com/9) is dedicated to the Cinque Terre and features American expat Amy Inman recounting life in her adopted home.

www.adr.it), and Milan's **Malpensa Airport** (MXP; tel. 02 232323; www.milanomalpensa-airport.com) are also possibilities.

Train

Train is the best way to arrive in the Cinque Terre. Intercity and regional trains from Rome (4 hours; €56-64), Pisa (1 hour; €12.90-16), Genoa (1.5 hours; €7.70-16), and Milan (3.5 hours; €20.55-29) all arrive in **La Spezia,** where you can connect to the local train to Riomaggiore (8-10 minutes) and all the Cinque Terre towns. **Levanto,** at the northern end of the five Cinque Terre towns, is also a transfer station to the local Cinque Terre line for trains coming from the north, such as Genoa or Milan.

Along the **local Cinque Terre line** that connects all the towns, trains arrive roughly every half hour and the entire end-to-end Cinque Terre journey is less than 15 minutes. Single tickets cost €5 (discounts available for ages under 12 and over 70); service starts at 4am and continues until midnight.

Cinque Terre Treno Card (tel. 39.018/776-2600;www.parconazionale5terre.it; 8am-3pm Mon.-Wed.) can be purchased as a one-day (€18.20), two-day (€33), or three-day (€47) unlimited ride pass for transportation to all the Cinque Terre towns, La Spezia, and Levanto, including hiking fees. Bus service from town to town is also included with the card, which is useful for reaching or coming back from the inland trails.

Ferry

www.navigazionegolfodeipoeti.it; 10:30am-5pm daily spring and summer

Ferries connect all the Cinque Terre towns except Corniglia in spring and summer and offer giornaliero, or day passes (€30). One-way tickets (€7-13) are also available.

Getting Back

Get home or to your next destination by train to Rome (via La Spezia) or Milan (via La Spezia or Levanto), both of which have major international airports. Genoa and Pisa, which are closer, also have international airports and a variety of train connections.

CONNECT WITH

- Rome, Florence, and Venice (page 139)
- Tuscany and Umbria (page 289)
- The Alps (page 648)

ALTA VIA 1: DOLOMITE HIGH ROUTE

Why Go: This route, with epic mountains, panoramic trails, and a distinctly un-Mediterranean diet, is an amazing and occasionally grueling trek through one of the most legendary alpine areas in Europe.

Number of Days: 9

Total Distance: 100 km (62 mi)

Seasons: Summer

Start: Lago di Braies

End: Agordo

The Dolomite Mountains are iconic alpine ranges in northeastern Italy whose beauty and geological particularity have earned them UNESCO World Heritage status. They were formed from carbonated minerals and have a distinct grayish tint that changes color throughout the day. The Alta Via 1 High Route weaves up and down picturesque valleys, majestic passes, and idyllic mountain lakes. It's sometimes narrow, often steep, rarely paved, and always scenic.

The Alta Via Dolomite High Route is a challenge. It requires hiking 5-7 hours per day on varied terrain at high altitudes. Along the way you'll meet hikers from around the world and bunk at informal rifugi lodges where food, bed, and beer are accompanied by a warm alpine welcome.

Navigating the Dolomites in summer is easy. Trails are marked with signs and red and white stripes painted on rocks and trees. Alta Via, known locally as la Classica, is indicated with the number 1 surrounded by a triangle. Long-distance hikers follow the Alta Via 1 from north to south for less elevation gain.

TOP 3

Starting your hike at **Lago di Braies,** a scenic alpine lake surrounded by pines and peaks (page 441).

Going underground into the unexpected World War I tunnels preserved at **Galleria Lagazuoi** (page 448).

Waking up above the clouds at **Rifugio Nuvolau** (page 450).

Lago di Braies to Rifugio Biella

Arrive by: Bus to Lago di Braies

Hiking Distance and Time: 6 km (3.7 mi) with 929 m (3,048 ft) ascent, 96 m (315 ft) descent; 3.5-4 hours

Trail: 1

★ 1. Lago di Braies

Lago di Braies is stunning. The water is an exotic aquamarine and reflects gray Dolomite mountain peaks. It's not a place you want to leave, and if you arrive early, you can head out on one of the **vintage wooden rowboats** (€19 for 30 minutes, €29 for 1 hour) moored to the lake's only dock. Be sure to stop in the lake's only souvenir shop to buy a Passaporto delle Dolomiti for gathering stamps at rifugi along the way.

After that it's a pleasant walk along the right bank through a pine forest to the opposite end of the lake, where cows graze in summer and the real journey begins.

2. Croda del Becco

From the lake, it takes over an hour to reach the top of the first steep incline from where you can spot Rifugio Biella in the distance. You can head directly to the lodge or take a secondary trail up to the Croda del Becco (2,818 m/9,245 ft).

Croda means spire in the local dialect and becco is beak. The Croda del Becco peak is your introduction to elevation. Once you climb above the tree line there are only rocks and wide-open spaces where eyes can wonder freely. The air is fresh and eagles glide overhead. The trail to the top is popular with day-hikers out

Lago di Braies

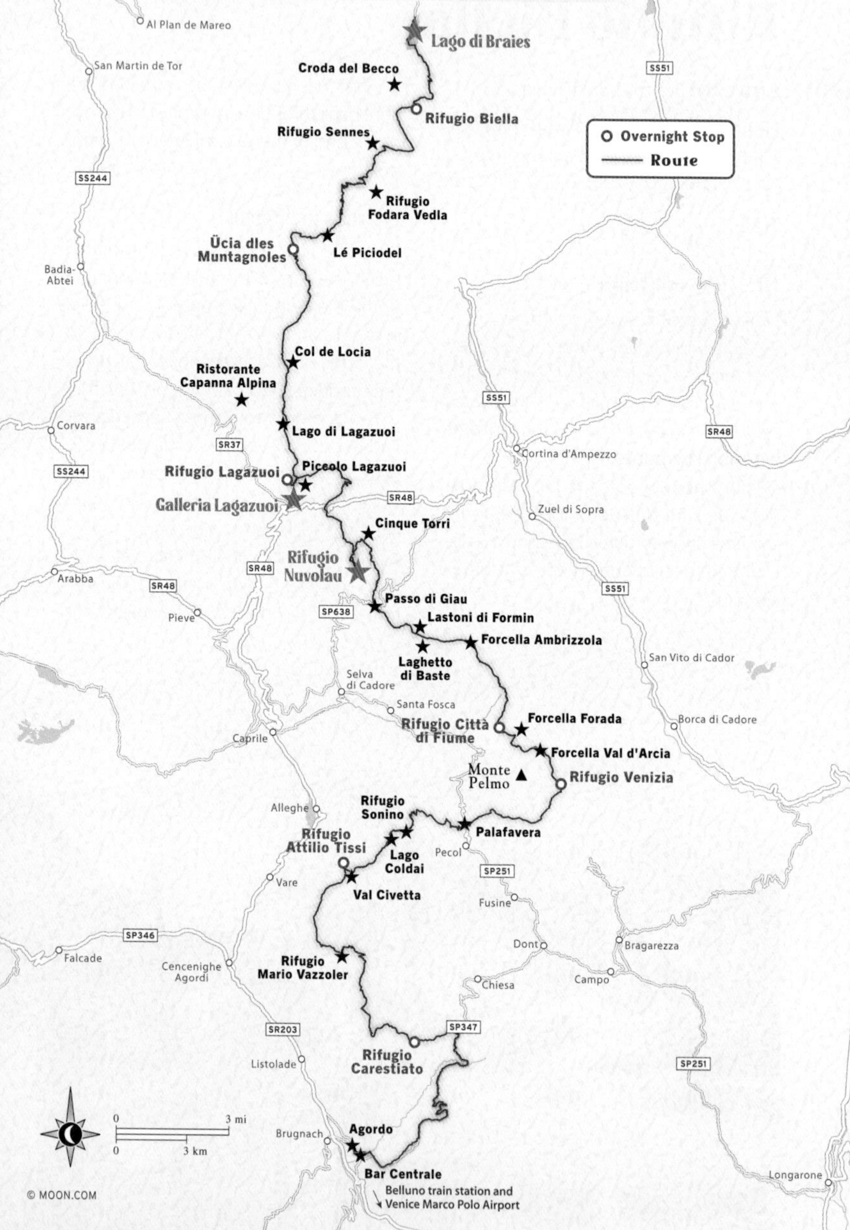
ALTA VIA 1: DOLOMITE HIGH ROUTE
Overnight Stop
Route
Lago di Braies
Croda del Becco
Rifugio Biella
Rifugio Sennes
Rifugio Fodara Vedla
Ücia dles Muntagnoles
Lé Piciodel
Col de Locia
Ristorante Capanna Alpina
Lago di Lagazuoi
Rifugio Lagazuoi
Piccolo Lagazuoi
Galleria Lagazuoi
Cinque Torri
Rifugio Nuvolau
Passo di Giau
Lastoni di Formin
Forcella Ambrizzola
Laghetto di Baste
Rifugio Città di Fiume
Forcella Forada
Forcella Val d'Arcia
Monte Pelmo
Rifugio Venizia
Rifugio Sonino
Palafavera
Rifugio Attilio Tissi
Lago Coldai
Val Civetta
Rifugio Mario Vazzoler
Rifugio Carestiato
Agordo
Bar Centrale
Belluno train station and Venice Marco Polo Airport
Al Plan de Mareo
San Martin de Tor
Badia-Abtei
Corvara
Arabba
Pieve
Selva di Cadore
Santa Fosca
Caprile
Alleghe
Pecol
Vare
Fusine
Dont
Bragarezza
Falcade
Cencenighe Agordi
Chiesa
Campo
Listolade
Brugnach
Longarone
Cortina d'Ampezzo
Zuel di Sopra
San Vito di Cador
Borca di Cadore
SS549
SS51
SS244
SR37
SR48
SP638
SP251
SP346
SR203
SP347
0
3 mi
3 km
© MOON.COM

Key Reservations

Don't show up unannounced and expect accommodation. Although there are dozens of **rifugi** (refuges) along the Alta Via 1 route, they're small and beds can be scarce in July and August when the trail is at its liveliest. It's important to know your travel dates and contact each rifugi 4-5 months in advance. A €20-30 deposit is usually required. Some hiking companies will do this for you. Camping is the adventurous option and eliminates the need for reservations, but it does get chilly at night and a tent adds extra weight to a pack.

This is not a last-minute route. It requires preparation. Get a good map like the **Dolomite UNESCO Map** (Tabacco) or a detailed trail guide like ***Trekking the Dolomites AV1*** (Knife Edge Outdoor), which is dedicated entirely to the Alta Via 1.

For what to pack, see the **packing list** for Tour du Mont Blanc (page 410).

for a taste of the high altitude you will experience over these nine days.

It's steep going through lunar-like terrain and requires the use of a ferrata (iron railing). These were installed to assist alpine troops during World War I and are common along the Alta Via. There's a cross near the top of the mountain and peaks in all directions. Sunsets are special in the Dolomites, and if you time it right you'll witness your first **enrosdira,** a phenomenon that tinges gray Dolomite rock shades of pink and orange at dusk and dawn.

3. Rifugio Biella

Tel. 043/686-6991; www.rifugiobiella.it; open June 20-Sept. 30; €25 bed, €10 breakfast

Rifugio Biella is a solid three-story refuge that has survived more than one storm since it opened in 1907. It's a good introduction to rifugio living and one of the most basic on the route, although fresh sheets are provided (not always a given). Rooms are dormitory style, with bunk beds and shared bathrooms equipped with Turkish toilets (otherwise known as squat toilets). The tap water isn't drinkable but they do sell bottled mineral water (€3.50). Showers are cold and ear plugs help filter out the snoring of fellow hikers.

Dinner is à la carte and consists of thick soups and traditional **canederli balls** made from bread and flavored with cheese and mushrooms. Breakfast is a hearty buffet with sweet and savory options that provide the necessary protein for hiking. Bag lunches are available upon request (ask the night before). Here you also get a piece of fruit, small dessert, and water.

Rifugio Biella

Sleeping Along the Alta Via

Don't expect five-star accommodations along the Alta Via. The only thing you'll find at this altitude are rifugi (refuges) and places to camp nearby.

RIFUGI

Rifugi are basic lodges located at strategic intervals that offer warm food and communal living. Some have private rooms, but most perks are missing—and sometimes so is the hot water. Then again, the important thing after 5-7 hours hiking is a friendly welcome, and rifugi are a sight for sore feet.

Don't be surprised by lack of televisions or spotty Wi-Fi. These are friendly, informal places where everyone gets to know everyone else. Outside there's always an incredible view, while inside comradery grows between hikers sharing stories and drinking beer.

It's important to reserve bunks as early as possible, as rifugi are reserved months in advance by eager hikers from around the world. Prices range from €30-40 for a bed to €60-80 for bed and half-board (dinner and breakfast), which is by far the better option.

DINING

The food at rifugi is filling and features traditional alpine favorites. Drinks are often home brewed, and the grappa liquor (70-120 proof, made from wine byproducts) must be sipped slowly unless you're doing shots. Breakfast varies at each rifugi, from sweet continental to savory buffets.

Most rifugi prepare packed lunches (€8-10), which come in handy on the trail. Otherwise, there are usually one or more refuges along each stage where you can stop for a sit-down lunch or light snack and a drink.

CAMPING

Camping is another option if you are willing to carry your gear and is permitted only within the vicinity of rifugi. If you set up anywhere else you risk being fined by park rangers. Tents must be pitched after sunset and removed before dawn to preserve the surroundings. Campfires are strictly forbidden, and everything else is basic common sense. Sleeping outdoors is an incredible audio experience and you'll be serenaded by an array of nocturnal birds and mini mammals. Although wolves are present in the Dolomites, they rarely roam above the tree line and avoid inhabited areas where hikers gather.

THE DOLOMITE PASSPORT

The Dolomite Passport, or Passaporto delle Dolomiti, can be a fun and rewarding souvenir. The passport is a little booklet that can be stamped at the rifugi where you stay along the hike. The booklet comes in five colors, costs €6.50, and can be purchased in advance from **Light Hunter** (www.lighthuntershop.com) or at the **gift shop** at the Lago di Braies. It might seem like a gimmick, and in some ways it is, but having it stamped at the refuges starts conversations and will remind you of this adventure in years to come. Inside there's information about the trail, emergency numbers, and blank pages for noting impressions, so bring a pen.

If you bring the stamped passport to the **Tourist Office** (Via Duomo 2) in Belluno, they'll even give you a free commemorative **Alta Via pin.**

DAY 2

Rifugio Biella to Ücia dles Muntagnoles

Hiking Distance and Time: 14 km (8.7 mi) with 565 m (1,854 ft) ascent, 830 m (2,723 ft) descent; 4.5-5 hours

Trails: 6, 7

1. Rifugio Sennes

S. Vigilio di Marebbe; tel. 047/464-6355; www.sennes.com; Jan. 29-Apr. 18 and June 4-Oct. 16

The Alta Via isn't a single continuous path and there are often several ways to reach the same destination. The first decision comes 10 minutes from Rifugio Biella, where you can follow a hardened dirt path over rolling shrubland or a gravel road through progressively greener landscape. Both are marked as the number 6 and lead to Rifugio Sennes about an hour away. It may be too early for lunch, but you can still enjoy a drink on the sunny terrace or just watch the horses grazing in the meadow nearby. Livestock roam free in these parts and cowbells make a familiar sound.

Sennes is a good stop if you're thirsty. You can pick up cold drinks for the road or take a seat and enjoy your first **Radler,** a refreshing mix of beer and lemonade. In the distance are some of the most dramatic peaks in the Dolomites. Each one has a name and locals recognize them like members of their own family. For everyone else there are apps that can identify the Croda Rossa (3,146 m/10,322 ft), Cristallo (3,221 m/10,568 ft), Sorapis (3,205 m/10,515), and Tofane (3,243 m/10,640 ft) in the distance.

2. Rifugio Fodara Vedla

Alpe di Fodara Vedla 2; tel. 348/853-7471; www.fodara.it; May 21-Nov. 1; €12-15

Continue from Rifugio Sennes on the 7 trail and follow signs for Rifugio Fodara Vedla, which is the halfway point of this stage. Unless you pick up a cestino (bag lunch) in the morning at your rifugio, you'll need to find somewhere to eat along the trail. Fortunately for famished hikers, there are always one or two rifugi between each

Regional Cuisine

Hiking burns calories and builds appetites. Fortunately, refuge kitchens serve hefty portions of alpine comfort food influenced by centuries of Austro-Hungarian traditions and prepared with ingredients grown and raised in nearby valleys. Alpine cooking has less to do with the Mediterranean diet Italy is famous for and more to do with simple dishes made with potatoes, smoked pork, bread, and apples—German-sounding recipes that have satisfied hikers for generations.

- **Schüttelbrot** is the quintessential mountain flatbread invented by shepherds who were away from home for long periods and needed something quick and easy to sustain them. It's baked from rye, sourdough, and cumin into a hard crunchy bread that remains edible for months and makes a tasty trail snack.
- **Speck** is the local version of prosciutto, or smoked pork thigh, spiced with salt, pepper, juniper, and bay leaves. It's aged for three months and has a strong meaty flavor that is a fixture of cold cut platters and the sandwiches refuges prepare for hikers every morning.
- **Grostle** is the local version of a full breakfast with sausage, sauerkraut, potatoes, onions, and eggs fried into a hearty all-in-one dish. It's not pretty, but it is tasty and filling. Although most common at breakfast, it's often also available at lunch and dinner.
- You can't travel the Alta Via without tasting **canederli.** This iconic dish originated in eastern Europe, and the local version is a mix of bread, milk, egg, onion, flour, and chives shaped into matzah ball-like dumplings. Canederli are filling and usually served in broth or flavored with mushrooms and speck. Nearly every cook has their own family recipe, which is a good reason to order them often.
- **Spätzle** is a gnocchi-like pasta dish made from wheat and water. Spinach and cheese are ingredients in the most popular version.
- Apples are everywhere in this region. It's hard to find a dessert that doesn't incorporate them in some way, and **strudel** is undoubtedly the most famous. **Apfelkiachel** is a lesser-known alternative consisting of apple slices dipped in batter and then fried, sprinkled with cinnamon or powdered sugar, and topped with whipped cream or ice cream. It's like a donut—only better.

stage. The menu at Fodora Vedla includes polenta and sausage, omelets, and plenty of potato dishes that can be washed down with local Forst (Forest) beer. They intentionally have no Wi-Fi, but the grazing cows and wooden huts scattered around the refuge are a fine substitute.

3. Lé Piciodel

The route continues through a forest to a paved road that zigzags its way down into the Fanes valley. There's another lodge at the bottom and plenty of day hikers and cyclists congregating around picnic tables. Six km (3.7 mi) up the trail is a small mountain lake, Lé Piciodel, that looks perfect for a summer dip. Lé Piciodel is chilly at best, even in August, but the water is pristine and you can dry off under the sun on the grassy banks in near solitude.

4. Ücia dles Muntagnoles

Localité Fanes 11; tel. 347/521-4753; www.muntagnoles.com; June 15-Oct. 18; €70 half board pp

There are four lodges near the end of this stage, but family-owned Ücia dles Muntagnole is the coziest with four rooms and two shared bathrooms (standard toilets). Dinner is served in a traditional alpine dining room with stufa (heater) and wood-paneled ceiling and walls. Entertainment involves board games, books travelers left behind, and homemade grappa flavored with mountain herbs. Breakfast is abundant with eggs, ham, bread, and as much coffee as you can drink. Afterward, you can start the day exploring the stream out back.

DAY 3

Ücia dles Muntagnoles to Rifugio Lagazuoi

Hiking Distance and Time: 11 km (6.8 mi) with 1,070 m (3,510 ft) ascent, 375 m (1,230 ft) descent; 5-5.5 hours

Trails: 10, 11, 20b, 20

1. Col de Lucia

Today is one of the most scenic and challenging stages of the entire route. Trail 20B is difficult but special and leads to Forcella del Lago (Lake Fork), Lago di Lagazuoi, and the legendary Scotoni Wall, the El Capitan of Italy. If 20B sounds beyond your hiking ability (you *can* do it!) take the longer and gentler 11 trail to Lago di Lagazuoi.

The Col de Lucia is less than two hours from Ücia dles Muntagnole and is reached by way of a long meandering valley that is green and pockmarked with boulders of all sizes and shapes. There are small streams and occasional fountain troughs with cold drinkable water. There are wooden benches where hikers sit to look out over pines and the Gruppo del Sella range in the distance. It's a steep way down, but sustenance is not far off.

2. Ristorante Capanna Alpina

San Cassiano; tel. 047/184-9418; 7am-9pm daily June 1-Oct. 1; €10.50-17

A sit-down lunch is a pleasant way to break up each stage and taste local dishes. The food at Capanna Alpina isn't fancy but it is filling, and dishes like eggs, potatoes, and speck, or polenta with sausage ragu and fontina cheese provide the energy for the second half of the journey. There are tables outside and strudel for dessert.

3. Forcella del Lago

The Forcella del Lago mountain pass is the highest point of the stage. It can be cold even in summer, and the closeness of the rock faces on either side is naturally imposing. The stone is streaked black as though it's been burned and could keep a geologist busy for months. Most hikers stop here to gaze down on the lake way below before slowly descending the

Ücia dles Muntagnoles

(top to bottom) Galleria Lagazuoi; Rifugio Lagazuoi; Rifugio Lagazuoi sauna; Piccolo Lagazuoi

steep switchbacks. The mountain sides are exposed to wind, rain, and snow that cause erosion and result in vast gravel washouts.

4. Lago di Lagazuoi

Lake Lagazuo, or Lech de Lagacio in the local Ladino language, is a glacial lake that is fed by underground springs and is surprisingly full of fish. It's the highest lake (2,180 m/7,152 ft above sea level) along the Alta Via, and depending on the season can vary significantly in diameter due to evaporation. It's shallow and the perfect spot to refresh after the challenging descent. It's also perfect for skipping stones, having picnics, and contemplating the gray mountain ranges that surround the lake. The **Scotoni Wall** is the most imposing of these and has been challenging alpinists since its sheer face was first climbed in 1909. On most days you can spot climbers inching themselves up one of the two bolted routes to the top.

★ 5. Galleria Lagazuoi

Galleria Lagazuoi is less than two hours away via a long steady climb through a barren landscape followed by a short descent. Somewhere along the way you'll cross the border between the Trentino and Veneto regions and meet fewer hikers along this section of the route. Don't let the tranquility fool you. During World War I, Lagazuoi was the scene of fierce fighting between Italian and Austrian alpine troops. Both sides dug into the mountain to survive, and the network of galleries and trenches they built have been restored and transformed into an open-air museum (open 24 hours; free).

There are various entrances to the galleries near Rifugio Lagazuoi and the possibility to rent helmets with flashlights. If you start from the top and work your way down, you can catch the **Lagazuoi Cable Car** (9am-5pm daily; €15 one-way, €21 round-trip, higher prices in Aug.) back up the mountain. The ride takes 15 minutes and offers extraordinary views over the Southern Dolomites and an endless horizon of peaks.

6. Rifugio Lagazuoi

Monte Lagazuoi; tel. 340/719-5306; www.rifugiolagazuoi.com; open year-round; 60 bed, 140 room with breakfast, dinner 30

Lagazuoi is the largest refuge on the Alta Via and is popular with day hikers who ride the cable car up from the valley below. There are private and communal rooms, which are booked months in advance. There's also a rare perk: an outdoor Finnish sauna, and €20 gets you all the heat you can stand, a bathrobe, and tokens for a hot shower. The Wi-Fi works and a hearty three-course meal is served for dinner. Pack lunches (€10) can be ordered the night before (recommended since there are no interim rifugi or restaurants on the next segment) and include a sandwich, fresh fruit, energy bar, and water.

7. Piccolo Lagazuoi

The Piccolo Lagazuoi (2,778 m/9,114 ft), or Little Lagazuoi, demonstrates the local sense of irony. There's nothing small about this mountaintop just 15 minutes from the lodge. It's a popular post-dinner jaunt and an absolute must for sunset seekers. There's a 360-degree view that includes the rocky mountain pass from whence you came and the green verdant valleys where you'll be heading tomorrow. It's easy to be moved by the infinite vista. A cross was erected here and hikers pile small rocks into delicate mounds.

DAY 4

Rifugio Lagazuoi to Rifugio Nuvolau

Hiking Distance and Time: 15 km (9.3 mi) with 635 m (2,083 ft) ascent, 810 m (2,657 ft) descent; 6-6.5 hours

Trails: 20, 401, 402, 404, 403, 412, 440

1. Travenànzes Valley

Set your alarm early and start the day with a sunrise. This is the longest stage of the route and cuts through the heart of the Dolomites. It isn't particularly arduous, and much of the way follows lightly trafficked paved roads through the lush pine forests of the Travenànzes Valley, a bucolic valley awash in brooks, streams, and tiny tributaries. The water is ice cold and the stony banks border meadows bursting with white alpine flowers. High mountains are all around, and most days you can spot climbers following the via ferrata (iron path) routes hammered into the rock face.

Travenànzes Valley

If you're feeling tired, hop-on the **Lagazuoi Cable Car** at the start of the trail, skipping the Grotta della Tofàna cave.

2. Grotta della Tofàna

This evocative cave is one of the few cavities in the Dolomites. It forms a spiral shape for more than 300 m (984 ft) and vaulting up to 10 m (33 ft) high. To access Grotta della Tofàna you have to walk along a ledge and hold on to cable railing. The cave is slightly off the main trail with some exposed passages inside that are better off faced with climbing equipment if you want to explore it fully. There are signs for the cave along the 404 trail, and the detour will only add an hour or so to your journey. You can enter the enormous entrance of the cave and walk around 10 yards before the light starts to fade; after that you'll need a flashlight or headlamp. Even without the equipment to explore deeper, the cave is worth a visit.

3. Cinque Torri

Rock climbing in the Dolomites began in the 1930s, and another short detour leads to the Cinque Torri, or Five Rocks, which is the perfect testing ground for amateur and expert climbers. This mini-mountain range consists of five tower-like outcrops with varied surfaces that burst out from the grassy hillside. The tallest (Torre Grande) is 170 m (558 ft) high while the runt of the bunch is barely 10 m (33 ft). There are a number of paths that crisscross and circumnavigate the unique formation. Walk around and get a close-up look at an alpine wonder and a last view of the Travenànzes Valley.

Here, too, you can save yourself some walking by taking the **Cinque Torri chairlift** to the rocks.

★ 4. Rifugio Nuvolau

Monte Lagazuoi; tel. 335/686-8066; www.rifugioaverau.it; June 11-1st Sun. in Oct.; €78 half-board

It's a gentle upward climb from the Cinque Torre to Rifugio Nuvolau that takes an hour to cover at a leisurely pace. The path is wide and hard from use but becomes progressively narrower and wilder. Near the end you'll need to choose your footing carefully and take frequent stops to enjoy the view. The final section follows the ridge line with dramatic drops on both sides and the refuge perched defiantly in the distance.

left, Cinque Torri; right, Rifugio Nuvolau

Neighboring mountain ranges are snow-capped even in summer and appear close enough to touch.

Rifugio Nuvolau was built on the peak of the same name in 1883 and has been managed by Sandro and his family for the past four decades. It's an exceptional stop both for the hospitality and spectacular light shows that occur at dusk and dawn. Every refuge comes with a view, but this is one is exceptional—you may find yourself standing above the clouds. The restaurant has the best wine list on the Alta Via. There are no showers, but they do prepare sandwiches for hikers heading off each morning.

DAY 5

Rifugio Nuvolau to Rifugio Città di Fiume

Hiking Distance and Time: 11 km (6.8 mi) with 260 m (853 ft) ascent, 915 m (3,002 ft) descent; 4.5-5 hours

Trails: 438, 443, 436, 458, 467

1. Passo di Giau

This stage provides a tantalizing range of alpine landscapes. You can get an exciting start to the day by following the via ferrata (cables route) or the easier paved route over the **Ra Gusela** mountain (2,595 m/8,514 ft). Either way, both routes meet up at the Passo di Giau, one of the widest and most stunning high passes along the Alta Via. The combination helps explain the road and the people who drive here for the view. **Colle Santa Lucia** is the highest point of the pass and a natural meeting place that gets crowded in summer.

There are often locally produced goods for sale on the side of the road, and the local tradition of woodworking means you may come across spoons, baskets, swords, stools, and traditional figurines that were hand-carved from pine.

2. Lastoni di Formin

Lastoni di Formin (2,670 m/8,760 ft) are part of the Croda da Lago-Cernera range and are among the most iconic formations in the Dolomites. According to legend, on the wedding day of a local queen plants began to bloom on the mountain and flowers were distributed to her subjects. You can simply admire this flat-topped behemoth or get a closer look via one of the side trails. It can get foggy and wet in spring, making the approach difficult, but the higher you go the better the view gets.

3. Laghetto delle Baste

Laghetto means small lake, but even that is an overstatement. Laghetto delle Baste is 183 m (600 ft) from the main trail, surrounded by a bog-like landscape, and it's worth the short detour. What's magic is the mountains reflecting off the water. From here the iconic **Monte Pelmo** and **Lastoni di Formin** ranges are clearly visible. It's perfect for a picnic and some mountain reflecting.

4. Forcella Ambrizzola

The dirt trail is easy and cuts through a grassy valley that's lush green in spring and gradually becomes browner. This is prime marmot habitat and these timid rodents have all the vegetation they need. You'll hear their high-pitched calls and may even spot some scurrying between burrows.

It takes about an hour and a half to reach the Forcella Ambrizzola (2,277

top, Passo di Giau; bottom, Lastoni di Formin

m/7,470 ft) fork from the Giau Pass, and the last section is the most dramatic. Here you walk near a long stretch of towering rock face that culminates with a narrow fork. It's an alpine meeting point with panoramic views of the Cortina d'Ampezzo range and the remnants of a medieval burial ground nearby.

5. Col della Puina

The final descent toward the refuge is down a dirt road, from where you can reach the Col della Puina (2,254 m/7,395 ft) peak. It's topped with a small wooden cross around which hikers lay rocks. It provides a close-up view of the gleaming Monte Pelmo. You can also check into the refuge first and hike to the top after dinner. The climb is simple and takes less than hour from the lodge.

6. Rifugio Città di Fiume

Loc Malga Durona; tel. 320/037-7432; www.rifugiocittadifiume.it; June 20-Sept. 20; €60-80 pp half-board

The end of the day is a long descent underneath tall pines all the way to Rifugio Città di Fiume, which is managed by the local chapter of the Italian Alpine Club (CAI). It's a no-frills refuge with thick walls, five dorm rooms, and two bathrooms where hikers line up to wash their clothes. A warm shower costs €3.50 and there's an electric outlet in each room. The kitchen doesn't offer an extensive menu, but there are vegan and vegetarian options along with alpine classics like mushrooms with polenta and cold cut platters served with chilled beer. They don't prepare packed lunches, but you can order a sandwich (€4.50) in the morning.

DAY 6

Rifugio Citta di Fiume to Rifugio Venezia

Hiking Distance and Time: 12 km (7.5 mi) with 580 m (1,903 ft) ascent, 990 m (3,248 ft) descent; 5.5-6 hours

Trails: 480, 472, 474

1. Forcella Foràda

Don't let the start of today's stage fool you. The initial flat section over an old mule track soon gives way to a daunting washout and a trail covered in loose gravel that can get slippery. It's a long, hard climb toward a Forcella Foràda and the Val d'Arcia pass.

The panorama up here is green and forested and unlike anything you've seen so far. There's a *Sound of Music* quality that makes it a perfect stop. It's probably too early for lunch, but you can rest along the path and use your binoculars. By carefully observing the unique color and shape of mountains, you can learn to recognize them.

As you go higher, though, the landscape becomes progressively barren the closer you get to the Foràda peak. Near the top it's just rock and the washout caused by thousands of years of erosion.

2. Forcella Val d'Arcia

You'll be hiking along the sloping side of the mountain for long stretches, and this is where those rugged climbing shoes and walking stick will come in handiest. Take it slow and stick to the narrow trail. Red arrows painted on bright white boulders point the way across a lunar landscape that makes everything else seem small.

Throughout there are incredible views of the northern slope of **Monte Pelmo,** which is a mountain unto itself and ringed by a forest of tall pines. The hard work continues through the saddle and down across steep gullies covered in loose rock, making this a tricky descent. There's a large outcrop and some ferrata sections that provide the grip needed to stay on course.

3. Monte Pelmo

Beautiful is an understatement for this monumental peak formed millions of years ago and situated at the crossroads of three valleys. It's one of the most characteristic reliefs in the Dolomites, with a concave shape that looks like a throne and which early inhabitants of the area attributed to the gods. The range is a constant companion on this stage, and the rock surfaces subtly change color throughout the day. Monte Pelmo is a popular destination for expert climbers who can see all the way to the Gulf of Trieste when they reach the top. The trail doesn't crest the mountain, but rather goes over the lower part of it.

4. Rifugio Venezia

Loc. Campi di Rutorto; tel. 04/369-684 or 320/010-3872; www.rifugiovenezia.it; June 18-Sept. 25; €27 bed, €60 half-board

Barbara, Valentino, and the enthusiastic staff at Rifugio Venezia know how to treat famished hikers—you won't wait long for cold beers and generous plates of cured meats to be served on their sunny terrace. It's not about plating here; it's about large portions of goulash and polenta. Sleeping arrangements are dormitory style. The Wi-Fi is weak and the only outlets are in the first-floor dining room. Sleeping bags or liners are recommended.

DAY 7

Rifugio Venezia to Rifugio Attilio Tissi

Lago Coldai

Hiking Distance and Time: 14 km (8.7 mi) with 850 m (2,789 ft) ascent, 650 m (2,133 ft) descent; 6-6.5 hours

Trails: 564, 556, 560

1. Palafavera

After leaving Rifugio Venezia, the first two hours are a downhill descent to Palafavera, the first sign of civilization in a long time. There's a small campground with a **mini market** (9am-6pm daily) where you can get all the ingredients for a picnic before hiking, or ride the **chairlift** (Val di Zoldo; https://skicivetta.com; 8:40am-5:15pm; €7 single or €10 roundtrip) as a shortcut up the mountain to the grassy plateau where dairy farmers bring their cows to graze in summer.

WATCH

Brothers of the Wind: It isn't a blockbuster, but this 2015 coming-of-age story, partially filmed in the region, depicts alpine beauty in nearly every frame. The Dolomites have appeared on film since the silent era and get significant screen time in ***Cliffhanger*** (1993) and ***Point Break*** (2015) as well.

Gino's Italian Express (season 7, episode 5): Gino D'Acampo has a great job. He travels around Italy discovering what makes the country special. In this episode, he heads to Bolzano and learns about strudel, cable cars, and local folklore.

READ

My Life at the Limit by Reinhold Messner: If you want to be inspired, read local legend Messner's memoir. He was first to climb all 14 mountains exceeding 8,000 m (26,000 ft) and first to complete a solo summit of Everest. He recounts his adventures in this interview-style autobiography.

LISTEN

Schuhplattln: This South Tyrolean circle dance combines clapping, stomping, slapping, and yodeling with rhythmic accordion playing. It's cheery and performed during local festivities.

2. Rifugio Sonino

Località Coldai; tel. 043/778-9160; www.rifugiocoldai.com

Majestic doesn't have to mean strenuous—a relief after the previous day's climb. From the trail, Palafavera is a continuous vision of the great northern wall of **Mount Civetta,** known as the "Wall of the Walls," for which locals have particular affection. The moniker is due to the legendary 4-km-long (2.5-mi) rock face believed to be the first ever Dolomite mountain to be climbed back in 1855.

The Sonino refuge was built in 1911 and lies at the northern end of the range, where you can look back down on the village of Palafavera. There is no outdoor seating, but no one minds if you order drinks and enjoy them outside.

3. Lago Coldai

The trail from Sonino heads up to the Coldài Fork and down the opposite side to a gravelly basin and Lake Coldai, a large lake by alpine standards and situated over 2,100 m (6,890 ft) above sea level. It's a remnant of a glacial flow that has been retreating ever since the ice age, and the name is a good indication of the water temperature. Evaporation and melting have increased significantly in recent decades, and glaciers are retreating throughout the Alps. That hasn't stopped marmots from making this their main watering hole, and if there aren't many hikers around you might spot these cautious mammals. They burrow into the hillsides nearby and are always on the lookout for golden eagles and peregrine falcons circling the skies above.

You'll also see red crossbills, a sparrow-like bird with a funny beak and chamois skillfully climbing the steep rock faces. On the ground there is an assortment of colorful wildflowers such as the perennial crocus, which is the harbinger of spring, and the electric blue campanula.

4. Rifugio Attilio Tissi

Località Col Reàn; tel. 347/593-1833; www.rifugiotissi.com; June-Sept.; €30 bed, €62 half-board

Just when you thought the views from a refuge couldn't get any better, along comes Attilio Tissi. There are photo ops of Mount Civetta on the cliff nearby, along with a wooden heart where hikers watch the sunset. Meals are simple but tasty, and the beer and homemade grappa foster good cheer among the hikers who hail from all continents. Wake up early to take advantage of the only shower (€5 for 5 minutes). Clouds can be above or below in the morning and the sunrise should not be missed.

DAY 8

Rifugio Attilio Tissi to Rifugio Carestiato

Hiking Distance and Time: 8 km (5 mi) with 555 m (1,821 ft) ascent, 430 m (1,411 ft) descent; 6-6.5 hours

Trails: 555, 554

1. Val Civetta

From Attilio Tissi, the trail heads south through the Val Civetta valley, where you'll enter in and out of an airy pine forest, cross dozens of slow-running streams, and have a constant view of Mount Civetta all the way to the next refuge. It's mostly flat or downhill along rugged terrain marked by large boulders and major washouts, which explains how mountains get smaller.

2. Rifugio Mario Vazzoler

Località Col Negro Di Pelsa; tel. 340/161-2828; June-Sept.; €12-15

Rifugio Mario Vazzoler is one of the most beautiful refuges of the bunch. It's the midpoint of this stage and an ideal stop if you're hungry. This is your last full day, after all, and should be celebrated with

Val Civetta

pappardelle sugo di cervo and a beer. Cervo is venison, better known as deer. They thrive in the Dolomites and are sustainably hunted so as not to overpopulate the area. Most of the ingredients served at the outdoor tables didn't travel far and are prepared following traditional alpine recipes. Don't leave without a slice of strudel.

3. Pian de le Taie and Torre Trieste

Beyond Rifugio Vazzoler, the path continues to the Pian de le Taie plane and the imposing Torre Trieste (2,458 m/8,064 ft), a jagged peak that gets its name from its tower-like appearance. It has attracted climbers since 1910 and BASE jumpers in more recent times. You can get close to the base, but unless you've brought serious climbing gear, you're better off admiring it from down below.

4. Rifugio Carestiato

Loc. Col dei Pas; tel. 0437 62949; www.rifugiocarestiato.com; €30 dorm bunk, €62 half-board

The last downhill section to Rifugio Carestiato shouldn't be underestimated: It requires firm footing and a fondness of heights. Once you arrive, you'll find that this is one of the rare refuges with a helipad, which hopefully you won't need. There's a great atmosphere in the communal area and fresh bread at dinner. The Wi-Fi works, English is spoken, and credit cards are accepted. In the evenings the fireplace gets lit and strangers become friends. It's the perfect place to spend your last night on the trail.

DAY 9

Rifugio Carestiato to Belluno

Hiking Distance and Time: 17 km (10.6 mi) with 1,266 m (4,154 ft) descent; 3.5-4 hours

1. Road to Agordo

It's all downhill on a narrow paved road where you'll have to get reacquainted with cars. It takes an hour to reach the main road and a couple more to arrive in Agordo, where your hike ends. The end of a journey is always a little sad, and it's true you could hike all the way to Belluno, but this is a pleasant end to an Alta Via adventure and provides enough time to get anywhere you need to go.

2. Bar Centrale

Piazza della Libertà 14; tel. 347/890-4052; 7am-10pm daily

If you aren't in a hurry, it doesn't take long to visit the sleepy mountain town of Agordo, and afterward you can order a spritz and toast the trip at Bar Centrale, located on the main square with outdoor tables and views of the surrounding mountains.

3. Belluno Tourist Office

Via Duomo 2; tel. 334/281 3222; 10am-1pm Tues. and Thur.-Fri., 10am-1pm and 2pm-5pm Sat.-Mon.

When you're ready to leave Agordo, the bus station is on the outskirts of town. Board bus 001 to Belluno. Half the people onboard are likely to be fellow hikers, and you may even notice some familiar faces. It gets even more crowded at the **La Pissa** stop, another Alta Via finish line, from which it takes about 20 minutes to reach Belluno where everyone gets off. Before you head off in a new direction, walk 10 minutes to the tourist office to collect your Alta Via pin as a symbol of the hike you just completed.

road to Agordo

TRANSPORTATION

Air

Venice's **Aeroporto di Venezia** (VCE; Via Galileo Galilei 30; tel. 041/260-6111; www.veniceairport.it) is the closest international airport to the start of the Alta Via 1.

Bus

The **Cortina Express bus** (www.cortinaexpress.it) departs from outside the Venice airport arrivals hall and runs to **Cortina D'Ampezzo** (2 hours; €20). From there, take **Südtirolmobil** (SAD; www.suedtirolmobil.info) bus 445 to **Dobbiaco Toblach bus station** (1 hour; €5). The SAD bus 442 from Dobbico runs to **Lago di Braies** (40 minutes; €5) and drops off near the Hotel Lago di Braies.

Given flight and bus schedules, you will likely need to spend the night either in Cortina, the Aspen of Italy, or Dobbiaco, which has a distinct Germanic vibe, before making it to Lago di Braies to start your hike.

Getting Back

Belluno is connected to Venice by regional **Trenitalia** train (www.trenitalia.com; 2 hours; €9). The Belluno train station is a 10-minute walk west of the Tourist Office.

CONNECT WITH

- Rome, Florence, and Venice (page 139)

CAMINO DE SANTIAGO

Why Go: Follow in the footsteps of history as you join trekkers from more than 190 nations on this famous pilgrimage through France and Spain.

Number of Days: 7

Total Distance: 115.5 km (72 mi)

Seasons: Spring to fall

Start: Sarria

End: Santiago de Compostela

The Camino de Santiago is both a sacred pilgrimage and an outdoor adventure. Its most historic route, the Camino Francés, begins in the town of Saint-Jean-Pied-de-Port in France and travels west for 780 km (485 mi) until it reaches the purported tomb of Saint James the Greater in Santiago de Compostela in Spain.

The most popular starting point, though, is Sarria. From here, in Spain's Galicia region, the final 100 km (62 mi) of the Camino leads through river valleys and mountains covered in ancient oak and chestnut forests. Along the way, you'll hear locals tell stories of meigas (white witches) with healing powers; try queimada, a heated elixir of well-being offered to pilgrims; and sample celebrated cheeses and seafood dishes of the region.

TOP 3

★ Standing at the hilltop **Castro de Castromaior**, a 2,400-year-old Celtic settlement with 360-degree views of the surrounding mountains (page 464).

★ Touring **Iglesia de Santa María de Melide** with the cheerful volunteer who can illuminate the history of the church (page 471).

★ Hugging the statue of Saint James on the high altar of **Catedral de Santiago de Compostela**, an emotional rite of passage for pilgrims ending their journey (page 473).

DAY 1

Sarria to Portomarín

Arrive by: Train to Sarria station

Walking Distance: 22.1 km (13.7 mi)

1. Sarria

Sarria's hilltop location and rich waterways made it a destination long before the Middle Ages. Modern Sarria has a pragmatic, industrial feel, and is set up with a wide range of good lodging options. The riverside is a nice place to gather for a snack or before-dinner drinks with friends, and the 13th-century **Iglesia de San Salvador** (Rúa do Castelo, s/n), with an appealingly primitive engraving of Christ over the entrance, is worth pausing to see. If you don't already have a pilgrim's credential, stop in **Iglesia de Santa Marina** (Plaza de Juan Lopéz, s/n; tel. 982-531-024) to get one.

As you begin your trek and head out of Sarria, you'll pass its **castle ruins** and cross the medieval **Ponte Áspera** bridge over the Celeiro river, traversing ancient oak forest until you reach the village of Barbadelo, 3.6 km (2.2 mi) away.

2. Iglesia de Santiago

Barbadelo; mass noon in winter and 1pm summer, usually Sun. and holidays, but also inquire in the village

Set 200 m (656 ft) off to the left of the Camino just as you approach the village of **Barbadelo,** Iglesia de Santiago is a worthwhile stop. The church's enigmatic engravings include a primitive Christ image with sun-like forms, which may harken to pre-Christian ideas about an all-important sun deity.

3. Panadería Peruscallo

More oak forest and sinuous roads through small farmsteads lie ahead, along with possible visits from a vocal donkey and a beautiful black stallion. After 6 km

Sarria

(3.7 mi), you can stop for a meal at the family-run Panadería Peruscallo, a farmstead abutting a café and bakery in the hamlet of **Peruscallo** (pop. 34).

4. Iglesia de Santa María

Continue to **Ferreiros** (pop. 27), which was a thriving pilgrim stop in the 12th century. Today, the tiny village still gathers around its most important feature, the 12th-century Iglesia de Santa María. The entire church preserves its 12th-century form, and the west entrance is especially ornate, with lions and other animal figures with animated faces and expressions.

5. Portomarín

Climb to the plateau overlooking Portomarín's river valley and then descend, crossing the river at the high, vertigo-inducing modern bridge into Portomarín. Take half an hour to visit Portomarín's two Romanesque churches, **San Nicolás** (Praza Condes de Fenosa; tel. 982-545-206; https://turismo.ribeirasacra.org; 11am-1pm and 4pm-7pm daily; free) and **San Pedro** (Traversía Circunvalación, 30; https://turismo.ribeirasacra.org; usually closed).

The highlight of Portomarín is the town's **arcaded passageways,** lined with many cheerful options for a glass or meal. Even though they are modern constructions, built in the 1950s and 1960s, they give the modern town a feeling of timelessness. **Posada del Camino** (Rúa Lugo, 1; tel. 982-545-081; €10-15), on the terrace overlooking Iglesia de San Nicolás, has a good menú del día or á la carte options.

Spend the night in Portomarín, where there are a few albergues as well as hotels.

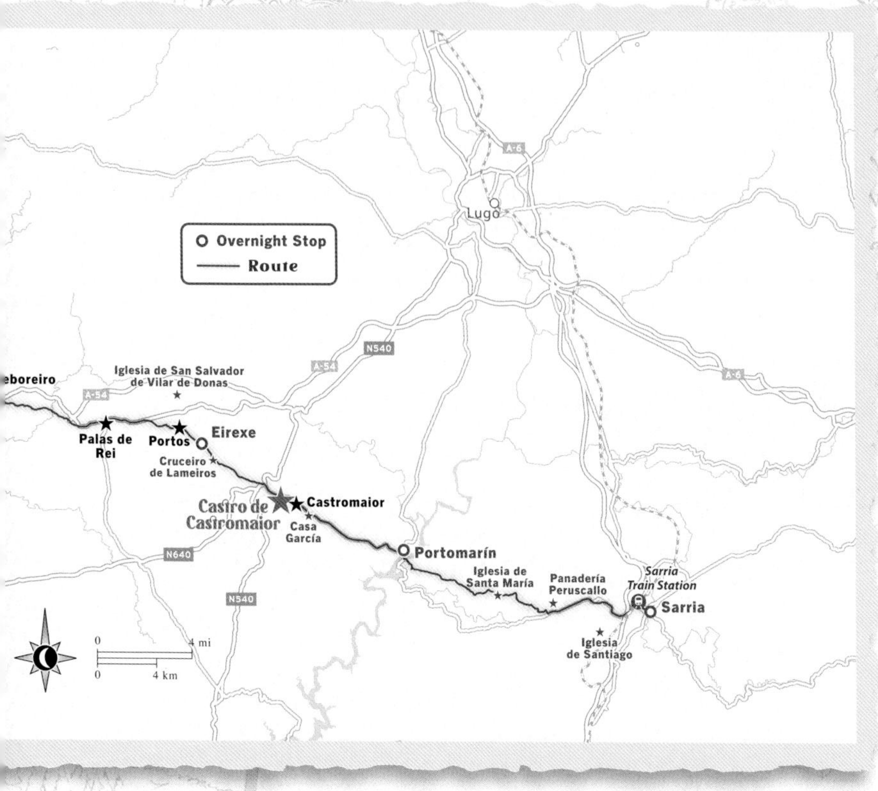

DAY 2

Portomarín to Eirexe

Walking Distance: 17.8 km (11 mi)

1. Casa García

Gonzar, 8; tel. 982-157-842; €4-11

Leave Portomarín, crossing a small tributary of the Belesar dam. Pass through oak and chestnut forest on the climb to the farm village of **Gonzar** (pop. 35; 7.8 km/4.8 mi from Portomarín). Stop for lunch at Casa García, immediately to the left at the village entrance. This café with an outdoor terrace churns out fresh omelets, sandwiches, salads, baked goods, and refreshments. A family

Portomarín arcaded passageways

Key Reservations

Part of the Camino's magic is letting each day unfold unplanned and savoring the chance to travel without making reservations. However, some people may prefer to avoid racing for a bed at the end of a day of walking, especially during the peak months (May-Sept.). You can reserve accommodations in advance or as you go.

of friendly calico and striped cats also share the space but go about their own business.

2. Castromaior

Continue a couple more kilometers (a little over a mile) to the small village of Castromaior (pop. 30). As you are about to leave Castromaior, look for the **Bar O Castro** (Castromaior, 11; €4-10) to the left, a great place to stop for a homemade dish of yogurt from local cow's milk or the patroness's fresh raspberry smoothie, both of which are delicious.

top, Portomarín; bottom, Iglesia de Santiago

★ 3. Castro de Castromaior

As you leave the village of Castromaior, follow signs to the Castro de Castromaior. It's just a slight, 200-m (656-ft) detour off the Camino (to the left), and it's one of the highlights of the entire route.

Some 2,400 years ago, on this hilltop, Iron Age peoples built a substantial castro (hilltop fortress) and enclosed it with a series of round fortifying walls. Archaeologists began excavating this castro in 2004, and though most of it is still under mounds of sediment and grass, the excavation has already revealed a large hill fort town, along with the walls that surround it.

The settlement's protective outer walls have yet to be excavated and are currently ring-shaped earthen mounds. You'll pass through each ring wall on a dirt path as you approach the protected settlement. Once you step through the inner wall's entrance and climb up to the center of the windy hilltop and castro, you will see why Iron Age peoples built here: a 360-degree view offers perfect visibility and yet the hilltop is practically unseen from below, offering its residents enhanced protection. From here, look for the excavated houses of the castro that lie within the innermost protective wall; you'll also be able to make out the outlines and homes still under the earth and of the other two walls encircling the Iron Age town.

Castro de Castromaior

Exit the site (a yellow arrow on a tree points the way). After a slight climb up and over the castro wall, you'll see the Camino—indicated by a visible iconic stone pillar with scallop shell—and soon you can rejoin the pilgrimage trail.

4. Cruceiro de Lameiros

Follow the path from there through fields and forest to the Cruceiro de Lameiros, an elaborate and expressive cross on the left side of the road, standing near an ancient and venerated oak. Both the cross and the oak tree are symbolic. You'll continue seeing oak trees—and at times cypress and olive—planted around churches and chapels all along the Camino. Veneration of oak trees has been a tradition from the Iron Age to Christianity, representing strength, wisdom, and transcendence.

Less than 1 km (0.6 mi) from the Cruceiro de Lameiros, you'll reach the village of **Ligonde** (km 76.4; pop. 168) with food and lodging options.

5. Eirexe

Just after Ligonde, the neighboring hamlet of Eirexe (pop. 3)—also spelled Airexe—is your stop for the night. Eirexe is just a small cluster of buildings in a grove of trees, reflecting the serene and self-sufficient life of farm, fields, and kitchen gardens.

At night, the **Restaurante Ligonde** (tel. 660-971-787; www.restauranteligonde.com; €10-12) becomes the center of village life. They serve a traditional pilgrims' menu—salad, soup, pasta, grilled fish, chicken, pork, or beef, and an array of desserts—and it's good, fresh home cooking.

Spend the night at **Pensión Eirexe** (Airexe, 18; tel. 982-153-475 or 650-965-873; five private rooms; €25-40), one of the Camino's best-run inns.

Other Starting Points

Walkers commence their journey at different starting points for a variety of reasons, some because they can only get one to two weeks off at a time, and others because of personal preferences for terrain and duration. **Sarria,** where this itinerary starts, is the single most popular starting point, with 50 percent of pilgrims starting here. It's the last easily accessible access point from which to start and still earn a Compostela. There are five other common starting points.

- **Saint-Jean-Pied-de-Port,** the Camino's official starting place, is the second most popular starting point. It takes 33-34 days to walk to Santiago de Compostela from here.
- Four percent of pilgrims start in **Roncesvalles,** which is still an early start but skips the rigorous mountain crossing from Saint-Jean-Pied-de-Port.
- **León** is home to a Gothic cathedral that imbues this midway starting point with medieval mood and mystery. From here, the third most popular place to start, it takes 14-16 days to reach Santiago.
- Five percent of pilgrims start in **Ponferrada,** which is home to a dramatic Templar Castle and is easy to access by train and bus.
- Santiago is 7-8 days from the dramatic mountaintop town of **O Cebreiro,** where 5-6 percent of pilgrims start.

DAY 3

Eirexe to Melide

Walking Distance: 22.6 km (14 mi)

1. Iglesia de San Salvador de Vilar de Donas

Usually noon-6:40pm Tues.-Sun. July-Oct., inquire with Palas de Rei's tourist office (tel. 982-380-001; www.concellopalasderei.es)

Depart Eirexe and soon arrive in the next village of **Portos,** where you can make a 2.2-km/1.4-mi (4.4 km/2.7 mi round-trip) detour to the Iglesia de San Salvador de Vilar de Donas. Only the chapel of this medieval monastery complex survives, but it still is considered one of the region's Romanesque gems. You'll find extensive and well-preserved 14th-15th-century Gothic murals, as well as a Gothic-arched west porch.

2. Palas de Rei

From Portos, the Camino meanders 5.4 km (3.4 mi) to Palas de Rei (pop. 3,326), a serious working farm town, with tractors rolling through and the occasional cow, donkey, chickens, and passing sheep herd.

As you enter Palas de Rei, you pass its most historic icon, the **Iglesia of San Tirso** (Travesía da Igrexa, s/n; mass 7pm Mon.-Sat., 12:30pm and 7pm Sun. and holidays). A church has stood on this spot, in one form or another, since the 9th century. The interior offers respite for anyone seeking a quiet retreat. Don't miss the sculptures: There's Mary standing on a big three-dimensional spiral, and Baby Jesus with a sandal dangling from his right foot.

For a place to eat, try **Mesón A Forxa** (Traversía da Igrexa, 2; tel. 982-380-340; €10-12).

3. Leboreiro

After several other hamlets, enter Leboreiro, a peaceful and pleasing village to walk through. The village church, **Iglesia de Santa María,** is dedicated to

Leboreiro

Pilgrim's Credential

A pilgrim's credential—**credencial del peregrino** in Spanish and **carnet de pélerin in French,** also known as your pilgrim passport—is what allows you to stay in albergues along the Camino. They typically cost €2, and you can order one online before leaving from a pilgrim association, such as the American Friends of the Camino (USA), Canadian Company of Pilgrims, Confraternity of Saint James (UK), Camino Society Ireland, Australian Friends of the Camino (Australia and New Zealand), and Confraternity of St. James South Africa. You can also pick one up at a number of places along the way, including at Sarria's Iglesia de Santa Mariña (Plaza de Juan Lopéz, s/n; tel. 982-531-024).

Getting your passport stamped at albergues, churches, and other landmarks is an important part of walking the Camino: You need a minimum of **two stamps per day** from the **last 100 km/62 mi** (or the last 200 km/124 mi if you're traveling by bicycle) to collect your **Compostela** (the certificate completing the pilgrimage) in Santiago de Compostela. Fortunately, practically every place on the Camino will have a stamp to offer. The locals really get into this tradition and love designing stamps for their businesses. Many will have them out front on the counter, but if you don't see one, be sure to ask.

When you arrive in Santiago de Compostela, take your credential to the pilgrim reception office to receive your Compostela. It's a jubilant moment.

Mary, who is said to have appeared in a nearby fountain one night, combing her hair. Take a few moments to study the church entrance, an unusual tympanum of appealingly primitive design.

4. Melide

On your way to Melide (5.7 km/3.5 mi from Leboreiro), where you'll be spending the night, you'll cross over two pretty stone medieval bridges, in Leboreiro and in Furelos. The area also teems with prehistoric remains, from 4,000-year-old burial mounds to Roman roads.

Melide also has more modern delights and boasts many culinary creations, including its creamy and delicious locally made cheeses, several types of bread, and a celebrated cookie called **melindres de melide,** which you will likely smell

Iglesia de Santa María

Albergues

There are hotels and pensiones (budget inns) along the Camino, but albergues (pilgrim dorms) are the traditional accommodations for pilgrims walking the Camino. Albergues are only meant for those walking or cycling the Camino and who have a credential (but don't sweat it—if you lose your credential, you can buy a new one and get it stamped at the albergue). Additionally, walkers get priority over cyclists. Many only allow cyclists to check in after 6pm, 3-4 hours after the albergue opens for walkers, and only if there are any beds left over.

TYPES

There are four general types of albergues:

- **Municipal** or **xunta:** Run by the town or village.
- **Parroquia** and **monasterio:** Run by a religious organization, either a local parish or a monastic order.
- **Privado:** Run by private individuals/families.
- **Asociación:** Run by nonprofit pilgrim associations, typically from different countries, and usually run by volunteers.

PRICING AND RESERVATIONS

Most albergues have set prices but some run on a **donativo** (donation) basis; try to leave at least €6 minimum if you can. Typically, municipal albergues are bare bones and the least expensive (around €8). Next in price are those run by parishes and associations (€6-12), followed by private albergues (€10-20), which offer more creature comforts. Most albergues of all types, except most municipal ones, offer an evening menú or communal meal (€10-14), and many also offer breakfast (€3-6).

It's possible to travel without reservations on the Camino, but during the peak months (May-Sept.), you may want to make reservations to avoid the "bed race" at the end of the day. You don't have to book any further ahead than for the next day.

WHAT TO EXPECT

Most albergues open in the afternoon and stay open until about 10pm, which is lights out, when everyone is expected to be in bed and quiet. Some even lock the doors, so it is good to observe the curfew.

When staying in an albergue, you will be sleeping in a room with other people, at times as few as 2-4, and at others, as many as 50, but on average, around 8-15 people. Almost all the albergues are mixed-gender dorms, though a few have separate women's and men's sleeping quarters. Many, especially the private albergues, also have private rooms that cost two to three times more than a dorm bed (€25-45). Beds are almost all twin size, and most are bunk beds. Bathrooms vary: Some are gender-mixed and others separate. Some have private shower stalls and others are open. (All have private toilets!)

WHAT TO BRING

If you plan to stay in albergues, you'll want to pack a light, small, quick-dry traveler's towel and either a light sleeping bag or sleeping bag sheet, depending on the season. Consider bringing flip-flops to wear in the shower.

before you see: The perfume of their key ingredient, anise, laces the air as you walk into town. Try them at **Panadería Tarrío** (Calle de San Antonio, 21), where you can also stock up on rustic breads and other picnic staples for the trail.

But what Melide is most famous for is the Galician specialty **pulpo á feira,** boiled octopus seasoned with sea salt, smoked paprika, and olive oil. There are two excellent places in town where you can try the dish: **Pulpería Garnacha** (Rúa Camiño Vello de Santiago, 2; tel. 981-507-347 or 605-883-268; www.pulperiaagarnacha.com; €10-25) and **Pulpería Ezequiel** (Cantón de San Roque, 48; tel. 981-505-291; www.pulperiaezequiel.com; €10-25). These communal and festive eateries offer plenty more to savor, even if octopus is not your thing.

DAY 4

Melide to Arzúa

Walking Distance: 13.9 km (8.6 mi)

★ 1. Iglesia de Santa María de Melide

Rúa Santa María, s/n; tel. 981-505-003; www.santiagoturismo.com; mass 11am Sun.

One km (0.6 mi) from the center of Melide, pause at a crown jewel of the Camino: the Iglesia de Santa María de Melide. This late-11th-century church preserves two ornate doorways on the south and west sides, and also has multicolored frescoes from the 12th and 15th centuries inside. The altar is an 8th-century Visigothic piece reused from an earlier chapel.

The church has a champion as well, an engaging volunteer, José Antonio, who opens the church for visits and guided tours when he is not working his full-time job (usually on holidays and weekends). Passionate about the Middle Ages, he will gladly discuss the church's earlier founda-

left, Arzúa; right, Iglesia de Santa María de Melide

tions, not only from the Visigoths, but further back to the Iron Age Celtic speakers who possibly also worshipped here.

2. Ribadiso da Baixo

Beyond the church, follow the tree-covered lanes and forest paths to the 13th-century **bridge** that leads into Ribadiso da Baixo, a hamlet of nine people. The village is home to the **Hospital de San Antón,** a restored pilgrims' hospital that dates back to 1523 and is now used as an albergue. **Mesón Rural Ribadiso** (€8-14) is a terrific café; for dessert, try the local semi-soft arzúa cheese with a dense slice of membrillo (quince paste).

3. Arzúa

Continue along country roads and a slight ascent until you reach the substantial town of Arzúa, an upbeat place famous for locally produced cow's milk **cheeses** (and a great place to try them). Stay the night in an albergue or pension here, dining at **Restaurante Casa Nene** (Rúa Cima do Lugar, 1; tel. 981-08-107; €30), where the cheese board for dessert will let you sample the best of Arzúa's cheeses.

DAY 5

Arzúa to O Pedrouzo

Walking Distance: 19.1 km (11.9 mi)

1. O Empalme de Santa Irene

From Arzúa, the Camino continues through bucolic countryside and tiny settlements. Make a point of being in O Empalme de Santa Irene (15.3 km/9.5 mi from Arzúa) in time for lunch at **Café O Ceadoiro** (O Empalme de Santa Irene, 18; tel. 981-511-348), a delightful roadside café with locally harvested and home-cooked meals popular with locals.

2. O Pedrouzo

A kilometer (about half a mile) after O Empalme de Santa Irene, pass through

O Pedrouzo

WATCH

The Way: This 2010 film was written by Emilio Estevez and stars his father, Martin Sheen, as a fictional father who has a personal reason for walking the Camino de Santiago.

READ

The Pilgrimage by Paulo Coehlo: The author (best known for *The Alchemist*) recounts his pilgrimage on the Camino de Santiago in this 1987 book.

LISTEN

"Tu gitana" by Luar na Lubre: Check out this group for traditional Galician music.

the hamlet of Santa Irene, and soon after a short detour leads to a good array of food and accommodation options in O Pedrouzo, where you'll be spending your last night on the trail. For a meal, try **Taste the Way** (Avenida de Lugo, 9; tel. 615-104-141; www.tastetheway.com; €4-30), a creative gourmet café with Galician-style omnivore and vegetarian dishes.

DAY 6

O Pedrouzo to Santiago de Compostela

Walking Distance: 20 km (12.4 mi)

1. Lavacolla

Your last day on the Camino continues through fragrant eucalyptus forest and proceeds to the historic village of **Lavacolla** (10 km/6.2 mi after O Pedrouzo). In medieval times, pilgrims washed their private parts in the freshwater stream here. There's an important metaphor to the ritual: to cleanse one's body in preparation to cleanse one's soul.

2. Monte de Gozo

Continue through a neighborhood on the outskirts of Santiago and climb toward Monte de Gozo, or Mount Joy. This is the 380-m-high (1,247-ft) historic hill from which medieval pilgrims first caught sight of Santiago de Compostela's cathedral spires and cried out with emotion, "Mont joie!" ("Mount Joy!"). You can still catch a glimpse of Santiago de Compostela from here, even though the tree cover at mid-distance blocks the cathedral spires.

★ 3. Catedral de Santiago de Compostela

9am-8:30pm daily; free

The path enters Santiago de Compostela on the west side of town at the neighborhood of **San Lázaro.** Way-markers along the streets lead you into the medieval center of the city and straight to the cathedral square, **Plaza de Obradoiro,** which faces the western entrance of the Catedral de Santiago de Compostela.

Regional Cuisine

Galicia's fertile landscape and proximity to the ocean translates into diverse and delicious foods from both land and sea.

CHEESE

The **tetilla** cheese, unmistakable from its breast shape (hence the name), is common across the Camino in Galicia. It is a creamy, medium-yellow, and semi-cured cheese with a buttery and mild flavor. A similarly shaped cheese known as **san simón** is firmer and smoked (traditionally with birch wood) and also ubiquitous across Galicia, easily found in just about every grocery and cheese shop. Semi-soft but dense and creamy cheeses from the **Palas de Rei, Melide,** and **Arzúa** area are famous. If you are lucky to be walking in autumn when locals make quince preserves, be sure to ask for the dessert of **queso con membrillo** (cheese with quince paste).

CALDO GALLEGO

Caldo Gallego, a pork and bean stew rich in dark leafy greens (collards, kale, or mustard tops/grelos), as well as potatoes, onions, and garlic, is ubiquitous in pretty much every bar, café, restaurant, and household, each chef putting a unique spin on this iconic dish.

SEAFOOD

Pulpo á feira—boiled octopus seasoned with Spanish paprika, sea salt, and olive oil and served on a wooden platter, accompanied with local white wine—is synonymous with Galicia. On the Camino, Melide is the most famous destination for pulpo á feira. Once here, you will pretty much find it offered almost everywhere and all chefs take pride in their pulpo.

Try all things from the sea here, such as **percebes** (gooseneck barnacles that look like dinosaur claws but harbor meat tasting like oysters crossed with lobster), eel (especially the braised eel, **lampera estofado**), and most especially, the scallops that give the Camino its symbol: the large ones are often called **vieiras,** and the smaller ones, **zamburiñas.**

CASTAÑAS

Before potatoes arrived in Iberia from the Americas, castañas or chestnuts were, and sometimes still are, used in the same way. During chestnut season (autumn and winter), you may find a creamy chestnut soup, **sopa de castaña,** on the menu, made from nuts gathered from the forests through which you walk. The chestnuts are boiled and shelled, sautéed in pork fat with onions and garlic, and then puréed and finished with a bit of wine or sherry vinegar and a drizzle of olive oil before serving.

PIMENTOS DE PADRÓN

In an order of these little green peppers, about one in 10 is hot and the rest are sweet. They are almost always sautéed in olive oil and served crispy and hot with a dash of sea salt.

DESSERT

Galicians make traditional crepes (**freixós** and **filloas** in Galician, and frisuelos in Spanish) that are similar to those found in Brittany, but usually served sweet, with a dusting of sugar. Among the most frequent desserts you'll be offered is the **tarta de Santiago,** a dense almond cake with a powdered-sugar sword of Santiago dusted on the surface.

WINE

Albariño, the effervescent dry white best known from the Rias Baixas along the coast, is one of more than a dozen grape varietals grown in Galicia. Three other celebrated growing regions, Valdeorras, Ribeiro, and Ribeira Sacra—which the Camino passes through just after Sarria—produce wonderful local wines as well. Other grape varietals worth looking for are **godello, dona branca,** and **palomino fino** for white wines and **mencia, garnacha, tempranillo,** and **loureira,** among others, for reds.

ORUJO

The local after-dinner drink, orujo, is made from the residue of pressed grapes, stems, and seeds left over after winemaking. Once distilled, orujo is offered three ways: straight as it is (a clear liquor), infused with locally harvest herbs (a yellow liquor), or infused with coffee (a dark brown liquor). It is mostly a homemade enterprise. Makers pride themselves on the quality, especially of their **orujo con hierbas,** orujo with herbs, selecting secret herbs that grow in the surrounding valley or mountain to alchemically transform the elixir. Orujo is believed to have healing medicinal properties and is often offered as a gift and a gesture of shared well-being. Orujo is also the key ingredient in the ritual brew called **queimada.**

left, Monte de Gozo; right, Pilgrims' Reception Office

Do as pilgrims have done over the past millennia: Enter the cathedral and deliver a long-awaited hug to Santiago on the high altar. Congratulations! You did it!

The cathedral stands on the hill where Santiago's tomb was discovered in the 9th century, buried there since the 1st century on an already known Iron Age and Roman-era burial hill. News of the discovery soon spread, and by the end of the 9th century, pilgrims were beginning to make their way from across Europe to Compostela. At first, a small church covered the tomb, but each century demanded a larger church.

Highlights of the cathedral are the **Pórtico de la Gloría** (one of the glories of medieval architecture on the Camino, by master builder Maestro Mateo), the main altar, Santiago's relics crypt, the **botafumeiro** (massive swinging incense burner), the 9th-century chapel of **Capilla de la Corticela,** and the four exterior facades of the cathedral, not to mention the exquisite stonework, Romanesque capital sculptures, and the curious stonemason's marks throughout.

4. Pilgrims' Reception Office

Rúa Carretas, 33; tel. 981-568-846; www.oficinadelperegrino.com; 10am-6pm daily

Perhaps the most important stop before or after you visit the cathedral is the pilgrims' reception office, **Oficina Acogida al Peregrino.** It's about a five-minute walk downhill and north of the cathedral to pick up your hard-earned Compostela. Before new measures were set in place, due to Covid-19, pilgrims simply could go to the pilgrims' reception office, stand in line (often quite long), and pick up their Compostela when it came their turn. Now, pilgrims are asked to register in advance on the reception office's website and obtain a number and a time to visit the pilgrim office to gather their certificate.

When it is your turn to go, take your stamped credential, wait in line in the order of your assigned number, and then step up to the counter to receive a beautiful illuminated certificate on ivory-toned

Catedral de Santiago de Compostela

paper in Latin inscribed with your name and the date. It is not mandatory, but you can make a small contribution (a few centimes to €1-2), if you wish, in return for your Compostela.

5. Celebrate in Santiago de Compostela

For a celebratory dinner, head to **Jardín Café Costa Vella** (Calle Puerta de la Pena, 17; tel. 981-569-530; www.costavella.com). Locals come to this spot, which has the feeling of a secret garden, for deep conversation, atmosphere, serene calm, and at times, live music.

Hotel Fonte de San Roque (Rúa Hospitaliño, 8; tel. 981-554-447; www.hotelfontedesanroque.com; 15 rooms; €40-80) is one of the most uplifting places to stay in Santiago de Compostela, with an exuberant staff who brighten each time you walk through the door. The rooms, with 19th-century decor, are fresh, inviting, and immaculate. If you want to treat yourself to a luxurious stay, try **Hostal de los Reis Católicos** (Praza do Obradoiro, 1; tel. 981-582-200; www.parador.es; 137 rooms; €150-300), a late-15th century pilgrims' hospital that today is an opulent accommodation.

DAY 7

Santiago de Compostela

1. Mercado de Abastos

Rúa das Ameás, s/n; tel. 981-583-438; www.mercadodeabastosdesantiago.com; 8am-2pm Mon.-Sat.

Start your morning in Santiago de Compostela at the Mercado de Abastos, one of the most distinctive and colorful markets in Spain. The market has both covered and open-air sections, the latter wrapping around the former over a space that covers a large city block. Here you can find everything you need for a picnic or souvenirs, from local cheeses (including tetilla), sausages, meats, fish, vegetables, seasonal fruits, and elixirs. Sellers of household goods, clothes, and crafts also set up on the perimeter.

Mercado de Abastos

2. Museo de las Peregrinaciones y de Santiago

Plaza de las Platerías, 2; tel. 881-867-401; www.museoperegrinacions.xunta.gal; 9:30am-8:30pm Tues.-Fri., 11am-7:30pm Sat., 10:15am-2:45pm Sun. and holidays; €2.40/€1.20 for pilgrims

Next, spend an hour in the Museo de las Peregrinaciones y de Santiago, an interactive and engaging museum dedicated entirely to the theme of pilgrimage, from its first occurrences in human society, to its manifestations across the globe, to the Camino itself.

Afterward, have a lively meal at **Casa Manolo** (Praza de Cervantes; tel. 981-582-950; www.casamanolo.es), which has been hailed as a pilgrim meeting place for over three decades. The ample three-course pilgrims' menu (€11, wine not included) highlights classic Galician home cooking.

3. Petróglifo de Castriño de Conxo

www.compostelarupestre.gal

In the afternoon, walk 2.6 km (1.6 mi) to

the outer edge of the old town to see the surviving 3,000-year-old petroglyph of Castriño de Conxo. It dates from the late Bronze Age or early Iron Age—attesting that this place was considered sacred long before the time of Saint James—and its impressive images are engraved on a large, gray granite rock face. The images show a hybrid bird/man with a human-sized bird body, outstretched wings, and a human head.

4. Evening Mass at Catedral de Santiago de Compostela

Return to the cathedral for evening pilgrims' mass, at 7:30pm daily. If you're lucky, you will get to see the massive incense burner, **botafumeiro,** in use.

Then, kick off the evening sampling the tapas, pinchos, and regional wines at the bars lining on the streets of **Rúas Franco, Nova, Vilar,** and **Raiña.** Finish the evening at **Café Casino** (Rua do Vilar, 35; tel. 981-577-503; www.cafecasino.gal) with a flaming cup of **queimada,** a heated concoction of spirits, sugar, coffee beans, and orange and lemon peels that's said to quemar (burn) out all bad karma and energy.

TRANSPORTATION

Air

The most common international airport to reach the Sarria is Madrid's **Adolfo Suárez Madrid–Barajas Airport** (MAD; www.aeropuertomadrid-barajas.com), which is well connected to Sarria by train (5-6 hours).

Santiago de Compostela's **Rosalía de Castro airport** (SCQ; www.aena.es/en/santiago-rosalia-de-castro.html) is the closest airport to Sarria and serves flights from within Spain and nearby European countries. From Santiago de Compostela, you can catch a train (2-3.5 hours) or a bus (2 hours) to Sarria.

Train

Spain's national rail, **RENFE** (www.renfe.com), connects Madrid to Sarria (5-6 hours from Madrid; €43-58; some trains to Sarria change in Ourense).

The **Sarria train station** (Rúa Calvo Sotelo, s/n) is 1.1 km (0.7 mi) north of the Camino, about a 20-minute walk.

Bus

The bus company **ALSA** (www.alsa.com) runs buses from Madrid to Pedrafita do Cebreiro, where you transfer to a **Monbus** (www.monbus.com) bus to get to Sarria (8-9 hours).

The **Sarria bus station** (Rúa Matías López, s/n) is 800 m (0.5 mi) north of the Camino where it enters Rúa Maior near Iglesia de Santa Mariña (Plaza Juan María López and Rúa Maior, 65), a 12-minute walk.

Getting Back

To get back to **Sarria,** Monbus runs a bus from Santiago de Compostela (2 hours; €7-14).

To get back to **Madrid** (5-6.5 hours; €45-58), you can take a train from Santiago de Compostela's RENFE station, which is 1.6 km (1 mi) directly south of the cathedral, a 20-minute walk. **ALSA** (www.alsa.com) also runs buses to Madrid's Barajas airport (9-14 hours; €49-72).

You can also catch a flight out of Santiago de Compostela's **Rosalía de Castro airport** to Madrid, Paris, London, and a few other major European hubs. The city airport **bus 6** runs nearly every half-hour to the airport with pickup points at the central Plaza de Galicia, near the historic city (35-45 minutes; €3). **Monbus** (www.monbus.es) also runs buses from the airport to the bus station next to Santiago's train station (15-30 minutes; €2).

- Barcelona and Madrid (page 99)
- The Douro Line (page 663)

ON THE WATER

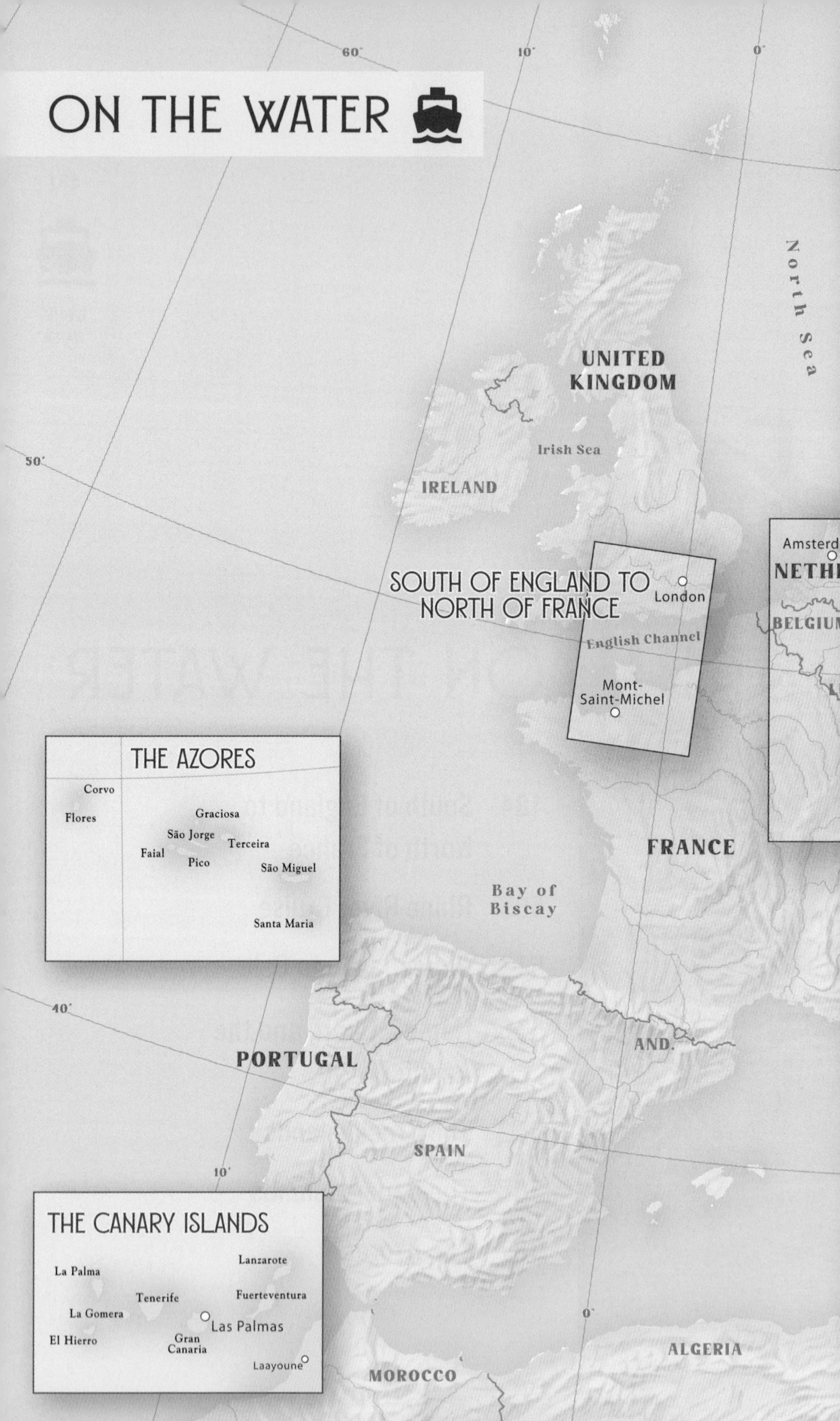

ON THE WATER
60°
10°
0°
North Sea
UNITED KINGDOM
Irish Sea
IRELAND
50°
SOUTH OF ENGLAND TO NORTH OF FRANCE
London
English Channel
Mont-Saint-Michel
Amsterd
NETH
BELGIU
THE AZORES
Corvo
Flores
Graciosa
São Jorge
Terceira
Faial
Pico
São Miguel
Santa Maria
FRANCE
Bay of Biscay
40°
PORTUGAL
AND.
SPAIN
10°
THE CANARY ISLANDS
La Palma
Lanzarote
Tenerife
Fuerteventura
La Gomera
Las Palmas
El Hierro
Gran Canaria
Laayoune
0°
ALGERIA
MOROCCO

ORWAY
FINLAND
COPENHAGEN
TO OSLO
Oslo
ESTONIA
RUSSIA
LATVIA
SWEDEN
ENMARK
LITHUANIA
Copenhagen
Baltic Sea
RUSSIA
BELARUS
POLAND
RHINE RIVER
CRUISE
GERMANY
UKRAINE
CZECHIA
SLOVAKIA
MOL.
AUSTRIA
HUNGARY
ROMANIA
ITZ.
SLO.
CROATIA
Black Sea
ITALY
BOS. &
HERZ.
SERBIA
BULGARIA
Adriatic
Sea
KOS.
MONT.
NORTH
MACEDONIA
NAPLES, CAPRI, AND
THE AMALFI COAST
Naples
Amalfi
ALBANIA
Aegean
Sea
TURKEY
GREECE
THE GREEK
ISLANDS
Athens
Santorini
Mediterranean Sea
TUNISIA
MALTA
10°
20°
30°
40°
50°
60°
© MOON.COM

SOUTH OF ENGLAND TO NORTH OF FRANCE

Why Go: The 185-km (115-mi) journey across the English channel takes you from one history-rich coastline to another.

Number of Days: 5

Total Distance: 885 km (550 mi)

Seasons: Spring

Start: London

End: Mont-Saint-Michel

On this trip, you'll visit the historic heartlands of two countries that had more than their fair share of influence in shaping the modern world. For all their apparent differences, there is much in common between Southern England and Northern France. Traveling their genteel back roads, rolling fields, and historic towns, not to mention the sea that divides them, offers fascinating insight into the strange nature of national borders, a glimpse of a vital aspect of Europe's soul, and all the plush comforts of two regions that have been inexorably connected through much of history.

TOP 3

Diving deep into Britain's naval history at the **Historic Dockyard** in Portsmouth (page 491).

Paying respects to the hundreds of Allied servicemen who gave up their lives for freedom on **Omaha Beach,** one of the D-Day landing beaches (page 495).

Catching sight of **Mont-Saint-Michel** towering majestically over a vast tidal plain (page 498).

SOUTH OF ENGLAND TO NORTH OF FRANCE

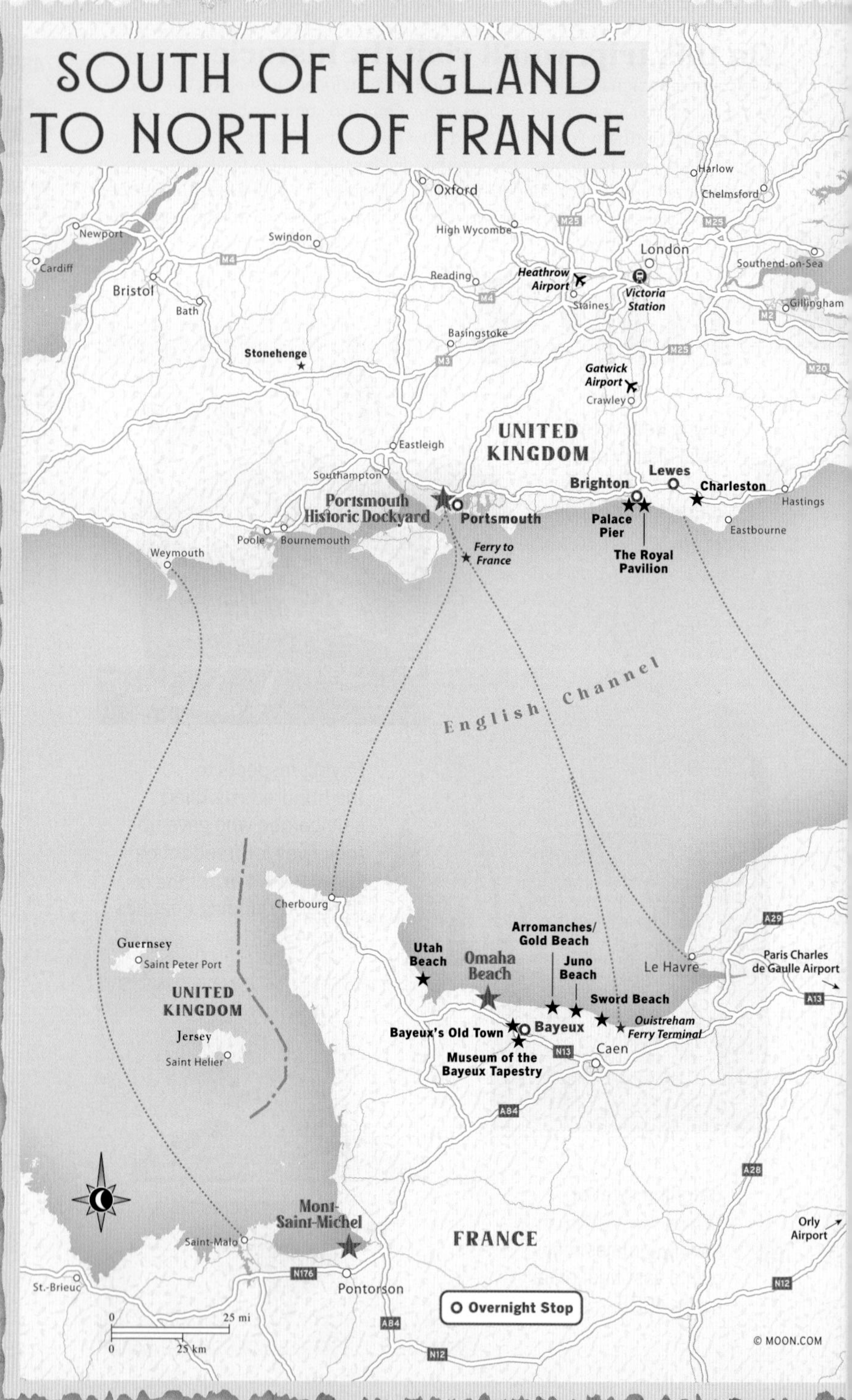

Harlow
Oxford
Chelmsford
High Wycombe
M25
Newport
Swindon
London
Cardiff
M4
Southend-on-Sea
Heathrow Airport
Reading
Victoria Station
Bristol
Staines
Gillingham
Bath
M4
M2
Basingstoke
Stonehenge
M3
M25
M20
Gatwick Airport
Crawley
UNITED KINGDOM
Eastleigh
Lewes
Southampton
Brighton
Charleston
Portsmouth Historic Dockyard
Portsmouth
Hastings
Palace Pier
Eastbourne
Poole
Bournemouth
Weymouth
Ferry to France
The Royal Pavilion
English Channel
Cherbourg
Arromanches/ Gold Beach
Utah Beach
Omaha Beach
Juno Beach
Guernsey
Saint Peter Port
Le Havre
Paris Charles de Gaulle Airport
A29
UNITED KINGDOM
Sword Beach
A13
Bayeux
Ouistreham Ferry Terminal
Jersey
Bayeux's Old Town
Saint Helier
N13
Caen
Museum of the Bayeux Tapestry
A84
A28
Mont-Saint-Michel
Orly Airport
FRANCE
Saint-Malo
N176
St.-Brieuc
Pontorson
N12
Overnight Stop
0
25 mi
0
25 km
A84
N12

London

Arrive by: Train to Victoria Station

1. Victoria Station, London

Victoria St.; tel. 0343 222 1234; https://tfl.gov.uk and www.networkrail.co.uk

Victoria train station is one of the world's great departure points, having been built to link London with England's south coast and, by extension, the rest of the world. Direct trains from Victoria to Lewes leave a little more than once every hour. Have breakfast at the nearby **Bill's Victoria** (6 Cathedral Walk, Cardinal Place; tel. 020 4512 6668; bills-website.co.uk/restaurants/victoria; 8am-11pm Mon.-Sat., 9am-10pm Sun.; Garden Plate breakfast £12.95), part of a restaurant chain founded in Lewes back in 2000, where the Garden Plate breakfast makes a great start to any journey.

Brighton

Where to Stay: Brighton seafront or Regency Square

Arrive by: Train from Victoria Station to Brighton Station (1.5 hours)

It's an easy shorthand to describe Brighton as a kind of London-on-sea, but reducing Brighton to just London's beach also misses much about its unique laid-back charm. With its fabulous Regency architecture, quirky backstreets, and tourist infrastructure that dates back to the very advent of tourism, the town overflows with its own character.

2. Brighton Waterfront Promenade

Take a casual stroll east along the embankment or the walkways on the beach itself.

Brighton waterfront promenade

Key Reservations

- Brittany Ferry from Portsmouth, England, to Ouistreham, France
- D-Day landing beaches tour

Brittany Ferry

Join the flow of other colorful meanderers, people-watching, architecture spotting, stopping in the bric-a-brac stores or looking out to sea.

3. The Palace Pier

Madeira Dr.; tel. 01273 609361; www.brightonpier.co.uk; 9am-9:30pm Mon.-Fri., 9am-10pm Sat.-Sun.; wristbands for all rides £30 for people over 1.2 m (4 ft) tall, £18 for shorter people

After about 10 minutes of walking, you'll come to Palace Pier, one of Brighton's most recognizable sights. Stretching out into the English Channel, this waterborne theme park opened in 1899. Complete with fairground rides like roller coasters and teacups, it really does look like a palace constructed over the sea.

It's a scientific fact (unverified) that England's national dish of fish-and-chips tastes 65 percent better when you eat it with a wooden fork, wrapped in greaseproof paper, facing the sea. There are a lot of great fish-and-chips places in Brighton, and Captains (9-10 lower promenade; tel. 07939 340458; www.captainsbrighton.co.uk; 10am-10:30pm daily, until 8pm in winter; mains from £10), at the foot of the pier, with a terrace straight on the beach, more than holds its own with all of them.

4. The Royal Pavilion

4/5 Pavilion Buildings; tel. 0300 029 0900; https://brightonmuseums.org.uk/royalpavilion; 9:30am-5:45pm daily Apr.-Sept., 10am-5:15pm daily Oct.-Mar.; adults £17, under 18 £10.50

Head north and inland up the Pavilion Parade—this is directly opposite the entrance to the pier, over a multipronged road junction. About five minutes along this, past the Old Steine Gardens you'll come to the Royal Pavilion. Constructed in the late 18th-early 19th century as a seaside residence for the then Prince Regent, who would go on to become King George IV, and modeled after the Mughal palaces of India, it's now a museum to the period when it was built. It consists of meticulously preserved rooms in the sumptuous Regency style,

top, the Palace Pier; bottom, the Royal Pavilion

SLOW IT DOWN: Brighton

With its 6-km-long (4-mi) beach, cosmopolitan restaurants, and lively nightlife, Brighton is an excellent place to stay for a few more days. Just be careful, or you may find yourself extending your trip indefinitely, seduced by what can only be called the Brighton state of mind.

- When the sun's shining there are few better things to do than pull up a picnic blanket and unfurl it on the pebbles of the town's **main beach.** The bustling vibes are unmatched, the nearby amenities plentiful, and the sea eminently swimmable—if a little cold.
- For those wanting a little pampering, why not book yourself into one of the many **luxury spas** in and around the town, like the one at the **Brighton Harbour Hotel** (64 Kings Rd.; tel. 01273 323221; www.harbourhotels.co.uk/brighton; treatments from £49 per person).
- Then, there are the town's many offbeat music venues, hosting gigs throughout the year—the beachfront **Brighton Music Hall** (Kings Road Arches, 127; www.brightonmusichall.co.uk) has an outdoor stage that really comes into its own over the summer months.
- There's also an embarrassment of good eating in town. Embrace the diversity of the modern British palate with a trip to the high-end grill **Salt Room** (106 Kings Rd.; tel. 01273 929488; https://saltroom-restaurant.co.uk), or go grazing at the recently rebuilt food market **Shelter Hall** (Kings Road Arches, Shelter Hall; tel. 07903 284511; https://shelterhall.co.uk).

but the building's main draw is probably its external appearance, garlanded it as it is by glorious domes direct from the English imagination of the East.

5. Shopping Tour of the Lanes

Heading along North Street (which actually runs the southern length of the Royal Pavilions grounds) will take you to The Lanes, a maze of narrow streets boasting a strong Bohemian feel along with a whole constellation of quirky, independent stores, from esoteric junk shops like the North Laine Bazaar (5, 5A Upper Gardner St.; tel. 01273 626634; www.northlainebazaar.com; 10am-5:30pm Mon.-Fri., 10am-6pm Sat., 11am-4:30pm Sun.) to real one-of-a-kind establishments. The best way to tackle them is without any plan in particular, just letting your nose guide you, surprise by surprise. As long as you remain within their rough bounds of North Street to the north, Ship Street to the west, Prince Albert Street to the south, and East Street to the east, you can't go wrong.

There are also plenty of pubs and bars where you can refuel or stop for dinner. Try Indian Summer (70 East St.; tel. 01273 711001; www.indiansummerbrighton.co.uk; 5pm-10:30pm Mon.-Fri., noon-10:30pm Sat.-Sun.; mains from £6) for award-winning food and flavors of the subcontinent.

DAY 2

Portsmouth

Arrive by: Train from Brighton Station to Portsmouth Harbour Station (1 hour 45 minutes)

★ 1. Portsmouth's Historic Dockyard

Victory Gate, HM Naval Base; tel. 023 9283 9766; www.historicdockyard.co.uk; 10am-5pm daily; 3-attraction ticket adults £34, children £24

One of the best attractions in the country offers deep, interactive insight into Britain's naval past with three prestige "exhibitions" in which visitors are invited to explore some of the most important historic ships ever to sail under the British flag. Here you'll visit Nelson's flagship, the **HMS *Victory;*** the steel 19th-century hulk of the **HMS *Warrior;*** and the restored wreck of Tudor battleship, the ***Mary Rose.*** Take the guided tours to really get the most out of the experience. There's also an on-site museum of naval history and several

Portsmouth

(top to bottom) shopping tour of the Lanes; Old Steine Gardens on the way to the Royal Pavilion; Portsmouth's historic dockyard; ferry to France

smaller exhibitions—more than you can easily cram into a full day, so plan your time wisely.

Afterward, have dinner at **The Ship & Castle** (90 Rudmore Square; tel. 023 9267 0998; www.shipandcastleportsmouth.co.uk; 11am-midnight Mon.-Fri., 11am-1am Sat., 11am-10:30pm Sun.; mains from £6.50), right next door to the ferry port. It overflows with authenticity—a real sailor's tavern that has been serving a final slice of English dining to people about to depart to the continent for years.

2. Ferry to France

The Brittany Centre, Wharf Rd.; tel. 330 159 7000; www.brittany-ferries.co.uk; £37-161

After being near the sea for so long, there's something exciting about setting out upon it, leaving Portsmouth the same way that hundreds of explorers and admirals have done before. Granted, the Brittany Ferries that sail every evening across the Channel may not quite be the HMS *Victory,* but there's still something stirring about standing out on deck, watching the lights of the British shore disappear, the salt smell of the sea in your nostrils and the wandering screech of seagulls in your ears.

Even better is arriving the next morning "on the continent," as the British say, the French shore greeting you from the horizon, a whole new country to explore. There are 2-4 sailings a day, depending on the time of year (more in the summer months), with the night boat leaving at 10:45pm and getting to France just before 7am the next morning. For this crossing, it's highly recommended that you book a cabin, which though more expensive, will leave you refreshed and ready to carry on your journey the next day without fuss. Cabins come in various shapes and sizes, all accommodating at least four people. The most luxurious come with a balcony and a complimentary continental breakfast, though even the least expensive are relatively spacious and comfortable, even if they don't necessarily have outside windows.

ADDING ON Stonehenge

The standing stone circle known as Stonehenge (Salisbury; www.english-heritage.org.uk/visit/places/Stonehenge; daily 9:30am-5pm; adults £22, children £13.20) is one of the UK's most famous and recognizable sights. The questions surrounding its origins and the unique lintel formation add to Stonehenge's attraction, with thousands of visitors every year making their way to the windswept Salisbury plain to see this Neolithic sight. The summer and winter solstices are especially popular times to visit: The stones seem to frame the setting sun on the former and the rising sun for the latter. Booking tickets ahead of time is recommended.

To reach Stonehenge, you have to travel through **Salisbury.** The soaring Gothic **Salisbury Cathedral** (Salisbury; www.salisburycathedral.org.uk; Mon.-Sat. 10am-4:30pm; adults £10, children £6-7) is the town's centerpiece, and it holds an original Magna Carta document.

GETTING THERE

From Portsmouth, it's possible to do a day trip to Stonehenge. From Portsmouth Harbour station, head to Salisbury via the Great Western Rail (www.gwr.com; direct 1.5 hours, change at Southampton 2 hours; £22). From Salisbury station, you can either take the hop-on, hop-off Stonehenge Tour bus (www.thestonehengetour.info; 30 minutes; adults £34, children £22.50) or the Connecting Wiltshire public bus (www.connectingwiltshire.co.uk; 30 minutes; adults £9.50, children £6.20) to reach the Stonehenge Visitors Center.

DAY 3

Caen

Arrive by: Ferry from Portsmouth Harbour to Ouistreham Ferry Terminal

1. Café Breakfast

The ferry arrives in the port of **Ouistreham,** a suburb of Caen, and to carry on your journey take a taxi (around €30) or the Twisto bus (12EX from the rue du Tour de Ville; www.twisto.fr; €2) into Caen's city center. You've just arrived in France! A stop at a café is in order; there are a number of them near Caen's train station where you can find your first authentic croissant and café noir with which to start the day. A good bet is the **Quai des Arts** (40 Pl. de la Gare; tel. 02 50 50 00 56; 8am-9pm Mon.-Fri., 11am-9pm Sun.). From there, hop on the train to Bayeux.

Where to Stay: Bayeux Town Center

Arrive by: Train from Caen Station to Bayeux Station (20 minutes)

2. Notre Dame Cathedral

Rue du Bienvenu; tel. 02 31 92 48 48; www.bayeux.fr/fr/decouvrir-bayeux/cathedrale-notre-dame; 9am-5pm daily Jan.-Mar., 8:30am-6pm daily Apr.-Jun., 9am-6pm daily Jul.-Dec.; free

Start your day in Bayeux at one of the great churches of France. With a towering, stark interior, this cathedral is also filled with light on account of large windows of clear glass that make up much of the church's transepts. Consecrated in 1077, the original structure was Romanesque, but it has been added to over the years in various different architectural styles. The most sustained period of additional building took place in the mid-13th century, and indeed, it was this period that gave the church most of its character.

Afterward, grab a bite in **Le Moulin de la Galette** (38 rue de Nesmond; tel. 02 31 22 47 75; 12:30pm-2:30pm and 7pm-9:30pm Fri.-Sat., 12:30pm-2:30pm and 7pm-9:30pm Sun.-Tues. and Thurs.; €6-17). There are few more picturesque places in Bayeux than this crepe restaurant, with its terrace over the River Aure. The restaurant can get very busy, so consider booking ahead or be prepared to wait for a table, especially on warm summer days.

3. Museum of the Bayeux Tapestry

13 bis Rue de Nesmond; tel. 02 31 51 25 50; www.bayeuxmuseum.com; 9am-6:30pm daily Mar.-Apr. and Sept.-Oct., 9am-7pm daily May-Aug., 9:30am-12:30pm and 2pm-6pm daily Nov.-Dec. and Feb.; adults €9.50, reduced €7.50, under 10 free

Time to take in the tapestry, a 70-m-long, 51-cm-wide (230-ft-long, 20-in-wide) length of embroidered fabric that

left, Notre Dame Cathedral; right, Bayeux

is effectively a 50-panel comic strip depicting the events surrounding William the Conqueror's successful invasion of England in 1066. This stands both as a remarkable work of art and a hugely instructive historical document, showing in visceral detail one of the most important events in European history. It offers a stunning illustration of Norman and Anglo-Saxon culture at the time of the conquest, including everything from ship-building techniques to hairstyles. Make sure to take advantage of the audio tour, which is free and really brings the story of the tapestry to life.

4. Bayeux's Old Town

After seeing the tapestry, take a casual stroll around Bayeux's back and front streets. From the **Quai de l'Aure** there's a nice view of the river, specifically the old water mill, which harkens back to the days when Bayeux was a center of the tanning and dyeing trade. Farther along, on the corner of the Rue Saint-Martin and Rue Cuisiniers, teeters an authentic **14th-century half-timber house.** It's a design common throughout northern France, though often only in reconstruction. There are plenty of fine townhouses, too, on the roads Franche, Ursulines, and Général-de-Dais, which are all worth a look on your way to the **Place Charles-de-Gaulle.** This refined public garden, dotted by trees and centered on a fountain, is a pleasant place to pause after your stroll before heading back into town for aperitif.

The aperitif is a venerable French institution, essentially consisting of an early evening drink and snacks. **Le Bouchon** (15 rue Maréchal Foch; tel. 02 31 92 06 44; www.lebouchon-cavebistrot.fr; 10am-5:30pm Mon., 10am-7:30pm Tues.-Thurs., 10am-9pm Fri.-Sat.), with its casual, bottle-lined interior and excellent platters of meat and cheese, is the perfect place to get acquainted with this custom.

DAY 4

The D-Day Landing Beaches

Arrive by: Car from Bayeux (30 minutes) or guided tour

The coast just north of Bayeux, and for roughly 40 km (25 mi) in either direction, was the site of one of World War II's most historic engagements and the largest military landing ever attempted: D-Day. In June 1944, this windswept length of shoreline became the first foothold that Allied forces were able to gain in Northern Europe, from which they began its bloody liberation, hastening the end of Nazi Germany and the war.

Today, the landscape remains sculpted by the brutality of war, and everywhere you look there are reminders, both incidental and deliberate, of the price paid by thousands of American, British, Canadian, and other Allied soldiers, fighting for freedom far from home. From international cemeteries to museums, to the careful preservation of certain battle sites, there is much on this beautiful coastline to inspire poignant reflection and to allow visitors to pay their respects.

★ 1. Omaha Beach

Plage, Vierville-sur-Mer

If there is any operation that stands in the forefront of peoples' minds for the terrifying slaughter that took place on the beaches of Normandy on June 6, 1944, then Omaha is it. This was one of the two

A Guide to the D-Day Beaches

D-Day beaches and the sights associated with Operation Overlord are spread across a very wide area. Indeed, just trying to see all the major battlegrounds in a single day provides a striking impression of the operation's scale. Sword Beach is farthest east, and from east to west are Juno Beach, Gold Beach, Omaha Beach, and Utah Beach, the westernmost invasion point. As a rule of thumb, it takes about half a day to explore one beach and its surrounds fully, thus a full day tour is enough for two.

SWORD BEACH

Lion Plage, Lion-sur-mer

This easternmost of the five Allied landing beaches, and the one situated closest to Caen, was assaulted by the British Third Infantry Division on D-Day. Today it is one of the most easily accessible of the beaches by public transport, with the small port town of Ouistreham nearby. This is where Sword's museums are located, including the **Musée du Mur de l'Atlantique le Bunker** (Avenue du 6 Juin, Ouistreham; tel. 02 31 97 28 69; https://museegrandbunker.com; 9am-7pm daily Apr.-Oct., 10am-6pm daily Nov.-Mar.; adults €8, reduced €6), dedicated to German coastal defenses, and the **Musée du No. 4 Commando** (Avenue du 6 Juin, Ouistreham; tel. 02 31 96 63 10; www.musee-4commando.fr; 10:30am-1pm and 1:30pm-6:30pm daily; adults €5, reduced €3), which tells the story of French commandos caught up in the invasion.

Nearby are the **Merville Battery** (Place du 9ème Bataillon, Merville-Franceville-Plage; tel. 02 31 91 47 53; www.batterie-merville.com; 9:30am-6:30pm mid-Mar.-Sept., 10am-5pm Oct.-mid-Nov.; adults €8, ages 6-14 €5, under 6 free), a museum surrounding a still-intact gun emplacement, and the **Memorial Pegasus** (Avenue du Major Howard, Ranville; tel. 02 31 78 19 44; musee.memorial-pegasus.com; 9:30am-6:30pm daily Apr.-Sept., 10am-5pm Oct.-mid-Dec. and Feb.-Mar.; adults €8, ages 8-17 €5.50, under 8 free), a museum and memorial dedicated to an operation to capture a bridge.

JUNO BEACH

2 Avenue du Château, Courseulles-sur-Mer

Juno Beach, located between the two British-attacked beaches and running from the village of Courseulles in the west to Saint-Aubin-sur-Mer in the east, was assaulted by a largely Canadian force. The beach itself is long and sandy, backed by houses and patches of scrub.

Most things to see here are located in Courseulles, including the **Juno Beach Centre** (Voie des Français Libres, Courseulles-sur-Mer; tel. 02 31 37 32 17; www.junobeach.org; 9:30am-7pm daily Apr.-Sept., 10am-6pm daily Mar. and Oct., 10am-5pm daily Feb. and Dec.; adults €7.50, reduced €6). This is not only a museum commemorating the events of Juno Beach, but also a cultural center dedicated to the entire Canadian experience of the Second World War in France and beyond.

GOLD BEACH

Arromanches les Bains

Located at the center of the five Normandy landing beaches, Gold Beach was taken by the British Army and is most notable for being the site of a floating harbor constructed soon after the invasion. Much of this remains today, with parts on the horizon looking like some vast art installation, and others dug in the sand of the beach, itself. Aside from these, there's the **Landing Museum** (Place du 6 Juin 1944, Arromanches-les-Bains; tel. 02 31 22 34 31; www.musee-arromanches.fr; 9am-7pm daily May-Aug., 9am-6pm daily Sept., 9:30am-12:30pm and 1:30pm-5:30pm Oct.-Dec. and Feb.-Apr.; adults €8.20, reduced €6). Notable for being the first museum dedicated to the Normandy landings anywhere along the coast (it opened June 5, 1954), it remains an excellent, digestible primer for teaching about D-Day.

OMAHA BEACH

Plage, Vierville-sur-Mer

One of two beaches assaulted by US forces, Omaha Beach (page 495) and the operation that took place here were immortalized by the photographs of Robert Capra, and then later realized in all its frenetic horror by Stephen Spielberg in the film *Saving Private Ryan.* At the nearby **Normandy American Cemetery and Memorial** (page 498), the serene white crosses lend the impression that this is American rather than French territory. **Pointe du Hoc** (page 498) was a fortified German area on a cliff between Omaha and Utah Beaches, which the US Army Ranger Assault Group captured by scaling the cliffs themselves.

UTAH BEACH

Pouppeville, La Madeleine

An American landing zone, this beach saw the fewest casualties sustained anywhere along the coast on D-Day. Today, visits focus on the part of the beach nearest the **Musée du Débarquement** (La Madeleine, Sainte-Marie-du-Mont; tel. 02 33 71 53 35; www.utah-beach.com; 9:30am-7pm daily Jun.-Sept., 10am-6pm daily Oct.-May; adults €8, under 15 €5, under 7 and WWII veterans free). This is among the best, most high-tech of the D-Day landing museums—it concentrates both on Utah and the broader operation. There's not a massive amount to see on the beach itself, but it bears perhaps the greatest similarity to how it might have appeared back in 1944.

BAYEUX SHUTTLE TOUR

tel. 9 70 44 49 89; www.normandy-sightseeing-tours.com; half-day tours from €65, full-day tours from €110

The best way to explore the D-Day beaches is to take a tour. On many of the beaches themselves there's not so much to actually see apart from sand and tussocks of grass, so a good tour guide can really help to bring the landscape's history alive. Bayeux Shuttle is one of the most applauded tours in the region. Be aware that the good reputation of this company is well-known, and as such, booking way in advance is highly recommended.

beaches assaulted by US forces, where the waves were at their most severe and where German resistance was strongest.

Today, Omaha is less built up than some of the other beaches; at the eastern end is the **Monument des Braves,** an abstract sculpture of straight and curving metal that thrusts from the sand like waves or the blades of swords. At high tide, their bases are submerged by the sea, bringing to mind the many soldiers who would have had to wade waist-deep toward Nazi gun emplacements on shore.

2. Pointe du Hoc

Pointe du Hoc, Cricqueville-en-Bessin; tel. 02 31 51 62 00; www.abmc.gov/cemeteries-memorials/europe/pointe-du-hoc-ranger-monument; 9am-6pm daily mid-Apr.-mid-Sept., 9am-5pm daily mid-Sept.-mid-Apr.; free

Make the short (15-minute) trip up to Pointe du Hoc, the remnants of a German fortification. What remains are undulations of bomb craters and mangled defense bunkers that serve as a haunting monument to the destructive powers of war.

Drive back toward Omaha Beach for a light seafood lunch at **La Sapinière** (100 Rue de la 2ème Division US, Saint-Laurentsur-Mer; tel. 02 31 92 71 72; www.la-sapiniere.fr; 12:30pm-2:30pm and 7:30pm-10pm daily; mains €16-20).

3. Normandy American Cemetery and Memorial

Colleville-sur-Mer; tel. 02 31 51 62 00; www.abmc.gov/cemeteries-memorials/europe/normandy-american-cemetery; 9am-6pm daily mid-Apr.-mid-Sept., 9am-5pm mid-Sept.-mid-Apr.; free

Nearby you will find this vast and hugely affecting cemetery where the massed ranks of headstones offer a whole other sense of scale to the conflict. The memorial inscriptions talk not of victory for its own sake, but of the noble sacrifice of the soldiers who fought to free the world of tyranny and never made it home.

After the long day, head back to Bayeux for dinner. **La Rapière** (53 rue Saint-Jean, Bayeux; tel. 02 31 21 05 45; www.larapiere.net; 6:30pm-9:15pm Mon.-Sat.; menus €36-49) offers the kind of rustic, home-cooked fare almost entirely sourced from local producers that people come to France to find. Expect rich and succulent variations on classic dishes of duck and veal, as well as the freshest local seafood.

DAY 5

Mont-Saint-Michel

Where to Stay: Grand Rue in Mont-Saint-Michel

Arrive by: Train from Bayeux Station to Pontorson Station (2.5 hours), then shuttle bus from Pontorson to Mont-Saint-Michel (20 minutes)

Because you can't very well visit the North of France without setting eyes on its most awe-inspiring sight, your next stop is the logic-defying, fantasy-realm cathedral island of Mont-Saint-Michel. A lonely rock rising from a vast tidal bay, it has been a place for Christian hermits since deep in the Dark Ages, and was consecrated as a religious site in the early 8th century. Following that, its architecture was added to until it became the Gothic marvel with a medieval village surrounding it that we see today.

★ 1. The Causeway

The shuttle from Pontorson will only take you as far as Mont-Saint-Michel's mainland tourist village; to get to the island itself, you need to get on one of the free shuttle buses. Or, better yet, walk across the causeway: Mont-Saint-Michel is in

the abbey

your sightline for the entire 30-minute walk.

This centuries-old pilgrimage sight has been called many things in its long history: "the jewel in France's crown," "the French pyramid," "wonder of the Western world," but no description can do justice to its majesty. Fantastic in the purest sense of the word, it seems to be more than mere physics that allow Mont-Saint-Michel to rise like a lonely mountain from its tidal bay. The Mont's iconic shape becomes more impressive the closer you get, as the complex tangle of old domestic housing, fortifications, and transcendent religious building is revealed.

2. The Grande Rue

Step through the main entrance in Mont-Saint-Michel's walls, and you'll see the tourist office to your left, while the citadel's main and only thoroughfare, the Grande Rue, extends off to your right. This climbs up, spiraling left past hotels, restaurants, and souvenir shops, toward the abbey, Mont-Saint Michel's main sight. It's a real gauntlet of tourist traps, where **La Sirène** (Grande Rue; tel. 02 33 60 08 60; 11:45am-3pm daily; €10) is one of the few places where you won't feel fleeced. Settle in for a crepe before tackling the abbey itself.

3. The Abbey

Abbaye du Mont-Saint-Michel; www.abbaye-mont-saint-michel.fr; 9:30am-6pm daily Jan. 2-Apr. 30, 9am-7pm daily May 2-Aug. 31, 9:30am-6pm daily Sept. 1-Dec. 31; adult €10, non-EU resident 18-25 €8, EU resident under 26 and non-EU resident under 18 free

Carry on to the abbey and buy tickets at the entrance, then the route up through the sight itself is obvious. A self-guided tour can take anywhere from 30 minutes to two hours, while one with a group should take about an hour. There are also audio tours (about 1 hour; €3) available when you buy your tickets.

4. Wander down the Ramparts

As well as being a pilgrimage center, Mont-Saint-Michel's naturally isolated position made it a military stronghold. The sturdy granite fortifications that ring the Mont were built between the 13th and 16th centuries; they became particularly important during the Hundred Years' War.

Mont-Saint-Michel Sights

Here is what you can expect to see at Mont-Saint-Michel—and a little bit of the history.

THE ABBEY CHURCH

With its transept crossing at the very pinnacle of the mount and its spire reaching toward heaven, a total height of 170 m (557 ft) above sea level, the abbey's church is Mont-Saint-Michel's symbolic heart and defines its iconic silhouette known around the world. Situated on an 80-m-long (262-ft) platform, built over preexisting crypts built into the spur of the rock, the building has its origins in the early years of the 11th century and combines a Romanesque nave and Gothic chancel.

LA MERVEILLE

Built over 17 years, La Merveille—literally "The Marvel"—consists of three layered levels, reaching up 35 m (115 ft) from the rock, and is supported by no less than 16 buttresses. Though the design is profoundly Gothic, there are hints here of the earlier Romanesque style on lower levels, where a somber simplicity still reigns. Below are descriptions of La Merveille's constituent parts.

- **The Cloisters:** Designed in the 13th century, Mont-Saint-Michel's cloisters consist of gallery arcades decorated in intricate carvings of both figures and foliage and a central garden, festooned with herbaceous plants. They're a reminder that this was once a sanctuary and site of calm.
- **The Refectory:** This hall is where Mont-Saint-Michel's monks sat down for their meals. There are tall, thin windows between each of the many arches that run its flanks, and a couple of long lines of austere wooden tables and benches offer a reminder of its original purpose. Built between 1211 and 1218, it was among the first rooms of La Merveille to be constructed.
- **The Knights' Hall:** Despite its militaristic name, this glorious space was used by the monks for reading and study. Characterized by a forest of evenly spaced stone pillars that bloom into a canopy of intricate vaulting, the room has otherwise been left bare, meaning you can really appreciate its interior architecture.
- **The Guests' Hall:** Dating from 1213, this hall received guests only of the most important stripe, including several French kings. A curtain of tapestries is hung in the center, designating half of the room as a dining hall and the other half a kitchen.
- **The Crypts:** The oldest parts of the abbey—pre-Gothic, even pre-Romanesque—the three crypts were only rediscovered at the close of the 19th century. With no natural light, cramped, and pressured by the sediments of history layered above, these, more than anywhere else on the Mont, feel like a step back in time. All the stone that surrounds them also serves to deaden noise from the outside world, and often compels visitors into silence, as though suddenly reminded they are walking through a religious institution.
- **The Great Wheel:** This human-size wooden hamster wheel dates from when Mont-Saint-Michel's abbey was being used as a prison from the 15th to the 19th centuries. Inmates would stand inside of it and walk to turn a cog and haul provisions up to their place of incarceration.

WATCH

Saving Private Ryan: The film that revolutionized how war was depicted on screen, *Saving Private Ryan* remains the most visceral depiction of D-Day, making it an ideal—if harrowing—accompaniment to any present-day trip to the Normandy beaches.

READ

Watching the English by Kate Fox: Written by anthropologist Kate Fox, this excellent and eminently readable primer to English customs and habits is enlightening no matter how well you think you might know them—even if you are English yourself.

Madame Bovary by Gustave Flaubert: One of the most influential books of all time, *Madame Bovary* effectively established the modern realist novel. Flaubert's tale about the misadventures of a dissatisfied housewife is also soaked in the textures of his native Normandy, flitting between Rouen and the region's countryside, both of which remain recognizable to this day.

LISTEN

"The Shipping Forecast": It may not make much sense, but this radio broadcast detailing the weather reports and sea forecasts for the coasts around the British isle is a national institution. Tuning in is an essential British ritual, and lets you know what you're in for when you cross the Channel yourself—listen to what they say about Wight.

They are well signposted on the exit and make for a good route back down to the base of the citadel, avoiding the human traffic of tourists climbing up the Grande Rue. You can get back to street level via a stairway, just before the King's Gate.

5. Walk out onto the Bay

As important to Mont-Saint-Michel's grandeur and unique history as any other part of the monument, this remarkable tidal bay oscillates from sea to vast mud flat and back to sea again throughout the year. Walk out here to experience its surreal, almost extra-terrestrial quality; it's a biosphere uncanny in its emptiness, and it feels by turns like some vast desert, or like the surface of a shallow sea. Note that while a meander here close to the village walls should be trouble-free, if you stray any farther than that, a guide becomes a necessary safety precaution, as the tides come in "faster than a galloping horse." For further information about tides, consult with the tourist office, either in the citadel itself or on the mainland.

It's well worth the expense of finding a hotel on the island, such as **La Mère Poulard** (Grande Rue; tel. 02 33 89 68 68; www.merepoulard.com; from €200 d), to experience it in the morning without the tourists. At sunrise, the Mont is at its empty best.

TRANSPORTATION

Air

The closest international hubs at either end of this journey are London and Paris.

England

- **Gatwick Airport** (www.gatwickairport.com): Located 47 km (29.5 mi) south of the city center, this is the best airport for this itinerary. It's actually on the same trainline that takes you to Lewes (www.southernrailway.com; roughly hourly; 30 minutes; £12), meaning you really can hit the ground running. If you're heading into London first, take either the Gatwick Express (www.gatwickexpress.com; 30 minutes; £12) or Southern Rail (30 minutes; £12).
- **Heathrow Airport** (tel. 0844 335 1801; www.heathrow.com): Located on London's outskirts, Heathrow is on the Piccadilly line of the Underground, from which you can transfer at Earl's Court to get to Victoria Station (https://tfl.gov.uk; 1 hour; £7). The Heathrow-Paddington Express (www.heathrowexpress.com; 15 minutes; £5.50-28) is faster and will take you to Paddington Station in London's northwest.

France

- **Charles de Gaulle** (www.parisaeroport.fr/roissy-charles-de-gaulle): Situated just to the north of the city, it's well connected to the center. The most straightforward route is the RER train network, Line B (1 hour; €10). Taxis have a flat rate of €60.

Boat

There are multiple connecting ferry ports along the coasts of Southern England and Northern France, all of which provide regular service throughout the year for motorists, foot passengers, and cyclists.

- **Brittany Ferries** (tel. 330 159 7000; www.brittany-ferries.co.uk) service the **Portsmouth-Caen route** (3 sailings daily; 6-7 hours; foot passengers from £30), as well as Dover-Calais (more than 30 sailings daily; 1.5 hours) farther east along the coast, Portsmouth-Le Havre (Apr.-Dec.; 4-5 hours), and Poole-Cherbourg (1 daily; 4.25 hours).

Train

There are good rail connections between all destinations suggested on this itinerary. In England, all the towns, including London, are linked by the **Southern Railway** (www.southernrailway.com). In France, destinations are linked by regional TER trains, under the umbrella of the French rail, the **SNCF** (www.sncf.com). Journeys should be swift and hassle free, and seldom cost any more than £30.

Luggage Storage

It's possible to stow your luggage Portsmouth Harbour ferry terminal.

Bus

To complete your trip to mainland Mont-Saint-Michel from Pontorson station in the Mont's gateway town, catch the **shuttle bus** (11 times daily; 7:35am-9:45pm; 20 minutes; €2.90) with "Mont-Saint-Michel" written clearly as its destination in its frontal display.

Car

While most of this trip can be done without a car, one can come in very handy if you wish to explore the D-Day beaches independently. Try **Hertz** in Bayeux (Total Station Route de Cherbourg, Departementale 613).

Getting Back

From Mont-Saint-Michel, take the shuttle back out to Pontorson, where you can catch a train to Paris. From Paris, you can take a train back to London via the Eurostar (tel. 01233 617575; www.eurostar.com; 2.5 hours; €39-300) or fly home.

- London and Paris (page 44)

RHINE RIVER CRUISE

Why Go: Crossing through six countries, this is the quintessential European river cruise. Sail through frozen-in-time medieval villages, lush forests, romantic castles, craggy cliffs, and snowcapped mountain peaks.

Number of Days: 8

Total Distance: 740 km (460 mi)

Seasons: Spring and fall

Start: Amsterdam

End: Basel

This river cruise begins in the vibrant cultural capital of Amsterdam with its picturesque canals, museums, and nightlife. From here, your longship will take you upriver, beginning in the Lower Rhine. Highlights here include the windmills and tulip fields of Kinderdjik, the High Gothic cathedral of Cologne, Germany, and the rolling vineyards nestled in the valleys of the Vosges Mountains. Continue through the half-timbered medieval villages of Rudesheim am Rhein up to the Middle Rhine, into the baroque architecture of Heidelberg, and on to the Upper Rhine, where you'll visit Strasbourg in the French Alsace region before sailing through the fairy-tale Black Forest and up into the Swiss Alps. Along the way, majestic castles are revealed at seemingly every bend of the river, and charming old towns showcase the rich heritage of the region.

TOP 3

★ Admiring a classic scene of windmills and polders at **Kinderdijk** and then learning about the marvel that is Dutch water management (page 505).

Climbing the south tower of the **Cologne Cathedral**, a High Gothic architectural masterpiece (page 507).

Delighting in the wonderfully cozy **beverages of the Rhine region** that are rightfully famous (page 513).

DAY 1

Amsterdam, Netherlands

After arriving in Amsterdam (likely via Schiphol Airport), transfer to the river cruise ship, which will also be your accommodation for the trip. If you have time to see Amsterdam before the ship sets sail, see **Amsterdam, Brussels, and Bruges** (page 81) for ideas on how to spend a few hours in the city.

DAY 2

Kinderdijk, Netherlands

TOP EXPERIENCE

★ 1. Kinderdijk

Nederwaard 1; www.kinderdijk.com; 9am-5:30pm daily Mar.-Oct., 10am-4pm daily Jan.-Feb. and Nov.-Dec.; summer adults €9, youth 5-17 €5.50, children 0-4 free, winter adults €4.50, youth €2

UNESCO World Heritage Site Kinderdijk, with its 19 picturesque windmills, is easily one of the most beautiful regions in the Netherlands, a perfectly preserved village dating back to the 13th century. Named after a folk tale called *Kinderdijk* (children's dike), about a child found floating in a cradle after the infamous Saint Elizabeth flood in 1421, this is an incredible place to learn about Dutch water management throughout history. The Dutch have long battled water encroaching on their land, and this complex system of windmills, pumping stations, polders, and sluices created in the medieval period has prevented flooding in the lowlands.

Depending on how much time you have, there are a couple ways to see this quintessential Dutch landscape.

Kinderdijk

RHINE RIVER CRUISE
English Channel
Amsterdam Centraal
Amsterdam
Haarlem
Amsterdam Airport Schiphol
NETHERLANDS
The Hague
Utrecht
Rotterdam
Arnhem
Kinderdijk
Ems River
Weser River
Osnabrück
Bielefeld
Münster
Middelburg
's-Hertogenbosch
Wesel
Dortmund
Eindhoven
Duisburg
Brugge
Antwerpen
Gartenstadt Meerer
Düsseldorf
Kassel
GERMANY
Gent
Dormagen
Cologne Cathedral
Cologne
Cologne Old City
BRUSSELS
BELGIUM
Maastricht
Lille
Bonn
Rhine
Liège
Giessen
Mons
Namur
Maas River
Charleroi
Neuwied
Basilica of St. Castor
Koblenz Old Town
Koblenz
Stolzenfels Castle
Wiesbaden
Frankfurt
Mosel River
Drosselgasse
Mainz
Rüdesheim am Rhein
Diekirch
LUX.
Arlon
LUXEMBOURG
Worms
Mannheim
Ludwigshafen
Heidelberg
Reims
Saarbrücken
Speyer
Metz
Beverages of the Rhine region
0
50 mi
0
50 km
Karlsruhe
Rhine
Nancy
Stuttgart
Strasbourg Cathedral
Strasbourg
Troyes
FRANCE
Colmar
Black Forest
Breisach
Freiburg
EuroAirport Basel-Mulhouse-Freiburg
Basel
Schaffhausen
Overnite Stop
River Cruise Route
Kunstmuseum
Zürich Airport
Zürich
SWITZERLAND
Biel
Zug
VADUZ
Luzern
© MOON.COM
BERN
Stans
Altdorf
Fribourg

Key Reservations

Some of the more popular river cruises sell out more than a year in advance, so plan accordingly. If you are a flexible traveler, sometimes you can find last-minute deals.

2. Biking the Windmills

Anyone can bike or walk past the windmills—many of which are still lived in and in active operation—and explore the 322 hectares (796 acres) without paying the entry fee. You can rent a bike just outside Kinderdijk at **Café De Klok** (Molenstraat 117; tel. 078 691 2597; www.deklok.com; 11am-closing daily; €8) to enjoy a scenic cycle through this landscape.

3. Windmills Up Close

The Kinderdijk admission ticket allows you to access two of the windmills-cum-museums and the visitors center. It also includes a 30-minute boat tour for a different perspective on the scenery.

DAY 3

Cologne, Germany

★ 1. Cologne Cathedral

Domkloster 4; tel. 22 117940555; www.koelner-dom.de; 6am-8pm daily; free

Towering over the old city of Cologne is the unmissable High Gothic masterpiece of the Cologne Cathedral. At a massive 157 m (515 ft) in height, this was the tallest building in the world for centuries. Begun in 1248, but not finished until 1880, this unrivaled place of worship was the work of a succession of builders who remained true to the vision of this cathedral. In 1996, the cathedral was named a UNESCO World Heritage Site, not least of all for its impressive medieval stained-glass windows and for the shrine

Cologne Cathedral

Cologne Carnival

On the 11th day of the 11th month at exactly 11 minutes past 11 o'clock, Cologne rings in its annual carnival, quite literally. At Alter Markt, the old bell dongs and dings in another year of festivities. This is one of the longest running carnivals in the world and lasts through Passover. The culmination of the celebration is a week-long street festival from Fat Tuesday through Ash Wednesday, just before Lent, and the Rose Monday Parade, where thousands of carnivalgoers dance and sing their way through the city.

of the Three Wise Men, a gilded triple sarcophagus believed to house the relics of the biblical Magi. For those who enjoy views from above, you can climb the south tower staircase, past Saint Peter's Bell (the largest and heaviest free-swinging bell in the world), and up about 100 m (330 ft) for panoramic views of the city.

2. Cologne Old City

Cologne's Old Town has an undeniable old-world charm with cobblestone streets and rustic alleyways. This pedestrian-friendly bit of Cologne invites you to discover local handicrafts and trades, particularly in the vibrant **Alter Markt** and **Heumarkt** plazas, which remain popular with residents of Cologne as well as visitors to the city. Locally brewed **Kölsch,** a light, crisp beer only brewed in Cologne, can be found in numerous Brauhauses nestled up against the pastel-colored houses. Getting turned around in the old city is a sort of rite of passage, so take it easy on the ale.

3. Farina Fragrance Museum

Obenmarspforten 21; tel. 22 13998994; http://farina.org; 10am-6pm Mon.-Sat.; €5

You have no doubt heard of "eau de Cologne." But did you know that this most famous of perfumes was invented over 300 years ago right here in Cologne? On a 45-minute tour, you will engage your olfactory senses as you discover the root of eau de cologne in the world's oldest working perfume factory. Discover more about the life of the founder, Italian Giovanni Maria Farina, and rest assured that by the end, you will be a perfume expert and know how to sniff out an imitation scent from the real-deal cologne from Cologne.

TO TAKE *Home*

In addition to the lovely beverages available along the Rhine, there are other unique gifts to evoke a trip to this region.

EAU DE COLOGNE

Small, discrete, and wonderfully scented, an authentic bottle of eau de cologne from Cologne makes the perfect gift or souvenir. Look for the bottles by Farina labeled as 1709 for the original perfume, which features notes of citrus, jasmine, and violet touched with sandalwood and olibanum. Small bottles can be had for as little as €6, while larger bottles, soaps, diffusers, and more can all be found in the **Farina Fragrance Museum** (page 508) and in various little shops throughout Cologne's old city.

CUCKOO CLOCKS

Once you see the skill and artistry that go into making a traditional Black Forest cuckoo clock, it is hard not to want to pack one home with you. The art of the cuckoo clock dates back to 1640, when during the cold, dark winter months, farmers would spend their time making clocks and carving little figurines to pass the time. The most classic Black Forest cuckoo clocks feature a railway and a guard's lodge with a pitched roof, among other wooden ornaments. Of course, the famous cuckoo clock is known for the distinct signal, every hour on the hour, that originates from a device that resembles a pair of miniature organ pipes. The more traditional movements are one- and eight-day winding movements, though there are battery-powered quartz movements as well.

To guarantee the most authentic Black Forest clock, you will want to look for clocks made by local manufacturers that are part of the **Black Forest Clock Association.** This membership is a guarantee that at least 90 percent of all the parts used in the clock originated in the Black Forest. Prices range from a couple hundred to thousands of euros, depending on the movements, craftsmanship, size, and materials used.

Koblenz, Germany

1. German Corner and Ehrenbreitstein Fortress

Konrad-Adenauer-Ufer; tel. 26 119433; open 24/7; free

At the meeting point of the Moselle and Rhine Rivers, the German Corner (Deutsches Eck) has long stood as a place of importance for controlling the waterways of this region. Long disputed between Germany and France, this is now a decidedly German port of call. A stoic 37-m (122-ft) statue of Kaiser Wilhelm I, the person responsible for the unification of modern Germany, stands watch over this impressive meeting point. From the German Corner, cable cars whisk you up and over the Rhine River to the Ehrenbreitstein Fortress, the second largest military fortress in Europe with commanding views over the rivers. For the brave of heart, cable car 17 has a glass-paneled floor for some breathtaking views over the Rhine and Koblenz, the city that spreads out from the German Corner.

2. Basilica of St. Castor

Kastorhof 4; tel. 26 131446; www.sankt-kastor-koblenz.de

Originally constructed in the 9th century, this is the oldest church in Koblenz and one of the oldest along the entire Rhine Valley. Located next to the German Corner, this is one of those can't-miss sites, with authentic Romanesque architecture, vaulted ceilings, and a rich history that spans centuries. Since its inception, this was the meeting point for emperors and kings to negotiate and settle disputes, including the Treaty of Verdun, which divided old Francia into three kingdoms, and was heavily involved in the earliest days of the Holy Roman Empire.

3. Koblenz Old Town

As if you could get enough of old-world Europe! Koblenz calls with its cobblestone streets and wonderfully charming plazas surrounded with buildings from the late Renaissance, early baroque, and

left, Koblenz Old Town; right, Stolzenfels Castle

MAKE IT Active

KOBLENZ: THE RHINE CASTLE TRAIL

From Koblenz, you can join the historic Rhine Castle Trail. Though this trail spans more than 191 km (118 mi), there is a wonderfully hilly 13-km (8-mi) stretch of trail that begins in Koblenz and ends in Rhens. This moderate hike takes you through some of the most beautiful, unspoiled nature of the Rhine River Valley. The hike usually takes around five hours, so make sure to pack snacks and plenty of water, particularly in the warmer months, and be liberal with the sunscreen!

Along the way, you will cross through **Denkmal Rittursturz,** a historical memorial with a commanding viewpoint over the river valley, and **Schloss Stozenfels.** You will also pass through other historic sites, including an old Celtic fort, a Roman temple, and an ancient Jewish cemetery. Finish your walk in Rhens, from which trains depart regularly for Koblenz, a quick seven-minute connection between the two towns.

BREISACH: HIKING THE BLACK FOREST

It is one thing to drive through the Black Forest, but another thing entirely to confront it on foot. Outside of the cold winter months, most cruise operators offer a hike through this historic forest. It's not necessary to join a group to hike, but it will ensure you meet up with your group on time and won't get left behind. For those more comfortable keeping their own time, a solo hike is easy enough to accomplish.

One lovely, manageable hike that goes into the forest starts from a well-marked trailhead at **Hofgut Sternen,** just north of the tiny town square. The trail takes you into the forest, past a gurgling river, and into the Ravenna Gorge. Here you will see a towering old stone arched bridge still used for the local railroad. The trail goes on a loop for 6.5 km (4.1 mi) throughout mostly flat terrain on a well-kept path, making this a moderate hike. All throughout you'll find the dense forest breaking into rolling meadows, which burst to life in the late spring, while hovering on the horizon are jagged mountain peaks.

more modern art nouveau periods. At **Jesuits Square,** still magically lined with gas lanterns and numerous, often humorously cheeky, statues, you can find the **Town Hall** (Rathaus), which dates from 1695, while the nearby **Florins Market** is home to the 12th-century Florins Church and Old Merchant's Hall.

4. Stolzenfels Castle

Schlossweg 11; tel. 26 151656; https://tor-zum-welterbe.de/de/schloss-stolzenfels; 10am-5pm Tues.-Sun. (hours vary slightly depending on season), closed Dec.; €5

Built on the ruins of a 13th-century fortress, the gleaming white 19th-century Stozenfels Castle is all fairy-tale magic and Prussian elegance at the pinnacle of the empire's influence and the epitome of the zeitgeist of Rhine Romanticism. From the outside, the castle gleams white, reflecting the sunlight off its bright exterior. It is easy to see that inspiration for this Gothic revival palace was taken from the nearby Rheinstein Castle and the more distant Bavarian folly of Maximillian II's Hohenschwangau Castle perched along

Germany's Romantic Road. Inside, the decor is resplendent with gilded, vaulted ceilings, giant public halls, and more murals than you can count. Make sure to take a stroll through the gardens before descending back down to the valley. Located south of the city, the castle is a 15-minute trip by car. Those up for an active day can walk here along the **Rhine Castle Trail** (page 511).

DAY 5

Rüdesheim am Rhein, Germany

1. Stroll the Drosselgrasse

If ye search for the olde worlde, here ye shal fynd it! With its half-timbered buildings, cobblestone lane, and centuries-old taverns dotting the quaint 14-m (472-ft) pedestrian thoroughfare in the middle of Rüdesheim am Rhein's Old Town, the Drosselgrasse makes for a delightful stroll that will transport you back in time. This is the perfect spot to have a light bite and to sample some of the region's heartiest cuisine, including Odenwälder Frühstückstäse (a light, yellowish soft cheese traditionally served with breakfast) and Nordhessiche Ahle Wurscht, a slowly matured raw pork sausage typical of the region.

Drosselgrasse

2. Niederwald Monument

Drosselgrasse

Take the Seilbahn Rüdesheim cable car a quick 10 minutes up to the hilltop monument of Niederwald. The monument itself was built between 1870 and 1880 to commemorate the unification of Germany under Kaiser Wilhelm I, whose carved relief meets you after the ascent. Though the monument is of interest, it is the views that are inspiring. From the cable car ride all the way to the monument itself, the Rhine curves on and around in, and castle towers dot distant hilltops while vineyards sprawl far into the distance.

3. Bruer's Rüdesheimer Schloss

Steingasse 10; tel. 67 2290500; www.ruedesheimer-schloss.com/en/wine-restaurant; 11:30am-9pm daily; €30

This four-star remodeled hotel is the place to break out from the all-inclusive river cruises and sample some of the local cuisine and taste some delightful vintages of local Rieslings and pinot noirs. The seasonal menu is varied, locally sourced, and highlights regional flavor profiles. The "Castle Duck" and a Riesling-infused cheese soup are two sure-fire crowd pleasers. The local estate was founded in 1880 with nearly 80 percent of its wine production dedicated to Rheingau's most traditional grape variety, Riesling. The wine list is expansive, with rare wines dating as far back as 1893.

★ Regional Beverages

You will encounter numerous specialty beverages along the Rhine. Here are a few that are sure to please.

- **Apfelwein:** Usually made from sweet apples, this German cider is most often thought of as a product of Frankfurt and the Hesse region. Styles do vary, though a dry, light, tart cider is most common. You'll see apfelwein throughout your journey along the Rhine, most often served in a diamond-patterned glass called a gerippte.
- **Asbach Uralt:** It was while living in Cologne in 1892 that Hugo Asbach first distilled this distinct brandy, aged in Limousin and German oak. Over a century later, the warm amber delight, with sweet notes of honey and vanilla, plums and chocolate, is warmed with a peppery nuance and enjoyed worldwide. Fun fact: Asbach had originally designated his distilled beverage as a cognac, but following the Treaty of Versailles, wherein a certain pride of terroir made what we know as cognac a strictly French beverage, Asbach was forced to change the name. He thus renamed his cognac what we know it as today: Asbach Uralt.
- **Glühwein:** Popular during the holiday season, particularly at Christmas markets, this warm, cozy concoction is a winter staple. Recipes differ among households and regions, but the basics are generally the same: dry red wine, cinnamon, anise, sugar, and orange. Brandy is a popular addition, as well as vanilla, ginger, cardamom, and even black pepper.
- **Kölsch:** Something of a hybrid between an ale and a lager, Kölsch is a top-fermenting beer, like an ale, though it is conditioned at cold temperatures, like a lager. The end result is a pale, slightly hoppy, bright beer that hits just the right note on a warm day. Kölsch should be served in a tall, thin cylindrical glass called a stange. Authentic Kölsch is brewed within 50 km (30 mi) of Cologne and has a protected geographical indication (PGI) status by the European Union.
- **Rüdesheim Coffee:** First introduced by German television chef Hans Karl Adam in 1957, Rüdesheimer Kaffee is made by first flambéeing a generous thimble of Asbach Uralt with sugar, partially evaporating the alcohol (emphasis on partially). Coffee is introduced and the whole thing is served in a tall, specially designed glass, topped with vanilla-perfumed whipped cream and delicate chocolate shavings.

DAY 6

Strasbourg, France

1. Strasbourg Cathedral

Pl. de la Cathédrale; tel. 3 88 21 43 34; www.cathedrale-strasbourg.fr; 8:30am-11:15am and 12:45pm-5:45pm Mon.-Sat.; free

From the Rhine, the towering Strasbourg Cathedral climbs into the sky. A masterpiece of High Gothic architecture, it is still one of the tallest cathedrals in the world at 142 m (465 ft) and the tallest structure built during the Middle Ages. From the exterior, the main entrance greets you with a series of delicately carved stone

ADDING ON Mainz, Germany

Bookworms and history buffs may want to find a way to get to Mainz, located 35 km (22 mi) farther east on the Rhine from Rüdesheim. Mainz was the home of Johannes Gutenberg, inventor of the 15th-century printing press, perhaps one of the single most important inventions of the last millennium. It was with Gutenberg's press that the written word, and education in general, was democratized because books became readily available to working people and not just the monied elite.

GUTENBERG MUSEUM

Liebfrauenpl. 5; tel. 61 31122503; www.gutenberg-museum.de; 9am-5pm Tues.-Sat., 11am-5pm Sun.; €5

In this museum, explore the evolution of the printed word and samples of newspapers of different ages. The real crown jewels here are the two original 500+-year-old Gutenberg Bibles, the priceless first-ever books printed by Gutenberg.

Following this bit of erudition, spend some time in Mainz's **old town,** taking in the German charm and the centuries-old **Mainz Cathedral** (Markt 10; tel. 61 31253412; www.mainz-dom.de; 9am-6:30pm Mon.-Fri., 9am-4pm Sat., 12:45pm-3pm and 4pm-6:30pm Sun.; free).

GETTING THERE

With a car, old town Mainz is a 45-minute drive from Rüdesheim. The closest train station is **Mainz Kastel** (45 minutes from Rüdesheim Bahnhof), across the river from the old town—a 20-minute walk or 10-minute bus ride.

statues in high relief while stone columns soar upward, seemingly weightless. Inside, the original stained-glass windows cast their colorful light over the faithful, tucked beneath the vaulted ceilings.

2. La Petite France

Ponts Couverts

Dating from the 16th and 17th centuries, the black-and-white timber-framed houses and shops are quintessentially Strasbourgian. Located on an island in the middle of the waterways surrounding the city, La Petite France is terribly charming. This is the sort of neighborhood where you want to stroll arm-in-arm with that special someone. During Christmas season, the charm is cranked up to a thousand with holiday cheer and decor to match.

3. Alsatian Wine Tasting

Get to know your Rieslings from your Gewurztraminers on an Alsatian wine tour that will take you from the bustling city of Strasbourg and busy Rhine Valley into medieval villages set against verdant vineyards that roll on as far as the eye can see. Some tour operators will couple wine tastings with bike tours of the region, with many offering e-bikes as an option to make keeping up a little easier. Wine lovers, consider arranging tours around October as many wine festivals, including the famous "vin nouveau," are held this time of year.

DAY 7

The Black Forest and Colmar, France

1. The Black Forest

Hofgut Sternen; tel. 76 52 90 11 61; www.blackforestvillage-shop.com; 9am-4pm Mon.-Fri.; free

Breisach, Germany, is the doorway to the fairy-tale Black Forest, made famous by *Grimm's Fairy Tales*. From Breisach, quite a few river cruises have an option to take a day trip into the Black Forest, which does live up to its eerie reputation.

In the middle of the forest is a tucked-away little village, **Hofgut Sternen,** which offers the possibility to see local glass blowing and a quick Black Forest Cake workshop, though it is the locally handcrafted **cuckoo clocks** that are impossibly charming and the real must-see here. The demonstration of how they work only takes 10 minutes or so, leaving you plenty of time to peruse.

2. Colmar Old Town

Colmar, on the other side of the river from Breisach, is a quaint half-timbered village with true Alsatian charm. It's a

left, Musée Bartholdi; right, Colmar Old Town

WATCH

Sherlock Holmes: Game of Shadows: This stylistic take on the world's most famous detective is fast-paced, but don't let the beautifully moody scenery of old Strasbourg pass you by.

READ

Grimms' Fairy Tales by Jacob and Wilheim Grimm: If you believe, as the brothers Grimm did, that the fairy tales of a country are particularly representative of said country, be prepared to be bewitched! Read the original versions from the early 19th century for the closest sense of the brothers' original intentions in writing and recording the sordid tales of the Black Forest and other corners of Germany.

Wine and War: The French, the Nazis, and the Battle for France's Greatest Treasure by Donald and Petie Kladstrup: Arguably, there is not nation prouder of its wine production than France. During World War II, as Germans washed over the Rhine River, winemakers did everything they could do protect this quaffable national treasure.

LISTEN

River Cruise Radio: If you are interested in river cruises and traveling by water, this is the podcast for you. Host Sherry Laskin interviews people throughout the industry and often has reviews of different companies, new ships, and some foodie experiences she's loved in her travels. Sherry is often a solo female traveler and speaks to that experience.

"Lonely River Rhine" by Bobby Helms: This classic 1960s tune of love, heartbreak, and tragedy is best enjoyed at sunset while cruising down the Rhine. What stories lurk below the surface?

common afternoon destination following a morning in the Black Forest. The requisite cobblestone streets and medieval buildings sprawl out around the central 13th-century Gothic **Saint Martin Church.** Unlike many other towns and villages in this part of Europe, Colmar was unscathed during World War II, and many of the buildings are bending under the weight of their unrestored history. The sherbet-colored buildings along the canals of Colmar's "Little Venice" are as fairy-tale beautiful as it gets.

3. Musée Bartholdi

30 Rue des Marchands; tel. 3 89 41 90 60; 10am-noon and 2pm-6pm Tues.-Sun.; €6.70

If you recall your US history, you may remember that the Statue of Liberty (or to give her full name, "The Statue of Liberty Enlightening the World,") was a gift from France to the United States and commemorated on Liberty Island in New York in 1886. The sculptor of this world-famous statue, Frederic-August Bartholdi, was born here in Colmar. Learn all about him, his creation of the Statue of Liberty, and some of his other great works at this museum.

As you walk around Colmar, if you look down, you will see little golden triangles placed in the cobblestones, etched with the likeness of the Statue of Liberty. These triangles take you on a walking tour of Colmar's old town, where you will encounter the Statue of Liberty, albeit a 12-m (39-ft) replica, in the middle of a grassy roundabout.

Basel, Switzerland

1. Kunstmuseum

St. Alban-Graben 16; tel. 61 206 62 62; www.kunstmuseumbasel.ch; 10am-6pm Tues.-Sun., until 8pm Wed.; 15CHF

Basel is the debarkation point for most Rhine cruises, usually arriving in the morning. Rather than rushing off to catch a flight home or to your next destination, spend some time in this Swiss city. Art lovers will want to head straight to Switzerland's premier art museum, which houses an impressive collection of great works from Rubens, Rembrandt, Renoir, Matisse, Van Gogh, Kandinsky, Miró, and others. Devote at least half a day to do this museum justice.

Stop in **Spoon** (Malzgasse 1; tel. +41 612741313; https://www.spoon-basel.ch; Mon-Fri 8am-2:30pm; €20) for lunch: Ein Löffel Gutes (a spoon of good) awaits you at this women-owned, health-conscious cafe with loads of locally sourced, seasonal legumes featured on the menu.

2. Basel Papermill

St. Alban-Tal 37; tel. 61 225 90 90; www.papiermuseum.ch; 11am-6pm Tues.-Fri., 1pm-5pm Sat., 11am-5pm Sun.; 15CHF

A 10-minute walk east from the art museum, the Basel Papermill engages all of your senses as you touch, hear, smell, see, and perhaps even taste a little bit of bookish history. Follow through the medieval papermill from handmade and cut paper to more modern bookbinding processes. Along the way, you can make your own paper, practice your longhand with a goose quill, hunt and peck on a classic typewriter, typeset your own name, and even create a unique marbled paper.

Basel Papermill

TRANSPORTATION

Air

Amsterdam Schiphol Airport (AMS; Evert van de Beekstraat 202; tel. 20 794 0800; www.schiphol.nl) is located about 20 km (12 mi) southwest of Amsterdam. It's 10-15 minutes by train to central Amsterdam and costs €4.50 one-way.

Train

Amsterdam Centraal (Stationsplein 15; tel. 030 751 5155; www.ns.nl; open 24 hours) train station is located in Amsterdam's city center.

Boat

There are dozens of operators running cruises along the popular Rhine River. During summer months, as many as 300 cruises depart each day! Nearly all companies use longships. The smaller ships hold 80-90 people, while the larger ships can hold more than 200 passengers. When making your reservations, it is almost as important to pay attention the type of ship you are reserving as it is the company. Some ships offer more amenities than others. Likewise, different companies offer different inclusions.

Rhine River

Though you will be sleeping in your cabin aboard the ship, not all ships have meals and beverages included. Some companies will offer various onshore excursions, from guided tours and hikes to free bike rentals, museum visits, wine tastings, and more. Here are a few companies that own and operate their own longships:

- **Croisi Cruises** (www.croisieuroperivercruises.com) is a French family-owned and -run river cruise operator that has been around for three generations. It's popular with European river cruisers and is a good value, though the staff is not always English-speaking.
- **Emerald Cruises** (www.emeraldcruises.com) is one of the best values in river cruising, offering many perks reserved for more expensive cruises. This is the best option for solo travelers, as they are one of the very few cruise companies offering single-cabin options.
- **KD Waterways** (www.k-d.com) is ideal for shorter cruises of 1-2 days exploring the Middle Rhine. These cruises are obviously less comprehensive than longer ones, but this is a good option for those in the region, on a budget, or looking for a last-minute tour possibility.
- **Tauck** (www.tauck.com) is one of the more boutique options with many immersive onshore experiences that add up to a deeper sense of discovery, though you will need deeper pockets to match.
- **Viking River Cruises** (www.vikingrivercruises.com) operates river cruises worldwide with the largest fleet, offering the most flexibility in terms of dates and times.

Getting Back

Across the river from Basel, the **EuroAirport Basel-Mulhouse-Freiburg** (Saint-Louis; tel. 3 89 90 31 11; www.euroairport.com) offers connections throughout Europe, though international direct flight offerings are limited. Swiss-run SBB (www.sbb.ch) runs one daily direct overnight train between **Basel SBB** station and Amsterdam (10 hours).

From Basel, you can also fly out of nearby **Zürich Airport** (Flughafen Zürich, Kloten, Switzerland; tel. 43 816 22 11; www.flughafen-zuerich.ch). Budget bus operator Flixbus (1 hour, twice daily; www.flixbus.com; €8) runs service from Basel direct to Zürich Airport. Train service (1 hour, 90-plus trains daily; www.sbb.ch; €30) is regular, though some trains require you to switch at stations en route. Look for direct service.

- London and Paris (page 44)
- Amsterdam, Brussels, and Bruges (page 81)
- Romantische Strasse (page 307)
- Holland Junction Network (page 377)
- Tour du Mont Blanc (page 405)
- The Alps (page 648)

COPENHAGEN TO OSLO

Why Go: An overnight ferry ride is a surprising and scenic way to connect these two Scandinavian capitals.

Number of Days: 7

Total Distance: 600 km (370 mi)

Seasons: Spring to fall

Start: Copenhagen

End: Oslo

Scandinavia holds a favorable reputation on the world stage, heralded for its high quality of life, yet the region and its capital cities have often remained off the beaten path, or at least down a side street, for many visitors to Europe. Neither Copenhagen nor Oslo has a Big Ben, Eiffel Tower, or Colosseum to conjure up iconic images in travelers' minds. What makes these two cities special isn't a particular sightseeing highlight, but rather the way of life, seen in the bike-friendly streets, the attention to design, and the value of coziness and comfort over hustle and bustle. Don't rush your visit to either city, and take your time to scratch under the surface. In a way, the slower pace that a boat takes to travel from one capital to the other is uniquely suited to traveling between them.

TOP 3

★ Experiencing what makes Copenhagen such a bike-friendly city by taking a ride over the **Cykelslangen** (Bicycle Snake) bridge (page 526).

★ Stepping into Shakespeare's world with a visit to **Kronborg Castle.** This iconic Danish castle jutting out from the coast is the setting of *Hamlet* (page 526).

Learning about the impact Nobel prizewinners have had on the world through the **Nobel Peace Center's** interesting and interactive exhibitions in Oslo (page 532).

Copenhagen

Where to Stay: Near Nyhavn or Kongens Nytorv

Arrive by: Plane into Copenhagen Airport

DAY 1

1. Nyhavn

Start your time in Copenhagen in Nyhavn. Lining a canal, this photogenic area is famous for its row of 18th-century pastel-colored houses. You'll also find an extensive selection of quayside restaurants and cafés, some of which are housed on boats.

2. Canal Tour with Stromma

Nyhavn; tel. 32 96 30 00; www.stromma.dk/kobenhavn; boat tours from 85 DKr

Don't lose any time getting out on the water. One of the largest tour groups operating in the city, Stromma offers a classic one-hour canal tour that passes by many of Copenhagen's popular sights, including the royal palace of Amalienborg, the Royal Library (a striking building known as the Black Diamond), and the statue of Hans Christian Andersen's The Little Mermaid. Tours leave from Nyhavn throughout the day.

Afterward, stop in for a New Nordic lunch and coffee at **Apollo Bar** (Nyhavn 2; tel. 60 53 44 14; http://apollobar.dk; canteen open noon-2pm Tues.-Fri., bar 8am-5pm Tues., 8am-midnight Wed.-Fri., 10am-midnight Sat., 10am-5pm Sun.; mains 85 DKr, students 45 DKr).

3. Round Tower

Købmagergade 52A; tel. 33 73 03 73; www.rundetaarn.dk; 10am-8pm daily; adults 25 DKr, children 5 DKr

Cross Kongens Nytorv (King's New Square) and walk 15 minutes to the Round Tower, a 42-m-high (138-ft) 17th-century tower smack in the middle of modern Copenhagen. The swirling, snail-like stone path up the tower is unlike anything else in European period architecture. Enjoy the view from the top of this essential Copenhagen sight.

4. Kastellet (The Citadel)

Gl. Hovedvagt, Kastellet 1; tel. 72 84 00 00; www.kastellet.dk; free

Walk 20 minutes to Kastellet, one of the best-preserved examples of a medieval star fortress in Europe. It's still used by the military, which occupies some of its buildings, but much of the Citadel is open to the public. Walk around the raised rampart, which provides views across the harbor and the surrounding historic buildings.

top, Nyhavn; bottom, Round Tower

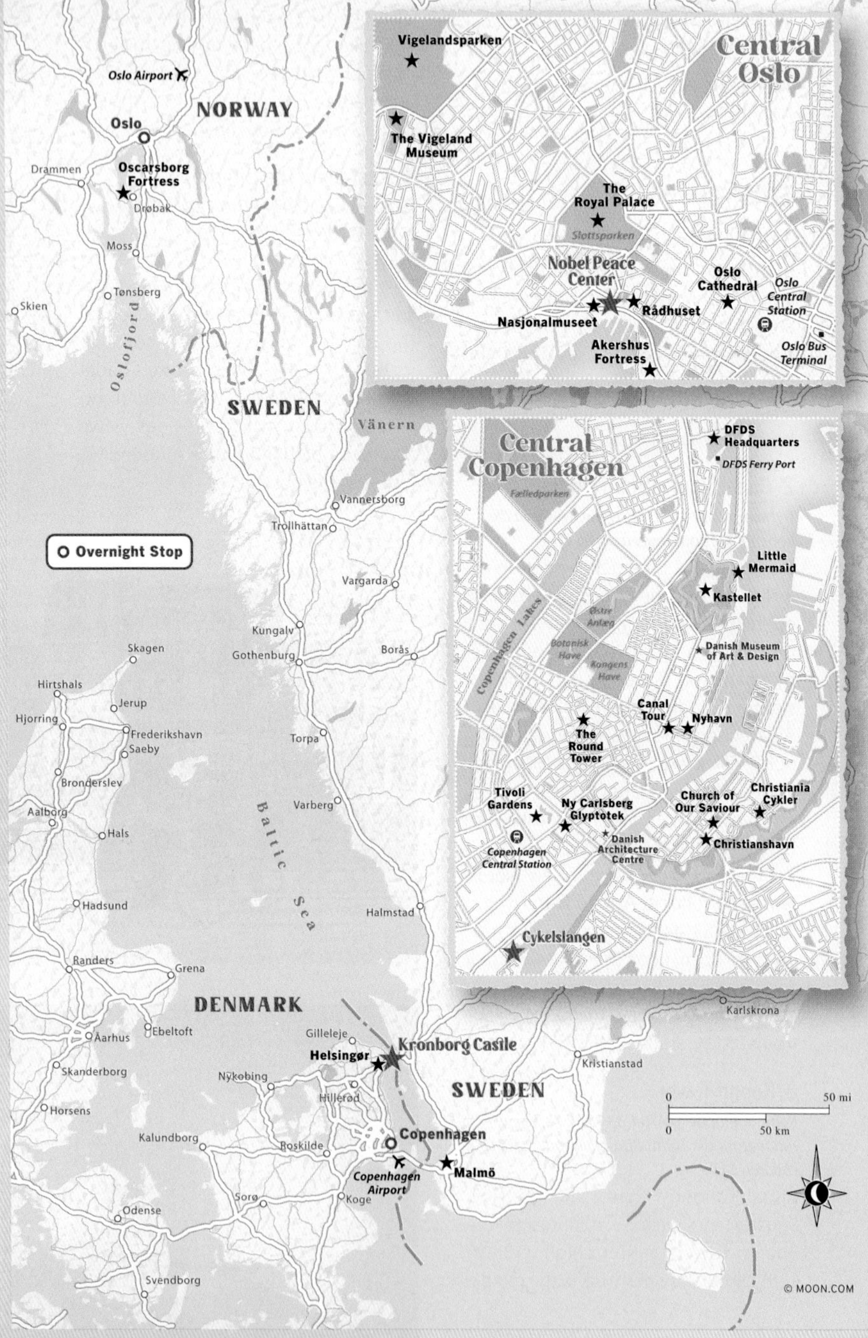

COPENHAGEN TO OSLO
Central Oslo
Vigelandsparken
The Vigeland Museum
The Royal Palace
Slottsparken
Nobel Peace Center
Nasjonalmuseet
Rådhuset
Oslo Cathedral
Oslo Central Station
Akershus Fortress
Oslo Bus Terminal
Central Copenhagen
DFDS Headquarters
DFDS Ferry Port
Fælledparken
Little Mermaid
Kastellet
Østre Anlæg
Botanisk Have
Kongens Have
Copenhagen Lakes
Danish Museum of Art & Design
Canal Tour
Nyhavn
The Round Tower
Tivoli Gardens
Ny Carlsberg Glyptotek
Copenhagen Central Station
Danish Architecture Centre
Church of Our Saviour
Christiania Cykler
Christianshavn
Cykelslangen
Oslo Airport
NORWAY
Oslo
Drammen
Oscarsborg Fortress
Drøbak
Moss
Tønsberg
Skien
Oslofjord
SWEDEN
Vänern
Vannersborg
Trollhättan
Overnight Stop
Vargarda
Kungalv
Gothenburg
Borås
Skagen
Hirtshals
Jerup
Hjorring
Frederikshavn
Saeby
Torpa
Bronderslev
Aalborg
Hals
Varberg
Baltic Sea
Hadsund
Halmstad
Randers
Grena
DENMARK
Karlskrona
Aarhus
Ebeltoft
Gilleleje
Kronborg Castle
Helsingør
Kristianstad
Skanderborg
Nykobing
Hillerød
SWEDEN
Horsens
0
50 mi
0
50 km
Kalundborg
Roskilde
Copenhagen
Malmö
Copenhagen Airport
Sorø
Koge
Odense
Svendborg
© MOON.COM

Key Reservations

COPENHAGEN

- Book your tickets on the **ferry** between Copenhagen and Oslo in advance.
- Reserve a table at popular **restaurants** 1-2 weeks in advance, and 2-3 months in advance for Michelin-starred restaurants.
- In high season, book **accommodations** and **tours** 2-3 weeks in advance.

OSLO

- Book your summer tour of the **Royal Palace** in advance.

Royal Palace

5. Little Mermaid

Langelinie; www.mermaidsculpture.dk; free

On the far side of the citadel, get your camera ready for a closer view of the Little Mermaid, which sits discreetly by the water at the beginning of the Langelinie promenade. This diminutive and easy-to-miss bronze statue was inspired by Hans Christian Andersen's fairy tale and is an iconic Copenhagen sight.

Restaurant Palægade (Palægade 8; tel. 70 82 82 88; https://palaegade.dk/frontpage; daily 11:30am-4pm and 6pm-midnight Mon.-Sat.; entrées 125-175 DKr) is a fine option to round off a day of classic Copenhagen sights: The Danish-inspired dishes served in a rustic setting are worth a little splurge. The restaurant is a 20-minute walk from the Little Mermaid.

Finish the day with a drink at legendary jazz bar **La Fontaine** (Kompagnistræde 11; tel. 33 11 60 98; www.lafontaine.dk; 8pm-5am Mon.-Sun. 8pm-5am), where live concerts take place every Friday, Saturday, and Sunday.

DAY 2

1. Christianshavn

In the morning, head to Christianshavn, a historic harbor area where cobbled streets, canals, and townhouses have retained their 17th-century layout. Start with coffee and croissant at **Kafferiet** (Wildersgade 26; tel. 20 20 85 77; http://kafferiet.dk; 7am-6pm Mon.-Fri., 7am-9pm Sat.-Sun.; from 25 DKr) on the corner of Torvegade, the main road through Christianshavn. Seat yourself at the window and watch the morning traffic of bicycling parents with their kids in trailers, suited officials on their way to ministry buildings, and international students heading to the library.

Head southeast on Torvegade to the canals, where you can take an easy walk

Scandanavian Design

Scandanavian deisgn is charactarized by clean, traditional lines; minimalism and simplicity; and a color palette inspired by nature. The style is also known for high quality in both architecture and design. Scandinavian home goods, furniture, and styles can be found in interior design magazines all over the world, and particular pieces like the egg chair, designed by Copenhagen native Arne Jacobsen, or buildings like the Oslo Opera House are instantly evocative of the style. When it comes to Scandanavian design, words like "minimalist" and "functional" are often used.

ARCHITECTURE

- Located in the striking new BLOX building on Copenhagen's quayfront, the **Danish Architecture Center** (BLOX, Bryghuspladsen 10; tel. 32 57 19 30; https://dac.dk; 10am-6pm daily and until 9pm Thurs.; adults 110 DKr, students 85 DKr, under 18 free) is a showcase for architectural design in Denmark and internationally.
- To get a taste of Danish design under one roof, visit the **Danish Museum of Art & Design** (Bredgade 68, Copenhagen; tel. 33 18 56 56; https://designmuseum.dk; 10am-6pm Tues. and Thurs.-Sun., 10am-9pm Wed.; adults 115 DKr, seniors 80 DKr, under 26 free).
- Norwegian design and architectural company Snøhetta won several awards for the **Oslo Opera House** (page 532).

SHOPS

- **Stilleben Niels** (Hemmingsensgade 3, Copenhagen; tel. 33 91 11 31; www.stilleben.dk; 10pm-6pm Mon.-Fri., 10am-5pm Sat.) Named by *Forbes* magazine as one of Copenhagen's top five design stores, this shop gives you a taste for bringing the clean Scandinavian style to your own home.
- **GUBI Store** (Møntergade 19, Copenhagen; tel. 53 61 63 68; www.gubi.dk; 10am-6pm Mon.-Fri., 10am-4pm Sun.): This luxurious design store with innovative, aesthetic lamps, chairs, and other furniture shows a prominent influence from the Arne Jacobsen functionalist school.
- **Høyer** (Jernbanetorget 6, Oslo; tel. 22 17 03 00; www.hoyer.no; 10am-8pm Mon.-Fri., 10am-6pm Sat.): Find upscale fashion and home goods right off Karl Johans Gate.
- **Illums Bolighus** (Haakon VIIsgate 10, Oslo; tel. 22 01 55 10; www.illumsbolighus.no; 10am-7pm Mon.-Fri., 10am-6pm Sat.): The go-to place for Scandinavian home goods in Oslo.

left, Christianshavn; right, Church of Our Saviour

among the winding streets, many of which are cobbled and connected by arched stone bridges. This area is quiet and picturesque with sailboats moored alongside the paths and plenty of nooks to explore.

2. Church of Our Saviour

Sankt Annæ Gade 29; tel. 32 54 68 83; www.vorfrelserskirke.dk; 10am-7pm Mon.-Sat., 10:30am-7pm Sun. and public holidays May-Sept., 10am-4pm Mon.-Sat., 10:30am-4pm Sun. and public holidays last week of Feb.-Apr. and Oct.-Dec. 15; church free, spire adults 50 DKr, children free

Visit the baroque Church of Our Saviour, a five-minute walk from the café. The real treat is climbing the 400 steps to (almost) the top of the 90-m-tall (295-ft) spire: The last 150 steps are actually on the outside of the spire, so you get a full 360-degree panorama as you go up. (Not recommended for those who are averse to heights.)

For lunch, enjoy a selection of herring and salmon smørrebrød, the classic Danish open-faced sandwich on rye bread, at the more than 150-year-old **Christianshavns Færgecafé** (Strandgade 50; tel. 32 54 46 24; https://faergecafeen.dk; lunch 11:30am-3:30pm Mon.-Sat., dinner 5:30pm-9:30pm Mon.-Thurs., 5:30pm-10pm Fri.-Sat. June-Sept., 5:30pm-9pm Mon.-Thurs., 5:30pm-10pm Fri.-Sat. Oct.-May; lunch from 72 DKr, smørrebrød from 82 DKr, dinner mains 189-235 DKr), a five-minute walk from the church.

3. Bike Rental at Christiania Cykler

Mælkevejen 83A; tel. 70 70 76 80; www.christianiacykler.dk; 9am-5pm Mon.-Fri., 11am-3pm Sat.; rental 450 DKr per day

Rent a classic three-wheeled Christiana cargo cycle, commonly seen with one or more children in the front being ferried around Copenhagen by a parent, for a uniquely Copenhagen way to experience this famously bike-friendly city. For information on Copenhagen's **"Super bike lanes,"** a coherent network of "fast" bicycle connections with easy-to-follow set routes that take you around the city, download the Cykelplanen app or visit the Supercykelstier website (http://supercykelstier.dk).

Started as a hippie squat in the 1970s after the departure of the Danish military from barracks north of Christianshavn, **Christiania** is an alternative, part-autonomous community that is run by consensus of the people who live there. The sign that used to hang above the entrance to Christiana read, "You are now leaving the EU," and encapsulates the vibe of the area, quite distinct from Christianshavn. The Christiana cargo cycles were developed by a resident of the enclave.

★ 4. Cykelslangen

Dybbølsbro, Kalvebod Brygge; free; S-Train Dybbølsbro

Christiana bike rented, you're ready to feel the wind on your face on a leg-powered trip around town. From Christiana, head south over to Islands Brygge and the Bryggebro bicycle and pedestrian bridge. This connects to the winding, bicycle-only Cykelslangen (Bicycle Snake) bridge, a hallmark of Copenhagen's bike-forward planning. The bridge stands up to 7 m (23 ft) above the harbor at its highest point, giving riders a unique vantage point. At the other end of the Cykelslangen is the neighborhood of Vesterbro.

5. The Copenhagen Lakes

Dronning Louises Bro or Peblinge Dossering; free

The Østerbro-Islands Bryggeruten super bike lane connects Cykelslangen to the Copenhagen Lakes. In summer, the lakeside paths hum with life as Copenhageners come out to jog, picnic, or people-watch on a bench. Paddle boats can be rented from **Kaffesalonen** (Peblinge Dossering 6; tel. 35 35 12 19; http://kaffesalonen.com/water-bike-rental; 10am-8:30pm daily; from 100 DKr for 30 minutes), close to the Dronning Louises Bro/Nørrebrogade connection.

On your way back to Christiana, be sure to take **Inderhavnsbroen,** the other bicycle-only bridge, to cross from Nyhavn to Christianshavn.

After returning your bike, head north to **Refshaleøen** (http://refshaleoen.dk; 30 minutes on foot or 20 minutes on the 2A bus), a former industrial area that's emerging as Copenhagen's new must-see destination, for dinner at the street market **Reffen** (Refshalevej 151; tel. 32 54 32 21; https://reffen.dk), and end the night with a craft beer at **Mikkeller Baghaven** (Refshalevej 169B; https://mikkeller.com; 1pm-11pm Mon.-Thurs., noon-midnight Fri.-Sat., noon-9pm Sun.).

DAY 3

★ 1. Kronborg Castle

Kronborg; tel. 33 13 44 11; http://kronborg.dk; 11am-4pm Tue.-Sun. Jan.-Mar., 11am-4pm daily Apr.-May, 10am-5:30pm daily June-Sept., 11am-4pm daily Oct., 11am-4pm Tues.-Sun. Nov.-Dec. (last admission 30 minutes before closing); June-Aug. adults 140 DKr, Sept.-May adults 90 DKr, under 18 free

Today is a day trip to **Helsingør** (Elsinore), where the colossal Kronborg Castle, the setting of Shakespeare's *Hamlet,* stands rugged and proud over the waters of the Øresund. Take a morning train from Copenhagen Central Station to Helsingør Station (1 hour), and then walk about 15 minutes to the castle. Along the way, be sure to look out over the water: The Swedish city of **Helsingborg** is visible on the other shore on most days. Nowhere else is the Øresund narrower than here.

After crossing the bridge over the moat, you'll be in the outer battlements of the castle itself, and you'll get a first view of the Renaissance and baroque influences on its construction. Reliefs, statues, and pillars decorate the entrance to the main courtyard, a spectacular, walled-in square of sandstone, towers, and narrow rectangular windows. From this courtyard, signposts direct you to all the attractions within the castle itself.

There is much to see, and at least a half-day is necessary to take in the castle and its grounds. Many spots at the castle are referenced in *Hamlet,* and these can be found if you look around (and use your imagination a little):

- On the castle **ramparts,** Prince Hamlet gets a shock when he meets

(clockwise from top) Kronborg Castle; Tivoli Gardens; bike rental at Christiania Cykler

ADDING ON Malmö

From Copenhagen, Sweden is less than an hour away by train. Malmö, Sweden, lies just across the Øresund from the Danish capital and is sometimes accused of becoming a pocket-sized Copenhagen. But Malmö remains a destination that offers something entirely different—different country, different language, different scale. The city's sights are very close to each other, and it is quite easy to navigate on foot.

Arrive by: Train to Malmö Station
Travel distance, time, and cost: 45 km (30 mi); 40 minutes from Copenhagen Central Station; 89 DKr one-way

1. MALMÖHUS CASTLE

Malmöhusvägen 5-8; tel. 040-34 44 37; https://malmo.se/museer; 10am-5pm daily; adults 40 SEK, students 20 SEK, under 19 free (Malmö Museer ticket)

Welcome to Sweden! After taking the train from Copenhagen, head for the 16th-century Malmöhus Castle and spend the morning exploring. The low, deep-red cannon towers and broad moat are the castle's most striking features. The castle's interior successfully conjures up medieval and Renaissance Sweden, with the king's antechamber, carved furniture, tapestries, portraits, and marble floors on the upper level, and the dark, stony dungeon below. There are also museums within the castle grounds, such as an aquarium, a dinosaur exhibition, and an art museum.

Walk 10 minutes to lunch at **Malmö Saluhall food market** (Gibraltargatan 6; tel. 040-626 77 30; www.malmosaluhall.se; 10am-7pm Mon.-Thurs., 10am-9pm Fri., 10am-5pm Sat., 11am-4pm Sun.; coffee/pastries from 30 SEK), an artisan food market in a converted warehouse near the harbor. You'll have a vast array of options.

2. TURNING TORSO

Lilla Varvsgatan 14; tel. 040-17 45 40

Hop on a bus or walk 20 minutes to the **Västra Hamnen** seafront promenade, where the centerpiece is the Turning Torso tower. Twisting its way 190 m (623 ft) into the Öresund coastal sky, it's unlike any other building

the ghost of his dead father. You can evoke this scene without having to go into the castle itself, as Kronborg's ramparts are outside the castle wall.

- In Act III, Hamlet and Gertrude's showdown takes place in the **Queen's Chamber** (located within the **King's Apartment** in the real castle), while Polonius listens in from behind a tapestry.
- In the **chapel,** in front of the altar, Claudius surrenders and admits to murdering the king.
- The dramatic climax in Act V Scene II was set by Shakespeare at "a hall in the castle": for this, see Kronborg's **grand ballroom,** located within the castle's royal quarters.

For an additional cost, you can also partake in a special castle tour that follows in the footfalls of Hamlet, Claudius, Ophelia, Laertes, and company: **"In Hamlet's Footsteps"** (year-round except June-Aug.) or **"In Hamlet's World"** (June-Aug. only).

Afterward, have a bite at **Elsinore Street Food** (Ny Kronborgvej 2; tel. 49

in either Malmö or Copenhagen, its white, neofuturist facades bending through seemingly impossible angles. It is a residential building and not generally open to the public, but the exterior is well worth seeing.

3. LILLA TORG

Head back to the Gamla Staden (Old City), where the most camera-friendly of many handsome spots is the cobblestoned Lilla Torg. Spend some time walking around the centuries-old wood-framed buildings.

4. FIKA AT LILLA KAFFEROSTERIET

Baltzarsgatan 24; tel. 040-48 20 00; www.lillakafferosteriet.se

Before leaving Sweden, be sure to do as the locals do and go for fika, the quintessentially Swedish daily afternoon coffee break. Although coffee is consumed at other times of the day, it is the crucial afternoon combination of coffee with a delicious, sweet cinnamon bun that makes fika the phenomenon it is. People at home, at work, or hiking in the mountains are very rigorous in making space in their schedules for the bittersweet afternoon break. Lilla Kafferosteriet, found in one of Malmö's oldest houses and offering variations on the sugary cinnamon bun, is the perfect place to try fika.

GETTING THERE

The quickest way to Malmö is by **DSB** train (www.dsb.dk) from either **Copenhagen Central Station** or **Copenhagen Airport.** The trip to Malmö's Central Station is a 25-minute journey from Copenhagen Airport or 40 minutes from Copenhagen Central Station. Tickets cost 89 DKr for a one-way ticket.

Crossing the **Danish-Swedish Border** is not as seamless as you would expect between two Schengen countries. Identification checks and border controls can happen on either side, so you will need to carry your passport. Sweden, like Denmark, does not use the euro, so you will need to exchange or withdraw some **Swedish kronor** (SEK).

20 02 01; http://vaerftetsmadmarked.dk; 11am-10pm daily, food stands close 9pm; entrées from 65 DKr), a street food market with about a dozen stalls offering everything from Argentinian steak sandwiches to fish and chips.

2. Helsingør's Old Town

Sudergade-Strandgade; Sophie Brahesgade-Stjernegade

Before going to Helsingør train station, spend some time wandering the well-preserved old city center, which survived a redevelopment of the 1960s and 1970s and retains a layout that has been in place since medieval times. The names of the streets here carry their own stories about the town's history: **Stengade (Stone Street)** was the well-to-do quarter where the first stone houses were built, and **Sudergade** was the shoemaker's street, the word *Suder* coming not from the Danish, but the Low German word for "shoe." One "block" south of Stengade, **Strandgade ("Beach Street")** is nearer the coast and was built at some point after the original old town. One street connecting these two parallel roads is **Gl. Færgestræde (Old Ferry Passage),** perhaps the most atmospheric in the entire old town of Helsingør, its cobbled stones still covering the ground the way they were in the Middle Ages.

3. Tivoli Gardens

Vesterbrogade 3; tel. 33 15 10 01; www.tivoli.dk; 11am-11pm Mon.-Thurs., 11am-midnight Fri.-Sun. Mar.-Sept., mid-Oct.-early Nov., mid-Nov.-Dec. 31; 100 DKr, ages 3-7 50 DKr, under 3 free

Back in Copenhagen, spend the evening at Tivoli Gardens, located in front of Copenhagen Central Station. One of Denmark's most popular attractions with locals and tourists alike, this amusement park opened in 1843 and includes the original wooden roller coaster known simply as the *Rutschebane* as one of its attractions. The park is magical at night when it is all lit up; you can even dance to a live swing band.

DAY 4

1. Morning of Copenhagen's Café Culture

Start your last morning in Copenhagen slowly with coffee and wienerbrød, the pastry known as a "Danish" in the United States or the United Kingdom. Enjoy them outside if the weather's fine or, in Copenhagen spring tradition (if it's warmish), even if it's not. In doing so, you'll be participating in Copenhagen's café culture, where locals linger for an hour or three catching up with a friend or even alone, getting some work done or reading a book.

Copenhagen has every type of café imaginable, from small independent roasteries to large chains to pastry and bread specialists. **Democratic Coffee** (Krystalgade 15; tel. 40 19 62 37; 8am-4pm Mon.-Fri., 9am-4pm Sat.-Sun.) prepares its baked goods on the premises, and there's seating and window space, so it's a good place to try doing as the Danes do.

2. Ny Carlsberg Glyptotek

Dantes Plads 7; tel. 33 41 81 41; www.glyptoteket.com; 11am-6pm Tues.-Sun., 11am-10pm Thurs.; adults 115 DKr, under 27 85 DKr, under 1 free, Tues. free (special exhibitions 60 DKr)

After breakfast, head to Ny Carlsberg Glyptotek, a supremely elegant museum that is home to the classics: Greek and Roman sculptures, Egyptian hieroglyphs, and paintings by Picasso and Monet. The sumptuous collection will get art lovers

left, DFDS Ferry; right, Ny Carlsberg Glyptotek

drooling from the moment they pass the resplendent columns and arches of the museum's entrance.

3. DFDS Ferry Port

Dampfærgevej 32; www.dfds.com; from €54; reserve in advance

And now, off to Oslo by ferry! The ferry departs daily at 3pm, and you'll want to be at port with a comfortable cushion before that time (last check-in at 2:45pm). As the ferry passes out of the Øresund, you'll see **Kronborg Castle** from a different angle. Enjoy the onboard dining for an additional cost, and then settle in as the boat plies its route toward Norway overnight.

Oslo

Where to Stay: The downtown area around Karl Johans Gate

Arrive by: Ferry from Copenhagen DFDS Ferry Port to DFDS Oslo terminal (17-19 hours)

DAY 5

The ferry will reach Oslo by 10am. If you wake up early, you can watch as the boat cruises through the **Oslofjord.** When you arrive, drop off your luggage at your hotel or in the lockers at Oslo Central Station (Jernbanetorget 1; https://oslo-s.no).

1. Royal Palace

Slottsplassen 1; tel. 22 04 87 00; www.kongehuset.no; only open in summer, by guided tour; adults 175 NKr, seniors and students 145 NKr, ages 6-18 125 NKr, under 5 free

Start your first day in Norway's capital by heading toward the Royal Palace, the official home of Norway's king and queen. Completed in 1849, it's a classic modern palace with a large balcony, six massive pillars in front, and 173 rooms inside. To go inside, you must purchase a ticket to join one of the interior palace **tours.** Otherwise, enjoy the surrounding place gardens, or **Slottsparken,** and its many sculptures.

Head out of the palace grounds along the main pedestrian street of **Karl Johans Gate;** you'll pass the grand Nationaltheateret and the Norwegian Parliament Stortinget buildings along the way to your next stop.

2. Oslo Cathedral

Karl Johans Gate 11; tel. 23 62 90 10; www.oslodomkirke.no; 10am-4pm Sat.-Thurs., 4pm-11:30pm Fri;. free

After 15 minutes, you'll reach the Oslo Cathedral, a beautiful baroque church dating back to 1697. The bell tower is the highlight of the exterior, with its symmetrical windows, big clock—Norway's oldest clock still in use—and several pointed spears around the bell itself. Pop inside to marvel at the original altar and pulpit, dating to 1699.

For lunch, walk five minutes to the **Royal Gastropub** (Østbanehallen, Jernbanetorget 1; tel. 21 08 22 72; www.royalgastropub.no; 11am-11pm Mon.-Wed.,

Oslo Cathedral

11am-12:30am Thurs.-Sat., noon-11pm Sun.; 239-300 NKr), a food hall in the oldest part of Oslo Central Station. The name of this restaurant comes from the fact that it's set in the king's former waiting room, from back when he primarily traveled to various parts of Norway by train.

3. Oslo Opera House

Kirsten Flaagstads plass 1; tel. 21 42 21 21; www.operaen.no

Just five minutes away you'll find the stunning Oslo Opera House. Opened in 2008, the building itself is spectacular; Norwegian design and architectural company Snøhetta won several awards for their work. Depending on whom you ask, the building can resemble a ship, a ski slope, or the zig-zag hairpin turns found on mountainsides all over Norway. You can walk on top of the building, where there are lovely views of the Oslofjord and the distinctive stretch of Oslo skyline known as the Barcode. It's worth joining a tour (1pm Sun.-Fri., noon Sat.) of the interior, too.

4. Akershus Fortress

grounds open 6am-9pm daily; free

From the Opera House, walk along the water for 20 minutes to Akershus Fortress. Perched on the top of a hill overlooking the Oslofjord, the fortress looks somewhat like a medieval castle from the outside, with the thick stone walls surrounding it. Inside the walls, however, it almost resembles a small village, with cobblestoned streets, several small houses and buildings, and lawn areas to relax on. It was originally built in the 1200s as a royal residence, and in the 1600s, the castle was expanded and the fortress walls were added.

Spend some time walking around the grounds, perhaps visiting the Norwegian Armed Fortress Museum, which covers the development of the Norwegian military from the 1400s up until today.

Nobel Peace Center

★ 5. Nobel Peace Center

Brynjulf Bulls Plass 1; tel. 48 30 10 00; www.nobelpeacecenter.org; 11am-5pm Thurs.-Sun.; adults 120 NKr, ages 12-18 50 NKr under 12 free

Your busy day of sightseeing continues at the Nobel Peace Center, a 10-minute walk along the bay. This museum and center are dedicated to the Nobel Peace Prize, winners throughout the decades, and the impact and legacy of their work. The exhibitions here are inspirational and interactive, and their aim is to inspire visitors to make small (and big) changes for a more peaceful world.

For dinner, there are several options in the upscale dockside neighborhood of Aker Brygge. Try **Entrecôte by Trancher** (Bryggetorget 10; tel. 22 44 44 60; https://trancher.no/aker-brygge; 5pm-10pm Wed.-Sat.; 245-525 NKr), a Norwegian take on a steakhouse, serving carefully selected cuts of meat.

DAY 6

1. Nasjonalmuseet

Brynjulf Bulls Plass 3; tel. 21 98 20 00; www.nasjonalmuseet.no; 10am-9pm Tues.-Sun.; adults 180 NKr, over 67 and 18-25 110 NKr, under 18 free

On your second day in Oslo have breakfast and head to the Nasjonalmuseet. This massive museum, the largest in the Nordics, is located on the Aker Brygge waterfront and offers state-of-the-art

WATCH

The Bridge: The Öresund (or Øresund) Bridge, which links Copenhagen and Malmö, Sweden, is featured in this hugely successful Scandinoir TV show. The dark atmosphere, quirky personalities of the characters, and the shared Scandinavian backdrop have captivated audiences since the show first aired in 2011, beginning with the gruesome, but no less symbolic, discovery of a body in two parts—one on each country's side of the bridge.

Henrik Ibsen plays: Works by Norway's most important literary figure include *Hedda Gabler, Peer Gynt,* and *A Doll's House* and are still being performed around the world today. The theater at the **Ibsen Museum** (Henrik Ibsens Gate 26, Oslo; tel. 40 02 36 30; https://ibsenmuseet.no) regularly stages performances of his plays.

The Worst Person in the World: This melancholy comedy-drama follows main character Julie as she navigates love, family, and career in modern-day Oslo. The Norwegian movie, released in 2021, is one of three films set in Oslo by director Joachim Trier.

READ

The Snowman by Jo Nesbø: This dark and violent crime novel by Norway's most successful author follows a police inspector as he tracks down a serial killer in Oslo.

Hans Christian Andersen fairy tales: Popular stories such as "The Ugly Duckling" and "The Emperor's New Clothes" were written by Danish author Hans Christian Andersen. The Little Mermaid statue, a tribute to another one of his tales, is an icon of Copenhagen.

exhibit rooms showcasing Norwegian art and design. There are several floors of permanent and non-permanent exhibitions, so check the website before your visit to decide what you'll want to see.

2. Rådhuset

Rådhusplassen 1; tel. 23 46 12 00; www.oslo.kommune.no/radhuset/#gref; 9am-4pm daily; free

Walk 10 minutes the Rådhuset, or city hall, a commanding redbrick building with two massive, distinctive front towers. Rådhuset's clocks boast Norway's largest chimes, which play different songs throughout the day, 7am-midnight. Oslo is woken up by "Morning Mood" by Edvard Grieg, while later in the day you may hear the themes from *Jurassic Park* or *Top Gun*.

Head to the Nationaltheateret subway station take the train one stop west to Majorstuen. Grab lunch at **Kverneriet** (Kirkeveien 64B; tel. 90 60 03 33; www.kverneriet.com; 4pm-9pm Mon., 4pm-10pm Tues.-Wed., 11am-10pm Thurs.-Fri., noon-10pm Sat., noon-9pm Sun.; 169-239 NKr), which serves great burgers and milkshakes right next to the station.

3. Vigelandsparken

open 24 hours; free

From Kverneriet, walk 10 minutes to the entrance of the famous, can't-miss sculpture park of Vigelandsparken. This is perhaps the most popular attraction in Oslo, and with good reason. Housed within **Frognerparken,** it's the largest sculpture park in the world created by one artist. In addition to carving, sculpting, and casting the sculptures, Gustav Vigeland also designed the layout of the park himself.

You'll find beautiful sculptures here, depicting everything from the frustrations of parenthood, to love between siblings, to vanity, grief, and anger. The largest of the sculptures, ***Monolitten*** (the Monolith) is both fascinating and slightly grotesque, as it displays human bodies twisted together to build a large stone column. The entire Monolith was carved from the same piece of stone. Another popular, though much smaller, statue is called ***Sinnataggen,*** depicting an angry little boy throwing a tantrum.

Vigeland Park is particularly busy on Sunday, when locals and visitors alike head to the park to get some fresh air, enjoy a walk with friends, or lounge on the grass.

4. Vigeland Museum

Nobels Gate 32; tel. 23 49 37 00; https://vigeland.museum.no; noon-4pm Tues.-Sun.; adults 100 NKr, children free

After a stroll through Vigelandsparken, head across the street learn more about the Norwegian sculptor behind it, Gustav Vigeland. The museum houses 1,600 additional sculptures as well as some of his drawings and wood carvings. The museum also puts on tours of Vigeland's apartment in Oslo, which has been kept with its original furnishings so you can get a glimpse into his life with his wife, Ingrid.

After your museum visit, walk to tram stop Frogner Plass and get on tram #12 back to **Majorstuen.** Stroll down Bogstadveien, a lovely shopping street. Grab dinner at **FYR Bistronomi** (Underhaugsveien 28; tel. 45 91 63 92; www.fyr-bistronomi.no; 5pm-midnight Mon.-Sat.; 155-215 NKr small plates), a gastronomic bistro at the other end of Bogstadveien.

DAY 7

1. Ferry to Drøbak

After a couple of days on dry land, it's time to get out on the water again on a day trip to Drøbak. The scenic boat ride to this quiet fishing town travels down the Oslofjord, giving you another chance at some of the views you might have missed on the way in from Copenhagen. Public ferry B21, operated by Ruter (www.ruter.no), leaves Aker Brygge in twice a day in the high season (June-Aug.), and on weekends only in April, May, and September. The journey takes around 1.5 hours and costs 114 NKr one-way.

2. Oscarsborg Fortress

Husvikveien; tel. 64 90 41 61; www.forsvarsbygg.no/no/festningene/finn-din-festning/oscarsborg-festning; open 24 hours; free

The main sight in Drøbak, this island fortress was once the winter harbor for the capital back when the inner Oslofjord used to freeze over, and has always been an important part of the protection of the city. The fortress is a massive, rounded stone wall shaped like a half moon when seen from the top, and the walls are thick enough to house a hotel and several museums, including the **Fortress Museum** (10am-5pm Mon.-Sun.; free) on the military history of the fortress, with a focus on the events of April 9, 1940 and the **Coastal Artillery Museum** (10am-5pm Mon.-Sun. summer) covering the history of the Norwegian Kystartilleriet. The fort you see today dates mostly to the 1800s, and played its most important role in World War II, when the German war ship *Blücher* was famously sunk by the torpedo battery in the early hours of April 9, 1940.

From Drøbak, there are several ferries to Oscarsborg daily (110 NKr round-trip), and the crossing takes around 10 minutes. The ferry leaves from Sundbrygga, about a 15-minute walk north from the B21 ferry terminal.

3. Drinks at Thief Roof

Landgangen 1; tel. 24 00 40 00; https://thethief.com/the-roof; Apr.-Sept.

After getting back to Oslo, end your stay in Norway with drinks at one of few rooftop bars in Oslo. The roof of the luxurious

Thief Hotel (open only in summer) is stylish and upscale, equally fun on warm or cold nights.

TRANSPORTATION

Air

- **Copenhagen Airport** (CPH, or Kastrup; Lufthavnsboulevarden 6; tel. 45 32 31 32 31; www.cph.dk) is about 10 km (6 mi) from the city center. A ride on the Metro to the city center takes 15 minutes and costs 17-20 NKr, and a taxi ride will likely take 20-30 minutes and cost 300 NKr or more.
- **Oslo Airport Gardermoen** (OSL; Edvard Munchs veg; tel. 64 81 20 00; https://avinor.no/flyplass/oslo) is about 50 miles from Oslo, a 40-minute drive. The airport express train FlyToget takes you directly to Oslo Central Station in 20 minutes (220 Nkr).

Train

- **Copenhagen Central Station** (Hovedbanegården, often abbreviated to Hovedbanen) is in the center of Copenhagen, across the street from Tivoli Gardens. Tickets can be booked via **DSB** (tel. 70 13 14 18; www.dsb.dk).
- **Oslo Central Station** (Oslo Sentralstasjon, Oslo S for short), located in Oslo's city center, is the main train station for Oslo. **Vy** (tel. 61 05 19 10; www.vy.no) is Norway's main railway company.

Bus

- In Copenhagen, buses leave and depart from the rather underwhelming **terminal,** which is no more than a road side with a series of bus stands, at **Ingerslevsgade.**
- The main bus station for Oslo is Oslo Bus Terminal (Schweigaards Gate; tel. 23 00 24 00; https://oslobussterminal.no), located in downtown Oslo a short walk from Jernbanetorget and Karl Johans Gate.

Public Transportation

Copenhagen

Copenhagen's public transportation system is comprehensive, consisting of bus and Metro systems as well as an overground network known as the S-tog (S-train). The **Rejseplanen app,** available in English, is a must-have for planning; official site **Din Offentlig Transport (DOT)** (https://dinoffentligetransport.dk) is also useful.

Oslo

Most of Oslo's sights are concentrated in the very walkable city center. The city also has a great public transit system, across the subway (called the T-bane), buses, and trams (trikk). All belong within the same network: Download the **Ruter Reise** app (www.ruter.no) to check schedules and find travel routes across the whole city. The logo for Ruter is a hashtag (#), and you will see it around the city indicating tram and bus stops, and where there are steps or walkways down to the subway.

Getting Back

Fly home from **Oslo Airport Gardermoen.** You can also get back to Copenhagen via a 6.5-hour drive (600 km/370 mi), 8-hour bus ride, or the return 19-hour ferry ride.

CONNECT WITH

- Copenhagen to Berlin by Bike (page 389)
- The Bergen Line (page 675)
- Lofoten (page 268)

NAPLES, CAPRI, AND THE AMALFI COAST

Why Go: Ply the waters between Naples, Capri, and the Amalfi Coast for some of the most beautiful views in Italy, or perhaps the world.

Number of Days: 7

Total Distance: 60 km (37 mi)

Seasons: Spring and summer

Start: Naples

End: Amalfi

When you think of la dolce vita, chances are the Amalfi Coast comes to mind. With pastel-hued homes clinging to the cliffs between mountain and sea, iconic beaches lined with colorful umbrellas, and postcard-worthy views in every direction, the Amalfi Coast is a bucket-list destination. This extraordinary region is a stunning combination of natural beauty, culture, and history, with a healthy dose of warm southern Italian hospitality.

Start in Naples, a pulsating city set to the soundtrack of buzzing scooters and Neapolitan songs, before catching a ferry to impossibly chic Capri. More ferry rides take you to Positano and Amalfi, with their quintessential charming villages, rocky beaches, and famous views. Just make sure to plan your trip in season (Easter-Oct.) when the ferries are running and everything is open.

TOP 3

★ Cruising on a boat around **Capri,** through turquoise blue waters and past stunning grottoes (page 545).

★ Hiking the **Pathway of the Gods,** the most breathtaking trail in a landscape famous for beautiful coastal views (page 546).

★ Finding your own personal paradise at **Santa Croce beach,** set in a secluded rocky cove (page 547).

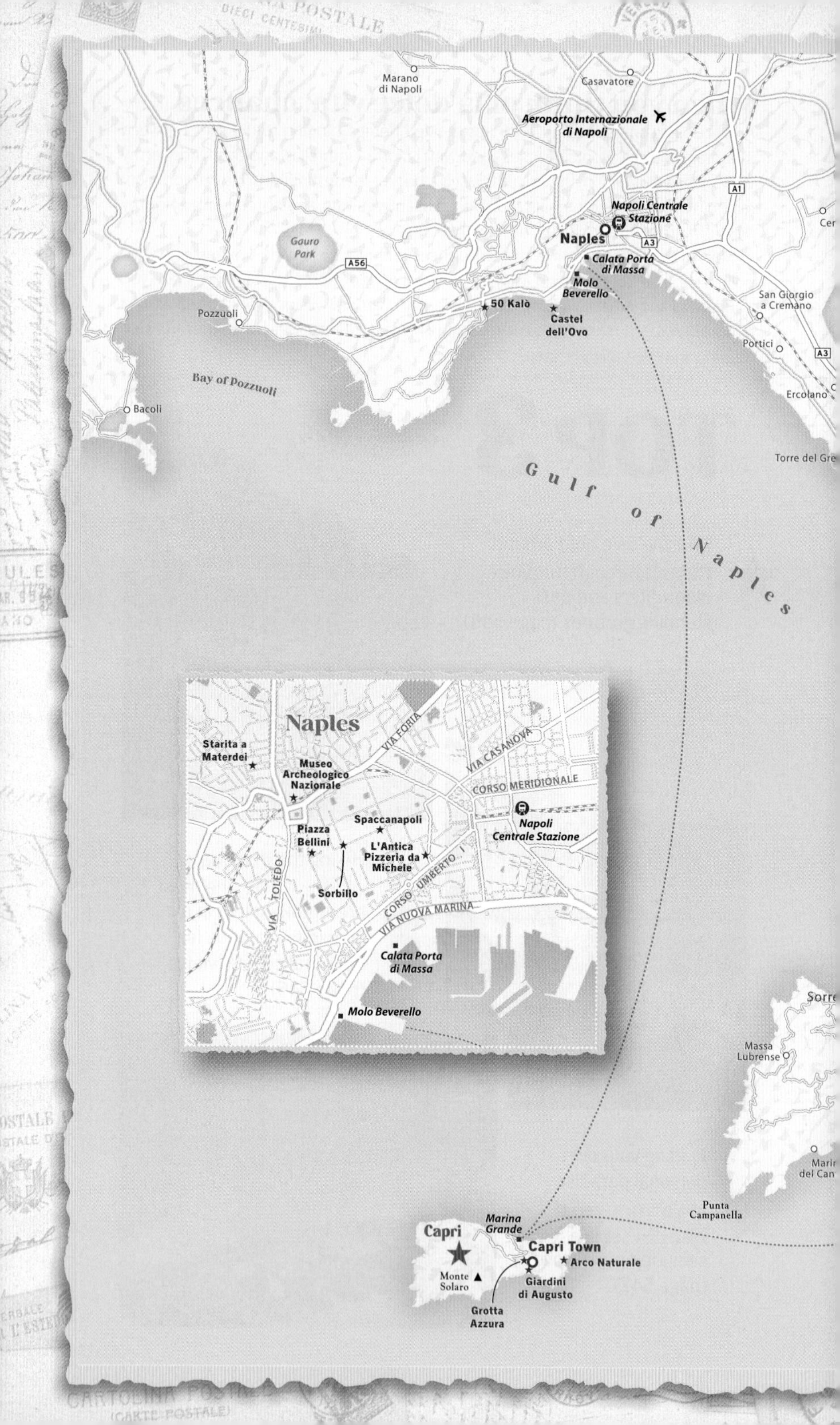
Marano di Napoli
Casavatore
Aeroporto Internazionale di Napoli
A1
Napoli Centrale Stazione
Naples
A3
Gauro Park
A56
Calata Porta di Massa
Molo Beverello
50 Kalò
Castel dell'Ovo
Pozzuoli
San Giorgio a Cremano
Portici
A3
Bay of Pozzuoli
Bacoli
Ercolano
Gulf of Naples
Naples
Starita a Materdei
Museo Archeologico Nazionale
VIA FORIA
VIA CASANOVA
CORSO MERIDIONALE
Napoli Centrale Stazione
Spaccanapoli
Piazza Bellini
L'Antica Pizzeria da Michele
Sorbillo
VIA TOLEDO
CORSO UMBERTO I
VIA NUOVA MARINA
Calata Porta di Massa
Molo Beverello
Massa Lubrense
Punta Campanella
Capri
Marina Grande
Capri Town
Arco Naturale
Monte Solaro
Giardini di Augusto
Grotta Azzura

NAPLES, CAPRI, AND THE AMALFI COAST

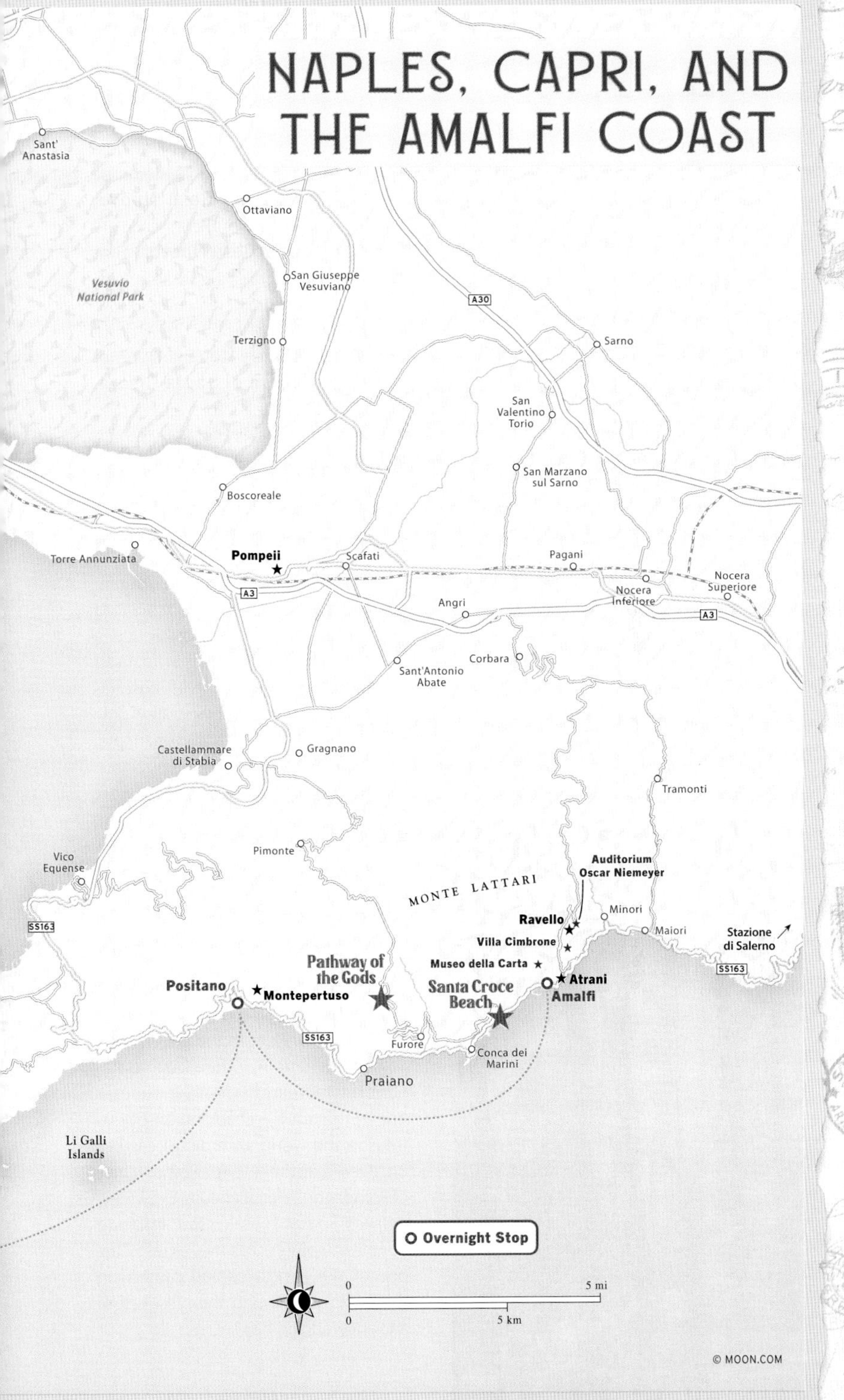

Naples

Where to Stay: San Ferdinando or Quartieri Spagnoli (Spanish Quarter) neighborhoods, which are close to the top sights and Molo Beverello ferry terminal

Arrive by: Plane to Capodichino Airport (Aeroporto Internazionale di Napoli)

DAY 1

1. Spaccanapoli

Via Benedetto Croce and Via San Biagio dei Librai, from Piazza Gesù Nuovo to Via Duomo

After arriving in Naples, get your bearings with a walk down Spaccanapoli in the most characteristic area of this energetic city. The street, whose name means "Split Naples," cuts a straight line through the historic center. Starting in Piazza del Gesù Nuovo, the street now is labeled Via Benedetto Croce, which then becomes Via San Biagio dei Librai until it crosses Via Duomo. Along this walk, you'll see many of the city's most important churches and historic monuments in a very short distance. Among them: the beautiful **Piazza del Gesù Nuovo,** with its ornate Spire of the Immaculate and the **Chiesa di Gesù Nuovo,** which is striking for its dark gray stone facade, which is almost completely covered with carved pyramid-shaped projections; and the monumental religious complex of the **Chiesa di Santa Chiara,** which includes a beautiful majolica-tiled cloister and the ruins of a Roman bath complex.

Spaccanapoli

2. L'Antica Pizzeria da Michele

Via Cesare Sersale 1; tel. 081/553-9204; www.damichele.net; 11am-11pm Mon.-Sat.; €5

Once you reach Via Duomo, you're tantalizingly close to L'Antica Pizzeria da Michele, easily the most iconic pizzeria in Naples. Everything here is focused 100 percent on the pizza in its most traditional form, and the menu offers only the classics: Margherita and marinara. Thanks not only to the divine pizza but also to Elizabeth Gilbert's book *Eat, Pray, Love*, you can expect to find a good line here most days.

3. Museo Archeologico Nazionale

Piazza Museo 19; tel. 848/800-288; www.museoarcheologiconapoli.it; 9am-7:30pm Wed.-Mon.; €10

Spend the afternoon at the world-class Museo Archeologico Nazionale (about a 20-minute walk from the pizzeria or a 10-minute metro ride from Duomo station). This museum is a must, as it houses one of the finest archaeological collections in the world, including treasures uncovered at the ancient Roman cities of Pompeii and Herculaneum. Exquisitely detailed Roman mosaics, awe-inspiring marble sculptures, and the Farnese Cup, one of the largest carved cameos in the world, are among the pieces from ancient world on display.

Key Reservations

MONUMENTS AND MUSEUMS

Unlike in other parts of Italy, the major sights in Naples, Capri, and the Amalfi Coast do not generally sell out. Large and small museums are now equipped with online booking systems or ticket booking partners, so booking in advance is possible—and might be convenient for popular sights like **Pompeii**—but usually not necessary.

RESTAURANTS AND HOTELS

Reservations for restaurants on the Amalfi Coast and Capri can be a good idea during the popular summer months. Booking ahead is necessary for **Caruso Roof Garden Restaurant** (Naples) and **Da Paolino** (Capri).

The Amalfi Coast and Capri are among the most popular travel destinations in Italy, so accommodations can fill up very quickly. It's wise to book ahead of time, especially if you're going to be traveling from July to August.

TRANSPORTATION

During the summer months, booking ferries ahead of time is recommended, especially on car ferries.

Pompeii

4. La Sfogliatella Mary

Via Toledo 66/Galleria Umberto I; tel. 081/402-218; 8am-8:30pm Tues.-Sun.; €1.80-2.50

This small bakery is located in the **Galleria Umberto I,** a shopping center with a soaring glass dome just south of the Municipio metro station—you'll likely catch the sweet scent of sfogliatella before you arrive. One of Naples's traditional desserts, the shell-shaped sfogliatella pastry has a citrus-infused ricotta filling and comes in two varieties: The classic sfogliatella riccia has a flaky crust, and the frolla variety has a soft short-crust pastry shell.

True Neapolitan Pizza

In 2017, the art of the Neapolitan Piazzaiuolo, or pizza maker, was added to UNESCO's list of Intangible Cultural Heritage of Humanity. It was a moment of great celebration in Naples, where the famous gastronomic delight is indelibly connected to the city's identity.

The most classic of Neapolitan pizzas is the **pizza Margherita,** which dates to 1889 when Raffaele Esposito made pizzas for King Umberto I and Queen Margherita di Savoia during their visit to Naples. The queen most enjoyed the pizza topped with tomatoes, mozzarella, extra virgin olive oil, and basil—to represent the green, white, and red of the Italian flag—and so Raffaele named the pizza in her honor. You'll find pizza Margherita on every pizzeria menu, along with the **marinara pizza** topped with tomatoes, oregano, garlic, and extra virgin olive oil (no cheese). These two pizzas are considered the most traditional. Naples is also famous for its pizza fritta (fried pizza): This is pizza that's topped with a variety of different fillings, like ricotta and salami, and then folded in half and deep fried.

Pizza in Naples is usually about the size of a large plate, considered an individual portion. Your pizza will not arrive presliced, so grab your knife and fork and dig in. It's not hard to find an excellent pizzeria, and here are some suggestions beyond **L'Antica Pizzeria da Michele** (page 540) to get you started.

- **Sorbillo:** Among Sorbillo's multiple locations around the city are a restaurant in the centro storico (Via dei Tribunali 32; tel. 081/446-643; www.sorbillo.it; noon-3pm and 7pm-11pm Mon.-Sat., closed mid-Aug.) and a seaside outpost (Via Partenope 1) with a view of the Castel dell'Ovo. Many of their branches specialize in pizza fritta.
- **50 Kalò** (Piazza Sannazzaro 201/b; tel. 081/192-04667; www.50kalo.it; 12:30pm-4pm and 7pm-12:30am daily): This pizzeria is not far from the Mergellina harbor.
- **Starita a Materdei** (Via Materdei 27/28; tel. 081/557-3682; www.pizzeriestarita.it; noon-3:30pm and 7pm-midnight Tues.-Sun.): This classic pizzeria also serves gluten-free pizza.

5. Castel dell'Ovo

Borgo Marinari; tel. 081/795-4592; www.comune.napoli.it; 9am-7:30pm Mon.-Sat. (closes 6:30pm in winter), 9am-2pm Sun.; free

After your snack, head down to the waterfront—being sure to stop and absorb the sweeping expanse of **Piazza del Plebiscito,** the largest piazza in Naples—to Castel dell'Ovo, a 15th-century castle that sits on a islet jutting out into the Gulf of Naples. Climb to the top for incredible views of the Gulf of Naples with Vesuvius and the island of Capri in the distance. At the end of the day, relax and watch the golden glow of sunset from the nearby **Caruso Roof Garden Restaurant** (Via Partenope 45; www.vesuvio.it/caruso; 1pm-3pm and 8:30pm-11pm Tues.-Sun.; reservations recommended; €24-30) at the Grand Hotel Vesuvio, which overlooks the gulf and the charming Borgo Marinari below.

Day Trip to Pompeii

DAY 2

Arrive by: Circumvesuviana train from Naples central train station to Pompeii Scavi-Villa dei Misteri (45 minutes)

1. Parco Archeologico di Pompei

tel. 081/857-5111; www.pompeiisites.org; 9am-7pm Tues.-Sun. Apr.-Oct., 9am-5pm Nov.-Mar.; €16

After getting off at the "Pompeii Scavi-Villa dei Misteri" stop, cross the street to the **Porta Marina** entrance. Before Mount Vesuvius erupted in 79 CE, Pompeii was a large Roman city. The volcanic eruption covered the city with pumice and ash, stopping every part of life in an instant and freezing Pompeii in time.

Plan on about three hours to see the highlights of the archaeological site and really experience what life was like in an ancient Roman town, stopping for a light lunch at the café on-site. Don't miss the experience of standing in the center of Pompeii's ancient **Amphitheater,** where gladiators once battled, or exploring the **Villa of the Mysteries,** named for its captivating and enigmatic frescoes.

2. Piazza Bellini

After returning to Naples, enjoy an aperitivo and people-watching in Piazza Bellini. The small square is a lively nightlife spot and is worth a visit to see the ancient Greek walls that are visible below a part of the piazza. For dinner, try a ragù-based dish at nearby **Tandem Ragù** (Via Giovanni Paladino 51; tel. 081/190-02468; www.tandemnapoli.it; 12:30pm-3:30pm and 7pm-11:30pm Mon.-Tues., 12:30pm-11:30pm Wed.-Sun.; €10-15). In Naples, ragù is essential. This tomato sauce is simmered for hours upon hours and enriched with various types of meat—and quite possibly a touch of magic.

Capri

Where to Stay: Capri town, the hub of activity on the island

Arrive by: Ferry from Molo Beverello in Naples to Marina Grande on Capri (1 hour)

DAY 3

1. Monte Solaro

Chairlift: Via Caposcuro 10; tel. 081/837-1438; www.capriseggiovia.it; 9:30am-4pm daily Mar.-Apr., 9:30am-5pm daily May-Oct., 9:30am-3:30pm daily Nov.-Feb.; €12

In the morning, head to the Molo Beverello, Naples's major ferry terminal, for the hour-long water crossing to the island of Capri. After heading into

Monte Solaro

Best Views

CAPRI

- **Giardini di Augusto:** Only a short stroll from the central Piazzetta, these gardens are easy to reach to enjoy a view of the Faraglioni rocks. The beautiful garden setting is an extra perk (page 544).
- **Monte Solaro:** Hands down, the finest view on Capri is from the island's highest point atop Monte Solaro. Hop on the chairlift for a scenic ride to the top to enjoy the 360-degree views over the island (page 543).

AMALFI COAST

- **Spiaggia Grande, Positano:** Standing on this beach, you get one of the best views of Positano and find out why it's called the Vertical City (page 547).
- **Pathway of the Gods, Positano:** This mountain trail offers breathtaking views of the coastline around Positano (page 546).
- **Villa Cimbrone, Ravello:** The view the from Terrace of Infinity is one of endless beauty (page 549).

Capri town to drop off your bags and get a quick bite, take a local bus or taxi up to **Piazza Vittoria** in Anacapri and hop on the chairlift to the top of Monte Solaro, the island's highest point. This is one of Capri's most majestic spots, and the views stretch all around the Gulf of Naples, from the Sorrentine Peninsula and Mount Vesuvius on the mainland to the islands of Ischia and Procida.

2. Arco Naturale

Make your way back to Capri town. The roughly 1.6-km (1-mi) walk to the dramatic Arco Naturale rock formation is well-marked: Start off in the bustling **Piazzetta,** the square that's the heart of town, and head east, following the signs for Arco Naturale. Down a series of steps, the craggy natural arch is located in a peaceful pine tree-studded landscape and creates a framed view of the sea. From there, go back up the steps, and follow signs for Gortta di Matermania, Via del Pizzolungo, and Via Tragara to reach **Belvedere Tragara** (about 1.6 km/1 mi from Arco Naturale) and an incredible view overlooking the famous **Faraglioni rocks.**

3. Giardini di Augusto

Via Matteotti 2; tel. 081/837-0686 (tourist office); www.cittadicapri.it; 9am-7:30pm daily Apr.-Sept., 9am-4pm in winter; €1

Giardini di Augusto is about a 15-minute walk from Belvedere Tragara. These lush gardens are planted across several terraces

with flora that are typical of Capri, like ginestra (broom), bougainvillea, cacti, and bird of paradise. However, the main draw here is the sweeping view from the edge of the garden of the Faraglioni rocks in one direction, and the bay of Marina Piccola in the other, as well as the zigzagging Via Krupp, carved into the mountainside. Next door, **Capri Rooftop** (Via Matteotti 7; tel. 081/837-8147; www.caprirooftop.com; 10am-2am daily mid-May-mid-Sept., 9am-midnight daily mid-Apr.-mid-May and mid-Sept.-Nov.) is perfect for a relaxed drink anytime of the day.

4. Caprese Dinner at Da Paolino

Via Palazzo a Mare 11; tel. 081/837-6102; www.paolinocapri.com; 7pm-11:30pm daily late Apr.-late Oct., also 12:30pm-2:15pm Apr.-May; €20-45

For dinner, head down to Marina Grande to one of Capri's most romantic spots. Da Paolino, which should be booked in advance, serves Caprese (Capri-style) specialties on an enchanting dining terrace nestled into a lemon grove. The fresh pasta with lemon sauce is a classic choice while dining under the lemon trees.

DAY 4 MORNING

★ 1. Grotta Azzura

tel. 081/837-5646; www.musei.campania.beniculturali.it; 9am-5pm daily Apr.-Oct., 9am-2pm daily Nov.-Mar., weather permitting; €14

Synonymous with Capri around the world and one of the island's most popular sights, the Grotta Azzurra (Blue Grotto) is a natural cavern on the north coast with deep, electric blue water that shimmers with a silvery glow thanks to the refraction of light from an opening below sea level. The entrance to the grotto is very small and can only be accessed by rowboats that hold up to four people. Visit the grotto in the morning, as wind or weather changes can occasionally make it inaccessible in the afternoon. Several group and private tour options are readily available from Marina Grande, often combined with a boat tour of the island. Afterward, have lunch and maybe do a little shopping before catching the mid-afternoon ferry (45 minutes) to **Positano.** Be sure to admire the view as the boat approaches the vertical city.

Positano

Where to Stay: Near Spiaggia Grande

Arrive by: Ferry from Capri's Marina Grande to Spiaggia Grande in Positano (45 minutes)

DAY 4 AFTERNOON

1. Spiaggia di Fornillo

Via Fornillo

After checking in to your hotel, head back down to Spiaggia Grande, and follow the scenic, cliff-hugging Via Positanesi d'America pathway over to Spiaggia di Fornillo, Positano's second-largest beach. It's quieter here than at Spiaggia Grande, and **Da Ferdinando** (tel. 089/875-365; 8am-8pm daily mid-May-mid-Oct.), a stabilimente baleare (beach club), rents sun beds and umbrellas. When you're ready to eat, just head up to the restaurant area overlooking the beach.

Spiaggia di Fornillo

(top to bottom) Pathway of the Gods; Montepertuso; Spiaggia Grande

2. Music on the Rocks

Via del Brigantino 19; tel. 089/875-874; www.musicontherocks.it; 10:30pm-4am daily Apr.-Oct.; price varies by event

This nightclub is literally on the rocks, as it's set in a cave carved out of the mountainside just steps from the sea. Head here for a night of music and dancing, a hot spot on the Amalfi Coast for more than 40 years, and it still attracts national and international DJs and musicians. There is a cover charge, but it varies depending on the events taking place.

DAY 5

TOP EXPERIENCE

★ 1. Pathway of the Gods

Piazza Paolo Capasso, Bomerano

Start the day early with a good breakfast at your accommodation before lacing up comfortable walking shoes, packing some water, and catching the bus from Positano up to Agerola. Get off in **Bomerano** to begin the Sentiero degli Dei, or the Pathway of the Gods, one of the most impressive and scenic walks on the Amalfi Coast. Passing along the mountains high above the sea, the trail is dotted with Meditteranean vegetation and offers panoramic views overlooking Praiano, Positano, and Capri in the distance. The 6-km (3.7-mi) walk takes 3-4 hours and ends in **Nocelle,** a frazione (hamlet) above Positano. Look for the granita stand in a small plaza down the steps headed to Positano—nothing will taste so good as that icy lemon or orange drink after the hike!

2. Montepertuso

From Nocelle, continue along the road to Montepertuso, another frazione, for a hearty lunch. Try **La Tagliata** (Via Tagliata 32B, Montepertuso; tel. 089/875-872; www.latagliata.com; noon-3:30pm and 7pm-10:30pm daily mid-Mar.-early Nov.; fixed-price menus €30-45 per person) for regional cuisine and views overlooking Positano and the coastline. If you have energy afterward, follow the steps that start near the restaurant Il Ritrovo and hike up to the pertuso (the Neapolitan word for hole) in **Monte Gambera,** which can be seen from far below and gives the village its name.

3. Spiaggia Grande

Via Marina Grande

Catch a local bus down to Positano and head down to the beach to give your legs a rest or go for a swim at the Spiaggia Grande, with the town's vertical stack of colorful buildings as the perfect backdrop. Have dinner at nearby **Ristorante La Pergola** (Via del Brigantino 35; tel. 089/811-461; www.bucadibaccolapergola.com; 8:30am-11pm daily Mar.-mid-Nov.; €20-50).

Amalfi

Where to Stay: Near Piazza Duomo

Arrive by: Ferry from Spiaggia Grande in Positano to Amalfi's Molo Pennello pier (25 minutes)

DAY 6

1. Museo della Carta

Via delle Cartiere 23; tel. 089/830-4561; www.museodellacarta.it; 10am-6:30pm Tues.-Sun. Mar.-Oct., 10am-4pm Tues.-Sun. Nov.-Jan.; from €4.50

Pack up and hop on a morning ferry to Amalfi, the namesake town of the coastline. After arriving at Molo Pennello, drop off your bags and visit the Museo della Carta to learn more about Amalfi's long tradition of papermaking. Located in a 13th-century mill near the top of town, the museum offers a rare look at how paper was made in Amalfi before industrialization.

2. Shopping along Via Lorenzo d'Amalfi

Museo della Carta sits near the northern end of Amalfi's main street, which begins at Piazza Flavio Gioia, close to the main ferry terminal. Near Piazza Flavio Gioia, the street is called Via Lorenzo d'Amalfi, changing names to Via Pietro Capuano, Via Cardinal Marino del Giudice, and Via delle Cartiere as it winds its way through town. Around Piazza Duomo, the street is lined with a wonderful array of shops. As you make your way back toward the harbor, you'll find plenty of places to find the Amalfi Coast's traditional crafts and products, such as handmade paper, limoncello and lemon-themed items, and ceramics. There will be plenty of spots for lunch as well; you can't go wrong with the authentic home cooking at **Trattoria Da Maria** (Via Lorenzo D'Amalfi 14; tel. 089/871-880; www.amalfitrattoriadamaria.com; noon-3:30pm and 5:30pm-11pm daily; €12-22).

★ 3. Santa Croce

Spiaggia di Santa Croce

In the afternoon, head to Molo Darsena (next to Molo Pennello) and look for the small boats marked either Da Teresa or Santa Croce to take you to one of the Amalfi Coast's most beautiful beaches. (You'll need to rent a sun bed and umbrella at the beach in exchange for the free ride.) Beneath a sheer cliff and surrounded by large rocks, this secluded beach feels like your own secret spot.

4. Sunset Aperitivo at Gran Caffè

Corso delle Repubbliche Marinare 37/38; tel. 089/871-047; www.bargrancaffeamalfi.it; 7:30am-1am Tues.-Sun. Oct.-Jan. and Mar.-July, daily Aug.-Sept.; €5-10

Return to Amalfi and watch the sunset accompanied by the sound of the sea with drinks at Gran Caffè, which overlooks Marina Grande beach. There's an extensive drink menu, but you can't go wrong with a classic spritz or their unique version with limoncello. For dinner,

TO TAKE Home

The warm colors and brilliant landscape of the Amalfi Coast region have long inspired artists, creating a strong local craft tradition and a laid-back yet chic sense of style when it comes to fashion. The diverse natural landscape and mild Mediterranean climate also support various plants and flowers. Shopping on the Amalfi Coast is truly a feast for the eyes, with lots of options if you want to bring home something special.

PAPER

The town of Amalfi has a long tradition of papermaking, which you can learn about at the **Museo della Carta** (page 547). In addition to the museum's gift shop, you can find paper goods at shops on or near Amalfi's main road, such as **La Scuderia del Duca** (Largo Cesareo Console 9; tel. 089/872-976; www.carta-amalfi.com; 10am-7pm daily Apr.-Oct., 10am-6pm Mon.-Sat. Nov.-Mar.) and **Karta Handmade** (Largo Cesareo Console 9; tel. 338/289-8170; 10am-7pm daily).

LEMON PRODUCTS

The Amalfi Coast's distinctive lemons grow on terraced groves along the coastline and are ubiquitous in the region's cuisine, from pasta sauces to desserts. **Limoncello,** the traditional lemon-infused liqueur, and other lemon-flavored goods are on tempting offer at Amalfi's **La Valle dei Mulini** (Via Lorenzo d'Amalfi 11; tel. 089/872-603; www.amalfilemon.it; 9:30am-10pm daily).

PERFUME

The flowers of Capri have inspired perfumes for decades—or even centuries, according to **Carthusia** (www.carthusia.it), the legendary parfumerie. There is a factory and multiple Carthusia outposts on the island, where you can pick up perfumes, soaps, lotions, and more.

HANDMADE SANDALS

Handmade sandals are a firm fixture on the Amalfi Coast and Capri. You can have a pair custom-made to fit while you wait at **Canfora** (Via Camerelle 3; tel. 081/837-0487; www.canfora.com; 9:30am-11pm daily Apr.-Oct., 10:30am-5pm daily Nov.-Mar.) on Capri or **La Botteguccia** (Via Regina Giovanna 19; tel. 089/811-824; www.labottegucciapositano.it; 9am-10pm daily Mar.-Oct.) in Positano.

keep the beach views going at nearby **Ristorante Marina Grande** (Viale della Regione 4; tel. 089/871-129; www.ristorantemarinagrande.com; noon-3pm and 6:30-10pm Wed.-Mon. mid-Apr.-mid-Nov.; €14-38).

Day Trip to Ravello

Arrive by: SITA-SUD bus from Piazza Flavio Gioia in Amalfi to Ravello's Galleria Nuova stop (25 minutes)

DAY 7

1. Ravello's Piazza Duomo

In the morning, take the bus to Ravello, located in the mountains above the Amalfi Coast. The heart of Ravello is Piazza Duomo, right in the center of town, where you'll find the town's largest church, great shopping and dining options, and the entrance to **Villa Rufolo** (tel. 089/857-621; www.villarufolo.com; 9am-sunset daily; €7), one of the two noted gardens in town (the other is Villa Cimbrone).

2. Auditorium Oscar Niemeyer

Via della Repubblica 12; tel. 089/857-096

A few minutes' walk from Piazza Duomo, the Auditorium Oscar Niemeyer is one of the few new constructions on the Amalfi Coast, given the area's designation as a UNESCO World Heritage Site. The sweeping curved roofline of the bright white building, which was inaugurated in 2010, is a strikingly modern addition to Ravello's cityscape. It's worth visiting, even if not for its status as a state-of-the-art concert venue.

3. Villa Cimbrone

Via Santa Chiara 26; tel. 089/857-459; www.hotelvillacimbrone.com/villa-cimbrone; 9am-sunset daily; €7

If you're hungry, backtrack toward Piazza Duomo for a bite to eat. Afterward, enjoy a leisurely 15-minute walk through Ravello to the Villa Cimbrone. The gardens make for peaceful wandering, but the show-stopper here is the **Terrace of Infinity,** where the waters of the Gulf of Salerno and blue sky blend into one breathtaking vista.

4. Walking from Ravello to Atrani

On the way back toward Piazza Duomo, you'll see a "To Atrani" sign pointing down some stairs. Follow the sign to hike down the valley on the western side of Ravello to the tiny town of Atrani, just east of Amalfi. Via San Cosma, a footpath that alternates between flat walkways and steps hugs the mountainside below Villa Cimbrone. Very steep steps lead down toward the sea through the Civita area of Ravello, just above Castiglione. Look for Via San Nicola near Civita, a gorgeous walk high above the Castiglione beach, that takes you directly down into Atrani. The 3-km (2-mi) walk takes about 1.5 hours.

Linger in Atrani for the evening. For your final night on the Amalfi Coast, it doesn't get much more romantic than **Le Arcate** (Largo Orlando Buonocore, Atrani; tel. 089/871-367; www.learcate.net; noon-3:30pm and 7pm-11pm Tues.-Sun. early-

Villa Cimbrone

WATCH

Beat the Devil: An entertaining and, at times, comic parody of a film noir, this 1953 movie was filmed in Ravello and various spots on the Amalfi Coast, and stars Humphrey Bogart, Jennifer Jones, and Gina Lollobrigida. Bogart's character teams up with a band of crooks to buy a uranium-rich piece of land in Africa. While they are waiting in Italy to depart for Africa, a series of encounters sets off a chain of unexpected events.

READ

Mamma Agata: Traditional Italian Recipes of a Family That Cooks with Love and Passion in a Simple and Genuine Way by Chiara Lima: Both a cookbook and the story of a family dedicated to traditional cooking on the Amalfi Coast, this book will enchant you with its photos and help you re-create the delicious recipes in your own home.

The House in Amalfi and Sailing to Capri by Elizabeth Adler: International bestselling author Elizabeth Adler has brought a charming combination of romance, intrigue, and love of travel to her two novels set on the Amalfi Coast and Capri. These are fun and light travel reading for a beach holiday.

LISTEN

"O Sole Mio," lyrics by Giovanni Capurro, music by Eduardo di Capua and Alfredo Mazzucchi: Conjuring the joy of the region's sunny days, this popular song is often thought of as quintessentially Italian, but the lyrics are actually in Neapolitan.

Mar.-mid-Nov.; €8-26). The outdoor dining area is situated under a series of arches (arcate), and when the weather is warm, a table right by the sea is the place to be. Don't worry about missing the bus: The walk back to Amalfi takes just 10 minutes. It's the perfect spot for toasting your trip to one of the most beautiful places on earth.

TRANSPORTATION

Air

Located about 6 km (3.7 mi) northeast of Naples city center, **Aeroporto Internazionale di Napoli** (NAP; Viale F. Ruffo di Calabria; tel. 081/789-6111; www.aeroportodinapoli.it), also referred to as Capodichino, is the main airport for the region. **Alibus** (www.anm.it) connects the airport with the city center.

Train

Napoli Centrale Stazione (Piazza Giuseppe Garibaldi; www.napolicentrale.it) is located in the heart of Naples at Piazza Garibaldi and is connected by metro to the histic center of the city.

Ferry

Ferries connect Capri to Naples year-round, and seasonally to the Amalfi Coast. Ferry service to and around the Amalfi Coast runs seasonally, from around Easter to the beginning of November.

- **Naples:** One of the busiest ports in Italy, Naples is well-connected by ferries from around the Gulf of Naples, such as Capri (1 hour; €23). **Molo Beverello,** near the Stazione Marittima, is the ferry terminal for most destinations, and the **Calata Porta**

di Massa is where larger passenger and vehicle ferries, including those from Capri, arrive.

- **Capri:** All ferries to Capri arrive at and leave from **Marina Grande.**
- **Positano:** Ferries arrive at, and depart from, the large cement pier on the western end of the **Spiaggia Grande** beach, with service to Capri (€22), as well as the town of Amalfi. Because there is no port and the pier is open to the sea, ferry service to Positano is dependent on good weather and sea conditions; stops in Positano can be limited or canceled if the sea is rough, a stronger possibility in the shoulder seasons of early spring or October.
- **Amalfi:** Right in the center of Amalfi's harbor is the **Molo Pennello pier** where the ferries arrive and depart. Along the western side of the pier, you'll find the smaller boats that travel to and from nearby beaches. The end of the pier is where the larger ferries from Positano (€9) and Capri dock.

Public Transportation

- **Naples:** The public transportation system in Naples, which includes metro, tram, bus, and three funiculars, is operated by ANM (Azienda Napoletana Mobilità; tel. 800/639-525; www.anm.it).
- **Capri:** Capri's public buses, operated by **A.T.C.** (tel. 081/837-0420), are pint-sized to match the island and connect all the main points on Capri, including Marina Grande, Capri town, Anacapri, Marina Piccola, Punta Carena, and the Grotta Azzurra.
- **Amalfi Coast:** Towns are well connected with buses operated by **SITA SUD** (tel. 089/386-6701; www.sitasudtrasporti.it) that run along the Amalfi Coast Road and to towns located higher in the mountains. Amalfi is a central bus hub along the Amalfi Coast Road, with the main bus lines running from Salerno to Amalfi and from Amalfi to Sorrento, which stops in Positano. Buses for Ravello depart from Amalfi.

Getting Back

The return trip to Naples by ferry (about €30), available only in season, takes about two hours; you would need to go to Capri first, and then transfer to a boat headed to Naples. You can also make the trip by bus and train; take the bus to Sorrento (about two hours) and get off in front of Sorrento's train station, and then transfer to the Circumvesuviana train back to Naples (about one hour); this route costs about €25 total. A taxi (about €110) is the fastest way to go—the ride is about one hour.

- Rome, Florence, and Venice (page 139)

THE GREEK ISLANDS

Why Go: Each Greek island has something special to offer, whether it's pristine beaches, traditional villages, ancient ruins, fine dining with a view, or a combination of all of the above.

Number of Days: 7

Total Distance: 286 km (179 mi)

Seasons: Spring to early fall

Start: Athens

End: Santorini

There are 6,000 Greek islands flung across the Mediterranean, about 200 of which are inhabited. Each offers a unique experience, from the lush forests of Samothrace to the glitz of Santorini. You'll find villages precariously carved into cliff sides, domed churches painted ochre, octopuses drying in the sun, and bodies of every shape and size lounging on the beach.

There are six major island groupings—Cycladic, Dodecanese, Northeast Aegean, Sporades, Ionian, Saronic—plus the islands of Crete and Evia. The Cycladic islands in the middle of the Aegean Sea include some of the most famous islands, such as Mykonos and Santorini, plus lesser-known picks like Naxos. Buy your ferry tickets and head to the Cycladics, where turquoise seas and whitewashed villages await.

TOP 3

★ Walking in the footsteps of the the original Olympians on a visit to **Delos Archaeological Site.** Just off Mykonos, stunning Delos is the mythological birthplace of Apollo and Artemis (page 559).

★ Lounging among the ruins on Naxos' **Alyko Beach,** where the main attraction is an abandoned beachside hotel that's been covered in frescoes and turned into an open-air art museum (page 562).

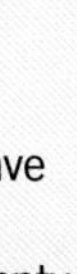

★ Rising early for **sunrise in Oia.** The best time to see Santorini's jewel is before the crowds have woken up, when the streets are mostly empty and bathed in a soft pink light (page 564).

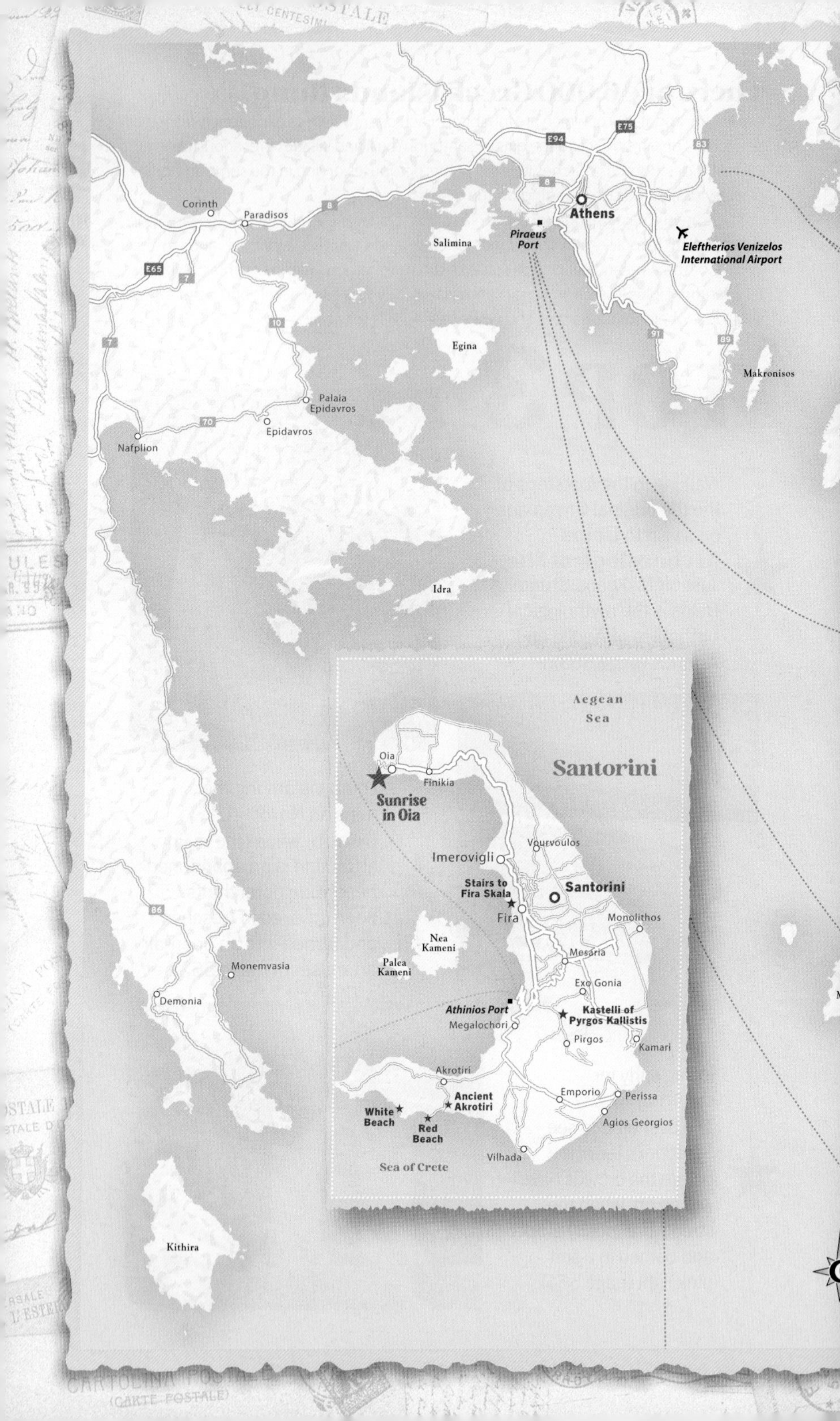
Corinth
Paradisos
Salimina
Piraeus Port
Athens
Eleftherios Venizelos International Airport
Egina
Makronisos
Palaia Epidavros
Epidavros
Nafplion
Idra
Aegean Sea
Santorini
Oia
Finikia
Sunrise in Oia
Vourvoulos
Imerovigli
Stairs to Fira Skala
Santorini
Fira
Monolithos
Nea Kameni
Palea Kameni
Mesaria
Exo Gonia
Athinios Port
Kastelli of Pyrgos Kallistis
Megalochori
Pirgos
Kamari
Akrotiri
Ancient Akrotiri
Emporio
Perissa
White Beach
Red Beach
Agios Georgios
Vilhada
Sea of Crete
Monemvasia
Demonia
Kithira
E94
E75
E65
83
8
7
10
70
86
91
89

THE GREEK ISLANDS

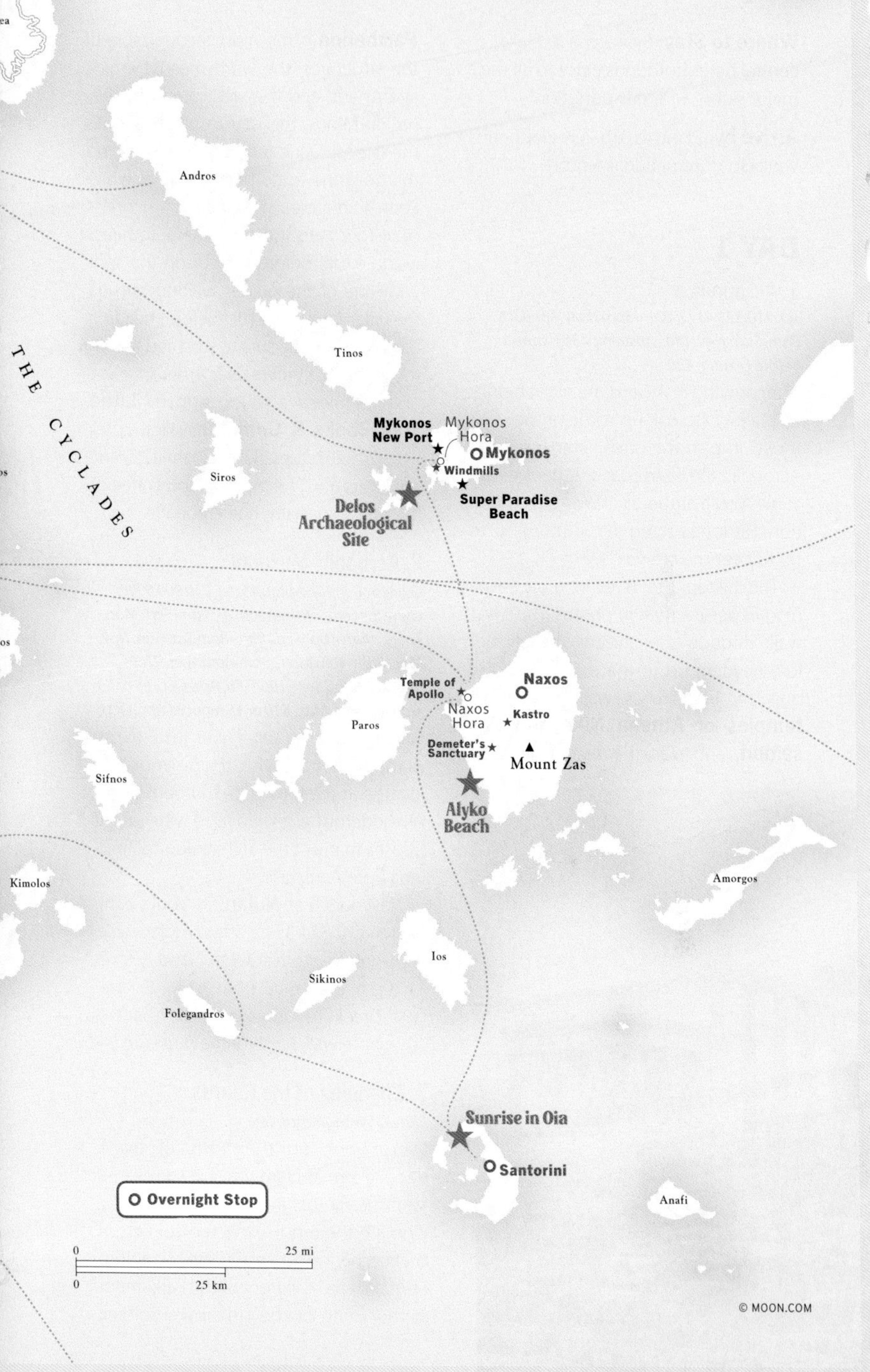

Athens

Where to Stay: Syntagma or Plaka, central neighborhoods close to all the major sights and transportation

Arrive by: Plane to Athens's Eleftherios Venizelos International Airport

DAY 1

1. Acropolis

Tel. 210 321 4172; 8am-8pm daily Apr.-Oct., 8am-5pm Nov.-Mar., last entry 30 minutes before closing; €20

After arriving in Athens the night before, take a day to soak up some of the city's most important sites, starting with Acropolis, the heartbeat of Athens—and, some would argue, all of Western civilization. Hit it first thing in the morning, to try to beat the crowds.

The hilltop site is even more stunning in person than in photos. You'll first walk through the ancient theater before heading up to the main site. You'll duck through arches, walk around the **temples of Athena Nike and Poseidon,** and past the sanctuaries. The **Parthenon** is the most recognizable of the structures; the word means "virgin's apartment" and it is dedicated to Athena Parthenos, the patron of Athens. It's the largest Doric temple in Greece (and the only one to be built purely of white Pentelic marble). There's such a richness of history here, it can be useful to hire a guide either beforehand or on the spot with one of the guides waiting outside the site (around €10). Before heading back downhill, be sure to stop and take in the incredible **views** over Athens.

Acropolis

If you need a snack, stop by **Little Tree Books & Coffee** (Kavalloti 2; tel. 210 924 3762; Tues.-Sun. 8:30am-12:30am; drinks from €2) for a pastry and coffee or the house specialty, hot lemonade.

2. Acropolis Museum

Dionysiou Areopagitou 15; tel. 210 900 0900; www.theacropolismuseum.gr; 9am-5pm Mon.-Thurs., 9am-10pm Fri., 9am-8pm Sat.-Sun. Nov.-Mar., 8am-4pm Mon., 8am-8pm Tues.-Thurs. and Sat.-Sun., 8am-10pm Fri. Apr.-Oct.; €5 or €3 reduced Nov.-Mar., €10 or €5 reduced Apr.-Oct.

Give context to what you just saw at Acropolis with a visit to this museum located at the foot of its southern slope. All modernist glass and filled with light, it houses many of the archaeological findings from Acropolis.

Have lunch at **Nolan** (31 Voulis Athina; tel. 210 324 3545; https://nolanverse.com/nolan; 1pm-5:30pm and 7pm-11:30pm Mon.-Sat.; from €14), a Japanese-Greek fusion experience that's a 10-minute walk north of the museum.

3. Changing of the Guards

Plateia Syntagmatos; free

Every hour, on the hour, of every day—even at 3am on Tuesday—the fantastically costumed evzones (guards), who are the most respected soldiers in Greece, perform an elaborate changing-of-guards ritual in front of the Parliament at the Tomb of the Unknown Soldier,

Key Reservations

MYKONOS

Book accommodations for popular Mykonos well in advance, and if you're visiting in high season, it's a good idea to make reservations for every night you go out. Reservations at **Bill & Coo** are a must.

NAXOS

Reservations are required at **Axiotissa.**

SANTORINI

Santorini is also crowded, so be sure to book accommodations far in advance.

CAR RENTAL

Book ahead of time if you want an automatic transmission car when renting on Naxos and Santorini.

Mykonos

which honors any Greek soldier who was ever killed in any Greek war.

4. Wine at Heteroclito

2 Fokionos and Petraki; tel. 210 323 9406; 12:30pm-midnight Mon.-Thurs., 12:30pm-1:30am Fri.-Sat., 6pm-midnight Sun.; glasses from €5

Start the evening with a glass of wine at this cozy spot that serves some of Greece's most interesting wines, originating from Crete to Macedonia. Before heading here, stop by **Zisis, Fish in a Cone** (Athinaidos 3; tel. 210 321 1152; www.zisisfish.gr; 1pm-7pm daily; from €3.80) for a preview of the seafood you'll encounter in the Greek islands. Try not to make it a late night, since you'll be catching an early ferry in the morning.

Mykonos

Where to Stay: Hora to be in the middle of the party, or just outside Hora for something quieter

Arrive by: Ferry from Piraeus in Athens to Mykonos New Port (2.5-4.5 hours)

DAY 2

1. Ferry to Mykonos

Your ferry to the Greek islands will leave from **Piraeus port,** which is 10 km (6 mi) southwest of central Athens. Head to Piraeus first thing in the morning and take the earliest possible ferry to Mykonos.

2. Wandering and Shopping in Hora Mykonos

After checking in your hotel, stroll through Hora—or Mykonos, as it's interchangeably called. This beautiful, bougainvillea-laced Cycladic town serves as the island's main port and capital. During the summer months, Hora Mykonos becomes something of a catwalk as people put on their best clothes and highest heels to sashay through the crowded streets.

Among the Greek islands, Mykonos stands out for its shopping. In town, Check out **Parthenis** (Alefkandra Square; tel. 228 902 2448; www.orsalia-parthenis.

Greek Cuisine

Greek cuisine focuses on simple, fresh ingredients, and slow-cooked foods preserved with olive oil. Common ingredients include olives, dairy (from goat, sheep, and cow's milk), whole grains, seasonal vegetables and fruit, fresh herbs and wild greens, fish, and meat (including goat, lamb, and beef). The national dish of Greece is bean soup, and therein lies a perfect truth: The simplest food is often the best.

MEZE AND SALADS

Most restaurants offer a selection of meze to start your meal; if you go to a tsipuradiko or ouzeri, you'll be served meze along with your drinks. It is also common to eat cheese at the start of the meal in Greece.

- **Tzatziki:** This dip made of strained yogurt, cucumber, and salt is usually served alongside fried vegetables or patties. (It's rare to order tzatziki alone to eat on bread; only tourists do this!)
- **Fava:** Pureed fava beans are often served with caramelized onions. Santorini is famous for having the best fava beans.
- **Saganaki:** This fried cheese is often served with a savory marmalade.
- **Horiatiki salad:** Also known as Greek salad, this is a simple combination of peppers, cucumbers, onions, tomatoes, olive oil, and olives (no lettuce!), served with a slice of feta cheese.

SEAFOOD

- **Kalamari:** This is squid, either fried or grilled; you'll sometimes find it stuffed.
- **Baccalaro:** Salty cod is usually served with potatoes and a pungent garlic sauce.

BAKED DISHES

- **Yemista:** In this dish, seasonal vegetables are stuffed with a mixture of rice and meat, sometimes served with avgolemono (an egg-and-lemon sauce that's similar to hollandaise).

com; daily 10am-10pm) for cool unisex clothing or **Ergon Mykonos** (F. Zoiganeli 23; tel. 228 902 8674; www.ergonmykonos.com; Orthodox Easter-Oct.; daily 11am-1am) for souvenirs and gifts.

3. Windmills

Perched on the outskirts of town (off Plateia Alefkandra) on a small hill looking out onto the sea, the windmills are iconic on Mykonos. They were built in the 16th century by the Venetians and were originally used for milling wheat. The location is beautiful, but it does get very crowded.

4. Sunset at 180 Degrees Sunset Bar Restaurant

Epar. Od Mikonou; tel. 695 195 6333; www.180.bar; hours depend on sunset time, open daily Apr.-Oct.

This bar is the best place to watch the sunset in Hora. Located above Hora, it offers—as its name suggests—an unobstructed view of Hora and the port. The best way to reach the bar is on foot (a steep, though short walk from Hora). Sit on one of the kilim-covered cushions and watch the sky turn blood orange.

For dinner, head down to **Baboulas**

- **Moussaka:** This is a layered vegetable dish with meat, eggplant, potatoes, tomato, and béchamel sauce.
- **Gigandes:** "Giant" beans are baked in a tomato sauce with herbs.
- **Spanakorizo:** A great vegetarian option, this is a mixture of rice, spinach, herbs, and lemon.

MEAT

You'll find plenty of baked and grilled options for meat, including:

- **Souvlaki:** These grilled skewers of meat are usually made with pork, though you'll also find chicken, beef, or lamb versions.
- **Soutzoukakia:** Spicy meatballs are served in tomato sauce.
- **Giovetsi:** In this dish, lamb is cooked in a clay pot.
- **Gyros:** Usually pork (but sometimes beef or chicken, or a combination), meat is cooked on a rotating spit that is sliced and eaten in sandwiches with pita bread and vegetables.

SWEETS

Greeks love their sweets, and you'll see plenty of pastry shops and bakeries dotting the islands.

- **Baklava:** This dessert is made of phyllo pastry swimming in honey and nuts (pistachio is considered the best).
- **Galaktoboureko:** This custard pie is made with phyllo and is often drizzled with an orange or lemon sauce.
- **Halva:** There are two types of halva in Greece: the dense confection made of tahini and sugar or honey and flavored with chocolate, vanilla, nuts, or dried fruit; and the cake halva, made of semolina flour. If it's being offered at a restaurant for dessert, it's probably the latter.

Ouzeri (Harborfront; tel. 228 907 8950; 6:30pm-midnight daily; from €12) for good, classic taverna food and ouzo.

DAY 3

★ 1. Delos Archaeological Site

Tel. 228 902 2259; 8am-8pm Mar.-Oct.; museum and site visit adults €12, over 65 €6, children free

Wake up early to take the 9am boat to Delos from the **Old Port.** Of all the beautiful and awe-inspiring archaeological sites in Greece, Delos might be the most important. It's the birthplace of twins Apollo and Artemis and is a UNESCO World Heritage Site. The small island is just a short boat ride from Mykonos, and visitors are allotted four hours to wander around this amazing piece of living history. Make sure to check out the Terrace of the Lions, the fantastic mosaics at the House of Dolphins, and the Sanctuary of the Foreign Gods.

Your boat will be back in time for lunch. Have a quick and healthy meal at **Nice n Easy** (Little Venice; tel. 228 902 5421; www.niceneasy.gr; 10am-1am daily Mar. 25-mid-Nov.; from €20) in Hora Mykonos.

2. Super Paradise Beach

Mykonos is Greece's most notorious party island, and you can dive into the frenetic vibe of a bacchanalia at the famous Super Paradise (or Super P) Beach. From the **Old Port,** you can take a water taxi directly there and spend the afternoon sipping champagne and dancing with beautiful people at **Jackie O Beach Club** (www.jackieomykonos.com; 9am-1am Apr.-Oct), an LGBTQ-friendly space.

3. Night Out at Scorpios

Paragas; tel. 228 902 9250; www.scorpiosmykonos.com; 11am-late daily Apr.-Oct.

Keep the party going at Scorpios, where you can have a wild night of dancing. Perhaps the chicest of the beach bars, Scorpios is where you come if you want to catch a glimpse of one of the Hadid sisters and any other model/celebrity of the moment. There's also a restaurant. You'll probably get back to your hotel sometime in the wee morning.

Naxos

Where to Stay: On the southwest coast, close to some of the best beaches

Arrive by: Ferry from Mykonos New Port to Naxos Hora (40-45 minutes)

DAY 4

1. Ferry to Naxos

It might be hard to get up, but try to take a morning ferry from Mykonos to Naxos. Boats dock in Naxos Hora; past the port, Hora village is a maze of twisting streets with steep stairs, heavy with bougainvillea and full of stray cats.

Have lunch at the port at **MezeMeze** (tel. 228 502 6401; 1pm-midnight daily year-round; from €7). Restaurants near the port can be touristy, but this is one of Hora's best seafood spots.

ferry to Naxos

2. Temple of Apollo

free

On an island full of beauty, the Temple of Apollo (also called **Portara,** or "door" in English) at the edge of Hora might be one of the more arresting sites. Walk 10 minutes from the port to the temple, which stands as a beautiful ruin with an archway.

3. Kastro

Though Kastro literally means "castle" in Greek, in Naxos it refers to the hilltop neighborhood established by Venetian Marco Sanudo back in 1207. Wander the neighborhood to find Venetian mansions, adorable narrow streets, and worthwhile sights such as the rectangular **Tower of Sanoudos,** the remnants of one of the 12 defense towers built by Sanduo.

When you're ready for dinner, head to **Doukato** (Old Town; tel. 228 502 7013; 6pm-1am daily, summer only; from €8). The cuisine is typical Greek with a focus on local ingredients and specialties such as gouna (sundried mackerel).

(clockwise from top) Delos Archaeological Site; Kastro; Temple of Apollo

MAKE IT Active

NAXOS

Hiking Mount Zas: The highest mountain in the Cyclades is thought to be where Zeus was brought to be birthed in order to escape the wrath of his father. There are two popular routes here: One is the well-marked, relatively easy 8-km (5-mi) loop from the church of Agia Marina. The other is the 6-km (3.75-mi) loop from Arai Spring next to Filoti. The views alone are worth the hike up here—you'll feel like you're floating above Naxos. For more information, see www.naxostrek.com.

MYKONOS

Bike tour with Yummy Pedals: A lot of Mykonos is actually farmland, and Yummy Pedals (2.7 km/1.7 mi north of Ano Mera; tel. 697 229 9282; www.yummypedals.gr; 2-hour tour from €50) offers mountain-biking tours through the backroads of the island. In addition to riding through the countryside, you'll learn about Mykonos's religious and cultural heritage. Rides end with a dip at the beach.

DAY 5

1. Sweet Treat at Kafeneio Galani

Tel. 228 503 2280; 7am-last customer daily summer, 8am-3pm daily winter; from €2.50

Rent a car and drive inland to the village of **Halki** to sample the best the best galaktoboureko (custard pie) on the island at Kafeneio Galani-To Spitiko Galaktoboureko. Mrs. Katerina's shop has been a hallmark of the village for more than 60 years. Afterward, stroll the labyrinth of whitewashed houses and cobblestone streets of this once-capital of the island.

2. Demeter's Sanctuary

Drimalia; tel. 228 503 2591; 8:30am-3:30pm Wed.-Mon.; adults €4, over 65 €2

From Halki, drive 15 minutes to Demeter's Sanctuary to pay homage to the goddess of fertility. These stunning ruins, which date to 530 BCE, have been so thoughtfully preserved that it's easy to imagine yourself actually in ancient Greece. Most of the original columns are still standing.

★ 3. Alyko Beach

Head back toward the coast, to the southwestern end of the island. At Alyko Beach, a series of coves create semi-private beaches before the white sand stretches out into a long strip. One of the best attractions isn't the sea at all, but rather a hotel from the 1960s that was abandoned midway through construction. A few years ago, an Athens-based graffiti artist came and painted incredible frescoes on the abandoned structure; the result is a stunning piece of free art. Bring your own snacks and water, and enjoy an afternoon of relaxation.

During the summer, the **F.B.I. food truck** (noon-8pm daily; from €4) is parked outside of Alyko Beach. The name stands for Food Beverage Ice Cream, and the brothers helming the truck do all three fantastically.

4. Dinner at Axiotissa

18 km (11 mi) south of Hora, Alyko; tel. 228 507 5107; 2pm-late daily Apr.-Oct.; from €8

For dinner, drive five minutes to Axiotissa,

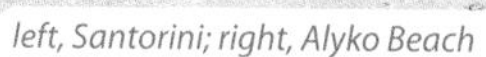

left, Santorini; right, Alyko Beach

the best restaurant on an island full of amazing food. This family-run taverna has a focus on fresh, local products, and the food is a modern, innovative take on classic Greek dishes. Reservations are required.

Santorini

Where to Stay: Oia or Imerovigli, at the north end of Santorini, for views of the caldera

Arrive by: Ferry from Naxos Hora to Athinios Port (2 hours)

DAY 6

1. Ferry to Santorini

Thousands of years ago, a cataclysmic volcano made Santorini what it is today: an architectural marvel of cave dwellings precariously perched on the lip of the red caldera. As you approach the island from the sea, the view of the red caldera is truly fantastic. Boats dock in **Athinios,** located on the western coast.

2. Relax at Your Hotel

Rent a car and drive 20-30 minutes north from the port to your hotel in **Oia** or **Imerovigli.** There are a few moments in life worth splurging on, and getting a room overlooking Santorini's caldera is one of them. Spend the rest of the day lounging poolside and marveling at the view. Here are a few places to choose from:

On The Rocks

Imerovigli; tel. 228 602 3889; www.ontherocksantorini.com; Apr.-Oct.; from €450 breakfast incl.

This small white-and-blue hotel, perched on

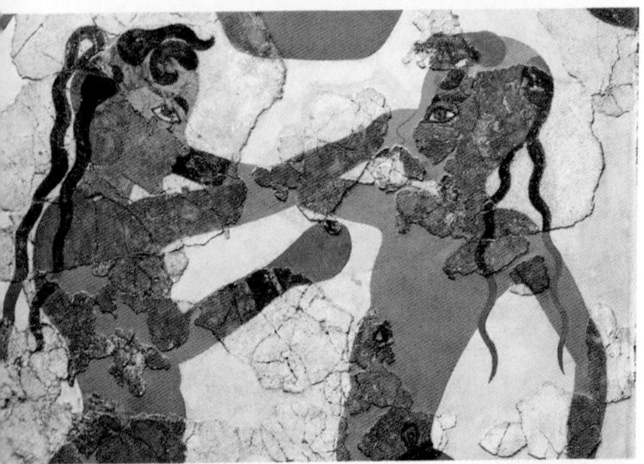

(top to bottom) Fira Skala; sunrise in Oia; Ancient Akrotiri; White Beach

the caldera, is charming and luxurious, with a great spa, pool, and beautiful balconies.

Divine Cave Experience

Imerovigli; tel. 228 602 4654; www.divinesuites.com; Apr.-Oct.; from €1,100 breakfast incl.

At Santorini's best-designed hotel, 10 suites have been carved out of the rock, resulting in an intimate cocoon that features private infinity pools and stunning sunset views.

Perivolas Hotel

Oia; tel. 228 607 1308; www.perivolas.com; May-Oct.; from €600 breakfast incl. (minimum stay 2 nights)

This cluster of white cave dwellings is absolutely sumptuous, and everything, from the bed to the couch to the shower, is harmoniously built in. Some rooms feature private pools.

3. Stairs to Fira Skala

When you need to stretch your legs, head to **Fira,** Santorini's busy capital city, and descend 600 steps to the small port of Fira Skala, one of the most beautiful walks around Fira. As you go down the steps, the sea is laid out before you, with little fishing boats bobbing in the water; to your back is the caldera. Take the **Santorini Cable Car** (www.scc.gr; 7am-9pm Apr., 7am-10pm May and Sept.-Oct, 7am-11pm June-Aug., 7:30am-6pm Nov. and Mar., 7:30am-4pm Dec.-Feb.; €6 one-way, luggage extra €3) back up the hillside.

Have dinner in Fira, right on the lip of the caldera, at **1500 BC** (tel. 228 602 1331 or 693 808 4878; www.1500.gr; 11am-1pm daily Apr.-Oct.; mains from €18).

DAY 7

TOP EXPERIENCE

★ 1. Sunrise in Oia

Surrounded by water on the northwest tip of Santorini, Oia might be one of the most beautiful villages in the world. The whitewashed houses carved into the red caldera, the sparkling blue hotel pools, and

WATCH

Mamma Mia (2008): This movie musical featuring ABBA songs is set on a fictional Greek island but was filmed on Skopelos, one of the Sporades islands.

Never on Sunday (1960): Starring the inimitable Melina Mercouri and set in the port city of Piraeus, this film spurred a so-called Greek fever that swept the United States after its release—and perhaps even inspired Jackie Kennedy to make a visit.

READ

Circe by Madeline Miller: This is a feminist retelling of the story of one of Greek mythology's most misunderstood nymphs, Circe, who was exiled to a Mediterranean island.

LISTEN

An important musical tradition in Greece is **rembetika,** or the Greek blues, which is tied to the artistry and struggles of the lower class and recently arrived refugees from Turkey. The opening credits to the movie *Pulp Fiction* include surf guitarist Dick Dale's rendition of the popular rembetika song **"Misirlou."**

the tiny alleyways snaking through the village make for a truly unique place. Oia can be packed with tourists, so to truly appreciate how beautiful the village is, get up early, when everyone else is still asleep and everything is bathed in a soft pink light.

2. Ancient Akrotiri

Akrotiri; tel. 228 608 1939; 8am-8pm Fri.-Wed. Apr.-Oct., 8:30am-3:30pm Thurs.; €12, reduced €6, children free

After returning to your hotel for breakfast, drive 35 minutes south to Akrotiri, Santorini's version of Pompeii. At once destroyed and preserved by a massive volcanic eruption in 1450 BCE, Akrotiri is a living reminder of the stunning contribution of the ancient Minoan civilization. Take your time walking through the streets of the ancient city. You'll see the crumbled walls of homes and shops, but also some objects—bed frames, pots, tiled floors, windows.

3. Red Beach

People seek out the beaches near Akrotiri mostly due to their colorful sands. Located 5 km (3 mi) south of Akrotiri, Red Beach, so called for the volcanic minerals in the sand, is a small and often very crowded slice of real estate. You'll have to walk down from the main road to get here, and be careful, as there are often falling rocks!

4. White Beach

Right next to Red Beach is a small cove called White Beach, a novelty mostly because the majority of Santorini beaches are black. (If you're driving, you'll need to head back into Akrotiri, as there is no connecting road between the two beaches.) It's less busy than Red Beach, and there's (usually) enough room to spread your towel if you don't want to splurge on a beach chair (€10).

If you get hungry while in Akrotiri, **Giorgaros** (just before the lighthouse, Akrotiri; tel. 228 608 3035 or 697 628 8301; www.giorgaros.com; noon-10:30pm daily year-round; from €10) is about a 15-minute drive from Ancient Akrotiri, Red Beach, and White Beach. They have everything from sardines to lobster, which can be ordered grilled or fried, and there's a glassed-in terrace that offers stunning views of the caldera from a distance.

5. Kastelli of Pyrgos Kallistis

daily; free

On the drive back to the north of the island, stop in **Pyrgos** for an evening stroll. The former capital of Santorini, Pyrgos is probably the best-preserved medieval settlement on the island—and one of its prettiest villages. Catch the sunset from the top of the village at Kastelli of Pyrgos Kallistis. The best preserved of the five Venetian castles dotting Santorini, this castle was built in the 13th century. Keep your eye out for the so-called "murder hole" (fonissa in Greek) above the door, where boiling water or oil was poured over the heads of would-be intruders.

Stay in Pyrgos for a fantastic dinner at **Selene** (Pyrgos village, far end of main car street; tel. 228 602 4395 bistro, 228 602 2249 fine dining; restaurant 7pm-11pm daily, bistro noon-11pm daily; bistro from €14, fine dining from €36), your last in the islands. There's a meze-and-wine bistro downstairs and a fine dining section upstairs, both located in a charming old house.

TRANSPORTATION

Air

- Athens is served by the **Eleftherios Venizelos International Airport** (ATH), which underwent a renovation in 2017. All major airlines fly through Venizelos, with many airlines now offering direct flights from the United States, Asia, and the Middle East. It's located 27 km (17 mi) east of the city center. To get to the city center from the airport, you can take a taxi (30 minutes), metro (40 minutes), or bus (1 hour).
- **Mykonos International Airport** (JMK; tel. 228 907 9000; www.mykonos-airport.com) is located 2 km (1.25 mi) south of the Hora, about a 10-minute bus or five-minute taxi ride.
- The **Santorini Airport** (JTR; tel. 228 602 8400; www.santoriniairport.com) is located on the central-east side of the island, 6 km (4 mi) east of Fira. There are regular buses to and from Fira's main bus station and the airport (20 minutes), and a taxi to Fira or Oia to the airport takes around 10 minutes.
- **Naxos** is served by a small airport (JNX), 3 km (2 mi) south Hora, best reached by taxi (10 minutes).

Ferry

Multiple companies run ferries to and between the Greek islands, including **ANEK Lines** (www.anek.gr), **Blue Star** (www.bluestarferries.com), **Grimaldi Lines** (www.grimaldi-lines.gr), **Hellenic Seaways** (www.hellenicseaways.gr), **Superfast Ferries** (www.superfast.com), and **Minoan Lines** (www.minoan.gr).

There is no official government-run website for Greek ferries, but there are several private websites where you can buy tickets. Sites like **www.ferryscanner.com, www.ferries.gr,** and **www.ferryhopper.com** are good options. If you are planning multiple trips to different islands, though, a tour operator can make the booking process much easier. **Priority Travel & Tourism** (Sofokelous stoa inside the alley; tel. 210 331 4476; www.prioritytravel.gr) in Athens is one good option. You can also buy tickets directly at the port, though it's better to do this only on return trips from more relaxed islands. (Navigating the ticketing at Santorini or even Piraeus is not for the fainthearted.)

Ports

- **Piraeus:** Located 10 km (6 mi) southwest of central Athens, this is the primary mainland access point for Mykonos, Santorini, and Naxos, as well as a number of other Greek islands.

- **Rafina:** Located 30 km (19 mi) east of Athens, this is the second port for boats headed to the Cycladic islands of Mykonos and Santorini.
- **Mykonos New Port:** Located 2 km (1.25 mi) north of Hora Mykonos, this is where most of the bigger boats dock, including the ferry from Athens (2.5-4.5 hours, depending on if you get a fast or slow boat; €32-65).
- **Mykonos Old Port:** Located 400 m (0.25 mi) north of Hora, Old Port is the place to catch boats to Delos and water taxis to Super Paradise beach.
- **Naxos:** Boats from Mykonos dock in Naxos Hora (35 minutes-1.5 hours; €10-85).
- **Athinios:** Located on the western coast, a 20-minute drive from Fira, this is the main port in Santorini, where boats from Naxos dock (2 hours; €40-100) and boats to Athens (Piraeus) depart (€50-100; 4-9 hours).

Car

A car is recommended for Naxos and Santorini, although finding parking in the latter is extremely difficult in the summer months. In Greece, driving is on the right-hand side of the road, and the **minimum driving age** in Greece is 18. On highways the **speed limit** is 120 km/h (75 mph); 90 km/h (56 mph) on country roads; 50 km/h (31 mph) in the city.

Car Rental

Most car rental places won't rent to you unless you're at least 21 years of age, and bigger cars will only be rented to those above the age of 23. Some ferries can transport cars, in addition to passengers, but note that car rental companies will not let you bring your rental car on ferries. Book automatic transmission vehicles in advance.

- **Naxos:** There are several car rental places along the port, or you can book ahead from **Naxos Auto Rent** (Galanado Village, 5.5 km/3.5 mi from Hora; tel. 693 099 3670; www.naxosautorent.com; 8am-11pm daily).
- **Santorini:** There are a few car rental places near the port. In Fira, try **Nomikos Travel** (tel. 228 602 3660; www.nomikoscarrental.com).

Bus

The Greek bus network is comprehensive and operated by **KTEL** (www.ktelbus.com), which manages the long-distance buses as well as island buses. Bus fares are fixed by the government and it remains one of the cheapest ways to travel (approximately €5 per 100 km/62 mi). Buy tickets ahead of time in the station.

In **Naxos,** the main bus station is opposite the main dock in the port (tel. 228 502 2291; www.naxosbuses.com). From there, buses run to Agios Prokopios-Agia Anna-Plaka and Plaka in the direction of Alyko Beach, but you'll need a taxi to get all the way there, as well as to Filoti-Halki. In **Santorini,** buses run to Fira, Oia, and Akrotiri.

Taxi

Taxis are available on every island, and there's a particularly heartwarming number of women taxi drivers on the islands. You don't need to tip drivers, but rounding up to the nearest euro is appreciated. It's best to carry small bills.

Getting Back

To get back to Athens from Santorini, you can take a ferry from Athinios to Piraeus (4 hours for the high-speed, 8 hours for regular ferry) or Rafina (5-6 hours for the high-speed). There are also flights from Santorini Airport to Athens and other major European cities.

- Transylvania (page 320)
- Paris to Bucharest (page 600)

THE CANARY ISLANDS

Why Go: Have a subtropical island vacation while still in Europe.

Number of Days: 5

Total Distance: 432 km (268 mi)

Seasons: Year-round

Start: Las Palmas de Gran Canaria

End: Los Cristianos, Tenerife

It may be hard to believe you're still in Europe when you dive into this subtropical destination, with wonderful year-round weather, some of the Atlantic's most exciting snorkeling, and Spain's highest point, the summit of El Teide.

A visit to three of the eight Canary Islands offers a range of adventures. Head out to sea and see whales bursting triumphantly from the waves; sip on a glass of banana wine; venture deep into Garajonay National Park, the world's largest pre-glacial forest; explore the old town of Santa Cruz de Tenerife; and visit San Sebastián de Gomera, Christopher Columbus's last stop before he crossed the Atlantic. Despite their geographical distance—located as they are off the coast of Morocco—the Canary Islands are well connected with major cities in Western Europe. This is the sort of destination that could be added on to just about any trip, particularly during the winter months, to get a bit of warm weather into your European travels.

TOP 3

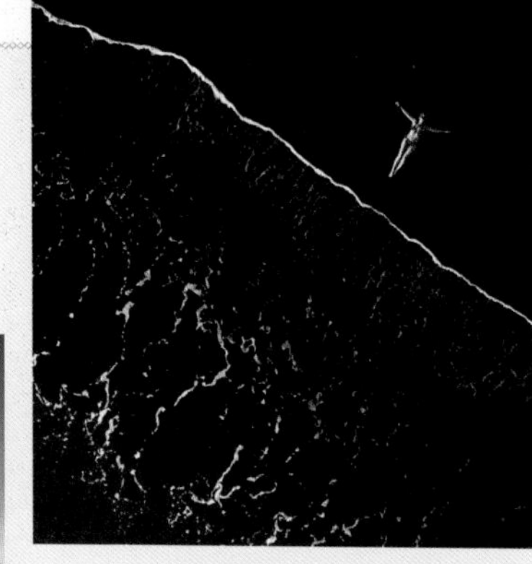

★ Laying down your towel on one of the Canary Islands' **best beaches** for an afternoon of sunbathing (page 574).

★ Journeying to the summit of **El Teide,** the tallest peak in all of Spain, whether by gondola or your own two feet (page 575).

★ Trekking through the dense, misty forests of **Garajonay National Park** (page 578).

THE CANARY ISLANDS

Overnight Stop

0 20 mi
0 20 km

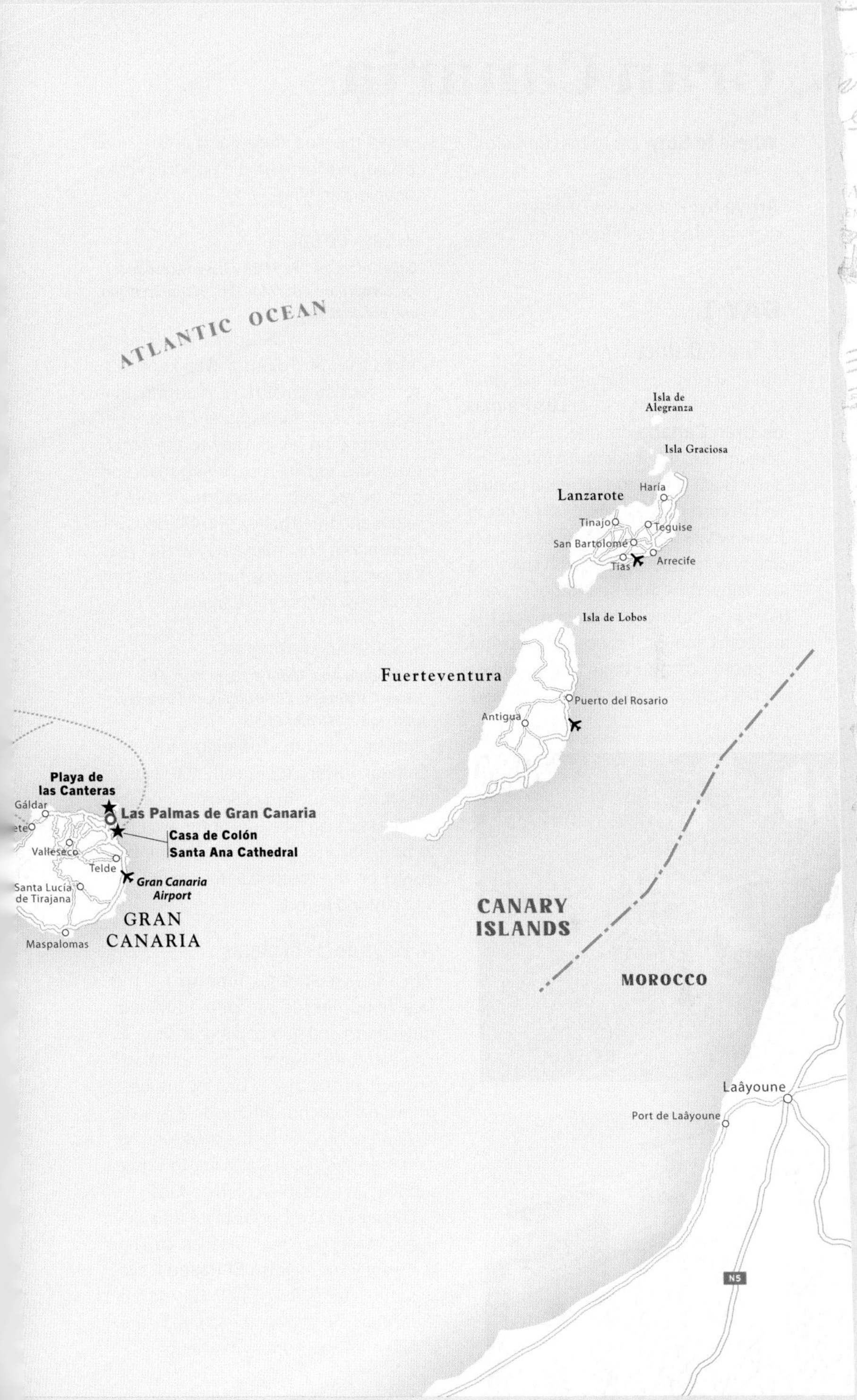

ATLANTIC OCEAN

Isla de Alegranza

Isla Graciosa

Lanzarote

Haría

Tinajo

Teguise

San Bartolomé

Tías

Arrecife

Isla de Lobos

Fuerteventura

Puerto del Rosario

Antigua

Playa de las Canteras

Gáldar

Las Palmas de Gran Canaria

Casa de Colón

Santa Ana Cathedral

Valleseco

Telde

Gran Canaria Airport

Santa Lucía de Tirajana

GRAN CANARIA

Maspalomas

CANARY ISLANDS

MOROCCO

Laâyoune

Port de Laâyoune

N5

Gran Canaria

Where to Stay: Las Palmas de Gran Canaria

Arrive by: Plane to Las Palmas de Gran Canaria Airport (Gondo Airport)

DAY 1

1. Triana District

After picking up your rental car, drive into the colonial-era city of **Las Palmas de Gran Canaria,** founded in the 14th century. The oldest and most interesting districts are Triana and Vegueta, located on the eastern coast of the city. Start in Triana, where narrow cobblestone streets give way to small plazas with gurgling fountains. You could spend hours wandering the colonial streets, perusing the museums and local shops, and looking for photo ops, and there are a number of coffee shops and restaurants tucked down the side streets and in the small plazas, providing ample opportunity for people-watching.

top, inside Casa de Colón; bottom, Casa de Colón

2. Casa de Colón

Calle Colón; tel. 928 31 23 73; www.casadecolon.com; 10am-6pm Mon.-Fri., 10am-3pm Sun. and holidays; €4

From Triana, walk south to Vegueta and Casa de Colón, a well-kept, historic former governor's mansion that once housed the explorer Christopher Columbus on his journey to the Americas while repairs were being made on one of his ships. Throughout the 13 salons and three patios, you will discover more about Columbus's stay while in Las Palmas, as well as the history of the city and the island of Gran Canaria.

3. Santa Ana Cathedral

Plaza Santa Ana; 10am-4:30pm Mon.-Fri., 10am-1:30pm Sat.; €2.40 adults, children free, south tower elevator €1.50

Next, step into the towering Santa Ana Cathedral, which took nearly 400 years to finish, hence the mix of Renaissance and neoclassical architecture. If the weather is nice, head up the elevator to the bell tower on the south side for views over the city and harbor.

4. Playa de las Canteras

After sightseeing, it's time to hit the beach; hop in the car for a 10-minute drive north and find parking as close as you can to the water. In the northeastern part of the city is one of the best municipal beaches in Europe, Playa de las Canteras. Known for the snorkeling off its shores, this beach is also fine for some sunning on the sable-colored sands.

This area is also a good place for a delicious dinner. For true Canarian cuisine at a great value, head to **El Paseo** (Calle Segunta 3; tel. 928 27 73 65; 8am-11pm Thurs.-Tues.; €15). The terrace with the sea view is a must, unless it's windy.

Key Reservations

ACCOMMODATIONS AND TRANSPORTATION

- Book **accommodations** as soon as possible, particularly in Santa Cruz de Tenerife, El Teide around Los Cristianos and Playa de las Américas, and on Gran Canaria. With limited availability, these locations do tend to fill up quickly, especially during the summer (June-Aug.), winter holidays (end of Dec.-early Jan.), and Carnival (Feb.).
- You should also arrange a **rental car** before your arrival. It's also a good idea to book **ferries** ahead of time, especially if you need a **bus transfer** through your ferry line.

ACTIVITIES

- Activities such as **whale-watching** and **hiking the summit of El Teide** should be booked weeks, if not months, in advance. Spaces for these experiences are limited and dependent on weather. Try to book these activities on the earlier end of your trip if possible, to allow for rebooking after potential cancellations.
- Call ahead to book a rum tasting tour at the **Destilerías Arehucas** on Grand Canary Island.

whale-watching

Tenerife

Where to Stay: Santa Cruz de Tenerife

Arrive by: Ferry from Agaete on Gran Canaria to Santa Cruz de Tenerife (2 hours, including bus transfer between Las Palmas and Agaete)

DAY 2

1. Museo de Naturaleza y Arqueología

Calle Fuente Morales; tel. 922 53 58 16; www.museosdetenerife.org; 9am-5pm Mon.-Sat., 10am-5pm Sun.; €5

Take an early ferry to Tenerife and drop your bags at your hotel in central Santa Cruz de Tenerife. Then, set out to the Museum of Nature and Archaeology, located within the charming backdrop of a remodeled hospital dating back to 1745. As you visit, you will see a rich, entertaining vision of the incredible natural heritage of the Canary Archipelago and the people who inhabited it before the Spanish conquest, the Guanches, who made their way to the Canaries from Morocco. Learn about the volcanic origins of these islands, and about the indigenous flora and fauna you'll soon see up close.

★ The Canary Islands' Best Beaches

The innumerable beaches dotting the coasts of the Canary Islands are enjoyable year-round, though some are more easily accessible than others. Some are beaches of pebble and rock, others are soft, black volcanic sand, and still others are graced with sand from the Sahara. And just as exciting as the beaches themselves is what you can find out in the water. Many Canary Island beaches are great places for snorkeling, renting a kayak or catamaran, or even taking scuba diving courses. Below are some of the best beaches you'll visit on this route.

- **Playa de las Canteras, Gran Canaria** (page 572)
- **Playa de San Telmo, Tenerife** (page 574)
- **Costa Adeje Beach, Tenerife** (page 578)

2. Municipal Market of Our Lady of Africa

51 Ave. de San Sebastián; tel. 922 214 743; 9am-2:30pm Tues.-Sun.; free

Nearby, the lively, open Municipal Market of Our Lady of Africa (Mercado Municipal de Nuestra Senora de Africa) has been a staple of Santa Cruz city life since 1943, set inside a salmon-colored colonial structure with an arcaded interior not unlike something you might find in Andalusia or even Morocco. Mounds of fresh seasonal fruits and vegetables, various meats, artisanal cheeses, and colorful flowers are readily available. Browse with a coffee from the simple café and choose from a number of local joints to buy supplies for a fresh, local lunch.

3. Parque Marítimo César Manrique

Avenida de la Constitución 5; tel. 922 22 93 68; https://parquemaritimosantacruz.es; 10am-6pm daily, until 7pm in summer; €5

The Parque Marítimo César Manrique along Santa Cruz de Tenerife's coast makes for a perfect afternoon in the sun. This maritime park was designed by one of the Canary Islands' favorite sons, artist and architect César Manrique. Centered around a main pool are umbrellaed sunloungers that face toward the ocean. Next to the maritime park is the unmissable **Auditorium of Tenerife** (https://auditoriodetenerife.com), designed by the Valencian architect Santiago Calatrava, obviously influenced by the Sydney Opera House in Australia.

DAY 3

1. Playa de San Telmo

Puerto de la Cruz

Get in a car and head out from Santa Cruz de Tenerife to the north side of the island. The coast here boasts dark, almost

Plaza de la Libertad, Garachico

black, volcanic-sand beaches, and one of the best is Playa de San Telmo, about a 30-minute drive. The rock pools at this beach make for some nice snorkeling with a good chance of seeing fish and even sea turtles. Or, if you want something a little more refined, **Lago Martiánez** (Av. De Cristobal Colón, Puerto de la Cruz) is a saltwater pool complex also designed by architect César Manrique.

2. Garachico

Farther down the coast (about 45 minutes from San Telmo), Garachico is considered one of Spain's prettiest towns. The town rose from the ashes, quite literally, after a volcanic eruption in 1706, which is why the entire old city is a well-preserved complex of 18th-century architectural delights.

Start at the **Plaza de la Libertad.** From here, you can check out the **San Francisco Convent** (9am-2pm and 4-6pm Mon.-Sat.; €2), which survived the volcanic eruption and has been repurposed into a small science museum on the history of Garachico, as well as the public library and municipal records. Across the plaza you can't miss the **Church of Santa Ana** (Iglesia Matriz de Santa Ana, Plaza de la Libertad; 9am-6pm Mon.-Sat.; free), largely destroyed by the volcanic explosion but rebuilt using the original plans. Along the Plaza de la Libertad are a number of cafés and small shops perfect for getting a quick bite or to take a seat for a bit of people-watching. On Sundays, there's a small village market (9am-2pm) that features handicrafts and local artisanal goods.

For lunch, pop into the bustling **Bodegón Plaza Casa Juan** (Calle Francisco Martínez de Fuentes 7; tel. 922 13 34 03; noon-5pm Fri.-Wed.; €10) for some traditional Canarian delights.

3. Icod de los Vinos

Wine lovers will know they're in for a treat in a place that has "Vinos" in its name, but first, pay your respects to the local dignitary, the 1,000-year-old **Dragon Tree** (dragon trees are indigenous to the Canary Islands) off Icod de los Vinos's main plaza. Then, it's off to the **Museo de Malvasia** (tel. 607 610 065; https://museomalvasia.com; €8), where you'll quickly get up to speed on all things to do with Canarian wines and liquors. A flight of five wines, including a taste of a regional Malvasia, is accompanied by mojo canarios, a pepper-based sauce that's a local specialty.

There are several good dinner spots here, but a local favorite is the **La Parada** (Rbla. Perez del Cristo 2; tel. 922 81 14 91; noon-4pm and 7pm-10pm, until 11pm weekends and holidays, closed Sun. afternoon and all day Tues.; €20), which serves up delicious traditional Canarian food. Head back to Santa Cruz de Tenerife for the night (1 hour from Icod de los Vinos).

DAY 4

★ 1. El Teide National Park

www.miteco.gob.es/es/red-parques-nacionales/nuestros-parques/teide

Pack your bags and check out of your hotel in Santa Cruz de Tenerife. This morning you'll strike out for Spain's tallest peak, El Teide, for unbeatable views of the island. El Teide is the third highest

Canarian Beverages

There are a number of iconic alcoholic beverages in the Canary Islands that you can try on your trip.

WINE

Although the subtropical climate might seem incongruous with winemaking, the mountains and wind patterns, as well as volcanic soil, of the Canary Islands create conditions that allow wine production. Gran Canaria, Tenerife, and La Gomera all have wineries and wine-tasting experiences, including **Museo de Malvasia** (page 575), which takes its name from the white wine grape grown in the islands.

RUM

What better way to start your trip than with a rum tasting? In the colorful old town of Arucas on Gran Canaria, head to the **Destilerías Arehucas** (Lugar Era de San Pedro 2; tel. 928 62 49 00; https://arehucas.es; 9am-2pm Mon.-Fri.; free). At over 100 years old, this distillery is one of the oldest rum cellars in all of Europe.

BANANA WINE

Banana plantations and farming have been a large part of the Canarian agroeconomy for more than six centuries. Though various banana liquors have been produced since time immemorial, often by families for their own consumption, the production of banana wine has recently started to be taken more seriously. You'll find "Platé," a surprisingly dry, crisp white wine, served in some of the local restaurants, but one of the best spots for a degustation is at **Casa del Platano** on Tenerife (Calle Hercules 4; tel. 922 812 213; http://casadelplatano.com; 11am-7pm daily; €5). Here you can see a variety of banana trees, and you can learn about the process of turning banana fruit into wine.

volcano in the world at 3,718 m (12,198 ft), and it and its surrounding natural park are a UNESCO World Heritage Site. Start your visit at the **El Portillo Visitor Center** (tel. 922 92 23 71; 9am-4:15pm daily; free), about a one-hour drive from Santa Cruz de Tenerife, to learn more about this immense volcano, and then take the Telefèrico gondola to the peak. At these heights, even on the warmest of days, you'll want to pack extra layers. Note that if the day is windy, the gondola will be closed.

If you're not up for ascending El Teide on foot, or you're unable to get a hiking pass, there's ample opportunity for light and moderate hiking and incredible views over this lunar-like volcanic landscape. To learn more about El Teide National Park, consider booking an experience with **Volcano Teide** (https://volcanoteide.com).

2. Whale-Watching with Whale Watch Tenerife

Tel. 634 35 18 56; https://whalewatchtenerife.org; departures 9:30am, noon, and 2:30pm Sat.-Tues.; €50

Continue your adventurous day on Tenerife with an afternoon whale-watching

MAKE IT *Active*: SUMMITTING EL TEIDE

Distance: 8.3 km (5 mi) one-way
Time: 6 hours
Elevation Gain: 1,368 m (4,488 ft)
Difficulty: Strenuous
Trailhead: Montaña Blanca (PK 40.2 on TF21)
Permit Reservations: www.reservasparquesnacionales.es
Information and Maps: www.miteco.gob.es/es/red-parques-nacionales/nuestros-parques/teide

PLANNING YOUR HIKE

Though you can easily summit El Teide with the help of the gondola, there is something infinitely more gratifying about doing the six-hour hike all the way up the summit. To hike up to the summit, you will need to make a **permit reservation** online in advance of your trip. Only 200 passes are given each day, making these very difficult to obtain at the last minute.

Make sure to leave early enough in the day to give yourself plenty of time to get up... and down... the mountain! There are three stages to this hike, with the first two stages being the most difficult.

STAGE 1

The best trail for hiking up begins at the foot of Montaña Blanca and continues over a well-signed, though largely desolate, volcanic region that feels a bit like hiking over Mars. After reaching the peak of Montaña Blanca, you will be at the halfway point of the hike, but the steepest slopes still lie ahead.

STAGE 2

On this stage, you will follow La Fortaleza (trail 11) from the Altavista Refuge to climb from the peak of Montaña Blanc to La Rambleta, the upper station of the cable car at an altitude of 3,555 m (11,663 ft). This is by far the most challenging part of the hike. The air becomes thinner as you ascend, with a good level of fitness required. Even hikers who are in excellent shape will want to stop for the occasional rest. While you catch your breath, keep an eye out for the Gallot's lizard and the flightless beetle (pimelia ascendens) that only live in the national park.

STAGE 3

From La Rambleta, it is a short jaunt up the Telesforo Bravo (trail 10) to the summit of El Teide. This is a 30 minute-1 hour hike that climbs a farther 173 m (570 ft) in elevation over a rocky 614-m (half-mi) piste. The distinctive smell of sulfur will remind you that you are atop a volcano, while the views will have you feeling like you are on top of the world.

THE DESCENT

To descend, you can catch the cable car down the mountain from La Rambleta. If you plan to descend on foot, you will want to allow for 4-4.5 hours to make the descent down the same trail you came up. Keep in mind that if you do take the cable car down, you will still have a short hike (3 km/1.5 mi) to the base of Montaña Blanc trailhead.

tour. There are a few whale-watching companies around the island, but most of them are concentrated around the harbor of **Costa Adeje,** on the western coast (2 hours from El Teide). Whale Watch Tenerife's excursions are led by English- and Spanish-speaking marine biologists, who will happily tell you all about the different species you will see on tour, from pilot whales and bottlenose dolphins to the local sea turtles that call Tenerife home. This is a great excursion for the whole family, ages 3 and up, and is done in a peaceful, respectful way. November-March is typically the best season for whale watching.

If you need a bite before heading down to the pier to meet your captain, have a quick lunch at **The Thirsty Turtle** (Avenida de España 2; tel. 922 27 11 16; 10am-1am daily; €15). Drop off your bags at your Costa Adeje accommodations beforehand, as well.

3. Costa Adeje Beach

Playa de Las Americas; free

After a big day of peak views and whale-watching, it's time to grab your towel and relax. This long stretch of sandy beach looks westward out over the Atlantic and to the distant island of La Gomera, your destination for tomorrow's adventure. Late afternoon is great for snorkeling, particularly on the north side of the beach at rock formations where all sorts of little crabs and fishes dart in and out the little nooks.

Stay at the beach for a guaranteed glorious sunset before heading via the waterfront walk for dinner at **Limoncello** (C. C. Litoral Maritimo 1; tel. 922 711 335; 1pm-11pm daily, no reservations needed; €25), where you'll find dishes such as seafood soup and scallop risotto. You might stay in Costa Adeje to avoid traveling back to Santa Cruz de Tenerife, only to come back to the west coast to the Los Cristianos port in the morning.

Day Trip to La Gomera

Arrive by: Ferry from Los Cristianos Port on Tenerife to San Sebastian de La Gomera Port (2 hours, including bus transfer from Santa Cruz de Tenerife to Los Cristianos)

DAY 5

1. Ferry to La Gomera

In the morning, catch the earliest ferry to La Gomera from Los Cristianos on the western coast of Tenerife. Keep your binoculars and camera handy; during the crossing, you may see breaching whales and dolphins leaping from the water playing the ferry's wake. The ferry will dock in **San Sebastian de La Gomera,** the capital of the island.

★ 2. Garajonay National Park

www.miteco.gob.es/es/red-parques-nacionales/nuestros-parques/garajonay

Garajonay National Park occupies 40 sq km (15 sq mi) in northern La Gomera and was declared a UNESCO World Heritage Site in 1986 due to its status as the world's largest pre-glacial forest. Most of

Garajonay National Park

the park is covered in laurel forests, not unlike those that would have been found in Europe throughout the Tertiary Period from 66 million years ago. The landscape feels fittingly primeval, with clouds and mists hovering on the peaks.

From San Sebastian de La Gomera, drive the GM2 road up into the park (21 km/13 mi; 30 minutes). From here, there are several well-marked turnouts, trailheads, and small, free parking lots to leave the car and explore. Hiking trails are often steep, winding through the mossy forests, opening occasionally to breathtaking, vertigo-inspiring views. For most abilities, the **Roque de Ojila circular trail** (moderate; 8.7 km/5.4 mi; 4 hours) makes for a half-day hike that highlights some of the best features of the park, with incredible views above the misty forest. Hiking this trail counterclockwise makes for a slightly easier ascent. Make sure to pack some snacks and plenty of water.

If you didn't pack a lunch, the **Restaurante Laguna Grande** (Ctra General, s/n Vallhermosa; tel. 922 69 50 83; 10am-6pm daily; €20) is conveniently located at the sight of several trailheads and connections. The **Juego de Bolas visitors center** (La Malmita, Agulo; tel. 922 477 222; www.miteco.gob.es/en/red-parques-nacionales/nuestros-parques/garajonay/guia-visitante/centros.aspx) is 3 km (1.9 mi) north of the park.

3. La Iglesia de la Asunción

Calle Real 24; tel. 922 870 303; 8:30am-6:30pm Mon.-Sat., 11am-8pm Sun.; free

After exploring the national park, head back down into San Sebastián de La Gomera, Christopher Columbus's last stop in 1492 before he famously crossed the Atlantic Ocean to the Americas. In town, La Iglesia de la Asunción is a must-see, and offers a pleasant, cool break on hot afternoons. This is where Columbus and his crew prayed before making the long crossing over the Atlantic. The church has seen a few expansions and rebuildings over the years, with the latest being in the 18th century following a fire, though the altar and nave remain from the earlier church. Outside, the lively main plaza often has licensed buskers performing traditional Canarian and Spanish dancing and music, as well as a number of cafés and restaurants. The last ferry to Los Cristianos usually departs at 5:30pm.

TRANSPORTATION

Air

- **Las Palmas de Gran Canaria Airport** (LPA; Autopista General del Sur; tel. 913 21 10 0; www.aena.es/es/gran-canaria.html), also known as Gondo Airport and Gran Canaria Airport, connects by bus and taxi with Las Palmas de Gran Canaria. The airport is located about 25 km (15.5 mi) south of the city. Iberia has daily direct flights from Madrid (3 hours).
- **The Tenerife South-Reina Sofía Airport** (TFS; Calea Bucurestilor nr. 224 E; tel. 212 041 000; www.aena.es/en/tenerife-sur.html), commonly known as the Tenerife South Airport, is connected by bus and taxi with the rest of the island of Tenerife. It's about 15 km (9 mi) east of Los Cristianos ferry port and 60 km (37 mi) southwest of Santa Cruz de Tenerife. Iberia has daily direct flights between Madrid and Tenerife South (3 hours). Note that most short flights connecting with other Canary Islands arrive/depart from **Tenerife North Airport** (TFN) on the other side of the island, though some airlines use this airport as well.

Ferry

Fred Olsen ferries (www.fredolsen.es) are the most convenient for this route, as they are generally the earliest out and the latest to return. The ferries are generally very punctual and have plenty of restrooms and lounging spaces for a comfortable crossing. If you rented a car, you can take it on the ferry, though it is

WATCH

The Whistlers: Though many otherworldly Hollywood blockbusters have been filmed here, from *Star Wars* to superhero films, only this 2019 Romanian crime thriller really delves into el silbo, the unique whistling language spoken by the inhabitants of the island of La Gomera.

READ

Dogs of Summer by Andrea Abreu: Set in Tenerife, where the author was born, this short novel about the intense best-friend relationship between two preteen girls evokes the island's heat.

LISTEN

"Isa de Tenerife" by Los Majuelos: The Canary Islands have developed a very distinct musical tradition. Perhaps the most distinctive music is the Isas, a variation of Jota found throughout Spain. Each island proudly has its own isa, with each having an accompanying dance. Perhaps the most popular of these is the Isa de Tenerife.

sometimes a bit of a tight squeeze. Use **Ferry Hopper** (www.ferryhopper.com) to book ferry passage ahead of time.

- **Agaete ferry port** (Puerto de Las Nieves s/n, Villa de Agaete, Gran Canaria): Fred Olsen ferries between Gran Canaria and Tenerife (80 minutes; from €54) use the port in Agaete, on the western coast of Gran Canaria. The ferry company offers a 25-minute bus ride from Las Palmas de Gran Canaria to Agaete that synchs with ferry departure times. Note that there are ferries from other companies running from the port in Las Palmas to Tenerife (2 hours).
- **Santa Cruz de Tenerife** (Puerto Santa Cruz de Tenerife, Muelle Ribera, first dock, Tenerife): The ferry terminal in Santa Cruz to Tenerife is close to the center of town, about a 15-minute walk to the Municipal Market of Our Lady of Africa.
- **Puerto Los Cristianos** (Muelle del Puerto de Los Cristianos en Arona): Located on the western coast of Tenerife, Los Cristianos is the port for ferries to/from La Gomera (1 hour; from €47). For those staying Santa Cruz de Tenerife, Fred Olsen offers a 1-hour bus to Los Cristianos that synchs with ferry departure times.
- **Port of San Sebastián de La Gomera:** This port is located on the eastern end of La Gomera and is the arrival point for boats from Tenerife.

Car

Car rental companies are available near airports and ferry terminals.

Getting Back

Get back to Las Palmas de Gran Canaria or Tenerife by retracing your ferry routes in the opposite direction. Binter Canarias runs flights from La Gomera Airport (GMZ) to Las Palmas de Gran Canaria (1 hour) and to Tenerife North Airport (30 minutes).

- London and Paris (page 44)
- Barcelona and Madrid (page 99)
- Sevilla, Córdoba, and Granada (page 117)

THE AZORES

Why Go: Sense the vastness of the Atlantic from some of Europe's most remote islands.

Number of Days: 7

Total Distance: 330 km (205 mi) in the Azores

Seasons: Late spring to early fall

Start: Lisbon

End: São Jorge

The Azores, a Portuguese archipelago of nine islands, float in the Atlantic more than 1,500 km (1,000 mi) from the nearest landmass. The remoteness doesn't quite hit home until you land on one of the islands, look around, and see endless sea from all sides. The heady fragrance of moist, fertile earth, sea salt, and hot basalt rock perfectly exudes the essence of the Azores, with their luxuriant landscapes, staggering volcanic features, and four-seasons-in-one-day weather.

With a range of direct flights from Lisbon, the Azores' biggest island, São Miguel is the unofficial main gateway to the archipelago. The islands of Faial, Pico, and São Jorge are nicknamed the Azores Triangle for their close proximity, and are conveniently connected by short ferry rides. Each of these islands is distinct and unique, and a trip encompassing all of them is a dynamic and rewarding way to get a taste of the Azores.

TOP 3

Viewing São Miguel Island's **Sete Cidades Lake** from every angle—going up to a gorgeous vista point or kayaking on the calm, greenish water (page 588).

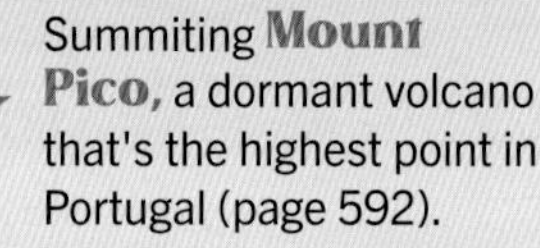

Summiting **Mount Pico,** a dormant volcano that's the highest point in Portugal (page 592).

Feeling the vastness of the ocean at **Rosais Point,** São Jorge's dramatic northwesternmost tip (page 594).

Lisbon

Where to Stay: Baixa neighborhood

Arrive by: Plane to Humberto Delgado Airport

DAY 1

1. Comércio Square

After you land and drop your bags off at your hotel, start your day in Lisbon in famous Comércio Square in the main downtown area. The formal entrance to the Baixa neighborhood, the **Triumphal Arch** (Rua Augusta 2; tel. 210 998 599; www.visitlisboa.com; 9am-8pm daily; viewing terrace €3) gazes over the square from its north side. Make sure you climb to the top for sweeping views of the plaza.

2. Santa Justa Elevator

Rua do Ouro; www.carris.pt; 7am-11pm daily Mar.-Oct., 7am-9pm daily Nov.-Feb.; €5.30 round-trip

A few streets back from the main square is the 19th-century wrought-iron Santa Justa Elevator, also called the Carmo Lift. This historical contraption transports passengers from Baixa up to the famous Bairro Alto neighborhood. Hop on and admire how the old-fashioned machinery comes to life, taking you to the viewing platform at the top.

3. Time Out Market Lisboa + Riverside Market

Avenida 24 de Julho 49; tel. 213 951 274; www.timeoutmarket.com/lisboa; 10am-midnight Sun.-Thurs., 10am-2am Sat.-Sun.

For lunch, hop on the Metro (from Baixa-Chiado to Cais do Sodré) to the bustling Time Out Market Lisboa, set back from the Cais do Sodré quay. This eclectic food hall, now run by the team behind the Lisbon edition of *Time Out* magazine, showcases the finest Portuguese products. The two-dozen-plus stands are allocated to chefs and restaurants handpicked by *Time Out*'s food writers.

4. Belém Tower

Av. Brasília; tel. 213 620 034; www.torrebelem.gov.pt; 10am-5:30pm daily Oct.-Apr., 10am-6:30pm daily May-Sept.; €6

Belém is a bright and breezy neighborhood west of downtown. Jutting into the Tagus River, Belém Tower is Portugal's most famous monument. Built in the early 16th century at the river mouth, the fortified

Comércio Square

THE AZORES

Graciosa

ATLANTIC OCEAN

Rosais Point

São Jorge Union of Agricultural and Dairy Cooperatives

Terceira

Faial

Velas

Fajã dos Cubres

Faial Caldera Volcanic Complex and Nature Reserve

Fajã da Caldeira de Santo Cristo

Pico Airport

Landscape of the Pico Island Vineyard Culture

Horta

Madalena

Horta Airport

São Jorge

Mount Pico

Pico

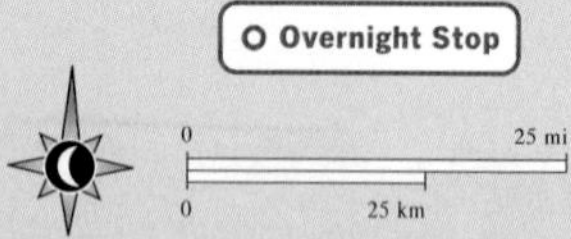

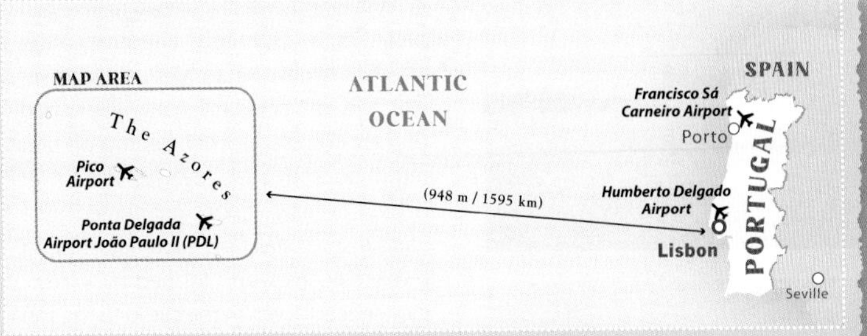

ATLANTIC

OCEAN

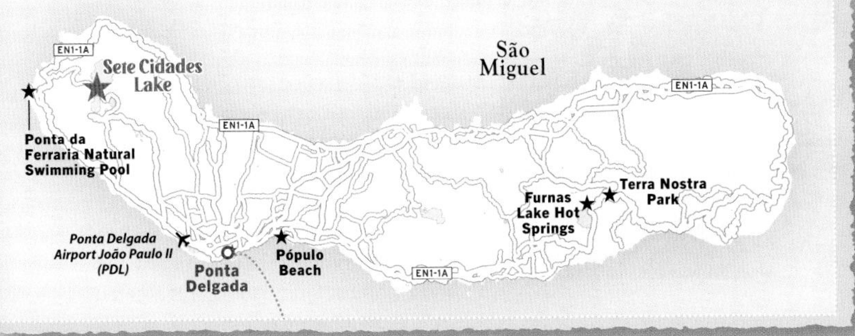

(top to bottom) Belém Tower; Pastéis de Belém; Ponta Delgada waterfront; Graça market

tower was both functional and ornamental, defending Lisbon from sea raiders and providing a ceremonial entrance to the city. The ornate white Manueline tower was the last and first sight sailors had of their homeland when setting off and returning from their voyages. The tower is built over five floors, connected by a narrow spiral staircase, each floor having lovely balconies, and topped by a viewing terrace. It's worth the climb to the top for views over the Tagus estuary and the Belém neighborhood's monuments.

To get to Belém from downtown Lisbon, take the commuter train headed to Cascais from Cais do Sodré.

5. Pastéis de Belém

Rua Belém 84-92; tel. 213 637 423; www.pasteisdebelem.pt; 8am-11pm daily; €5

No visit to Lisbon is complete without a taste of the humble, iconic pastel de nata custard tart. It can be found throughout Portugal, but Belém is its birthplace. Pastéis de Belém started making the delectable tarts, here called pastel de Belém, in 1837, following a secret recipe. The buttery pastry contains a creamy, eggy filling, slightly caramelized top, and a sprinkling of cinnamon. Afterward, catch the train back to Cais do Sodré, and head to the Alfama neighborhood, about a 20-minute walk east.

6. A Night of Fado at Parreirinha de Alfama

Beco do Espírito Santo 1; tel. 218 868 209; www.parreirinhadealfama.com; 8pm-1am Tues.-Sun.; minimum per person €40, cash only

Fado is one of Portugal's best-known genres of traditional music. Often associated with darkened backstreet taverns in early 19th-century Lisbon, fado features singers (fadistas) intoning tales of longing and daily hardships of the era, with songs ranging from mournful and melancholic to upbeat and jovial. Established in 1939, Parreirinha is one of Lisbon's oldest and most popular fado haunts. It is located in the Alfama neighborhood, widely believed to be the birthplace of fado.

Key Reservations

ACTIVITIES

- Be sure to pack an old swimsuit since the soothing, rust-colored waters at São Miguel's **Terra Nostra Park** can turn it orange.
- Reserve in advance for a wine-tasting and guided tour at the **Landscape of the Pico Island Vineyard Culture Interpretation Center.**
- Book your Pico whale-watching trip with **Espaço Talassa** ahead of time.
- If it's on your bucket list to summit **Mount Pico,** the highest point in Portugal, be sure to reserve in advance at the **Mountain House,** as the number of people allowed on the mountain at any one time is limited.
- If you plan to visit **São Jorge Union of Agricultural and Dairy Cooperatives** on a day other than Tuesday or Thursday, call at least one day ahead to make an appointment.

RESTAURANTS

Reservations for the most popular restaurants, particularly those famous for local specialties or those that feature fado, are highly recommended year-round.

- **Lisbon:** Parreirinha de Alfama
- **São Miguel:** Restaurante Miroma
- **Pico:** Cella Bar

Mount Pico

TRANSPORTATION

- Reserve your **car rentals** well in advance, as they sell out in peak seasons, especially summer (July-Aug.).

São Miguel

Where to Stay: Ponta Delgada

Arrive by: Plane from Lisbon Airport to Ponta Delgada Airport (2 hours)

DAY 2

1. Ponta Delgada Waterfront

Take an early morning flight from Lisbon to Ponta Delgada on São Miguel, the Azores' biggest island and main gateway. Get your bearings by exploring wonderfully historic Ponta Delgada, São Miguel's biggest town. Start at the 16th-century **Fort of São Brás** (Rua Engenheiro Abel Ferin Coutinho 10; tel. 296 304 920; www.monumentos.gov.pt; 10am-6pm Mon.-Fri.; €3), today occupied by the Portuguese Navy and a museum dedicated to Azorean military paraphernalia. Head east to the striking old **City Gates,** at the entrance to **Gonçalo Velho Cabral Square.** An age-old local saying goes that those who walk through the gates twice will return to São Miguel, while those who walk through three times will return and stay. Be sure to look down upon entering the square: The cobblestone pattern is as intricate as a tapestry, with its ornamental knots, twists, and stars.

2. Graça Market

Rua do Mercado; tel. 296 282 663; 7:30am-6:30pm Mon.-Wed., 7:30am-7pm Thurs., 7am-2pm Fri.-Sat.

Stop at this local market, which is full of the island's intriguing local produce. Products to take home include cheeses and honey, hand-rolled cigars, and the famous Gorreana tea, organic green and black teas grown right here on São Miguel at Europe's only tea plantation.

3. Furnas Lake Hot Springs

Furnas Lake shore; tel. 296 588 019; open 24 hours daily; €2

Pack an old swimsuit and towel, and pick up your car. From Ponta Delgada, drive along the southern coast east toward Furnas, about 50 minutes away on the EN1-1A. Your first stop is the Furnas Lake hot springs, with its bubbling geysers and fumaroles where the local specialty **cozido das Furnas** is cooked. In the early morning, huge steel pots of this local stew are lowered into the ground and covered, then left for several hours to cook before being removed, loaded into waiting vans, and zipped off to nearby restaurants. To see the pots getting lifted out, visit around noon.

Taste this unique geothermal gastronomy at **Restaurante Miroma** (Rua Dr. Frederico Moniz Pereira 15, Furnas; tel. 296 584 422; 9:30am-9:30pm daily; €15), near the center of Furnas, a short 10-minute drive east from the lake. Afterward, stroll among the geysers bubbling in **Calderas Square.** The square is surrounded by little stalls selling corn on the cob cooked in the boiling underground water, another local specialty.

top:, Sete Cidades Lake; bottom, Ponta da Ferraria natural swimming pool

4. Terra Nostra Park

Rua Padre Jose Jacinto Botelho Furnas; tel. 296 549 090; www.parqueterranostra.com; 10am-6pm daily; adults €8, ages 3-10 €4

The paradisiacal Terra Nostra Park gardens are a 20-minute walk west of Calderas Square. If there were a paradise on earth, it might look like this park, a captivating Eden of sprawling gardens, shady tree-covered walkways, babbling streams, lily-covered ponds, and a big pool of hot, rusty-red spring water that soothes aching muscles and joints. Have a soak in this historic pool, initially built in 1780.

5. Seaside Dinner at Bar Caloura

Rua da Caloura 20, Água de Pau, Lagoa; tel. 296 913 283; noon-9:30pm daily; €15

On your way back to Ponta Delgada, stop at the idyllic Bar Caloura, in the tiny village of Água de Pau on the island's southern coast, for a romantic and scenic drink and seafood meal.

DAY 3

★ 1. Sete Cidades Lake

EN9-1A; tel. 296 249 016; http://parquesnaturais.azores.gov.pt; open 24 hours; free

This morning head straight to the Sete Cidades (Seven Cities) Lake, the Azores' most famous vista, located on the western end of the island. Five km (3 mi) long and 12 km (7 mi) around, Sete Cidades is the largest freshwater lake in the Azores; it's technically two large twin lakes in the crater of a giant dormant volcano. Surrounded by vibrant vegetation, the lakes are connected by a narrow, bridged strait and are locally called "Green Lake" and "Blue Lake," differing in how they reflect the sun.

Stop first at the **Grota do Inferno viewpoint** (Rua Ribeira do Ferreiro 117, Candelaria) for one perspective, then make the short drive west to the **Vista do Rei viewpoint** (Road 9-1 142; tel. 917 189 250), which offers the most iconic views of the lake. To get up close and personal with the lake, rent a kayak from **Garoupa Canoe Tours** (Sete Cidades; tel. 917 158 701; www.garoupa.pt; open 24/7; from €10). After working up an appetite, grab lunch at lakeside **Green Love** (9-1 23, Sete Cidades; tel. 296 915 214 or 914 229 699; 9:30am-6pm Mon.-Thurs., 9:30am-9:30pm Fri.-Sun.; €15).

2. Ponta da Ferraria Natural Swimming Pool

Rua Padre Fernando Vieira Gomes; open 24 hours daily; free

Back in your car, drive west toward the coast for a quick dip in the ocean. At Ponta da Ferraria, volcanic hot water and refreshing seawater merge in a natural rock pool.

3. EN1-1A Scenic Drive

Follow the EN1-1A around the western tip of the island, through traditional little coastal villages like **Mosteiros,** home to one of São Miguel's most popular black sand beaches, and **Capelas.** End up at **Rabo de Peixe,** which translates to "fish tail," a typical fishing village. Explore the streets lined with colorful houses and the port to absorb the charm of these picturesque seaside villages.

4. Pópulo Beach

Estrada Regional do Pópulo, São Roque; open 24 hours daily; free

Cut south across the island on the EN3-1A to Rua Duarte Borges to get to the black-sand Pópulo Beach, just east of Ponta Delgada on the island's southern coast, for a memorable sunset drink at one of the many beach bars, such as the fantastic **Sunset Beach Restaurant & Bar** (Canada do Borralho, Pópulo Beach; tel. 911 050 309; 8am-2am Thurs.-Fri., 8am-1am Sat.-Wed.; €15).

Faial

Where to Stay: Horta

Arrive by: Plane from Ponta Delgada Airport to Horta Airport (1 hour)

DAY 4

1. Faial Caldeira Volcanic Complex and Nature Reserve

open 24 hours daily; free

Take an early morning flight from Ponta Delgada to Faial, picking up a rental car when you arrive. Stop at the **Horta Municipal Market** (Rua Serpa Pinto; tel. 292 202 074; www.cmhorta.pt/index.php/servicos-municipais/mercado-municipal; 6:30am-7pm Mon.-Fri., 6:30am-1pm Sat.-Sun.) to grab some fresh produce for a picnic lunch, and then drive out to see Faial's famed landmark, the gargantuan 2-km-wide (1-mi), 400-m-deep (1,300-ft) crater known as the Caldeira. Located in the very middle of the island, the monumental caldera is truly staggering. It's an immense geological formation carpeted in varying shades of green fuzz, with soaring sides that encircle the flat crater bottom, creating dramatic and breathtaking—almost prehistoric—scenery. Enjoy the bird's-eye island views as you trek around the rim (8 km/5 mi round-trip; 3 hours), and stop at the **Caldera viewpoint** for the best vantage point of the cauldron.

2. Monte da Guia

Head back to central Horta and take a pleasant 45-minute walk to Monte da Guia, the volcanic outcrop overlooking the town. Spend the first part of the morning here, making sure to get a picture from the **Monte da Guia viewpoint.** You can gaze over Horta and enjoy excellent views to the islands of Pico, São Jorge, and Graciosa, surrounded by infinite sea.

3. Jetty Murals

As you walk back toward town, stop by the colorful murals decorating the jetty facing the Marina. It has become something of a tradition for visiting sailors to paint a mural before departing, and each tells a story or conveys a message from the hundreds who pass through every year.

4. Peter Café Sport

Rua José Azevedo 9; tel. 292 392 027; www.petercafesport.com; 8am-1am daily

Head back to Horta for an evening in this quirky sailors' town. Make sure to have a gin and tonic or cold beer in the legendary Peter Café Sport bar—there's a saying among sailors that if you visit Horta and don't come here then you haven't actually visited Horta. Every inch of the interior is covered with nautical paraphernalia**.** It's a lively place and also home to arguably the largest and most beautiful private collection of scrimshaw (the art of engraving on bone or ivory) in the world. For dinner, try nearby **Canto da Doca** (Rua Nova; tel. 292 292 444; noon-2:30pm and 7pm-11pm daily; €15), where fresh fish and meats are cooked on sizzling lava stones.

Pico

Where to Stay: Madalena

Arrive by: Ferry from Faial's Horta Port Terminal to Madalena on Pico (30 minutes)

DAY 5

1. Landscape of the Pico Island Vineyard Culture

Interpretation Center: Rua do Lajido Santa Luzia; tel. 965 896 313; 10am-1pm and 1:30pm-5pm Tues.-Sat. Nov. 1-Mar. 31, 10am-1pm and 2pm-6pm daily Apr. 1-Oct. 31; €3

In the morning, catch the car ferry to make the short crossing between Horta and the town of **Madalena** on Pico. From the ferry terminal, drive 10 minutes northeast to the Landscape of the Pico Island Vineyard Culture, where you can learn about the island's distinctive winemaking practices. Pico's wine grapes grow within currais, pens formed by woven grids of low basalt rock walls, to protect the vines from harsh sea air and regulate their temperatures. So unique and characteristic is this lattice-like landscape that it has been classified a UNESCO World Heritage Site. Drive around or wander among the currais, and visit the Vineyard Culture Interpretation Center to see historic artifacts linked to the island's winemaking. If you reserve in advance, you can enjoy a wine-tasting and guided tour.

2. Whale-Watching

Pico's pristine waters make whale-watching off the island stand out in an archipelago with some of the best whale-watching in the world. The species spotted vary from season to season, but may include sperm whales, blue whales, fin whales, sei whales, and humpback whales, as well as bottlenose and Risso's dolphins. Most whale-watching trips depart from **Lajes do Pico,** on the south coast of the island—try **Espaço Talassa** (tel. 292 672 010; www.espacotalassa.com; from €39), one of the first whale-sighting tour companies on the island. Give yourself at least an hour before your tour to make the drive from the northwest side of Pico.

From Whaling to Whale-Watching

The Azores archipelago is today one of few places on the planet that unreservedly showcases its whaling tradition, warts and all. While the activity has long been eradicated in this part of the world, its heritage remains ingrained in the region, clear for all to see. Most islands have statues or monuments alluding to the islands' former lifeblood; old wooden whale boats are proudly restored and used as showpieces in museums or regattas; and festivals celebrate time-honored whaling traditions. Today, the waters around the Azores continue to attract cetaceans, making the islands a premier whale-watching destination.

A WHALING TRADITION

Whaling arrived in the Azores from the Americas in the late 18th century, when large American ships began to explore the untapped bounty of whales in the cool blue waters off the islands. Azoreans learned their whaling techniques from the visiting Americans, and it rapidly became a key pillar for the local economy and an intrinsic part of the archipelago's culture.

Whales swam so close to the shores of the Azores that they could be spotted from land in vigias (lookout stations). Whalers used rudimentary techniques and equipment, like hand-thrown harpoons and open wooden rowboats, to kill the huge mammals, which were then tied to the boats with ropes and towed back to land to be transformed into lucrative by-products. Fat was transformed into oil and exported to be used as fuel and lubricant, and in cosmetics; bones were ground and used as fertility treatments. Whaling in the Azores was officially banned in 1982, with the ban fully implemented in 1986. Famously, the last whale in the Azores was killed in 1987 as a protest from a few staunch whalers from Pico.

You can see how the whaling tradition is preserved in the Azores at a few spots in the Azores Triangle:

- **Monte da Guia:** A number of little buildings linked to whaling, such as vigias and an old processing factory that houses the **Porto Pim Whaling Station Museum** (www.oma.pt), still flank the mount outside Horta on Faial (page 590).
- **Lajes do Pico:** The **Whaler's Museum** (www.museu-pico.azores.gov.pt) focuses on the heritage and culture of the former Azorean whaling industry.

TRANSITION TO CONSERVATION

As tourism crept into the Azores, the region gradually established itself as one of the foremost whale-spotting sites on the globe. Tourism has thrived hand in hand with marine conservation, with preservation replacing profitability. Today, the Azores' waters provide a safe haven for over 20 species of whales that can be spotted year-round, one of the most magical experiences on offer in the Azores. **Lajes do Pico,** formerly a hub for the whaling industry, is now considered the archipelago's whale-watching capital (page 590). **Ponta Delgada** (page 587) is also a great base for a whale-watching trip.

3. Petiscos at Tasca O Petisca

Avenida Padre Nunes da Rosa; tel. 292 622 357; www.facebook.com/tascapetisca; 10am-3pm and 6:30pm-midnight Mon.-Sat.; €15

Head back to Madalena after your tour, and have an early dinner. Specializing in traditional regional tapas, or snack dishes (petiscos), O Petisca was the first restaurant of its kind on the island. Seafood, island beef, local breads, and homemade desserts are among the specialties at this busy and popular eatery. Tuck in early tonight, to rise bright and early to conquer the iconic Mount Pico the next day.

DAY 6

★ 1. Mount Pico

Mountain House admission center open 24 hours May 1-Sept. 30, 8am-8pm Mon.-Thurs., Fri. 8am-Sun. 8pm uninterrupted Apr. and Oct., 8am-6pm daily Nov. 1-Mar. 31; €15

Its soaring, conical outline rising voluptuously from its base is unmistakable. The highest point in Portugal, Mount Pico's summit stands at 2,351 m (7,713 ft) above sea level, double the height of any other peak in the Azores. Pico actually has a double peak: The top of the mountain is capped by a huge crater, Pico Grande, on which sits another little cone, Pico Pequeno. Mount Pico calls to hikers worldwide, but it's not for the fainthearted. However, the breathtaking 360-degree views at the top, even on the way up, are the ultimate reward.

Having registered in advance for the climb and reserved a guide (see the Advance Reservations callout), head off bright and early for Mount Pico with a backpack holding essentials like a windbreaker, snacks, and water. The starting point is the **Mountain House** (Caminho Florestal 9, Candelária; tel. 967 303 519), where you can get information about the route as well as learn about the history and geology of the mountain. This hike is a daylong job, taking 7-8 hours to complete.

2. Celebratory Dinner at Cella Bar

Rua Da Barca; tel. 292 623 654; 4pm-midnight Mon.-Fri., noon-late Sat.-Sun.; €20

After scaling Pico, head back to Madalena and reward yourself with dinner and drinks at the stunning Cella Bar. Housed within a futuristic-looking, award-winning wooden building attached to a traditional stone house, this bar boasts a magnificent beachside setting, perfect for a sunset cocktail.

São Jorge

Where to Stay: Velas

Arrive by: Ferry from Madalena, Pico, to Velas on São Jorge (2 hours)

DAY 7

1. Ferry to São Jorge

Take the morning ferry between **Madalena** and **Velas,** São Jorge's main town, for a quick one-night stay on the third island in the Azores Triangle. You'll likely arrive in late morning. Stop at **Café Restaurante Velense** (Rua Conselheiro Doutor José Pereira; tel. 295 412 160; 8am-1am daily; €10), located next to the quay, and lunch on local specialties, such as cheese, fresh prawns, and lapas (limpets).

2. São Jorge Union of Agricultural and Dairy Cooperatives

Canadinha Nova, Beira (4 km/2 mi north of Velas); tel. 295 438 274 or 295 438 275; www.lactacores.pt; 9am-5:30pm Mon.-Fri.; €1.50, tours Tues. and Thurs. or by appointment

A classified, controlled island product, the famous São Jorge cheese is a semi-hard, tangy cheese made from unpasteurized cow's milk. Located a five-minute (3.6-km/2.2-mi) drive north of Velas, this agricultural and dairy cooperative

Made in the Azores

The Azores' unique position in the middle of the Atlantic means they have their own microclimate, making it possible for many crops that wouldn't have much of a chance on the Portuguese mainland to flourish here. On their way between the Old and New Worlds, explorers, settlers, traders, and sailors brought and left seeds and starters for various foodstuffs, which today are among the products that the Azores are known for.

CHEESE

Arguably the most famous Azorean product, cheese from the islands is justifiably famous, produced by cows that roam the archipelago. You'll find it in almost every restaurant and market, and it's possible to visit factories where the cheese is made on many islands, including the **São Jorge Union of Agricultural and Dairy Cooperatives** (page 592).

WINE

Though mainland Portugal has a formidable winemaking tradition, wine from the Azores holds up, if only for its uniqueness. Grown in basalt stone pens to protect it from the sea air and battered by changeable weather, Azorean wine is known for its salty, minerally notes. The majority of wine from the archipelago comes from the celebrated **Landscape of the Pico Island Vineyard Culture** (page 590).

TEA

On São Miguel's northern coast, the **Gorreana Tea Plantation** (just off EN1-1A road, Maia; tel. 296 442 349; www.gorreana.pt; 8am-7pm Mon.-Fri., 9am-7pm Sat.-Sun.; free) specializes in green and black teas, a perfect souvenir to take home from your trip.

PINEAPPLES

This South American transplant grows smaller and sweeter in the Azores. São Miguel is the largest producer; you can see for yourself where these tropical fruits grow at the **Augusto Arruda Pineapple Plantation** (Rua Doutor Augusto Arruda; tel. 296 384 438; www.ananasesarruda.com; 9am-6pm daily; free), just outside Ponta Delgada.

TUNA

The **Santa Catarina Tuna Factory** (Santa Catarina Indústria Conserveira, Rua do Roque, 9, Calheta; tel. 295 416 220; www.atumsantacatarina.com; 8:30am-5pm Mon.-Fri.; €3.90) on São Jorge cans locally caught tuna according to artisanal methods used by the old cannery masters. The fish is caught using sustainable pole-and-line methods and canned by local women using traditional techniques. The **tins** themselves are lovely little mementos of the island, thanks to their retro, vintage look.

produces the distinctive cheese, staying faithful to its historic roots, which date back to the 16th century when it is believed the famous cheese was developed by the Flemish people who settled in the area around Topo, the island's southeasternmost point. Guided tours around this industrial, pungent-smelling factory include a tasting and wind up in the gift shop and café, which also sells the cheese to take away.

3. Fajã dos Cubres and Fajã da Caldeira de Santo Cristo

Known as the Island of the Fajãs, São Jorge is famous for its fajãs, or flat coastal lava plateaus. Locals love to talk about their fajãs and debate over which fajã is the best—São Jorge is said to have over 70. On the north coast and accessible by car, Fajã dos Cubres is one of the most beautiful fajãs on the island and an important waterfowl habitat—it's the perfect fajã to visit for bird-watchers.

If you have the energy for more hiking, take the lovely, 4-km (2-mi) hike from Fajã dos Cubres to the magical Fajã da Caldeira de Santo Cristo, which can only be reached on foot. One-way, it takes about an hour, and your reward is a beautiful spot that sits at the foot of the Santo Cristo Caldera and is hugged by sweeping green cliffs. The waves that close in around the fajã are famous among surfers. The natural lagoon here is also the only spot on the island where local clams are cultivated and picked. **O Borges** (Rua Ribeira; tel. 918 650 613; 7am-midnight daily; €20) is the place to try this delicacy close to the source.

★ 4. Rosais Point

After visiting one or both fajãs, drive out to dramatic Rosais Point, São Jorge island's most northwesterly tip. An isolated, rugged spot where vertiginous 200-m-high (700-ft) cliffs form a sharp point over the Atlantic and an eerie old abandoned lighthouse complex stands, Rosais Point provides incredible views of the neighboring islands of Pico, Faial, and, on a good, clear day, Graciosa, and even Flores.

5. Restaurante Fornos de Lava

Hotel Os Moinhos, Travessa de S. Tiago, Santo Amaro; tel. 917 394 977; www.osmoinhos.com; noon-3pm and 6pm-11pm daily; €20

End the day with more stunning views and dinner at this lovely restaurant. The food is an intriguing fusion of Azorean and Galician cuisine, and big bay windows show off Pico and Faial—a view that recaps your trip.

TRANSPORTATION

Air

The primary way to get to the Azores is by plane, via **Lisbon** (Humberto Delgado Airport; LIS) or **Porto** (Sá Carneiro International Airport; OPO) on mainland Portugal. It's possible to fly to **São Miguel** (Ponta Delgada Airport; PDL), **Pico** (Pico Airport; PIX), and **Faial** (Horta Airport; HOR) directly from mainland Portugal.

Flights between Lisbon and **São Miguel** are short (around 2 hours; €100) and offered by TAP, SATA, and Ryanair. SATA also operates daily nonstop flights to **Faial** from São Miguel (1 hour; €150). It's also possible to fly to **São Jorge** (São Jorge Airport; SJZ) from São Miguel with SATA (1 hour).

Ferry

Pico, Faial, and São Jorge are connected by relatively short and year-round ferry routes. These ferries usually can also carry vehicles, meaning you can rent a car on one island and take it to another. **Atlanticoline** (tel. 707 201 572; www.atlanticoline.pt) runs the ferries between the islands.

- **Horta Port Terminal Passenger Ferry, Faial** (Avenida 25 de Abril; tel. 292 292 132; https://portosdosacores.pt): Six daily departures to Pico Madalena (30 minutes; €5).

- **João Quaresma Maritime Ferry Terminal, Pico** (Rua dona Maria da Glória Duarte; tel. 292 623 340; www.atlanticoline.pt): Ferries from São Jorge (2 hours; €10-16) and Faial (30 minutes; €5) sail to this port in Madalena, Pico's main town, on the island's northwestern tip.
- **Velas Ferry Terminal, São Jorge** (tel. 295 432 225; http://marinas.visitazores.com/marinas/velas): There are three or four weekly crossings between Madalena, on Pico, and Velas (2 hours; €10-16 one-way).

Car

On the islands themselves, it's easiest to rent a car to get around.

São Miguel

A half-dozen rental companies operate at Ponta Delgada Airport. Local companies such as **Autatlantis** (tel. 296 205 340; www.autatlantis.com) and **Micauto** (tel. 296 284 382; www.micauto.com) have offices in Ponta Delgada's city center and offer competitive rates. Reserve a car well in advance, as they sell out in peak seasons, especially summer.

Faial

Companies including **Ilha Verde Rent a Car** (tel. 292 392 786; www.ilhaverde.com) and **Europcar** (tel. 918 611 766; www.europcar.pt) can be found on Horta waterfront and at the airport, or try a local company, like **Auto Turística Faialense** (Rua Conselheiro Medeiros 12; tel. 292 292 308; www.autoturistica-faialense.com).

Pico

You can rent a car at the Pico Airport in Bandeiras, or ask for the vehicle to be dropped off and picked up from your hotel. Companies range from international names like **Europcar** (www.europcar.com) to local companies such as **Rent-a-Car Oásis** (www.rentacaroasis.com).

São Jorge

Pick up and drop off a car at the São Jorge airport or from a vehicle rental branch in Velas town, or on the harbor from companies such as **Ilha Verde Rent a Car** (www.ilhaverde.com), **Sixt Rent a Car** (www.sixt.pt), **Autatlantis** (https://autatlantis.com), and **AzoreanWay Rent a Car** (https://azoreanwayrentacar.com).

Public Transportation

Public transport is patchy on the islands but is cheap and easy for getting around Lisbon.

Lisbon's **Metro** (www.metrolisboa.pt) has four main lines—Green, Yellow, Red, and Blue. The Red Line runs from just outside the airport's main entrance and connects with the Green Line at Alameda station, which runs to the Baixa and Cais do Sodré riverfront, and ends at the Blue Line, at the São Sebastião station. A journey from the airport to downtown Lisbon (€1.25) requires one transfer and takes 20 minutes.

Getting Back

From São Jorge, catch the ferry back to Faial (with a stop in Pico), which takes about 2 hours total. From Horta Airport on Faial, there is at least one direct flight daily to Lisbon (2.5 hours) with Azores Airlines. However, on some days, the ferry might arrive too late to make the Lisbon flight, in which case an overnight on Faial would be required. You could also fly from São Jorge to São Miguel (1 hour) for and fly back to the mainland from there.

- Barcelona and Madrid (page 99)

CLASSIC RAIL TRIPS AND MORE

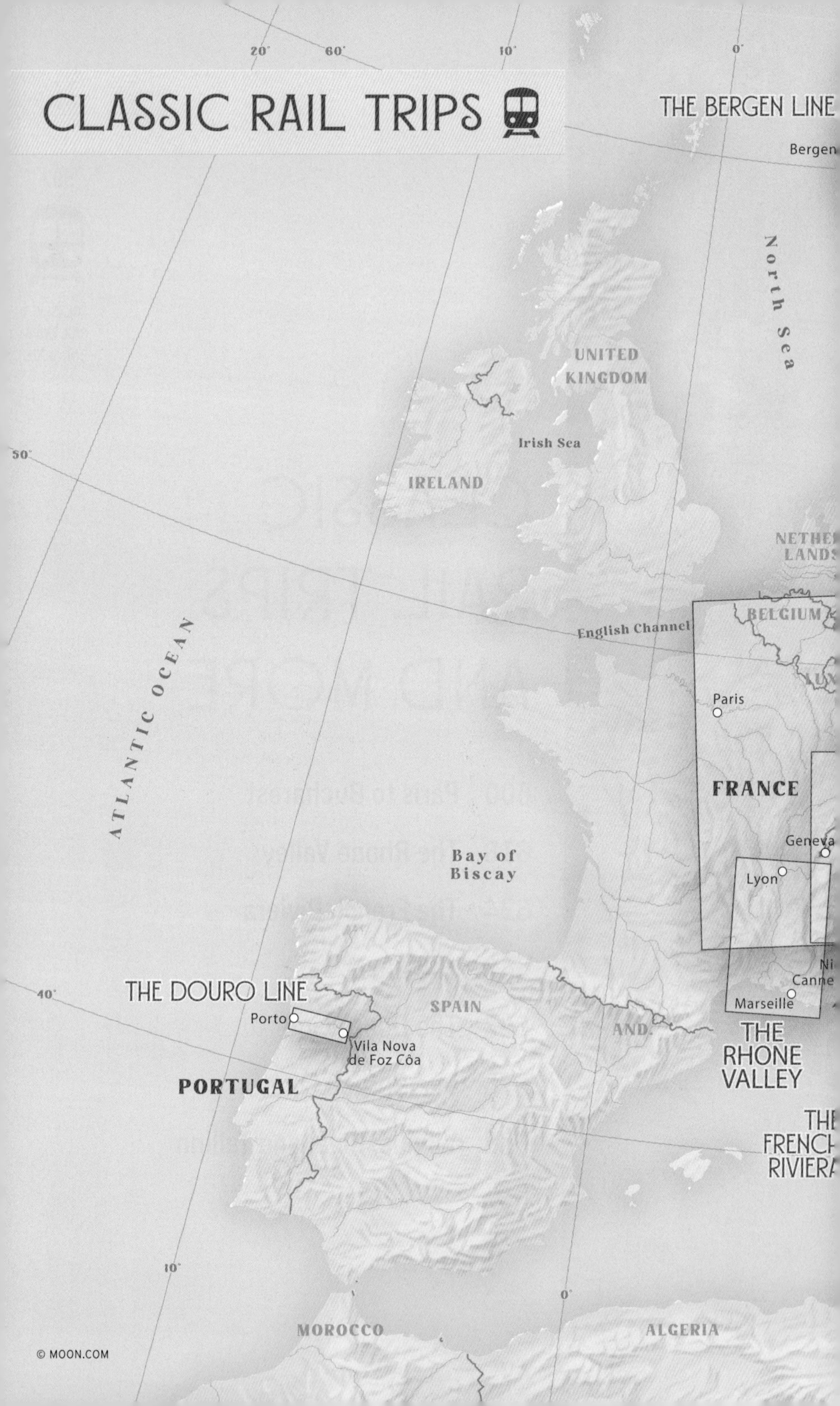

CLASSIC RAIL TRIPS

THE BERGEN LINE

Bergen

North Sea

UNITED KINGDOM

Irish Sea

IRELAND

NETHERLANDS

BELGIUM

English Channel

Paris

ATLANTIC OCEAN

FRANCE

Geneva

Lyon

Bay of Biscay

THE DOURO LINE

Porto

Vila Nova de Foz Côa

SPAIN

AND.

Cannes

Marseille

THE RHONE VALLEY

PORTUGAL

THE FRENCH RIVIERA

MOROCCO

ALGERIA

20° 60° 10° 0° 50° 40° 10° 0°

FINLAND
ORWAY
VILNIUS, RIGA
& TALLINN
Oslo
Tallinn
ESTONIA
RUSSIA
LATVIA
Riga
SWEDEN
LITHUANIA
ENMARK
Baltic Sea
RUSSIA
Vilnius
BELARUS
POLAND
PARIS TO BUCHAREST
UKRAINE
ERMANY
CZECHIA
SLOVAKIA
rasbourg
Munich
Vienna
MOL.
Budapest
ROMANIA
AUSTRIA
HUNGARY
VITZ.
THE ALPS
SLOV.
CROATIA
Milan
Bucharest
ALY
BOS. & HERZ.
SERBIA
BULGARIA
Black Sea
Adriatic Sea
KOS.
MONT.
NORTH MACEDONIA
ALBANIA
Aegean Sea
TURKEY
GREECE
TUNISIA
Mediterranean Sea
MALTA

PARIS TO BUCHAREST

Why Go: This classic rail voyage follows the route of the Orient Express, the quintessential European Tour. For lovers of riding the rails, this is a bucket list voyage par excellence.

Number of Days: 11

Total Distance: 2,300 km (1,430 mi)

Seasons: Year-round

Start: Paris

End: Bucharest

This is a "grand tour" of Europe in the truest sense. Your journey begins in Paris and heads due east on the rail adventure of a lifetime, following the path of the original Orient Express Railway chugging across the entire continent of Europe. On this voyage, you will pair Parisian charm with a crisp Bourgogne chardonnay, enjoy the quaint medieval Bavarian cities with hearty German lager, feast on rich Viennese chocolates while you marvel at opulent palaces, delight in delectable Hungarian classics, and taste Romanian hospitality in all its many flavors. Should you choose, you could opt to continue by train to its most popular terminus: Istanbul. This makes for a true cross-continental adventure.

TOP 3

Wandering Strasbourg's **La Petite France** neighborhood, a fairy tale of 16th- and 17th-century buildings (page 606).

Sipping a boot of lager at the **Hofbräuhaus** in Munich, the quintessential German beer hall experience, full of lighthearted fun with music and dancing year-round (page 608).

Celebrating your arrival in Bucharest with a stroll down **Victory Avenue** (page 612).

Antwerp
BRUSSELS
BELGIUM
Lille
Cologne
Dresden
GERMANY
Frankfurt
PRAGUE
LUXEMBOURG
Paris Charles de Gaulle Airport
Paris
Bateaux-Mouches
Orly Airport
Metz
Nürnberg
Stuttgart
La Petite France
Strasbourg
Ulm
Munich
Hofbräuhaus
Rosenheim
Salzburg
Linz
AUSTRIA
FRANCE
Zürich
BERN
SWITZERLAND
Geneva
Lyon
ITALY
LJUBLJANA
Milan
Venice
Turin
Genoa
0 100 mi
0 100 km
© MOON.COM

PARIS TO BUCHAREST

Overnight Stop
Rail Route

Kraków
Lvov
POLAND
ZECHIA
UKRAINE
MOLDOVA
SLOVAKIA
Vienna
BRATISLAVA
Győr
Tatabánya
Budapest
Szolnok
Cluj-Napoca
HUNGARY
Békéscsaba
Alba Lulia
Brașov
Deva
ZAGREB
REPUBLIC OF SERBIA
ROMANIA
Henri Coandă International Airport
Ploiești
CROATIA
Bucharest
Victory Avenue
BOSNIA AND HERZEGOVINA
BELGRADE
To Istanbul

left, Pont Alexandre III, Paris; middle, Vienna; right, Széchenyi Baths, Budapest

Paris, France

Arrive by: Plane to Charles de Gaulle or Paris Orly

DAY 1

This grand journey starts in Paris, and you could spend an untold number of days in the City of Light before hopping on the train. For three days of ideas, see **London and Paris** (page 44), and if that's not enough, here are a few more options.

1. Musée de l'Orangerie

Jardin Tuileries; tel. 01 44 50 43 00; www.musee-orangerie.fr; 9am-6pm Wed.-Mon.; €12.50, free 1st Sun. each month

Get here first thing in the morning to enjoy minimal crowds as you wander around the Impressionist masterpiece the Water Lilies cycle by Claude Monet. These eight larger-than-life paintings, each over 2 m (6 ft) tall and as long as 91 m (300 ft), grace the walls of the top floor of this museum. The play of natural light from the skylights above and the flowing architecture, shaped in the form of the infinity sign, make for a breathtaking display. Don't sleep on the impressive permanent collection on the floor below either; Picasso, Renoir, and more are well-represented.

top, Musée de l'Orangerie; bottom, Pont Alexandre III

2. Pont Alexandre III

Take a stroll on Paris's most iconic bridge, the Pont Alexandre III. This beaux arts-style bridge, a memorial to the Franco-Russian Alliance of 1892, features decorative art nouveau lamps as well as numerous statues and reliefs of two nymphs on either side of the bridge. Immense gilt-bronze statues anchor each corner of the bridge, adding a grandiosity to the whole. The views across the Seine to the Eiffel Tower, the Louvre, the Hôtel des Invalides, and countless other Parisian highlights, should not be missed.

3. Les Invalides

Place des Invalides; www.invalides.org

The domed building towering over the other side of the bridge is Les Invalides, a military hospital and residence for war veterans built by Louis XIV in 1670. Today it also houses the Musée d'Armée, a military weapons and uniforms museum. Walk around the grounds, and then stroll west in search of lunch. A good pick is **La Fontaine de Mars** (129 Rue Saint-Dominique; tel. 01 47 05 46 44; www.fontaine-de-mars.com; noon-3pm and 7pm-11pm Mon.-Fri., 12:30pm-3:30pm and 7pm-11pm Sat.-Sun.; €22-39), a charming bistro-style restaurant serving southwestern French cuisine that can boast Barack Obama as one of its customers.

Key Reservations

- If you plan on traveling with the Eurail pass, you need to book the pass before arriving to Europe.
- Though not strictly necessary, it is a good idea to book accommodations ahead of time, particularly during European holidays and summer months.
- Some museums and sites require reservations. For others, though reservations are not necessary, they can help you skip the lines and save time. See also **London and Paris** (page 44) and **Prague, Vienna, and Budapest** (page 184) for reservations needed when visiting Paris, Vienna, and Budapest.

Belvedere Palace

4. Bateaux Mouches River Cruise

Port de la Conférence, Pont d'Alma; tel. 01 42 25 96 10; www.bateaux-mouches.fr; daily cruises every hour; €15

See the major Parisian monuments on the classic Bateaux Mouches river cruise. The boat cruises up the Seine, passing the Louvre and ornate Hötel de la Ville before turning at the Arab World Institute. From here, it goes down the Seine, passing by the Ile de la Cité for a close-up view of the Notre Dame Cathedral before continuing past the Musée d'Orsay to the Eiffel Tower.

5. Happy Hour at Montparnasse Tower

33 Av. du Maine; tel. 06 03 93 81 82; 5pm-2am Mon.-Sat.; €10

Amazingly laid-back, this little watering hole is a favorite for locals, couples, and travelers in-the-know. After all, these are the best views in all of Paris. Take your time, watch the sunset, and sip on a chilled Agwa de Bolivia, Apero, or fresh mojito. Happy hour goes until 10pm (11pm on weekends).

Afterward, if the weather cooperates, walk over to the plant-filled terrace at **La Closerie des Lilas** (171 Blvd. du Montparnasse; tel. 01 40 51 34 50; www.closeriedeslilas.fr; noon-1:30am daily; €25), and kick off an evening meal with a plate of oysters. If you're looking for Parisian brasserie ambience with a 1920s vibe, this is the place. At least Hemingway thought so. Be sure to check out his plaque at the bar, where he wrote parts of groundbreaking first novel *The Sun Also Rises.*

Bateaux Mouches river cruise

THE LOST GENERATION

In case you didn't know it, Paris in the 1920s was a thing. After World War I, after the French franc was devalued and prohibition took hold in the United States, writers, artists, musicians, and more descended on Paris, many of them settling in the 5th and 6th arrondissements on the Left Bank. Because of the weak franc, Paris was amazingly inexpensive, and while jazz-infused music echoed down the boulevards and the champagne poured endlessly, the array of artistic talent magnetized to this one spot was immeasurable, perhaps unmatched in history. For a few years, within walking distance, these are just a few of the people who called Paris home: Ernest Hemingway, F. Scott Fitzgerald, T. S. Eliot, Josephine Baker, Pablo Picasso, Henry Tanner, Salvador Dalí, Henri Matisse, Georges Braque, Cole Porter, Amedeo Modigliani, Alice B. Toklas, Igor Stravinsky, James Joyce, and many more.

However, it was **Gertrude Stein,** an American writer, art dealer, and longtime companion to Alice B. Toklas, who was the true tastemaker. It was her discerning eye and ear that elevated greatness. Stein moved to Paris in 1902 and made it her home for the rest of her life. After World War I, with North America and Europe struggling to understand how such a war could happen, it was clear that the somewhat stodgy Edwardian values before the war were no longer serving the greater good. It was this break, in many ways, alongside the flappers, jazz, and incessant traveling, that led Gertrude Stein to famously exclaim to Hemingway, "You are all a lost generation."

Strasbourg, France

Where to Stay: Near the Cathedral

Arrive by: Train from Paris Gare de l'Est to Gare de Strasbourg (2 hours)

DAY 2

1. Grande-Île

Leave Paris in the morning to arrive in Strasbourg with the better part of the day free for sightseeing. After stashing your bags at your hotel, head over to Grande-Île, which makes up the city's historic center. The centerpiece here is the **Strasbourg Notre Dame Cathedral** (Pl. de la Cathédrale; tel. 03 88 21 43 34; www.cathedrale-strasbourg.fr; 8:30am-11:15am and 12:45pm-5:45pm Mon.-Sat.; free), the pinnacle of High-Gothic architecture, quite literally! In fact, the 142-m-high (465-ft) spire made this the tallest building in Europe until the 19th century. Some of the highlights include the medieval facade with hundreds of intricate figures, the delicate stained-glass rose window, and the Renaissance astronomical clock.

★ 2. La Petite France

Off the western end of Grand-Île is La Petite France, Strasbourg's most picturesque neighborhood. Meander around the black and white timber-framed houses and shops that all date from the

The Orient Express

The dream of Belgian-born Georges Nagelmackers, inspired by trains he witnessed on his trip to the United States in the 1860s, was to connect all of Europe with quick, luxurious trains. It took Nagelmackers over two decades to see his dream come to life, but when the first Orient Express train departed the Gare de l'Est in **Paris,** it was an immediate success.

Over the 1880s, Nagelmackers continued expanding the train route from the original terminus in Giurgui, a small town just south of Bucharest in Romania, to Varna, Bulgaria, and eventually all the way to **Istanbul** in 1891, when the Orient Express grew to its greatest fame.

Over the years, the routes of the Orient Express have changed from that original route, with different services and routes being added, connecting different European capitals, such as London, Athens, Milan, Venice, and Trieste. On all these runs by Nagelmackers's company, Compagnie Internationale des Wagon-Lits, Nagelmackers prided himself on having the fastest, most luxurious train in the world. By the 1930s, the Orient Express was at the height of its popularity, renowned for its comfort, unparalleled service, and haute cuisine.

Though sadly Nagelmackers's company did not survive, you can still enjoy the ambiance of the original Orient Express in restored train cars decked out in all of their 1920s art deco glory. Owned by luxury staple the **Belmond Group,** the new Orient Express company (www.orient-express.com) offers limited service connecting Europe, if your pockets are deep enough. This is modern, high-end luxury with eye-watering prices to match.

16th and 17th century. Cozy up to **Chez l'Oncle Freddy** (9 Rue des Moulins; tel. 03 88 22 08 14; www.chezlonclefreddy.com; 11:30am-10pm daily; €18) for a lunch of classic Alsatian dishes like tarte à l'oignon and mushroom spaetzele, best paired with a local wine, like a riesling, or an Alsatian pale lager.

3. Covered Bridges

Ponts Coverts; open daily 24 hours; free

As you wander, you will notice four large towers that form a set of three bridges, which were built in the 14th century as ramparts to protect the city. As the name suggests, they were originally covered to protect people in times of siege. Today, the only siege is a commercial one, with travelers enjoying the cobblestone streets and the giftshop owners displaying some of Alsace's finest, particularly during the festive Christmas season, perhaps the best time of all to visit Strasbourg.

4. Drinks at Les Berthom Strasbourg

18 Rue des Tonneliers; tel. 03 88 32 81 18; www.lesberthom.com; 5pm-midnight Sun.-Mon., 5pm-1:30am Tues.-Thurs., 5pm-2:30am Fri., 3pm-2:30am Sat.; €8

Belly up to the bar, or rather, the Stammtisch in the local lingo, and sample some of the finest local beers from the Alsace region in this microbrewery.

Munich, Germany

Where to Stay: Near Munich Central Station

Arrive by: Train from Gare de Strasbourg to Munich Central Station via Stuttgart (4 hours without sightseeing in Stuttgart)

DAY 3

1. Stop in Stuttgart

You will change trains in Stuttgart, so why not spend a couple of hours to check it out? This little-visited German town has a surprising amount to offer. In an hour, you can see a few sights in the old city right near the train station—just head south. Highlights include the Palace Square, where you will see the baroque New Palace, reminiscent of the Louvre, while a stroll through the Oberer Palace Gardens isn't complete without a selfie by the Schicksalsbrunnen Fountain.

When you get hungry, enjoy local Swabian cuisine full of rustic, rich, hearty favorites at **Wirtshaus Lautenschlager** (Lautenschlagerstraße 24; tel. 0711 252 412 60; www.wirtshaus-lautenschlager.de; 11:30am-11pm Sun.-Thurs., 11:30am-1pm Fri.-Sat.; €20). Dig into fresh egg pastas, like spätzle noodles and maultaschen dumpling wrappers. On warm days, the fresh lemonade in the upstairs terrace can't be beat. Then, board the next train to Munich.

★ 2. Hofbräuhaus

Platzl 9; tel. 089 290 136 100; www.hofbraeuhaus.de/de/hofbraeuhaus.html; 9am-midnight daily; €20

If you took some time to explore Stuttgart, you'll probably arrive in Munich a

left, Stuttgart; right, Hofbräuhaus

TO TAKE Home

A traditional **beer stein** (or variously "humpen," "steinkrug," or "seidl" in the local lingua franca, er, Deutsch) is a beautifully crafted, artisanal thing of Bavarian beauty, whether you are fan of ales and lagers, or just like pretty things. However, finding the perfect stein is something of an art in and of itself.

Beer steins are generally cylindrical, though they do come in more rounded shapes. They could be made of clay, glass, or porcelain, with strong handles—you need a strong handle when gripping a liter or more of your favorite beer. One of the biggest steins hold over 32 liters (8 gallons) of ale. The best ones are hand-painted, often with tin or brass decorative elements and reliefs.

One of the better places to choose your own stein is the **Hofbräuhaus** tavern (page 608), which sells a variety of authentic steins and is popular with tourists and locals alike. In fact, many locals choose to purchase their steins here, where they are stored in the tavern for regular use. It is a custom hundreds of years old.

little too late to go into any sights, but you can strike out on foot to explore the **Old Town,** about a 15-minute walk from the station. At dinnertime, head to Hofbräuhaus. Experience the cradle of Bavarian tavern culture and genuine gemütlichkeit (warm friendliness) in the world's most famous tavern. This three-story beer hall is a true institution. In fact, groups of friends have regular tables that they visit daily. The oldest such table has been held for 70 years now! Hundreds of personal beer steins and mugs of regulars are held in the safe. Expect local music and dancing, a great night out filled with more than the occasional "prost!"

If you went straight to Munich without stopping for a few hours in Stuttgart, head up to **Alte Pinakothek Museum** (Barer Str. 27; tel. 089 23805 216; www.pinakothek.de; 10am-8:30pm Tues.-Wed., 10am-6pm Thurs.-Sun.; €7) before dinner. This world-class museum holds 700 works spanning greats from Raphael and Leonardo da Vinci to Titian, Dürer, El Greco, and so many others.

DAY 4

1. Dachau Concentration Camp

Alte Römerstraße 75, Dachau; tel. 08131 66 99 70; www.kz-gedenkstaette-dachau.de; 9am-5pm daily; free

Pay your respects at the Dachau Concentration Camp while standing witness to one of the darkest periods in human history: the Holocaust. To get to Dachau, take the S2 train from Munich to Dachau (25 minutes). Disembark at Dachau and take the 726 bus in the direction of Saubachsiedlung (7 minutes). Get off at Dachau KZ-Gedenkstätte and walk the last couple of minutes to the camp.

It's best to purchase a day pass from the MVV München website (www.mvv-muenchen.de; €9.30) from Zone M1, which will allow you round-trip access on the train from Munich as well as the bus in Dachau. English-language guided tours are given twice daily (11am and 1pm; 2.5 hours; €4, reservations required) and highly recommended. On a guided tour, you receive necessary insight to this chilling, heartbreaking moment in time.

2. Munich Farmers Market

Viktualienmarkt 3; tel. 089 89068205; open 24 hours; free

Head back to Munich the same way you arrived (via the 726 toward Dachau and then the S2 train to München) and flock into the Viktualienmarkt. This 200-year-old farmers market is popular with both locals and travelers alike. There are over 100 stalls for you to sample an array of local specialties, from hearty soups to steaming pretzels, and wash it all down with a lager (of course!). You can even pick up a bouquet of fresh-cut flowers for that special someone. Spend the best part of the afternoon here, hobnobbing, people-watching, snacking, and meandering through one of the more mesmerizing neighborhoods in Munich.

top, Munich Residence; bottom, Marienplatz

3. Munich Residence

Residenzstraße 1; tel. 089 290671; www.residenz-muenchen.de; 9am-6pm Apr. 1-Oct. 15, 10am-5pm Oct. 16-Mar.; €9

Spend the rest of the day at the palatial Munich Residence. Use the free audio guide to make the most of your tour of this largest of museum complexes in Bavaria. The art collection spans from the Renaissance, into the baroque, rococo, and neoclassical, though what is perhaps most impressive is the extensive Antequarium, an ornate Renaissance hall, built by Duke Albrecht V from 1568 to 1571 to house his collection of antique sculptures.

End the day with dinner of heaping plates of classic German food at **Nuernberger Bratwurst Gloeckl am Dom** (Frauenplatz 9; tel. 089 2919450; www.bratwurst-gloeckl.de; 10am-8:30pm Tues.-Wed., 10am-6pm Thurs.-Sun.; €20). Sausages are served with your choice of side dish: sauerkraut, horseradish, or potato salad.

DAY 5 MORNING

1. Marienplatz and Rathaus Glockenspiel

Marienplatz 8; tel. 089 23300155; open 24 hours; free

Before leaving for Vienna, stop in Marienplatz, the town square, a vibrant, pedestrian-only zone full of shops and wonderful old-world architecture. Pay special attention to the Gothic town hall and the famous Rathaus Glockenspiel, a relatively new addition to the town square, built in 1908, but one of Munich's most lighthearted attractions. Get here a little before 11am for a bit of glockenspiel gawking as the daily 15-minute performance begins.

The performance is divided into two halves on the glockenspiel, the total of which involves 43 bells and 32 life-size figures reenacting two stories of Bavarian lore. The top half tells the tale of the eye-wateringly expensive 1568 marriage of the Bavarian Duke Wilhelm V to Renata of Lorraine that lasted for 18 days; while the bottom half tells the story of the 16th-century plague and how the barrel makers jolly dance—the Schäfferstanz, thought to be the last original guild dance of Germany—brought people joy. The daily song ends with a golden rooster quickly chirping three times to signal the end.

Vienna, Austria

Where to Stay: Historic Center or the Hofburg area

Arrive by: Train from Munich Central Station to Vienna Westbahnhof station (4 hours)

DAY 5 EVENING

From Munich to Vienna, opt for the private **West Bahn** double-decker trains over those run by the state operator, OBB. If you stay to watch the glockenspiel performance, you'll likely arrive in Vienna in the late afternoon or evening. If you need a bite to eat when you reach Vienna, try **Café Heuer** (Treitlstraße 2; tel. 01 8900590; www.heuer-amkarlsplatz.com; 11:30am-1am Tues.-Sat.; €25). Locally sourced legumes and carefully selected viands are crafted in true Viennese fashion. Meat lovers will want to try the Viennese-style fried chicken. Following dinner, hang out in the vibrant beer garden and soak in the nightlife.

DAYS 6-7

Spend two days in Vienna taking in grand palaces, engrossing museums, and, of course, the classical music the city is known for by following the itinerary in **Prague, Vienna, and Budapest** (page 184).

Hofburg, Vienna

(top to bottom) Liberty Bridge, Budapest; Hungarian Parliament, Budapest; Village Museum, Bucharest; Romanian Athenaeum, Budapest

Budapest, Hungary

Where to Stay: Jewish Quarter or Inner City

Arrive by: Train from Vienna's Wien Hauptbahnhof to Budapest Keleti (2.5-3 hours)

DAYS 8-9

The next stop on your eastward journey is Budapest. You'll find yourself going back and forth across the Danube as you follow the recommendations in **Prague, Vienna, and Budapest** (page 184). At the end of your second day, board the overnight train to Bucharest.

Bucharest, Romania

Where to Stay: On or around Victory Avenue

Arrive by: Overnight train from Budapest Keleti to Gara de Nord in Bucharest (15-20 hours)

DAY 10

★ 1. Victory Avenue

Calea Victorei; open 24 hours; free

Arrive in Bucharest around midday. After storing your luggage at your hotel, savor your own personal victory for having followed the Orient Express all the way to the "Paris of the East" with a visit to Bucharest's answer to the Champs Élysées. A visit to Bucharest isn't complete without a stroll down this grand boulevard, which features lots of baroque architecture dotted with little museums, quaint parks, Orthodox churches, and high-end shops with the latest fashions imported from Paris.

Romanian Cuisine

Romanians have two sayings related to their cuisine: "The best fish is pork" and "The best vegetable is meat." Vegetarians beware. Like much of the Balkan region, the Romanian diet is meat-heavy. Here are a few traditional specialties to try when you're in Bucharest.

- **Chiftele:** Also called "parjoale," these are authentic Romanian meatballs.
- **Mamliga:** Though it's known as the "dish of Romania," you likely know this by another name: polenta, a combination of cornmeal mush and butter.
- **Mucenici:** Served in homes throughout the country on March 9 for the orthodox Christian celebration of the Feast of the 40 Martyrs, this is an amazingly vegan-friendly dish that is half pasta, half soup, with a savory-sweet taste filled with walnuts and a touch of sugar.
- **Sarmale:** Grilled meat wrapped in cabbage; it is usually served with polenta, cream, and chili pepper.
- **Shepard's Bulz:** Grilled or pan-friend polenta is stuffed with butter and sheep cheese and rolled into balls, often topped with ham or bacon. And yes, Bulz means exactly what you think it means.
- **Zacusca:** This eggplant and red pepper dip has loads of paprika goodness.
- **Papanasi:** Either fried or boiled, these cheese-stuffed donuts are topped with jam and smetana, a type of local cream cheese that is lower in fat content than the cream cheese eaten in the United States.

2. Dinner at Caru' cu Bere

Strada Stavropoleos 5; tel. 726 282 373; www.carucubere.ro; 9am-midnight Sun.-Thurs., 9am-2am Fri.-Sat.; 70 Lei

If you only have one night in Bucharest, this is the place to be. The "Beer Wagon" has been serving up traditional Romanian food and drinks for over 130 years. On a hot summer night, cool down on the patio with a fresh draft of the house beer. For dinner: slow-roasted pork knuckle with braised cabbage and grilled minced-meat rolls. With dinner there is nearly always music and dancing, making this a festive night.

ADDING ON Istanbul

Time allowing, take the Orient Express all the way to its terminus: Istanbul, where East meet West. A riotous cacophony of bazaars is set against a backdrop rich with history. Once in Istanbul, you can decide whether to spend a couple of days or slow it down and spend a couple of weeks! Must-see sights include:

GRAND BAZAAR (KAPALI ÇARŞI)

Near Beyazit, Sirkeci, or Üniversite tram stops

The Kapalı Çarşı is a mind-boggling collection of over 4,000 businesses. Souvenirs, leather, jewelry, clothing, carpets, copper, and anything else that might interest tourists can be found here. Roughly 65 pedestrian streets traverse this domed structure, which is accessed through 22 gates.

TOPKAPI PALACE (TOPKAPI SARAYI)

Sultanahmet, Eminönü; tel. 0212 512-0480; 9am-6pm Wed.-Mon.; 320TL

Serving as the seat of the Ottoman government, the imperial residence, and as the location of the Sultan's legendary harem, the ornate Topkapı Palace housed more than 4,000 people in its heyday. Now a museum, it contains one of the rarest collections of porcelain, as well as the mythic 86-carat Spoonmaker's Diamond.

HAGIA SOPHIA (AYASOFYA)

Sultanahmet Square; tel. 0212 522-1750; open 24 hours; free

The Ayasofya was commissioned by Emperor Justinian I in the 6th century as a means to establish his claim to the imperial throne of Byzantium. The basilica remains to this day one of the largest testaments of faith and architectural might on the globe—it's a UNESCO World Heritage Site and almost made the list for the New Seven Wonders of the World.

DAY 11

1. Parliament Palace

Strada Izvor 2-4; tel. 733 558 102; http://cic.cdep.ro; 9am-5pm daily Mar.-Oct., 10am-4pm Nov.-Feb.; 40 Lei

If you were to summarize this palace in a single word, it would be "immense." The Guinness Book of World Records lists this structure as the largest, most expensive, and heaviest administrative building on the entire planet. Though it looks very old-world, in truth this was built in 1984 while Romania was under communist rule. Because of this, most Romanians disdain this building for its communist symbolism, though this is undeniably the single biggest tourist draw to the city. Remember to bring your passport for admittance.

For lunch, walk over to **Hanu' Beralilor Casa Oprea Soare** (Strada Poenaru Bordea 2; tel. 729 400 800; https://hanuberarilor.ro; 8am-11pm Sun.-Wed., 8am-midnight Thurs.-Sat.; 50 Lei), about 20 minutes from the Parliament building. Try some Romanian classics, like pork ciobara and mici, while the papansi pairs splendidly with a pint of the local lager, Ursus.

2. Village Museum

Şoseaua Pavel D. Kiseleff 28-30; tel. 213 179 103; http://muzeul-satului.ro; 10am-6pm daily; 20 Lei

Step back in time at the quaint Village Museum in the King Mihai I Park (about 30 minutes by bus from the restaurant). Here you will see the regional specialties of Romania from the different towns and

BLUE MOSQUE (SULTANAHMET CAMII)

Sultanahmet Square; www.sultanahmetcamii.org; 8:30am-one hour before dusk, closed for 90 minutes of prayer time Sat.-Mon., closed 2 hours during Fri. noon prayers; free

Completed in 1617, this mosque was commissioned by Sultan Ahmet in an effort to outdo the Ayasofya. It's widely considered to be the epitome of Byzantine and Ottoman mixed architecture. Light from the 260 glass windows floods the cavernous space and bounces off more than 21,000 hand-painted blue Iznik tiles to create a bluish haze, hence its nickname.

GETTING THERE

From the Bucharest Gara de Nord station, the train continues on to Istanbul. The daily overnight train run by **Bosphorus Express** departs at 11pm with tickets starting around €50. However, the train does not feel quite express at a run time of 18.5 hours. Book your tickets online with Romania's national rail service, **CFR** (www.cfrcalatori.ro). Choose "Halkali" as your destination.

You will arrive to Istanbul at the **Istanbul Halkali Station,** about 25 km (15 mi) outside of central Istanbul. From Halkali, you connect with the city center by the suburban train (about 30 minutes). Trains from Halkali leave for Istanbul about every 15 minutes and cost around €2.

To return home, fly out of **Istanbul Airport** (www.istairport.com), located a 30- to 45-minute drive from the city center. Buses and shuttles, as well as taxis, connect the airport and the city.

villages dotting the countryside. They are all brought together here in a celebration that is as popular with the locals as it is with visitors. Over 300 houses, annexes, churches, and other installations feature a rich array of pottery, textiles, furniture, and other artisanal objects from around the country.

3. Romanian Athenaeum

1, Strada Benjamin Franklin 1-3; tel. 213 152 567; http://fge.org.ro; hours vary; free

Don't miss out on the spectacular Romanian Athenaeum, perhaps Bucharest's most beautiful neoclassical building. Built in the late 19th century, the concert hall is today home to the George Enescu Philharmonic Orchestra—fitting, as this was the place where George Enescu first performed his seminal Romanian Rhapsody in 1903. In the Big Hall, there is an impressive fresco by Costin Petrescu depicting scenes from the history of Romania. Try to see a performance here—a lovely way to end your epic trip.

TRANSPORTATION

Air

Paris

Paris is served by two major international airports.

- **Charles de Gaulle** (Roissy-en-France; tel. 33 1 7036 3950; www.parisaeroport.fr/roissy-charles-de-gaulle) is 35 km (22 mi) north of the city and well-connected with the city center by the RER train, bus, and

WATCH

Before Sunrise: This 1995 romantic drama follows follow Jesse (Ethan Hawke) and Céline (Julie Delpy) on a Eurail train to Vienna. They spend a fateful night together, with Vienna taking center stage throughout. This is the first installment of the *Before* trilogy; the second, *Before Sunset,* takes place in Paris, while the third, *Before Midnight,* takes us to the Greek islands.

READ

Black Girl in Paris by Shay Youngblood is the story of a young Black girl from Alabama who travels to Paris to follow in the steps of the American writer James Baldwin.

European Rail Timetable (ERT): Published every 2-3 months since 1872, this is a must read for train enthusiasts. Find print and digital editions on the European Rail Timetable website: www.europeanrailtimetable.eu.

Murder on the Orient Express by Agatha Christie: A detective fiction classic unfolds on the Orient Express train as it is lodged in a snowstorm in Eastern Europe, unable to budge, trapping all the passengers onboard when the murder happens. Not to worry, Detective Hercule Poirot is on the case.

LISTEN

"First Paris-Istanbul Run of the Orient Express" on ***This Day in History Class*** with host Tracey V. Wilson: This short podcast tells the story of this first historic journey (https://omny.fm/shows/this-day-in-history-class/first-paris-istanbul-run-of-the-orient-express-oct).

taxi. Most flights from North America connect with Charles de Gaulle.

- **Paris Orly** (Orly; tel. 0 892 56 39 50; www.parisaeroport.fr/orly) is 20 km (12 mi) south of the city and, like Charles de Gaulle, well-connected with the city center. Flights from around Europe often connect here.

Bucharest

To do this trip in the opposite direction, fly into Bucharest.

- **Henri Coanda International Airport** (Calea Bucurestilor nr. 224 E; tel. 212 041 000; www.bucharestairports.ro), commonly known as the Otopeni Airport, is connected by bus, taxi, and rail. The **780 Express Bus** (24/7, every 40 minutes at night; magnetic card 7 Lei, good for one round-trip) connects the airport with the Gara de Nord train station while the **783 Express Bus** connects with the city center. The **train** (24/7, runs every 40 minutes at night; www.cfr.ro; 7.7 Lei) connects Henri Coandă Airport and the Gara de Nord in 20 minutes.

Other Cities

Major airports are also found in **Munich** (page 319), **Vienna** (page 203), and **Budapest** (page 203).

Train

Each country has its own rail network. Purchasing the **Eurail Pass** is the easy way of using the trains throughout Europe. If you plan in advance, purchasing point-to-point tickets can often be less expensive; however, you will be tied into specific departure times.

Paris and Strasbourg

In France, you will use the **TGV** (www.sncf-connect.com; 10 or more trains daily), France's storied high-speed train operator. The TGV connects from Paris through Strasbourg and to Stuttgart. Trains to Strasbourg leave Paris from the **Gare de l'Est** train station (Rue du 8 Mai 1945; www.garesetconnexions.sncf/fr/gare/frpst/paris-est; multiple trains daily; 2 hours; €110), located about 20 minutes northeast of the Louvre by Metro. In Strasbourg, trains arrive at and leave from the **Gare de Strasbourg** (Pl. de la Gare), just west of Grand-Île and a 20-minute walk to the Cathedral.

Stuttgart and Munich

German trains are run by **DB** (www.bahn.de; 20 or more trains daily), where you can purchase a ticket easily. From Strasbourg, this itinerary suggests heading to Munich via Stuttgart (3 trains daily; 4 hours without sightseeing in Stuttgart; €80-140). **Stuttgart Central Station** (Arnulf-Klett-Platz 2; www.bahnhof.de/bahnhof-de/bahnhof/Stuttgart-Hbf-1038338) is located close to the major sights, and you'll arrive at **Munich Central Station** (Bayerstraße 10A; tel. 1806996633; www.bahnhof.de/bahnhof-de/bahnhof/M-C3-BCnchen-Hbf), west of Old Town and a 20-minute walk to Marienplatz.

Vienna

From Munich to Vienna, the double-decker trains run by the private firm **West Bahn** (https://westbahn.at; 4 daily trains) often make more travel sense than those run by the state operator, **OBB** (www.oebb.at; 10 or more trains daily), particularly if you are purchasing tickets for point-to-point travel. In Vienna, trains arrive to the **Wien Westbahnhof** train station (Europaplatz 2/3; www.bahnhof-citywienwest.at; 4 hours; €40-61), about 10 minutes west of the historic center by subway. Note: When searching for tickets to Vienna, it helps to know that the Austrian name of Vienna is "Wien."

Budapest

Departing from Vienna, **Railjet** (www.railjets.com; 4 daily trains) and **Regiojet** (https://novy.regiojet.cz; 4 daily trains) offer high-speed rail service into Budapest. From Vienna, you embark at the **Vienna Central Train Station** (Am Hbf 1; www.oebb.at). You will arrive to Budapest at either the **Budapest-Kelenföld** (Budapest, Péterhegyi út 5; www.mavcsoport.hu/mav-start/belfoldi-utazas/vasutallomas/budapest-kelenfold), which is a bit outside of the city center, or the **Budapest-Keleti** (Budapest, Kerepesi út 2-4; www.mavcsoport.hu; 2.5-3 hours; €13-30), which is more central.

Bucharest

From Budapest to Bucharest, you will want to take the overnight train operated by **CFR** (www.cfrcalatori.ro; 5 or more daily trains; €30-40) as this is an unavoidable 15- to 20-hour slow train ride. Trains leaves from the Budapest-Keleti train station and arrive to the **Gara de Nord** (www.metrorex.ro) in Bucharest. Note: You leave the Schengen area on the crossing into Romania. Expect the train to stop for about an hour while a customs officer boards the train and walks through the cars to scan passengers' passports.

Getting Back

To get back to Paris, head to Bucharest's **Henri Coanda International Airport,** which has daily direct flights to the French capital. There are also flights to other European cities, where you can connect to a flight back home.

CONNECT WITH

- London and Paris (page 44)
- Romantische Strasse (page 307)
- Transylvania (page 320)
- Rhine River Cruise (page 503)

THE RHONE VALLEY

Why Go: Some of the best food on Earth, well-preserved sites from antiquity, sunshine, and wine: All of this is linked by France's broad and beautiful Rhone River.

Number of Days: 6

Total Distance: 375 km (230 mi)

Seasons: Spring and fall

Start: Lyon

End: Marseille

Among the continent's mightiest rivers, the Rhone has been a great highway of European culture and trade since ancient times, bringing Greek learning in from the coast to touch the Celtic interior. Countless layers of history have formed the towns that cling to its banks, and the swath it cuts through the natural landscape is regal and dramatic. It makes a perfect route along which to build a journey, from the reserved gastronomic mecca of Lyon down through the bucolic beauty of Provence to the shabby coastal ebullience of Marseilles, passing olive groves, Roman ruins, and dramatic gorges in between.

TOP 3

Feasting on the **gastronomy of Lyon,** the cradle of French cuisine (page 623).

Delving into the story of the Avignon Papacy amid impressive Gothic architecture and intricate frescoes at the **Palais des Papes** (page 626).

Watching for wildlife on a **safari tour of the Camargue,** the marshy wetlands formed where the Rhone meets the sea (page 630).

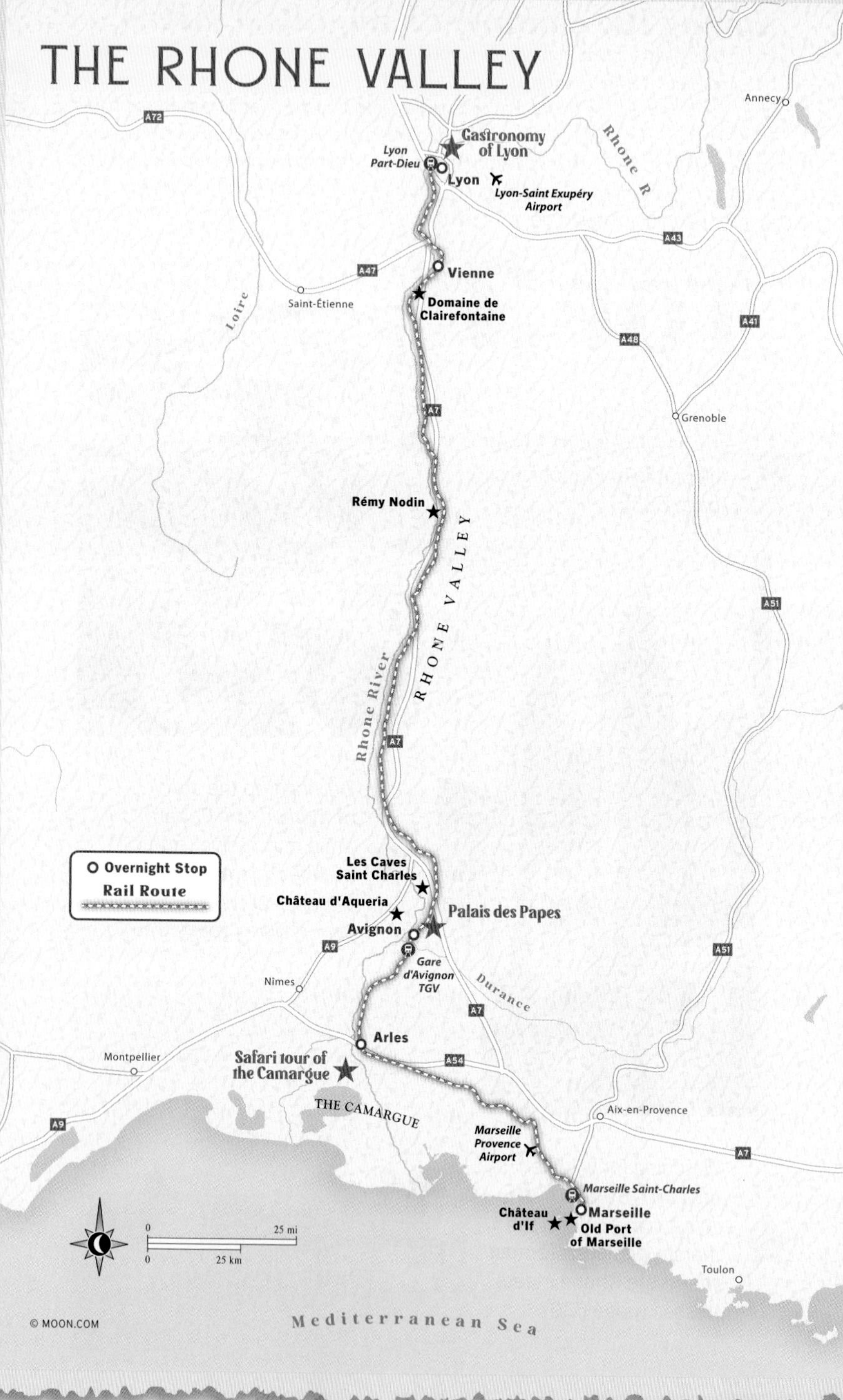
THE RHONE VALLEY
A72
Gastronomy of Lyon
Lyon Part-Dieu
Lyon
Lyon-Saint Exupéry Airport
Annecy
Rhone R
A43
A47
Vienne
Saint-Étienne
Domaine de Clairefontaine
Loire
A41
A48
A7
Grenoble
Rémy Nodin
RHONE VALLEY
A51
Rhone River
A7
Overnight Stop
Rail Route
Les Caves Saint Charles
Château d'Aqueria
Palais des Papes
Avignon
A9
Gare d'Avignon TGV
Nimes
Durance
A51
A7
Arles
Montpellier
Safari tour of the Camargue
A54
THE CAMARGUE
A9
Aix-en-Provence
Marseille Provence Airport
A7
Marseille Saint-Charles
Château d'If
Marseille
Old Port of Marseille
0
25 mi
0
25 km
Toulon
© MOON.COM
Mediterranean Sea

DAY 1

Lyon

Where to Stay: Presqu'Ile to be close to the main sights and shops

Arrive by: Plane to Lyon-Saint Exupéry Airport or train to Lyon Part Dieu

There are many things to recommend Lyon—its refined Old Town, its handsome museums, its 2,000 years of history—but the primary concern of any sensible visitor to France's third largest city should be its food.

1. Machon at Le Meunière

11 Rue Neuve; tel. 04 78 28 62 91; www.lameuniere.fr; noon-2pm and 7:30pm-9:30pm Tues.-Sat., machon 9am Tues.-Sat.; from €20

Established by the city's silk workers who would gather either before or after their grueling shifts, machon is not for the fainthearted, consisting of cottage cheese, beef tripe, and pork scratchings, washed down by a couple of glasses of light red wine (yes, for breakfast; welcome to France!). Still very much practiced by locals, this ancient Lyonnaise breakfast tradition will help you hit the gastronomic ground running. Hard. Le Meunière is one of the few bouchons (simple restaurants serving workers) in the city that offers it most mornings; book in advance.

2. Musée des Beaux Arts

20 Pl. des Terreaux; tel. 04 72 10 17 40; www.mba-lyon.fr; 10am-6pm Wed.-Mon.; adults €8, ages 18-26 €4, under 18 free

Don't tell the Parisians, but this may actually be the single best museum in France. Just a short walk north of Le Meunière, its collection is rich and varied, with works by the likes of Monet, Van Gogh, and Picasso, as well as sarcophagi from ancient Egypt and statuary from ancient Athens, but it's also not so impossibly vast that you can't get a decent feeling for it within the space of a 3-4-hour visit.

For lunch (if you're even hungry after the machon), grab a sandwich at **Gourmix** (112 Cr Charlemagne; tel. 04 78 92 57 52; www.facebook.com/GourmixLyon;

left, Musée des Beaux Arts, Lyon; right, Lyon's Old Town

Key Reservations

- **Restaurants:** Make reservations at Le Meunière in Lyon and the restaurants by chef Jean-Luc Rabanel in Arles.
- **Tours:** The Safaris Camargues Alpilles tours are by advance reservation only.

the Camargue

11:30am-3pm and 6:30pm-10pm Mon.-Sat.; menus from €10). They sell slider-sized sandwiches stuffed with locally sourced filling, from fresh veggies if you're feeling healthy to foie gras if you're not.

3. Traboules of Old Town

Head west over the **Pont de la Feuillée,** crossing not the Rhone but the river that connects with it here, La Saône. This will take you into Lyon's Old Town, a Renaissance-era district famous for its cobbled streets, terracotta-tiled roofs, and most of all, its courtyards and the covered passageways between them known as traboules. **Rue Saint-Jean** is the old town's main thoroughfare, linking Place du Change with Place Saint-Jean. The traboules, once used by silk merchants as shortcuts to move their heavy wares around the city, honeycomb the surrounding buildings. There are said to be more than 400 in total, though only 40 are open to the public. The longest stretches from 54 Rue Saint-Jean and tunnels through four houses to 27 Rue du Bœuf and is a good place to start exploring. To spot this one, and others, look for lion's head signs, which mark traboules' openings.

4. Dinner at Café des Fédérations

9 Rue Major Martin; tel. 04 78 28 26 00; https://restaurant-cafedesfederations-lyon.fr; noon-2pm and 7pm-9:30pm Mon.-Sat., noon-2pm Sun.; menu €29

After a quick trip back to your hotel to refresh, head out again for what will almost certainly be one of the highlights of your trip: dinner at Café des Fédérations, a Lyon institution. From the wood paneling of its exterior to its red gingham napkins, the whole place positively exhales authenticity—and the food! It's rich, copious, and sure to reward the adventurous diner. Try the tête de veau; seriously, you won't believe cow's head could ever taste so good.

The Gastronomic Capital of France

From butter-sautéed potatoes to lovingly cured sausages, viscous wines, and angelic desserts, Lyon has been building its gastronomic reputation for at least 500 years and is the best place to eat anywhere on Earth. The first thing you should do on getting here is loosen your belt!

In France, Lyon is located at the crossroads between north and south, between butter and olive oil, cream and tomato, grape and grain. And more than that, it's on the confluence of two major European rivers, a trading hub and a bottleneck of flavors since its very founding. Add to that, the almost uncanny abundance of its surrounding farmland—from the chickens of Bresse to the vineyards of Burgundy—and you start to get an idea of why Lyon's kitchens seem of an otherworldly quality.

★ LYONNAISE SPECIALTIES

To sample the richness of Lyonnaise cuisine, try some of these specialties—and be sure to wash it all back with a few glasses of Burgundy wine!

- **Lyonnaise potatoes:** potatoes pan fried with onions, butter and parsley
- **Pike quenelle:** a lightly set dumpling of creamed fish
- **Paté en croute:** paté in pastry
- **Rosette de Lyon:** a kind of dried sausage
- **Grenouilles à la Lyonnaise:** frogs' legs fried with onions, butter, and parsley
- **Gras-double:** tripe cooked with onions

DAY 2

Lyon

1. St. Antoine Market

Quai Saint-Antoine; 6am-1pm daily

Before starting your journey down the Rhone, check out Lyon's largest outdoor food market on the banks of the River Saône. A fantastic bazaar of regional delights, it's a great place for tourists to explore, as well as a thriving, practical part of the city. Gourmet options abound as do hot food stalls, making it great for a morning snack and for stocking up for a picnic later in the day.

St. Antoine Market

(top to bottom) Vienne; Temple of Augustus and Livia; Abbaye de Saint-André-le-Bas

Vienne

Where to Stay: Near the city center, or at a hotel in the countryside like Domaine de Clairefontaine

Arrive by: Train from Lyon Part Dieu to Vienne train station (20 minutes)

Hop on the train down to the ancient commune of Vienne, less than 40 km (25 mi) south of Lyon. Once the capital of the Gallic Allobroges people, it later became a major hub for the Roman Empire and remains festooned with an embarrassment of ruins.

2. Picnic in the Jardin de Ville

10B Boulevard Asiaticus; tel. 04 74 78 30 00; 9am-5pm Mon.-Sat., 9am-6pm Sun.; free

If you've managed to hold off snacking on your market haul so far, Vienne's Jardin de Ville offers a great spot for a picnic. Less than 183 m (600 ft) from the train station, it's a smartly maintained green space that incorporates some of the town's Roman ruins as part of its decoration.

3. Walking Tour of Vienne

https://guideprovence.net/activities/vienne-guided-tour; €150 per group (up to 30 people)

Vienne is overflowing with history; get the most out of its important sights by booking a private walking tour. During a two-hour tour, your guide will explain the story behind locations like the stunning Roman **Temple of Augustus and Livia,** the amphitheater (which still hosts select concerts), the circus, and the **Abbaye de Saint-André-le-Bas,** among others. Even better, you can time the tour to end just in time for aperitif.

4. Domaine de Clairefontaine

105 Chemin des Fontanettes, Chonas-l'Amballan; tel. 04 74 58 81 52; domaine-de-clairefontaine.fr; from €61 per night

Take a taxi to this hotel and restaurant complex in the countryside just beyond Vienne's limits. With the oldest parts of its main building constructed in the 17th century, this is a great place to relax after

Rhone Valley Wineries

The second largest wine producing region in France, the Rhone Valley (at least in its south) has produced grapes since at least the 4th century BCE. It's a region of two distinct characters, with the granite of the north limiting growers to just one grape variety (Syrah), while the limestone of the south allows for a much wider variation. That said, the climate is broadly similar throughout—dry, hot, and often windy—and there is a prevailing belief in the unity of the region, which leads people to regard all its wines as sharing a particular essence.

As a general rule, due to the hot climate, Rhone Valley wines tend to possess concentrated fruity flavors reminiscent of New World wines and that are currently popular in the English-speaking world. A trip to any vineyard for a tasting and a tour is always a rewarding experience. The region around Lyon has only a few options. Farther south there's a whole glut of vineyards with open doors; check out www.ruedesvignerons.com to see which one best suits you. Make sure to book ahead for any of these experiences, and it goes without saying, but if you are going to enjoy one of the free tastings, be prepared to buy a few bottles when it's done.

NEAR LYON

- The family-run organic wine estate **Rémy Nodin** (Domaine La Beylesse, 1 Av. du 8 Mai, Saint-Péray; tel. 04 75 40 35 90; www.remy-nodin.fr; 10am-noon and 2pm-7pm Tues.-Sat.; tastings €15, tours €30) just to the west of Valence is an excellent choice.

NEAR AVIGNON

- One of the most beautiful wineries in the region is the **Château d'Aqueria** (Tavel; tel. 04 66 50 04 56; www.aqueria.com; 8am-12:30pm and 1:30pm-5:30pm Mon., 10am-1pm and 2:30pm-6:30pm Tues.-Sat.; tasting and tours free) not far from Avignon. Founded in 1919 and still run by the same family, this winery offers tasting, tours, and meals from the sumptuous chateau at the center of the estate.
- If you want something high-end, head to the village of Châteauneuf-du-Pape, surrounded by vineyards responsible for the famous label of the same name. **Les Caves Saint Charles** (10 Rue des Papes, Châteauneuf-du-Pape; tel. 04 90 39 13 85; fr.cave-saint-charles.fr; 10am-6pm Mon.-Sat.; tasting free) is one of the best places to sample the elixir. On a visit to this 13th-century cellar, master sommelier Guy Bremond will walk you through some of the best tastings anywhere in France.

a day in the city. There is both food and accommodation here to suit all budgets, with one of the two on-site restaurants boasting a Michelin star—a very different, more refined dining experience than what you have experienced so far.

DAY 3

Avignon

Where to Stay: Within the walls of Avignon's historic center

Arrive by: Train from Vienne train station to Gare d'Avignon Centre (2.5 hours)

Your train ride to Avignon features views of the pastel hills of Provence out in the distance. The seat of the Catholic popes for six turbulent decades in the 14th century, this small town was once a rival to Rome, and its grandeur from those days still dominates its character and skyline.

1. Les Halles Food Market

18 Place Pie; tel. 04 90 27 15 15; www.avignon-leshalles.com; 6am-2pm Tues.-Sat.

This covered market is like a window into the French soul. The pride that each of the market traders takes in the produce and the care with which it is arranged speak to the French people's enduring relationship with the land and their cuisine.

★ 2. Palais des Papes

Place du Palais; tel. 04 32 74 32 74; www.palais-des-papes.com; 10am-6pm daily; adults €12, under 18 €6.50

Following a conflict between the French crown and Rome, the Papal enclave was forcibly moved from the Vatican to Avignon for almost 70 years in the 14th century. Designed to house and protect those who held the position of pope in this time, the Palais des Papes grew into one of the largest, most important examples of Gothic architecture anywhere in the world. Utterly dominating the skyline of Avignon, it's an absolute must-visit, being in the top 10 most popular tourist sites in France. Along with its breathtaking

Palais des Papes

Rhone River Cruises

Another option to get around the Rhone Valley, one that predates cars, trains, or even roads, is to take to the river itself. Experience the landscape as the original inhabitants of the region would have done, enjoying the leisurely unfolding of the riverside scenery, uncluttered by highway modernity, and creeping up slowly on the various ancient towns, allowing them to reveal themselves to you just as they would have in centuries past. The Rhone is far too treacherous a river to navigate alone, but a whole slew of cruise firms offers all-inclusive packages with days in port at towns along the river.

ON THE CRUISE

On these cruises, much of the traveling is done while you sleep in well-appointed cabins, and guided tours are put on at various destinations on the way. There are even vineyard tours on which you are bused away from the river for afternoons of tastings, where there's no concern over who's going to be the designated driver! Two of the biggest players in the river cruise market are **Viking** (www.vikingrivercruises.com) and **CroisiEurope** (www.croisieurope.com), but there are many others.

ITINERARY CHOICES

Once you've chosen a provider, the main choice is which direction you want to go. Cruises run north to south as well as south to north, with the former option marginally more highly recommended—that way you'll be chasing antiquity and the heat. Otherwise, you just have to decide how long you want to be onboard. All cruises cover more or less the same distance—from Lyon down to the Camargue—but some do it with more stops over seven days, and some are three-day trips with fewer stops.

scale, it's also a place of hypnotic artistic detail in its chapel ceilings and frescos. More than anything, though, it's the story of the Avignon Papacy—a tale of feuding kings and the conflict between Earthly and heavenly power—that really gives this vast palace life. Take advantage of the information tablets offered or even book into a guided tour. Expect visits to take around two hours.

3. Pont Saint-Bénézet

Boulevard de la Ligne; tel. 04 32 74 32 74; 10am-6pm daily; €4

Ten minutes down some steps from the Palais des Papes is (probably) the most famous bridge in France. Avignon's Pont Saint-Bénézet was once-upon-a-time (the 12th century) the only bridge spanning the Rhone anywhere south of Lyon, making the town a major medieval transport hub and bringing it plenty of trade, culture, and riches. Today only half the bridge remains, and you can walk out onto it for a small fee to get good views of both the wildlife on the river and the Palais des Papes behind you.

4. Place des Corps Saints

For dinner, there are few better places in town than the shady Place des Corps Saints. Not as touristy as the squares closer to the Palais des Papes, it's characterized by a central fountain and a 14th-century church. It is ringed by several decent restaurants, and **Le Moliere** (68 Place des Corps Saints; tel. 06 74 74 00 53; le-moliere-avignon.business.site; 9am-4pm and 6pm-10pm daily; menus from €14), with its seasonal Mediterranean flavors, is among the best.

DAY 4

Arles

Where to Stay: Historic Center

Arrive by: Train from Avignon Centre to Arles train station (15-20 minutes)

Arles is a laid-back little town with a big history and strong sense of its own identity. The self-described Capital of the Camargue (the beguiling delta-land of the Rhone just to the south) and a longtime refuge for artists, most famously Vincent Van Gogh, is a town with powerful links to its surrounding countryside and a cosmopolitan feel.

1. Les Arènes

1 Rdpt des Arènes; tel. 0 891 70 03 70; www.arenes-arles.com; 9am-6pm; adults €9, reduced €6

Easily Arles' most imposing building and arguably the most important one for understanding the town's history and soul, the Roman arena looms into view just after you've past through the old city walls (themselves, a five-minute walk south from the train station, down the Avenue Paulin Talabot). Once a scene of gladiatorial combat, the 1st century CE building

left, LUMA; right, Les Arènes

NAME CHECK: Vincent Van Gogh

In February 1888 Van Gogh arrived in Arles from Paris, drawn by the clear light and bright colors. He dreamed of living in an artist's commune, and in May he rented the yellow house that was to become the subject of one of his pictures. In October fellow artist Paul Gauguin came to live with him. In December they fought and Van Gogh slashed off his ear. He was then admitted to a hospital in Arles. The people of Arles petitioned to have Van Gogh thrown out of town, and he moved to Saint-Rémy-de-Provence where he entered a mental hospital. There he spent a year before moving to Auvers-sur-Oise outside Paris, where he shot himself.

During this time in Provence, Van Gogh painted 350 works. *The Night Café, Sunflowers,* and *Yellow House* are just three of the works that changed the art world forever. Though the people of Arles once kicked Van Gogh out of town, they are proud of him now. The artist's legacy can be seen all over the area, not to mention throughout France:

- **Fondation Van Gogh** (35 rue du Dr Fanton, Arles; tel. 04 90 93 08 08; www.fondation-vincentvangogh-arles.org; 11am-6pm Tues.-Sun.; €9, reduced €7, ages 12-18 €4): Founded in the spirit of the artist's desire to create an artistic community, this old hôtel particulier usually has a few Van Gogh originals on display.
- **Le Café Van Gogh:** This café, though not necessarily a culinary highlight of Arles, is featured in *Café Terrace at Night* (page 630).
- **Van Gogh Walking Tour:** Follow signposts throughout Arles marking the spots where 10 seminal paintings were completed (page 630).
- **Musée des Beaux Arts, Lyon:** Like many major art museums, Lyon's fine arts museum displays some of Van Gogh's works (page 621).

was requisitioned as a fortress during the Dark Ages but has since been restored to accommodate something approximating its original purpose, hosting bullfights and other seemingly anachronistic events throughout the year. Even when there's no event taking place, walking its cavernous hallways and looking on the spooky wide expanse of its sands offers an uncanny window into history. Visits shouldn't last much more than an hour.

2. Lunch in the Parc des Ateliers

35 Avenue Victor Hugo; tel. 04 65 88 10 00; www.luma.org/en/arles/visit-us/eating-and-drinking-on-the-parc-des-ateliers.html; 10am-6pm Wed.-Mon.; free

Try not to get too distracted by the other Roman and medieval architecture as you wander the 15 minutes to the other side of Arles where the LUMA and its adjoining Parc des Ateliers awaits. It ought to be time to grab lunch in the latter, a garden landscaped in postmodern styles, now home to the workshops of numerous visiting artists and rotating exhibition halls accessible with tickets to the LUMA. There are four eateries to choose from at various price points, each serving modern takes on Italian and/or local cuisine.

3. LUMA

35 Avenue Victor Hugo; tel. 04 65 88 10 00; www.luma.org; 10am-6pm Wed.-Mon. 10am-6pm; free

Founded in 2013 by a Swiss billionaire, housed in a building designed by

Café Van Gogh

star-architect Frank Gehry, and home to an impressive collection of contemporary art, the LUMA is easily the most important thing to happen to Arles' art scene since Van Gogh decided he liked the look of the night sky here over the Rhone. It's a great place to get lost for a couple of hours, with a particular highlight being Christian Marclay's *The Clock*, a film installation guaranteed to move even the most cynical critics of contemporary art.

4. Le Café Van Gogh

11 Place du Forum; www.restaurant-cafe-van-gogh-arles.fr; 9am-midnight daily; pastis €4

Instantly recognizable from one of Van Gogh's most famous paintings, the café on Arles' Place du Forum is still going strong. A bit overpriced when it comes to eating, it remains an excellent, atmospheric terrace where you can enjoy an aperitif before heading on to one of the better, albeit not immortalized, restaurants nearby, like **Galoubet** (18 Rue du Docteur Fanton; tel. 04 90 93 18 11; noon-2:30pm and 7:30pm-9:30pm Tues.-Sat.; €16-22), a cozy bistro featuring local classics prepared using seasonal ingredients.

DAY 5

Day Trip to the Camargue

Land of white horses, black bulls, and pink flamingos, the Camargue is where the Rhone fractures into a delta and finally makes its way into the sea. It's also one of the most enchanting, mysterious landscapes anywhere in Europe, characterized, by its colorful wildlife, windswept vastness, and unique local culture. With its salty wind and large resident population of mosquitos, don't mistake it for a seaside resort (which some of the tourist industry in its towns pretends it is), though it makes a great day trip from Arles.

★ 1. Safaris Camargues Alpilles

Pickup point outside Arles Tourist Office, 9 Boulevard des Lices, Arles; tel. 04 90 93 60 31; www.camargue.com; €40

The Camargue covers 930 sq km (359 sq mi), one-third of which is marshland or inland water. Various companies offer educational safaris that take you in an open-topped Land Rover into the undiscovered Camargue for a couple of hours or a whole day. You'll enjoy wildlife spotting (bulls, horses, and flamingos) as well as an excellent introduction to the culture of the Camargue, from rice growing to bull herding. It is simply the best way to gain insight into the Camargue in a short amount of time. In half a day, you will see more wildlife and learn more about the culture of the Camargue than you would on your own in a week. Tours of varying lengths (2 hours, 4 hours, or full day) are available.

2. Van Gogh Walking Tour of Arles

www.arlestourisme.com/en/visits-of-arles.html; 1:30pm daily; €12 or free with downloadable map

When you return to Arles, stretch your legs on a self-guided walking tour of Arles through the lens of Vincent Van Gogh's work. Signposts on the walk mark where these and other seminal paintings were completed. Pick and choose the places you're interested in: There are 10 different spots in all, and completing the circuit, depending on how long you stop and stare, takes around three hours.

If you want a blowout meal, the restaurants of chef Jean-Luc Rabanel are perfectly suited to provide. If your budget's up to it, head to two Michelin-starred **Greenstronome** (7 Rue des Carmes; tel. 04 90 91 07 69; www.rabanel.com; menus from €95), where platters of sumptuously prepared, organic, vegetable-led cuisine await. Reservations are essential.

DAY 6

Marseille

Where to Stay: Vieux Port, close to all the sights

Arrive by: Train from Arles train station to Marseille-Saint-Charles Station (1 hour)

Marseille, which began life as a small Greek trading settlement in 600 BCE, is today a big, brash, multicultural, graffiti-splattered metropolis and port.

1. Le Panier

Get an introduction to the city in the neighborhood of Le Panier, Marseille's oldest quarter, about a 20-minute walk from the train station. It's an atmospheric area to shop with its mix of cobbled narrow streets and walls covered in street art.

For a light breakfast, stop at **Cup of Tea** (1 rue Caisserie; tel. 04 91 90 84 02; www.facebook.com/Cup-of-Tea-168429123172778; 9:30am-7pm Mon.-Sat.; cakes €3.50).

2. MuCEM

7 Promenade Robert Laffont; www.mucem.org; 11am-6pm Wed.-Mon.; €9.50 or City Pass

Make your way down out of Le Panier and walk 15 minutes to the **Euroméditerranée project,** an area of quays near the old port that were redeveloped in 2013. This neighborhood is dominated by the MuCEM building, as much an architectural statement as a museum. It's a futuristic glass box, clad in a web-like concrete skin that architect Rudi Riciotti claims was inspired by the ocean floor. You can walk around the building for free—the exhibits inside don't quite live up to the outside. Make sure to cross the futuristic-looking bridges that connect

top, Le Panier; bottom, MuCEM

WATCH

Plus Belle la Vie: This soap opera set in a fictional part of Marseille is the longest running show of its genre in France. The episodes are filmed on location in Marseille and at the show's studios in the city's 3rd arrondissement.

***At Eternity's Gate*:** Filmed in Arles, this 2018 movie stars Willem Dafoe as Vincent Van Gogh and attempts to capture the light and shade of the painter's time in Provence.

READ

Two Towns in Provence by M. F. K. Fisher: American writer M. F. K. Fisher was a laureate of gastronomy, and this book, which is actually two books in one, describes her experiences in and around the markets and producers of Aix-en-Provence, as well as cooking overlooking the old port of Marseille.

LISTEN

"La Marseillaise" by Claude Rouget de Lisle: Written in 1792, the French national anthem acquired its name and popularity thanks to a unit of soldiers from Marseille singing the song as they entered Paris the same year.

the box to Fort Saint-Jean and on from there to the the Vieux Port.

For lunch, have fresh fish at **Au Bout du Quai** (1 avenue Saint-Jean; tel. 04 91 99 53 36; noon-2:30pm and 7:30pm-10:30pm Wed.-Mon., noon-2:30pm Sun.; €15-30), a 10-minute walk from MuCEM.

3. Château d'If

Depart from 1 Quai de la Fraternité, Vieux Port; tel. 04 96 11 03 50; www.frioul-if-express.com; half hourly 6:30am-8:30pm June-Aug., hourly 6:30am-8:30pm out of season; €10.80 one island stop, €16.20 two island stops, reduced €12 and €8, Château d'If €5 supplement

Walk around the port to the Vieux Port to catch the boat to Château d'If. The most famous of the four Iles de Frioul, thanks to Alexandre Dumas's story of *The Count of Monte Cristo,* is the Isle of If. Dumas's fictional hero Edmond Dantes was imprisoned for 14 years in the Château d'If before escaping and taking revenge for his imprisonment. This was an actual prison, not just a literary one, and the cells with iron bars and grafitti scribbled on the walls leave no doubt as to the desolation felt by prisoners here. A more uplifting experience is the view over the water back toward Marseille. Allow at least half a day to visit the prison.

4. Vieux Port

When you get back to the mainland, enjoy the atmosphere of the city with a stroll around the old port, which is ringed by restaurants and cafés and is home to many sights. Don't miss Norman Foster's **L'Ombrière,** an arresting art installation, 48 m (157 ft) long and 22 m (72 ft) wide, composed of mirrored sheets hanging over the Qaui de Rive Neuve. The effect is reminiscent of that of Chicago's Bean sculpture (formally known as Anish Kapoor's *Cloud Gate*).

5. Jardin du Pharo

Finish the day with a walk in the Jardin du Pharo, a park with views of the old port. High on the headland, this magnificent garden houses the Palais du Pharo, which was intended as a residence for Napoleon Bonaparte, though he never actually lived there. On the lawn in front of the Palais is a moving monument to sailors lost at sea in World War I.

Le Chalet du Pharo (58 Boulevard

Charles Livon; tel. 04 91 52 80 11; www.le-chalet-du-pharo.com; noon-2:30pm and 7:30pm-9:30pm Mon.-Sat.; €19-34) is a good spot for dinner. Enjoy the view and contemplate everything you've seen along the Rhone.

TRANSPORTATION

Air

- **Lyon-Saint Exupéry Airport** (www.lyonaeroports.com): France's third-largest airport sits 18 km (11 mi) southeast of the city center. To get into town, the Rhôneexpress tram service runs at least every half hour and takes 30 minutes into the heart of Lyon (€9.50). A taxi (€50-55) also takes about 30 minutes, traffic depending.
- **Marseille Provence Airport** (www.marseille.aeroport.fr): This international airport (no direct flights to the United States) is 27 km (17 mi) northwest of the French port town; 25 minutes by train (€10) or 30 minutes by taxi (€50). It's about one hour by train from Arles (€13).

Train

France's famous high speed TGVs makes the travel time from one side of the country to the other overland very nearly the same as flights (less if you consider getting too/from airports). Regional trains are slower but stop in some of the smaller towns skipped by the TGV. Access tickets to both through **SNCF** (www.sncf-connect.com), France's national rail company.

- **Lyon Part Dieu** (5, Place Charles Béraudier): In the eastern side of the city; a 20-minute bus ride takes you to Presqu'Ile, a peninsula formed by the Saône River to the west and the Rhone River to the east where many major sights are located. From Paris to Lyon on the TGV is two hours (from €30).
- **Vienne train station:** Located in the city center, within walking distance to most sights. Regional trains connect Lyon to Vienne (20 minutes; €16-30).
- **Avignon Centre** (Boulevard Saint-Roch): This station is in the center of Avignon, just outside the town walls and near all the sights in the historic center. It's a 15-minute walk to Palais des Papes. It only serves regional trains, such as those from Vienne (2 hours; from €32) and Tain-l'Hermitage (1.5 hours; from €25).
- **Avignon TGV** (Avenue de la Gare): Southwest of the city center, this station serves TGV trains, such as those from Lyon (1.5 hours; from €34). Transfer to a regional train to reach Avignon Centre (5 minutes).
- **Arles train station** (Avenue Paulin Talabot): Located a short walk from the center (10 minutes to the Roman arena), this station serves regional trains, such as those from Avignon Centre (15 minutes; from €9).
- **Marseille-Saint-Charles Station:** Located northeast of the Vieux Port (10 minutes by public transit), this station serves both regional and TGV trains. From Arles, catch a regional train (1 hour; from €17).

Getting Back

You can take the TGV from Marseilles back to Lyon (1 hour 45 minutes; from €60), or back to Paris, arriving at Gare de Lyon (3 hours; from €75). Or, fly home from Marseille Provence Airport.

CONNECT WITH

- London and Paris (page 44)
- The French Riviera (page 634)
- The Alps (page 648)

THE FRENCH RIVIERA

Why Go: A convenient train line makes travel along the coast of the French Riviera easy. Visit the sandy beaches, glamorous hotels, and world-class museums of Nice, Monaco, Antibes, and Cannes.

Number of Days: 4

Total Distance: 80 km (50 mi)

Seasons: Year-round

Start: Nice

End: Cannes

Mentioning the French Riviera conjures up visions of seafront promenades, film festivals, sports cars, turquoise waters, and superyachts. That's not too far off—except it's also a global center for high-tech development, a pioneer in eco-friendly practices, and home to pine forests, nature reserves, museums, and Roman ruins.

The entire French Riviera is only 180 km (111 mi) long, but it is packed with amazing scenery and sights. A rail network runs along the Riviera from Marseille to Ventimiglia across the Italian border, servicing all the major towns except Saint-Tropez. Hop on the train for a tour of some of the Riviera's most famous cities: Nice, Monaco, Antibes, and Cannes.

TOP 3

★ Joining the stream of joggers and cyclists on the **Promenade des Anglais,** Nice's iconic seafront boulevard (page 640).

★ People-watching on **Place du Casino,** the center of Monaco's amazing spectacle of glamorous denizens and expensive cars (page 640).

★ Sipping a drink as the sun sets at a **beach bar in Juan-les-Pins** (page 645).

THE FRENCH RIVIERA
M6202
A8
Cagnes-
sur-Mer
D2085
Overnight Stop
Rail Route
D6185
A8
Mougins
Antibes
Antibes
Marché Provençal
Musée Picasso
Plage de
la Salis
A8
D6285
Beach Bar in
Juan-les-Pins
Gare SNCF
de Cannes
Cannes
La
Croisette
Le Suquet
Old Town
Plage de
la Croisette
Île Sainte-
Marguerite
Réserve biologique dirigée
de l'Ile Sainte-Marguerite
© MOON.COM
Île Saint-
Honorat

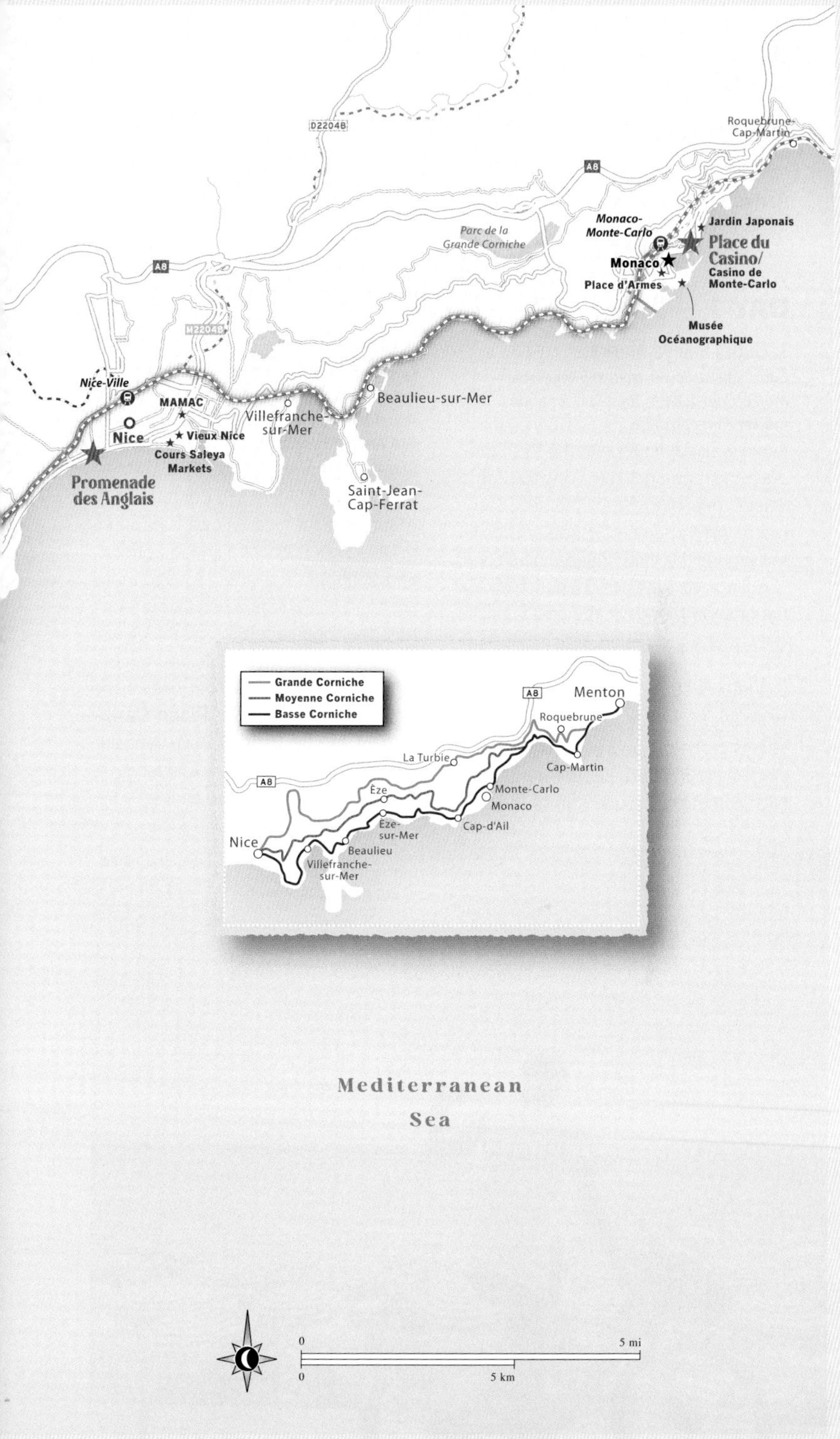

D2204B
Roquebrune-
Cap-Martin
A8
Monaco-
Monte-Carlo
Jardin Japonais
Place du
Casino/
Casino de
Monte-Carlo
Parc de la
Grande Corniche
Monaco
Place d'Armes
Musée
Océanographique
A8
M2204B
Nice-Ville
MAMAC
Nice
Vieux Nice
Cours Saleya
Markets
Promenade
des Anglais
Villefranche-
sur-Mer
Beaulieu-sur-Mer
Saint-Jean-
Cap-Ferrat

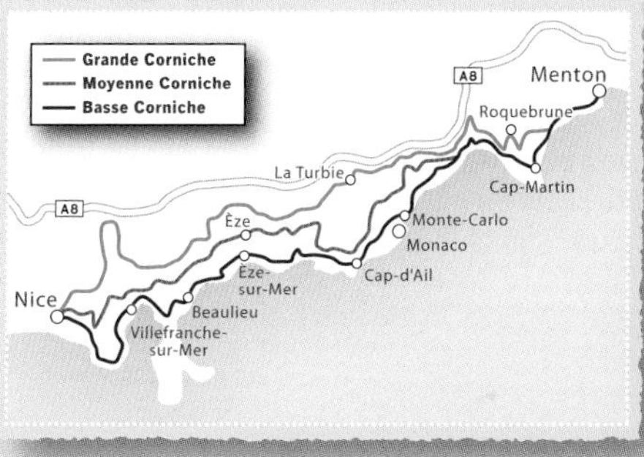

Mediterranean
Sea

Nice

Where to Stay: Vieux Nice or the Carré d'Or

Arrive by: Plane to Nice-Côte d'Azur Airport

DAY 1

1. Cours Saleya Markets

Cours Saleya; flower, fruit, and vegetable market 6am-1:30pm Tues.-Sun., antique market 7am-6pm Mon.

Begin your day in Nice at the fresh produce and flower markets along the Cours Saleya, one block from the sea. Every morning, thousands of visitors and locals mill around the stalls, squeezing fruit and haggling over the price of a bunch of carnations. On Mondays, the area is taken over by antique dealers.

2. Vieux Nice

Walk away from the sea into the narrow streets of the old town, Vieux Nice, for a wander around the neighborhood. Vieux Nice is the picturesque hub of the city, where bars, art galleries, boutiques, and ice cream parlors coexist inside ancient doorways and vaulted rooms.

For breakfast or a slice of cake, head to **Marinette** (13 Rue Colonna d'Istria; tel. 04 93 88 29 52; www.restaurantmarinette.fr; 8am-7pm Wed.-Sun.; breakfast €9).

3. MAMAC

Place Yves Klein; tel. 04 97 13 42 01; www.mamac-nice.org; 11am-6pm Tues.-Sun. Nov.-Apr., 10am-6pm Tues.-Sun. May-Oct.; adults €10, under 18 and students free

Stroll 10 minutes to the MAMAC (Museum of Modern and Contemporary Art of Nice), the most enjoyable museum in Nice. Four floors of paintings, photos, and sculptures from the 1950s to today are housed in a huge, airy building. Don't miss the roof garden for great views of the city and the whole Baie des Anges.

Have a seafood lunch at one of the many restaurants on the **Place Garibaldi—Café de Turin** (5, Place Garibaldi; tel. 04 93 62 29 52; www.cafedeturin.fr; 8am-10pm daily) is a good choice.

Promenade des Anglais

Key Reservations

Booking accommodations in advance is essential during the summer; even in the spring and fall, the best locations can be fully reserved many months in advance. For the Monaco Grand Prix or Cannes Film Festival, hotels raise their prices considerably, and hotels and guesthouses fill up six months in advance. From October to April, it is possible to wait until the last minute to decide on accommodations, but beware that many hotels close during this period, even in Nice and Cannes.

Hotel Le Negresco, Nice

LES CORNICHES

Heading east out of Nice you'll find some of the Riviera's oldest, most glamorous resorts: **Villefranche-sur-Mer, Beaulieu-sur-Mer,** and **Saint-Jean-cap-Ferrat,** home to casinos, luxury hotels, and some of the most expensive villas in the world. Even if you don't quite qualify as a member of the jet set, it's a delight to rent a car and drive along Les Corniches, the three thrilling coastal roads twisting through the mountains east of Nice, stopping here and there at a beach or café.

The three roads run parallel to the coast linking Nice to Menton: one beside the sea (the Basse Corniche, or the Corniche Inférieur), one halfway up the mountains (the Moyenne Corniche), and one perched on the edge of the clifftop (the Grande or Haute Corniche).

BASSE CORNICHE

Traffic on the Basse Corniche can slow to a standstill in the summer, but it's an entertaining journey, snaking through the Riviera's top resorts, casinos, and grand hotels. The Basse Corniche passes through Villefranche-sur-Mer, Beaulieu-sur-Mer, Èze-sur-Mer, Cap-d'Ail, and Monaco.

MOYENNE CORNICHE

The Moyenne Corniche was constructed in the 1920s when the area began to take off as a vacation destination. It's wider and popular with motorcyclists; it passes through long tunnels, over viaducts, and through Èze.

GRANDE CORNICHE

The Grande Corniche is the highest and most spectacular of the coastal routes. The hairpin bends and thick vegetation make it a popular ride with sports-car enthusiasts and cyclists—although the first savagely steep incline as you leave Nice gets rid of all but the hardiest of riders. The Grande Corniche eventually arrives at **La Turbie** and its huge Roman monument, **La Trophée des Alpes.** Occasional rockfalls and mudslides can cause the Grande Corniche to close for a few days (sometimes weeks), but it is a thrilling drive.

★ 4. Promenade des Anglais

The promenade des Anglais is the wide, sweeping boulevard that flanks the Mediterranean along Nice's seafront. It's the first place visitors see when they arrive in Nice, and it takes you past some of the city's most celebrated buildings. The palm-tree-lined promenade is always full of dog walkers, cyclists, joggers, rollerbladers, and holidaymakers. It's a place for early-evening cocktails, car racing, busking, and people-watching, yet it's also a place of tragedy: a new plum-colored surface was laid and barriers put up after the Nice terrorist attack in July 2016.

The best time to stroll along the promenade des Anglais is at dusk. For a glamorous beachside dinner, try **Le Galet** (3 promenade des Anglais; tel. 04 93 88 17 23; www.galet-plage.fr; 8am-12:30am daily; mains €15-25).

Day Trip to Monaco

Arrive by: Train from Nice Ville station to Monaco Monte-Carlo station (25 minutes)

DAY 2

1. Place d'Armes

When you arrive in the city-state of Monaco, head to Place d'Armes, which is surrounded by early-morning market stalls and is a nice place for breakfast or a coffee. It's a 15-minute walk from the train station. As you walk, you'll notice that there's nowhere else in the world quite like Monaco. There's no graffiti or litter, just a lot of police officers making sure millionaires get home safely to their yachts or micro-apartments.

Musée Océanographique

2. Musée Océanographique

Avenue Saint-Martin; tel. 93 15 36 00; www.oceano.org; 10am-6pm daily Oct.-Mar., 10am-7pm daily Apr.-June and Sept., 9:30am-8pm daily July-Aug.; adults €11/€16 (low/high season), ages 13-18 and students €7/€12, ages 4-12 €5/€8

From the place d'Armes, walk up the steep slope to the top of **Le Rocher** (a 15-minute walk), the medieval town, on a huge outcropping of rock jutting out into the Mediterranean. Here, visit the Musée Océanographique, arguably the best museum on the Riviera. The baroque-revival oceanography museum focuses on marine conservation and education. Its aquarium has more than 100 tanks holding 6,000 marine species. Perhaps its most impressive display is in the salle de la baleine (whale room), which has an 18-m (59-ft) whale skeleton hanging from the ceiling.

Walk back downhill to **Port Hercule** and have lunch at the **Quai des Artistes** (4 quai Antoine Ier; tel. 97 97 97 77; www.quaidesartistes.com; daily noon-2:30pm and 7:30pm-11pm; mains €18-32) brasserie on the western flank of the port.

★ 3. Place du Casino

Walk past the lines of superyachts and Monaco's famous Olympic-size outdoor swimming pool. Continue up the hill on the other side of the port to the Place du Casino, the centerpiece of Monte-Carlo. Here, crowds gather for family

MAKE IT Active

The Riviera coast is an attractive destination itself, and the surrounding steep hills and beautiful waters are ideal for getting outside.

NICE

Nice Port to Mont Boron Hike

Hiking Distance: *4.2 km/2.6 mi round-trip*
Hiking Time: *2 hours*
Difficulty: *Easy*
Information and Maps: *Nice tourist office*
Trailhead: *La Réserve restaurant, 60 Boulevard Franck Pilatte*

This easy hike is a great way to get acquainted with the lay of the land around Nice. You'll pass Belle Epoque villas as you climb Mont Boron, and the hike ends at a 16th-century fort on top of the hill.

Cycling

Nice is a popular destination for cyclists of all levels, and cycling is a smart, pleasant way to travel around the city. For people who enjoy a gentle ride, there's a wide, flat cycle path alongside the seafront promenade. Serious amateurs and pro cyclists tend to head east up the Haute and Moyenne Corniches toward Menton and Italy.

Water Sports

Head to the beach or the port where outfitters can set you up with waterskiing, wakeboarding, stand-up paddleboarding, kayaking, Jet Skiing, scuba diving, and more.

MONACO

Monte-Carlo to La Turbie Hike

Hiking Distance: *6.5km/4mi one-way*
Hiking Time: *3.5 hours*
Difficulty: *Moderate*
Information and Maps: *Monaco tourist office*
Trailhead: *Monaco Monte-Carlo railway station*

Starting at the Monaco train station, make your way up to the village of La Turbie and its famous Roman monument, the **Trophée des Alpes,** taking in the **Tête de Chien** (a rock named for its resemblance to the head of a dog) and incredible views of the coast.

CANNES

Cycling

The long, steep ascents from the town heading north and the proliferation of traffic do not make Cannes ideal for bikes, but cycling along the coast is fun and popular, and there are intermittent dedicated cycling paths in both directions.

Îles de lérins

For a wild and often almost deserted swimming experience among the rocks, take the ferry from Cannes to one of the Îles de Lérins, where the water is bright turquoise and the pine forest touches the beach.

Luxury Hotels

In the famous Riviera resort towns, many hotels are out of the price range of the average traveler, but they are glamorous enough to be sightseeing destinations in themselves. They're worth walking by or peeking into, perhaps even splurging at one of their luxurious restaurants before returning to your more reasonable accommodation for the night.

NICE

- **Le Negresco** (37 Promenade des Anglais; tel. 04 93 16 64 00; www.hotel-negresco-nice.com) is probably the most recognizable building in Nice, and it's the Belle Epoque showpiece of the promenade des Anglais.
- The extraordinary facade of the **Hyatt Regency Palais de la Méditerranée** (13 Promenade des Anglais; tel. 04 93 27 12 34; https://nice.regency.hyatt.com) is probably the most magnificent example of art deco architecture in Europe.
- Irish writer James Joyce began his near-indecipherable work *Finnegans Wake* in **Hotel Suisse** (15 Quai Rauba Capeu; tel. 04 92 17 39 00; www.hotel-nice-suisse.com) in October 1922. The entrance has changed, but the ginger and cream facade remains the same.

MONACO

- **Hotel de Paris** (Place du Casino; tel. 98 06 30 00; www.hoteldeparismontecarlo.com) is one of the world's most prestigious (and expensive) hotels. It's been undergoing renovations since October 2014, but the main facade facing the Café de Paris remains intact, as do the entrance, shopping arcade, and restaurants.
- **Hotel Hermitage Monte-Carlo** (Square Beaumarchais; tel. 98 06 40 00; http://fr.hotelhermitagemontecarlo.com) is just a casino-chip's throw from the Hotel de Paris. A carved Belle Epoque facade, a huge winter garden atrium designed by Gustave Eiffel, and a drink at the Crystal Bar will feel like something out of a fairy tale.

photoshoots and selfies alongside the expensive sports cars and vintage convertibles on Monte-Carlo's most famous roundabout.

To do some people-watching, grab a table on the enormous terrace of the **Café de Paris** (Place du Casino; tel. 98 06 76 23; www.montecarlosbm.com/fr/restaurant-monaco/le-cafe-de-paris; 8am-2am daily; mains €29-54). It has a huge choice of snacks and meals, too.

4. Casino de Monte-Carlo

Place du Casino; tel. 98 06 21 21; http://fr.casinomontecarlo.com; 2pm-late daily, identification required, tours 9am-1pm daily Oct. 1-May 1; adults €12, ages 13-18 €8, ages 6-12 €6, May 2-Sept. 30 adults €17, ages 13-18 €12, ages 6-12 €8

Everyone should pay a visit to the Monte-Carlo Casino, even if just on an afternoon tour. This is the world's most famous casino. Go just for a look or to try your luck at one of the many games.

- **Hotel Monte-Carlo Bay** (40 Avenue Princesse Grace; tel. 98 06 02 00; www.montecarlobay.com) is more a resort than a hotel, with the feel of a film set from a '60s-style beach party.
- **Fairmont Monte Carlo** (12 Avenue des Spélugues; tel. 93 50 65 00; www.fairmont.com/montecarlo), built into the rock behind Monaco's casino, is a glamorous monster of a hotel.

ANTIBES

- **Hotel du Cap-Eden Roc** (Boulevard John F. Kennedy; tel. 04 93 61 39 01; www.oetkercollection.com; mid-Apr.-mid-Oct.) is so majestic, even Jay Gatsby may have glanced at the price list. The hotel's sumptuous buildings are set on huge swaths of lawns and gardens at the southwest corner of the Cap d'Antibes. The legendary list of guests includes Kirk Douglas, Greta Garbo, and Marc Chagall.

CANNES

- The **International Carlton Cannes** (58 Boulevard de la Croisette; tel. 04 93 06 40 06; www.carlton-cannes.com) is one of the most sumptuous of Cannes's palace hotels. It's the seat of the Cannes Film Festival jury and the location for many film shoots, including Alfred Hitchcock's *To Catch a Thief.*
- **Hotel Martinez** (73 Boulevard de la Croisette; tel. 04 93 90 12 34; www.hotel-martinez.com) is the art deco gem of La Croisette, a palace dedicated to luxurious stays. At over €40,000 per night, the hotel's penthouse suite, with a 500-sq-m (5,300-sq-ft) decked terrace just below the neon Martinez sign, is one of the three most expensive hotel suites in the world, reputedly with Picasso and Matisse original paintings on the walls.

5. Jardin Japonais

Walk 10 minutes to the Jardin Japonais, one of Monaco's most restful green spaces. The gardens were created in 1994 in accordance with the principles of Zen design by Yasuo Beppu; the gardens feature a pond with koi fish swimming under water lilies and lotus flowers, islands, decked walkways, bamboo water features and hedges, a waterfall, teahouse, stone lanterns, red bridges, and a Zen garden.

Have a Chinese dinner across the street at **Song Qi** (7 Avenue Princesse Grace; tel. 99 99 33 33; www.song-qi.mc; noon-2:30pm and 7:30-11pm daily; mains €29-€120). If you have time, walk back up to the Place du Casino and finish the evening at the **Buddha Bar** (Place du Casino; tel. 98 06 19 19; www.montecarlosbm.com/en/bar-nightclub-monaco/buddha-bar-monte-carlo; 6pm-2am Tues.-Sun.), one of the top locations for a pre- and post-casino drinks. Just be sure to get back to the train station in time for the last train to Nice.

Antibes

Where to Stay: In or near Old Town

Arrive by: Train from Nice Ville station to Antibes station (20-30 minutes)

DAY 3

1. Marché Provençal

Cours Masséna; tel. 04 22 10 60 01; 6am-1pm daily June-Sept., 6am-1pm Tues.-Sun. Sept.-May

Begin the day at the covered Marché Provençal in the Old Town, a 10-minute walk from the train station. Antibes's market is one of the region's best fresh produce sources, with local fruit and vegetable stalls, cheese, fish, charcuterie, and flowers mixed up with tables of lavender honey, nougat, and barrels of olives. At lunchtime in the high season, the area is washed down and replaced by modern art, sculpture, and handmade jewelry. The high roof keeps the place nice and cool in the summer.

2. Musée Picasso

Place Mariejol; tel. 04 92 90 54 26; www.antibes-juanlespins.com/culture/musee-picasso; 10am-1pm and 2pm-6pm Tues.-Sun. mid-Sept.-mid-June, 10am-6pm Tues.-Sun. mid-June-mid-Sept.; adults €8, reduced €6, under 18 free

Next, walk two minutes to the Musée Picasso. The château that now houses this museum was built on the remains of a Greek encampment. Pablo Picasso visited the museum in 1946 and was offered to take part in a workshop; he turned the first floor into a studio and eventually presented the town with 23 paintings, 44 sketches, and a further 78 ceramics. Later, the collection was enlarged by donations from Jacqueline Picasso, the artist's last wife. The museum also houses important works by some of the 20th century's most notable painters and sculptors.

For lunch, **Le P'tit Cageot** (5 Rue du Dr Rostan; tel. 04 89 68 48 66; www.restaurantleptitcageot.fr; Mon.-Tues. and Thurs.-Sat. noon-2pm and 7pm-10pm; mains €19) is a good pick.

3. Plage de la Salis

Boulevard James Wylie; limited parking in the Parking Salis or Parking du Ponteil

Spend the afternoon sunbathing on Plage de la Salis, Antibes's most popular beach. The narrow beach has thick,

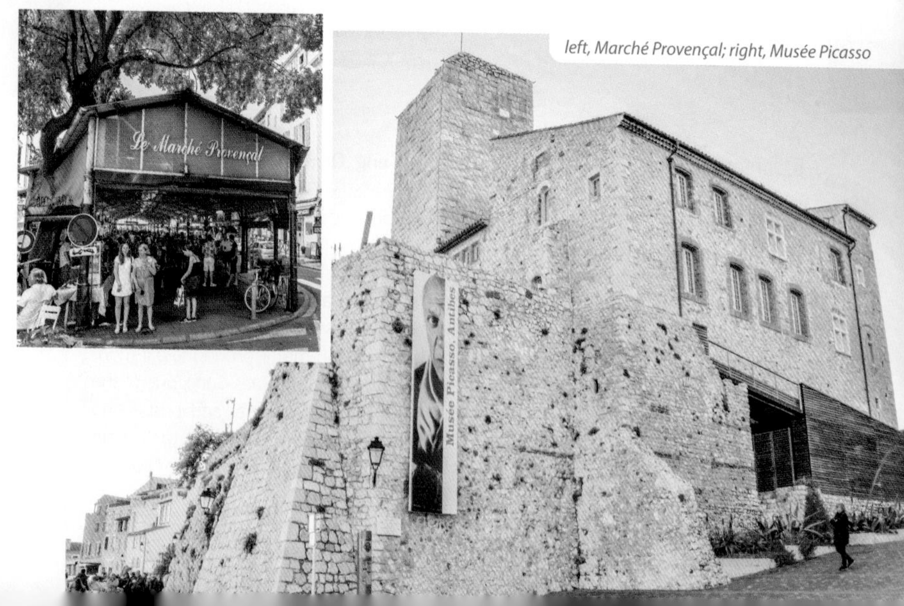

left, Marché Provençal; right, Musée Picasso

golden sand and three snack bar/beach kiosks open April-September.

★ 4. Beach Bar in Juan-les-Pins

There's no better way to end the day than with a drink and a view of the ocean. Juan-les-Pins, just a 20-minute walk or 5-minute taxi ride from Antibes, is home to a line of beach bars along one of the best strips of sand in the French Riviera. There are many spots to choose from, but **Plage Le Colombier** (4 Blvd. Edouard Baudoin; tel. 04 93 61 24 66; www.hotelhelios.fr; beach service 9am-6pm daily, lounge bar and evening restaurant service 6:30pm-11:30pm Apr.-Sept. and Oct.; mains €15-42) is a good choice, serving pasta, fresh fish, steaks, and more, as well as drinks.

Day Trip to Cannes

Arrive by: Train from Antibes station to Cannes station (10 minutes)

DAY 4

1. Le Suquet Old Town

After you arrive in Cannes, wander through the steep, narrow cobbled streets of Le Suquet old town, Cannes's most touristy district, built into a hill overlooking the pleasure boat marina. The buildings originally housed fishermen and are now full of bars, restaurants, and gift shops. Head to the summit for great views of the Baie de Cannes.

2. Bouillabaisse Lunch

For lunch, treat yourself to bouillabaisse. This traditional fish soup from Marseille was originally prepared using the humble rascasse (scorpion fish) that fishermen were unable to sell to restaurants. Now, bouillabaisse is prepared all along the Riviera, usually at the more expensive restaurants. It is usually served for two people and often requires pre-booking (24-hours' notice).

Bistrot Gourmand (10 Rue du Docteur Pierre Gazagnaire; tel. 04 93 68 72 02; www.bistrotgourmandcannes.fr; noon-2pm and 7pm-10pm Tues.-Sat., noon-2pm Sun.; mains €15-26) serves the fish stew, along with other delicious local fare.

3. La Croisette

After lunch, go for a walk along Boulevard de la Croisette, a wide seafront roadway with sandy beaches on one side, designer shops and palatial hotels on the other. The promenade starts behind a seafront park, the **Square Hahn,** which features an old-fashioned carousel.

4. Plage de la Croisette

Boulevard de la Croisette; limited parking on La Croisette

If you fancy an afternoon at the beach, head to Plage de la Croisette. The 800-m (2,600-ft) beach beneath La Croisette is one of the most famous strips of sand in the world, having appeared in hundreds of Film Festival photos. It runs from the Palais des Festivals in the west to Port Canto in the east, with public sections at both ends and the main expanse in front of all the large hotels given over to private beach clubs.

Have dinner at one of the eateries on the pedestrianized **Rue Meynadier; Aux Bons Enfants** (80 Rue Meynadier;

Boulevard de la Croisette

Cannes Film Festival

Le Palais des Festivals, 1 Boulevard de la Croisette; www.festival-cannes.com; May

For two weeks in May, Cannes is overtaken by the biggest event in the south of France, with full hotels, full car parks, full restaurants, and increased security. If you want to be there during the festival, you need to book a hotel room at least six months in advance. However, the rewards are considerable—photo opportunities of stars on red carpets, blissfully warm evenings, late-night screenings, and chance access to enjoy private views and parties in hillside villas.

Beside the official selections, there are special screenings, a classics festival, a shorts festival, and **cinéma de la plage,** screenings that are open to the public at 9:30pm on the beach. A huge screen is erected on the beach near the Palais in front of several hundred deck chairs, and tickets are available free of charge in the tourist office on the day of the screening.

www.aux-bons-enfants-cannes.com; noon-2pm and 7pm-10pm Tues.-Sat.; three-course evening meal €31) offers one of the most authentic and satisfying dining experiences in the city.

TRANSPORTATION

Air

Most travelers to the French Riviera from North America will arrive at **Nice-Côte d'Azur Airport** (www.nice.aeroport.fr), which is only 6 km (4 mi) from the center of the city. Tram line 2 takes passengers directly into the center or to the port area in 20 minutes (€1.50). There is also a bus to the center of town (25 minutes; €1.50), and taxis take 15-25 minutes (€30).

Train

To get to the French Riviera by train, there are direct **TGV fast trains** from Paris (Gare de Lyon) to Cannes, Antibes, and Nice via Marseille. The train is fast until Marseille, where it switches to the slower, coastal track. Journey time from Paris to Nice is around six hours.

To get between the French Riviera towns, the comfortable, efficient French **TER rail network** runs along the Riviera between Marseille and Ventimiglia just across the Italian border. It services Nice, Monaco, Antibes, and Cannes, as well as other towns.

Stations

- **Nice Ville** (Avenue Thiers; 5am-12:30am daily): Nice's main train

WATCH

To Catch a Thief: Alfred Hitchcock's classic 1955 romantic thriller starring Cary Grant and Grace Kelly was filmed all along the Riviera seafront.

READ

Tender Is the Night by F. Scott Fitzgerald: Inspired by the author's own time on the Riviera in the company of wealthy US socialites the Murphys, Fitzgerald's 1934 novel details the high life and mental demise of American couple Dick and Nicole Driver, who rent a villa in the south of France.

LISTEN

Jazz music is an integral part of the Riviera experience, and the cities of Nice and Juan-les-Pins have big jazz festivals every July. Trumpeter Miles Davis recorded the album ***1969 Miles—Festiva de Juan Pins*** at Juan-les-Pins's Jazz à Juan festival in in 1969.

station, with service to **Monaco** (every 30 minutes; 25 minutes; around €4) and **Antibes** (every 30 minutes; 20-30 minutes; around €5), is about a 20-minute walk north of Promenade des Anglais.

- **Monaco Monte-Carlo railway station** (Place Sainte-Dévote; tel. 377 93 10 60 05): Located close to the France-Monaco border, this station is a 15-minute walk to Place du Casino.
- **Antibes station** (Gare SNCF, Avenue Robert-Soleau; www.oui.sncf): This station is about a 15-minute walk to the Picasso Museum.
- **Cannes SNCF railway station** (Gare de Cannes, Rue Jean Jaurès; tel. 0892 35 35 35; www.oui.sncf). Cannes's station has a sparkling concourse on Rue Jean Jaurès, five blocks from the sea. From Antibes, the ride (every 30 minutes) takes 15 minutes and costs €3-5.

Bus

The Riviera's main towns are also connected by coaches with bus stations (gares routières) usually centrally located (except in Nice, whose bus station is in Riquier, 3 km/1.8 mi from the main Place Masséna, though connected by tram line). Zou (https://zou.maregionsud.fr) has information on buses.

Getting Back

Cannes is 27 km (16 mi) from **Nice-Côte d'Azur airport** (www.nice.aeroport.fr). **Airport Express Bus 210** (tel. 0800 06 01 06; www.niceairportxpress.com; journey time 50 minutes; €22 single, €33 return, under 12 €5) stops at Cannes railway station (approx. two buses per hour 8am-8pm).

From **Cannes SNCF railway station** (Gare de Cannes, Rue Jean Jaurès; tel. 0892 35 35 35; www.oui.sncf), travel time to **Nice** is 25 minutes (€6.10). Direct trains to **Paris** take 5.5 hours.

- Cinque Terre (page 423)
- The Rhone Valley (page 618)

THE ALPS

Why Go: Winding through the snowcapped peaks of the Swiss and Italian Alps, this scenic rail voyage connects you through three diverse European cities.

Number of Days: 6

Total Distance: 560 km (348 mi)

Seasons: Summer

Start: Geneva

End: Milan

Begin this rail adventure in Geneva, Switzerland. This centuries-old city boasts plenty of great food and history, though its privileged geography, hugging the coast of expansive Lake Geneva and nestled in the Swiss Alps, will really take your breath away. From Geneva, you leave the French-speaking region of Switzerland for the German-speaking north and the economic capital of Zürich. The Golden Pass train ride is one of the most picturesque in all of Europe, passing Swiss lakes and snowcapped mountains. Zürich is a vibrant, fast-paced city that manages to straddle that fine line between big-city bustle and relaxed hospitality. From Zürich, enjoy another gorgeous train ride, this time on the Bernina Express, which takes you south, from the Swiss Alps and Italian Alps to magnificent Milan. The Milanese are famous for their high style and busy metropolitan lifestyle, though they are also known as Italy's aperitivo culture par excellence.

TOP 3

★ Geeking out on Swiss watchmaking, a painstakingly detailed art, at **Patek Phillipe Museum** (page 651).

★ Riding the **Bernina Express** through the Alps, one of the most spectacular, picturesque train voyages in the world (page 657).

Quietly absorbing ***The Last Supper*** by Leonardo da Vinci, one of the Italian High Renaissance master's most impressive works (page 659).

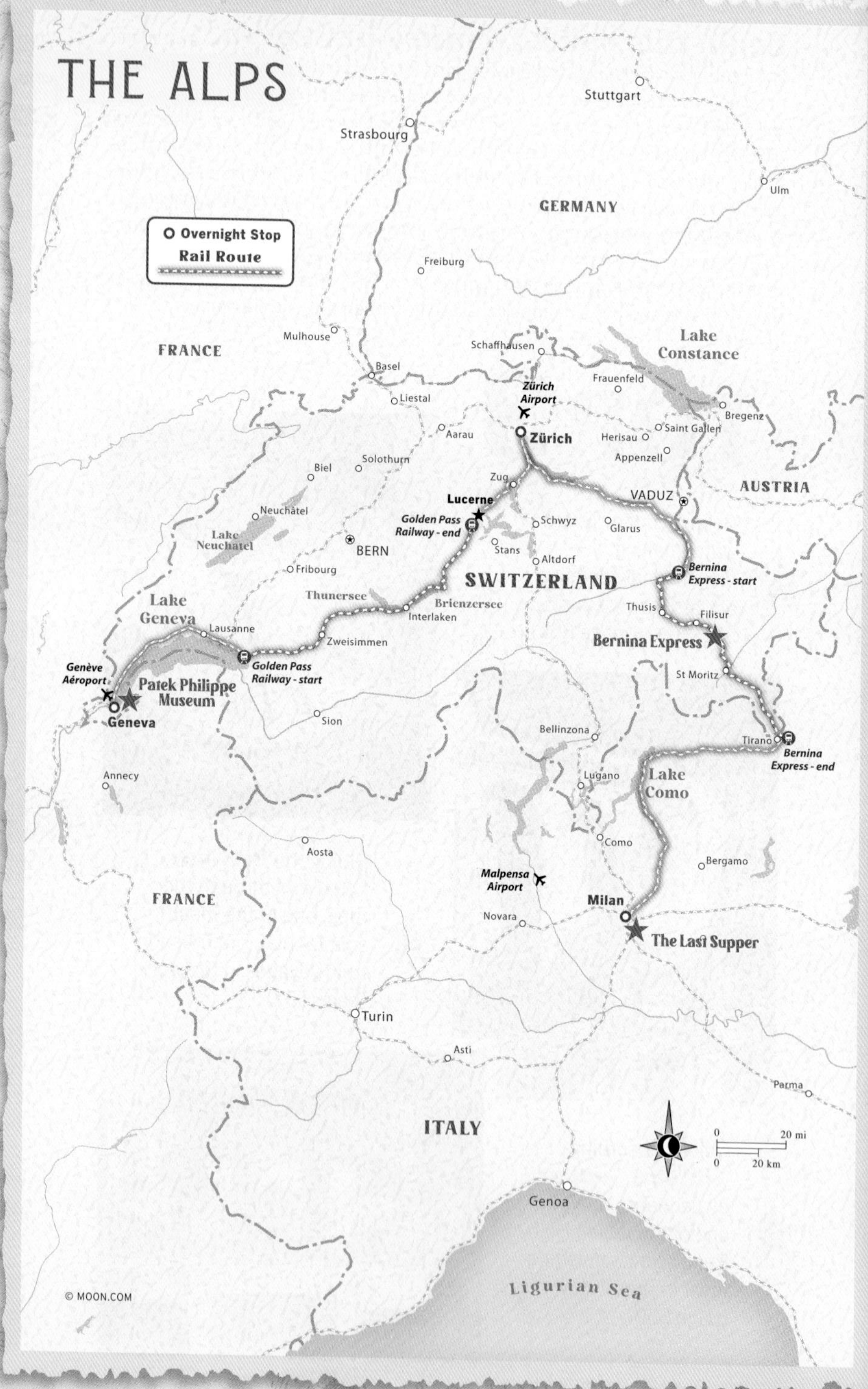
THE ALPS
Overnight Stop
Rail Route
Stuttgart
Strasbourg
Ulm
GERMANY
Freiburg
FRANCE
Mulhouse
Schaffhausen
Lake Constance
Basel
Liestal
Zürich Airport
Frauenfeld
Bregenz
Aarau
Zürich
Herisau
Saint Gallen
Appenzell
Solothurn
Biel
Zug
VADUZ
AUSTRIA
Lucerne
Neuchâtel
Golden Pass Railway - end
Schwyz
Glarus
Lake Neuchatel
BERN
Stans
Altdorf
Fribourg
SWITZERLAND
Bernina Express - start
Thunersee
Brienzersee
Interlaken
Thusis
Filisur
Lake Geneva
Lausanne
Bernina Express
Zweisimmen
Golden Pass Railway - start
St Moritz
Genève Aéroport
Patek Philippe Museum
Geneva
Sion
Bellinzona
Tirano
Bernina Express - end
Lugano
Lake Como
Annecy
Como
Aosta
Bergamo
Malpensa Airport
FRANCE
Milan
Novara
The Last Supper
Turin
Asti
Parma
ITALY
0
20 mi
0
20 km
Genoa
Ligurian Sea
© MOON.COM
CARTOLINA POSTALE
(CARTE POSTALE)

Geneva, Switzerland

Where to Stay: Geneva's Old Town, walking distance to nearly everything in the city

Arrive by: Plane to the Geneva Airport or train to the Geneva Train Station

DAY 1

1. La Place du Bourg-de-Four

Place du Bourg-de-Four, open 24 hours; free

Geneva's oldest public square is in the heart of its Old Town. Lined with upscale shops and cafés, this is the place to feel the distinct French influence on Geneva. Interestingly, two castles used to sit on either side of the square, though both have long been demolished, one in the 13th century and the other in the 18th century.

2. St. Pierre Cathedral

Cathedral de Saint-Pierre; tel. 22/311 75 75; www.cathedrale-geneve.ch; 9:30am-6:30pm Mon.-Fri., 9:30am-4:30pm Sat., noon-6:30pm Sun.; free (12 CHF for access to the tours and attached archaeological site)

Nearby, this cathedral is something of an oddity. Though it was built in the Gothic tradition of the 12th century, the interior has been stripped of nearly all decoration because the cathedral was the adopted home of John Calvin, one of the leaders of the Protestant Reformation. The clean whitewashed walls of the inside make for a distinct juxtaposition, not only with the church's exterior but also with other European cathedrals that have remained ornate Roman-Catholic houses of worship.

3. Picnic at Jardin Anglais

Jardin Anglais; open 24/7; free

Either pick up your picnic fixings at a local grocery store or head over to **Three Kids Bagel** (Rue du Vieux-Collège 10bix; tel. 22/311 24 24; www.threekids.ch; 11am-3pm Mon.-Sat.; 12 CHF). Take a seat and enjoy the views over Lake Geneva and the Jura Mountains bordering the north of the city. At the park, be sure to take a moment to appreciate the **Flower Clock.** Originally planted in 1955, the fusion of horology and horticulture features plants, shrubs, and flowers that change seasonally.

★ 4. Patek Phillipe Museum

Rue des Vieux-Grenadiers 7; tel. 22/707 30 10; www.patek.com; 2pm-6pm Tues.-Fri., 10am-6pm Sat.-Sun.; 10 CHF

Walk 20 minutes south to this museum. There are few crafts more closely associated with Switzerland than precise watchmaking. Take a tour through the last five centuries of Swiss horology, with exhibits on everything from firing colorful enamel to hand-assembling automatic watch movements with thousands of moving parts.

top, La Place du Bourg-de-Four; bottom, Jardin Anglais

Key Reservations

GENEVA

- In Geneva, the **Geneva City Pass** (www.geneve.com/en/plan-a-trip/geneva-city-pass) should be purchased before your arrival. This pass gives you free or discounted access to many of the museums and experiences throughout the city as well as public transportation. Often a 24-hour Geneva City Pass is offered for free with your hotel reservation, a fantastic value.
- Book a ticket to **Palais des Nations** a month or more in advance.

ZÜRICH

- There always seems to be a conference happening in Zürich, which quickly fills the most centrally located hotels. Be sure to book your **accommodation** ahead of time.

MILAN

- Book tickets for ***The Last Supper* mural** directly online from Vivaticket (www.vivaticket.com), or by phone (tel. 02/9280-0360) as far in advance as possible.

TRANSPORTATION

Book the following train tickets in advance:

- **Montreux-Zweisimmen** portion of the Golden Pass
- **Bernina Express**

Palais des Nations

5. Fondue and Raclette at Auberge de Savièse

Rue des Pâquis 20; tel. 22/732 83 30; www.aubergedesaviese.com; noon-11pm daily; 35 CHF

Tuck into woody rustic chalet charm in this local restaurant specializing in fondue and raclette, two French-Swiss classics. As a traveler, you will be forgiven your indiscretion in eating raclette (a winter dish for locals) out of season. If you have never enjoyed raclette before, you may go home needing to get all the accoutrements to make this dish of grill-melted cheese over potatoes at home.

MAKE IT Active

GENEVA

Lake Geneva: There are many ways to explore Geneva's expansive Lake Geneva in a more active fashion. If you have the Geneva City Pass, you can take advantage of free **paddleboard or pedal boat** rental with your pass at **Bains des Paquis** (page 653). Pack along your waterproof camera for some unbeatable views over Geneva, the lakes, and the mountains.

MILAN

Lake Como: The third-largest lake in Italy, Lake Como has been the destination for the wealthy since the Roman age. The lakeshores, set against the backdrop of the towering Alps, make for a spectacular landscape. Despite its posh reputation, the Lake Como area offers plenty of active pursuits, from sailing to hiking. In **Varenna** (accessible by 1-hour train ride from Milan; €6.70 one-way), an unpretentious town on Lake Como's eastern shore, you can take a guided canyoning excursion with **Alto Lario Guide** (tel. 333/673-5419; www.altolarioguide.com; 7am-11pm Apr.-Sept.; €60 per person, equipment included).

DAY 2

1. Palais des Nations

Parc de l'Ariana; tel. 22/917 12 34; www.ungeneva.org; 8:30am-5pm Mon.-Fri.; 16 CHF

It's not every day you get to visit the headquarters of the United Nations. Some of the highlights include the Human Rights and Alliance of Civilizations room decorated by Miquel Barcelò, Ariana Park, and discovering the intricacies of collateral, international cooperation. This is one you should book a month or more in advance as spots do fill up quickly. Tours last approximately one hour. Arrive 30-45 minutes before your scheduled tour time to make sure you have plenty of time for security checks. Passports are required for entry.

2. Bains des Paquis

Quai du Mont-Blanc 30; tel. 22/732 29 74; www.bains-des-paquis.ch; open daily, hours vary according to weather; 50 CHF

Spend your last afternoon in Geneva exploring this famous, beach-lined man-made peninsula. Named for their public baths, this peninsula jets out into Lake Geneva (or Lac Léman, as it's known in French). For lunch, settle into **La Bouvette des Bains** (Bains des Paquis; tel. 22/738 16 16; www.buvettedesbains.com; 7am-11pm daily; 15 CHF), which offers a bright seasonal menu highlighting some of the region's fruits and legumes.

Afterward, join locals in their favorite summer pastimes, swimming and sunbathing, on the beaches and protected swimming areas of this peninsula. Beyond the beaches, the public Turkish-style baths provide another glimpse into the local culture and are well worth the price of admission (60 CHF).

For dinner, you can try more fondue at **Les Gruyérien** (Boulevard de Saint-Georges 65; tel. 22/320 81 84; www.bucheronne.ch; 6:30-11:30pm Tues.-Sat.; 30 CHF). Forgo the cheese this time and opt for the Fondue Bûcheronne. The chef carefully selects the best cuts of beef and other meats especially for this carnivorous delight.

Zürich, Switzerland

Where to Stay: Centrally located Altstadt, also known as District 1 and Old Town

Arrive by: Train from to Geneva Gare Cornavin to Zurich Hb (3 hours direct, 7 hours via the Golden Pass)

DAY 3

1. The Golden Pass

www.goldenpass.ch; 6 hours; from 38 CHF

You could take a fast train from Geneva to Zürich and arrive three hours later, but why rush through the alpine beauty? The six-hour, three-leg (sometimes four) Golden Pass journey starts in **Montreux** on the eastern side of Lake Geneva (1 hour by train from Geneva; from 30 CHF), where you can board the Golden Pass Panoramic train, which has large panoramic windows, or Golden Pass Belle Epoque train to **Zweisimmen.** From there, you transfer to the train to **Interlaken** (sometimes there is an additional change at Spiez), the town beautifully nestled between Lake Brienz and Lake Thun. At Interlaken, you switch trains to reach **Lucerne,** the end of the Golden Pass route. Along the way, you'll pass lakeside scenery, alpine meadows, and quaint villages. At Lucerne, hop on an intercity train for the ride to Zürich (1 hour; from 25 CHF).

2. Dinner at Zeughauskeller

Bahnhofstrasse 28A; tel. 44/220 15 15; www.zeughauskeller.ch; 11:30am-11pm daily; 40 CHF

When you arrive, head to your hotel to freshen up. Then, start your visit to Zürich with one large mug of ale and a generous plate of wienerschnitzel in the city's most storied eatery. Built in 1487, this large, rustic beer hall—much like ones you might find in Germany—was originally the local zeughaus, or "arsenal storehouse" where artillery and weapons were kept. Since 1926, this has been a peaceful, sociable, if not somewhat rowdy eatery welcoming guests from around the world in typical, hospitable Swiss fashion. It's a fun night out for travelers and Zürchers alike.

Old Town

TO TAKE Home

Swiss-made goods are widely regarded as being well-made and sturdy, with the high attention to detail expected of expert-level craftspeople and artisans. You can be assured that whatever you purchase in Switzerland will last you a lifetime—unless it is chocolate. That might not survive your trip back home! Here are a few things to consider picking up as a souvenir or a gift.

- **Swiss Army Knife:** Besides chocolate, the handy, multitool Swiss Army Knife is perhaps the item most closely associated with Switzerland. You will want to look for the classic **Victorinox,** the original maker of the Swiss Army Knife; just remember to pack it in your checked bag for any flights.
- **Brienz woodcarving:** Located just a couple of hours south of Zürich, the small village of Brienz has been carving intricate wood sculptures since the 19th century. The most ubiquitous sculptures you will find are palm-sized animals and typical Alpine scenes featuring the people of the region in traditional dress.
- **Swiss-made watches:** Not every Swiss-made watch is a Rolex, though you will find plenty of luxury shops carrying that and other high-end brands. Look out for classic pieces by **Mondaine,** which not only carries watches at affordable price points, but also offers watch face designs with miniature clocks of the Swiss Railways.
- **Swiss chocolate:** What says Switzerland more than chocolate? Though brands like Lindt and Toblerone are easily found, stop by **Sprunglï** (Bahnhofstrasse 67, Zürich; tel. 44/212 17 02; www.spruengli.ch; 8am-7pm Mon.-Fri., 9am-6pm Sat.), where they have been crafting fine chocolates and other confections since 1859.

Sprunglï

DAY 4

1. Kunsthaus Zürich Art Museum

Heimpl. 1; tel. 44/253 84 84; www.kunsthaus.ch; 10am-6pm Tues.-Sun.; 23 CHF

The art movement of Dada, the first real international art movement, began in Zürich, forging the way for the Surrealists and other movements to follow. Unsurprisingly, this museum has the world's largest Dada collection. Kunsthaus also has the world's largest collection of Edvard Munch paintings outside Norway, with over a dozen in the permanent collection. Works by Mondrian, Picasso, Rembrandt, Rubens, Van Gogh, and a large gallery of Claude Monet's impressionist paintings are just a few of the other highlights.

top, Grossmünster Cathedral;
bottom, Bahnhofstrasse

2. Grossmünster Cathedral

Grossmünsterplatz; tel. 44/250 66 51; www.grossmuenster.ch; 10am-6pm daily; free

Of the churches and cathedrals in Zürich, none are as symbolic of the city as Grossmünster. This 12th-century, iconic Romanesque cathedral is topped by two towers, dubbed "salt and pepper." The cathedral itself, with its vaulted ceilings and stained glass, is impressive, though you will want to pay the 5 CHF to climb the "salt and pepper" towers for some incredible views over the city.

A 10-minute walk away, **Haus Hiltl** (Sihlstrasse 28; tel. 44/227 70 00; http://hiltl.ch; 7am-10pm Mon.-Thurs., 7am-11pm Fri., 8am-11pm Sat., 10am-10pm Sun.; 20 CHF), purportedly the oldest vegetarian restaurant in the world, has offered a wide variety of vegetarian and vegan dishes since 1898. Even non-vegetarians might reconsider their dietary choices after a meal here!

3. Bahnhofstrasse

Bahnhofstrasse; open 24 hours; free

Zürich's current high-end shopping strip was once the city moat. It's strange what 150 years can do! Today, you can find all of the luxury labels and high-end boutiques associated with everything Swiss and European, particularly the more known watch brands. It would be a shame to come to all the way to Zürich and not do at least a little window shopping for what Zürich is well known for.

4. Old Town

Spend the rest of the afternoon exploring the Old Town on foot. There are a number of smaller side streets and charming alleyways to discover, alongside some of the world's most high-end luxury goods. This is Zürich, after all! Be sure to make a quick stop by the **Fraumunster Church** (Münsterhof 2; tel. 44/221 20 63; www.fraumuenster.ch; 10am-6pm daily Mar. 1-Oct. 31, 10am-5pm daily Nov 1.-Feb 28.; 5 CHF) to admire the Expressionist stained-glass windows of Marc Chagall. Consider a ferry ride out over Lake Zürich and perhaps the cable car up to the Felsenegg viewpoint.

Afterward, have dinner at **Raclette Stube** (Zähringerstrasse 16; tel. 44/251 41 30; www.fondue-stuben.ch; from 5:30pm Mon.-Fri., from 1pm Sat.-Sun.; 35 CHF). Grill your Swiss raclette cheese at your table and carefully pour it over your bread, baby potatoes, or charcuterie.

Milan, Italy

Where to Stay: Porta Nova, close to the main sights with tons of restaurants and bars at your doorstep

Arrive by: Train from Zurich Hb to Milano Centrale (3 hours 20 minutes direct, 7 hours via the Bernina Express)

DAY 5

TOP EXPERIENCE

★ 1. Bernina Express

www.rhb.ch/en/panoramic-trains/bernina-express; twice daily, 4.5 hours; panorama train from 83 CHF, reservations required

Between Zürich and Milan, too, there are high-speed trains that zip between the cities in a little over three hours, but take the Bernina Express instead. A bucket-list experience for some, this UNESCO World Heritage listed journey travels at the highest elevation of any train route through the Alps with amazing scenery along the way. Departing from **Chur** (1 hour 15 minutes from Zürich; 27-40 CHF), it winds through 55 tunnels and across 196 bridges as it makes its way along the stunning 122 km (76 mi) to **Tirano,** Italy. Passengers are seated in panorama cars with large view-friendly windows. There are a number of stops en route; between

NAME CHECK: Leonardo da Vinci

Undoubtedly you have heard the name Leonardo da Vinci. You are likely familiar with the *Mona Lisa* hanging in the Louvre in Paris, and maybe you studied the proportions of his *Vitruvian Man* in school. Leonardo is a name as synonymous with the Italian Renaissance as Michelangelo and Raphael, two of his contemporaries. However, da Vinci was not always met for the life of an artist. When he came to Milan in 1482, he came with the understanding that he would work for the Duke of Milan as an engineer and weapons designer. The mention of him being an artist of any merit was in passing.

Over the next few years, da Vinci wrote in his notebooks, creating various inventions and curios that would mark his genius. He wrote in a special mirror script in his journals, which included sketches of scientific ideas, and studied the human form in intense detail. The lifelike quality of his drawings and sketches was unparalleled. The Duke of Milan gave various commissions to da Vinci to perform, from creating floats for local pageants to drawing plans for sculptures and structures that were never completed.

It would be over a decade before da Vinci would receive the commission that would become his first masterpiece, ***The Last Supper.*** It is this mural that cemented da Vinci's reputation as a master artist and unrivaled genius, perfecting the use of a vanishing point to create three-dimensional space on a two-dimensional surface. In addition to *The Last Supper,* Milan holds da Vinci's **Codex Trivulzianus,** a 55-page manuscript he wrote in the effort to improve his literary education in the Trivulziana Library at **Castello Sforzesco** (page 659).

Bernina Lagalb and Alp Grüm, the train ascends to its highest point, 2,253 m (7,390 ft) above sea level, at **Ospizio Bernina.** Tirano, at the end of the line, is connected to Milan by regional train (2.5 hours; €10-13).

Note that once you get off in Italy (Tirano is the only Bernina Express stop in Italy), euros are used, not the Swiss franc.

2. Navigli

Navigli district; www.turismo.milano.it

If you start your Bernina Express ride in the morning, you should arrive in Milan in the afternoon with enough time to check into your hotel and get ready for aperitivo, a true Milanese experience. Starting at 5pm or 6pm, and sometimes lasting throughout the night, aperitivo is a special offered by bars and cafés where buying a drink for €10-20 comes with appetizers and small bites. Other Italian cities have adopted the aperitivo culture, but Milan is still considered the capital.

The Navigli district, where colorful buildings and two canals make it one of the most charming parts of Milan, is one of the most popular neighborhoods for aperitivo and nightlife. The two canals, the **Naviglio Grande** and the **Naviglio Pavese,** are lined with restaurants, bars, galleries, and shops. Start at **Mag Cafè** (Ripa di Porta Ticinese, 43; tel. 02/3956-2875; 7:30pm-1:30am daily), where the house cocktails are made with fresh ingredients, accompanied by aperitivo snacks

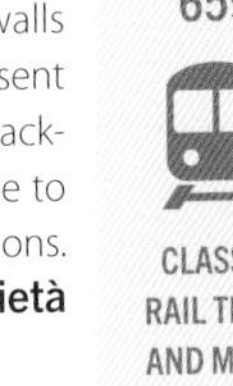

of cheese and charcuterie. For a dinner of classic Milanese cuisine—risotto Milanese, osso buco, and a cotoletta alla milanese (veal cutlet) so big that it overflows your plate—look no further than **La Madonnina** (Via Gentilino, 6; tel. 02/257-2998; www.facebook.com/lamadonninamilano; noon-2:30pm Mon.-Sat., 8pm-10:30pm Wed.-Sat.; entrees €10-12).

DAY 6

★ 1. *The Last Supper*

Piazza Santa Maria delle Grazie, 2; tel. 02/9280-0360; https://cenacolovinciano.vivaticket.it; 8:15am-7pm Tues.-Sat., 2pm-7pm Sun.; adults €15, 18 and under free

Santa Maria delle Grazie church holds one of Milan's most prized possessions, Leonardo da Vinci's 15th-century *The Last Supper* fresco. Although a majority of the church was destroyed by Allied bombing during World War II, the fresco, protected by heavy sandbags, survived. While the room in which it is displayed is fairly small, quiet, and dark, Leonardo's fresco is nothing less than astonishing, depicting the scene from the Gospel of John, in which Jesus is sitting down to supper with his 12 disciples and telling them that one would soon betray him. Put your camera away and spend your 15 minutes taking in every single color and detail, especially the restored colors of the clothes on Jesus and the disciples.

Booking is absolutely mandatory here, and tickets should be purchased well in advance. Due to the fresco's fragility, visitors are only allowed into the viewing room 30 at a time for 15 minutes.

2. Castello Sforzesco

Piazza Castello; www.milanocastello.it; castle 7am-7:30pm daily, museums 9am-5:30pm Tues.-Sun.; castle and museums adults €10, over 65 €8, under 18 free

Head northeast, and after about 10 minutes' walk, you'll reach 15th-century Castello Sforzesco, built by Francesco Sforza, the fourth Duke of Milan and the founder of the famous Milanese Sforza dynasty. Comprising a number of walls and moats for defense, it's an ever-present reminder of historical Milan amid a backdrop of modernity and today is home to several civic museums and art collections. Visit the **Museum of Rondanini Pietà** to see Michelangelo's last sculpture.

3. Duomo di Milano

Piazza del Duomo; tel. 02/7202-3375; www.duomomilano.it; cathedral 8am-7pm daily, rooftop terraces 9am-7pm daily; cathedral adults €3, terraces adults €9 on foot or €13 by elevator, children and students €4.50 on foot or €7 by elevator

Walk 15 minutes southeast into the Piazza del Duomo, the very heart of Milan. Here, the dominating presence of the Duomo di Milano, the pride and joy of Milan, seems to breathe life into the rest of the city. The Duomo, built in the Gothic style, is Italy's largest church (some mistakenly believe that title goes

top, Navigli; bottom, Bernina Express

to St. Peter's Basilica, but is actually in the State of Vatican City, a separate country) and the third largest in the world. Constructed over a period of nearly six centuries, its five broad naves and 40 intricately designed and delicately detailed pillars can be viewed for a fee from the **roof.** Follow the marked paths and stairways to view Milan's skyline from all angles, and to experience the Piazza del Duomo from a bird's-eye view.

If you need to eat beforehand, grab lunch from **Terrazza Aperol** (Via Ugo Foscolo, 1; tel. 335/735-6773; https://ilmercatodelduomo.it/terrazza-aperol; 11am-11pm daily; drinks €10-20) at the four-story **Galleria Vittorio Emanuele II,** the world's oldest active shopping mall, which sits on the north side of Piazza del Duomo

4. Via Montenapoleone

Via Montenapoleone

From the Duomo, walk east along Coros Vittorio Emanuele II to Piazza San Bablia, which is at the foot of Via Montenapoleone. Milan's iconic Via Montenapoleone is a narrow street lined with the flagship stores of Italy's most popular and exclusive brands, as well as boutiques of famous Italian designers and shoemakers. Even if you only plan to window shop, stop into a store simply to take in the experience. You'll see some of the world's most lavish brands: Gucci, Prada, Armani, Dolce & Gabbana, and Fendi. While Via Montenapoleone's upscale and extravagant character may appear to invite only patrons of the same ilk, all are welcome.

5. La Scala

Via Filodrammatici 2; tel. 02/88-791; www.teatroallascala.org; box office 10am-6pm Mon.-Sat., noon-6pm Sun.

Italy's most famous opera house, La Scala (Teatro alla Scala) also mounts performances of La Scala Theater Ballet, Theater Chorus, and Theater Orchestra. Many of the world's most iconic opera singers have performed at La Scala since its opening in 1778. It is internationally considered one of the leading opera and ballet theaters in the world. If you can, spend your last evening at a performance here, where the atmosphere is akin to stepping into another time.

For a pre-show meal, try **Ristorante**

Duomo di Milano

WATCH

***Sister*:** This 2012 French-language drama by French-Swiss director Ursula Meier follows a young boy who makes a living by stealing from the wealthy at a ski resort in Geneva. The main character and his older sister live in a housing complex below the luxury resort.

READ

Frankenstein by Mary Shelley: One of the most influential horror stories of all time is almost entirely set in Geneva.

Hausfrau by Jill Alexander Essbaum: In this intense psychological thriller, Anna Benz is an American expat living with her family in the suburbs of Zürich. She has problems adjusting to the Swiss way of life, and when her coping mechanism fails her, tragedy strikes.

LISTEN

***Rigoletto*:** Get inspired to visit Milan's La Scala, the world's most famous opera house, where opera master Guiseppe Verdi composed many of his best-known works.

Emilia e Carlo (Via Giuseppe Sacchi, 8; tel. 02/862-100; noon-3pm and 7pm-11pm Mon.-Fri.; entrées €20-45), a classic Italian restaurant with a large menu of appetizers and first courses.

TRANSPORTATION

Air

All three of the main cities on this route have international airports with direct flights to and from countries outside Europe.

- **Geneva International Airport** (GVA; www.gva.ch): Located 6 km (4 mi) northwest of Geneva. A free airport train takes about six minutes and connect the airport with downtown.
- **Zürich Airport** (ZRH; tel. 0900 300 313; www.flughafen-zuerich.ch): Located 10 km (6 mi) from Zürich. A free airport train takes about 10 minutes to connect with downtown Zürich.
- **Milan Malpensa Airport** (MXP; tel. 02 232323; www.milanomalpensa-airport.com): About 50 km (31mi) northwest of central Milan; 45-60 minutes to Milano Centrale via Malpensa Express train (€12 one-way).

Train

Geneva, Zürich, and Milan can be reached by high-speed trains from a number of cities, both domestic and international. In Switzerland, **SBB** (www.sbb.ch) is the national operator; it's **Trenitalia** (www.trenitalia.com) in Italy, although **Trenord** (www.trenord.it) runs trains in Lombardy, including the line between Tirano and Milan and the Malpensa Express to Milan's airport.

- **Geneva Gare Cornavin:** (1201 Geneva; www.sbb.ch): Geneva's recently renovated main train station is on the northwest corner of the old city, just a five-minute walk to downtown. Leave from here to reach **Montreux,** the beginning of the Golden Pass train route (1 hour; from 30 CHF).

- **Zurich Hb** (Bahnhofpl, www.sbb.ch): Located on the northside of the old city, next to the Swiss National Museum. Trains from Geneva arrive here (3 hours; 85-150 CHF), as do trains from Lucerne (1 hour; from 25 CHF). Leave from here to reach **Chur** (1 hour 15 minutes; 27-40 CHF), where you board the Bernina Express.
- **Milano Centrale** (Piazza Duca d'Aosta, 1; www.milanocentrale.it): Located 3 km (1.8 mi) northeast of the city center, conveniently connected by metro line 3 (7 minutes). Trains from Zürich arrive here (3 hours 20 minutes; from €80), as do the Malpensa Express (45-60 minutes; €12) and trains from Tirano (2.5 hours; €10-13).

Public Transportion

Geneva

Geneva's **UNIRESO** (www.unireso.com) public transport system is a diverse, interconnected mix of trams, buses, boats, and commuter trains. The most common single ticket costs 3 CHF, is transferable between transport, and is valid for 60 minutes. If you are staying at a hotel or hostel in Geneva, you are entitled to a free public transport card for the length of your stay.

Zürich

The **ZVV** (www.zvv.ch) runs the interconnected public transport system of Zürich, which uses a mix of buses, trams, trains, boats, and cable cars. Single ride tickets are 4.40 CHF and are valid for one hour. The **Zürich Card** (1 day 27 CHF, 3 days 53 CHF) is a good value as it offers not only free unlimited travel on public transportation, but also free or reduced admission to 43 museums.

Milan

Milan's public transportation system, operated by **ATM** (Azienda Trasporti Milanesi; www.atm.it) is arguably the best and most efficient of its kind in Italy and is by far the most economical way to travel around. The city is covered by metro, buses, and trams. A single ride via any public transportation mode is €1.50, with a ticket valid for 90 minutes.

Getting Back

From Milan, it's easy to get back on a train to Zürich (3 hours 17 minutes; from €80) or Geneva (4 hours; from €110). Alternatively, fly back to your point of origin or on to your next stop from Milan's Malpensa Airport.

CONNECT WITH

- Tour du Mont Blanc (page 405)
- Alta Via 1: Dolomite High Route (page 439)
- Rhine River Cruise (page 503)
- The Rhone Valley (page 618)

THE DOURO LINE

Why Go: The Douro Line is one of Europe's best rail journeys. The route goes through tunnels and passes vineyards and picturesque towns as it hugs the curves of the Douro River across Northern Portugal.

Number of Days: 4

Total Distance: 200 km (120 mi)

Seasons: Summer and fall

Start: Porto

End: Vila Nova de Foz Côa

With verdant landscapes, medieval villages, and majestic mountains, Northern Portugal is invigorating. Its defining feature is the Douro River, flowing westward through the rugged landscape to the Atlantic at the region's biggest city, Porto. The Douro Line railway follows the curves of the river through the Douro Valley, from Porto in the west to the town of Pocinho in the east. The scenery around every bend is breathtaking, changing with the seasons from luxuriant green in spring to gold and copper in autumn. Along the way, you can make stops to ride a historic steam train, taste delicious wine, and see prehistoric art.

TOP 3

Tasting port in Vila Nova de Gaia, where famous makers of the fortified wine share the history of the drink for which this region is famous (page 669).

Tracing one of the most scenic stretches of the Douro River on the **Douro Historic Steam Train** (page 670).

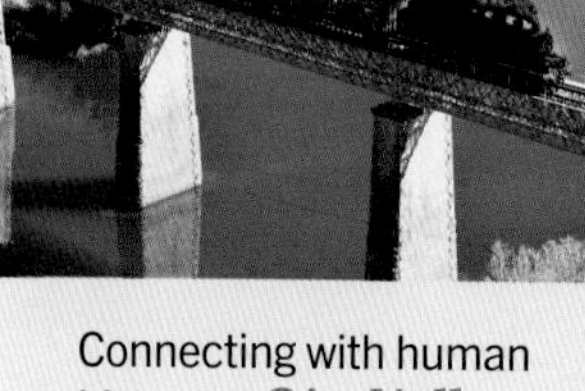

Connecting with human history at **Côa Valley Archaeological Park**, an open-air gallery of Paleolithic art along the Portuguese-Spanish border (page 673).

DAY 1

Porto

Where to Stay: Downtown to be centrally located

Arrive by: Plane to Porto's Sá Carneiro International Airport or train to Porto Campanhã

1. Bolhão Market

Rua Formosa (main ground floor entrance); tel. 223 326 024; 8am-8pm Mon.-Fri., 8am-6pm Sat.

The unrefined charm of Portugal's second city is part of its allure. Shabby in parts, sophisticated in others, Porto is down-to-earth, relaxed, and endearingly genuine. Porto's best-known export, port wine, is reason enough to visit the city, but there's plenty of sightseeing to keep you busy as well.

Start your time in Porto at the bustling Bolhão Market. Located inside an impressive neoclassical building, the market is packed with stalls run by farmers, butchers, and fisherfolk.

Next, walk a few minutes down the main Rua de Santa Catarina shopping street to the famous belle epoque **Majestic Café** (Rua de Santa Catarina 112; tel. 222 003 887; www.cafemajestic.com; 9:30am-11:30pm Mon.-Sat.; €15) for a snack of coffee and cake.

2. Livraria Lello

Rua das Carmelitas 144; tel. 222 002 037; www.livrarialello.pt; 9:30am-7pm daily; entry €5, deductible from any book purchase

Walk 10 minutes to the Livraria Lello bookshop. A frontrunner for the title of most beautiful bookshop in the world, the building features a sweeping crimson central staircase and a spectacular stained-glass skylight. Besides books in several languages, the shop has a café upstairs that sells coffee, port wine, and cigars. Livraria Lello served as J. K. Rowling's inspiration for the Flourish & Blotts bookshop in the Harry Potter novels, and the small shop is so popular, especially with Harry Potter fans, that long queues form at the door. Tickets can be bought online or from a shop just around the corner.

For lunch, walk five minutes to **Petisqueira Voltaria** (Rua Afonso Martins Alho 109; tel. 223 256 593 or 913 885 252; noon-10pm Thurs.-Tues.; €12). Order the

Livraria Lello

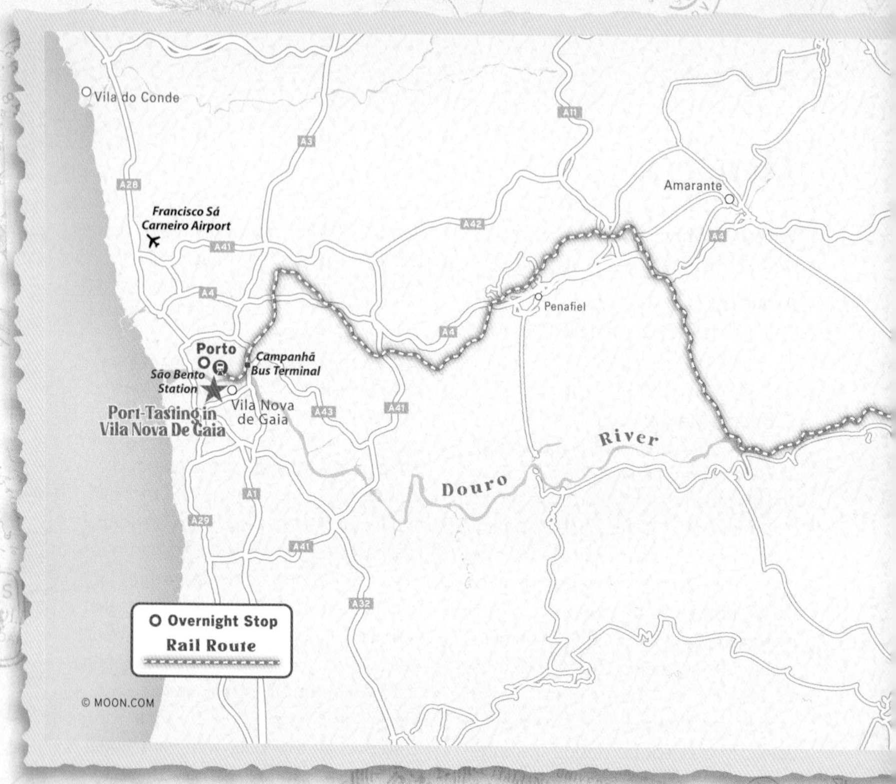

Vila do Conde

Amarante

Francisco Sá Carneiro Airport

Penafiel

Porto

Campanhã Bus Terminal

São Bento Station

Port-Tasting in Vila Nova De Gaia

Vila Nova de Gaia

Douro River

A28 A3 A11 A42 A41 A4 A43 A1 A29 A32

Overnight Stop

Rail Route

© MOON.COM

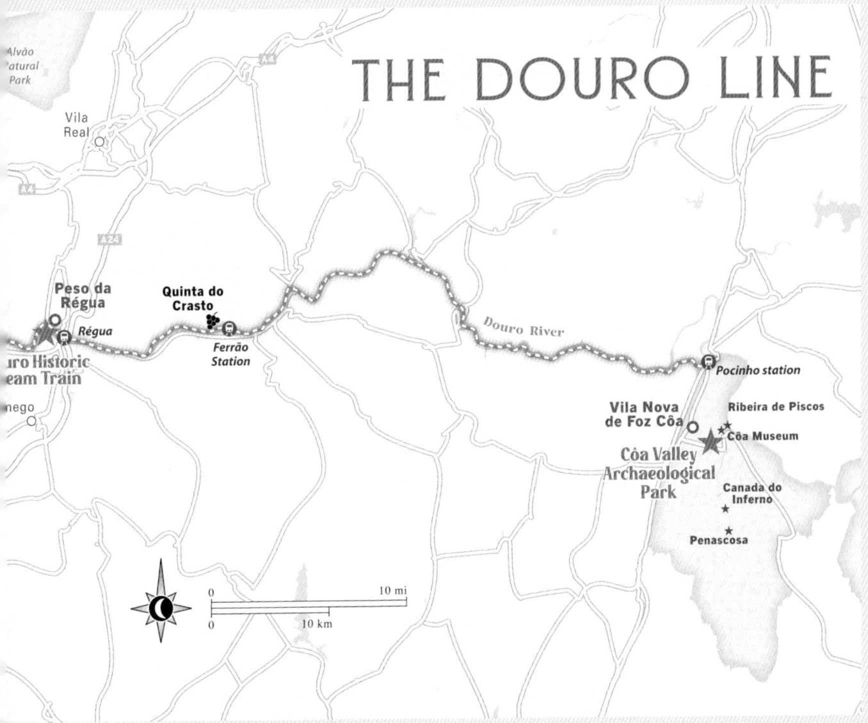

THE DOURO LINE

Alvão
Natural
Park
Vila
Real
A4
A24
Peso da
Régua
Régua
Quinta do
Crasto
Ferrão
Station
Douro River
Pocinho station
uro Historic
eam Train
nego
Vila Nova
de Foz Côa
Ribeira de Piscos
Côa Museum
Côa Valley
Archaeological
Park
Canada do
Inferno
Penascosa
0
10 mi
0
10 km

left, castle near Vila Nova de Foz Côa; middle, Porto River; right, Bolhão Market

Key Reservations

- **Train tickets** are often cheaper if booked in advance online (www.cp.pt).
- Lunch at **Tasca da Quinta** in Régua.
- Time your trip with the **Douro Historic Steam Train,** which only runs Saturdays June-October and Sundays July-October.
- Reserve your tour of **Quinta do Crasto** wine estate, night visit to **Penacosa,** and other guided tours of **Côa Valley Archaeological Park** in advance.

Quinta do Crasto

francesinha, a monster signature sandwich comprising a stack of meats, smothered in melted cheese and a beer sauce, often topped with a fried egg. It's not for the fainthearted, but it's a must in Porto.

3. Vila Nova de Gaia

Afterward, walk down to the river and cross the iconic **Dom Luís I Bridge** to Vila Nova de Gaia, the center of port wine–making in Porto. Visit the cellars of **Cálem** (Av. Diogo Leite 344; tel. 916 113 451; https://tour.calem.pt; from €15) for a tour and tasting of their port wine. Cálem is a 15-minute walk from Petisqueira Voltaria.

4. Porto Riverfront

Cross the bridge again back into Porto and round the day off with a sunset stroll along Porto's charismatic riverfront area, with its mishmash of colorful houses. It's particularly lovely at night. Stop for dinner at **Taberna dos Mercadores** (Rua dos Mercadores 36; tel. 222 010 510; 12:30pm-11pm Tues.-Fri. and Sun., 12:30pm-3:30pm and 7pm-11pm Sat.; €20), a romantic spot for a cozy meal.

São Bento Railway Station

DAY 2

Porto

1. São Bento Railway Station

Praça Almeida Garrett; tel. 707 210 220; www.cp.pt

Although there are fewer departures than from Porto Campanha, begin your rail journey on the Douro Line at São Bento. More than just a railway station, São Bento is a piece of history. It features a stunning U-shaped atrium clad floor-to-ceiling in 20,000 hand-painted traditional Portuguese azulejo tiles that depict scenes from Portugal's history, such as the Conquest of Ceuta in 1415.

★ Port-Tasting in Vila Nova de Gaia

Deep, rich, fortified port wine has become an ambassador for Portugal as a whole. Port wine must be produced in Northern Portugal, and authentic port is produced exclusively in vineyards in the Douro Region, demarcated in 1756, with mostly native grape varieties. It is transported downriver and aged in barrels stored in cellars such as those in Vila Nova de Gaia, just over the Douro River from Porto.

VARIETALS

Generally enjoyed as a dessert drink, the best-known port is typically ruby red in color. **Ruby** is the younger, lighter, fruitier variety, while **tawny** varieties are older and nuttier. Exceptional **vintage** port is produced only from the finest harvests and aged for long periods in oak casks. **Rosé** and **white** varieties have recently given the wine a trendy makeover as an ingredient of white port and tonic, a popular summer cocktail.

VILA NOVA DE GAIA PORT WINE CELLARS

Some of Portugal's oldest port companies were founded by British mercantile families in the 17th and 18th centuries and are still run by their descendants. Most of the lodges offer guided tours in English, culminating in a tasting session.

- **Cálem** (page 668): Founded in 1859, Cálem is one of Portugal's signature ports. Tour options include tastings, food, and even fado performances.
- **Sandeman** (Largo Miguel Bombarda 47; tel. 223 740 534; www.sandeman.com; from €14): Globally renowned since 1790, tours of the magnificent 200-year-old cellars include a 1790 vintage visit, an Old Tawnies tour, and a Port Wine and Chocolate experience.
- **Taylor's** (Rua do Choupelo 250; tel. 223 772 973; www.taylor.pt; €15): Producing port since 1692, Taylor's is among Portugal's oldest port houses. Audio-guided tours provide information in 11 languages.

If you'd like more guidance, **Porto Walkers** (tel. 918 291 519; www.portowalkers.pt; from €27) takes groups on half-day walking tours that include a trio of different lodges. Knowledgeable guides teach you about the origins of port, and even how to sample the drink properly.

Peso da Régua

Where to Stay: In town, a few streets back from the riverfront

Arrive by: Douro Line train from Porto's São Bento Railway Station to Régua train station (2 hours)

2. Douro Museum

Rua Marquês de Pombal; tel. 254 310 190; www.museudodouro.pt; 10am-5:30pm daily; €7.50, includes a glass of port

Surrounded by stepped terraces covered in lacy vines, Peso da Régua, commonly abbreviated to just Régua, is at the center of wine country. Not as picturesque as nearby towns, hardworking Régua is important in the port wine trade as a crossroads for shipping. The riverfront lacks charm, but if you wander a few streets back, you'll find a quaint, authentic town.

Alight the train at Peso da Régua, and walk west about 20 minutes to get to the town center and the Douro Museum. To get a feel for local winemaking culture and history, spend an hour here. The exhibits, featuring short films, vintage photos, and even a rabelo boat, take you through the process, from growing and harvesting to fermenting and shipping. The building, 18th-century Casa da Companhia Velha, was once the headquarters of the Royal Company of Vine-Growers from the Alto Douro Region, the oldest company in Portugal.

Located behind the museum, **Tasca da Quinta** (Rua do Marquês de Pombal 42, ground floor; tel. 918 754 102; 7pm-10pm Tues.-Fri., 12:30pm-2:30pm and 7pm-10pm Sat., 12:30pm-2:30pm Sun.; €15) is perfectly situated for a lunch of Portuguese tapas. Make a reservation; it's hugely popular with both visitors and locals.

top, Régua; bottom, Douro Historic Steam Train

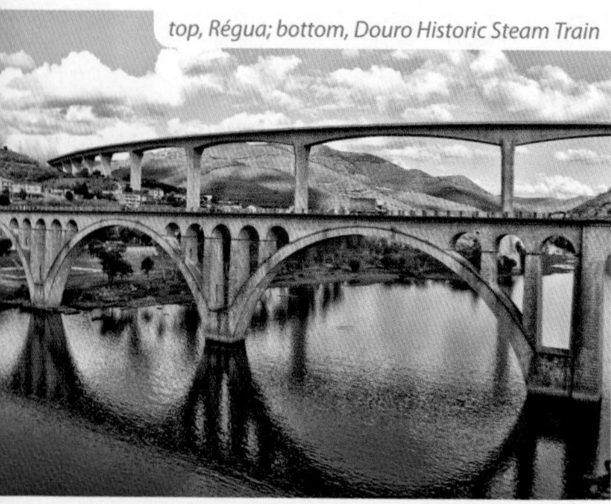

★ 3. Douro Historic Steam Train

Tel. 707 210 220; www.cp.pt; round-trip 3-hour rides Sat. afternoon June 4-Oct. 29, Sun. afternoon July 3-Oct. 9; adults €45, ages 4-12 €22.50

Make sure your trip to Régua falls on a Saturday or Sunday so you can take the three-hour round-trip on the Douro Historic Steam Train. This is not only a train ride, but also a trip back in time—the vintage steam train dates to 1925. You'll cross rickety bridges, pass through atmospheric countryside and provincial villages, and stop in ornate old stations. This stretch between Peso da Régua and the town of Tua is one of the most scenic along the Douro. Trips include onboard entertainment courtesy of local folk singers as well as a glass of port wine.

You'll return to Régua for the evening. For dinner, head to **Cacho D'Oiro** (Rua Branca Martinho 5050; tel. 254 321 455; www.restaurantecachodoiro.pt; noon-3pm and 7pm-10:30pm daily; €15), hidden at the end of a small dead-end street. Its traditional menu is complemented by a selection of Douro wines.

The Wines of the Douro Valley

The beating heart of Portuguese viticulture, the Douro's deep valleys are flanked by steep terraced vineyards that step prettily down the hillsides toward the languid Douro River, which carves its way through the region. Covering close to 250,000 hectares (620,000 acres), the distinctive landscape is stunning, protected from the humid Atlantic winds by the mountainous topography. Winters can be bitterly cold, while summers are arid and hot, climactic extremes beneficial for grape-growing. The soil here is made up mostly of slate-like schist rock, which is rich in nutrients and excellent at retaining humidity. The region is a UNESCO World Heritage Site.

GRAPES AND WINE VARIETALS

The Douro Valley is home to scores of different grapes, more than 80 indigenous varieties, chosen to suit the varying types of terrain and exposures. As a general rule, port wine grapes are thicker-skinned and hardier than other varieties, making them better suited to the valley's dry conditions. While the Douro's whites can be a lovely surprise, the region is best known for its reds, the most famous of which is, of course, port wine.

The most popular red grape varieties are the touriga nacional, touriga francesa, tinta roriz, tinta barroca, and tinto cão. These varieties are renowned for being intense and robust, often blended with other national and international varieties. Port grapes provide depth, a strong tannin structure, and rich, fruity, or floral aromas. Rabigato, gouveio, viosinho, and malvasia fina are the most common whites.

BEST WINERIES

The Douro Valley is full of renowned wine estates; many are also centers of gastronomy and architecture.

- **Quinta da Pacheca** (Rua do Relógio do Sol 261; tel. 254 331 229; www.quintadapacheca.com; 10am-7pm daily): Located a few kilometers from Peso da Régua, this preeminent 18th-century manor wine estate overlooks the Douro River and was one of the first to bottle its own brand of wine.
- **Quinta do Crasto** (page 672): With idyllic vistas over the Douro River, family-run Quinta do Crasto is a centuries-old estate whose name sits alongside regional heavyweights and embodies the essence of Douro winemaking.
- **Quinta do Vallado** (Vilarinho dos Freires; tel. 254 323 147; www.quintadovallado.com; 9am-7pm daily): Another of the best-known names in Douro wine production, Quinta do Vallado is a historic estate with a contemporary look and feel.

Ferrão

Arrive by: Douro Line train from Régua train station to Ferrão station (20 minutes)

1. Quinta do Crasto

Gouvinhas; tel. 254 920 020; www.quintadocrasto.pt; 9am-1pm and 2pm-6pm Mon.-Fri.; from €20

Hop back on the Douro Line for a quick ride to the Ferrão station, and head to your reservation at Quinta do Crasto wine estate. It's a 45-minute walk from the Ferrão train station, but the Quinta can pick up visitors.

Quinta do Crasto has roots stretching back to 1615. The vast estate comprises 135 hectares (334 acres)—74 hectares (183 acres) of which are vineyards—and produces 1.4 million bottles of wine and port per year. At its heart is a century-old farmhouse. Visits include guided tours (available in English) with wine-tastings, which can also include lunch or dinner and boat trips on the Douro River. Guests are invited to enjoy a dip in Quinta do Crasto's famous infinity pool, designed by Portuguese architect Eduardo Souto de Moura, or just take in the stunning view over the valley from the poolside.

Vila Nova de Foz Côa

Where to Stay: Center of Vila Nova de Foz Côa where there are a few properties

Arrive by: Douro Line train from Ferrão station to Pocinho station (1 hour), then taxi to Vila Nova de Foz Côa (10 minutes)

Vila Nova de Foz Côa

2. Night Visit of Penascosa

tel. 279 768 260 or 965 778 799; https://arte-coa.pt; hours vary based on sunset time; €20, reserve in advance

At the end of the Douro Line is Pocinho station, but the main attraction here is farther south: **Côa Valley Archaeological Park,** where Paleolithic engravings are preserved. Vila Nova de Foz Côa, a short cab ride south of Pocinho, is the closest town to the archaeological park.

A night visit to the Penascosa site of the park is an unforgettable experience. A guide in an all-terrain vehicle takes you to Penascosa, where nighttime provides the best conditions for viewing the Paleolithic carvings. Under flickering light, the drawings appear to move. The two-hour tours depart from the park reception center in Castelo Melhor, 15 minutes by taxi from Vila Nova de Foz Côa.

Back in town, have dinner at **Aldeia Douro** (Rua Dr. José Augusto Saraiva de Aguilar 19; tel. 279 094 403; 11am-3pm and 6:30pm-10:30pm Wed.-Sun.; €15), a restaurant and wine bar serving regional cuisine.

WATCH

***The Strange Case of Angelica*:** Directed by Porto-born filmmaker Manoel de Oliveira, this playful, charming movie is about a photographer who falls in love with a ghost. It's set in Peso da Régua and the surrounding Douro Valley.

READ

Night Train to Lisbon by Pascal Mercier: This well-known thriller-mystery-romance, later made into a movie starring Jeremy Irons, unfurls in Portugal, showcasing the romantic allure of Lisbon.

LISTEN

Fado: Portugal, especially Lisbon, is known for this moving, soulful genre. Fado is often associated with backstreet taverns where singers, the fadistas, accompanied by guitars and violas, entertain crowds with ballads of longing and daily hardships. Check out **Amália Rodrigues,** the Queen of Fado.

DAY 4

Day Trip to Côa Valley

Arrive by: Taxi from Vila Nova de Foz Côa to Côa Museum (10 minutes)

★ 1. Côa Valley Archaeological Park

tel. 279 768 260 or 965 778 799; https://arte-coa.pt; guided tours €16, reserve in advance

Vila Nova de Foz Côa became an archaeological hot spot in the 1990s with the discovery of thousands of mystifying rock engravings along the Côa Valley, depicting animals, hunters, weapons, and abstract images. The Côa Valley Archaeological Park was created to manage and protect the most important Paleolithic art collection in the world, with more than 60 sites in 17 km (10.5 mi) of the valley. The earliest drawings in the Côa Valley are believed to date back more than 20,000 years.

There are three main rock art sites, with guided tours offered for each: **Canada do Inferno** (departs in the morning from the Côa Museum; 1.5-2 hours); **Ribeira de Piscos** (departs in the morning from the Côa Museum; 2.5 hours; involves some challenging walking); and **Penascosa** (departs in the afternoon

Côa Valley Archaeological Park

and evening from park reception center in Castelo Melhor; 1.5 hours). Each stop includes a guided walk. Since you did Penascosa the night before, choose between the other two based on the level of activity you'd prefer.

2. Côa Museum

Rua do Museu, Parque Arqueológico do Vale do Côa; tel. 279 768 260 or 279 768 261; 10am-1:30pm and 2pm-5:30pm Tues.-Sun.; museum €7

After your guided tour, visit the state-of-the-art Côa Museum for a more detailed insight into prehistoric artwork. The museum is located at the gateway to the park, on one of the slopes where the Douro and the Côa Rivers meet. Over four floors, exhibits explore the valley through multimedia, photography, and images of the engravings. Objects unearthed during excavations in the valley are also showcased. Have dinner at the museum's modern **restaurant** and wine bar.

After your visit, return to your accommodation in Vila Nova de Foz Côa for the night. The next day, take a taxi back to Pocinho train station for your trip back to Porto.

TRANSPORTATION

Air

Porto's **Sá Carneiro International Airport** (OPO; tel. 229 432 400; www.aeroportoporto.pt) has daily flights from dozens of European destinations year-round as well as regular direct flights from Canada, the United States, South America, and Africa. Located in Maia, the airport is 10 km (6 mi) north of Porto city center and served by the **Metro** (www.metrodoporto.pt) light rail and tram system to central Porto (30 minutes; €2.55).

Train

Douro Line

The national rail service, **CP** (tel. 707 210 220; www.cp.pt), operates the Linha do Douro (Douro Line), which connects Porto in the west to Pocinho in the east. The full journey takes around 3.5 hours and costs €14 one-way. The Douro Line train runs several times a day, starting from Porto's São Bento or Campanhã stations, and less frequently on weekends and holidays.

Stations

- **Porto Campanhã** (Rua Pinheiro de Campanhã, Largo da Estação) station, located on the eastern outskirts, is Porto's main train station. From here there are connections to Porto city center by train (5 minutes; €1) and bus (15 minutes; €1-2).
- **São Bento Railway Station** (Praça Almeida Garrett) is Porto's historic urban station in the heart of the city center.
- **Peso da Régua Train Station** (Largo da Estação) is a 20-minute walk east of the town center and is a stop on the Douro Line and the start of the Douro Historic Steam Train. From Porto, trains run every two hours from Porto's Campanhã station (2 hours; €7-14).
- **Ferrão station** is the gateway to the Quinta do Castro wine estate. The Douro Line stops here two stops after Régua (20 minutes; €2.15).
- **Pocinho station** is the end of the Douro Line, eight stops after Ferrão (1 hour; €5.55).

Getting Back

The ride from Pocinho train station back to Porto takes 3-4 hours (€14).

CONNECT WITH

- Camino de Santiago (page 459)
- The Azores (page 581)

THE BERGEN LINE

Why Go: Experience Norway's dramatic landscapes, from famous fjords to mountaintop plateaus, on a scenic train ride between Oslo and Bergen.

Number of Days: 4

Total Distance: 500 km (310 mi)

Seasons: Late spring and summer

Start: Oslo

End: Bergen

The Bergen Line, or Bergensbanen, is one of the most scenic railway journeys in Norway—maybe in all of Europe. It connects Oslo and Bergen, Norway's two largest cities, crossing the Hardangervidda mountain plateau and hugging the edges of rivers and fjords along the way. The ride between Oslo and Bergen takes about seven hours nonstop, but if you pause in towns along the way—and even take a detour on another scenic railway line—you'll be able to enjoy more of what this region has to offer: stunning fjords, mountaintop hikes, extreme sports, historic sights, meals and brews fit for Vikings, and much more.

TOP 3

★ Riding the **Flåm Railway,** a one-hour train trip that serves up natural beauty and engineering marvels (page 677).

★ **Cruising the Nærøyfjord** from Flåm to Gudvangen, a quintessential experience in Norway (page 681).

Floating up to the top of Mount Hanguren on **Voss Gondol** (page 681).

DAY 1

Oslo

Where to Stay: Near Oslo Central Station

Arrive by: Plane to Oslo Airport Gardermoen

Wake up in Oslo, and head to **Oslo Central Station** (Oslo Sentralstasjon, or Oslo S for short) in the morning to embark on your Bergen Line rail journey. If you have time in Oslo before the train ride, see **Copenhagen to Oslo** (page 519) for what to see and do.

Myrdal

Arrive by: Bergen Line train from Oslo Central Station to Myrdal mountain station (5 hours)

1. Bergen Line to Myrdal

www.vy.no; four daily departures; 350-1,000 Kr

The first leg of your Bergen Line trip is the five-hour ride from Oslo to Myrdal. Leaving Oslo, the train first passes through the city of Drammen and follows along the **Drammenselva** river before skirting the shores of two lakes, **Tyrifjorden** and **Krøderfjorden.** The train passes through forests in **Flå,** home to a sanctuary for bears and other wild animals, and climbs up to 794 m (2,600 ft) above sea level to reach the ski resort town of Geilo.

From here, the route crosses the **Hardangervidda mountain plateau** and its national park, where you'll see spectacular nature—and sometimes extreme weather. Expect mountain lakes, peaks, and vast flats. In the winter, you might want to wear sunglasses, as the entire area is bright white with snow. In both winter and summer you might catch a glimpse of reindeer, as there are over 9,000 of them living on the plateau.

About 30 minutes before you arrive in Myrdal, you may recognize the scenery around the train station in **Finse:** Scenes from ***Star Wars Episode V: The Empire Strikes Back*** were filmed in the snow here. This is also the railroad's highest point, at 1,222 m (4,000 ft) above sea level.

★ 2. The Flåm Railway

A-Feltvegen 11; tel. 57 63 14 00; www.norwaysbest.com/no/flamsbana; 500 Kr

In Myrdal, you'll be switching from one scenic rail line to another. The one-hour ride on the Flåm Railway, one of the most beautiful rail journeys in the world, connects Myrdal's mountain station with the village of Flåm and one of Norway's most famous fjords, the **Aurlandsfjord.** Along the way, the train travels through the lush **Flåm Valley,** climbing up along mountainsides, across rivers, and through tunnels. It's not only beautiful—it's also a feat of engineering. Along the 20-km (12-mi) journey, the train passes through 20 tunnels, 18 of them made by hand.

Flåm

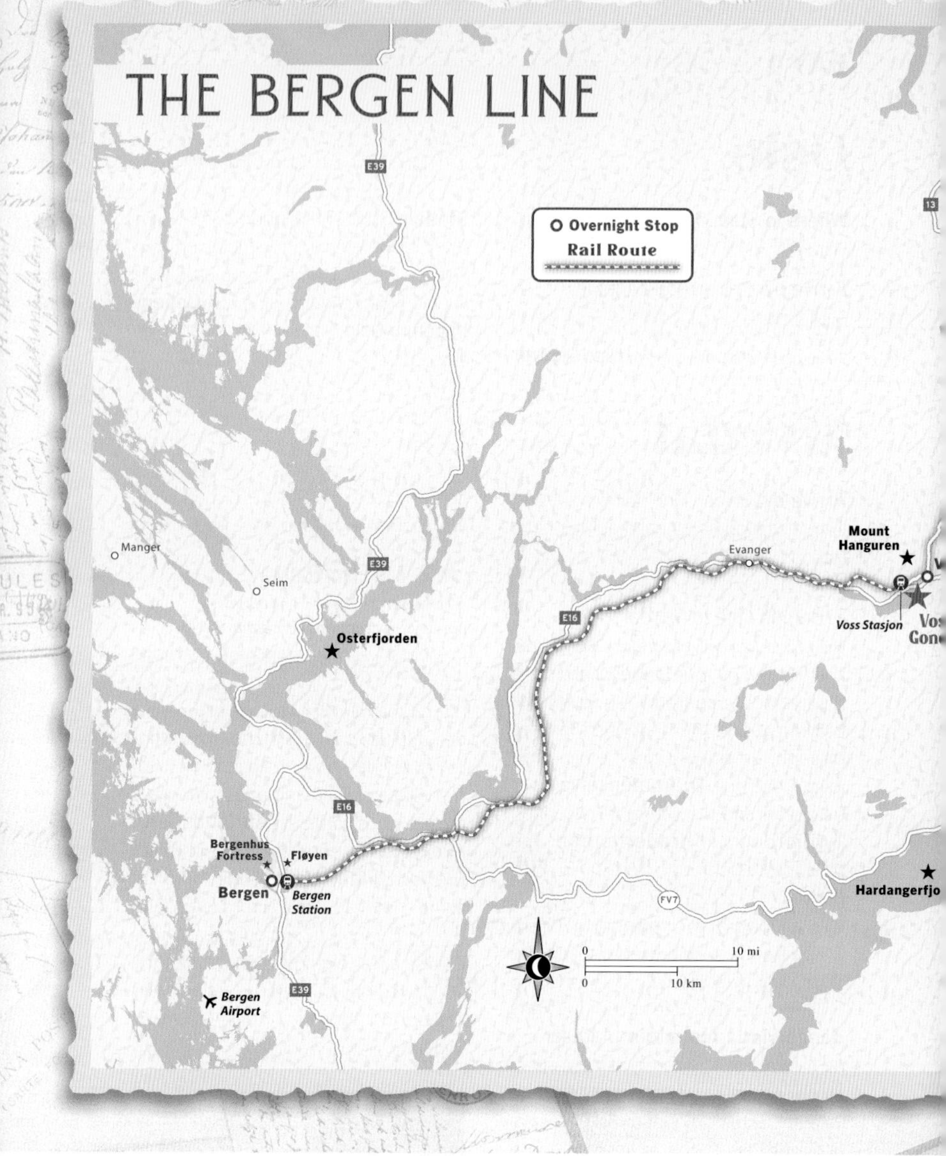

Flåm

Where to Stay: Flåm, along the fjord

Arrive by: Train from Myrdal mountain station to Flåm station (1 hour)

3. Fjord Sauna

Vikjavegen 4; tel. 90 93 41 59; www.fjordsauna.no; daily May-Sept., weekends and selected weekdays Oct.-Apr.; 325 Kr for 1.5 hours

It will be mid- to late afternoon by the time you arrive in Flåm, a picturesque village at the end of the Aurlandsfjord. Check into your hotel, and then head to this floating sauna, a five-minute walk

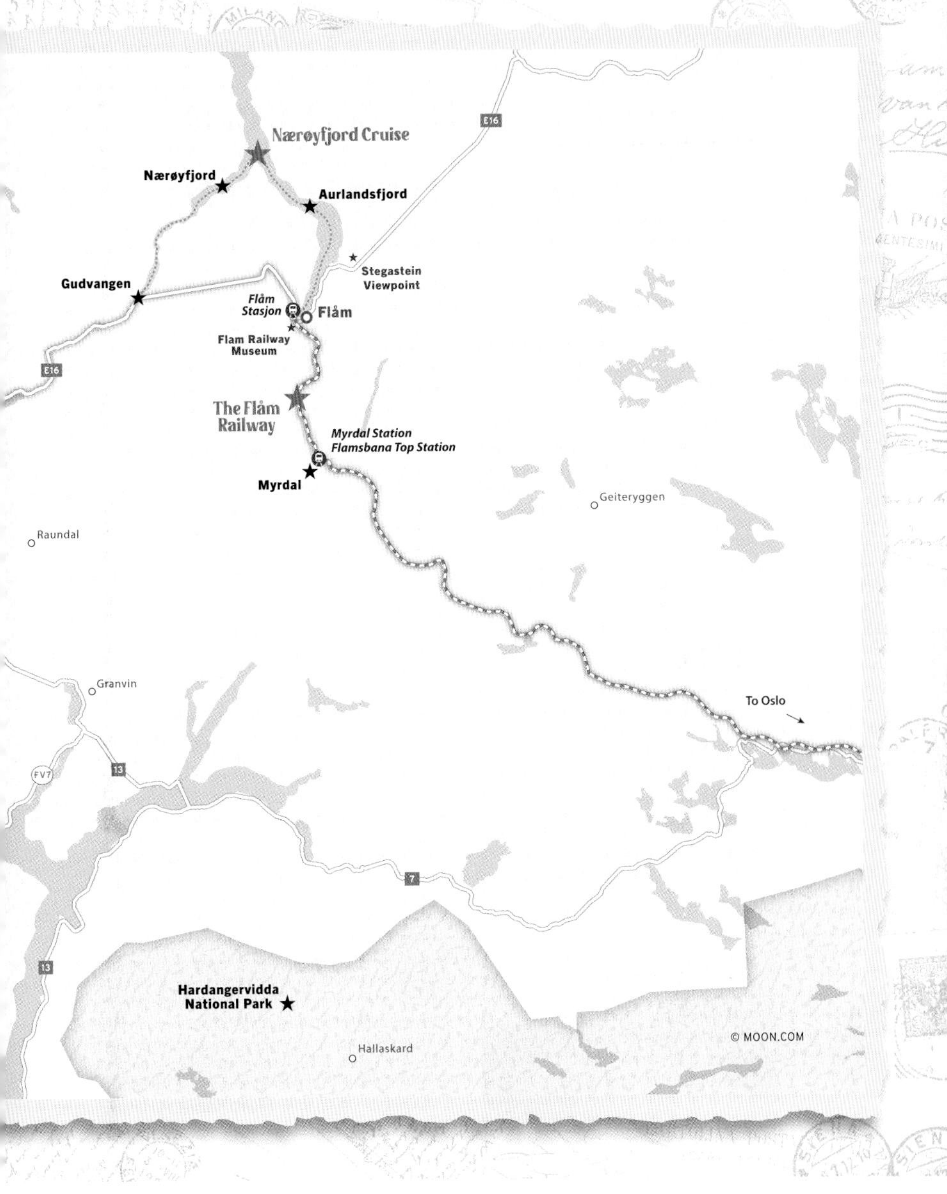

from the Flåm train station, to unwind after your day of train travel. With the Aurlandsfjord as a stunning backdrop, relax inside the hot sauna, and then go for a refreshing dip in the waters of the fjord. You can either join the open sauna time slots or book a private session. The sauna seats up to 12 people, and there is a small changing area outside.

4. Ægir Restaurant and Brewpub

A-Feltvegen 23; tel. 57 63 20 50; www.aegirbryggeri.no; daily 6pm-9pm, open from 1pm in the summer; 190-665 Kr

After your sauna experience, have dinner at this local brewery that makes award-winning beer sold all over Norway and is also a pub/restaurant. It's located in a stave church-style building right

Key Reservations

- Reserve your train tickets on the **Bergen Line** in advance for the best price; the cheapest tickets often sell out quickly. Also reserve your **Flåm Railway** and **tours** from Flåm ahead of time, to ensure optimal timing and connections.
- Make reservations for dinner at **Pergola** in Bergen.

on the docks of Flåm, and the atmosphere inside is rustic and warm. From the second floor, you can look through a large window to see the brewing process in action. The main event on the Viking-themed menu is the Ægir Viking Plank, a five-part tasting menu paired with a selection of beer.

DAY 2

Flåm

1. Stegastein Viewpoint

Bjørgavegen 83, Aurland

Located at 650 m (2,130 ft) above sea level, the Stegastein Viewpoint is one of the most spectacular views of the Aurlandsfjord. Perched on the edge of a mountain above the fjord, this dramatic wooden platform has a glass fence and gives the illusion of dropping off at the end, due to the rounded shape of the front of the structure. The panoramic view of the fjord will take your breath away.

Stegastein Viewpoint

From Flåm, the viewpoint is a 30-minute drive up the winding roads of Aurlandsfjellet mountain. Several **bus tours** (tel. 57 63 14 00; www.norwaysbest.com/no/ting-a-gjore/bussruter/stegastein-utsiktpunkt; daily departures; 360 Kr) depart from Flåm daily. The bus tour gives you 30 minutes at the top to gaze at the view and take photos.

For a light meal in Flåm before boarding the first morning bus to the Stegastein Viewpoint, head to **Flåm Bakery** (Stasjonsvegen; tel. 99 20 26 04; www.norwaysbest.com/no/overnatting-og-restauranter/flam-bakery; 8am-5pm daily), which sells fresh pastries and bread.

When you return to Flåm, head to **Flåm Marina** (Vikjavegen 4; tel. 57 63 35 55; www.flammarina.no; 160-360 Kr), a dock restaurant serving international dishes for lunch and dinner. The main event here is the view, so try to get a table outside if you can.

★ 2. Nærøyfjord Cruise

Pier 1-3; tel. 57 63 14 00; www.norwaysbest.com/no/ting-a-gjore/fjorder/fjord-cruise-naeroyfjord; daily departures year-round; 540 Kr

In the afternoon, you're headed to one of the main events that most people come to Norway to experience: a fjord cruise. The two-hour ride from Flåm to Gudvangen sails out through the Aurlandsfjord and into the Nærøyfjord, a UNESCO World Heritage Site. Along the 17-km (10.5-mi) length of Nærøyfjord, you will pass by abandoned farms and villages (such as Bakka and Dyrdal, where no one lives anymore), steep mountains, and cascading waterfalls. At its narrowest, the distance from one side of the fjord to the other is just 250 m (820 ft), making it the world's narrowest fjord. The dramatic landscape of the Nærøyfjord is not only what put it on the World Heritage list, but also what inspired the scenery in Disney's movie ***Frozen.***

To return to Flåm, take a shuttle bus arranged through your cruise company (20 minutes; 115 Kr), although you can also sail back along the same two-hour route. For dinner, **Arven Restaurant** (Nedre Fretheim; tel. 57 63 14 00; www.norwaysbest.com/no/overnatting-og-restauranter/arven-restaurant; 7pm-9pm daily; 190-320 Kr) in the Fretheim Hotel serves a seasonally changing menu. Through the large glass windows, you have views of the village and fjord outside.

DAY 3

Voss

Where to Stay: Voss is a small town, so nearly everything is within walking distance

Arrive by: Bus from Flåm station to Voss station (1 hour 10 minutes)

If you have time before you leave Flåm for Voss, start your day with a visit to the free Flåm Railway Museum (Stasjonsvegen 8; tel. 57 63 14 00; www.norwaysbest.com/no/inspirasjon/theflam-railway-museum).

★ 1. Voss Gondol

Evangervegen 5; www.vossresort.no; tel. 47 00 47 00; 10am-8pm daily; 425 Kr for a return ticket

Voss

Norway's Fjords

To many travelers, the fjords are the highlight of Norway. The most dramatic fjords are in western Norway; this is where you'll find cascading waterfalls, steep mountains, and scattered villages. While there are many fjords around the country worth visiting, these are the most accessible from along the Bergen Line.

NÆRØYFJORD AND AURLANDSFJORD

The Nærøyfjord and the Aurlandsfjord are two arms of the larger Sognefjord. Both offer dramatic landscapes, but the Nærøyfjord is especially famous—it's a UNESCO World Heritage Site. Flåm is the town at the southernmost tip of the Aurlandsfjord, and the Nærøyfjord's counterpart is the town of Gudvangen. In addition to a **Nærøyfjord cruise** (page 681), there are a couple other ways to experience these two fjords up close.

- Going on a **FjordSafari** (Inner Harbour; tel. 99 09 08 60; www.fjordsafari.no; daily departures; 790 Kr) from Flåm is an exhilarating option. The ride is via a rigid inflatable boat (RIB) that seats up to 12, and the driver also functions as a guide. There are a handful of tour options, from 1.5 to three hours, and along the way, you might spot eagles, porpoises, and seals.
- **Njord** (Flåm Beach; tel. 91 32 66 28; www.seakayaknorway.com; daily tours June-Sept.; 970 Kr) offers kayaking adventures departing from the beach in Flåm. Their three-hour guided trip is beginner friendly.

HARDANGERFJORD

Just east of Bergen, you'll find the less-famous—though still dramatic—Hardangerfjord.

- To explore the Hardangerfjord at a leisurely pace, opt for the **Fjord Cruise Hardangerfjord** (tel. 57 63 14 00; www.norwaysbest.com/no/

Take the bus from Flåm to Voss, arriving in the early afternoon. The scenery along the bus route is dazzling. Once in Voss, drop off your bags, put on some hiking shoes, and head to Voss Gondol.

Opened in 2019, Voss Gondol whisks passengers from the center of Voss up to the top of **Mount Hanguren:** from 0 to 818 m (2,680 ft) above sea level in just nine minutes. It's Northern Europe's largest gondola, and the journey up is breathtaking. At the top, you'll find plenty of hiking trails.

Before setting off on a hike, have lunch at the mountaintop **Hangurstoppen Restaurant** (Hangurstoppen; tel. 47 00 47 00; www.vossresort.no/restaurant/hangurstoppen-restaurant; 10am-4pm Sun.-Thurs., 10am-9pm Fri., 10am-8pm Sat.; 149-269 Kr). The restaurant's large windows offer great views of the mountains

ting-a-gjore/fjorder/fjord-cruise-hardanger; daily departures June-Sept; 540 Kr round-trip). The cruise stops in the towns of Odda, Tyssedal, Nå, Børve, Aga, and Lofthus three times a day, and the full ride from Odda to Lofthus is 1.5 hours. To explore these towns, you can hop on and off the boat. Odda is a 2-hour 45-minute drive from Bergen.

- **Hardangerfjord Adventure** (Hardangerfjordvegen 613; tel. 93 20 44 17; https://hardangerfjord-adventure.no; 990 Kr for the Basic Fjordsafari) is the place to go for rigid inflatable boat (RIB) tours. The tour options include the fjord- and landscape safari, which takes you to the village of Botnen—only accessible by boat—at the end of Fyksesundet, an arm of the Hardangerfjord. Trips depart from Øystese, a 1.5-hour drive from Bergen.
- **Hardangerfjord Active** (www.hardangerfjordactive.com; 550 Kr/person per kayak), located in Lutro, a 2.5-hour drive from Bergen, rents kayaks if you want to paddle along the edge of the fjord. There are no guided tours on offer, so you need some previous experience.

OSTERFJORDEN

Lesser-known Osterfjorden is one of the closest fjords to Bergen, located in the Modalen municipality north of the city.

- **Rødne** (tel. 51 89 52 70; https://rodne.no/fjordcruise/fjordcruise-til-mostraumen) offers a fjord cruise from Bergen to Mostraumen. Leaving from Zachariasbryggen, right by the Bergen Fish Market, this small-vessel cruise travels along the Osterfjorden and lasts around 3.5 hours. In addition to seeing the beautiful western Norwegian landscapes on this trip, you might also get to see some coastal wildlife, such as seals and eagles.

outside, and the seasonal menu features fresh ingredients and Norwegian produce.

2. Hanguren Panorama Trail

Distance: *1 km/0.6 mi*
Hiking Time: *30 minutes*
Difficulty: *Easy*
Trailhead: *Mount Hanguren Gondola Station*
Maps and Information: *www.vossresort.no/opplev/fotturar*

Starting at the Mount Hanguren Gondola Station, this easy trail goes in a loop at the top of the mountain, following a wheelchair- and stroller-accessible gravel path, with a panoramic view of Voss and the surrounding mountains.

Have dinner at your hotel, and make it an early night.

MAKE IT Active

Voss is known as the **Extreme Sports Capital of Norway.** The claim to fame comes from Voss's location near mountains that are perfect for snow sports, paragliding, and BASE jumping, as well as near rivers with white-water rafting. Every summer the town hosts **Ekstremsportveko,** the world's largest extreme sports festival. The following activities around Voss are sure to get your adrenaline pumping.

skydiving over Voss

SKIING

Hit the slopes at **Myrkdalen Resort** (Klypeteigane; tel. 47 47 16 00; www.myrkdalen.no; ski season mid-Nov.-May; day pass 485 Kr) or **Voss Resort** (Bavallsvegen 227; tel. 47 00 47 00; www.vossresort.no; ski season Nov.-Apr.; day pass 565 Kr).

CLIMBING

The **Wild Voss Climbing Experience** (Skjerpestunet 5; tel. 93 48 40 41; www.wildvoss.no; daily late May-late Oct.; 1,790 Kr per person) offers guided rock-climbing trips. The **Voss Active High Rope & Zipline Park** (Vossestrandvegen; tel. 56 51 05 25; www.vossactive.no/high-rope-zipline-park; daily mid-June-Aug., weekends May-mid-Oct.; 796 Kr) is an outdoor climbing and zipline park that's fun for the whole family.

SKYDIVING

At **VossVind Indoor Skydiving** (Oberst Bulls Veg 28; tel. 40 10 59 99; https://vossvind.no; noon-8pm Tues.-Sat., noon-6pm Sun.; 1,399 Kr per person for 4 flights) you can soar inside a wind tunnel. For the real deal, **Skydive Voss** (Flyplassvegen 135; tel. 56 51 10 00; www.skydivevoss.no; daily Apr.-Sept.; 4,890 Kr per jump) offers tandem jumps with experienced skydivers.

HANGLIDING AND PARAGLIDING

Check out **Voss Hangliding and Paragliding** (Flyplassvegen 135; www.vosshpk.no; hours vary; 2,400 Kr per flight) to fly through the air on a tandem paragliding experience.

WHITE-WATER RAFTING

Voss Active (Nedkvitnesvegen 25; tel. 56 51 05 25; www.vossactive.no; 2 daily departures May-mid-Oct.; 1390 Kr per person) offers white-water rafting on the Stranda or Raundal Rivers.

DAY 4

Bergen

Where to Stay: Bryggen, central to most sights and various restaurant offerings

Arrive by: Bergen Line train from Voss station to Bergen station (1.5 hours)

1. Bergen Line to Bergen

www.vy.no; daily departures

At the train station in Voss, get back on the Bergen Line for the final leg of the rail journey, the one-plus-hour ride to Bergen. On this stretch, you're truly surrounded by the famous landscapes of the western fjords. As the train passes in and out of tunnels, the views continue to awe.

2. Bergenhus Fortress

55 54 63 87; www.forsvarsbygg.no/no/festningene/finn-din-festning/bergenhus-festning; 6am-11pm Mon.-Sun.; free

Bergen, the second largest city in Norway, is a popular base for exploring the fjords. However, the city is also a destination in itself, with a well-established cultural scene and a growing number of great restaurants and nightlife options.

When you arrive in Bergen, drop off your bags at your hotel, and then head first to Bergenhus Fortress, one of the best kept fortresses in Norway and one of the oldest. Construction of the fortress began in the early 1500s, around the already standing Håkonshall. It has a long history as the seat of kings and bishops, and it's still an active military site today.

Inside the fortress area, which consists of walled cobblestoned streets and squares, don't miss **Håkonshallen** (tel. 55 30 80 30; https://bymuseet.no; 10am-4pm daily Jun.-Aug., 11am-2pm daily Sept.-May; adults 120 Kr, under 17 free). Built between 1247 and 1261, Håkonshallen ("the hall of Håkon") was the residence and banquet hall of King Håkon Håkonsson and was the site of many important events, including the creation of Norway's first set of common laws. Also worth visiting is **Rosenkrantztårnet,** or the Rosenkrantz Tower (tel. 55 30 80 30; https://bymuseet.no; 10am-4pm daily June-Aug., hours vary Sept.-May; adults 120 Kr; under 17 free), considered the most important Renaissance monument in Norway.

3. Bryggen

Next, walk five minutes to what is perhaps Bergen's best-known sight, Bryggen. The 17 colorful buildings along the dock, along with alleyways behind them, are a UNESCO World Heritage Site. This is where Bergen's first settlements were located, and where the city's importance as a trade port grew. The bay of Vågen sheltered ships from the worst of the North Sea weather, and thus the area became a natural meeting point for traders and sailors from Northern Norway and the rest of Europe.

The building facades make for a great photo op, and once you head into the

Bryggen

WATCH

Frozen: Disney's 2013 animated movie is set against the spectacular scenery of Norway. The fictional kingdom of Arendelle is set in the Nærøyfjord, and the town features architectural details inspired by Bryggen in Bergen.

READ

Kristin Lavransdatter by Sigrid Undset: This epic trilogy set in 14th-century Norway earned writer Sigrid Undset the Nobel Prize in Literature in 1928. The strong, relatable female protagonist and vivid historical details make the long read worth it.

LISTEN

Bergen is home to a small but notable indie pop scene. Bands to check out include **Kings of Convenience** and **Röyksopp.**

wooden alleyways, you'll find shops and cafés, as well as the **Bryggens Museum** (Dreggsallmenningen 3; tel. 55 30 80 30; https://bymuseet.no; 11am-5pm daily May-Aug., hours vary in low season; adults 120 Kr, under 17 free), where you can learn more about Bergen's history as an important trading port. In the crowded summer months, bars fill the square in front of Bryggen with tables and chairs, so you can enjoy a beer in the sun.

For truly authentic Norwegian food, walk two minutes along the docks to **Bryggestuene** (Bryggen 11; tel. 55 30 20 70; www.bryggeloftet.no; noon-11pm daily; 325-495 Kr). Be sure to try the fish soup, the restaurant's signature dish.

4. Mount Fløyen

After lunch, either walk up Mount Fløyen (45 minutes uphill), or take the **Fløybanen** funicular to the top. Both the trailhead and funicular are a three-minute walk from Bryggen.

Mount Fløyen is located right in Bergen's city center, and locals and visitors alike enjoy making their way to the top to enjoy the view. At the summit, you'll find a restaurant, café, ice cream kiosk (open in summer), playground for children, ropes course, and several easy hiking trails.

5. Night Out in Bergen

After hiking (or taking the funicular) back down to the city, head to **Pergola** (Nedre Korskirkeallmenningen 9B; tel. 55 01 86 73; 4pm-midnight Mon.-Fri., 2pm-midnight Sat.) for dinner, located a three-minute walk from the funicular. This hidden Italian restaurant offers a simple menu—pizza or charcuterie boards—as well as the largest collection of wine in Bergen. It's a good idea to make reservations here.

For a drink after dinner, **Dark & Stormy** (Kong Oscars Gate 12; www.darkandstormy.no; 5pm-1am Tues.-Thurs., 4pm-2:30am Fri.-Sat.), a tropical-themed bar that will make you forget you're in Norway, is just around the corner.

TRANSPORTATION

Air

- **Oslo Airport Gardermoen** (OSL; Edvard Munchs veg; tel. 64 81 20 00; https://avinor.no/flyplass/oslo) is Norway's main international airport, as well as its main domestic hub. To get from Gardermoen to the city center, the airport express train FlyToget

(https://flytoget.no; 20 minutes; 220 Kr) takes you directly to Oslo Central Station.

- **Bergen Airport Flesland** (BGO; Flyplassvegen 555; tel. 67 03 15 55; https://avinor.no/bergen-lufthavn), Bergen's international airport, is located 18 km (11 mi) outside the city center. You can travel between the airport and the city center via light rail on ByBanen (www.bybanen.no; 40 minutes; 32-64 Kr) or bus on FlyBussen (www.flybussen.no; 30 minutes; 75-120 Kr). Flights from outside Europe usually require at least one stop.

Train

Norway's national rail company is **Vy** (tel. 61 05 19 10; www.vy.no).

The Bergen Line

www.vy.no; four daily departures; 350-1,000 Kr

Traveling from Oslo to Bergen, the Bergen Line has four daily departures, one of which is an overnight train. Ticket prices vary—the cheapest tickets often sell out quickly—but it is possible to ride the entire route for as little as 349 Kr. Most likely you will be paying around 700-900 Kr, though in peak season it can cost as much as 1,050 Kr. The nonstop ride from **Bergen to Oslo** takes seven hours.

The Flåm Railway

A-Feltvegen 11; tel. 57 63 14 00; www.norways-best.com/no/flamsbana; 370 Kr one way, 500 Kr return

The Flåm Railway has 4-10 daily departures, depending on the season. At the southern end is Myrdal, which is a stop on the Bergen Line; at the northern end is Flåm, right on Aurlandsfjord. There are a few stops between Myrdal and Flåm, but most visitors take the one-hour ride from end to end.

Stations

- **Oslo Central Station** (Jernbanetorget 1; tel. 81 50 08 88; https://oslo-s.no), aka Oslo S, is centrally located in Norway's capital city, just a five-minute walk to the Oslo Opera House.
- **Myrdal station** is a transfer station between the Bergen Line and the Flåm Railway, with arrivals and departures of the two lines generally coordinated for easy transfers. The ride from Oslo to Myrdal is about five hours.
- **Flåm station** (A-Feltvegen 11; tel. 57 63 14 00) is located within a three-minute walk to the ferry terminal, where fjord tours depart, and is an easy distance from sights, restaurants, and hotels.
- **Voss station** (Stasjonsvegen 5) is centrally located in the small town and is a stop on the Bergen Line. From Myrdal to Voss, it's about a 46-minute ride (64-85 Kr).
- **Bergen Station** (Strømgaten 4) is the end of the Bergen Line. It's centrally located in the city, about a 15-minute walk to Bryggen.

Bus

Vy buses (tel. 61 05 19 10; www.vy.no) serve most major cities and destinations in Norway, including Flåm to Voss (1 hour 10 minutes; 215 Kr) and Gudvangen to Voss (1 hour; 150 Kr). The bus between Gudvangen and Flåm can be arranged with your fjord cruise.

Getting Back

To get back to Oslo, you can take the Bergen Line in the opposite direction, which takes seven hours. Flying from Bergen to Oslo takes one hour.

CONNECT WITH

- Lofoten (page 268)
- Copenhagen to Oslo (page 519)

VILNIUS, RIGA, AND TALLINN

Why Go: Combining the vibrant, youthful capital cities of the former Soviet Baltic states, this is a wonderful urban adventure into a lesser-visited corner of Europe for those looking for something a bit off Europe's more well-trod city trails.

Number of Days: 7

Total Distance: 610 km (380 mi)

Seasons: Late spring to early fall

Start: Vilnius

End: Tallinn

Over the course of a week, experience a thousand years of Baltic history. This journey begins in the sprawling Lithuanian capital of Vilnius, with a day trip to a nearby castle. Next, you'll travel through the hip weekender getaway of Riga, Latvia, aka the "Venice of the Baltics," where you can also learn about the long history of the Baltic states at the Occupation Museum. Your trip ends in Estonia in the city of Tallinn, known for its incredibly well-preserved medieval Old Town.

A continuous rail trip connecting these three cities is something of a vision of the future: 870-km-long (540-mi) Rail Baltica is being constructed to link them by train—and beyond to Warsaw, Berlin, and all of Europe. Until then, traveling to all three cities plus Helsinki combines train, bus, and ferry.

TOP 3

Day-tripping from Vilnius to **Trakai Island and Castle** to combine a fairy-tale experience with plenty of lakeside activities (page 694).

Exploring Riga on a **canal cruise** for a new perspective to this old city (page 698).

Strolling through the cobblestone of **Tallinn's Old Town,** the most well-preserved medieval town in all of Europe (page 699).

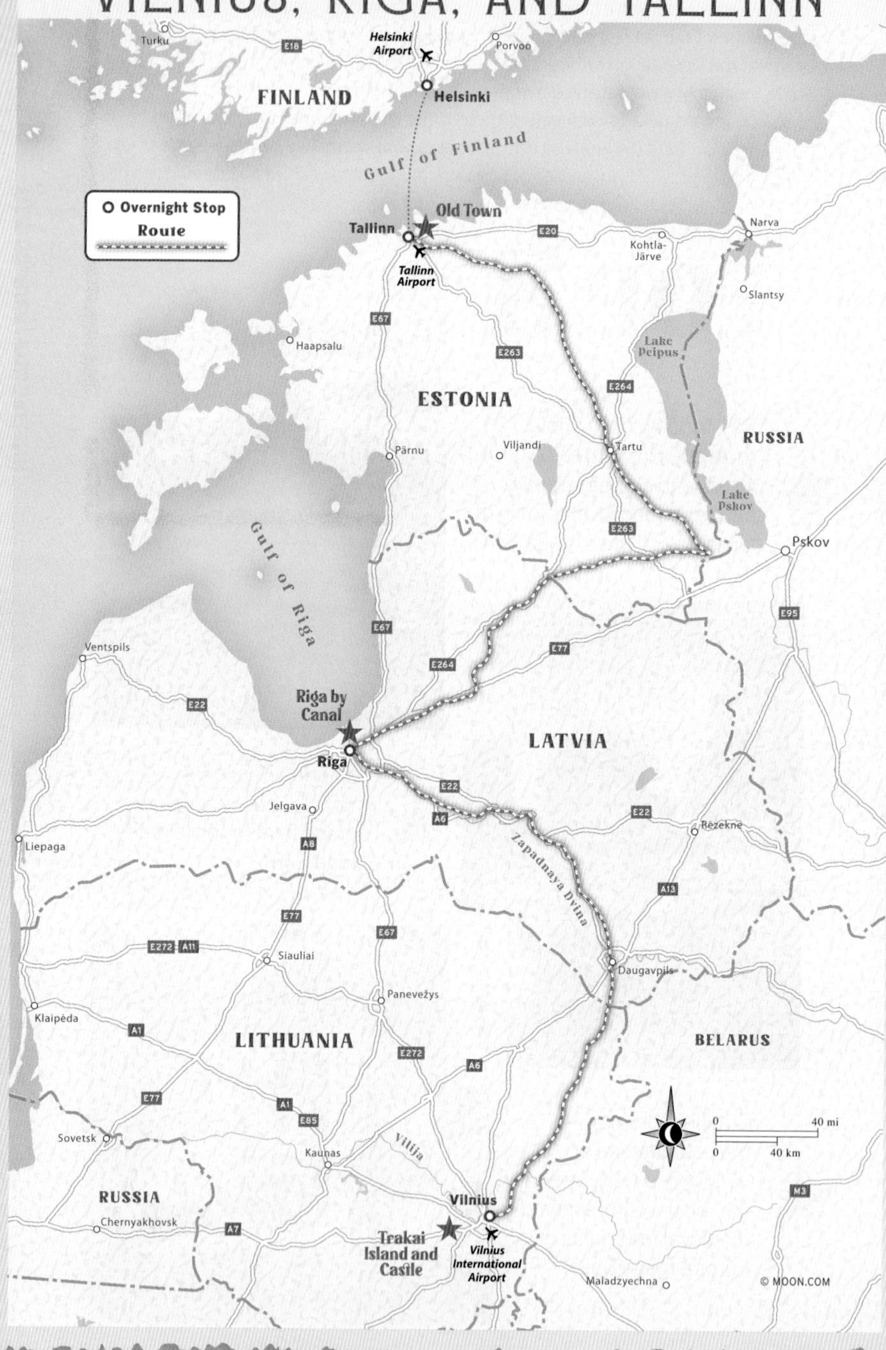

VILNIUS, RIGA, AND TALLINN
Overnight Stop
Route
Turku
Helsinki Airport
Porvoo
E18
FINLAND
Helsinki
Gulf of Finland
Tallinn
Old Town
Tallinn Airport
E20
Narva
Kohtla-Järve
Slantsy
Haapsalu
E67
E263
Lake Peipus
E264
ESTONIA
RUSSIA
Pärnu
Viljandi
Tartu
Lake Pskov
Gulf of Riga
E263
Pskov
E95
E67
E77
Ventspils
E264
Riga by Canal
E22
LATVIA
Riga
E22
Jelgava
A6
E22
Rēzekne
Liepaga
A8
Zapadnaya Dvina
A13
E77
E67
E272
A11
Siauliai
Daugavpils
Panevežys
Klaipėda
A1
LITHUANIA
BELARUS
E272
A6
E77
A1
E85
Sovetsk
Kaunas
Vilija
0
40 mi
0
40 km
RUSSIA
Vilnius
M3
Chernyakhovsk
A7
Trakai Island and Castle
Vilnius International Airport
Maladzyechna
© MOON.COM
CARTOLINA POSTALE

Vilnius

Where to Stay: Old Town for the most charming, central location in Vilnius

Arrive by: Plane to Vilnius International Airport or by train to the Vilnius Railway Station

DAY 1

1. Gediminas Hill and Tower

Gedminas Hill; https://lnm.lt; tower 10am-8pm daily; free, €6 access to tower

At a height of 48 m (157 ft), this is one of the tallest points in Vilnius. Begin your exploration of this hip European capital with 360-degree views looking down over the historic Old Town and the juncture of the Neris and Vilnia Rivers. Though access to Gediminas Hill is free, the Gediminas Tower is part of the Lithuanian National Museum. The tower is the last remaining piece of a 15th-century castle built by the Grand Duke of Lithuania, Vytautus, and is the symbol of the city. The tower houses a permanent exhibition exploring the architecture, armaments, and iconography of Vilnius's history.

2. Palace of the Grand Dukes of Lithuania

Katedros a. 4; tel. 52620007; www.valdovurumai.lt; 10am-6pm Tues.-Sun.; €10

Next, visit this ambitious reimagining of the "lower castle" that stood here from the 13th to the 17th century, when it was destroyed by invading Russian forces. It is thought that the original castle, though begun in the 13th century, was added to over the years, making for a mishmash of various architectural styles, ranging from the Gothic to the baroque. This hodgepodge of styles has been faithfully re-created here. Concerts are typically held on the grounds throughout the year. The palace itself features armaments and reconstructed palatial interiors.

3. Vilnius Cathedral

Šventaragio g.; tel. 52611127; www.katedra.lt; 7am-7pm daily; free

Pope John Paul II, upon visiting the cathedral, dubbed it a shrine "in which the heart of the Lithuanian nation beats." Venerated by Catholics around the world, the gleaming white Vilnius Cathedral is a vision of purity. Over the centuries, there have been many religious buildings here; the current cathedral was built in the 18th century. The cathedral contains the relics of St. Casimir, Lithuania's patron saint, and is also the final resting place for many Lithuanian nobles and bishops. The Sapiega Madonna painting gracing the Goštautas Family Chapel dates from the 16th century and is a popular focal point of prayer for the faithful. Be sure to visit the vaults to admire the oldest mural in the country.

top, Gediminas Hill and Tower; bottom, Palace of the Grand Dukes of Lithuania

Key Reservations

- If you are staying in **hostels,** be sure to book ahead, particularly in summer months.
- When your stay overlaps with a weekend, secure those **accommodation** reservations ahead of time as well, particularly in Riga. Note that Riga is a party town; read the reviews of lodgings to make sure the night noise level is acceptable to you, especially on weekends.
- In Vilnius, make a reservation at hot spot restaurant **Amandus.**

For lunch, settle in at **Edno Dvaras** (Pilies g. 16; www.etnodvaras.lt; 11am-midnight daily; €20) and dive into a plate of cepelinai (potato dumplings) while people-watching.

4. Old Town

After lunch, stroll Pilies Street, the main touristic pedestrian thoroughfare in the middle of Vilnius's Old Town. This is one of the largest, most intact medieval towns in all of Europe. You will walk through hundreds of years of architectural history in just a few short steps, from the Gothic to the Renaissance; the **Church of St. Johns** and **Vilnius University** are two of the many standout buildings. You will also want to make sure to stroll down **Literatų Street.** As the name suggests, this little street commemorates Lithuania's poets and writers. You'll find plenty of coffee shops and bars in Old Town to take a rest and soak it all in. This is one of those magical corners of Europe where, if you just squint past the modern marketing, you can take a trip through history.

Save a visit to **St. Anne's Cathedral** (Maironio g. 8; tel. 67674463; 11am-7pm Tues.-Sun.; free), located on the eastern edge of Old Town, for the end of the day. When the sky is clear and the sun low on the horizon, the entire redbrick structure emits a warm, flame-like feel. It is said that 33 different varieties of brick were used to give this Gothic masterpiece its unique texture where the light plays off the slightly different red tones of the clay.

For dinner, seek out **Stikliai Tavern** (Gaono g. 7, tel. 52649580; www.stikliai.com; noon-11pm daily; €15), which offers up outstanding traditional potato pancakes (bulviniai) to pair with your ale.

DAY 2

1. Halès Market

Pylimo g. 58; tel. 52625536; www.halesturgaviete.lt; 7am-6pm Tues.-Sun.; free

There is maybe no better way to explore a new culture than through its food and local markets. Head to the Halès Market, just north of the railway station, and peruse the seasonal fruits and veggies. Eavesdrop into the local Lituanians as they haggle, banter, and barter in equal turns, a sort of singsong soundtrack to your exploration. There are tons of specialty stalls and bistros to try local favorites, such as kastinys, a garlic cheese spread. This makes for the perfect place to find a tasty lunch.

2. Vilnius Museum

6 Vokiečių St.; https://vilniausmuziejus.lt; 3pm-7pm Tues.-Fri., 11am-7pm Sat.-Sun.; €4

After lunch, dive into a little local history at the Vilnius Museum. Opened in 2021, the museum was designed with both locals and travelers in mind. A few times a year, the exhibits change, each one casting a different light on the city through stories, both famous and not-so-famous.

Traditional Lithuanian Cuisine

You will be forgiven if you are not up with traditional Lithuanian cuisine. This hearty meat-and-potatoes fare features lots of root veggies and unsurprisingly shares DNA with its sister Baltic countries as well as with other parts of Central and Eastern Europe. Here are a few things to try while you're visiting.

- **Bulviniai:** Imagine a sandwich made of mashed potatoes and you will have some idea of what a bulviniai is. Potatoes on the outside and meat (or other) filling on the inside, it goes well with a beer, of which the Lithuanians are generally quite fond.
- **Cepelinai:** Perhaps the most "national" of the national dishes, this zeppelin-shaped potato dumpling is typically filled with meat and gravy, though these days many vegetarian and vegan options can be found using cheese, mushrooms, and other fillings.
- **Keptal Duona:** This is what you get when you take black bread, cut it in strips, rub it with garlic, fry it in olive oil, and top it with cheese. It's the go-to bar snack for Lithuanians enjoying a pint with friends.
- **Šaltibarščiai:** This delightfully bright, pink beetroot soup is served cold, like a gazpacho, and is most popular in the summer.
- **Šakotis:** Dubbed the "tree cake," this distinctively shaped treat is a must at any Lithuanian celebration… or as an afternoon pick-me-up for the kids and kids at heart.

3. Mo Museum

Pylimo St. 17; https://mo.lt; 10am-8pm Wed.-Mon.; €9

Put your finger on the pulse of the modern Lithuanian art scene. With more than 6,000 pieces, the museum holds one of the largest collections of the country's art from the 1960s to the present day. Heck, you can include the museum itself as one of those works of art. It truly is a stunning example of contemporary design and has won several architecture awards.

4. Republic of Užupis

Užupis District; open 24 hours; free

Keep on the Bohemian vibe and dive into the self-proclaimed "Republic of Užupis," a bit of a tongue-in-cheek, let's have some fun, sort of republic (about a 20-minute walk east from the Mo Museum). Here, you can listen to their national anthem and read the Constitution of the Republic of Užupis posted at Paupio Street, 3a. They even have their own currency, the EuroUžas. The currency is issued in denominations of one with each EuroUžas holding the established exchange rate of exactly one pint of beer, as it has since the currency first appeared on the market in 2003. Needless to say, it is a fun neighborhood to explore and enjoy a refreshment at one of the many bars and pubs lining the streets. Head down to **Spunka** (Užupio g. 9-1; tel. 65232361; www.spunka.lt; 3pm-10pm daily; €2), a funky, eclectic local favorite featuring many local craft beers on its menu.

For dinner, there are a lot of options around Užupis, ranging from Italian-style pizzas to shawarma sandwiches. These can do in a pinch, but if you want to treat yourself, head to Chef Deivydas's newest creation, **Amandus** (Užupio g. 22; tel. 67541191; www.amandus.lt; 7pm-11pm Wed.-Sat.; €105, reservations highly recommended). Here, the friendly staff happily leads you through various Latvian flavor profiles in each course of the tasting menus. Vegetarian options are available, though it's a good idea to ask ahead.

Day Trip to Trakai

Arrive by: Bus from Vilnius Bus Station to Trakai Bus Station (30 minutes)

DAY 3

★ 1. Trakai Island Castle

Kęstučio g. 4, Trakai; tel. 52855297; https://trakaimuziejus.lt; 10am-7pm daily, hours vary seasonally, closed Sun. Mar.-Feb.; €8-12, depending on season

Make your way for a fun day trip to the historic Trakai Castle, situated on a picture-perfect lake. Any time of year, this is a treat, whether in the ice and snow or beneath sunny summer skies. The restored 14th-century castle was once the home of the Dukes of Lithuania. Take the 300-m (984-ft) wood bridge and cross into storybook Latvian history. Discover the history of Trakai and its palatial digs. Start your day early as possible from to beat the summertime crowds.

2. Trakai Village

After the castle, head into the charming village of Trakai. The colorful village plunges you into rural Lithuanian life. There are more than a few options for drinks and dining, though many will be closed in winter months. No matter the time of year, the cozy rustic confines of **Senoji Kibininė** (Karaimų skg. 41B; tel. 65908033; www.kibinas.lt; 10am-10pm daily; €10) are a welcomed respite. Take advantage of the outdoor seating if the weather cooperates.

3. Kibinai Baking Course

Kybylar Restaurant; Karaimy St. 29; tel. 61291322; www.kybynlar.lt; 1-1.5 hours; €10

There is nothing quite like rolling up your sleeves and making a local specialty to bring yourself closer to a culture and its traditions. The storied kibinai rolls, small meat or vegetable-stuffed pastries, were

left, Trakai village; right, Trakai Island Castle

MAKE IT Active

No matter the time of year, **Lake Galvė** offers up some great action for those looking to get moving. In the winter, you can enjoy ice skating, cross-country skiing, or even paragliding over the frozen lake with Trakai Island Castle making an impossibly beautiful backdrop. Summertime brings opportunities for swimming in the lake, as well as rowing and other water sports—not to mention the 18-km (10-mi) round-trip scenic lakeside bike ride from Trakai peninsula to Užutrakis Manor—making this a hot spot for locals and travelers alike.

- **Bike tours and rentals:** Velo Takas (tel. 61845727; https://velotakas.lt) has regular bikes and electric bikes, making touring on two wheels a cinch.
- **Canoeing:** Wet Weim Adventure Company (tel. 66238238; www.wetweim.com) offers private guided rowing tours around the lake with certified guide Janis.
- **Ice skating:** Several of the little shops around Trakai offer inexpensive ice-skating rentals for €3-5.
- **Paragliding:** Arcus Flying School (tel. 699 53878; www.paragliding.lt) offers classes for all levels.

brought to Lithuania from Turkey. Known as the karaims, these Turkish people gave Trakai its most beloved savory pastry.

Afterward, head back into Vilnius, and have dinner in Old Town. Try a light, bright, veggie-filled dinner at **The Urban Garden** (Jono Basanavičiaus g. 3; tel. 61460292; www.theurbangarden.lt; 8:30am-7pm Mon.-Fri., 9am-7pm weekends; €12).

Riga

Where to Stay: Centrally located Old Town of Riga

Arrive by: Bus from Vilnius Bus Station to Riga Central Bus Station (4 hours)

DAY 4

1. House of the Black Heads

Rātslaukums 7, Centra rajons; tel. 67043678; https://melngalvjunams.lv; 10am-5pm Tues.-Sun.; €8 (with coffee) or €9 (with sparkling wine)

After the half-day bus ride from Vilnius, put your bags down, settle in, and then venture out. The elaborate guild hall of the House of the Black Heads makes for a rich introduction to Riga's UNESCO World Heritage listed Old Town. Originally built by merchants in 1334, the house has undergone some renovations over the years, each seemingly more elaborate than the last. The ballrooms are of significant note, feeling very much like Versailles in their grand elegance.

If you need a bite to eat, check out the sprawl of bars and restaurants in the area. Whatever you do, save some room for

Art Nouveau 101

Art nouveau is a movement of art and architecture that took place throughout Europe and North America around the turn of the 20th century. The artists, painters, sculptors, architects, and designers of this movement drew their inspiration from nature. The works of this period can be best recognized by their general organicism. In other words, art nouveau works look as though they could occur in the natural world.

The overall thrust of the art nouveau movement was to bridge the chasm between so-called "fine art" (painting and sculpture) and the applied arts, such as interior design, textiles, architecture, etc. The thought was to unify the visual aesthetic of a space, thus inspiring and perhaps even uplifting the population. Art nouveau, as a movement, was relatively short-lived; it enjoyed its height of popularity during the Belle Epoque, 1890-1910.

Architect Antonio Gaudí is probably the most extreme example of this with his striking masterpiece, the **Sagrada Família** in Barcelona, the most well-known example of this school, though much more conventional works in the art nouveau school can be seen throughout many **European capitals**, from London to Brussels to Prague, including some of the older Metro station entrances dotted around Paris.

The densest concentration of art nouveau architecture exists in central **Riga** where approximately one-third of all the buildings are designed in this distinctive style. Amazingly, even though Latvia was still very much developing its own identity as a nation during art nouveau's aesthetic reign, most of the buildings were designed and built by Latvians. Influenced by their time studying in Austria, Germany, and Finland, these Latvians brought their own unique twist to the stylistic apartment blocks that largely make up this quarter.

Riga Black Magic (Kaļķu iela 10, Centra rajons; tel. 67222877; www.blackmagic.lv; 11:30am-8pm daily; €5), where you can dive into some delicious chocolatey local confections as well as try Riga Black Balsam, a strong, 24-herb liquor championed locally for its health benefits and, on cold days, poured generously into hot coffee.

2. Three Brothers' Museum

Mazā Pils iela 19, Centra rajons; tel. 67037900; www.archmuseum.lv; 9am Mon.-Fri., closing hours vary; free

On your way to the Three Brothers' Museum, take your time and stroll around the Old Town a bit, taking in the **art nouveau architecture** for which it

left, Three Brothers' Museum; right, Swedish Gate

is famous. Along the way to the museum, you'll pass the hulking Riga Cathedral as well as Riga City Hall. The iconic Three Brothers' takes its name from the three houses abutting one another. These three houses are the oldest residences in Riga. Legend has it that they were built as a family succession, though in different eras throughout the Middle Ages. The museum focuses on the architecture of Riga, but ironically, it is perhaps the architecture of the museum itself that is most interesting.

3. Swedish Gate

Atgriežu iela, Centra rajons; open 24 hours; free

While the sun is low in the sky, make your way to the Swedish Gate. Built in 1698, this is the last remaining of the eight gates that once provided access into Riga through its fortification wall. At sunrise and sunset, the gate would be opened and closed, though these days you'll always find it open. Interestingly, the town's executioner was once in charge of this particular gate and would hang a rose to mark each beheading. Now that your appetite is primed, head to the nearby restaurant **Zvierdu Vārti** (Torņa iela 4-1a, Centra rajons; tel. 29414503; https://zviedruvarti.lv; 10am-10pm Mon.-Fri., 11am-10pm Sat.-Sun.; €15) for lamb soup, black pudding, and potato pancakes. They are to die for. Just don't tell the executioner.

4. Nightlife in Old Town

Riga is a very popular weekend destination for Europeans, as it is inexpensive and full of bars and nightclubs. Before heading out for the evening, you'll want to make sure to have plenty of energy for the night ahead. **Lido** (Krāmu iela 2, Centra rajons; tel. 29289507; www.lido.lv; 11am-10pm Mon.-Fri., 11am-11pm weekends; €15) is a local chain offering up fresh, traditional Latvian food. The decor is a bit hokey, to say the least, but the shashlik (Latvian BBQ) is dependably delicious and is just the thing to kick the night off.

DAY 5

1. Freedom Monument

Bastejkalna Park; open 24 hours; free

In the morning, make your way to the Bastejkalna Park and the Freedom Monument, the symbol of Riga. Financed entirely by public donations, the statue was unveiled in 1935. Its three golden stars at the top represent Latvia's three historic regions. Its base is inscribed with "For the Fatherland and Freedom." Though the ceremony is not as elaborate at the one at Buckingham Palace, there is a changing of the guards here every hour.

★ 2. Canal Cruise

City Canal, Centra rajons; tel. 25911523; www.rigabycanal.lv; 10:30am-7pm daily; €18

Head over the canal to board a relaxing one-hour cruise through Riga. You'll take an old wooden boat through the Riga City Canal and up the Daugava River, with a view of the Latvian capital's main sights. A free, informative audio guide in English will tell you a bit more about Riga's history as well.

3. Riga Central Market

Nēģu iela 7, Latgales priekšpilsēta; tel. 67229985; www.rct.lv; 7:30am-6pm daily; free

Hop off the canal boat and walk south 15 minutes to Riga Central Market. You have never experienced a market quite like this. As it is housed beneath not one, but five zeppelin hangers, the word "sprawling" does not do the Riga Central Market justice. You could spend an entire day here meandering through the various sellers, sampling Latvian traditional cuisine ogling the seasonal legumes, and arranging a bouquet of flowers. Or you could pick up a bottle of homemade vodka to go with that herring and sauerkraut, and head down to the river for a waterfront picnic.

canal cruise

4. Occupation Museum

Latviešu strēlnieku laukums 1, Centra rajons; tel. 67229255; https://okupacijasmuzejs.lv; 10am-6pm daily; €5

It is impossible to travel through the Baltics and not feel some of the weight that the Soviet Union left behind. Together, Estonia, Latvia, and Lithuania share a similar story of occupation, though perhaps no people share that burden so brutally as the Latvians. Of course, it wasn't just the Soviets who once occupied the Baltics in the 20th century. The Germans once pushed the Soviets out and controlled this region. The culmination of this shared story of occupation is housed here, giving you a vital sense of what it must have been like to live under the thumb of these brutal regimes. Understanding their story, you will better appreciate their joy of life.

5. St. Peter's Church

Reformācijas Laukums 1, Centra rajons; tel. 67181430; 10am-6pm Tues.-Sat., noon-6pm Sun.; €3, tower access, including church €9

Located in the middle of Old Town, this church has been witness to centuries of history. First mentioned in documents dating back to 1209, this former cathedral has been partially destroyed and rebuilt over years of violent struggle in the Baltics. The tower, at 72 m (236 ft), was once the tallest wood structure in all of Europe. The tower is accessed by elevator and offers breathtaking panoramic views over Riga and the powerful Daugava River.

Tallinn

Where to Stay: Tallinn's Old Town

Arrive by: Train from Riga Train Station to Tallinn Train Station with a transfer in Valga (10 hours)

DAY 6

If you leave Riga mid-morning, you'll be on the train all day, arriving in Tallinn around 9pm. For a hearty meal after all that travel, duck into **Restaurant Ratasakaevu 16** (Rataskaevu 16; tel. 6424025; http://rataskaevu16.ee; noon-11pm Sun.-Thurs.; noon-midnight Fri.-Sat.; €30), about 10 minutes away on foot, and settle in for a properly medieval feast featuring everything from oven-baked beetroot tartare to braised elk.

DAY 7

★ 1. Old Town Square

Raekoja plats; open 24 hours; free

While Vilnius has the largest intact medieval town and Riga is famed for its art nouveau, Tallinn has made its own mark by having the best-preserved medieval city in all of Europe. Smaller in footprint than Vilnius, the medieval walls of Tallinn are still intact. It is even possible to take a short walk on the ramparts. Pay a quick visit to the Town Hall, right on the square, to begin.

2. Alexander Nevsky Cathedral

Lossi plats 10; tel. 6443484; http://tallinnanevskikatedraal.eu; 9am-7pm daily; free

This still functioning cathedral dominates the Tallinn skyline from **Toompea Hill,** the highest point of Old Town. After Estonians won their freedom, they had originally planned to destroy the cathedral as it was seen as a tasteless show of Soviet hubris. Luckily for us, they left it standing. No photos are allowed of the ornate interior, but even the outside is pretty incredible. Come back in the evening for spectacular night views over Tallinn.

3. St. Catherine's Passage

Vene 14a, Kesklinna linnaosa, Kesklinna; open 24 hours; free

Named for the local church of the same name, St. Catherine's Passage is a typically medieval street that has been atypically well preserved. The cobblestone streets seem to crawl right up the walls and high above to the city gates. At the bottom of the alley is the access to walk part of the medieval walls that once guarded the city from marauders. For a light bite and something to drink, **Restoran Controvento** (Vene 12; tel. 6440470; www.controvento.ee; noon-11pm daily; €15) serves Italian food, which might seem odd for Tallinn, but it is the only restaurant along the passage. Enjoying an authentic Italian meal while sitting on this medieval passage is a must.

Old Town square

ADDING ON Helsinki

Finland's trendy capital city of Helsinki is a short two-hour ferry ride away from Tallinn, making it a natural connection to keep exploring Europe or even to visit as a day trip from Tallinn, where accommodations are considerably less expensive. Helsinki is known for its cutting-edge architecture, saunas and spas, hip Finnish design, and contemporary arts scene. Here are a few things to see and do in Helsinki:

Helsinki Cathedral

- **Helsinki Cathedral** (Unioninkatu 29; tel. 923406120; www.helsinginseurakunnat.fi; 9am-6pm daily; free): The most iconic building in Helsinki, the cathedral looms large over the city and is visually stunning, though the inside is quite austere. If pressed for time, you can skip a visit to the interior.
- **Kampii Chapel** (Simonkatu 7; 505781136; www.kampinkappeli.fi; 10am-6pm daily; free): Located right in the middle of Helsinki's trendy shopping district, this chapel is a space not only for quiet contemplation, but also to take in some of Finland's finest architecture and design.
- **Regatta Cafe** (Merikannontie; tel. 404149167; https://caferegatta.fi; 9am-9pm daily; €25): This charming café on the waterfront is popular with travelers and locals alike, and makes for a great lunch stop.
- **Suomenlinna Fortress and Island** (tel. 295338410; www.suomenlinna.fi; free): A short ferry ride from Helsinki brings you to this UNESCO World Heritage fortress and stunning island. Step back into the history of Finland. English-language tours available once daily (€12) during summer months.
- **Sauna:** When in Helsinki, one must sauna! There are numerous spas and saunas to choose from, usually starting around €15 for two hours. The modern **Löyly Helsinki** (Hernesaarenranta 4; tel. 961286550; www.loylyhelsinki.fi; hours vary, usually 10am-10pm or later; €20) is conveniently located on the southern edge of Helsinki.

GETTING THERE

Eckerö Line (www.eckeroline.com) runs ferries to Helsinki (12 daily; 2 hours; €34) from Tallinn's **Old City Harbor** (Sadama 25, Tallinn), which is an easy walk from Old Town. To make the most of your day in Helsinki, take the 6am ferry from Tallinn. Ferries arrive in Helsinki at **West Harbor** (Tyynenmerenkatu 14), which is connected to the city center by trams.

top, Helsinki; bottom, Suomenlinna Fortress and Island

(top to bottom) Alexander Nevsky Cathedral; Tallinn's Old Town; St. Catherine's Passage

4. Chocolate Workshop at Chocolala

Chocolala; Suur-Karja 20; tel. 55654333; www.chocolala.ee; 11am-7pm; from €15, depending on length of workshop

Make your own Estonian chocolates! Like citizens of so many other cold countries, Estonians love a good chocolatey treat to keep warm in the cold months. Try your own hand at making deliciously gorgeous chocolates. Workshops range from one to five hours, depending on what you want to do. You could try anything from making a chocolate lollipop (1 hour) to making your own chocolate bars from cocoa beans (5 hours), though this will require you to stop in for a couple of hours the following day.

5. Dinner and a Show at Troika

Raekoja plats 15; tel. 6276245; https://troika.ee; noon-11pm daily; €25

After heading back to Toompea Hill for the evening views, have dinner at Troika. Sure, it's more than just a little touristy, but it's still a lot of fun. This restaurant serves up traditional Russian hospitality, which is code for austere, as well as traditional Russian food that has had such an influence throughout the Baltics. From "Bear Dumplings" to Solyanka, a Russian meat soup, be prepared for a cozy meal. Roughly twice an hour there is a dancing performance in traditional Russian garb. With good food at a decent price and entertainment to boot, what's not to love?

TRANSPORTATION

Air

Vilnius International Airport (VNO; Rodūnios kl. 10A; tel. 61244442; www.vilnius-airport.lt): There are connections to Vilnius throughout Europe through carriers including popular low-cost airlines like Ryan Air and Wizz Air. From the United States, Canada, and elsewhere overseas, plan on having a layover, though ticket prices are generally much less expensive than those to other destinations around Europe. To connect with

WATCH

***The Singing Revolution*:** This is an inspiring documentary directed by James Trusty and Maureen Castle Trusty about the power of song to overthrow an empire. Amazingly, the Estonian revolution that succeeded in freeing the country from Soviet rule was powered by song.

READ

A History of the Baltic States by Andres Kasecamp: When we think of East meeting West, we typically think of Turkey or Morocco. This book will introduce the Baltics as another joining of Eastern and Western cultures while covering the many years struggling under oppressive rule these three Baltic countries share.

LISTEN

"Estonia Explained" by EER News (https://news.err.ee) is an English-language podcast diving into Estonian culture and history.

Vilnius Old Town, take the #88 bus (every 30 minutes; 15 minutes; €1).

Train

- **Vilnius Train Station** (www.traukiniobilietas.lt): This station is located just under 1 km (half a mile) south of Old Town, so you can walk into town from the train station if you are traveling light. The #7 bus connects with Old Town and runs every 20 minutes or so throughout the day.
- **Riga Train Station** (www.pv.lv): The Riga Train Station hugs the southern edge of Old Town. Most travelers will be fine walking to/from their accommodations, though taxis are available.
- **Tallinn Baltic Station** (Toompuiestee 37; https://elron.ee): The Tallinn Baltic station, the main station, is about a 10-minute walk to Old Town. There is no direct train from Riga; you will transfer at Valga, Estonia (10 hours with stop in Valga; from €15).

Bus

- **Vilnius Bus Station** (Sodų g. 22; www.autobusubilietai.lt): Buses to Trakai (more than 40 daily; 30 minutes; €0.65) and buses to Riga (4 hours; around €20) depart from this station, located next to the train station.
- **Riga Bus Station** (Latgale): Buses from Vilnius arrive at the Riga bus station, which is near Rigas Central Market.

Getting Back

The quickest way back to Vilnius is to fly from the **Tallinn Airport** (TLL; tel. 6058888; www.tallinn-airport.ee; 1 hour). **AirBaltic** (www.airbaltic.com) flies nonstop in that direction. You can also fly home or to your next destination from Tallinn, which usually involves a connection for anywhere outside Europe, or from **Helsinki Airport** (HEL; www.finavia.fi), which has a few direct flights outside Europe.

- Berlin, Warsaw, and Krakow (page 162)

ESSENTIALS

PASSPORTS AND VISAS

In order to enter countries within the **Schengen Zone,** the world's largest free travel zone that includes many European countries, travelers holding a valid passport from North America, the UK, or Oceania will need to make sure it is valid for at least 6 months days from the time of your departure and have a few blank pages for stamps. An automatic 90-day visa is granted on arrival. Countries not part of the Schengen Zone that are covered in this book include Bulgaria, Croatia, Ireland, England, Montenegro, Morocco, Romania, Scotland, and Turkey. Each of these countries has its own policies, in some cases requiring an e-visa.

In case of a lost, misplaced, or stolen passport, contact your country's embassy immediately. Generally, an emergency passport and/or travel documents can be reissued with 24-48 hours. Consulates and embassies for the US, Canada, UK, Ireland, New Zealand, and South Africa can be found in most countries in capital and larger cities, such as Paris, Munich, and Vilnius. Be sure to look up the closest consulate or embassy for you and save that information in case you need to replace your passport.

Border Crossings

Travel between countries in the Schengen Zone does not necessitate a passport or other identification, though you should always travel with your identification. In the Schengen Zone, other than perhaps a change of language, you won't necessarily even notice that you are traveling from country to country. There is a noticeable absence of customs or passport controls. If you are crossing in or out of

entering Switzerland from France in Mon Idée

EU, Schengen, Eurozone . . .

With so many countries in a small area, many with long histories of military conflict and distrust—politically, economically, and even socially—boundaries and groupings can be confusing in Europe. There are several organizations at work that travelers should be aware of.

EUROPEAN UNION

Founded in 1958 to foster cooperation between nations regarding trading and economy post World War II, the European Union initially included only six member states: Belgium, France, Germany, Italy, Luxembourg, and the Netherlands. This formed the basis for today's EU, which now includes 27 countries: Austria, Belgium, Bulgaria, Croatia, Cyprus, Czechia (formerly the Czech Republic), Denmark, Estonia, Finland, France, Germany, Greece, Hungary, Ireland, Italy, Latvia, Lithuania, Luxembourg, Malta, the Netherlands, Poland, Portugal, Romania, Slovakia, Slovenia, Spain, and Sweden.

SCHENGEN ZONE

Named for the town of Schengen, Luxembourg, where the original treaty was signed in 1985, the Schengen Zone are a collection of countries in Europe that have agreed to open borders and passport-free travel. Though most of the countries in the EU are part of the Schengen Zone, not all are. Ireland and Cyprus are not part of the Schengen Zone while Bulgaria and Romania are not full members, so passport controls are in effect to cross in/out of these countries. Iceland, Liechtenstein, Norway, and Switzerland are full members of the Schengen Zone, so if coming to/from another Schengen Zone country, you will not go through passport control, even though these countries are not members of the European Union. Though not strictly part of the Schengen Zone, visa-free travel has been extended to the micronations of Vatican City, Monaco, San Marino and Andorra as well.

EUROZONE

There are 20 countries that are part of the EU and share Euro currency. While Denmark has opted not to participate, others have yet to meet the criteria. Vatican City (Rome), Andorra, Monaco, and San Marino have adopted the Euro as their currency, though they are not, strictly speaking, part of the Eurozone or EU.

EUROPE ECONOMIC AREA (EEA)

Yet another series of agreements and treaties, the Europe Economic Area (EEA) allows for citizens of EU member states, as well as Liechtenstein, Norway, and Switzerland, to live and work without need of a visa or other paperwork in partner countries.

UNITED KINGDOM OF GREAT BRITAIN AND NOTHERN IRELAND

Including England, Scotland, Wales (the countries that comprise Great Britain) and Northern Ireland, this area known commonly as the UK is no longer part of the EU or EEA following the so-called Brexit on February 1, 2020. The UK was never part of the Eurozone. You will go through border controls and customs when crossing the border to/from the UK from EU member states, though there are no border controls within the UK. In a separate deal with Ireland, the UK and Ireland have free travel for their citizens as part of the Common Travel Area. As such, there is a selective passport check in place to verify citizenship. You may be asked to show your passport traveling between Ireland the UK, though not always.

the Schengen Zone, you will go through passport control and customs check.

AIRLINES AND AIRPORTS

The overwhelming majority of travelers from outside Europe arrive to the continent by air. Once in Europe, getting around by local and high-speed trains is a hassle-free, inexpensive, more environmentally friendly way to travel, though low-cost budget airlines do exist and are sometimes the only logical option to connect destinations.

Major Carriers

Every major carrier has some presence or partnership with European connections. The following carriers offer routes between North America and Europe: Aer Lingus, Air Canada, Air France, American Airlines, British Airways, Delta, Iberia, ITA Airways, KLM, Lufthansa, TAP Air Portugal, and United Airlines. For routes between Australia/New Zealand and Europe, Emirates, Qantas, Qatar Airways, and Virgin Australia are major carriers. For routes between South Africa and Europe, Emirates, Ethiopian Air, Lufthansa, and Swiss Air are major carriers.

Major Hubs

Depending on your airline and point of departure, you will likely connect with one of these major European hubs. Below you can find the major hubs with their corresponding cities and airport codes. Particularly for flights connecting through London and Paris, make sure to check if you have an airport change in the city.

- **Amsterdam, The Netherlands:** Amsterdam Airport Schiphol (AMS)
- **Barcelona, Spain:** Barcelona-El Prat (BCN)
- **Copenhagen, Denmark:** Copenhagen Airport (CPH)
- **Dublin, Ireland:** Dublin Airport (DUB)
- **Frankfurt, Germany:** Frankfurt am Main International Airport (FRA)
- **Istanbul, Turkey:** Istanbul Atatürk Airport (IST)
- **Lisbon, Portugal:** Lisbon Portela Airport (LIS)
- **Madrid, Spain:** Adolof Súerez Madrid-Barajas Airport (MAD)
- **Paris, France:** Charles de Gaule (CDG) and Orly (ORY)
- **London, UK:** Heathrow (LHR) and Gatwick (LGW)
- **Munich, Germany:** Munich Airport (MUC)
- **Oslo, Norway:** Oslo Airport Gardermoen (OSL)
- **Rome, Italy:** Leonardo da Vinci-Fiumicino Airport (FCO)
- **Zürich, Switzerland:** Zürich Airport (ZRH)

Budget Airlines

There are numerous budget airline carriers with new ones seeming to pop up and go out of business every year. Some of the more stable companies are Air Baltic, EasyJet, Norwegian Air, Ryanair, Transavia, Vueling, and Wizz Air. To keep costs low, these airlines all employ various tactics that generally reduce comforts and amenities associated with the flying experience. Do not expect free snacks or entertainment and expect to pay for literally everything other than your seat. Additionally, many of the routes that these airlines fly make use of smaller airports. Pay close attention to what airports you connect with and how these airports connect with major cities.

Luggage Restrictions

One of the more difficult parts of navigating the budget airlines experience is dealing with the various luggage restrictions. For the most part, expect to pay for checked luggage. If traveling carry-on only, attendants are often strict and will weigh and measure bags they believe to be over the airline's limit. Charges will often amount to triple (or more!) the cost of your ticket to check luggage or pay for "oversized" carry-on luggage.

TRAINS

For most travelers, nothing says "Europe" like traversing the continent by train. Getting around Europe by train is very easy. Nearly all major cities are served by multiple trains with various destinations each day. Stations for the most part are well-signed and generally located in downtown urban areas. Trains are famously punctual in countries such as Germany and Switzerland. Though perhaps a tad less punctual in other parts of Europe, trains still provide some of the most reliable, enjoyable, eco-friendly ways to travel from place to place. Prices do fluctuate with seasons and demand. It pays to book some key tickets in advance. Prices tend to increase closer to departure, though tickets are usually readily available the day-of, except for peak holidays.

High-Speed Trains

High-speed trains reach speeds of 321 km/h (200 mph); they are also comfortable and eco-friendly. Service on high-speed trains is offered in Italy, France, Germany, Spain, Sweden, Switzerland, The Netherlands, and the UK. All high-speed trains have choices of two or three different ticket levels (economy, business, and first class) and offer clean, quick, punctual service with amenities such as charging stations, Wi-Fi access, and other onboard services.

High-speed trains connecting individual countries include:

- **France:** TGV (France)
- **Spain:** Alvia, Altaria, AVE, Euromed
- **Italy:** Le Frecce
- **UK:** Javelin

High-speed train companies connecting multiple countries include:

- **Eurostar:** Belgium, France, The Netherlands, and UK
- **ICE:** Austria, France, Germany, Switzerland, and The Netherlands
- **Railjet:** Austria, Germany, Hungary, and Switzerland
- **RENFE-SNCF:** France and Spain
- **TGV-Lyria:** France and Switzerland
- **Thalys:** Belgium, France, Germany, and The Netherlands

Additionally, low-cost high-speed services offered by Avlo (Spain) and OUIGO (France and Spain), though with more limited connections, are making headway into the high-speed rail lines.

Regional and Local Service

All countries also have slower regional and local services that connect with smaller towns and villages. These trains are the heart and soul of European travel. Where the high-speed trains whisk you from urban center to urban center, these trains run at slower speeds, often along some of the most scenic routes in Europe, giving you time to take in the view. Regional trains are most often used by locals and provide a great chance to meet Europeans as you travel throughout the continent. Most regional and local services offer first and second class tickets, though they will not have a restaurant car, so be sure to plan accordingly. Nearly all countries have multiple rail companies that offer regional services. Italy alone has more than 60 companies operating local train lines.

Eurail Pass

For those looking to connect multiple train trips together, the **Eurail pass** (www.eurail.com) can be a great value (though not always) and must be purchased before your departure. There are different pass levels available (budget, economy, and premium) with different degrees of flexibility. Make sure to choose the best type of train pass for yourself. In some countries, like France, you will need to notify the train company ahead of time to reserve your seat, and you might have to pay a premium for your reservation. Passes also vary in length and combination; the most popular tickets allow you to travel a certain number of days over a specified period (i.e., unlimited travel for 7 days, midnight-midnight, within a month) while other passes give you unlimited travel for periods ranging from 15 days to 3 months. Prices start around €200. A ticket for unlimited first-class travel for a 3-month period runs just over €1,300.

CARS AND DRIVING

For the road trips outlined in this book, most travelers will need to rent a car. These routes take you into the countryside and through smaller villages and towns, but you may need to negotiate larger urban centers along the way. GPS navigation is nearly always optional in car rentals, though Google and Apple maps apps work fine throughout Europe. In urban centers, particularly, these driving aids can help you travel unfamiliar roads and interpret signage. Driving overall is as safe as it is back home, though you will be less familiar with the roads and streets, so pay attention and practice good defensive driving techniques.

Renting a Car

You will find local and international car rental agencies at all airports as well as in the downtown areas of large cities. Most agencies offer unlimited distance, though you will want to read through the rental agreement. Throughout the **Schengen Zone,** you will be able to drive freely. If you are planning to take your rental car out of the Schengen Zone, it is best to inquire ahead of time about the possibility. It may not be allowed, or you may need additional insurance.

In order to **rent a car,** you will need to provide a valid **driver's license** and **passport.** Specifics vary slightly from country-to-country. Most companies will require the driver to be 25-70 years old. Drivers younger or older may have to pay a higher insurance premium or may not be allowed a car rental. Insurance is a must, as is a valid credit card. If you wish to add a driver to the car, there is often a €10-15 per day surcharge.

You likely do not need an **International Driver's Permit.** The requirements for this are vague and generally not put into practice. I have rented cars for over 20 years in over a dozen countries in Europe, many of which supposedly require this document. Despite being pulled over numerous times (speeding... always speeding!) and receiving a few fines, to date, not a single police officer or car rental agent has ever requested this of me. That said, it might be worth the $20 to you to travel with complete piece of mind. In the United States, contact **AAA** (www.aaa.com/vacation/idpf.html) to request your International Driver's Permit.

The average cost of a vehicle rental varies according to season, location, vehicle type, and distance traveled. Expect to pay €25 or more per day, minimum, for your vehicle rental. The larger rental companies will allow you to drop off the vehicle in a different country from where you picked it up, though you will pay an extra fee for this (usually around €400 if connecting through major cities).

Automatic transmissions are becoming more commonplace, though manual transmissions are still the rule of thumb throughout Europe and usually cost less to rent. Make sure your rental car is something you are comfortable driving. If at all possible, rent an electric or hybrid car. This will not only reduce your carbon footprint, but also will save you money at the pump.

Savvy travelers with a long road trip ahead should consider leasing a car. If you plan on renting a car for more than a couple of weeks, leasing a new car is often less expensive than a traditional car rental. **Renault Eurodrive** (www.renault-eurodrive.com) in the US has information and plans.

Fuel

Cars in Europe will run on unleaded, diesel, or electricity. Make sure you understand what to put in your gas tank or how to charge your car before leaving the car rental agency. Unleaded and diesel are sold by the **liter** throughout Europe with prices generally twice that of North America. Budget and plan accordingly. Electric charge stations are easily found throughout Western Europe.

Tolls

Nearly all the freeways or autoroutes in Europe leverage tolled access. Tolls can range from as little as €1 to €10 or more, depending on time and season. There are three main types of tolls found in Europe: traditional road tolls paid at a booth, a vignette allowing for travel on a particular road network, and electronic tags that pay automatically when passing a gate or other pay control. Many toll booths accept credit and debit cards, though sometimes it is easier to pay in cash. It is a good idea to travel with a handful of euros in change for this reason. For countries running on the vignette system (such as Hungary), the vignette is included with your car rental. In other places in Europe, you may opt for an electronic sensor that will automatically charge your toll fee.

Rules of the Road

In the United Kingdom, the driver sits on the right side of the car and drives on the left side of the road. The rest of Europe is the same as North America, with the driver on the left side of the car, driving on the right side of the road.

All distance and speed markers are in kilometers. The standard speed limits are 50 km/h (31 mph) in urban areas, 90 km/h (56 mph) on rural roads, and 120 km/h (75 mph) on expressways, freeways, and autoroutes. It should go without saying that you should pay attention to the speed limits, which are marked with a bold number within a red circle.

Pay special attention to road signs. Though some signage can be found in English, most signage throughout Europe is in the local language.

Traffic Mitigation

Some cities, such as Paris and London, will have periods when downtown areas are closed to vehicular traffic, or to access the city you will have to pay a hefty charge.

Throughout Europe, you will encounter roundabouts and rotaries. Roundabouts are single lane circular connections of two or more roads where you turn right to merge onto the circle, progressing clockwise until your exit on the roundabout. A rotary is a multiple lane roundabout, generally with quite a few exits. Rotaries can be confusing to navigate, even for the most seasoned of drivers, and are where most traffic accidents happen throughout Europe. Luckily these are of the fender-bender variety as most drivers are traveling at lower speeds to navigate the rotary.

Parking

Parking garages in major cities are clearly marked with a capital P. In urban centers, parking in garages can be expensive, often costing €5 or more an hour. Street parking is nearly always metered. Some streets will reserve parking only for locals who pay for local passes. Parking on these streets should be avoided, as the risk of ticketing and towing is extremely high.

Road Conditions

The autoroutes covered in this guide are well maintained. Do keep in mind that in the cities, roads are often narrow and romantically bumpy with cobblestones. Weather, particularly snow and heavy rains, can have an adverse effect on roads, particularly in mountainous regions.

Via Michelin (www.viamichelin.com) is a good resource for updated traffic and road condition information. It can be used throughout Europe.

FERRIES AND BOATS

Ferries

Ferry services over large bodies of water, such as the Mediterranean and English

Channel, have regular hours throughout the year, though other crossings, particularly in the Baltic and North seas, are seasonal. Passengers with sensitive stomachs should consider taking an over-the-counter motion sickness medicine prior to setting sail, especially if the seas are stormy. In the summers and holidays, ferries are often at capacity.

There are many ferry companies operating different and overlapping passages throughout the continent. Prices vary dramatically throughout the year, depending on demand. Some ferries are passenger-only, while others serve a mix of commercial traffic and tourism. **Ferry Hopper** (www.ferryhopper.com) is a popular resource for up-to-date ferry information and to book passage.

You will be able to drive a car onto most ferries (though a few are for passengers only). Check with your car rental company about their rules and regulations before taking a rental car on any ferry service.

Cruises

River cruises and cruise ships operating around Europe require reservations ahead of time. Some of the best ships and companies often sell out months, if not years, in advance of setting sail. These ships are generally larger, so seasickness is less of a concern. The river cruises will generally be very smooth with little noticeable pitch or roll. A cruise can be a fantastic way to connect points of travel in Europe, though it does require a bit more prior planning and commitment.

BICYCLE

Biking throughout Europe is quite practical. It is often easy to rent bikes through **bike share programs** in the major cities. Programs such as Vélib in Paris, Donkey Republic in Berlin, Bicing in Barcelona, and Santander Cycles in London make it easy to pick up and drop off a bike for short connections. Bike sharing provides a greener, and more interesting, way to get from place to place in these major cities.

The entirety of Europe is geared for bikes. From bike lanes in urban spaces to well-marked countryside roads, and the general respect of local denizens, European biking infrastructure ensures a pleasant ride. In urban spaces, you can expect to find dedicated bike lanes and parking. Along the more popular biking paths crisscrossing the continent, you will find restaurants and lodgings catering to cyclists.

If you are planning to travel on one of the longer bike routes, bike rentals are readily available. For bike rentals, most major train stations in Western Europe have bike rental counters. Often you can arrange to have your bike dropped off in another location so you don't have to backtrack.

Another option is to purchase a bike in Europe. Famously, Belgium, France, The Netherlands, and Germany are all fantastic places to purchase a secondhand touring bicycle in great condition. Particularly for long excursions, it may make sense to pack your own bike.

Bicycles can be taken on trains. However, traveling by train with your bicycle can sometimes pose difficulties. In general, it is best to travel with your two wheels during off hours and in slower travel seasons. Your bike can nearly always travel for free if you can fold or disassemble your bike into a soft traveling case that is no larger than 135 x 85 x 30 cm (53 x 33 x 12 in). Other trains, such as the Eurostar, offer a registered luggage service. Some train companies, such as the TGV in France, will leverage a €10 fee for bike storage.

Cities vary on this, but in general stick to the buses if you need to transport your bike. Subways generally are not that bike-friendly, to say nothing of the trying to navigate the bustling underground public transportation infrastructure with your two wheels! In practice, you'll generally be riding around so you won't usually be using public transportation. If you do, be sure to ask the bus driver where to put your bike. The bus should have a front or back bike rack.

Depending on what kind of cyclist you are and your familiarity with navigating different urban areas, you may or may not feel comfortable getting around on two wheels in the bustling traffic. Regardless, if you are riding, wear a helmet, keep an eye out on the traffic, and be considerate of others. Bike theft is one of the more common petty thefts in Europe, so do lock up. Do be aware that some cities will have pedestrian-only zones where bikes are not allowed.

ON FOOT

Whether you are exploring urban landscapes or trekking the Alps, on any trip to Europe, one thing is certain: There will be walking. Most of Europe is perfectly walkable. In fact, every year people take slow travel seriously and walk across the entire continent.

Make sure to pack proper footwear and take care of your feet. Nothing will put a damper on your European excursion like sore, blistered feet. If you are primarily traveling on foot, pack accordingly. Keep your backpack as light as possible.

The urban spaces of Europe were meant for walking. Whether you're traipsing down the Champs Elysées or linking arms with a friend down Parizksa Street, you'll likely spend quite a bit of time exploring historic city centers on foot. Rules vary from country to country, though as a general rule of thumb you should stick to the sidewalk and cross in the crosswalks. Jaywalking is a fineable offense in most countries. Also, be aware of cyclists, bike lanes, and traffic.

Most cities now have some sort of reclaimed pedestrian-only neighborhood, or will sometimes close down all wheeled traffic in part of a city to give pedestrians the right of way. In historic neighborhoods, there are often parts with narrow (or non-existent) sidewalks. This is generally charming, though it can pose logistical problems for those with mobility issues.

Walking throughout Europe is safe, but as anywhere else, you should be aware that pickpockets and scam artists will target people who look like tourists. Be mindful of dark alleys and places where you feel unsafe. Listen to your intuition. For most people, the two biggest concerns about exploring Europe on foot are blisters and poor air quality. Masks are not just for COVID—feel free to wear one when air quality is poor, which often happens in summer months. Your lungs will thank you later.

ADVANCE RESERVATIONS

Though not entirely necessary, you will probably feel most comfortable if you have reserved a few things ahead of time, particularly during peak season when travel demand is high. Beyond your **plane tickets,** you will likely want to have **accommodations** in priority destinations reserved a few months ahead. This is particularly true of smaller, popular destinations, such as the Cinque Terre in Italy or Geneva. Cities like Barcelona and Paris occasionally host conferences and events that can make accommodations either difficult to find or very expensive.

Make sure to **book your key experiences** before traveling. Many of the experiences you want to have, from kayaking with sea turtles in the Canary Islands to visiting the Alhambra in Granada to wine tasting in Tuscany, are quite popular and will generally sell out well in advance. Other activities, such as particular hiking trails in many **national parks,** might require that you **apply for a day pass.** These passes are often limited to a certain number per day, and you will have better luck if you book early.

If you are a museum-goer, skip the line and purchase a **museum pass** or **city**

pass. These are available in most cities and can provide great value.

WHAT TO BRING

Pack great walking shoes. Inevitably, no matter what sort of travel you have in mind in Europe, you will end up walking… a lot. Beyond this, you will want to pack for the weather, and that means layers. Europe is a vast continent filled with microclimates. It is best to be prepared.

Keep all necessary medication in your carry-on luggage. Make a list of the generic names of your medication (not brand names) with you in case you need refills. Generic names can be understood by most pharmacies throughout the continent.

You will probably be traveling with some electronics (phone, laptop, tablet, watch, and/or camera). Most can be charged directly with the 220-240 volt electric system found in Europe. England, Scotland, and Ireland have a three-pin system while continental Europe has a two-pin system with round pins. You will only need these two plug adaptors; leave behind the electric converters for 220-240 to the 110-volt system found in North America. If you are considering packing a hair dryer or other non-convertible electronics, it's probably not worth the hassle.

WI-FI, GPS, AND ELECTRONICS

Wi-Fi and GPS are readily available throughout Europe in accommodations, museums, restaurants, and tourist centers. You will want to check with your cellphone provider about **international roaming,** and consider purchasing an international plan, the cost of which has plummeted in recent years. While using the Internet to access subscription-based services, a VPN may be necessary. If you have an unblocked cell phone, it's worth purchasing a SIM card in Europe for your travel. This will give you a local phone number and local data coverage. Most carriers in Europe have pay-as-you-go plans. If you have a dual-SIM phone, it is also possible to download an e-SIM for your travel. This can be a very easy, cost-effective solution to keep connected while in Europe.

Traveling with a smartphone can be a lifesaver. The GPS function will allow you to navigate unfamiliar city streets, and having local data makes it simple to keep in touch with family back home, find opening hours of local sights, and research and reserve restaurants that fit your taste and budget.

Nearly all electronics you travel with can be charged with the local electric system. If you do not have a plug adapter, you can find one at nearly any airport, train station, or electronics store.

MONEY AND CURRENCY

Throughout Europe, you will easily be able to use your **debit or credit cards,** though you will want to use cards with the chip. **Contact your bank and card issuers** before traveling to avoid holds being put on your cards as you are traveling internationally. Copy the **toll-free international phone number** of your card issuer or save it in your phone in case there are problems with your debit or credit cards.

Much of Europe has a shared currency, **the Euro** (EUR). You will be able to withdraw cash (10s, 20s, and 50s) from cash machines, though you should pay attention to the **currency exchange rate** (www.xe.com) and fees charged by the local bank and your home bank.

Other currencies you may encounter include: UK Pound Sterling (GBP), Bosnia and Herzegovina Mark (BAM), Bulgarian Lev (GBN), Czech Koruna (CZK), Denmark Crone (DKK), Hungarian Forint (HUF), Icelandic Krona (ISK), Moroccan Dirham (MAD), Norwegian Krone (NOK), Poland Zloty (PLN), Romanian Leu (RON), Turkish Lira (TRY).

HEALTH AND SAFETY

Generally speaking, Europe is a safe travel destination, with no health issues specific to the region, low crime rates, reliable transportation networks, and a well-established tourism infrastructure.

Vaccination Requirements

There is no requirement to show proof of vaccinations for traveling to Europe. It is recommended that you have updated hepatitis A and B vaccines, as well as influenza, COVID-19, and measles, mumps, and rubella. Typhoid and rabies vaccinations may be recommended in some cases.

Covid-19

European countries no longer have special requirements around COVID-19, though, of course, you should check before traveling for any global or local health emergency that might impact your travel.

Emergencies and Getting Care

If you find yourself anywhere in the EU and have an emergency, dial **112.** For most countries, this is the phone number for emergency services. In Switzerland, dial 117 (police), 144 (ambulance), or 118 (fire). Hospitals and emergency rooms can be found in nearly all larger towns and all cities. In case of emergency, your home insurance generally won't cover medical expenses while you're overseas. It's a good idea to carry comprehensive travel coverage, if only for medical emergencies. However, most countries subsidize their healthcare, so even if you do pay out of pocket, it will likely be the equivalent of your deductible anyway.

Health Issues

People with severe asthma or other lung-related allergies should know that air pollution is the biggest environmental health risk throughout Europe. This is accentuated in the urban centers and often occurs in the summer months. Pay attention to current air quality conditions, and use a mask when it makes sense.

Crime

Though Europe is safe in most respects, crime still exists. For most travelers, the biggest threat is petty theft. You can deter thieves by using a crossbody purse with a zipper and wearing coats and pants with zippered pockets (great for wallets). If you plan to walk around with your camera, or you are a digital nomad and have your laptop with you, use a day bag or backpack that locks.

Visitors to Europe should familiarize themselves with local laws and customs to avoid unintentionally breaking the law. Though public nudity and drug use are accepted or decriminalized in much of Europe, this isn't the case everywhere. Noticeably, there is no "1st Amendment Right" in Europe. In many countries there are strict, enforceable laws against hate speech and speech that incites violence.

LANGUAGE

The European Union recognizes 24 official languages. You likely know at least a few words in some of the more popular ones, such as French, Spanish, German and, of course, English. Generally speaking, English can get you around quite well throughout most of Western Europe and the Scandinavian countries, though the farther east you head, the fewer English speakers you will find outside of tourist hubs.

Making matters more linguistically diverse, though the EU might recognize 24 languages, it's believed that more than 200 languages are actually spoken in Europe! Basque, Icelandic, Gaelic, Catalan, and Flemish are just a few of the other languages you might hear while traveling the continent.

Wherever you travel, try to learn at least a few words of the local dialect, as this shows a level of respect and interest. Particularly if you learn some of the less commonly heard languages, you will likely find yourself forging friendly bonds that will add another cultural dimension to your travels.

Prioritize learning to say the following:

- Hello
- Please
- Thank you and you're welcome
- This and that (so helpful when you are pointing!)
- Yes and no
- Water
- Where is ________ (fill in the blank)
- Bathroom
- How much is
- Numbers 1-100
- Your city/country is beautiful

For travelers with life-threatening allergies or other medical concerns, carry a printed copy of your specific allergy or medical condition along with emergency treatment in each language you'll be encountering on your journey.

TRAVEL TIPS

Solo Travel

It sometimes feels like Europe was meant to be discovered by solo travelers. Hostels, shared train cars, and even car ride programs seem tailor-made to introduce solos to other travelers and locals. For safety, practice basic common sense and be aware of your surroundings. If you are interested in meeting other solo travelers or locals, check out the local Meet Up site (www.meetup.com) and Tours by Locals (www.toursbylocals.com), both of which have a diverse set of themed excursions and events, from photography walks to secret singles-only dinners.

Female Travelers

For women traveling, whether alone or in groups, Europe will be at least as safe as your hometown. Use the usual precautions you take at home. Stay alert and keep an eye on your drink, particularly if you are solo.

LGBTQI+ Travelers

Western Europe is largely regarded as one of the most progressive places to travel and live for people in the LGBTQI+ community. Same sex marriage is legal throughout the European Union, from charming Porto to modern Helsinki. Though most cities are quite progressive with active communities, in rural regions acceptance is sometimes less reliable. It may be best to keep PDA to a minimum in these typically more conservative spots. A few good resources are: **Nomadic Boys** (https://nomadicboys.com), **Queer in the World** (https://queerintheworld.com), **Mister B&B** (www.misterbandb.com), and the **International LGBTQ+ Travel Association** (www.iglta.org).

Travelers of Color

Travelers of color may experience some form of discrimination or racism, though it may be subtle, in countries that have considerable populations of immigrants from Sub-Saharan Africa, such as France and Italy. For more reading, check out **Travel Noire** (https://travelnoire.com), **Black and Abroad** (www.blackandabroad.com).

Travelers with Disabilities

All of the trips in this guide can be done by those with disabilities, though you will need to plan ahead. There are challenges in traveling Europe, particularly for those using a walker or wheelchair. Sidewalks are often narrow or sometime non-existent, particularly in the oldest parts of the cities.

Public subway systems often lack access. If you will be using public transportation, buses are often better equipped to help those with wheelchairs and other needs. In general, people are kind and are happy to help out when asked. Do not be afraid to ask for a hand if needed.

Many accommodations have few rooms designated for those with disabilities. Be sure to reserve your accommodations ahead of time to guarantee your reservation at an acceptable room.

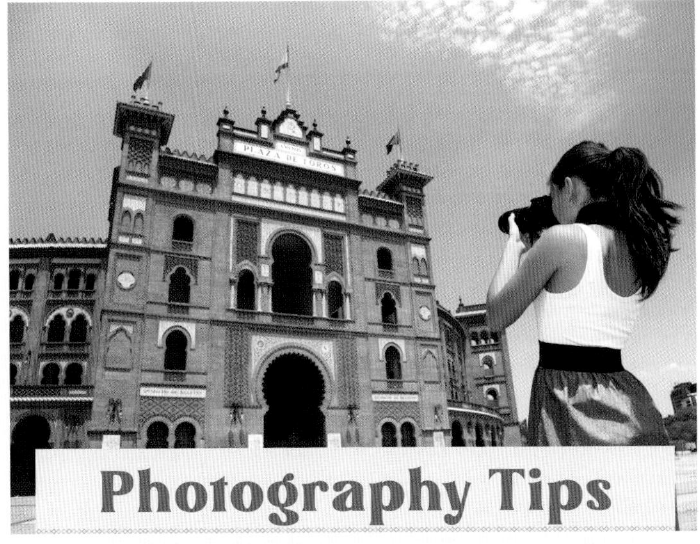

Photography Tips

- Learn the ins and outs of your camera before you travel. This will make taking memorable pictures that much easier.
- Ease the burden. Prioritize a light, versatile kit.
- Keep your gear clean, particularly your lens. Editing photos is easier without having to remove water or dust spots from your images.
- Have a spare battery and SD cards handy.
- Be aware. Your gear can make you a target for petty theft.
- Take photos of the monuments and sites, but don't forget the funny moments, foodie spots, and other things that make your travel special.
- Take lots of photos. Use your down time in the evenings or while in transit to filter what you like and don't like.
- Strike out early in the morning for great light and fewer crowds.

dations ahead of time to guarantee your reservation at an acceptable room.

Most museums and historic sites offer free or reduced entrance fees for disabled visitors and their companions. Priority access with no wait times are common, though you will want to check prior to arrival.

Travel specialists, such as **Easy Access Travel** (https://easyaccesstravel.com) or **Travel for All** (https://travel-for-all.com), will help you experience Europe to its fullest.

Traveling with Kids

An entirely different Europe opens wide to those traveling with children. Get to know the family-friendly side of the continent. Prioritize time spent in some of Europe's fantastic public parks. Watch as your children have their own cultural-immersion experience, playing in sand or chasing other kids around. Most, though not all, cafés and restaurants will have set child menus and child seats.

When traveling by rail or car with children, the trick is to keep them occupied.

Have plenty of activities on hand to keep them busy. For most kids, keeping their own travel journal is a great way to have them interact on their own terms with your travel. They can write journal entries, draw pictures, tape important ticket stubs, include important maps, and if you are traveling with an instant film camera, even insert their own instant photos.

When traveling by train, walk your child up and down the aisles and explore the mysteries of the dining car, observe the surrounding countryside, and draw portraits of other train passengers. If you're going by car, be sure to stop often enough to let the little ones run off all their energy. Keep snacks and water handy.

Before your go, prepare your kids for travel. Your local library is a great source of age-appropriate material for children. Little Passports (www.littlepassports.com) offers monthly subscriptions for kids aged 3-10 with hands-on activities, stories, and science experiments to help young ones develop their curiosity about the world. You can also help your children begin to learn some foreign phrase basics. Also, eat out at international restaurants that reflect where you will be going, or cook your own European food to prime the kids for your upcoming trip.

Senior Travelers

Seniors with a decent level of fitness will easily be able to follow any of the routes outlined in this guide. If you are considering renting a car, be aware that most car rental companies have an upper age limit, usually 70. Beyond 70 years of age, you may have to pay for supplemental car insurance.

Before traveling, be sure to understand how your medical insurance works overseas. Medicare in not valid in Europe. Travel insurance is extremely useful, though you should make sure you understand the terms of your policy. Pack extra medication and any dietary supplements. Though you can refill these in Europe, it is a hassle. You will need to know the generic name of your medicine as opposed to its brand name. Medicine and supplements in Europe may come in a different form than you are used to.

In Europe, many museums and sites offer discounts of 10 percent or more for persons ages 60 and up. In the UK, look for signs reading "concessions," while in other parts of Europe, "pensioner's rates" is more common. People of all ages find that an active day of sightseeing is best followed by a quiet day to recharge. Listen to your body and take a little downtime at a local café people-watching and experiencing local culture like the locals.

AARP (www.aarp.org/travel) has a variety of articles, advice, and information for senior travelers.

SEASONALITY

Seasonal weather throughout Europe differs drastically from north to south, east to west. Take this into consideration when planning and packing for your tour. In this guide, **fall** is defined as September-November, **winter** is December-February, **spring** is March-May, and **summer** is June-August.

Fall

Months: *Sept.-Nov.*

As the temperatures begin to dip and the leaves change colors, road trips and long train rides open over vast expanses of the European countryside. The long days of summer in the Nordic countries quickly give way to long sunsets, shorter days, and cooler temperatures. The beaches of the Mediterranean retain their summer glow well into October while, at the same time, the mountain peaks and much of Eastern Europe may witness their first snow fall. Temperatures across the continent will be temperate, though autumn storms are to be expected. Though cooler, November is often a great season to visit for those looking for fewer crowds.

Perfect time for: London and Paris; Prague, Vienna, and Budapest; Bordeaux and the Pyrenees; Tuscany and Umbria; Cinque Terre (hike); Camino de Santiago (hike); The Greek Islands; The Canary Islands; The French Riviera; Paris to Bucharest.

Winter

Months: *Dec.-Feb.*

Days are shorter and darker all around, though this is felt more the farther north you go, and the chances of cold, heavy snow become more likely. In countries like Iceland or Finland, hope for a glimpse of the aurora borealis, as there will be as little as 3-4 hours of daylight. The farther south you travel, though temperatures will be cooler and days shorter in winter, the effect is less obvious. In Spain, Italy, and Greece, nighttime temperatures can dip close to freezing, but daytime temperatures remain mild. In Central and Eastern Europe, snowy, freezing temperatures are the norm, while in the Canary Islands, you can still enjoy days at the beach. Throughout the continent holiday markets will be in full swing through the New Year, serving up warm, spiced wine and other beverages to keep your spirits up.

Perfect time for: Barcelona and Madrid; Sevilla, Córdoba, and Granada; Rome, Florence, and Venice; The Alps.

Spring

Months: *Mar.-May*

Spring in the southern regions of Europe, from Portugal, along the Mediterranean coast through to Turkey, is nearly perfect weather for travel—sunny and warm, with little rainfall. As you head northward into Europe and away from the coasts, temperatures can still be quite cold, particularly at night. As the weather warms, snowfall gives way to rain. In higher climes and northern countries, snow can still be expected throughout May.

Perfect time for: Amsterdam, Brussels, and Bruges; Berlin, Warsaw, and Krakow; Romantische Strasse; The Magistrala Coastal Road; Holland Junction Network (bike); Alta Via 1: Dolomite High Route (hike); Rhine River Cruise; South of England to North of France; The Douro Line.

Summer

Months: *June-Aug.*

Temperatures rise as the days lengthen. In the most northern reaches of Europe you can experience 24 hours of sunlight. Areas along the Mediterranean and Atlantic are warm, though temperate. Farther inland, heatwaves can be a real concern, particularly as most businesses and accommodations are not air conditioned. Stifling temperatures in cities like Paris, Rome, and Madrid are to be expected. Some local businesses close for much of August. When the snow thaws and roads open, this is the only viable time for some itineraries outlined in this guide, such as those that traverse mountain passes or cross the North Sea. The Copenhagen-Berlin bike tour, Tour du Mont Blanc trek, and Iceland's Ring Road are routes that can only be accomplished in summer.

Perfect time for: Edinburgh and Glasgow; Copenhagen to Oslo; Zagreb, Ljubljana, and Trieste; Vilnius, Riga, and Tallinn; Iceland's Ring Road; Causeway Coast; The North Coast 500; Transylvania; Dublin and the Wicklow Way (hike); England's Lake District (hike); Copenhagen to Berlin by Bike; Tour du Mont Blanc (hike); The Rhone Valley; The Azores; The Bergen Line; Lofoten.

Tourist Seasons

Mid-June-August and December-early January are considered the **high season** for nearly every destination in Europe. Expect longer lines, bigger crowds, and less availability for accommodations and tickets, so advance planning pays off. Typically, you will also find longer days, sunnier weather, more events, and more services. The winter holiday season makes up for its lack of sun and warm weather with lots of events and holiday markets. Europeans love to travel the continent as well. Any weeks in the year that coincide with holidays and school vacations tend to create mini-high seasons in the shoulder seasons of the spring and fall.

Early January-early March tends to be **low season** for much of Europe. With cooler, if not downright cold, temperatures throughout the continent, more focus tends to be on indoor activities. Accommodations may shutter for this time in some locations to do repairs and upkeep. Services outside of major cities can be limited. If you do not mind bundling up, this can be a wonderful way to experience Europe as a local.

The **shoulder seasons of** September-mid November and early March-early June tend to be great times to travel most of Europe. Accommodations are open, crowds are not at their highest peaks, and the weather, though variable, is generally better than it is deep into winter. You will still find several events and normal travel services will be open. For extremely popular countries like Italy and France, shoulder seasons are still quite busy and discounted rates associated with less-busy seasons are harder to come by.

SUSTAINABLE TRAVEL

Public Transit

Many of the routes outlined in this guide make heavy use of public transportation systems. In cities, you will be able to take advantage of quick, efficient subways, overland trams, and electric or hybrid buses. When you are traveling from city-to-city, avoid flying; the railway systems are comfortable, punctual, and often the best way to connect locations. Though you can pay for each voyage on a mode of public transportation individually, it is often less expensive to purchase packs of tickets or city passes.

Vehicle Energy Efficiency

If you are renting a car, choosing a hybrid or electric car is not only easier on your travel budget, but also better for the environment. The road trips in this guide minimize any backtracking, which will help lower fossil fuel usage. Maintain the proper tire pressure and use cruise control where appropriate to further help reduce emissions. Also, don't speed—maximum fuel efficiency for most passenger vehicles occurs at around 80 km/h (50 mph), and the faster you go above that, the less efficient your trip becomes.

Reusable Containers

One of the biggest wastes in travel are plastic bottles. The water throughout Europe is drinkable. Pack a large water bottle to keep hydrated and fill up at your accommodations or the numerous public fountains. You can travel with water purifiers or a filter if you have a sensitive system. In Paris, you can even find sparkling water at the public fountains. If you are a coffee or tea drinker, a thermos or washable travel mug is a must.

Travel with an over-the-shoulder collapsible bag. These fold up into a small square that is easy to pack away, and can be great on-the-go for shopping, picnics, the beach, and more. If you use plastic bags, keep them to reuse or as emergency rain gear either for yourself or your electronics.

Recycling Centers

Recycling is compulsory throughout Europe, though that's not always obvious on public transportation. Recycling bins are easily spotted in urban areas, train stations, and airports. Pack out any plastic, paper, and aluminum for recycling when hiking and biking.

Meal Planning

The EU has agreed to reduce food waste by 30 percent in 2025 and 50 percent by 2030. You can do your part by eating at local restaurants that employ a farm-to-fork business model. Throughout Europe, portion sizes tend to be smaller, which creates less waste. Avoid international restaurant chains. When food shopping for camping, road trips, long train trips, and hikes, buy in bulk when possible.

For more information, explore the European Commission website to combat food waste: https://ec.europa.eu/food/safety/food_waste/eu-food-loss-waste-prevention-hub/.

Fair Wages

No matter the size of your travel budget, try not to cut corners with guides, drivers, and other services. Paying a fair, or even above-market wage, particularly in less affluent regions, goes a long way to help local economies thrive. Websites, such as www.toursbylocals.com, are great ways to connect with locals, pay a fair wage directly for a service, and have a memorable experience.

Clean Energy Certifications

To further reduce your carbon footprint, look for businesses that abide by the European Energy Certificate System (EECS, www.aib-net.org/eecs) wherever possible. This is a guarantee of origin that the business or service is using renewable energy. In the United Kingdom, the Renewable Energy Guarantee Origin (REGO) serves the same purpose. Particularly for accommodations, these certifications are difficult to find. Also look for properties that make generous use of solar and wind turbine and do your part to reduce energy waste by limiting cooling, heating, and hot water usage.

Different regions have their own eco certification noting a certain adherence to clean energy and other environmentally sensitive practices. Here is a list of the most important by region:

- **Europe:** ECOTEL certification by HVS EcoServices
- **European Union:** Eco-Label for Tourist Accommodation Services (ELTAS)
- **European Union:** Green Key
- **Germany:** DEHOGA
- **Austria:** Hotel Label
- **Scandinavia:** Nordic Swan Ecolabel
- **Catalunya, Spain:** Catalan Emblem

Supporting Local Businesses

You will have a much better, much more local experience in Europe the more you spend time with local businesses, from the shops you frequent to your local café. Take a moment to dive into a specialty wine or cheese shop, explore the crafts in the local markets, check out the boutique watchmakers in Switzerland and pick up that handknitted wool sweater in Iceland. Keep it local, and you will have memories and souvenirs that will last a lifetime.

Water Conservation

Here are a few tips to help you use less water on your travels.

- Do a full load of laundry instead of several small ones.
- Don't take a bath, and take shorter showers.
- Use dry shampoo to extend the time between hair washings.
- Try to stay more than one night at accommodations, and keep the "do not disturb" sign on the door to lessen unnecessary cleanings.
- Reduce your meat consumption or eat completely vegan or vegetarian. Beef, in particular, is a water-heavy protein source.
- Pack your own water bottle, as using your own water bottle will save on plastic, and you will be less likely to waste drinking water. Interesting fact: it takes more than one bottle of water to make one plastic bottle to transport your water.
- Search for ecotourism options where available.

Energy Conservation

Besides conserving water, consider the following to reduce your energy consumption as well and lessen the overall impact on the climate while traveling. Many of these tips can be practiced at home as well.

- Turn off the lights, TV, computers, fans, and other energy sources in your hotel

or other accommodation when you are not using them.
- Keep heating and air conditioning use to a minimum.
- Reuse towels and sheets.
- Use public transportation whenever possible.
- Eat local. You'll enjoy better food and the satisfaction of knowing that less energy was used to transport your food.

Conserve energy at home during your trip by unplugging your entertainment. TVs, DVD players, game consoles, and cable boxes all use power when plugged in, even if they are turned off. Turn down your water heater.

Offsetting Your Carbon Footprint

If you are interested in reducing your carbon footprint, you can eat less meat, walk more, bike more, and use travel companies and tour operators that donate part of their proceeds to carbon offsetting programs. Also consider enrolling in one of the programs listed below to further offset the carbon cost of your travel.

- **Atmos Fair:** www.atmosfair.de—Specifically for offsetting air travel.
- **Sustainable Travel International:** https://sustainabletravel.org—Geared specifically toward travel professionals.
- **Terra Pass:** https://terrapass.com—Easy to use with programs for different levels of carbon offsetting.

ACCOMMODATIONS

Whether you are using a traditional hotel, a long-term rental, or a B&B, or even if you plan on camping for your European adventure, you should reserve your accommodations first, before you book anything else on your itinerary, including your plane tickets. The earlier you make a reservation, the more likely it is that you will have the type of accommodation you want for your dates at the very best price. Planning ahead here can really save you lots of money, stress, headache, and time.

Although booking accommodations through online travel agencies is very convenient, independently owned properties generally earn more when you book directly with them.

Hotels

Across Europe you will find a mix of hotels, from large chains like Westin, Hilton, and Sofitel, to boutique establishments priding themselves on originality, as well as more budget-oriented joints. You can generally find availability at the large chain hotels, but often boutiques and even budget hotels offer something more authentic. Particularly during the high season, you should reserve hotel rooms well ahead of time. Of the large hotel chains, both the Hilton and Fairmont hotel chains are making great strides in being more environmentally conscious.

Bed-and-Breakfasts

Over the past decade, cozy B&Bs have become more popular throughout Europe, particularly in Western Europe. Be sure to reserve well in advance as B&Bs have limited guest rooms. There is perhaps no better way to experience the hospitality of a place and discover its culture than to have a friendly chat over a delicious local breakfast. You can expect warm, attentive, personalized service at B&Bs throughout Europe, though English is not always spoken.

Camping

Camping in Europe is different from camping in North America. In Europe, campsites are often family-owned and -run, and offer a wide range of amenities, from swimming pools and wellness centers, to activities for children and even restaurants. There are also glamping options in most countries that generally offer an adult-oriented experience. On some of the walking routes described in this guide, you could opt for tent camping, though you should be sure to understand rules, regulations, and safety issues before setting out as these vary from country to country.

Throughout Europe, laws vary widely on wild camping. In some countries, such as Italy, wild camping is strictly illegal. In other countries, such as Estonia, Finland, Norway, Sweden, and Scotland, wild camping isn't only legal, it is encouraged. Many countries, such as France, Spain, and Portugal have confusing laws regarding wild camping, so it is best to inquire ahead. For popular treks, such as the Camino de Santiago and the Tour du Mont Blanc, there are a mix of places where wild camping is possible and where it is prohibited by local law.

Vacation Rentals

Vacation rentals offered with companies such as **Airbnb** (www.airbnb.com), **VRBO** (www.vrbo.com), and **HomeAway** (www.homeaway.com), or regional companies that manage privately owned properties, are a popular option for those looking to slow down their travel and have a more local experience. Vacation rentals offer a number of benefits for travelers. They are generally less expensive, often in local neighborhoods, and have kitchens and laundry facilities. You can expect to find essentials, such as linens, basic kitchen tools, and Wi-Fi, though you might be responsible for providing everything else. Rental properties are less consistent and not as secure as other accommodations. In popular cities, vacation rentals have also had an adverse effect on the local economy and face strong regulations from government agencies and, in many cases, from less-than-friendly neighbors who have grown tired of short-term vacationers in their apartment buildings.

Hostels

For solo travelers, hostels offer a great place to mingle and find like-minded travel companions. They're also among the more budget-friendly accommodations you can find throughout Europe. Hostels are generally found in urban areas. You can request a single room or dorm-style accommodation. There are often women-only dorms, though not all of the time. Expect to share bathrooms, kitchens, and common areas. Do reserve ahead of time to guarantee your space, as popular hostels tend to fill up. **Hostel World** (www.hostelworld.com) and **Europe Hostels** (www.europeanhostels.com) have the most comprehensive hostel listings.

Homestays

Homestays offer another way to interact with local culture. You will share residence with a homeowner and need to abide by your host's house rules; this might mean that smoking is prohibited (or allowed) throughout the home, or that there is a strict curfew. Homestays are not only an opportunity for cultural exchange, but also for a monetary or service-based exchange. **Homestay** (www.homestay.com) is the go-to resource throughout Europe.

Farmstays

None of the routes covered in this guide allow for a farm stay, though if you want to slow it down, a farm stay is a great way to meet locals, touch the local soil, and get some fresh air. Most farmstays in Europe tend to veer upmarket. **Farmstay Planet** (www.farmstayplanet.com) is a great resource. If you want to spend a week or more working on a European farm or sustainable agriculture project, check out Work Away (www.workaway.info).

INSPIRATION AND RESOURCES

Suggested Reading

Alone Time: Four Seasons, Four Cities and the Pleasures of Solitude by Stephanie Rosenbloom. With Paris, Florence, Istanbul, and New York as backdrops, the author embarks on a journey to discover the physical and mental health benefits of solo travel.

A Time of Gifts—On Foot to Constantinople by Patrick Leigh Fermor. The first of a three-volume classic memoir chronicling the author's 1933/34 walk across the European continent from Hook Island in the UK to Istanbul, Turkey.

Gears for Queers by Abigail Melton and Lilith Cooper. A relatable cycling book following the highs and lows of a visibly queer couple as they bike from the Netherlands on a meandering path that ends in Spain.

The Art of Travel by Alain de Botton. Using artists and writers as a launching pad, this is a book exploring the fundamental inspiration that leads us to travel. A modern philosophical travel treatise.

Europe in the Looking Glass by Robert Byron. Three young, inexperienced travelers take off on a road trip crossing Europe between the Great Wars. In turns erudite, humorous, and heartfelt.

Not Cool: Europe by Train in a Heatwave by Jules Brown. A delightful travel memoir that finds the joy of adventure in some of the least favorable circumstances.

Suggested Movies

A Good Year by Ridley Scott. A workaholic Wall Streeter obsessed by money inherits his beloved uncle's estate in the slow moving countryside of Provence, where he rediscovers a love for life.

Angst Essen Seele Auf by Rainer Werner Fassbinger. This '70s-era prize-winning classic ushered in new age of German cinema. The story tackles the complexity of Germany through the lens of an older German woman who has fallen in love with a Moroccan man.

The Before Trilogy by Richard Linklater. Together, this romantic trio of films make up a modern classic, where the settings star alongside the clever dialog. An encounter that begins on a train and on the streets of Vienna in a single night *(Before Sunrise)* later resumes in Paris *(Before Sunset)* and then Greece *(Before Midnight)*.

Breathless by Jean-Luc Goddard. Modern cinema begins here. Follow an on-the-run criminal and his American girlfriend through Paris on this action-packed jazzy art film that will leave you buzzing.

The Bourne Identity by Doug Liman (and sequels). Follow Jason Bourne in this action-packed spy thriller franchise that is largely set against the backdrop of iconic European locations. In a similar vein, many James Bond movies are set at least partially in Europe.

L'Auberge Espagnole by Cédric Klapisch. Follow a young Frenchman on his study-abroad adventure to the vibrant city of Barcelona where people of all nationalities and backgrounds meet for a life-altering experience.

National Lampoon's European Vacation by Amy Heckerling. A comedic family road trip through Europe starts in the UK before crossing to France, Germany, and Italy.

Off the Rails by Jules Williamson. In honor of a friend who has died, three longtime friends in their 50s take the rail journey of a lifetime, turning tragedy into a heartfelt comedy full of lost passports and train strikes.

The Girl on the Bridge by Patrice Leconte. This '90s black-and-white French film follows a couple through their carnival journey across Europe, from Paris to the French Riviera, Italy, and Istanbul. This movie is at once sexy and funny, tense, witty, and contemplative.

Suggested Podcasts

The Europeans (https://europeanspodcast.com) hosted by Katy Lee and Dominic Kraemer. The focus here is on the untold stories from people around Europe, particularly concerning culture and politics.

Extra Pack of Peanuts (https://extrapackofpeanuts.com) hosted by Heather and Travis Sherry. Listen for tips and tricks for budget travelers, maximizing frequent flyer miles, and traveling light.

A Girl's Guide to Traveling Alone (www.girlsthattravel.com) hosted by Gemma Thompson. Experienced solo women travelers provide a mix of travel inspiration coupled with real-world guidance on safety and the benefits of travel.

Zero to Travel (https://zerototravel.com) hosted by Jason Moore. For those looking to be location-independent while traveling, this podcast features interviews with travel experts and personalities.

The Thoughtful Travel Podcast (www.notaballerina.com) hosted by Amanda Kendle. Featuring interviews with bloggers, photographers, and authors, this podcast focuses on ethical travel.

Travel with Rick Steves (www.ricksteves.com/watch-read-listen/audio/podcasts) by Rick Steves. America's most popular travel personality, Rick Steves, provides his unique perspective on some his favorite European spots and experiences.

Suggested Websites

RE:European Stories (www.arte.tv/en/videos/RC-013956/re-european-tories/) by ARTE. This ongoing series from Arte inspires through its stories of Europeans, highlighting regional specialties and issues, from organized begging to sexy underwear.

Rome2Rio (www.rome2rio.com). Although not specific to Europe, this amazing website can tell you how to get between any two places in the world.

Eurail (www.eurail.com). Not only can you purchase your Eurail pass here, but also this website offers a wealth of planning information, such as train routes in each country.

European Rail Timetable (www.europeanrailtimetable.eu). Available in print or digital form, this book is just what it says; it hearkens back to an earlier time—and is still just as useful.

INDEX

A

B

C

D

E

F

G

H

I

J

K

L

M

QR

S

T

UV

WXYZ

LIST OF MAPS

Front Map

City Hopping

Road Trips

Outdoor Adventures

On the Water

Classic Rail Trips and More

PHOTO CREDITS

Front Matter

4 top to bottom © Ekaterinabelova | Dreamstime.com, © r.classen | Shutterstock, © muratart | Shutterstock; 5 © Apolinariy | Shutterstock; 6 © TTstudio | Shutterstock; 8 © Ekaterinabelova | Dreamstime.com; 9 © Fyletto | Dreamstime.com; 10 top © Antonel | Dreamstime.com; 10 bottom © Daryl Mulvihill | Alamy Stock Photo; 11 © Dmitry Morgan | Shutterstock; 12 © H368k742 | Dreamstime.com; 13 top © Michelangeloop | Dreamstime.com; 13 bottom © Carmengabrielafilip | Dreamstime.com; 14 top © Alerizzo78 | Dreamstime.com; 14 bottom © Mustang79 | Dreamstime.com; 15 top to bottom © cowardlion | Shutterstock, © Lostsomewhereinfrance | Dreamstime.com, © Sangapark118 | Dreamstime.com, © arkantostock | Dreamstime.com, © Julialav | Dreamstime.com; 16 © Frederik Jegsen | Shutterstock; 17 left © Yellowind | Dreamstime.com; 17 right © Adisa | Dreamstime.com; 18 © Awwwisme | Shutterstock; 20 © Sun_Shine | Shutterstock; 22 left © Denisbelitsky | Dreamstime.com; 22 right © Krivinis | Dreamstime.com; 23 © Araraadt | Dreamstime.com; 24 © Olganiekrasova | Dreamstime.com; 25 © peresanz | Shutterstock; 26 © SAKhanPhotography | Shutterstock; 27 © Wirestock | Dreamstime.com; 28 © smpoly | Shutterstock; 30 © Poike2017 | Dreamstime.com; 31 top © Dreamer4787 | Shutterstock; 31 bottom © S.Borisov | Shutterstock; 32 top to bottom © minnystock | Dreamstime.com, © minnystock | Dreamstime.com, © Tommyandone | Dreamstime.com, © Blunker | Dreamstime.com; 33 © Icenando | Dreamstime.com

City Hopping

40 © Audio und werbung | Shutterstock; 44 © Vwalakte | Dreamstime.com; 45 top to bottom © AlenaKravchenko | Dreamstime.com, © Jiggotravel | Dreamstime.com, © Petr Kovalenkov | Shutterstock; 48 © Audioundwerbung | Dreamstime.com; 49 © Aiisha | Dreamstime.com; 50 top © Irstone | Dreamstime.com; 50 bottom © Roland Nagy | Dreamstime.com; 53 top to bottom © Sborisov | Dreamstime.com, © Kiev.Victor | Shutterstock, © shawnwil23 | Shutterstock; 54 © Sampajano_Anizza | Shutterstock; 55 top © Fazlyeva Kamilla | Shutterstock; 55 bottom © Lucas M Peters; 58 top to bottom © Lucas M Peters, © Lucas M Peters, © Andersastphoto | Dreamstime.com, © Lucas M Peters; 61 top to bottom © Aliaksandrkazlou | Dreamstime.com, © Lucas M Peters, © Outline205 | Dreamstime.com; 63 © TungCheung | Shutterstock; 65 © Marazem | Dreamstime.com; 66 top to bottom © Chubable | Dreamstime.com, © Gjbphoto8 | Dreamstime.com, © Martingaalsk | Dreamstime.com; 67 © Shaiith | Dreamstime.com; 70 © Felixkiel | Dreamstime.com; 71 top to bottom © Oceanwhisper | Dreamstime.com, Jenifoto406 | Dreamstime.com, Martinmates | Dreamstime.com; 72 © Barmalini | Dreamstime.com; 73 © Oleksii Sidorov | Shutterstock; 75 © Tomas1111 | Dreamstime.com; 76 © Salvador Maniquiz | Shutterstock; 77 top © Jennifer622 | Dreamstime.com; 77 bottom © Electropower | Dreamstime.com; 78 © Magdanatka | Shutterstock; 79 top © Barmalini | Dreamstime.com; 79 bottom © Electropower | Dreamstime.com; 81 © Dennisvdwater | Dreamstime.com; 82 top to bottom © Anry | Dreamstime.com, © Seregalsv | Dreamstime.com, © Seregalsv | Dreamstime.com; 83 © Ntsmedia | Dreamstime.com; 86 © Jeafish | Dreamstime.com; 87 top

to bottom © Siraanamwong | Dreamstime.com, © Cebas1 | Dreamstime.com, Niserin | Dreamstime.com; 88 © Kitleong | Dreamstime.com; 90 © Bert e Boer | Shutterstock; 92 top to bottom © Emicristea | Dreamstime.com, © Seregalsv | Dreamstime.com, © Artjazz | Dreamstime.com, © Mathes | Dreamstime.com; 94 © Haveseen | Dreamstime.com; 96 left © Alexsalcedo |Dreamstime.com; 96 right © Emicristea | Dreamstime.com; 97 © Olena Znak | Shutterstock; 99 © Scorpionka | Dreamstime.com; 100 top to bottom © Perszing1982 | Dreamstime.com, © Inbj | Dreamstime.com, © Sepavo | Dreamstime.com; 101 © Seregalsv | Dreamstime.com; 104 © Mail2355 | Dreamstime.com; 105 left © Marcorubino | Dreamstime.com; 105 right Tomas1111 | Dreamstime.com; 106 © Mitzobs | Dreamstime.com; 107 © Yasonya | Dreamstime.com; 109 © Sirjohnnyray | Dreamstime.com; 110 top © Arsenie Krasnevsky | Shutterstock; 110 bottom © Yasonya | Dreamstime.com; 112 top to bottom © Noppasinw | Dreamstime.com, © Krivinis | Dreamstime.com, © Laudibi | Dreamstime.com, © Dimbar76 | Dreamstime.com; 114 top © Onlyfabrizio | Dreamstime.com; 114 bottom © Dobledphoto | Dreamstime.com; 117 © Taiga | Dreamstime.com; 118 top to bottom © Daanholthausen | Dreamstime.com, © Mmeeds | Dreamstime.com, © Master2 | Dreamstime.com; 119 © Javarman | Dreamstime.com; 123 top to bottom © Radiokafka | Dreamstime.com, © Lviani | Dreamstime.com, © Amina Lahbabi-Peters; 124 © leonov.o | Shutterstock; 125 left © Mayabuns | Dreamstime.com; 125 right © Anibaltrejo | Dreamstime.com;126 © MisterStock | Shutterstock; 127 © RedonePhotographer | Shutterstock; 129 © Graham King | Shutterstock; 130 top to bottom © Corluc | Dreamstime.com, © Malajscy | Dreamstime.com, © Viledevil | Dreamstime.com; 131 © Christiaenhector | Dreamstime.com; 132 © Neftali77 | Dreamstime.com; 134 top © Mathes | Dreamstime.com; 134 bottom © Bpperry | Dreamstime.com; 135 left © Alerizzo78 | Dreamstime.com; 135 right © Fevredream | Dreamstime.com; 136 © Flydragonfly | Dreamstime.com; 137 top © Jiss | Dreamstime.com; 137 bottom © Lenor | Dreamstime.com; 139 © muratart | Shutterstock; 140 top to bottom © Viacheslav Lopatin | Shutterstock, © Umberto Shtanzman | Shutterstock, © amw213 | Shutterstock; 141 © Tomas1111 | Dreamstime.com; 144 © Resul Muslu | Shutterstock; 145 top to bottom © Vladimir Sazonov | Shutterstock, © Juliengrondin | Dreamstime.com, © Pyty | Shutterstock; 146 top © Chanclos | Shutterstock; 146 bottom © ecstk22 | Shutterstock; 147 © PhotoSunnyDays | Shutterstock; 149 left © Catarina Belova | Shutterstock; 149 right © Taras Zheplinskyi | Shutterstock; 151 top © kavalenkava | Shutterstock; 151 bottom © ChiccoDodiFC | Shutterstock; 152 © Fatih Deniz Karacali | Shutterstock; 153 left © Valery Bareta | Shutterstock; 153 right © Jon Chica | Shutterstock; 154 © Oh Yesss | Shutterstock; 155 © Ingus Kruklitis | Shutterstock; 156 top to bottom © lapas77 | Shutterstock, © Viacheslav Lopatin | Shutterstock, © elxeneize | Shutterstock, © Anna Yordanova | Shutterstock; 157 © francesco de marco | Shutterstock; 159 top to bottom © canadastock | Shutterstock, © Katvic | Shutterstock, © Ivanchik | Shutterstock; 162 © Noppasinw | Dreamstime.com; 163 top to bottom © Ncn18 | Dreamstime.com, © Photokanto | Shutterstock, © Stefanozaccaria | Dreamstime.com; 166 © minnystock | Dreamstime.com; 167 © Agnes Kantaruk | Shutterstock; 169 top to bottom © Jovannig | Dreamstime.com, © Pixelklex | Dreamstime.com, © Tomas1111 | Dreamstime.com; 170 top to bottom © Zoom-zoom | Dreamstime.com, © Magann | Dreamstime.com, © Wongkaer | Dreamstime.com, © Sborisov | Dreamstime.com; 171 © spass | Shutterstock; 172 © Carlosftw | Dreamstime.com; 173 left © Draghicich | Dreamstime.com; 173 right © Sergey Kelin | Shutterstock; 174 © Marina Datsenko | Shutterstock; 175 © Photokanto | Shutterstock; 176 © Marekusz | Dreamstime.com; 177 top © Rosshelen | Dreamstime.com; 177 bottom © Lucavanzolini | Dreamstime.com; 178 © Malajscy | Dreamstime.com; 180 © Anitabonita | Dreamstime.com; 181 top to bottom © Bbsferrari | Dreamstime.com, © Agneskantaruk | Dreamstime.com, © Revoc9 | Dreamstime.com; 183 © minnystock | Dreamstime.com; 184 © Masterlu

| Dreamstime.com; 185 top to bottom © Alzamu | Dreamstime.com, © Tommyandone | Dreamstime.com, © H368k742 | Dreamstime.com; 188 © Bbsferrari | Dreamstime.com; 189 © Emicristea | Dreamstime.com; 190 top to bottom © Ioannis7 | Shutterstock, © Stock Holm | Shutterstock, © Kirk Fisher | Shutterstock; 191 © Maksym Kapliuk | Shutterstock; 192 top to bottom © Noppasinw | Dreamstime.com, © Pyty | Shutterstock, © Millafed-otova | Dreamstime.com, © TTstudio | Shutterstock; 193 left © Pytyczech | Dreamstime.com; 193 right © Smiltena | Dreamstime.com; 195 top to bottom © Maciejbledowski | Dreamstime.com, © Tomas1111 | Dreamstime.com, © Madrugadaverde | Dreamstime.com; 196 top © Andreykr | Dreamstime.com; 196 bottom © Jjfarq | Dreamstime.com; 197 © Pascaldeloche | Dreamstime.com; 198 © Mazzzur | Dreamstime.com; 199 left © Zol-tangabor | Dreamstime.com; 199 right © Genitchka | Dreamstime.com; 200 © Izabela23 | Shutterstock; 201 © Serrnovik | Dreamstime.com; 202 top © Sorincolac | Dreamstime.com; 202 bottom © Rosshelen | Dreamstime.com; 203 top © Martinkimla37 | Dreamstime.com; 203 bottom © Andreihrabun | Dreamstime.com; 205 © Serrnovik | Dreamstime.com; 206 top to bottom © Rumata7 | Dreamstime.com, © Robert3133 | Dreamstime.com, © Bepsphoto | Dreamstime.com; 207 top © Biserko | Dreamstime.com; 207 bottom © Ivansmuk | Dreamstime.com; 211 top to bottom © Alexeys | Dreamstime.com, © Phant | Dreamstime.com, © Izzzy71 | Dreamstime.com; 212 © Serrnovik | Dreamstime.com; 213 © Erix2005 | Dreamstime.com; 215 top © Vojkoberk | Dreamstime.com; 215 bottom © Dohtar87 | Dreamstime.com; 217 top © xbrchx | Shutterstock; 217 bottom © weniliou | Shutterstock; 218 © Giannit | Dreamstime.com; 219 © Moritzbobbel | Dreamstime.com; 220 top to bottom © Philfreez | Dreamstime.com, © Giuseppemasci | Dreamstime.com, © Rosshelen | Dreamstime.com, © Kasto80 | Dreamstime.com; 221 © Emanuel Glavina | Shutterstock; 222 © Finn stock | Shutterstock

Road Trips

224 © StevanZZ | Shutterstock; 228 © Pilat666 | Dreamstime.com; 229 top to bottom © Smallredgirl | Dreamstime.com, © Mandritoiu | Dreamstime.com, © Cimbala9 | Dreams-time.com; 232 © Mariiakan | Dreamstime.com; 233 © 36clicks | Dreamstime.com; 234 © Marcin Kadziolka | Shutterstock; 235 left © Jojjik | Dreamstime.com; 235 right © Piboon | Dreamstime.com; 236 left © Luisleamus | Dreamstime.com; 236 right © Tomas1111 | Dreamstime.com; 237 © minnystock | Dreamstime.com; 239 top © Sasha64f | Dreamstime.com; 239 bottom © Dudlajzov | Dreamstime.com; 240 top © minnystock | Dreamstime.com; 240 bottom © Tatonka | Dreamstime.com; 242 © Sergey Didenko | Shutterstock; 246 © Nahlik | Shutterstock; 247 top to bottom © Adamico | Dreamstime.com, © Lauz83 | Dreamstime.com, © Nahlik | Dreamstime.com; 250 left © Matthi | Dreamstime.com; 250 right © Puripatl | Dreamstime.com; 251 top © Jqnoc86 | Dreamstime.com; 251 bottom © Nahlik | Dreamstime.com; 252 © Ingridsil | Dreamstime.com; 256 © Lostsomewherein-france | Dreamstime.com; 257 top to bottom © thereBeAName | Shutterstock, © Grafxart | Dreamstime.com, © Adfoto | Dreamstime.com; 261 top © Gilliankennett05 | Dreams-time.com; 261 bottom © Cja176 | Dreamstime.com; 262 © Reimar | Shutterstock; 265 © Fotograf9 | Dreamstime.com; 268 © Dibrova | Dreamstime.com; 269 top to bottom © Lillitve | Dreamstime.com, © Rudi1976 | Dreamstime.com, © Rolf52 | Dreamstime.com; 272 © Skazzjy | Dreamstime.com; 274 © Stefano Zaccaria | Shutterstock; 276 © Rusel1981 | Dreamstime.com; 279 © Rosshelen | Dreamstime.com; 280 top to bottom © Rosshelen | Dreamstime.com, © Samael333 | Dreamstime.com, © Marktucan | Dreamstime.com; 281 left © Pixemac | Dreamstime.com; 281 right © Rosshelen | Dreamstime.com; 283 © Telly | Shutterstock; 284 © Coventryrobin | Dreamstime.com; 286 top to bottom © 2circles | Dreamstime.com, © Marktucan | Dreamstime.com, © Alexuhrin95 | Dreamstime.com, ©

Leavi1 | Dreamstime.com; 289 © Rosshelen | Dreamstime.com; 290 top to bottom © minnystock | Dreamstime.com, © Radiokafka | Dreamstime.com, © minnystock | Dreamstime.com; 291 left © Stevanzz | Dreamstime.com; 291 right © Radiokafka | Dreamstime.com; 294 © minnystock | Dreamstime.com; 295 © Evgord | Dreamstime.com; 296 top to bottom © Sborisov | Dreamstime.com, © Photogolfer | Dreamstime.com, © Daliu80 | Dreamstime.com, © Donyanedomam | Dreamstime.com; 297 © Elena.Katkova | Shutterstock; 298 © Zwawol | Dreamstime.com; 300 © Wjarek | Dreamstime.com; 302 © Shaiith | Shutterstock; 303 © Antonella865 | Dreamstime.com; 304 top to bottom © Camarneiro91 | Dreamstime.com, © Alessandrogiamello65 | Dreamstime.com, © Xantana | Dreamstime.com, © Ilfede | Dreamstime.com; 306 © Digitalsignal | Dreamstime.com; 307 © Mojolo | Dreamstime.com; 308 top to bottom © Irakite | Dreamstime.com, © Aspesyvtsev | Dreamstime.com, © Lolik | Dreamstime.com; 309 top © Shoter | Dreamstime.com; 309 bottom © Scanrail | Dreamstime.com; 311 © Naumenkoaleksandr | Dreamstime.com; 312 © Moritz Klingenstein | Shutterstock; 313 © Mirosk | Dreamstime.com; 314 © Frank Wagner | Shutterstock; 315 left © Kyolshin | Dreamstime.com; 315 right © Schwarzenberger46 | Dreamstime.com; 316 © Jblackstock | Dreamstime.com; 320 © Pilat666 | Dreamstime.com; 321 top to bottom © Jojjik | Dreamstime.com, © Outchill | Dreamstime.com, © Lenutaidi | Dreamstime.com; 323 left © Jojjik | Dreamstime.com; 323 right © Mitzobs | Dreamstime.com; 324 © Emily Marie Wilson | Shutterstock; 325 © Corinro | Dreamstime.com; 326 top © Fotokon | Dreamstime.com; 326 bottom © Emicristea | Dreamstime.com; 328 © Calinstan | Dreamstime.com; 330 © Romaniainspo | Dreamstime.com; 331 © Jason475 | Dreamstime.com; 332 top to bottom © Dennisvdwater | Dreamstime.com, © Xbrchx | Dreamstime.com, © Serrnovik | Dreamstime.com; 33 left © Graphiapl | Dreamstime.com; 33 right © Sangapark118 | Dreamstime.com; 336 top © Janoka82 | Dreamstime.com; 336 bottom © Susybaels | Dreamstime.com; 338 © Svandor82 | Dreamstime.com; 339 © Lexlero | Dreamstime.com; 340 top to bottom © Jojjik | Dreamstime.com, © Topdeq | Dreamstime.com, © Chrisjbabcock88 | Dreamstime.com, © Daliu80 | Dreamstime.com; 343 left © Liseykina | Dreamstime.com; 343 right © Rudi1976 | Dreamstime.com; 344 top © Steveheap | Dreamstime.com; 344 bottom © Baiad13 | Dreamstime.com; 346 © Rpulham | Dreamstime.com; 347 © Sergii Figurnyi | Shutterstock; 348 © Dvrcan | Dreamstime.com

Outdoor Activities

350 © S-F | Shutterstock; 354 © Pablesku | Shutterstock; 355 top to bottom © Lordignolo | Dreamstime.com, © Sakhanphotography | Dreamstime.com, © Lokono | Dreamstime.com; 359 © Vershinin89 | Shutterstock; 360 © Freeskyline | Dreamstime.com; 362 © AllaStasy | Shutterstock; 364 © Danoz619 | Dreamstime.com; 365 © Gaid Kornsilapa | Shutterstock, © Whitcomberd | Dreamstime.com, © Drewrawcliffe | Dreamstime.com; 367 top © Bpisiolek | Dreamstime.com; 367 bottom © Khrizmo | Dreamstime.com; 368 left, 368 right © Kitleong | Dreamstime.com; 370 top to bottom © Lostsomewhereinfrance | Dreamstime.com, © Andrewroland | Dreamstime.com, © Whitcomberd | Dreamstime.com, © Adeliepenguin | Dreamstime.com; 372 © Davedt | Dreamstime.com; 374 left © Zambezishark | Dreamstime.com; 374 right © Travelwitness | Dreamstime.com; 377 © Mihaiu | Dreamstime.com; 378 top to bottom © Apinna1990 | Dreamstime.com, © Neirfy | Dreamstime.com, Digikhmer | Dreamstime.com; 379 © Madrabothair | Dreamstime.com; 381 © Bjoern Wylezich | Shutterstock; 382 © Martin Bergsma | Shutterstock; 383 © top Hypnocreative | Dreamstime.com; 383 bottom © Sergii Figurnyi | Shutterstock; 384 © Vyychan | Dreamstime.com; 385 left © Digikhmer | Dreamstime.com; 385 right © Hit1912 | Shutterstock; 386 © Arty Om | Shutterstock; 389 © minnystock | Dreamstime.com; 390 top to bottom © Stig Alenäs | Dreamstime.com, © Balipadma | Dreamstime.com, © Rosshelen | Dreamstime.com; 391 top © Mail2kristinamoeller | Dreamstime.com; 391 bottom © Hubertus45, CC BY-SA 3.0; 393 © Gesturgis | Dreamstime.com; 394 © ClarkandCompany | istock.com; 396 top to bottom © Aldorado10 | Dreamstime.com, © Gesturgis | Dreamstime.

com, © Mapics | Dreamstime.com, © Haraldmuc | Dreamstime.com; 398 © guentermanaus | Shutterstock; 399 © DRpics24 | Dreamstime.com; 401 left © Edella | Dreamstime.com; 401 right © Karinhamich | Dreamstime.com; 403 © Krugli | Dreamstime.com; 405 © Panaramka | Dreamstime.com; 406 top to bottom © Delstudio | Dreamstime.com, © Goalie4 | Dreamstime.com, © Jojjik | Dreamstime.com; 407 © Sander van der Werf | Shutterstock; 409 left © Elenaphotos | Dreamstime.com; 409 right © Francoisroux | Dreamstime.com; 410 © Wirestock Creators | Shutterstock; 411 © Icenando | Dreamstime.com; 412 © Zdenek Matyas Photography | Shutterstock; 413 © Gumbao | Dreamstime.com; 414 top to bottom © Mikkeell | Dreamstime.com, © Icenando | Dreamstime.com, © Icenando | Dreamstime.com, © Mikkeell | Dreamstime.com; 415 © Michele Vacchiano | Shutterstock; 416 © Tomaszavadil87 | Dreamstime.com; 417 © Aishe | Shutterstock; 418 left © Jeromeperdriolle | Dreamstime.com; 418 right © Philipimage | Dreamstime.com; 419 © Walking Nature World | Shutterstock; 421 © Ganztwinspics | Dreamstime.com; 423 © Baarssen2 | Dreamstime.com; 424 top to bottom © Rechitansorin | Dreamstime.com, © Duncanpond | Dreamstime.com, © Travnikovstudio | Dreamstime.com; 425 © Olga Gavrilova | Shutterstock; 428 left © Maudem | Dreamstime.com; 428 right © Fravalenti92 | Dreamstime.com; 430 © Massimilianofinzi | Dreamstime.com; 431 © Gabriele Del Dotto; 432 © Simon Dannhauer | Shutterstock; 434 left © Rechitansorin | Dreamstime.com; 434 right © Sangapark118 | Dreamstime.com; 436 © Ekaterina Iatcenko/Shutterstock; 439 © Jojjik | Dreamstime.com; 440 top to bottom © Azgek | Dreamstime.com, © Caterinapuhali | Dreamstime.com, © Daniloforcellini | Dreamstime.com; 441 © Dajahof | Dreamstime.com; 443 © Gooddenka | Dreamstime.com; 444 © Giuma/Shutterstock; 446 © OlgaBombologna | Shutterstock; 447 © Zakaz86 | Dreamstime.com; 448 top to bottom © imagoDens | Dreamstime.com, Alistair Black | Shutterstock, © Dashat5 | Dreamstime.com, © Aagjedejong | Dreamstime.com; 449 © Alviseziche | Dreamstime.com; 450 left © Lucianbolca | Dreamstime.com; 450 right © Akakshu | Dreamstime.com; 452 top © Rolandbarat | Dreamstime.com; 452 bottom © Tomas1111 | Dreamstime.com; 454 © Karlosxii | Dreamstime.com; 456 © Tulda | Dreamstime.com; 458 © TeleMakro | Dreamstime.com; 459 © Marbom | Dreamstime.com; 460 top to bottom © Wirestock | Dreamstime.com, © Bepsphoto | Dreamstime.com, © Avictorero | Dreamstime.com; 461 © Mytravellessons | Dreamstime.com; 463 © Lkonya | Dreamstime.com; 464 top © Max8xam | Dreamstime.com; 464 bottom © Bepsphoto | Dreamstime.com; 465 © Ruben Perez Gil/Shutterstock; 466 © Elena Marzo/Shutterstock; 467 © Mondan80 | Dreamstime.com; 468 © Alfonso de Tomas | Shutterstock; 469 © bepsy | Shutterstock; 470 © Pedro Rufo | Shutterstock; 471 left © Mondan80 | Dreamstime.com; 471 right © Copito5 | Dreamstime.com; 472 © Writer | Dreamstime.com; 474 © Mytravellessons | Dreamstime.com; 476 left © Avictorero | Dreamstime.com; 476 right © Avictorero | Dreamstime.com; 477 © Samael333 | Dreamstime.com; 478 © Annegordon | Dreamstime.com

On the Water

480 © Nick N A/Shutterstock; 484 © F11photo | Dreamstime.com; 485 top to bottom © Garryuk | Dreamstime.com, © Smithore | Dreamstime.com, © minnystock | Dreamstime.com; 487 © Stanko07 | Dreamstime.com; 488 © Steve Mann | Shutterstock; 489 top © Designerandanimator | Dreamstime.com; 489 bottom © Arsty | Dreamstime.com; 490 © Clickos | Dreamstime.com; 491 © Sterling Images | Shutterstock; 492 top to bottom © David Molina | Dreamstime.com, © DimplePatel | Shutterstock, © Donsimon | Dreamstime.com, © Micko | Dreamstime.com; 493 © Abdoabdalla/Shutterstock; 494 left © Trudywsimmons | Dreamstime.com; 494 right © Massimosanti61 | Dreamstime.com; 496 © Wimseyed | Dreamstime.com; 499 © Mefunak | Dreamstime.com; 500 © Rparys | Dreamstime.com; 503 © Oktober64 | Dreamstime.com; 504 top to bottom © Jojjik | Dreamstime.com, Elenafetisova | Dreamstime.com, © Littleny | Dreamstime.com; 505 © Garrett1984 | Dreamstime.com; 507 © Zwawol | Dreamstime.com; 508 © YALCIN KAHYA |

Shutterstock; 509 © iceink | Shutterstock; 510 top © Gunold | Dreamstime.com; 510 bottom © Freesurf69 | Dreamstime.com; 512 © Mirosk | Dreamstime.com; 513 © cktravels.com/Shutterstock; 514 © Marcociannarel | Dreamstime.com; 515 top © Vanstaseghem13 | Dreamstime.com; 515 bottom © Murasmelania | Dreamstime.com; 517 © Mdurson | Dreamstime.com; 518 © Julia Lav/Shutterstock; 519 © Artmediafactory | Dreamstime.com; 520 top to bottom © Newparton | Dreamstime.com, © Rpbmedia | Dreamstime.com, © Stefanozaccaria | Dreamstime.com; 521 top © Acrogame | Dreamstime.com; 521 bottom © Ixuskmitl | Dreamstime.com; 523 © Gbruev | Dreamstime.com; 524 © Robert309 | Dreamstime.com; 525 left © Tomalv | Dreamstime.com; 525 right © Krugli | Dreamstime.com; 527 top to bottom © Rpbmedia | Dreamstime.com, © Martesero | Dreamstime.com, © Fightbegin | Dreamstime.com; 528 © Diego Grandi/Shutterstock; 530 left © Jeancliclac | Dreamstime.com; 530 right © Lirajoggi2016 | Dreamstime.com; 531 © Lowpower225 | Dreamstime.com; 532 © Nstanev | Dreamstime.com; 536 © Rudi1976 | Dreamstime.com; 537 top to bottom © Gstoyanov3 | Dreamstime.com, © Antonel | Dreamstime.com, © Kristinadrozdphotography | Dreamstime.com; 540 © 22tomtom | Dreamstime.com; 541 © Arcady31 | Dreamstime.com; 542 © V. Matthiesen | Shutterstock; 543 © Erix2005 | Dreamstime.com; 544 © Tenedos | Dreamstime.com; 545 © Solarisys13 | Dreamstime.com; 546 top to bottom © Massimobuonaiuto | Dreamstime.com, © Cmoswitzer | Dreamstime.com, © Erix2005 | Dreamstime.com; 548 © VIREN DESAI | Shutterstock; 549 © Chiyacat | Dreamstime.com; 552 © Zicksvift | Dreamstime.com; 553 top to bottom © Patrickwang | Dreamstime.com, Costas1962 | Dreamstime.com, © Jojjik | Dreamstime.com; 556 © Scaliger | Dreamstime.com; 557 © Kesu01 | Dreamstime.com; 558 © Deyangeorgiev | Dreamstime.com; 560 © Johnnyboy9591 | Dreamstime.com; 561 top to bottom © Ibyte | Dreamstime.com, © Milangonda | Dreamstime.com, © Milangonda | Dreamstime.com; 563 left © Smallredgirl | Dreamstime.com; 563 rigth © Costas1962 | Dreamstime.com; 564 top to bottom © Littledesire | Dreamstime.com, © Kaspiic | Dreamstime.com, © Lefpap | Dreamstime.com, © Smallredgirl | Dreamstime.com; 568 © Benophotography | Dreamstime.com; 569 top to bottom © Vladstar | Dreamstime.com, © Photobaisa | Dreamstime.com © Paop | Dreamstime.com; 572 top © RudiErnst | Dreamstime.com; 572 bottom © Lfortuin | Dreamstime.com; 573 © Hanohiki | Dreamstime.com; 574 © marako85 | Shutterstock; 575 © Hdamke | Dreamstime.com; 576 © barmalini | Shutterstock; 578 © Cmoswitzer | Dreamstime.com; 581 © Klaravlasakova | Dreamstime.com; 582 top to bottom © Daliu80 | Dreamstime.com, © Rvdschoot | Dreamstime.com, © Neristefano | Dreamstime.com; 583 © Dariakulkova | Dreamstime.com; 586 top to bottom © Tomas1111 | Dreamstime.com, © Matimix | Dreamstime.com, © Daliu80 | Dreamstime.com, © Esinel | Dreamstime.com; 587 © Mathiasrhode | Dreamstime.com; 588 top © Vickyspaenhoven | Dreamstime.com; 588 bottom © Ggfoto | Dreamstime.com; 591 © Hdamke | Dreamstime.com; 593 © Paop | Dreamstime.com

Classic Rail Trips

596 © Leonid Andronov | Shutterstock; 600 © Zoltangabor | Dreamstime.com; 601 top to bottom © Frantic00 | Dreamstime.com, © Rosshelen | Dreamstime.com, © Gianliguori | Dreamstime.com; 602 left © Lucas M Peters; 602 right © Datsenkomarina | Dreamstime.com; 603 © Jarino47 | Dreamstime.com; 604 top © fokke baarssen | Shutterstock; 604 bottom © Premier Photo | Shutterstock; 605 top © Jojjik | Dreamstime.com; 605 bottom © Frantic00 | Dreamstime.com; 606 © Everett Collection | Shutterstock; 607 © StelianPavalache | Dreamstime.com; 608 left © Begepotam | Dreamstime.com; 608 right © Tigger76 | Dreamstime.com; 609 © Hel080808 | Dreamstime.com; 610 top © Alejandra7139 | Dreamstime.com; 610 bottom © F11photo | Dreamstime.com; 611 © Areinwald | Dreamstime.com; 612 top to bottom © Zoltangabor | Dreamstime.com, © Tomas1111 | Dreamstime.com, © Sorincolac | Dreamstime.com, © Mbsstudio222 | Dreamstime.com; 613 © romeovip_md | Shutterstock; 614 © Seqoya | Dreamstime.com; 618 © Vwalakte | Dreamstime.com; 619 top to bottom © Hypnocreative | Dreamstime.

com, © Bunyos | Dreamstime.com, © Laraugrin | Dreamstime.com;621 left © Pjworldtour | Dreamstime.com; 621 right © Ladiras81 | Dreamstime.com; 622 © Phbcz | Dreamstime.com; 623 top © prochasson frederic | Shutterstock; 623 bottom © Newparton | Dreamstime.com; 624 top to bottom © Wallaceweeks | Dreamstime.com, © Keitma | Dreamstime.com, © Milosk50 | Dreamstime.com; 625 © Meandering Trail Media | Shutterstock; 626 © Kyolshin | Dreamstime.com; 627 © proslgn | Shutterstock; 628 left © LongstockingPippi | Dreamstime.com; 628 right © Sorincolac | Dreamstime.com; 629 © wjarek | Shutterstock; 630 © Tupungato | Shutterstock; 631 top © Olrat | Dreamstime.com; 631 bottom © Honmako1 | Dreamstime.com; 634 © Bareta | Dreamstime.com; 635 top to bottom © Bareta | Dreamstime.com, © Liligraphie | Dreamstime.com, © Travel-Fr | Shutterstock; 638 © Bareta | Dreamstime.com; 639 © Kitleong | Dreamstime.com; 640 © Sphraner | Dreamstime.com; 642 © Anton_Ivanov | Shutterstock; 644 left © Eddygaleotti | Dreamstime.com; 644 right © VVShots | Dreamstime.com; 645 © Swetlanafotos5588 | Dreamstime.com; 646 © Iurii Dzivinskyi/Shutterstock; 648 © CHEN MIN CHUN | Shutterstock; 649 top to bottom © Spettacolare | Dreamstime.com, © Viacheslav Lopatin | Shutterstock, © Giorgio65 | Dreamstime.com; 651 top © Rosshelen | Dreamstime.com; 651 bottom © Ppohudka | Dreamstime.com; 652 © Hypnocreative | Dreamstime.com; 654 © Gevisions | Dreamstime.com; 655 © Boris-B | Shutterstock; 656 top © Xantana | Dreamstime.com; 656 bottom © Bogdan | Dreamstime.com; 658 © Giorgio65 | Dreamstime.com; 659 top © Goncharovaia | Dreamstime.com; 659 bottom © Viacheslav Lopatin | Shutterstock; 660 © Janwehnert82 | Dreamstime.com;; 663 © Dimaberkut | Dreamstime.com; 664 top to bottom © Barmalini | Dreamstime.com, Phbcz | Dreamstime.com, © Ribeiroantonio | Dreamstime.com; 665 © Mikeltrako | Dreamstime.com; 666 left © Homydesign | Dreamstime.com; 666 right © Wirestock | Dreamstime.com; 667 © Zts | Dreamstime.com; 668 top © Irakite | Dreamstime.com; 668 bottom © Altezza | Dreamstime.com; 669 © Barmalini | Dreamstime.com; 670 top © Vector99 | Dreamstime.com; 670 bottom © Phbcz | Dreamstime.com; 671 © PIXEL to the PEOPLE | Shutterstock; 672 © Wirestock | Dreamstime.com; 673 © Makoshark2 | Dreamstime.com; 675 © Scanrail | Dreamstime.com; 676 top to bottom © Krishna.Wu | Shutterstock, © Chulanga | Shutterstock, © Ladiras81 | Dreamstime.com; 677 © Schitikoff | Dreamstime.com; 680 © Cookelma | Dreamstime.com; 681 © Marco Saracco | Shutterstock; 682 © Andrey_Fokin | Shutterstock; 684 © Sinesp | Shutterstock; 685 © Nikolais | Dreamstime.com; 688 © Zhan1999 | Dreamstime.com; 689 top to bottom © Proslgn | Dreamstime.com, © Ronstik | Dreamstime.com, © Arcady31 | Dreamstime.com; 691 top © Photobeps | Dreamstime.com; 691 bottom © Nikolpetr | Dreamstime.com; 693 © Sergii Koval | Shutterstock; 694 left © Pillerss | Dreamstime.com; 694 right © Proslgn | Dreamstime.com; 696 © Curiosopl | Dreamstime.com; 697 left © Curiosopl | Dreamstime.com; 697 right © Gbruev | Dreamstime.com; 698 © Ynos21 | Dreamstime.com; 699 © Arcady31 | Dreamstime.com; 700 © Finestock | Shutterstock; 701 top © Finn stock | Shutterstock; 701 bottom © Oleksiy Mark | Shutterstock; 702 top to bottom © Photoweges | Dreamstime.com, © Boris Stroujko | Shutterstock, © Madrugadaverde | Dreamstime.com

Essentials

704 © Chatdesbalkans | Dreamstime.com; 705 © artjazz | Shutterstock; 715 © Maridav | Shutterstock;

TEXT CREDITS

Alexei J. Cohen contributed Rome, Florence, and Venice (adapted from *Moon Rome, Florence & Venice,* third edition); sections of Zagreb, Ljubljana, and Trieste; Tuscany and Umbria; Cinque Terre; and Alta Via 1: Dolomite High Route.

Chris Newens contributed London and Paris, Bordeaux and the Pyrenees, England's Lake District, South of England to North of France (sections adapted from *Moon Normandy & Brittany*), and sections of The Rhone Valley.

CITY HOPPING

Text for Edinburgh and Glasgow adapted from *Moon Scotland,* first edition, by Sally Coffey. Text for Amsterdam, Brussels, and Bruges adapted from *Moon Amsterdam, Brussels & Bruges,* first edition, by Karen Turner. Text for Barcelona and Madrid adapted from *Moon Barcelona & Madrid,* first edition, by Jessica Jones. Text for Prague, Vienna, and Budapest adapted from *Moon Prague, Vienna & Budapest,* second edition, by Jennifer D. Walker and Auburn Scallon.

ROAD TRIPS

Text for Iceland's Ring Road adapted from *Moon Iceland,* third edition, by Jenna Gottlieb. Text for Causeway Coast adapted from *Moon Ireland,* third edition, by Camille DeAngelis. Text for The North Coast 500 adapted from *Moon Scotland,* first edition, by Sally Coffey. Text for Lofoten adapted from *Moon Norway,* first edition, by Lisa Stentvedt. Text for The Magistrala Coastal Road adapted from *Moon Croatia & Slovenia,* fourth edition, by Shann Fountain Alipour.

OUTDOOR ADVENTURES

Text for Dublin and the Wicklow Way adapted from *Moon Ireland,* third edition, by Camille DeAngelis. Text for Holland Junction Network adapted from *Moon Amsterdam, Brussels & Bruges,* first edition, by Karen Turner. Sections of Copenhagen to Berlin by Bike adapted from *Moon Copenhagen & Beyond,* first edition, by Michael Barrett. Text for Camino de Santiago adapted from *Moon Camino de Santiago,* second edition, by Beebe Bahrami.

ON THE WATER

Sections of Rhine River Cruise adapted from *Moon Amsterdam, Brussels & Bruges,* first edition, by Karen Turner. Text for Copenhagen to Oslo adapted from *Moon Copenhagen & Beyond,* first edition, by Michael Barrett and *Moon Norway,* first edition, by Lisa Stentvedt. Text for Naples, Capri, and the Amalfi Coast adapted from *Moon Amalfi Coast,* second edition, by Laura Thayer. Text for The Greek Islands adapted from *Moon Greek Islands,* second edition, by Sarah Souli. Text for The Azores adapted from *Moon Azores,* first edition, by Carrie-Marie Bratley.

CLASSIC RAIL TRIPS AND MORE

Sections of The Rhone Valley adapted from *Moon Provence,* first edition, by Jamie Ivey. Text for The French Riviera adapted from *Moon French Riviera,* first edition, by Jon Bryant. Sections of The Alps adapted from *Moon Milan & Beyond,* first edition, by Lindsey Davison. Text for The Douro Line adapted from *Moon Portugal,* second edition, by Carrie-Marie Bratley. Text for The Bergen Line adapted from *Moon Norway,* first edition, by Lisa Stentvedt.

MAP SYMBOLS

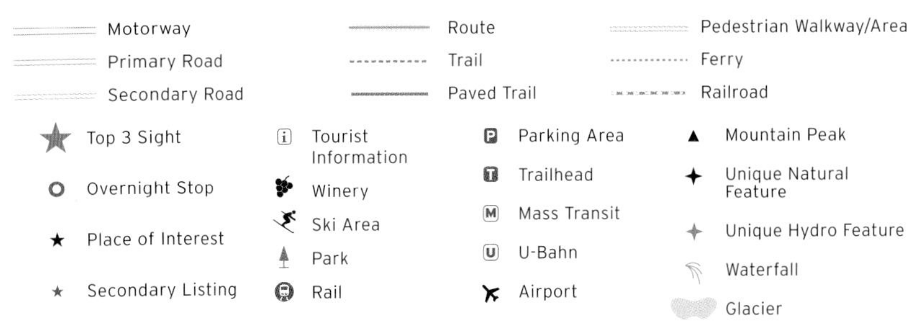

CONVERSION TABLES

°C = (°F - 32) / 1.8
°F = (°C x 1.8) + 32
1 inch = 2.54 centimeters (cm)
1 foot = 0.304 meters (m)
1 yard = 0.914 meters
1 mile = 1.6093 kilometers (km)
1 km = 0.6214 miles
1 fathom = 1.8288 m
1 chain = 20.1168 m
1 furlong = 201.168 m
1 acre = 0.4047 hectares
1 sq km = 100 hectares
1 sq mile = 2.59 square km
1 ounce = 28.35 grams
1 pound = 0.4536 kilograms
1 short ton = 0.90718 metric ton
1 short ton = 2,000 pounds
1 long ton = 1.016 metric tons
1 long ton = 2,240 pounds
1 metric ton = 1,000 kilograms
1 quart = 0.94635 liters
1 US gallon = 3.7854 liters
1 Imperial gallon = 4.5459 liters
1 nautical mile = 1.852 km

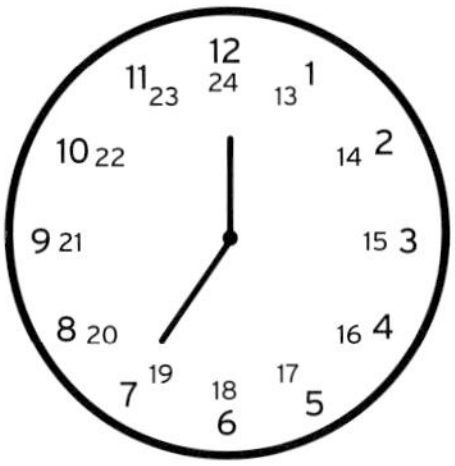

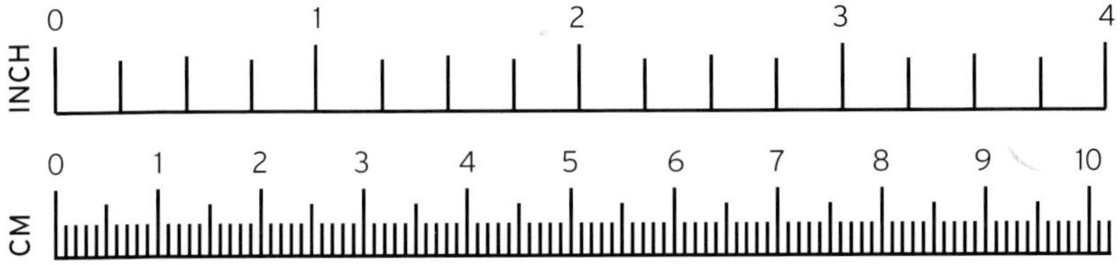

12 24 1 13 2 14 3 15 4 16 5 17 6 18 7 19 8 20 9 21 10 22 11 23

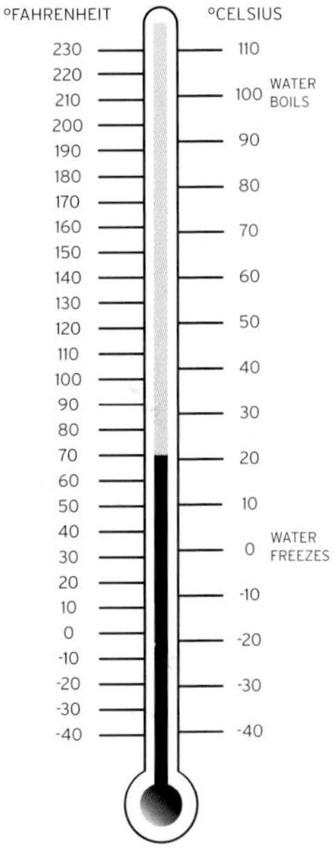

°FAHRENHEIT: 230 220 210 200 190 180 170 160 150 140 130 120 110 100 90 80 70 60 50 40 30 20 10 0 -10 -20 -30 -40

°CELSIUS: 110 100 WATER BOILS 90 80 70 60 50 40 30 20 10 0 WATER FREEZES -10 -20 -30 -40

INCH 0 1 2 3 4

CM 0 1 2 3 4 5 6 7 8 9 10

MOON GRAND EUROPEAN JOURNEYS

Avalon Travel
Hachette Book Group
1700 Fourth Street
Berkeley, CA 94710, USA
www.moon.com

Editors: Grace Fujimoto, Megan Anderluh
Managing Editor: Hannah Brezack
Copy Editor: Barbara Schultz
Graphics Coordinator: Kathryn Osgood
Production Coordinator: Suzanne Albertson
Cover Design: Faceout Studio, Molly von Borstel
Interior Design: Tabitha Lahr
Map Editor: Kat Bennett
Cartographers: Mark Stroud (Moon Street Cartography), Karin Dahl, John Culp
Indexer: Greg Jewett

ISBN-13: 978-1-64049-754-2

Printing History
1st Edition — February 2024
5 4 3 2 1

Front cover photo: retro sky @ Valentin Agapov/Shutterstock; Vltava river and old city center @ DaLiu/Shutterstock

Printed by APS